CACTI

A GARDENER'S HANDBOOK
FOR THEIR
IDENTIFICATION AND CULTIVATION

By

PROFESSOR J. BORG, M.A., M.D.

*Late Professor of Natural History
in the Malta University*

With a biography of the Author

By

BEATRICE BORG

London
BLANDFORD PRESS

First Published (by Macmillan & Co. Ltd.) 1937
Second Edition (Completely revised and enlarged) 1951
Reprinted . . 1956
Third Edition (enlarged) 1959

Made and printed in Great Britain by
S. TINSLEY & CO. LTD., Manor Farm Road, Alperton, Middlesex.

CACTI

Respectfully Dedicated
to the Members of
The Cactus and Succulent Society
of Great Britain

This

A
t

The late PROFESSOR J. BORG, M.A., M.D.

INTRODUCING THE AUTHOR

Professor John Borg, M.A., M.D., who died in Malta, the land of his birth, in 1945, at the age of 72 years, was a botanist of great repute, an indefatigable scientific worker, a prolific writer, an inspiring teacher, and a great philanthropist.

He studied Science and Medicine at the University of Malta, where he graduated M.A. in 1894 and M.D. in 1898.

Medicine was his profession, and he practised it most conscientiously and gave early proofs of a brilliant career, but his great love of Nature was a stronger attraction for him; so much so that, in 1900, he accepted the onerous duties of Superintendent of Public Gardens; in 1919 he became Superintendent of the Department of Agriculture, and in 1921 he was offered, and accepted, the Professorship of Natural History at the University of Malta.

Under his direction public gardening and agriculture in Malta underwent a complete overhaul: existing gardens were systematized, new gardens were opened, experimental farming was established, plant pathological work was introduced.

A list of some of his many publications is appended; it starts with a "Catalogue of Plants cultivated in St. Antonio Gardens"—the biggest public garden in the island—published two years before young Borg had left his University, and ends with a crowning publication on "Cacti" of which the present is a second and revised edition. Professor Borg had just finished the compilation of this revised edition at the time of his death. Cactus growing, in many cases from seed, was a life-long hobby with him; he personally tended a most extensive and comprehensive collection of Cacti and Succulents, which he donated to the Botanic Garden of the Royal University of Malta in the last days of his life.

Professor Borg added lustre to the chair of Natural History at the Royal University of Malta; his "Cultivation and Diseases of Fruit Trees," "Gardening in Malta," and "Descriptive Flora of the Maltese Islands" were all penned during his tenure of the professorship and they stand as a monument to his great erudition. His Manuscript on "The Phlegraean Fields" involving a very thorough and painstaking research is so far unedited. On his retirement he was appointed a Professor Emeritus and his services as Examiner in Botany and Zoology were retained up to his death.

The Royal University of Malta is also indebted to Professor Borg and his wife for a complete Herbarium of Local Indigenous Plants, a Research Microscope and Accessories, a £4,000 Scholarship Fund, and a Bronze Bust of Professor Borg himself, presented by his wife.

S. L. VELLA
Professor of Biology,
Royal University of Malta

5

LIST OF PUBLICATIONS
BY PROFESSOR JOHN BORG, M.A., M.D.

1896 CATALOGUE OF PLANTS CULTIVATED IN ST. ANTONIO GARDENS

1899 IL BIEDJA TAL MARD TA L'AGRUMI

1901 DISEASES OF THE ORANGE TREES AND THEIR TREATMENT

1908 THE PERIODICAL PHENOMENA OF PLANT LIFE IN MALTA

1911 REMAINS OF PREHISTORIC FLORA IN MALTA

1915 AGRICULTURE AND HORTICULTURE IN MALTA ⎰ In "Malta and
      FISHERIES IN MALTA   ⎱ Gibraltar"

1918 SEMINA IN MALTA DI PRODOTTI ORTICOLI ED AGRICOLI

1919 CLIMBING PLANTS. THE CULTIVATION OF BULBS, PALMS AND
      CYCADS

1920 COLTIVAZIONE DEL BANANO IN MALTA

1922 CULTIVATION AND DISEASES OF FRUIT TREES

1925 GARDENING IN MALTA

1927 DESCRIPTIVE FLORA OF THE MALTESE ISLANDS

1929 IL BIEDJA TAD-DWIELI AMERICANI

1932 SCALE INSECTS OF THE MALTESE ISLANDS

1936 TRACES OF THE QUATERNARY ICE AGE IN THE MALTESE ISLANDS

1937 CACTI. A GARDENER'S HANDBOOK FOR THEIR IDENTIFICATION

PREFACE TO THE FIRST EDITION

Growers of Cacti too often feel that there is a dearth of literature in a popular form on the cultivation and knowledge of these plants, and that the present revival of Cactus culture all over the world was not assisted in English-speaking countries by any considerable development of popular horticultural literature in this direction. Since the publication of "Cactus Culture for Amateurs," by William Watson, Curator, Royal Botanic Gardens, Kew, first published in 1889, which went through five editions, no other popular work on Cactaceae has been published in England until 1933, when Mrs. Vera Higgins, M.A., published her very interesting "Study of Cacti," which, besides much valuable cultural information, contains a general classification with descriptive characters of all the genera, as laid down by Britton and Rose. The "Cactus Book," by A. D. Houghton, published in America in 1930, gives good cultural directions and a classification of genera according to Britton and Rose, to which are added comprehensive lists of species recommendable to the grower. The enterprising firm of W. T. and H. E. Neale, of Meeching Rise Nurseries, Sussex, has also published an admirably illustrated and descriptive catalogue of "Cacti and Other Succulents," to which are added by way of introduction valuable cultural directions. Watson's work, although no doubt very useful and informative at the time when it was published, was too limited in scope, and is now too much out of date to be a real guide to the grower and amateur in the identification of his plants. On the other hand, "The Cactaceae," by Britton and Rose, in every respect a work of very high botanical standard, is too costly, too voluminous (4 volumes), and too technical to meet the needs of the mere grower and amateur. It was also, until lately, unfortunately out of print, and difficult to procure, but a reprint made under the auspices of the American Cactus Society is now available.

In the present work, after a few introductory chapters of a general character conveying elementary knowledge on the cultivation of Cacti, as well as on their structure, a general classification is given, with concise but full descriptions of the genera of Cactaceae and of most of the species in cultivation, along with their varieties. Most of the new species are also included, so that the gardener and amateur will find that there are very few species of any importance which are omitted, and that a gap in English horticultural literature has

7

been adequately filled up. Out of a total of about 1,576 species belonging to this family, over 1,187 species, besides varieties and forms, are described in the present work, and mention is also made of the latest discoveries. It is written in clear and popular language, with the least possible use of technical terms, and it is hoped that it will be of material assistance in fostering the rising tide of popularity which this very interesting family of plants is now enjoying.

My thanks are due to Messrs. Friedrich Adolph Haage, Junior, of Erfurt, for their courtesy in allowing reproduction of the illustrations in this book from a selection of photos kindly supplied by them, and also for the loan of the block for the frontispiece.

J. BORG

MALTA, *April*, 1937

The firm of W. T. and H. E. Neale referred to in the above
Preface is, of course, now known as W. T. Neale and Company
Ltd. and is operating from Franklin Road, Worthing, Sussex.

8

PREFACE TO THE SECOND EDITION

The favour with which the first edition of this book has been received by Cactus-growers and amateurs has induced me to revise the text for a second edition. The few inaccuracies which had crept in unavoidably in the preparation of the first edition have been corrected, and descriptions of 312 other species have been added, thus bringing the total number of species described to 1,500. The new genera *Haageocereus*, *Spegazzinia* and *Chilenia* have been included in the classification, as it appears that they are now being more generally accepted. The genera *Opuntia*, *Cephalocereus*, *Notocactus*, *Parodia*, *Echinopsis*, *Lobivia* and *Rebutia* have been rearranged and classified, in order to further assist the reader in the identification of the species.

The number of illustrations has been increased by eighteen plates, each showing two species, carefully selected for some outstanding character.

In the first edition the specific name was written with a capital initial letter only when it is the name for a person used in the possessive. In this edition I am complying with the International Rules by writing all specific names derived from names of persons or genera with a capital initial letter. This course, although not free from objection, has now the sanction of usage.

I am using again the Centigrade scale of temperature, whenever necessary for cultural directions, but in order to avoid possible confusion on the part of the gardener, in each case I am also giving the equivalents in the Fahrenheit scale.

J. BORG

MALTA, 1945

LIST OF ILLUSTRATIONS

THE LATE PROFESSOR J. BORG, M.A., M.D. *Frontispiece*

11

CONTENTS

A PRELIMINARY TALK ON CACTACEAE

ECHINOCACTUS INGENS
An old specimen in its native habitat

PLATE I

A PRELIMINARY TALK ON CACTACEAE
I.
INTRODUCTION

The *Cactaceae* are essentially, and almost exclusively, natives of America, and extend from the comparatively cold regions of the north-eastern United States down to Chili and Patagonia; but their classical home, where they are most numerous in forms and in numbers, is the Mexican region, including Mexico, Texas, New Mexico, Arizona, Southern California and Lower California. The Cactaceae are therefore a peculiarity of the Flora of America, and with the exception of a few and unimportant species of *Rhipsalis*, found in West Africa, and also in East Africa, Madagascar, the Comoro Islands, Mauritius and Ceylon, they are also exclusive to that Continent and to its Islands. Several species of *Opuntia* have become extensively naturalized in other countries through human agency. Thus *Opuntia Ficus-indica*, in many forms, *O. Opuntia*, and *O. amyclaea* are naturalized in the Mediterranean region, where *O. Ficus-indica* was originally introduced as a fruit tree. Other species, such as *O. tomentosa*, *O. aurantiaca*, *O. Dillenii*, etc., have become naturalized, and are now invading and alarming pests, over vast districts of Queensland and other parts of Australia, as well as in India and other countries. With the exception of the *Bromeliaceae* (the Pine-apple family), there is no other important family of plants which is so emphatically exotic in character. Cacti, like Bromeliads, are natives of the New World, and like them too, they are unmistakeably a comparatively recent evolution.

Many tropical Cacti live in the low-lying and very warm valleys and plains of Central America and the West Indian Islands down to Brazil, in the full blaze of the tropical sun. Other species of the same regions prefer the half-shade of neighbouring trees and shrubs, or of the rank vegetation which dries up during the recurrent periods of drought. The *Mountain Cerei* (*Oreocereus*) and species of *Borzicactus*, *Cleistocactus* and *Haageocereus* inhabit mostly the rocky and arid slopes of the Andes in Ecuador, Peru and Bolivia. Certain species of *Opuntia* and *Mammillaria* are covered with snow in winter, in the arid or semi-arid districts of Arizona, Utah and Colorado. Species of *Maihuenia*, and the interesting globular-jointed species of *Opuntia* are peculiar to the temperate regions of Bolivia, Argentina and Patagonia. Many species of *Lobivia* and *Rebutia*, and also of *Gymnocalycium*, etc., inhabit the sandy or alluvial plains and hills of Argentina, Bolivia and Paraguay, where the dry grass affords some covering or half-shade from the burning sun during the dry season, when the soil mostly becomes cracked and sun-baked. Others are epiphytic, living on the mossy trunks of trees in tropical or sub-tropical forests, or on ledges of rock in deep ravines, such as species of *Zygocactus*,

B

Schlumbergera, Epiphyllum (Phyllocactus), Rhipsalis, etc., and accordingly they require shade, along with warmth, and a soil rich in humus and rather moist, but always free from stagnant humidity.

This freedom from stagnant moisture is an invariably essential condition for the successful cultivation of Cactaceae, but while many species are able to thrive well in the poorest and most arid soil, others require a rich loamy soil with abundant moisture, at least during the growing period. Thus *Pyrrhocactus umadeave*, known also as *Friesia umadeave*, an interesting globular species from the rainless desert region of the Gran Chaco in Northern Argentina, thrives in perfectly dry sand and is only watered by the heavy dews and occasional showers which fall at certain seasons, and soon rots off if planted in moderately good soil and watered even sparingly. Many species of *Mammillaria* inhabiting the prairies of North America, and species of *Rebutia* inhabiting the pampas of South America, often in somewhat marshy localities, are occasionally inundated in the rainy season, followed by a period of drought and rest, during which they become much shrivelled, but do not seem to suffer from this mode of life. More or less the same happens to the Organ-pipe Cactus (*Myrtillocactus geometrizans*) of Mexico, whose thick stems become very much shrivelled in the dry season, but soon become plump again a few days after the commencement of the rainy period, and then the plant imbibes water with such avidity, that often the tissues burst and long deep wounds are developed along the stems and branches, which however rarely become the seat of infection and rot.

The gigantic species, such as *Carnegiea gigantea*, better known under its old name of *Cereus giganteus*, of Arizona, Sonora, and southwestern California, and *Pachycereus (Cereus) Pringlei*, native of Sonora and Lower California, as well as other species of *Pachycereus, Lemaireocereus* and *Machaerocereus*, and many species of large flat-jointed *Opuntia*, grow in colonies often of considerable extent, comparable to forests, in regions where a long period of drought is followed by another long period of torrential rains. After the first rains the plants which had become much shrivelled, as a result of the dry condition of the soil, the scorching heat of the sun from a cloudless sky, and the loss of water stored in their tissues, become plump and full in a few days, and soon start growing and flowering. With the gradual cessation of rainy weather and the increasing dryness of the soil, the new growth becomes seasoned and prepared to enter upon a long period of rest, during which very little, if any, growth is made.

Many species of *Mammillaria, Lemaireocereus, Pachycereus*, etc., and particularly of *Echinocactus* and *Cephalocereus*, have a poorly developed root-system, in proportion to the size and age of the plant. Thus most species of *Echinocactus* thrive very well in pots of a diameter hardly exceeding that of the plant, and even a still more restricted space is often advisable. In their native haunts these plants live mostly in stony shallow soils, or in narrow crevices, on the ledges of rock along the sloping sides of valleys. The Old Man Cactus (*Cephalocereus senilis*) lives in the dry, shaly, and arid slaty formations of the states of Hidalgo and Guanajuato in Mexico, and its growth is very slow, so that an imported plant about 25 cm. high, may well be over 25 years old. Its subsequent development is faster, although always comparatively slow. Under cultivation growth may be quicker, though not so sturdy as in its native country, and strong plants are known to make a growth of about 10 cm. in one year; but the tall pillars of this species in the hot valleys of the state of Hidalgo, reaching a height of 10 m. or more, with a stem of about 30 cm. in diameter at the base, cannot be less than 200 years old. In other species of *Cephalocereus* growth may be faster, but their root-system is invariably weak, even in the case of species which normally grow in moderately good soil, or which grow better in half-shade than in full sunshine.

The globular-jointed Opuntias (sub-genus *Sphaeropuntia* or *Tephrocactus*) such as *O. diademata*, *O. Turpinii*, *O. sphaerica*, *O. aoracantha*, *O. riojana*, *O. platyacantha*, etc., mostly natives of S. America, and the growth of which is usually slow, have also a weak root-system, and require little space for its development. On the other hand, the flat-jointed Opuntias (sub-genus *Platyopuntia*), particularly the species attaining a large size, have a very powerful root-system, and although they may be satisfied with the poorest soil, they are huge feeders, and make rapid growth when conditions are favourable. With the exception of a few species, such as *O. clavarioides*, *O. vestita*, *O. Verschaffeltii*, *O. teres*, *O. cylindrica*, *O. stapeliae*, etc., which prefer half-shade, all Opuntias thrive better in full sunshine and in exposed situations.

In this connection it should be borne in mind that, with very few exceptions, Cactaceae have no leaves, or rather have only leaves of a very fleeting character, the functions of the leaf being performed by the green stem, which is stiff, and therefore when fully developed is hardly responsive to heliotropic stimulus. For this reason, plants which have been kept long in the shade or half-shade, should be gradually and cautiously accustomed to the full action of the sun, especially during the hottest hours of the day. The same explanation applies in the case of not a few species, which definitely dislike a change of position, and therefore when moved from one place to another, the side of the plant which was directed towards the north, and therefore shaded, should not be too suddenly exposed to the direct action of the sun by turning towards the south. Even in case of plants kept more or less permanently under a glass shed, it is well to stick to this precaution, otherwise unsightly scorchings may result.

II.

THE CACTACEAE

To the difference of temperament and culture, as well as to the vagaries of fashion, may be ascribed the vast difference with which the cultivation of Cacti and of Succulents in general, was and is looked upon by the cultivator and by the general public. Many growers still look upon these plants with aversion, perhaps not unmingled with wonder and with awe, much as they would look on the collection of strange animals in the Zoo. To them the strange and often uncouth appearance of the plants, as well as their defensive armament, often formidable and trying to handle, seem to afford sufficient ground for dislike. On the other hand, to those who have become accustomed to these plants, that which to the uninitiated has only seemed grotesque, has become original and picturesque, with a peculiar beauty and attraction of its own, imparted by the strange aspect of the plant, and often by the unique magnificence of the flowers, hardly paralleled by other similar productions of the Vegetable Kingdom. They have learned to appreciate the beauties of Nature in its infinite variations; they have ceased to look upon these plants with terror, or as mere curiosities, but as a permanent source of interest and admiration, and they speak with pride and enthusiasm of their collections, which they are ever anxious to increase and improve.

Apart from the justifiable enthusiasm of the growers and collectionists, the Cactaceae and Succulents in general are certainly not less worthy of cultivation and study than any other class of plants. The cultivation of Orchids presents an almost parallel case. Vast quantities of Orchids, chiefly of tropical and subtropical species, were and are still being imported into Europe, and Orchid-hunters have scoured the primeval forests and the wooded hillsides of tropical America, southern Asia and the Eastern Archipelago in the hunt for new species to stock the hothouses of Europe. But the Orchid was always considered as the aristocrat, or rather the plutocrat, of flowers, and its cultivation on an ambitious scale was therefore reserved to the owners of fat purses. This drawback does not exist in the case of Cactaceae and Succulents. Not only are imported plants cheap enough and well within the reach of everybody, many species are easily raised from seed, or propagated by cuttings or offsets, by the grower himself. To this last quality may be ascribed the fact that, although their cultivation may have suffered the usual ups and downs attendant on the moods of fashion or of popularity, it was never allowed to be entirely banished from gardens of even quite modest pretensions.

The cultivation of Cacti was started in Europe on a large scale in the first part of last century, when French importers placed on the market in Paris and London vast quantities of Cacti, of many species not before seen in Europe. Belgian and German growers also imported considerable quantities, chiefly from Mexico, with the result that extensive collections were soon formed which afforded ample material for study to botanists such as Pfeiffer, Engelmann, the Prince of Salm-Dyck, Labouret, and Lemaire, who described the new species, although their descriptions were often incomplete, as many species, naturally of slow development, made no haste to flower in Europe. There are also the valuable contributions of Monville, Saglion, Houllet, Celsius, J. A. Purpus, Martius, Weber, Link, Otto, Ehrenberg, Zuccarini, Spegazzini, and more recently of Berger, Borzi and Riccobono besides many others who have added greatly to our store of knowledge of this interesting family of plants.

However, the study of Cactaceae and their classification began to take definite form with the standard work of Dr. Karl Schumann ("Gesamtbeschreibung der Kakteen," 1898-1903), and this author's classification, along with that of Lemaire, was and is still largely accepted by subsequent writers. With the great epoch-making work of Dr. N. L. Britton in New York and Dr. J. N. Rose in Washington: "The Cactaceae—Descriptions and Illustrations of Plants of the Cactus Family" (*The Carnegie Institute of Washington, Washington,* 1919-1923, 4 volumes in 4to), the study of Cacti may well be said to have had its crowning glory, as these authors working on the spot, have had the great advantage of much fresh material, which was denied to their predecessors. Since the publication of this work many new species have been discovered and studied, chiefly through the enterprise of German explorers and botanists, such as Boedeker, Haage, Kupper, Werdermann, Backeberg, Frič, Blossfield, etc.

Britton and Rose have adopted the fundamental classification of their predecessors, but have created a considerable number of new genera, founded mostly on the characteristics of the flower. To the genera created by them, others have been added by more recent German authors, such as : *Aztekium*, created by Boedeker in 1929, for *Aztekium Ritteri*, originally included under *Echinocactus; Obregonia* created by Frič in 1923 for *Obregonia Denegrii*, an intermediate species; *Neowerdermannia* also created by Frič for *Neowerdermannia Vorwerkii*, another intermediate species; *Encephalocarpus* created by Berger in 1928 for *Encephalocarpus strobiliformis* formerly included under *Ariocarpus;* and still more recently the new genera *Haageocereus, Chilenia, Spegazzinia, Bridgesia* (or *Chileniopsis*), and *Islaya* created by Backeberg, and *Neogomesia* created by Castaneda in 1941.

The recent work of Ernst Schelle, "Kakteen," and that of Dr. Alwin Berger, "Kakteen," both in German, have contributed much to popularize the cultivation of Cacti, especially in Central Europe, and in particular Berger's work is justly spoken of as "the little Schumann." Berger has also presented us with other very valuable works on Succulents, viz.: "Succulent Euphorbias," "Mesembryanthemums and Portulacaceae," "Crassulaceae," "Stapeliae and Kleiniae," and the classical monograph of the genus *Agave*.

III.
GENERAL ORGANOGRAPHY OF THE CACTACEAE

The histology or internal minute structure of Cacti is beyond the scope of this work, but a few notions on the outer structure or conformation of the various organs, or *organography*, is necessary to understand the descriptions of the species, although it is my object to avoid technical terms as much as possible, and to give the descriptions a thoroughly popular form.

The Cactaceae are dicotyledonous phanerogamic plants—that is.

their embryo on germination has two primary leaves or *cotyledons*, which are well developed and fleshy in the *Pereskieae* and *Opuntieae*, but are very minute and scale-like in the third sub-family or tribe *Cereeae*. Being dicotyledonous plants, the stem of Cacti shows the fundamental qualities of dicotyledons in general, that is, it has a well-marked and complete *cambium* or generative zone, by which the stem increases in diameter, and owing to which *grafting* is possible. On the other hand, in *monocotyledons*, plants germinating with only one cotyledon (Palms, Bamboos, Liliaceae, Orchids, etc.), and also in Ferns, the cambium is enclosed in each vascular bundle, and does not form a complete ring around the stem, and therefore in these plants grafting cannot be performed with success.

The Cactaceae are shrubs or perennial herbs, annual species being non-existent, with more or less fleshy stems, usually jointed, and with a green bark. The leaves are rarely perfect and permanent, but are generally absent, or rudimentary, or fugacious, or reduced to mere minute scales. There are no *stipules*, and the buds are *geminate* or in pairs, and super-imposed, that is, the lower bud developing into spines, and the upper, from which the flowers or the branches are produced, is often surrounded by a cushion of hairs or stinging bristles or *glochids* (*glochidium;* plural *glochidia*). Both buds are often very close together, forming one single round or oval *areola*, as in *Opuntia*, *Cereus*, *Echinocereus*, *Echinocactus*, etc.; or they may be separate, the upper bud, either naked or hairy or furnished with bristles, being found in the *axilla* or *axil* of a well developed *tubercle* or *wart*, on the top or tip of which is found the lower bud, generally furnished with spines (*Mammillaria*, *Coryphantha*, *Cochemiea*, etc.). Although the flowers and branches are developed normally from the upper bud in the axilla of the tubercle, in certain circumstances, as will be seen later on, it is possible for a new branch or stem to develop from the spiny lower bud on the tip of the tubercle.

The flowers are usually regular or *actinomorphic*. They are irregular or *zygomorphic* in *Zygocactus*, *Epiphyllanthus* and *Cleistocactus*. They are usually axillary and solitary, occasionally terminal, and are always hermaphrodite, with the exception of *Mammillaria dioica* and of a few species of *Opuntia*, in which the male plant bears larger flowers with an abortive pistil. The perianth is multiple: the calyx is superior, usually petaloid or coloured, often indistinguishable from the corolla, which is made of numerous delicate petals in two or more whorls, distinct, or forming a tube. Stamens inserted at the base of the corolla, very numerous, the outer being longer, all with filiform filaments, and with two-celled introrse anthers. The ovary is inferior, one-celled, with parietal placentas, with a simple style and as many stigmas or rather lobes of stigma, as there are placentas. Ovules numerous, anatropous. Fruit a berry, smooth or spiny, one-celled, umbilicate, rarely a dry capsule (*Pterocactus*); albumen wanting or very scanty.

The following is a summary description of the various organs:
The *Root* is typically tapering and branching; but of course is

22

multiple or fascicled in plants raised from cuttings or offsets. It is sometimes thick and conical, like that of a beet, in species of *Coryphantha, Lophophora, Ariocarpus, Encephalocarpus, Aztekium,* and in many species of *Mammillaria* and *Echinocactus* (*Gymnocalycium, Frailea, Neoporteria*). It is, or becomes, multiple and tuberous like that of a Dahlia in species of *Pterocactus, Wilcoxia, Peniocereus* and a few other species. It is thickened and nodose in certain species of *Opuntia*.

The *Stem* is hardly fleshy in species of *Pereskia* and *Pereskiopsis,* and is then almost like that of other plants, except for the fact that it is furnished with typical areoles and spines. It is jointed and very fleshy in species of *Opuntia* and *Nopalea,* being flat and oval or elongated in *Nopalea,* and is either globular or oval, cylindrical or flattened in species of *Opuntia,* and if flattened may be round or disc-like, or more or less ovate or elongated, always with *aereolae* or *areoles,* all round on both surfaces. The stem of *Epiphyllanthus* has very small oval, flattened joints, furnished with small areoles, like an *Opuntia*. *Zygocactus* and *Schlumbergera* have flat, leaf-like, truncated joints, with areoles at the top and along the side edges, but the flowers are borne on the long areole at the top. In *Epiphyllum* (*Phyllocactus*) the stem is flattened and leaf-like, much elongated, branching along the sides and at the top, and the flowers are produced mostly from the areoles along the sides The stem is jointed and globular or oval in the pretty *Arthrocereus* (*Cereus*) *microsphaericus* or *C. Damazioi.* It is columnar, erect and fluted or ribbed, or winged and angular in the large columnar *Cerei* which sometimes attain gigantic size, and is then either solitary or branched from the base or at some distance above ground. It is winged in *Hylocereus,* the stem showing a triangular transverse section, with broad wing-like ribs. In the genus *Trichocereus* it is erect and thick, with many ribs and branched from the base. It is columnar and erect in the genus *Cephalocereus,* or rarely prostrate, often branched above ground, with many ribs or with only 4 to 10 in the more slender species, and usually with tufts of hairs on the upper areoles; and these tufts of hair or wool become more abundant and longer on that part of the stem where flowers are produced, hence called the *cephalium* or rather *pseudocephalium* or head. In the genus *Cactus* or *Melocactus* the stem is globular or oval or elongated, with many spiny ribs, and when fully grown develops at the top a peculiar structure, densely covered with wool and bristles, on which the flowers are borne year after year. To this structure the term *cephalium* is more properly applied.

In the genera *Echinopsis, Rebutia, Lobivia, Echinocactus* (in a broad sense), *Astrophytum* and *Lophophora,* the stem is globular or ovoid or cylindrical, very fleshy, usually with many ribs, acute or rounded, straight, wavy, or spiral, more or less notched, with areoles and spines, and the flowers are borne on the areoles at the top or at the sides. In *Astrophytum* and most species of true *Echinocactus* and *Ferocactus* the stem is mostly solitary, and becomes branched only secondarily, when the growing top is injured. In other species, as well as in most species of *Coryphantha, Mammillaria, Cochemiea, Lobivia, Rebutia, Lophophora,* etc., it branches or produces offsets at the base and sides, or may even branch dichotomously, forming large solid clumps.

In *Dolichothele, Coryphantha, Mammillaria, Cochemiea, Mamillopsis, Escobaria,* etc., the stem is covered all over with *warts* or *tubercles,* which may be oval or conical or angular or cylindrical. These tubercles in reality represent the petiole or leaf-stalk of the abortive leaf, and as in the case of typical leaf-stalks, the bud is represented by the upper areole which is situated in the axil of the tubercle, from which flowers, branches or offsets are produced, and is often furnished with wool or hairs or bristles. In *Coryphantha* this areole or bud is situated in a groove on the upper side of the tubercle. The lower areole is situated on the top of the tubercle and is furnished with spines or bristles, and often also with wool. This areole on the tip of the wart is not a true bud, but in certain circumstances is transformed into an adventitious bud, and may give origin to branches, offsets or new plants. In these cases it is by no means rare to be able to propagate the plant by planting these tubercles as cuttings. This happens frequently in the case of species of *Dolichothele, Mammillaria plumosa, M. Schiedeana* and others. In *Neowerdermannia* both areoles exist in the axil of the wart, so that the tuft of spines and the flowers seem to be inserted between the warts, but in reality both the upper and lower areoles are united to form one areole in the axil of the wart, some way up the stem, so that it looks as if it were inserted between two warts. In *Encephalocarpus* and *Obregonia* the globular stem is furnished with short leaf-like scales, and in *Ariocarpus* the tubercles have a leaf-like fleshy appearance. In these cases there are no areoles with spines, although in *Obregonia* the spines exist and soon drop off, but in the axil of the tubercles there is always a bud-producing areole, from which issue the flowers at the top of the stem.

In *Leuchtenbergia principis* the tubercles are very much elongated and prismatic, up to 12 cm. or more in length, with both areoles joined together at the tip of the tubercle, the lower or outer areole being furnished with long papery spines, and the upper or inner bears the exquisite large yellow flowers. In this case the stem may branch either dichotomously or by the formation of adventitious buds at or near the base. Here again the long prismatic tubercles are really modified leaf-stalks (petioles) or even modified branches and in certain circumstances, when cut and planted, may give origin to a young plant, from the inner or flower-bearing areole.

The stem of *Opuntia* is always a typical joint, whether it is globular, or cylindrical, or flattened. The *joint* is therefore a stem which when properly formed ceases to grow at the apex, but continues to grow in size and thickness until it reaches its full development, and then the rudimentary fleshy cylindrical leaves drop off, and the spines grow to their full size. The joint continues to grow at the apex in the cristate forms and in a few species with cylindrical stems, such as *Opuntia pachypus, O. cylindrica,* etc. The joint produced at the very *apex* of a flat joint is very generally flattened at right angles to the flat surface of the joint on which it grows; the surface of the joints produced from the areoles along the margin being usually more or less in continuity with the surface of the joint which produced them.

However, the term *joint*, is also correctly applied to the branches of *Cerei* in general, or even to the various portions of the stem, produced in successive seasons or years, and showing a more or less marked constriction at the spot where growth had commenced. This is particularly noticeable in the stems and branches of species of *Hylocereus* and *Heliocereus*, but the same arrangement exists also in most other allied genera.

The *Leaf* is fully developed and more or less leaf-like and permanent in the genus *Pereskia* and also in *Pereskiopsis*. In certain Opuntias, such as *O. subulata*, it is large, fleshy, cylindrical or awl-shaped, and almost permanent. In other species (*O. imbricata*, *O. versicolor*, *O. floccosa*, *O. vestita*, *O. neoarbuscula*, etc.), the leaf is more or less of the same shape, but much smaller, and drops off when the joint is fully developed. In *O. Verschaffeltii* and *O. teres* the leaf is also small, but persists almost until the following spring. The leaf is fugacious or entirely missing in many other species of *Opuntia*, and is missing or reduced to very minute scales in most other species of Cactaceae. In fact, in most Cacti the leaf is of no importance whatever for the purposes of identification.

The *Spines* are absent in a few speceis of Cactaceae, and then their place is usually taken by bristles or hairs. Species of *Ariocarpus*, *Encephalcarpus*, *Lophophora*, *Aztekium*, *Astrophytum myriostigma* and *A. asterias*, as well as some speceis of *Opuntia*, species of *Epiphyllum*, *Zygocactus*, *Rhipsalis*, etc., are practically spineless. In Cactaceae the spine is an epidermic or superficial production. and is not connected with the woody tissues of the plant. It is therefore not a *true spine*, but a *thorn*, equivalent to the thorn of the Rose; but although incorrect, I am retaining the term spine, now very generally adopted in popular parlance.

Spines are of two types. The real spines, which according to the species, may be of any length from less than $\frac{1}{2}$ cm. to 15 cm. or more, may be of various shapes, flexible or even papery in texture, or very stiff and almost as hard as iron. They may be acute and needle-like, or almost blunt, cylindrical, flattened, prismatic or angular, subulate or awl-shaped, tortuous, arched, or hooked at the tip, smooth or rough or striated longitudinally, or ringed transversely, sheathed or even barbed. They may be glassy or diaphanous, or of various shades of white, yellow, grey, brown, purplish, red and black, or even zoned in various colours. Their function is mainly defensive against grazing animals, but they are useful also for the dissemination of the species, the plants or stems or joints being easily transported over wide areas by the animals to which they may become attached. They undoubtedly afford some shelter to the plant from the scorching rays of the sun, their shadow continually moving across the stem, between sunrise and sunset. They are also a protection from hail, which may injure the stem and especially the tender growing apex, and in many cases they are also a very good protection against the ravages of snails, slugs, and many small herbivorous animals and insects. However, they afford no protection against Scale-insects and other minute parasites which attack many species of Cacti.

As already mentioned true spines are developed exclusively on the outer or lower areole or bud. On the inner or upper areole or true bud, just above the spines, are developed hairs which are flexible and silky or woolly in character, or bristles more or less stiff. Very stiff bristles, very irritating and penetrating, and often long and stiff enough to simulate spines, called *glochids*, are generally grouped together in bundles or cushions in the upper part of the areoles of *Opuntia*, and of species of the same sub-family or tribe *Opuntieae*. In the flowering season the flower bud emerges from the centre of this tuft of bristles, just above the spines. These bristles, stiff and penetrating and usually miscalled spines, easily attach themselves to the skin, causing at first a great deal of discomfort and irritation, but very generally they leave no after effects, and if they cannot be seized with a pair of pincers, they may be scraped off close to the skin, and in a few days they will grow out and disappear. Occasionally they give origin to minute pustules, which soon disappear when just touched with tincture of iodine. In some *Opuntias* these bristles may be quite large, stiff and spine-like, and up to $1\frac{1}{2}$ cm. long, and then they are just as formidable as spines, but are less prone to attach themselves to the skin and clothes, as bristles which are only 1 to 3 cm. long.

The ribbon-like and papery productions from the areoles of certain globular-jointed species of *Opuntia* (*O. diademata,O. Turpinii, O. platyacantha*, etc.), often up to 10 cm. long, are not real spines, and their significance is still a matter for discussion. They appear to be hairs, or rather single rows of long hairs, knitted together into a flat ribbon-like production, after the manner of the *ramenta* of the stems of Ferns. They are more freely produced from the areoles on the upper part of the joint, from which other joints originate. They are curios and also quite ornamental. Although these species of *Opuntia* have no spines, they have the usual tufts of bristles, more or less reddish in colour, deeply embedded in the substance of the joint, and just showing above the surface.

To the beginner and sometimes to older growers as well, the spines and bristles of Cacti are often a terror and a tiresome object of aversion. No doubt on this account many species are usually awkward to handle, particularly in the operations of planting and transplanting. For this purpose a pair of good leather gloves is recommended, and also the use of suitable tongs, by which the plant can be taken up and kept in position for planting. The tongs may be of iron or brass, with shafts 25 to 30 cm. long, and twice arched, the smaller arch near the tip, about 5 cm. long, and a larger arch just below it, about 12 cm. long, so that when the shafts are closed together, they will enclose two oval spaces, to hold stems or joints of varying size. I have found these metal tongs very useful, and more practical than the clumsy wooden pincers usually supplied by nurserymen on the continent.

The *Flower*. The perianth of Cactaceae is never sharply differentiated into calyx and corolla. The outer segments representing the sepals of the calyx, are very generally coloured and petaloid in character, externally passing off into a series of bracts, which may be green or sometimes coloured, and internally passing off into whorls of broader segments representing the petals. The segments of the perianth may be joined together only at the base, or they may be united together for some length, forming a tube of varying shape and length. They may be rounded, or lanceolate, acute or obtuse or acuminate, entire or toothed, or even frilled and almost feathery at the margin. The colour may be white, yellow, orange, pink, red, dark crimson, purple, violet, pale violet, or brownish, always with a beautiful metallic sheen, which is almost peculiar to the Cactaceae and Mesembryanthemaceae or Ficoideae, but is met with also in the Portulacaceae and in certain Ranunculaceae. The ovary is inferior, that is the flower with all its parts is inserted on the top or crown of the ovary, which occasionally is smooth, but very generally is covered with areoles, bracts, spines and hairs. It is generally round or oval, in certain species becoming elongated at maturity. The stamens are always very numerous, inserted at the base of the corolla, mostly on long slender filaments, with introrse anthers. The pistil is also filiform, about as long as the stamens or longer, and is surmounted by the stigma, which may be green or whitish, but is often of a lively colour, and is always divided into elongated pointed lobes, usually disposed star-like.

The *Fruit* is very generally a one-celled berry made of as many carpels as there are lobes in the stigma, with an equal number of parietal placentas. It is a dry capsule in the genus *Pterocactus*. The fruit in *Opuntia, Epiphyllum, Mammillaria*, etc., is indehiscent, but has a septifragous dehiscence in many species of *Cereus, Echinocactus, Astrophytum, Echinopsis*, etc. The seeds are generally large in *Opuntia*, but are often quite small or minute in other genera, and in the dehiscent species they are quickly preyed upon and spirited away by ants. In certain species the seeds are somewhat corky; in others (*Astrophytum*) they are boat-shaped or cap-shaped, oval and excavated; in others (*Opuntia*) they are round or flat, or kidney-shaped and hard; in *Pterocactus* they are winged. In size the flowers vary considerably, from the minute, mostly whitish flowers of *Rhipsalis*, often less than 1 cm. broad, to the enormous blooms of *Selenicereus Macdonaldiae, S. pteranthus, S. grandiflorus* and many others.

The fruit of many species is edible, and in none is it poisonous or even noxious taken in moderate quantities. The fruit of the cultivated forms of *Opuntia Ficus-indica*, the common prickly pear, is well known and appreciated in most subtropical countries. But for the presence of its objectionable seeds, it would be hard to beat as a nourishing and refreshing fruit. The surplus production is largely used for fattening cattle and pigs. There are several varieties varying in shape, colour and sweetness, and there are varieties with very few seeds, or with very small blackish abortive seeds. Other species of *Opuntia* cultivated as fruit trees, are: *O. streptacantha* or *O. cardona*, and *O. tuna*. The fruit of *Carnegiea gigantea*, the *Saguarro*, is relished as a delicacy by the natives; so also is the large fruit of *Hylocereus undatus* and of other species of *Hylocereus* and *Cereus*. The small bluish olive-shaped berries of *Myrtillocactus geometrizans* are regularly sold in the markets of Mexico under the name of *garambullos*. The red fruit of *Epiphyllum Ackermannii* and other varieties of Epiphyllum has a pleasant aromatic flavour and is diuretic. The small red fruits of *Mammillaria prolifera* and other species have a marked flavour of strawberries, along with a pleasant acidity.

The joints of *Opuntia Ficus-indica*, being almost spineless, are extensively used as fodder in subtropical countries, where the supply of green fodder in summer is always precarious. The few spines are easily rubbed off, or scorched over a fire. For this reason the plants of the prickly-pear close to the farmyards are often more valued for this reserve of green fodder than for the fruit itself.

The stems of *Selenicereus grandiflorus* and other species contain a glucoside, which, in the shape of an extract or tincture, is a diuretic and has a powerful tonic action on the heart. The flat mushroom-like stems of *Lophophora* (*Anhalonium*) *Williamsii* are topped and the tops dried and a string passed through, like a necklace, and are or were sold in the markets of Mexico under the name of *peyotle* or *mescal-buttons*, *mescal* meaning a mushroom, to which the topped stem is very similar. At certain Mexican or Aztek festivals these mescal buttons were moistened or cooked and eaten, for their powerful exhilarating and afterwards narcotic action, not unlike that of *Cannabis indica* or hasheesh, a practice which is now rightly prohibited by law. This narcotic action is due to the presence of alkaloids in the soft tissues of the plant, viz: lophophorine, mescaline and anhalonine. The name *mescal* or mushroom had long baffled those who were trying to find out the plant which produced it. They had long searched for a fungus, until they found that it was a spceies of Cactus.

The largest and finest flowers of the Cactaceae are mostly nocturnal. They bloom at sunset and display all their glory in the dark hours of the night, and droop and fade away at dawn—a pitiful reminder that "a thing of beauty" is not necessarily "a joy for ever." The flower of other species of *Cereus* remain in bloom for one day or even two days. Most species of *Echinocactus*, *Astrophytum*, *Echinocereus* and *Mammillaria* last in bloom for several days, the flowers closing up at night and expanding again in the morning. The flowers of *Epiphyllum* (*Phyllocactus*) remain in bloom for 3 to 5 days, those of *Nopalxochia* for about one week, and the flowers of *Zygocactus*, *Schlumbergera* and *Epiphyllanthus* last for eight days or more. The flowers of species of *Rebutia* and *Lobivia*, with their gaudy colours, last for several days; and the large trumpet-like flowers of *Echinopsis*, often delicately perfumed, last for about two days, unless killed off during the day by the scorching sun.

Like other plants, Cacti are of course propagated by seed, and this method of propagation is now extensively adopted for most species by continental nurserymen, as well as by many amateurs. In the case of many species of *Echinocactus*, etc., which rarely or never produce offsets, the only possible method of propagation on a large scale is by sowing. In other cases, Cacti can be propagated by offsets (*Echinopsis, Rebutia, Mammillaria* etc.) or by suckers or branches arising from the base (*Echinocereus, Trichocereus, Bergerocactus*, etc.), or by cuttings of the stem (*Cereus, Selenicereus, Lemaireocereus, Cleistocactus*, etc.). The *Opuntias* are easily propagated by seed, or by a portion of the stem with two or more joints, or with only one joint. In fact, a joint of *Opuntia Ficus-indica*, thrown on a heap of stones and rubbish, given good conditions of climate, will not fail to root and attain fruiting size in two or three years. In some cases propagation is also easily effected by cuttings or pieces of the roots, such as the thick nodose roots of *O. macrorrhiza* and other species, and also the roots of certain species of *Cereus, Echinocereus, Trichocereus, Myrtillocactus, Bergerocactus, Peniocereus, Pterocactus*, etc. From the areoles of the fruit of several species of *Opuntia* other fruits may develop, and often also small globular joints. These eventually drop off and soon take root and grow into young plants.

The stamens of most species of *Opuntia* and of many species of *Echinocactus, Mammillaria* and *Coryphantha* exhibit the phenomenon of irritability in a remarkable manner. These flowers mostly open only during sunshine and close again as soon as the sun ceases to shine directly on them, or even in cloudy weather, to reopen as soon as the sun comes out again. When these flowers are quite open the stamens spread out towards the petals. If the stamens are touched by an insect, or by the finger, during sunshine, they move quickly upwards and close upon the pistil, to expand again a few minutes after the cause of irritation has ceased. This phenomenon or irritability of the stamens is shared by many other plants in various manner. Thus in *Sparmannia africana*, a shrub from South Africa, the red and yellow stamens, which are erect in full sunshine, expand and become reflexed on the petals as soon as they are touched.

THE CLIMATE

Owing no doubt to their succulent nature, and to the absence of tender foliage, most species of Cacti are able to tolerate without much inconvenience lower temperatures than those obtaining in their native haunts. In fact, with the exception of the purely tropical species inhabiting the lowlands in tropical America, all Cacti will thrive well in the open air in Malta and along the southern shores of the Mediterranean and even in Sicily, southern Italy, Greece, the south and south east of Spain, and along the favoured districts of the French and

CACTI

Italian Riviera. The gardens at La Mortola have become famous for their large collections of Cacti and Succulents, and for the size and beauty of the specimens which are cultivated there in the open, with little or no protection in winter.

However, even in the favoured localities above mentioned, an open glass shed, constructed in a sheltered and sunny situation, is always useful for the protection of plants which are not yet perfectly established, or which are yet too young and tender, or which are tropical or subtropical species, which would be adversely affected even by a few days of rigorous weather in winter. These sheds serve also the useful purpose of protecting the plants from injury by a passing shower of hail, and of course plants thus sheltered can be much better regulated as regards the amount of water which they should have during the resting period of winter, than plants kept in the open and liable to be repeatedly soaked through by rain. On the other hand, repeated showers of rain offer the advantage of washing off from the soil the excess of soluble alkaline salts, which are usually present in small quantities in spring and well water, and which by the periodical watering throughout the summer, may accumulate in the soil to a dangerous extent.

Under these glass sheds, even if shaded off from the sun, the temperature may rise in summer to over 40°C. = 104°F., when the thermometer in the open, but in close proximity, may not show more than 30°C. = 86°F. In cold dull weather in winter the temperature in the shed may go down to 7° or 6°C. = 44 3/5° or 42 4/5°F., for a few days; but even in a short spell of frosty weather, the protection of the shed from cold winds and from the dispersal of heat by radiation is always sufficient to ward off any danger of frost in the clear frosty mornings of early spring, particularly if the plants are kept rather dry as they should be during their period of rest. The size and type of the shed will depend on the amount expended on it, and the size and quality of the collection which it is proposed to house. However, it is always advisable to make use of thick glass (at least ⅛ inch, or 3 to 4 mm.), which is less liable to be damaged by cats, the fall of twigs, etc. The glass should be properly shaded off from April to October. The usual method is to whitewash it on the outside, and there are in commerce green shadings to mix with the lime. These however are objectionable in the case of a shed meant for Cacti, as they obstruct the light too much. For the same reason the use of matting, or other shading material, is objectionable, except when used only by night and in the early morning, to prevent loss of heat by radiation. In the case of an open shed it is possible to whitewash the roof on the inside, as there is no danger that the light will be too much obstructed by the growth of unicellular algae in the moisture which may collect on the glass as a result of condensation of vapour in a closed greenhouse. Cacti sheltered under glass are liable to suffer from attacks of Scale-insects much worse than those kept in the open, and frequent sprayings with a suitable insecticide are necessary throughout the winter.

Glazed garden frames are also very useful where only small collections are kept, and instead of having large garden frames which may be inconvenient to handle, it is better to have several frames, 1 to 1½ m. wide, by 1½ to 2 m. long and 50 to 60 cm. high at the back. These frames should be opened by day in sunny weather in winter, to allow the evaporation of excessive moisture and the renovation of stale and humid air. For the rearing of seedlings, and the wintering of newly rooted cuttings and newly potted young plants in general, these frames will prove indispensable, even to those who have already large and well-appointed glass structures at their disposal.

In colder climates the frames will have to be stood on a hotbed, or some other arrangement made to secure a moderate but steady supply of heat. In such climates a glass shed would only be useful as a temporary shelter during late spring and early autumn. In fact, the shed would be too open and cold in winter, and in the warm and sunny summer months full exposure in the open, is generally speaking, far more beneficial to the growth and health of the plants than any shelter. Therefore in cold climates, or rather in climates with a severe and frosty winter, the construction of a suitable glass-house becomes imperative, unless the shed is constructed with movable glazed sides, which can be put on in winter. An ordinary lean-to greenhouse, if available, erected along a sheltered wall, with proper arrangements for ventilation, will do very well for the cultivation of Cacti, and is easily transformed into a serviceable hothouse by installing a small heating apparatus, just enough to raise the temperature by 5° to 10°C. = 9°F., during the coldest period of the year. For very tall or bulky specimens it is advisable to have another smaller but high-roofed house, for which special heating arrangements will have to be provided. It is not agreed what would be the minimum nightly temperature permissible in winter, which of course must vary according to the native country of the plants, as well as according to their size and condition. Resting plants can bear lower temperature than growing plants or plants which have not yet matured their growth. But a minimum temperature of 9°C. = 48 1/5°F. would be quite safe for all purposes. A fall of temperature below 8°C. = 46 2/5°F., is dangerous, especially if continued for several nights with clear frosty weather outside, or unless the thermometer rises to at least 10°C. = 50°F., for some hours during day time.

However, it should be remembered that there is quite a large number of Cacti which, during their resting period, will tolerate unscathed temperatures as low as, or below, the freezing point. In their native habitat these species are frequently covered with snow during winter. For these species a cool house, or even an open shed, will be sufficient, but of course this arrangement will not do for the subtropical and tropical species, which are easily affected by cold, or even if exposed to a cold wind for some time. Thus *Opuntia phaeacantha, O. Howeyii, O. Rafinesquei, O. rhodantha*, etc., are perfectly hardy in the cold winter, of Central Europe; but *O. microdasys, O. Herrfeldtii, O. rufida*,

O. Scheeri, etc., are liable to suffer severely if kept too much in the open, in the mild winters of the Mediterranean region.

In winter, and during the entire period of rest, all Cacti should be kept comparatively dry at the roots, and only just enough water given occasionally to prevent the soil and roots from getting thoroughly dry. The plants may be lightly syringed twice or thrice a week, and the occasion may be availed of now and then to apply by means of the syringe some medicated spray, containing a solution of some suitable insecticide or fungicide, both as a preventive and curative measure, as plants kept under glass, whether a shed, a greenhouse or a frame, are more prone to suffer from outbreaks of all sorts of pests and diseases than plants kept in the open air. Insect parasites, particularly Scale-insects, and also microbic and fungous diseases, are apt to be more troublesome than usual in late summer and autumn, and therefore the plants when taken into shelter should have a thorough cleaning and disinfection. Winter-flowering Cacti, such as *Zygocactus*, must continue to be watered regularly as long as they continue in bloom.

Before taking in the plants under glass in autumn, water should be withheld gradually after the middle of September, and all new growth allowed time to mature. In the process of "maturing" many plants will become somewhat shrivelled, but if not excessive, this shrivelling is only a sign that the year's growth is properly matured, and need not cause any alarm.

As a rule Cacti do not show signs of a revival of vegetative activity until spring is well advanced. In a few cases growth is started, at first very slowly, when the open air temperature stands at 12°C. = 53 3/5°F. The temperatures under glass during sunshine at midday hours will be then from 18° to 20°C. = 64 2/5° to 68°F. Most Cacti will start growth with an outside midday temperature of 15° or 16°C. = 59° to 60 4/5°F., and growth becomes active with a temperature of 20°C. = 68°F., and over. Many species of *Selenicereus*, etc., do not start growth before the close of May, when the thermometer stands at 24°C. = 75 1/5°F., and even then the first sign of vegetative revival consists in the slow formation of flower buds, along with a return of the stems to their former plumpness. It is only towards the close of June, with an open air temperature of about 28°C. = 82 2/5°F., that the development of the flower-buds becomes rapid, and new growth is also started. In the hottest days of summer, with a blazing sun in a cloudless sky, and a temperature of 30° to 35°C. = 86° to 94°F. in the shade, growth is often retarded, and sometimes the stems turn yellowish or develop scorchings which disfigure the plant, and later may become the seat of canker or rot. This is particularly noticeable in plants which normally prefer half-shade, and therefore these plants should be shaded off, or better, transferred to the half-shade of tall trees.

In continental Europe, as well as in England, Cacti and indeed all plants, are considered *hardy* if they can resist a few degrees of frost in the open. Of course, all these plants are also hardy in southern

Europe, where severe frost is rare or unknown, but many species which are perfectly hardy in southern Europe, have no chance of surviving the winter in the open in central and northern Europe. Even in southern Europe certain Cacti, such as *Selenicereus grandiflorus, S. Pringlei*, etc., which are normally quite hardy, if allowed to remain in open and exposed situations in exceptionally severe winters, may suffer considerable injury or be killed off altogether. These injuries usually become manifest in early spring, when the danger of a passing frost is mostly over; and for this reason it is always safer to give these plants the shelter of a glass shed or they may be placed along a sheltered wall or around the stem of tall leafy trees in sunny situations protected from cold winds.

Most epiphytic species requiring half-shade and a moist atmosphere during their resting period under glass are more in need of moisture in the atmosphere than of moisture at the roots, and the glass should be well shaded off. Species of *Zygocactus, Epiphyllanthus* and *Rhipsalis* will thrive well in permanent shade. On the other hand, a moist atmosphere, expecially if associated with moisture at the roots, will cause many other tropical and subtropical species to perish.

V
THE SOIL

It is essential that the soil for Cacti in general should be porous and permeable. The presence of stagnant humidity, especially in the case of plants in pots, is bound to result in disaster, often in less than a week, the plant apprently turgid and healthy rotting off with astonishing rapidity. For species inhabiting the pampas of South America, which are occasionally inundated in the rainy season, the use of a loamy soil, with the addition of a little clayey material is permissible, and indeed advisable, provided that the pot is well drained. Almost all species of Cacti thrive well in a porous calcareous soil, and there is a great number of species for which a calcareous soil is necessary. The lime in the calcareous material to mix with the soil, should not be in a readily soluble or cretaceous form. Lime mortar from old buildings, or hard limestones, or marble, or even crushed valves of oysters or other shell-fish, roughly powdered and passed through a sieve to remove the fine dust, provide an excellent material to add to the soil; so also is the rough sand or gravel collected in valleys passing through a district of hard limestone. A granitic material or gneiss roughly powdered, or river sand or gravel, or powdered half-baked bricks, might constitute a considerable part of the soil. To this a good allowance of fine garden loam, which always contains some clayey material, may be added, along with a suitable proportion of calcareous matter above referred to. Some old leaf-mould, thoroughly rotted, should always enter in varying proportions into the composition of the soil. Instead of leaf-mould, or along with it, it is possible and often advisable to make use of cow manure, provided that it is thoroughly rotted and in a powdery condition. This is obtained by leaving the manure exposed

C

to the action of the atmosphere for at least one year, occasionally spraying it with water and turning it over, until all traces of fermentation have disappeared. Manure thus treated, especially if it is 2 or 3 years old, besides losing all further power of fermentation, will lose also the greater part of the volatile nitrogen compounds which it contained, and becomes identical with old leaf-mould.

Fermenting organic material in any shape, including liquid manure, is a fertile source of trouble, when used in the cultivation of Cacti. Chemical fertilizers should also be avoided, especially for plants grown in pots, but small quantities of superphosphates, or of basic slag, or of powdered phosphatic rock may be given. Bone meal which contains also a good percentage of salts of ammonia, might be used, but very sparingly, or in very small repeated doses. It should be remembered that the humus of the leaf-mould, or of old manure, mixed with the soil, will fix the small quantity of atmospheric nitrogen necessary for the normal growth of the plant, and any attempt to force a quicker growth by an excess of nourishment, is generally resented by Cactaceae, and often proves disastrous. It is an excellent plan to have the soil thoroughly mixed and watered, and allowed to become mellow and mature for a period of about six months before using it. If sea-shore gravel or sand is used, for want of better material, it should be thoroughly washed and allowed to stand in fresh water for some time, frequently changing the water.

A word of warning is necessary in regard to the use of powdered brick or powdered charcoal. Instrinsically these are excellent materials, but should be used always mixed with other ingredients. A layer of charcoal dust or of brick dust sooner or later becomes impervious to the roots and also acts as a sponge retaining much water. Possibly, there is also a chemical reason for this action, as charcoal is known to absorb and fix atmospheric and telluric ammonia, which is gradually transformed into nitrates, which of course may mean an excessive storage of fertilizing material. A small quantity of crushed charcoal or of charcoal dust, mixed with the soil, helps to keep it porous and sweet, and is a very good preventive for acidity and sourness, and a recognized check on the development of worms.

The following are the various types of soil recommended:

Pereskia. Any good garden loam, 3 parts; old manure and crushed old mortar or limestone gravel, 1 part of each, and a small quantity of crushed charcoal.

Opuntia, Nopalea, Grusonia, Maihuenia. For *Nopalea* and for cylindrical and flat-jointed species of *Opuntia*, 2 parts good garden loam, 1 part crushed bricks or grit, 1 part crushed old mortar or limestone gravel, 1 part old manure and some crushed charcoal. A few species require a more sandy soil. For the globular-jointed species of *Opuntia*, and also for *Grusonia* and *Maihuenia*, garden loam and sand (or grit) 2 parts of each; limestone gravel or crushed old mortar, old manure and leaf-mould 1 part of each, and some crushed charcoal.

Wilcoxia, Machaerocereus, Bergerocactus, Rathbunia. Sand 3 parts, garden loam 2 parts, limestone gravel leaf-mould (or manure) 1 part of each, and some charcoal dust.

Arthrocereus, Heliocereus, Leocereus and *Peniocereus.* Sand and leaf-mould 2 parts of each; limestone gravel, finely crushed brick and powdered charcoal, 1 part of each.

Cleistocactus, Espostoa, Oreocereus, Borzicactus, Haageocereus, Binghamia. Garden loam 2 parts, sand, old mortar or limestone gravel and leaf-mould or manure 1 part of each, and some crushed charcoal.

Cereus, Cephalocereus, Pachycereus, Lemaireocereus, Harrisia and other Cereanae. Garden-loam 2 parts, old mortar or limestone gravel, leaf-mould or manure 1 part of each; some crushed charcoal may be added.

Hylocereus, Mediocactus. A soil rather rich in humus. Garden loam, sand, crushed bricks, leaf-mould and manure, 1 part of each. Some charcoal dust should be added. *H. undatus, H. trigonus* and others need less humus. Other species such as *H. Purpusii*, etc., and *Deamia* may have sand and leaf-mould 2 parts of each, crushed brick, manure and crushed charcoal 1 part of each.

Selenicereus, Aporocactus. Garden loam 2 parts, sand, limestone gravel or crushed old mortar, leaf-mould and manure 1 part of each. *Aporocactus* is best grafted on *Selenicereus.*

Echinocereus. Garden loam, sand, limestone gravel, leaf-mould and manure 1 part of each. A few species require more leaf-mould, others such as *E. Engelmannii*, require more sand and limestone gravel.

Austrocactus, Chamaecereus, Rebutia, Lobivia. Same as *Echinocereus*, with more sand and some crushed charcoal. Peat may partly replace leaf-mould.

Echinopsis. Garden loam 2 parts, sand or limestone gravel, leaf-mould and manure 1 part of each. For certain species (*E. calochlora* etc.), the compost should have 2 parts of sand to 1 part of loam. The addition of a little crushed charcoal is always useful.

All *Echinocactanae* dislike a too nourishing soil. Two good composts are the following: (*a*) sand 3 parts, garden loam 2 parts; hard limestone chips or grit or crushed bricks, limestone gravel, leaf-mould and manure 1 part of each; (*b*) garden loam and sand 2 parts of each, crushed bricks, crushed old mortar and manure or leaf-mould 1 part of each. Some roughly crushed charcoal should be added.

Species of *Stenocactus* require a little more leaf-mould, and species of *Ariocarpus* more sand.

Astrophytum, Echinomastus, Gymnocalycium. Sand 3 parts, limestone gravel or crushed old mortar, garden loam, leaf-mould or manure, 1 part of each. For *Astrophytum* the proportion of limestone gravel and garden loam may be increased and that of sand reduced. A little charcoal dust may be added.

Thelocactus, Neolloydia, Cochemiea and *Coryphantha.* A soil predominantly sandy and gritty, viz: 2 to 3 parts sand and grit, 1 part crushed old mortar or limestone gravel, 1 part garden loam and

1 part manure or leaf-mould. For *Neobesseya* and *Escobaria*, the soil may be more calcareous and less sandy.

Mammillaria. Garden loam 2 parts; sand, crushed old mortar or limestone gravel, leaf-mould or old manure, 1 part of each. For a few species the soil should be more sandy, for others more calcareous.

The *Epiphyllanae* (*Epiphyllum*, etc.), require a nourishing soil, rich in humus, made up of garden loam, sharp sand, crushed bricks, leaf-mould and old manure, 1 part of each. Some finely crushed charcoal or charcoal dust should always be added.

For *Rhipsalis* and allied genera, the compost may be made of equal parts of leaf-mould and sharp sand or finely crushed bricks, with the addition of some old manure and charcoal dust.

It is not to be supposed that the composition of these composts is absolute, and the grower may find it advisable and even necessary to vary the proportions according to circumstances, remembering that, in general, plants kept under glass for a considerable part of the year, require a more open soil and a heavier proportion of leaf-mould than plants kept in the open and in full sunshine. The main points to be considered are that the soil should be perfectly porous, and never allowed to become water-logged or boggy and sour, fairly rich in hard calcareous matter, and not too nutritious. It is not rare to see Cacti thriving very well in a mixture of two parts of sand or gravel to one part of old leaf-mould, with just a little powdered old mortar to supply the small quantity of lime required for the growth of the plant and the proper development of the spines. In whatever compost they are planted, it is always safer to keep the Cacti rather on the dry side, as if the roots do not become completely dry, they do not suffer in any way by withholding water. On the other hand, a soil which keeps moist, or which form a green coat or crust on the surface, is either badly drained or unsuitable, and should be changed without delay. Another type of soil to be avoided is that containing too much soluble salt of any description, especially common salt (chloride of sodium). Cacti planted in these alkaline or saline soils, after a brave but futile attempt to establish themselves, will rot off at the roots and soon perish altogether. There are very few species of Cacti, which owing to the close proximity of the sea in their native haunts, are able to tolerate without much injury, an excessively alkaline or saline soil.

It is useful to subject the soil to sterilization by heat, before using it for plants in pots. This precaution is still more advisable if the soil is not new, but has been wholly or partly used for the cultivation of other plants and particularly of Cacti and Succulents. The soil may be packed, somewhat moist, in closed metal cylinders, with two or more small openings for the exit of vapour and gases, and the cylinders are placed in an oven and brought to the temperature of boiling water for about one hour. By this means all insects and fungi, as well as their eggs and spores, are killed off, and the soil being cooled, and afterwards watered and exposed to the action of the air for at least ten days, may be stored in the pot shed for use when required.

In favourable climates Cacti are very suitable for planting out in the open ground, and particularly for planting in rockeries. For this purpose a site should be selected, sloping more or less steeply towards the south or the east, and well sheltered from cold winds. If the soil happens to be too stiff and unsuitable, it should be changed, and the site thoroughly drained by spreading out a subsoil of crocks, stone chips, rubbish or shingle or thick gravel, to a depth of 10 to 20 cm., the finer material being placed on the top. On this a specially selected or specially prepared soil is spread out to a depth of 30 to 45 cm. For a selection, the soil should be sandy and porous, well mixed with gravel or grit, and with much hard calcareous material roughly powdered, or crushed old mortar, with the addition of a liberal allowance of well-rotted leaf-mould or old cow-manure, or a mixture of thoroughly consumed mould from the garden refuse heap along with some old manure.

The laying out of the walks and of the masses of rocks forming the rockery, is a matter for the personal taste of the individual, and in this task much ingenuity is often exhibited, resulting in the formation of quite picturesque rockeries, very tastefully arranged. Preference is given to naturally weathered pieces of rock, irregular and of unequal size, and in building up the mounds or hillocks ample spaces should be left between the stones, where the plants could be inserted. It is advisable to have the upper surface of the stones sloping inwards, so that the rain may percolate deeply to the roots. The craggy weather-worn surface rocks from a limestone formation are often selected for this purpose, and indeed are very attractive, but the many holes, crevices and pockets which they usually have, although pretty to see, offer so many lurking places for snails and slugs, which may afterwards become a source of trouble. For this reason, also, the rock-work should be embedded for a few centimetres into the soil, in order that these molluscs, as well as wood-lice and millepedes, may find no place where they can hide. The spaces left between the pieces of rock are filled with soil, and in them the smaller Cacti and other Succulents may be planted. The presence of tall trees need not be considered as a disqualification in selecting a site for the construction of a rockery, provided that their foliage be not too thick to unduly shade off the ground, and provided that their stems be tall enough to allow a free circulation of air, and to admit a proper action of the sun's rays.

VI
PLANTING AND POTTING

The best time for planting and potting is just at the commencement of the growing season in spring, with an outdoor temperature of at least 14° or 15°C. = 59° or 60 4/5°F., and it is important that the condition of the soil be not too wet, and in any case it is always safer to place some dry soil beneath and around the plant. Planting in a dry soil entirely free from any fermenting material becomes a necessity if the roots have been damaged during the operation of transplanting, and in that case water should be withheld altogether for some days, to allow time for the wounded tissues to dry and heal, and for some time afterwards very little water should be given,—just enough to keep the soil very moderately moist, in order to promote the formation of new roots. Water may be given more freely later on, when the temperature is rising, and the new growth is developing. In many cases, particularly in the case of imported plants, the roots are so much damaged that they have to be cut clean off, close to the stem. This should be done always with a sharp knife, so that the cut will result in a neat wound, which heals more quickly and is less liable to become infected and start rot. A little charcoal dust over the fresh wound, and again when planting, helps to ward off infection.

Plants in pots may be transplanted at any time during spring and summer, even if growth is already started. The pots should be well baked, but porous. Any glazing or painting on the outside is sure to interfere with the proper exchange of air and the aeration of the roots, and therefore glazed or painted pots should be discarded altogether. As to shape or form, it is important to make use of pots well open at at the mouth or top. Pots with the diameter at the bottom only slightly smaller than that at the top should not be used. Pots so shaped are more difficult to drain properly, and retain moisture much longer, and Cacti planted in them are liable to become pot-bound in such a manner that the pot has to be destroyed in repotting. The roots of many Cacti have a marked tendency to adhere to the sides of the pot, particularly if the surface is somewhat uneven or rough. The use of new pots is always preferable, but old pots need not be discarded if they are well washed inside and outside, and afterwards well dried in the sun, or better heated in an oven, or otherwise disinfected. In transplanting Cacti it is a safe rule to use pots which are only just larger than those in which the plants had been growing. The hole or holes at the bottom should be so made as to secure the immediate draining off of all surplus water.

Long pots may be used only for species with long tapering or beet-like roots, such as species of *Ariocarpus, Lophophora*, and certain species of *Echinocactus, Thelocactus* and *Coryphantha*. On the other hand, shallow pots or pans may be used for many species of *Mammillaria, Echinocereus, Rebutia*, etc., and are also very convenient for transplanting and rearing seedlings, and for purposes of propagation generally.

The pots should be filled for about one-third with crocks or other drainage material, the larger curved pieces to be placed on the holes and bottom, and the whole topped over by a thin layer of thick gravel or shingle or crocks broken into shall pieces. Any other drainage material may be used, such as pieces of old mortar, broken bricks, chips of hard calcareous stone or marble, either alone or mixed with bits of charcoal. The scope is to keep the soil in the pot well open and drained, and therefore powdered material, such as powdered bricks or crocks, powdered charcoal and the finer sorts of gravel are un-

38

suitable, and far from facilitating drainage, may prove a source of danger. Cinders and spongy lava chips should not be used, as the roots may penetrate into them, and then get bruised or broken in repotting. The soil may be placed in the pot either directly on the crocks, or the uppermost layer of small crocks may be lightly covered by a thin layer of roughly broken peat.

If it is found that the roots have become pot-bound, it is advisable to break off the pot with a sharp blow, instead of risking damage to the plant in trying to take it out and save the pot. The plant to be repotted or transplanted into the open ground, should be kept rather dry in order that it may easily come off the pot with its ball of earth; the crocks at the bottom should then be removed with care, so as not to injure the roots, and if these have become quite pot-bound, the crocks man be removed by turning them out carefully with a pointed wooden stick. The plant should be replanted just as deep down as it was in its previous pot. It must never be planted at a higher level, and never lower down, except in special circumstances, such as if the plant happened to have its upper roots exposed or in case the stem was leaning too much on one side. The soil should be pressed down firmly around the ball of roots; or if there was no such ball and the roots were free, the soil may be well shaken down all round the pot. The stem should be planted as much as possible in a vertical position, and for aesthetic reasons is usually made to occupy a central position in the pot. However, experience has shown that small plants and seedlings, and also cuttings, are best planted close to the sides of the pot, as the young roots at once reach the side of the pot, spread out immediately and grow better and are less liable to rot from occasional excess of moisture. This practice of planting Cacti along the sides of the pot is now very generally adopted by nurserymen, and there is ample proof that the plants make quicker and healthier growth. In all cases dry soil should be used for repotting, or at least just enough moist not to lose the powdery condition of dry soil. Unless the soil is in a perfectly dry condition, newly potted plants should not be watered for two or three days, but just lightly sprayed once or twice a day, and placed in shade for about one week, and afterwards in half-shade for at least an equal period.

Imported Cacti, which had to be "matured" or "cured" before packing for shipment on a long voyage, generally arrive in a very shrivelled condition. On arrival they should be unpacked immediately, cleaned of all dead roots and dead parts and placed on a shaded shelf in the shed or greenhouse. They are arranged in a single layer, and preferably upside down,—that is with their roots upwards, as commonly practised for imported Orchids. There they may be allowed to remain for two to four days, spraying them once a day, or twice if the temperaature is already high and the atmosphere too dry. They may then be planted in a dry soil, and watered at once, if they had no new wounds on the thick roots, and generally they become well established in three to six weeks, and soon they become plump again, and start growing if the temperature is still favourable for growth. The practice of placing them in a shaded garden frame on a hotbed is also commendable, as they become established more quickly, but great care must be taken to ventilate the frames regularly, by day, to prevent the air from getting dangerously charged with humidity. In any case, the shading should not be dispensed with until the plants have become well established, and then they may be gradually accustomed to the sunshine, by removing the shading for a few hours every day, at first only in the morning or in the afternoon, shading again during midday hours.

In potting or repotting Cacti it is a safe rule to select the pots just large enough to contain the plant. Pots which are too large have two disadvantages. When watered they retain too much moisture, and retain it too long, so that it is a constant danger to the plant, and the drainage is also more liable to become clogged and imperfect. Moreover, the roots take too long to reach the sides of the pot and to spread along them, and this means a delay in growth and a further delay in flowering. The root-system of many Cacti (*Cephalocereus*, *Echino-cactus*, etc.) is astonishingly poor and undeveloped, and consequently growth is rather slow. These plants may well remain for four or five years in the same pot, without needing repotting, and indeed with the exception of the flat-stemmed Opuntias, which usually have a powerful root-system, there are very few Cacti which may require repotting every year or every two years.

Whatever care may be taken by the grower, accidents may happen, perhaps more than with any other class of plants, and a certain percentage of failures is sure to occur, particularly in the case of the more delicate or exacting species. With all due care in potting and cultivation, and with all due attention to keep down microbic diseases and insect pests, numerous seedlings, and also valuable plants and grown-up specimens, not easily replaceable, are often lost, and it is hardly fair to charge the grower with ignorance or carelessness. The grower should not allow himself to be discouraged by these occasional set-backs. Indeed, if all Cacti imported in Europe during the last sixty years had lived and prospered, the landscapes of Europe would have been more Mexican in character than the landscapes of Mexico.

VII
WATERING AND SPRAYING

Rain-water, whenever obtainable, should be preferred for watering and spraying Cacti, and indeed all other plants. It is out of place to point out here how rain-water in sufficient quantity can be collected and stored in underground tanks and reservoirs. Rain-water which had run over the surface of the ground, and become contaminated and unfit for drinking, has lost none of its qualities for watering or irrigation, unless it has become charged with alkaline or other salts dissolved on its way along the ground. In the absence of pure rain-water, water obtained from wells or springs may be used, provided that it does not contain more then mere traces of chloride of sodium and other alkaline salts. Water containing more than 1 per 1000 of chloride of sodium is already objectionable, and should be avoided altogether if the quantity of salt held in solution amounts to more than 3 per 1,000, or if it is too much charged with carbonate of lime. In any case, the water to be used for watering or spraying, should be allowed to stand for some hours in a butt or other receptacle in the greenhouse or shed, or in full sunshine, to become well aerated and to acquire the same temperature as the plants and the surrounding atmosphere. To water or spray the plants with water appreciably colder would induce a chilly condition in the roots and tissues of the plant, which may cause a check to the growth, and may also predispose the plant to the attacks of fungous diseases.

Watering is best done early in the morning at sunrise, or before the plants have had time to become heated by the sun; and the next best is late in the afternoon, about one hour after the sun had ceased to shine directly on the plants and these have had time to cool. The same rules apply for spraying and syringing. To water or spray in full sunshine is always dangerous and should be avoided altogether.

Water should be given only when necessary. The dry condition of the surface of the soil in the pot is not a sufficient reason to think that the soil lower down is dry and requires watering. Just one-half centimetre to one centimetre below the surface the soil may be still moist, and in a far better condition to promote the activity of the roots than it was immediately after watering. The fact that Cacti, being leafless plants, do not wilt their foliage as a sign that they are in need of water, is no doubt often a puzzling question to the beginner, but on the other hand, there is reassurance in the thought that whereas other plants with wilting foliage will soon die unless watered at once, Cacti even in real need of water will not greatly suffer if watering is postponed for a day or two. Until one has acquired a practised eye in this matter, it is safer to precede the watering by a superficial stirring of the soil, which will reveal at once whether the plant is or is not in need of water. When, although the surface of the soil looks dry, there is still a narrow margin of moist soil around the rim of the pot, that is sufficient proof that the pot is still moist, and watering should be postponed for one or two days, and even more in the case of large pots.

For many reasons, there can be no hard and fast rule as to the incidence of watering. On the whole, plants in a shed or in a greenhouse, are watered once a week in winter, and twice a week or even on alternate days in summer, and the same may be said in regard to plants in the open air in the shade or half-shade. During the dry and warm days of summer, plants grown in small pots and placed in full sunshine, may need watering almost daily. Large plants in comparatively small pots, or with a strong root-system will require watering more frequently; but those with weak roots or planted in rather large pots, should be watered only at long intervals in autumn, in winter and in early spring, and if placed in shade or half-shade, not more than once a week in summer. Certain species may require more moisture at the roots, particularly during their growing and flowering period. It is a sound practice, when watering Cacti in summer, to drench them thoroughly, so that a certain quantity of surplus water may come out of the drainage holes, and drain off with it any excess of salts, which if allowed to accumulate in the soil, may prove injurious.

Occasional waterings with dilute liquid manure were formerly recommended, and in some cases and under proper management have given good results, provided that drainage is always perfect and the manure has been previously thoroughly fermented; but the practice is often attended with too much risk to be safely recommended as a matter of routine.

In watering *Echinocacti*, *Echinopsis*, *Lobivias*, *Rebutias*, *etc.*, it is very important not to pour the water over the plant, as the depression at the top of the stem may retain sufficient water to cause the growing top or heart to rot off, particularly if the watering is done in the evening, and the water is retained in the depression overnight. Indeed, water should never be poured on the stems of any species of Cacti, except in spraying or syringing, unless one is sure of a speedy evaporation.

Spraying, or more properly syringing, is best done early in the morning. It should be done always very lightly, just enough to cover the plant with dew-like drops, without causing them to run together and trickle down the stem. Plants under glass or otherwise shaded off, may be syringed at any time of the day, but the water must have stood for some time in the shed or in full sunshine to get warm and avoid a chilling effect on the plants. Syringing is done preferably on days when watering is not due, but plants kept indoors in a dry atmosphere may be syringed every day in summer, and this to a great extent may replace watering.

During their resting period in winter, Cacti kept under glass should be watered very little or none at all. In most cases it is a sound rule to water only once a month, and then the plant should be thoroughly watered by the drenching or plunging in water. During the period of rest, the roots are quite inactive, and just enough moisture is necessary to prevent them from drying off altogether.

VIII
SOWING AND CARE OF SEEDLINGS

Strictly speaking, all Cacti can be grown from seed, but the seedlings of many species grow so slowly, and take so long to reach a convenient size, that they do not compensate the trouble and care bestowed upon them. However, there are numerous species which, under proper care, grow quickly enough, and in two or three years develop into quite nice plants. Nurserymen usually concentrate their attention on these last, as a sound commercial proposition, and rarely trouble themselves with the propagation by seed of the slow-growing species. As will be seen later on, the new method of seedling-grafting enables the grower to push on the growth of these slow-growing species to a remarkable extent.

A PRELIMINARY TALK ON CACTACEAE

Cacti can be sown successfully at any time from April to October, but it is advisable to wait until the rising temperature in the shade has reached 21°C. = 69 4/5°F. Seed sown earlier, or at a lower temperature, takes much longer to germinate, and may fail to germinate later when the requisite degree of warmth is reached. The hard seeds of species of *Opuntia* will germinate more quickly if soaked in warm water for two or three days before sowing. The seeds of Cacti will keep better if preserved in their husk or dried berry, but whether preserved in the husk or not, seed which is properly matured and kept dry in paper packets, will retain its germinating power for at least two years. Of course fresh seed germinates far more quickly and evenly, than seed which has been kept for some months or for one year.

The seed is best sown in pans or shallow pots, filled with small crocks for one-third or one-half of their depth. The soil for most species may consist of equal parts of old leaf-mould and sand, with the addition of powdered brick, or grit, or hard limestone gravel, a little garden loam to give consistency, and some charcoal dust. The pans or pots are filled with this soil up to three or four cm. from the brim, and the soil is evenly levelled and moderately pressed down with a piece of wood. The seed is then evenly distributed on the surface and pressed down into the soil. The seeds of species of *Opuntia* may be covered with a layer of the same soil to a depth of $\frac{1}{2}$ to 1 cm., according to its thickness, but the seed of other Cacti should not be covered at all with soil, but simply pressed down, and then covered with a thin layer of thick sand or coarse gravel or shingle, not more than 3 mm. thick. The seed of epiphytic species and of species with minute seeds may be mixed with a little loam, moistened, and daubed on a soft thin paper, about the size of the pan or pot, and then the paper is applied with the seed-bearing surface on the soil, pressed down and covered with a thin layer of gravel as mentioned. Watering should be done by placing the pan or pot in water, just deep enough not to allow the water to flow in over the sides. Subsequent watering is done by repeating the operation, whenever necessary, or by spraying or syringing very lightly, so as not to disturb the covering layer of gravel, and the soil should be kept permanently moist until germination is well advanced. Until the seed has well germinated the pan should be covered with a sheet of paper if the sowing is done in a greenhouse, or with a shaded pane of glass if the sowing is done in a shed or in the open. In some cases, and when quite fresh seed is sown, germination will take place within eight days, but is sometimes delayed for three weeks or more, and a few seeds will go on germinating successively for a year or more after sowing.

The seedlings of *Opuntia, Nopalea, Grusonia, Pereskia* and *Maihuenia*, develop on germination a fleshy stem with two well-marked, lanceolate, fleshy cotyledons, and in a comparatively short time the plumule between the cotyledons starts to grow into the characteristic stem of the species, with this difference, that the young stem is not a joint, but a true stem, which goes on growing in length during the first year, but after the first winter resting period may either continue to grow in length, or may break out laterally into joints.

Seedlings of *Selenicereus* have well marked triangular fleshy cotyledons; those of certain species of *Cephalocereus* and *Cereus* have thicker and more fleshy stems and smaller cotyledons. In other species the stem is oval and very fleshy, surmounted by two small jointed cotyledons, which become abortive or are absorbed as soon as the plumule develops into a tiny stem. In most species of *Echinocactus*, *Astrophytum*, etc., the thick oval stem of the germinated embryo terminates in two knobs, which represent the residue of the cotyledons; and in species of *Mammillaria*, *Coryphantha*, etc., of which the germinated embryo looks like a diminutive green pellet, there is hardly any trace of cotyledons, and the primordial stem is pushed up through the top of the pellet, at the opposite end of the radicle.

The development of seedlings is far from being equal in all species. Most species of *Opuntia*, with the exception of the globular-jointed species (*Tephrocactus* or *Sphaeropuntia*,) develop quickly enough, and are always sufficiently strong to be potted off singly when one year old. Certain species of *Mammillaria*, such as *M. elegans*, *M. Hahniana*, *M. rhodantha*, *M. Pringlei*, etc., may have a diameter of 1 to 2 cm. in about 12 months, and can also be potted off singly. Growth is also quick in *Astrophytum* and in certain species of *Echinocactus*, as well as in many species of *Cereus*, *Cephalocereus* and *Echinocereus*. On the other hand, it is very slow in many species of *Mammillaria*, *Rebutia*, *Lobivia*, *Haagea*, *Echinopsis*, etc., and therefore these species are well calculated to exercise the patience of the grower. Seedlings of *Zygocactus*, *Epiphyllum*, *Oreocereus* and *Leuchtenbergia* make fairly quick growth.

During their more or less slow development the seedlings of Cacti are very much exposed to the ravages of slugs and snails, of wood-lice, of many insects, and particularly to the devastating infection of fungi and microbes. It is comparatively easy to protect them from slugs and snails, and as regards other parasites, resort must be had to frequent syringing with insecticides (such as *purpusol*), and with fungicides (such as *chinosol*). The use of chinosol or some other safe but efficient fungicide as a protective treatment for seedlings should be adopted as a matter of routine throughout the year, and particularly in late summer and autumn. The inquisitive robin, and other small insectivorous birds, may occasionally visit the pans of seedlings kept in the shed or in the open, and unprotected by a pane of glass. These birds pick up quantities of seedlings and throw them about, probably mistaking them for insects.

It is not advisable to pot off the young seedlings too soon. The larger they are, the greater their chance of survival. It is therefore advisable not to pot them off singly until they are 1½ to 2 cm. in diameter, and in the case of *Cerei* and tall-growing species, unless they are 4 or 5 cm. high. Only very small pots should be used for the purpose, that is, pots not more than 5 or 6 cm. in diameter. Some thick gravel or shingle is placed at the bottom to secure good drainage, and the soil should consist of the same compost as that used for the grown up plant, but with the addition of a little more leaf-mould. The soil in the seed pan is allowed to become somewhat dry, so that the seedlings can be transplanted with greater ease, without injuring the rootlets. The seedling is planted either at the centre of the pot, or better close to the side, so that the rootlets may soon spread over the porous inner surface of the pot and reach the gravel at the bottom. The seedlings are then placed in a shaded frame and allowed to remain dry for one day before watering, which is best done by spraying. It is important to replant the seedlings neither deeper nor more superficially than how they stood in the seed pan.

It is sometimes necessary or convenient to plant the seedlings several together in larger pots, but these should be of a shallow pattern or pans, 10 to 15 cm. in diameter, and the seedlings are best planted along the side of the pot, 3 to 4 cm. apart. In about two years the seedlings planted in small pots, as above mentioned, will have made sufficient progress to be transferred into larger pots, and indeed will be already nice plants of commercial size, showing all the characteristics of the species to which they belong; and the same may be said in regard to the seedlings planted several together into larger pots, which of course must now be potted off separately.

It is often necessary to transplant seedlings when they are quite small, and not more than a few months old. This happens whenever the seed has been sown too thickly or the seedlings are too overcrowded, and have little chance of development unless they are properly distanced. The seedlings are transplanted into other seed pans, filled with a compost of the same type; the compost is pressed down firmly, and the seedlings are pricked off carefully with a penknife and replanted at regular distances, 2 to 3 cm. apart, all over the surface of the pan, including the sides. Their subsequent care is the same as that of seedlings in the original seed pans; but as the rootlets are always more or less injured during the operation, it is advisable to spray with chinosol solution immediately after watering. Occasional sprayings with chinosol solution, to be always performed after watering, and not before, should be continued for all seedlings, until they become strong enough to resist microbic infection. If the seedlings are not too overcrowded, owing to faulty sowing, they should not be disturbed, as their growth does not suffer from a little overcrowding.

IX
PROPAGATION BY CUTTINGS AND OFFSETS

Propagation by cuttings and offsets is at once a convenient and ready way of propagating most species of Cactaceae, and is also the only manner available of propagating valuable hybrids. There are a few species which, having a solitary short stem, cannot be propagated in this way, and there are also tall-growing species which do not branch readily unless topped, and the grower who has a fine tall specimen will hesitate before he is persuaded to top it, in order to use the topped part as a cutting, and in the hope that the stump will throw up side branches to be used later on for propagation.

Spring and summer,—that is from May to September,— is the best time to propagate by cuttings and offsets, but even in midwinter cuttings will not fail to strike root if allowed to dry for ten days or more before planting, and afterwards placed in a warm frame and kept rather dry. It is important that the frame or shed where rooting cuttings are placed should be warmer than the place where the original plant had stood at the time when cuttings were taken. It is also advisable to take the cutting with a bit of heel from the old stem, whenever this can be done without danger to the stem. Cuttings should be made always with a sharp knife, in order to have a clean cut. Breaking off a branch, in woody species, and then trimming off the wound of the cutting, is sometimes done; but this practice invariably results in a deep and lacerated wound of the stem, which is dangerous at all times, and particularly so in autumn and winter, when the wound heals with difficulty, and is liable to become the seat of extensive rot or gangrene. Offsets and suckers arising from the base of the stem or a little above it. should only be cut in summer. At other seasons of the year the wound made on the stem is likely to develop rot, and many a nice specimen is thereby lost.

The cuttings duly prepared are placed in an airy and well shaded place for a period of three days to one month or more, according to the size of the cutting and the time of the year, the time being longer in spring, and shorter during the warmest period of summer. For delicate species the soil should consist either of pure sharp sand or mixed with a little old leaf-mould; but for most species the same compost as used for grown up plants may be used for rooting cuttings. All cuttings must be shaded off until they are well rooted,—that is, until they become plump again or start to make new growth,—and in the meantime water should be given very sparingly, even during summer.

Cuttings of *Opuntia, Nopalea, Grusonia, Maihuenia, Epiphyllanthus, Zygocactus, Schlumbergera*, etc., must consist of at least one joint; cuttings of two or more joints are better, as the lower joint which will be buried in the soil for one-half or one-third of its length, being about one year older, will be more mature and strikes more easily. *Opuntia brasiliensis, O. bahiensis* and *O. argentina* have a tall cylindrical stem or leader, and flat-jointed side branches; cuttings made of these flat joints will strike root as usual, but often fail to throw up a leader.

Cuttings of *Cerei*, including *Monvillea, Harrisia, Selenicereus*, etc., may be made by dividing the stem into convenient lengths, allowing them to dry for three days to three weeks according to season, and then planting them separately in small pots in a very sandy soil with a little old leaf-mould or old cow manure and some grit or gravel. They are kept rather dry until rooted. Thick-stemmed *Cerei* (*Pachycereus, Lemaireocereus, Piptanthocereus*) should be allowed to dry for a longer period, until the wound is well healed, and it is always better to take the cuttings at a joint, where the stem is constricted. Cuttings of the branching species of *Cephalocereus, Espostoa, Myrtillocactus, Neoraimondia*, etc., are dealt with in like manner. Cuttings of species of *Hylocereus*, which have triangular-jointed stems, should consist of one or more joints, the cut being made across the narrowest point between one joint and another. It should be remembered that in any case the smaller the wound, the sooner it heals, and the chance of infection is less. Cuttings of certain species, such as *Pachycereus Pringlei, P. pecten-aboriginum*, etc., root with difficulty, often requiring more than a year to be properly rooted.

The branching species of *Mammillaria, Lobivia, Rebutia, Pelecyphora, Solisia*, etc., are easily propagated by division of the rootstock. Thus large clumps can be divided into smaller clumps, or even into separate heads. Of course in order to do this the original large specimen, representing the growth of many years, has to be sacrificed, and this is a serious objection with amateurs, who naturally prefer to have two or three large specimens of exhibition size, than many smaller plants. This objection may be partly met by removing only a few heads from the original clump, and the occasion may be availed of to reduce the clump to a more regular shape. This operation must always be done in summer. In all these cases, the wounds made both on the mother plant and on the cutting are mostly large, and therefore should be made as neatly as possible and properly dried, and watering must be done most carefully for some time afterwards, in regard of both the mother plant and the cuttings taken from it. These cuttings are rooted in sand, or sand mixed with leaf-mould and a little charcoal dust, and are placed in a warm but well-shaded frame.

Cuttings of *Epiphyllum* are best taken across the broad part of the flat stems, as plants grown from such cuttings sucker and flower more freely. Cuttings of *Epiphyllum* and *Rhipsalis* are easily rooted in a mixture of sand and leaf-mould.

Species of *Trichocereus, Cleistocactus, Borzicactus, Echinocereus, Mila*, etc., producing suckers or branching from the base or from the lower part of the stem, are best propagated by separating the suckers when they have reached a length of at least 10 cm., and success is all the better assured if the suckers have already some rootlets of their own. They are best separated with a sharp-pointed knife, and a clean cut made. The subsequent treatment is the same as mentioned for *Mammillaria* and *Lobivia*, with this reminder, that the process for drying and healing the wounds should be always carefully attended to. It is also to be remembered that as these species naturally delight in full sunshine, the cuttings should be left in the shade only long enough to root properly.

Most species of *Echinopsis* are easily propagated by means of the offsets which are produced all round the stem and nearly up to the top. These offsets are allowed to reach a diameter of at least 3 cm. and then they are easily knocked off or cut off, and potted off forthwith. Under ordinary treatment they rarely fail to strike root; indeed in some instances (*E. nigricans*, etc.), the offsets develop rootlets when they are yet attached to the mother plant, and hardly more than 1 cm. in diameter. Certain species rarely or never produce offsets, and these can be propagated only by seed. Many species of *Malacocarpus, Notocactus, Gymnocalycium, Coryphantha*, may be propagated in the same way, by means of the offsets or suckers thrown up around the base or the lower part of the stem.

Cuttings unavoidably made out of season, late in autumn or in winter, require very careful treatment in the matter of drying or seasoning for planting. They should be placed on an airy and shaded shelf in the shed or greenhouse for a period of two weeks to one month or more, according to the thickness of the stem, and then planted in a dry sandy soil, with the addition of a little leaf-mould, and placed in a warm sunny frame and kept dry for a few days more. At first just enough water is given to moisten the soil around the cutting, and subsequent waterings should be at long intervals, of one week or more, and never abundantly, but may be syringed lightly about twice a week.

A few species which have a large fleshy root, mostly branched like the roots of a Dahlia, such as *Pterocactus* and *Peniocereus*, can be propagated by division of the rootstock and offsets, as well as in the ordinary way by cuttings of the stem. The division of the rootstock is a delicate and hazardous operation, and had better not be attempted, as these plants are so easily propagated by cuttings or by grafting. The separated offsets, after being allowed to dry for a few days on an airy and shaded shelf, are planted in a mixture of equal parts of sand, leaf-mould, powdered brick with the addition of some loam and old mortar. They are stood in a warm shaded frame and kept rather dry, until new growth is well started. The nodose roots of certain species of *Opuntia*, as well as the underground suckers of *Bergerocactus Emoryi*, can be used in the same manner for the purposes of propagation.

It is well known that many species of Crassulaceae, etc., are easily propagated by means of leaves which, separated from the stem and planted or simply placed on the soil develop adventitious buds and roots at the point where their vascular bundles were connected with those of the stem. In like manner the warts or tubercles of certain species of *Mammillaria* and *Dolichothele*, and of *Leuchtenbergia principis*, which are in reality leafless petioles, may develop adventitious buds and grow into new plants. It is not to be expected that every tubercle thus planted will produce a new plant; but tubercles which are cut off neatly with a sharp penknife, properly dried and seasoned in the shade, and planted in pure sand in a shaded frame, will yield a good percentage of small plants, which however take a long time to grow, and therefore this method of propagation for the species of Cacti above mentioned, is hardly of practical value.

X
PROPAGATION BY GRAFTING

Grafting affords a popular and very useful method of propagation, although strictly speaking grafting does not imply an increase in the total number of individual plants, but rather the transformation of a number of individuals of one species into individuals of other species or varieties, both the stock and the scion retaining unaltered all their distinguishing characteristics.

Theoretically any species of Cactus can be grafted on another Cactus, but apart from the fact that strong-growing species cannot be grafted successfully on species with slender stems and of weak growth, there is also the question of greater or less affinity, which is a sufficient explanation of what is so frequently noted in practice, viz: that one species unites better and thrives better when grafted on one stock than on another. There is also the other difficulty, likewise frequently met with, viz: that the scion may unite quickly and well on one type of stock, but fails to thrive so well on a stock of the same species but of a different type. Cases are also not unknown in which a scion grafted on a given type of stock unites well and at first thrives very well, but after a short time ceases to grow and gradually perishes, and the stock may even perish along with the scion, for no apparent reason whatever.

It is a general rule that when a weak-growing species is grafted on a stock of a strong-growing species, the weak growing species improves markedly in vigour and, on the other hand, the strong-growing stock shows signs that the vigour of its root-system is weakened. A strong-growing species grafted on a weak-growing species very generally has its growth greatly weakened, but there is rarely any marked increase in the vigour of the root-system of the species used as stock.

Cacti are never propagated by *budding*, although this operation is possible in theory, and in many cases quite practicable; but satisfactory results are obtainable only in a few instances, and at any rate grafting is far more practicable, and good results are far better assured. Of course, in the case of Cacti, budding is only a reduced form of grafting, in which one or more buds with a small piece of the stem attached to it is inserted in an equivalent cavity made neatly in the stem of the stock, and tied rather tightly for about ten days.

Although fundamentally the same, the forms of grafting vary according to the type of scion and stock, and reference is here made only to those forms which are in general use and which have proved entirely satisfactory in practice.

Selenicereus, *Aporocactus*, *Wilcoxia* and other slender-stemmed species, with a cylindrical or almost cylindrical stem, are grafted by *wedging*. The scion is cut in the shape of a wedge and is inserted in a cleft made across the topped end of the stock, which may consist of another species of *Selenicereus* of vigorous growth, and among these the most recommendable is perhaps *S. Macdonaldiae*, but other species, such as *S. hamatus*, *S. Kunthianus*, *S. pteranthus*, etc., also give good

D

results as stock. This graft may take the form of an *inverted wedge*,—
that is, the top of the stock is cut as a wedge, which is inserted in a
cleft made across the lower end of the scion, or better in a wedge-
shaped cavity made on the cut lower end of the scion to fit on the
wedge-shaped top of the stock. It is not at all necessary that the
diameter of the scion be equal to that of the stock, but it is convenient
not to have it larger. Should the stock be too slender to receive the
wedge-shaped end of the scion without undue pressure and risk of
breaking, it is advisable to practise upon it a V-shaped hollow of the
same length as the wedge on the scion, but slightly narrower, so that
when the scion is inserted, the cut sides will be applied somewhat
tightly on the sides of the hollow. The scion is best inserted in the centre
of the stock, so that the vascular bundles of the core of the stem of
both stock and scion may come in contact, but this precaution is by
no means necessary. It is, however, very recommendable that the edge
of the wedge should reach down to the bottom of the cleft or the
V-shaped hollow made in the stock, in order to secure a perfect union
and sturdier growth. In all these cases the scion is kept in place by
means of a slender spine driven across both scion and stock. The spine
may be allowed to remain in place for about eight days in summer,
and for a longer period in winter, and may then be removed by turning
it round and pulling it out.

Species and varieties of *Zygocactus, Epiphyllanthus, Epiphyllum*
(*Phyllocactus*) and *Schlumbergera* do very well when grafted on
Selenicereus Macdonaldiae or on *S. hamatus*. They are also grafted with
good results on *Cereus triangularis* and on flat-jointed species of
Opuntia, chiefly *O. Ficus-indica*. However *Schlumbergera, Chiapasia*
and most species of *Epiphyllum* and *Nopalxochia* thrive best on *Cereus
triangularis*. Grafting on the species of *Hylocereus* is done by slitting
the upper part of the margin of one or more ribs or wings, and
inserting deeply in each of the clefts thus made a scion cut like a thin
wedge, to be kept in place by means of a slender spine passed from side
to side across both stock and scion. Sometimes a pin is used instead
of a spein, but a pin rusts too quickly, and should be pulled out after
two or week days, otherwise the rust left in the wound may provoke
the development of rot. For this use in grafting the sheathed or barbed
spines of many species of *Opuntia* are objectionable, and the long and
slender, but stiff spines of various species of *Cereus, Trichocereus* and
Cephalocereus are to be preferred, and should always be wiped on a
clean cloth, or pricked deeply into a large joint of a prickly pear or
common species, before insertion in place to fix the scion to the stock.

Chamaecereus, Pterocactus, Peniocereus, Wilcoxia and the slender-
stemmed cylindrical species of *Opuntia*, may be grafted on rooted
joints of *O. Ficus-indica* or other species, or on rooted cuttings of
Cleistocactus or *Nyctocereus*. The lower $\frac{1}{2}$ to 1 cm. of the scion is
peeled off with a penknife and a neat cut made at the end. A hole a little
wider than the thickness of the scion and 1 to $1\frac{1}{2}$ cm. deep, is made at
or near the apex of the joint used as stock, or on the cut surface of the

topped *Cerei*, and all broken up tissue removed carefully from the hole, using for this purpose the narrow blade of the penknife. The scion is then inserted deeply into the hole, and if necessary kept in place with a spine.

For the grafting of *Cephalocereus*, thick-stemmed *Cerei*, *Oreocereus*, *Espostoa*, *Browningia*, as well as for most species of *Echinocactus*, *Coryphantha*, *Lobivia*, *Melocactus*, etc., the best stock and most in use is *Trichocereus macrogonus*, *T. Spachianus*, *T. Schickendantzii* and *Harrisia Jusbertii*, the first and last being preferable for thick-stemmed scions. The graft is made by a clean horizontal cut across the top of the stock, and another clean horizontal cut is made across the base of the scion, both cut surfaces are joined together, giving to the scion as much as possible a central position, so that the core of both stock and scion may be in contact. The scion is kept fixed to the stock by a moderate pressure, exercised either by tying down the scion with a string, which is passed over the scion and underneath the pot, or by some other means which may be found convenient. Another ligature made crosswise or at right angles to the first is often necessary to keep the scion well in place. In order that the string or other material may not press unduly on the top of the scion, it is advisable to put a small folded piece of cloth, or a bit of lint on the top of the scion before tying down. The ligature or other mode of pressure may be allowed to remain for about one month, to secure a perfect union, but it is often possible to remove it earlier. It is generally advisable to trim back or bevel the ends of the cut ribs of both stock and scion, in order that their projecting ends may not interfere with the close union of the scion to the stock. The cut ends of stock and scion instead of being horizontal, may be inclined at an angle of 45°, and this fluted graft or tongue-graft will permit the scion to be tied directly to the stock, as is often done when grafting certain fruit trees, and the additional ligature over the scion and underneath the pot will ensure a more perfect union, which may be still further secured by sticking a long slender spine horizontally through both scion and stock.

Instead of making a clean horizontal cut, the lower end of the scion may be cut in the shape of a cone or an inverted pyramid, and inserted in a corresponding cavity made into the upper end of the stock. The scion is then tied down in the usual manner. This form of grafting, besides ensuring a more perfect union, also prevents any accidental movement of the scion when the pot is moved or hit or otherwise handled, and is particularly useful when grafting globular or oval-jointed *Opuntias* on the stocks above mentioned or on other species of Opuntia. There is also the inverse process by which the cone or the pyramid is practised on the stock and the corresponding cavity made at the base of the scion. Instead of a ligature, it is often more practicable to make use of a bit of copper wire, curved V-shaped, and pressed down firmly across the scion and down into the soil. A piece of lint placed over the scion will prevent possible injury by the wire. Union will take place in about one week.

Very slender-stemmed species, such as the cylindric-stemmed *Rhipsalis*, may be grafted on practically any species of Cactus. They are best grafted by puncturing, or burrowing into, the upper or growing end of the stock (and in this case the horizontal cut is not needed), and inserting the lower end of the scion, which has been deprived of the epidermis or outer bark. Flat jointed species of *Rhipsalis*, such as *R. rhombea, R. Houlletiana*, etc., are dealt with exactly like species of *Zygocactus*, and the same remark applies in the case of *R. paradoxa* and *R. trigona*, although of course most species of *Rhipsalis*, as well as the pretty *Rhipsalidopsis rosea*, grow just as well on own roots and are rarely grafted. Here it is worth while to point out that those species of *Rhipsalis* which normally throw up straight wand-like leaders and have flat-jointed side branches, should be propagated by cuttings of the leaders, as plants raised by rooting or grafting the side branches rarely throw up leaders and usually have a poor development.

Continental nurserymen very generally graft species and varieties of *Zygocactus* and *Schlumbergera* on rooted cuttings of *Pereskia grandifolia* and *P. aculeata*. However, experience has shown that in southern Europe these grafts on *Pereskia*, made in the open air, although they unite well, do not thrive well, and never grow into such magnificent specimens, often over 60 cm. across, bearing annually several hundreds of flowers, as they do when grafted on *Selenicereus Macdonaldiae* or on *Cereus triangularis* or *Hylocereus undatus*.

Opunia clavarioides is grafted successfully on flat-jointed species such as *Ot. Ficus-indica* and also on *Harrisia Jusbertii* and *H. pomanensis*, etc. The graft is made as in the other round-stemmed species.

The flat-jointed *Opuntias* are best grafted on the stronger flat-jointed species. The graft is made by cutting the scion,—which should consist of one joint, and never of more than two joints,—wedge-like on the flat sides, but close to the base of the joint, and inserting this edge deeply into a wedge-shaped cut, made by removing an equivalent or slightly thinner wedge across the central part or apex of the stock, so that when grafted the flat sides of the scion shall be at right angles to the flat sides of the stock. The wedge end of the scion is deprived of all trace of epidermis which may still be attached and is inserted deeply into the cut, down to the bottom, in order to obtain a quick and perfect union, and the scion may be fixed in place by inserting a long slender spine through the upper edge of the stock and across the scion. By smearing a little loamy mud on all exposed cut parts of the stock and scion in this graft, and in grafts of similar nature, evaporation is excluded or moderated, and excessive shrinkage is thereby avoided. This excessive shrivelling may cause the scion which was intimately in contact with the stock, to become separated, notwithstanding the presence of the spine to hold it in place, and of course this will cause the graft to fail.

The seedlings of many species of Cacti (*Notocactus, Malacocarpus, Gymnocalycium, Parodia, Frailea, Porfiria, Lobivia, Rebutia*, many species of *Mammillaria*, etc.), usually grow too slowly, but by the new method of grafting seedlings, their growth is pushed on very remarkably, so that grafts one year old are often as large as seedlings 4 or 5 years old. Moreover as seedlings are very liable to perish during the first year of their life, by grafting them when still very young, this danger is greatly reduced and almost entirely eliminated. These seedlings are best grafted in late spring and in fine dry weather, when they are about one year old, and the stock may consist of larger and older seedlings of more robust species, or any other stock of suitable size, raised from cuttings or offsets. The stock, whatever it may be, is topped neatly across the central axis, and the seedling is likewise cut across just above the root, where the stem is at least 3 mm. thick. The cut is made with a very sharp and clean penknife, and the graft or scion is placed centrally on the topped stock. There are several devices how to keep the small scion firmly in place for one to three days, until it is perfectly united to the stock. The following method is both simple and effective. A soft cork or a piece of soft rubber, or some other resilient material, such as the pith of *Ferula communis* or of *Agave americana*, cut into pieces 1 to 1½ cm. thick and 2 to 3 cm. long, is used for the purpose, and a very shallow depression is scooped at one end, to place on the scion and gently press it down. At the other end is fixed a curved bit of wire, the free and longer end of the wire to be inserted deeply into the soil, to press down the cork and keep it in place.

Grafts made during the period from October to April inclusively, which in our climate corresponds to the period of cold and rest, are very liable to rot and fail. If it is necessary, occasionally, to graft during this period, is is important to place the graft in the warmer atmosphere of a good frame or of a hothouse, so as to start to some extent, an active action of the roots, and to avoid wetting the graft with sprayings. Later on when the days become warmer and longer, the graft may be removed to its place in the shed.

As a rule it is not advisable to start grafting unless the day temperature in the shed or greenhouse, at least for several hours of the day, stands at 18°C. = 64 2/5°F.; indeed for most species the optimum of temperature for grafting appears to be between 20° and 25°C. = 68° and 77°F., in the open air, with a temperature of about 30°C. = 86°F., in the shed or the greenhouse during the day, although higher temperatures do not seem to be in any way detrimental to the success of the operation. Much more important is the degree of humidity in the atmosphere, a rather dry condition of the air being conducive to an early healing of the wound and exposed surfaces, and to a perfect union of the graft. Oh the other hand, an atmosphere with over 70° of humidity is dangerous, particularly in late summer and early autumn, when south and south-easterly winds, hot and laden with moisture, create favourable conditions for the development of rot or gangrene in fresh wounds on all succulent plants. Even in a greenhouse or frame, an atmosphere with 70° of humidity constitutes a menace, and immediate ventilation become necessary.

XI
CRISTATE FORMS AND OTHER MONSTROSITIES

The more common forms of Cactus monstrosities met with in commerce, are the so-called "cristate" forms. These consist very generally of malformations due to the phenomenon of fasciation, a phenomenon common to many other plants, by which the terminal or growing point or bud divides and sub-divides itself into numerous buds, resulting in very irregular and often grotesque growths. Fasciated plants often produce flowers, but these are generally reduced in size, and are usually defective or malformed, seldom producing fertile seeds; and the fertile seed may reproduce the same fasciation, or the seedling may revert to its normal condition. Moreover fasciated or cristate Cacti quite often revert to their normal growth, wholly or partly. Cristate forms are therefore propagated exclusively by grafting or by cuttings, and at present a collection of Cacti is hardly considered complete without a few examples of fasciation.

There are few species of Cacti which are not known to be liable to fasciation, and beside the few scores of cristate species and varieties obtainable from dealers, there are many others which are met with in a wild state, but have not yet found their way to the commercial grower. Other sorts, being too large and unwieldy, are somewhat difficult to propagate by cuttings, and still more so by grafting. Obvious examples of these last are the large cristate forms of species of *Echinocactus*, and the not less wonderful fasciation of *Cephalocereus senilis* and *Carnegiea gigantea*. Others are of more convenient size, and being also more easily propagated by cuttings or by grafting, are preferred by nurserymen and growers.

The fasciation may be either *irregular*, developing from all buds around the stem, and in this case the resulting monstrosity will consist in an uneven growth, developing into a rock-like mass; or may develop along one diameter only, from the marginal buds, and the stem will then develop into a fan-like growth, which becomes more or less wavy and irregular with age, often growing into numerous convolutions like the coils of a snake. Common examples of the first case are the monstrosities of *Cereus peruvianus*, *C. pitahaya*, *C. formosus*, *C. chalybaeus*, *Trichocereus candicans*, *Cephalocereus senilis*, *C. Palmeri*, etc. Examples of the second case are the cristate forms of *Rebutia minuscula*, and other species of *Rebutia* and *Lobivia*, many species of *Echinopsis*, most species of *Mammillaria*, *Aporocactus*, *Notocactus scopa*, *N. Graesneri*, *Cephalocereus niger*, etc. To the same type belong generally the monstrosities of species of *Echinocereus*, and of species of *Opuntia*, such as *O. bernardina*, *O. cylindrica*, *O. vestita*, *O. floccosa*, *O. clavarioides*, etc., in which the growing axis goes on developing more or less fan-like, and later become pleated into folds, occasionally reverting to the original type. Other monstrosities of the same fan-like convoluted type are those of *Lophophora Williamsii*, *Pelecyphora aselliformis*, *Astrophytum asterias*, etc. In *Opuntia microdasys* the joint becomes very much elongated and much more narrow than in the normal type, with more numerous, smaller, and thickly-set areoles. A similar case was noted in the crimson-fruited variety of *O. Ficus-indica*. However, these last two cases of monstrosity may be due to a fungous infection, similar to that resulting in the development of the so-called "witches brooms," common on many forest trees.

A peculiar type of fasciation, or rather monstrosity, is presented by *Lophophorus Schottii*, in which the central or terminal bud goes on growing, with a complete derangement of the ribs, which are reduced to irregular and prominent tubercles, each bearing a bud, the plant when sufficiently old throwing up similar branches from the bases this branching occurring much sooner than in the normal type. As pointed out by Backeberg, *Cereus Mieckleyanus* Weingt. imported from Mexico some years ago as a rare spineless *Cereus*, is only another monstrous form of *Lophophorus Schottii*. An interesting fasciation of *Chilenia castaneoides*, *Browningia candelaris*, etc., is that in which the rows of areoles become almost continuous in very regular spirals.

In certain species of *Mammillaria*, such as *M. Parkinsonii*, *M. Karwinskiana*, *M. rhodantha*, etc., an initial stage of fasciation is generally the prelude to a normal form of ramification typical of those species. The plant shows the beginning of fasciation, which ends in the stem dividing dichotomously, and the process is repeated until the plant grows into a large mass with numerous heads, which remain united together on one stem, and never develop own roots, unless they are cut off and planted separately. Occasionally the process of division into two heads remains incomplete, and then the plant goes on developing as an example of fasciation, growing into a huge mass of intricate convolutions.

The fasciated forms of the large-growing species of *Cereus*, etc., are commonly propagated by cuttings in the usual way. The small-growing forms of other species may be propagated in the same manner, but are more commonly grafted on some strong-growing stock, such as species of flat-stemmed *Opuntia*, *Trichocereus macrogonus*, *T. Spachianus*, *Harrisia Jusbertii*, *H. Bonplandii*, *Cereus peruvianus*, etc., and the graft is made according to one of the methods already described, preference being given to one method or another, according to circumstances. That usually practised for the flat cristate forms is the wedge-shaped graft, in which the scion is cut into a broad wedge, forming a right angle or an obtuse angle, and is applied to, and tied down on, a similar shaped cavity or notch made on the top of the stock. In this case the scion is usually cut so that the edge of the wedge is at right angles to the plane of the fasciated crest, but this is by no means an invariable rule.

These monstrosities or cristate forms are often created artificially by the grower. The usual method consists in injuring the tip or terminal bud of the growing stem or joint in such a manner as to induce it to take a fasciated form, which once started, usually becomes permanent. This is done either by a cut carefully made across the centre of the bud, dividing it in two, with a sharp penknife or a razor blade, to a depth of about 5 mm.; or by pricking the bud with the point of a penknife, or with a needle or a long spine, to about the same depth. Of course, very often the operation merely results in the death of the terminal bud and the formation of side shoots of normal form, but now and then the desired cristate form is obtained.

The inclusion or otherwise of these cristate forms in a private collection is, of course, a matter for the personal liking of the grower. They are abnormal forms, and therefore more grotesque and curious than really beautiful; and being unnatural,—that is, a malformation or deviation from the normal type,—they are sometimes disliked even by persons who are keen enthusiasts of Cacti. But they are always interesting and instructive, and therefore few collectionists will long continue to ignore them altogether.

XII

HYBRIDIZATION

Natural hybrids are not unknown among the Cactaceae, and usually they have the valuable quality of coming true from seed. Thus *Astrophytum ornatum* is generally considered as a natural hybrid between *A. myriostigma* and an *Echinocactus*, its straight long yellow or brown spines, and its very acute ribs pointing to a species of *Ferocactus*, possibly *F. glaucescens*, as one of its parents, while all the other characters are those of *A. myriostigma*. It presents considerable variations in the number and shape of its ribs, just like *A. myriostigma*, and also in the colour and length of its straight spines, and in the abundance or scarcity of the characteristic white dots of star-like hairs which cover its body, and are of the same nature as those of *A. myriostigma* and *A. capricorne*. The finest variety is var. *Mirbellii*, with a body rather depressed at the top, and densely covered with silvery white dots, ribs numerous, acute and somewhat notched, and long, thick, straight, straw-coloured or golden yellow spines. It comes mostly true from seed, very few seedlings developing into other forms of *A. ornatum*. The soft, long, more or less incurved spines of *A. capricorne*, are reminder of those of *Stenocactus coptonogonus*, and it is not unlikely that the species, with its varieties, is itself a hybrid of *A. myriostigma* with *S. coptonogonus*.

Stenocactus multicostatus has typically a very large number of narrow, very acute and straight or wavy ribs, of a deep green colour, densely pleated together, with two to four short soft flattened brownish spines, arranged crosswise; but there are numerous varieties, with fewer ribs and with longer and less papery spines, passing gradually into *S. hastatus*, *S. arrigens*, *S. lamellosus*, *S. crispatus* and *S. gladiatus* these being considered more or less as distinct species. There is however a marked affinity between these species and their varieties, and *S. phyllacanthus* and other species, so that the suspicion is justified that they may be merely hybrids of *S. multicostatus* and *S. phyllacanthus*, etc.

So also *Ferocactus latispinus* (*Echinocactus corniger*) is very similar to *F. nobilis* or *F. recurvus*, and is possibly a natural hybrid between

A PRELIMINARY TALK ON CACTACEAE

F. recurvus and *F. crassihamatus* (*E. Mathssonii*) or even *F. Fordii.*
The general aspect of *F. melocactiformis* (*E. electracanthus*) has points
of marked similarity with that of *F. rafaelensis* and *F. echidne.*

Opuntia puberula is generally considered as a hybrid of the lovely
O. microdasys with an unknown species. Varieties of *O. microdasys* are
the splendid var. *albispina*, the large-jointed var. *pallida*, and the very
pretty var. *minima* or *minor.* On the other hand var. *rufida*, often
considered as a variety of *O. microdasys*, is probably a distinct species,
or even a hybrid with *O. Herrfeldtii.*

It is more than likely that several well-known species of *Selenicereus*
listed by nurserymen are natural hybrids, or at any rate well-defined
variations. On the other hand certain varieties listed as such by
nurserymen are obviously distinct species, and have little in common
with the supposed typical form of the species.

Bigeneric hybrids, natural and artificial, are by no means unknown.
Thus *Aporocactus Mallisonii* is evidently a hybrid between *A. flagelliformis* and a species of *Cereus*, possibly *Heliocereus speciosus* and
Phyllocactus Ackermannii is known to be an artificial hybrid raised
in England between an *Epiphyllum* and *H. speciosus.*

There is often a considerable range of variation in regard to the
thickness, length and colour of the stem, the number and shape of the
ribs, the size and even the colour of the spines, and the size and colour
of the flowers. This variation is noticed not only in the same species,
but also in the same plant under different cultural conditions, whether
the plants are grown in full sunshine, or in half-shade, or in the shade,
and particularly when grown in soils of different composition. Thus,
plants grown in highly calcareous and gritty soils develop spines much
longer and thicker than those grown in soils in which calcareous
matter is scarce. Indeed, contrary to the statement frequently met
with in books on the cultivation of Cacti, not only the flat-stemmed
Opuntias, but also many species of *Piptanthocereus*, *Trichocereus*,
Pachycereus, *Lemaireocereus* and *Cephalocereus*, will develop new and
stronger spines, even from old parts of the stem, when they are transferred into a soil rich in lime. These variations, being simply due to
the conditions of environment in which the plant is grown, of course
do not constitute a *variety*, or even a *race*, in a botanical sense; but
they are often disconcerting and misleading, frequently leaving one
in doubt as to the correctness of the description under which the plant
was first described and made known to science.

In the matter of artificial hybrids, the exertions of horticulturists
were mainly, and until recently almost exclusively, directed to the
production of flowers of an improved type, both in size and colour,
and for this reason hybridizations were and are still mostly made
between species and genera of Cactaceae producing large and showy
flowers or flowers with some desirable quality, day-flowering species
being preferred. The first and most important bigeneric crosses were
obtained between the day-flowering *Heliocereus speciosus* and the
day-flowering species of *Epiphyllum* (*Phyllocactus*), these last being

usually the female parent, and a large number of beautiful hybrids were raised, often very richly flowering, producing flowers in a considerable range of colours, and in every way superior to those produced by the parent plants. Good results from crossings and sowings of *Zygocactus truncatus* were also obtained, but in this case one or two natural variations or hybrids were also available. So far no satisfactory results have been obtained from crossings of *Zygocactus* with *Schlumbergera* or of this last with species and varieties of *Epiphyllum* and *Nopalxochia*, possibly owing to the different flowering season. Crossings and sowings of the large night-flowering species of *Selenicereus* have so far not given very good results, although there appear to be unusual possibilities in the range of the size and colouring of the flowers and also in the varying type of their perfume. There are however some notable natural hybrids, and the frequent sowings which are now being made by nurserymen, as well as by amateurs, may well result in raising quite a good number of valuable variations and forms of these very interesting species.

The beauty and size of the flower of the large-flowering Cacti are no doubt a strong incentive to obtain new forms by crossing; but it is also true that many species bearing small flowers are no less remarkable on the score of the characters of their stem, of their ribs or of their spines and hairs, and it is not unlikely that by crossing made on a wider range than hitherto many interesting new forms will be created. It is also possible by means of well conducted hybridizations to raise forms more hardy and more amenable to cultivation than the parent stock. Recent attempts at crossing between the various species of *Astrophytum* have resulted in a large number of hybrids with stems of remarkable beauty, many of which come true from seed.

The artificial crossing of flowers is always very enchanting, and has enriched our gardens with innumerable hybrids very much superior to the types from which they are derived, and has moreover proved of incalculable economic importance by the improved sorts of fruits, vegetables and farm crops which it has called into being. In the case of Cacti the process of hybridization is particularly easy. The flowers still in bud, but just before blooming, are slit longitudinally on one side by means of a penknife or a small pair of scissors, and all the stamens with their anthers, which are not yet expanded, are cut off and removed with the scissors, or picked off with pincers, and some anthers still unexpanded or just expanded taken from the species or variety which it is proposed to use as the male parent inserted in the female which is to serve as the female parent, and from which all its own stamens had been removed, and placed on or around the stigma. The flower thus pollinated is again closed up and tied to prevent it from blooming, and is enclosed in a bag of tissue paper or of cheese cloth, to prevent any possible access of other pollen. Many of these crossings will fail to set, particularly in the case of night-flowering Cacti, which last in bloom only for one night, and then only for a few hours, and this failure on their part is generally ascribed to the dry condition of the stigma, which prevents the quick germination of the pollen falling upon it. To modify this dryness of the stigma, it has been recommended to moisten the stigma with a camel's hair brush dipped in water in which a few drops of honey have been dissolved immediately before use. However, I have succeeded, almost always, in inducing fertilization, by tying rather tightly the petals over the bunch of stamens, placed on and around the stigma, as in this simple manner evaporation is greatly reduced, and the stigma retains all its natural moisture. By this means I have invariably succeeded to effect cross fertilization between species of the large night-flowering species of *Selenicereus*. It is important to mark each fertilized flower with the name of the plant which has supplied the pollen, and the resulting berry should be allowed to remain on the plant until perfectly ripe, and then the seed can be collected and sown immediately, or if the season is unfavourable, made into a paper packet, and kept at hand until required.

Night-flowering species can be hybridized with day-flowering species, or *vice versa*, by reserving the mature stamens from the day-flowering species or, as the case may be, from the night-flowering species, for a few hours until required for pollination. The stamens are collected very carefully, shaking them as little as possible, and are packed in oiled paper, to be used at the right moment. Pollen thus preserved will keep well for three days or more.

Hybridization of species belonging to genera too far apart, and therefore with little affinity, cannot be expected to yield good results. Thus, it would be useless to try to cross an *Opuntia* with the pollen of a *Cereus*, or *vice versa*, or an *Echinocactus* with a *Mammillaria* or an *Epiphyllum*. An *Opuntia* may be crossed with another *Opuntia* of the same section, etc. In other words there must be some degree of relationship or affinity, otherwise crossing between two highly specialized types, which are both too far evolved along different lines from the original type, is sure to yield no practical result. Thus it is difficult to admit, as stated by Beguin that *Harrisia Jusbertii*, could have been a hybrid obtained by crossing *Harrisia Bonplandii* with an *Echinopsis*.

CLASSIFICATION
(A Foreword)

The genus *Cactus* (from the Greek KAKTOS = cactos, an un-determined spiny plant of the old Hellenes, probably a thistle) was originally established by Linnaeus to include the few species of Cactaceae then known to science. During the second half of the eighteenth century many more species were introduced in Europe, the need of greater discrimination became evident, and Miller re-established the four genera *Pereskia, Opuntia, Cereus* and *Cactus*, which were already used in a generic sense by Tournefort, prior to Linnaeus. Subsequent important additions to the number of genera were made in the first half of the nineteenth century by De Candolle, the Prince of Salm-Dyck, Pfeiffer and Lemaire, during which period the cultivation of Cacti has had its first period of popularity. When, in 1898, Dr. Karl Schumann published his Monograph of the Cactaceae, the number of genera had increased to twenty-one. Schumann's admirable classification was soon adopted very generally, and in more or less modified form, is still greatly in vogue with continental writers, but even Schumann himself recognized that several of his genera are too comprehensive in character, and more in the nature of groups, and that a further study with more ample material would lead to more reliable conclusions. Before the publication of Schumann's Monograph, Lemaire in 1868 had already outlined a more rational Classification, the more salient features of which have been embodied in Schumann's work.

In the magnificent work "The Cactaceae," by Britton and Rose published in 1919-1923, the number of genera was increased to one hundred and twenty-four. Many of the sub-genera or sections given by Schumann and others were raised to generic status, and other genera created. This work was at once accepted as the standard systematic study of Cactaceae, an honour which it has well deserved. Further botanical explorations, chiefly in South America, have recently resulted in the discovery of a large number of new species, some of which could not be classified under the genera established by Britton and Rose. Hence a number of new genera have been created, chiefly by Berger, Boedeker and Backeberg in Germany. The new genera are the following: *Andena* Frič, *Armatocereus* Backbg., *Arthrocereus* Berger, *Aztekium* Boedeker, *Bridgesia* Backbg., *Brittonia* Houghton, *Chilenia* Backbg., *Chileniopsis* Backbg., *Epiphyllanthus* Berger, *Erythrorhipsalis* Berger, *Friesia* Frič, *Haagea* Frič, *Haageocereus* Backbg., *Islaya* Backbg., *Mediolobivia* Backbg., *Microspermia* Frič, *Morawetzia* Backbg., *Neowerdermannia* Frič, *Notocactus* Berger, *Obregonia* Frič, *Pseudoespostoa* Backbg., *Porfiria* Boedeker, *Pyrrhocactus* Berger, *Spegazzinia* Backbg., *Stephanocereus* Berger, *Weingartia* Werd.

CLASSIFICATION OF CACTACEAE

Without entering into a discussion on their relative merits, here it is enough to say that several of these new genera do not appear to be justified even from a purely systematic standpoint, let alone the fact that they only help to increase the confusion, already pushed too far, in the mind of the gardener and amateur. Accordingly, in this work the new genera *Andena, Armatocereus, Bridgesia, Chileniopsis, Brittonia, Friesia, Haagea, Islaya, Microspermia, Morawetzia, Pseudoespostoa, Stephanocereus* and *Weingartia* have been omitted altogether, or only mentioned as synonyms. There is a growing suspicion, perhaps not altogether unfounded, that as in other families of the Vegetable Kingdom so also in Cactaceae, the original conception and value of a generic name are being too easily departed from by systematic botanists. There is little doubt that several of the new genera are so ill-defined, and the characters on which they are founded are so uncertain or unimportant, that very often the same species is classified under different genera by expert botanists, and if the experts are themselves frequently at a loss, we may just imagine the plight of the gardener and amateur.

The classification adopted in this work is practically the same as that of Britton and Rose, with only a few modifications, but of course with the addition of the recognized new genera, and of the new species which have been discovered since 1924. Two of the genera created by Britton and Rose, viz: *Arrojadoa* and *Hickenia* have been eliminated; the first is reduced to a subgenus of *Cephalocereus*, and the second is passed to synonymy. Therefore the number of genera accepted in this work now stands at one hundred and thirty-four. The more recent classification proposed by Backeberg in 1933 has many points in its favour, but it offers much scope for controversy, and very likely will have to be considerably modified before general acceptance.

The following is a recapitulation of the Tribes, Sub-Tribes and Genera which are being dealt with in this work.

CLASSIFICATION OF THE CACTACEAE

A = Number of species included in each genus.
B = Number of species described in this work.

	A	B
Tribe I. Pereskieae		
Pereskia	19	6
Tribe II. Opuntieae		
Pereskiopsis	11	6
Quiabentia	3	3
Pterocactus	6	6
Tacinga	2	2
Maihuenia	5	5
Opuntia	302	280
Nopalea	7	7
Grusonia	1	1
Tribe III. Cereeae		
Sub-Tribe I. Cereanae		
Cereus	26	23
Monvillea	12	12
Arthrocereus	3	3
Cephalocereus	76	65
Facheiroa	1	1
Espostoa	4	4
Browningia	2	2
Oreocereus	5	5
Stetsonia	1	1
Jasminocereus	1	1
Escontria	1	1
Corryocactus	3	3
Pachycereus	10	6
Dendrocereus	1	1
Machaerocereus	2	2
Brachycereus	1	1
Leptocereus	8	4
Eulychnia	4	4
Lemaireocereus	23	20
Erdisia	4	4
Bergerocactus	1	1
Leocereus	4	4
Wilcoxia	5	5

Peniocereus	..	..	..	..	..	2	2
Nyctocereus	..	..	..	..	..	5	3
Acanthocereus	..	..	..	..	..	12	7
Heliocereus	..	..	..	..	..	7	7
Trichocereus	..	..	..	..	..	30	26
Binghamia	..	..	..	..	..	8	6
Harrisia	..	..	..	..	..	19	13
Borzicactus	..	..	..	..	..	16	13
Haageocereus	..	..	..	..	..	8	7
Cleistocactus	..	..	..	..	..	15	13
Carnegiea	..	..	..	..	..	1	1
Rathbunia	..	..	..	..	..	4	4
Zehntnerella	..	..	..	..	..	1	1
Lophocereus	..	..	..	..	..	1	1
Myrtillocactus	..	..	..	..	..	5	5
Neoraimondia	..	..	..	..	..	1	1
Neoabbottia	..	..	..	..	..	1	1

Sub-Tribe II. *Hylocereanae*

Hylocereus	..	..	..	..	..	18	18
Selenicereus	..	..	..	..	..	25	24
Wilmattea	..	..	..	..	..	1	1
Deamia	..	..	..	..	..	1	1
Mediocactus	..	..	..	..	..	2	2
Weberocereus	..	..	..	..	..	3	3
Werckleocereus	..	..	..	..	..	2	2
Strophocactus	..	..	..	..	..	1	1
Aporocactus	..	..	..	..	..	6	6

Sub-Tribe III. *Echinocereanae*

Echinocereus	..	..	..	..	..	78	61
Chamaecereus	..	..	..	..	..	1	1
Austrocactus	..	..	..	..	..	2	2
Rebutia	..	..	..	..	..	35	13
Mediolobivia	..	..	..	..	..	11	4
Lobivia	..	..	..	..	..	70	48
Echinopsis	..	..	..	..	..	36	34

Sub-Tribe IV. *Echinocactanae*

Denmoza	..	..	..	..	..	2	2
Ariocarpus	..	..	..	..	..	7	7
Neogomesia	..	..	..	..	..	1	1
Encephalocarpus	..	..	..	..	..	1	1
Obregonia	..	..	..	..	..	1	1
Lophophora	..	..	..	..	..	3	3
Aztekium	..	..	..	..	..	1	1
Copiapoa	..	..	..	..	..	9	9
Pediocactus	..	..	..	..	..	1	1

CACTI

Toumeya	..	..	..	..	..	1	1
Epithelantha	..	..	..	..	..	1	1
Neoporteria	..	..	..	..	..	13	13
Chilenia	..	..	..	..	..	3	3
Arequipa	..	..	..	..	..	3	3
Oroya	..	..	..	..	..	1	1
Matucana	..	..	..	..	..	1	1
Hamatocactus	..	..	..	..	..	3	3
Strombocactus	..	..	..	..	..	4	4
Leuchtenbergia	..	..	..	..	..	1	1
Stenocactus	..	..	..	..	..	32	26
Ferocactus	..	..	..	..	..	34	34
Echinomastus	..	..	..	..	..	7	7
Gymnocalycium	..	..	..	..	..	50	40
Echinocactus	..	..	..	..	..	9	9
Homalocephala	..	..	..	..	..	1	1
Astrophytum	..	..	..	..	..	4	4
Eriosyce	..	..	..	..	..	3	3
Malacocarpus	..	..	..	..	..	12	10
Notocactus	..	..	..	..	..	25	17
Pyrrhocactus	..	..	..	..	..	7	7
Parodia	..	..	..	..	..	28	23
Spegazzinia	..	..	..	..	..	3	3
Frailea	..	..	..	..	..	15	11
Mila	..	..	..	..	..	3	3
Sclerocactus	..	..	..	..	..	2	2
Utahia	..	..	..	..	..	1	1

Sub-Tribe V. Cactanae

Discocactus	..	..	..	..	..	7	3
Cactus	..	..	..	..	..	30	22

Sub-Tribe VI. Coryphanthanae

Ancistrocactus	..	..	..	..	..	3	3
Thelocactus	..	..	..	..	..	27	27
Neolloydia	..	..	..	..	..	5	5
Mamillopsis	..	..	..	..	..	2	2
Neowerdermannia	..	..	..	..	..	1	1
Cochemiea	..	..	..	..	..	5	5
Coryphantha	..	..	..	..	..	56	54
Neobesseya	..	..	..	..	..	7	7
Escobaria	..	..	..	..	..	11	7
Bartschella	..	..	..	..	..	1	1
Porfiria	..	..	..	..	..	1	1
Pelecyphora	..	..	..	..	..	2	2
Solisia	..	..	..	..	..	1	1
Dolichothele	..	..	..	..	..	3	3
Mammillaria	..	..	..	..	..	210	174

CLASSIFICATION OF CACTACEAE

Sub-Tribe VII. *Epiphyllanae*

Zygocactus	1	1
Epiphyllanthus	3	3
Schlumbergera	2	2
Epiphyllum	17	17
Disocactus	2	2
Chiapasia	1	1
Eccremocactus	1	1
Nopalxochia	1	1
Wittia	2	2

Sub-Tribe VIII. *Rhipsalidanae*

Erythrorhipsalis	1	1
Rhipsalidopsis	1	1
Pfeiffera	1	1
Acanthorhipsalis	3	1
Pseudorhipsalis	2	2
Lepismium	4	4
Hariota	3	3
Rhipsalis	60	51

Total number of species	1,752
Total number of species described in this work	1,500

E

TRIBE I. PERESKIEAE

Leafy shrubby Cacti. Seed coat thin and brittle. Cotyledons large, and hypocotyl hardly succulent.

PERESKIA (L.) Plumier

In commemoration of N.C.F. de Peirese, latinized Peireskius. More frequently written *Peireskia*, and sometimes also *Peirescia* and *Perescia*.

Stems hardly succulent, soon becoming woody, very spiny. Leaves large, well formed, somewhat fleshy, permanent, or more or less dropping off during the period of rest. Areoles large, woolly, spiny. Flowers stalked, solitary, or in clusters or panicles, with short leaf-like bracts. Floral leaves separate and spreading. Fruit fleshy. Seeds numerous, with a thin brittle brown or black seed coat.

Includes about 19 species, native of tropical America, mostly only of botanical interest, but a few are ornamental and deserve cultivation. They are also often used as stock chiefly for grafting *Zygocactus, Epiphyllanthus, Schlumbergera, Rhipsalis* and *Rhipsalidopsis.*

Pereskia aculeata Mill. = *Cactus Pereskia* L. = *P. peireskia* Karst. Florida to West Indies, Mexico and Argentina. A climbing or rampant shrub, 2 to 10 m. long. Areoles with 1 to 3 short hooked spines; upper areoles on old stems developing many long straight dark brown spines, 2 to 3 cm. long. Leaves 5 to 10 cm. long, elliptical, pointed, short-stalked, with a prominent midrib. Flower whitish, $2\frac{1}{2}$ to 4 cm. broad, in large clusters, strongly perfumed. Fruit yellow, spiny. This is the only species with spiny fruits.

Var. **rubescens** Pfeiff. = *P. rubescens* Pfeiff. = *P. Godseffiana* Hort. A pretty variety with leaves variegated red. Other forms, originally described as species, are var. *lanceolata* Pfeiff., var. *longispina* Haw., var. *latifolia* Salm-Dyck, var. *rotundifolia* Pfeiff., and var. *brasiliensis* Pfeiff.

Pereskia saccharosa Griseb. = *P. amapola* Weber. Paraguay and Argentina. An erect shrub, with erect branches, about 6 m. high. Leaves lanceolate, dark green, acute, short-stalked, keeled, fleshy, 8 to 12 cm. long. Areoles large, with numerous straight spines up to 5 cm. long. Flowers about 8 cm. broad, pink, borne in clusters. Fruit roundish, about 4 cm. long, with leaf-like bracts.

Pereskia grandifolia Haw. = *P. grandiflora* Hort. = *P. bleo* Hort. non DC. Brazil : also grown as a hedge plant in tropical America. An erect shrub 2 to 5 m. high, with thick and very spiny stems. Leaves ovate, pointed at both ends, short-stalked, 8 to 15 cm. long, and 3 to 4 cm. broad, fleshy. Areoles at first spineless, soon developing 1 or 2 almost black spines up to 5 cm. long, later developing other spines. Flowers about 4 cm. broad, borne in clusters, of a beautiful pink, with lanceolate obtuse petals. Fruit small, pear-shaped, green.

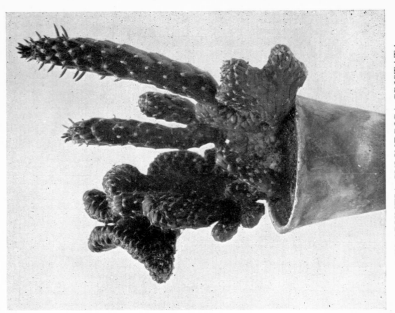

(b) OPUNTIA CYLINDRICA CRISTATA

(a) PERESKIA GODSEFFIANA

PLATE II

(b) OPUNTIA VERSCHAFFELTII

(a) OPUNTIA VESTITA

PLATE III

PERESKIEAE

Pereskia Bleo DC. Columbia and Panama. A tall erect shrub, up to 7 m. high. Stems reddish and spineless when young, later passing to green, and developing 5 or more spines on each areole. Leaves elongated, up to 20 cm. long, and 4 to 5 cm. broad, thin, with a leaf-stalk 2 to 3 cm. long. Flowers in clusters, short-stalked, about 4 cm. broad, of a lively pink. Fruit round, about 4 cm. thick, pale yellow, with short bracts.

Pereskia Conzattii Br. et R. Mexico (Oaxaca). A tall erect shrub, much branched, 8 to 10 m. high. Leaves almost round, short-stalked, 1 to 2½ cm. long. Areoles with several spines, 2 to 3 cm. long. Fruit pear-shaped.

Pereskia autumnalis Rose = *Peireskiopsis autumnalis* Eichl. Guatemala and Salvador. A tall erect shrub, up to 9 m. high, with a very spiny stem, brown when young. Leaves glossy green, roundish, fleshy, short-stalked, abruptly pointed, 4 to 8 cm. long. Areoles with 1 to 3 strong spines, 3 to 4 cm. long. Flowers mostly solitary, orange red, 4 to 5 cm. broad. Fruit round, about 4 cm. thick, pale yellow, with short bracts.

TRIBE II. OPUNTIEAE

Trees, shrubs and bushes, with hard seeds, sometimes winged. Cotyledons well developed, and hypocotyl slightly fleshy. Areoles with glochids. Leaves flat and large in the lower genera, cylindrical and fugacious in the higher genera. Fruit round, oval or fusiform, often proliferous.

Includes the genera *Pereskiopsis, Quiabentia, Pterocactus, Tacinga, Maihuenia, Opuntia, Nopalea* and *Grusonia*.

PERESKIOPSIS Br. et R.

Stem erect, with many slender twigs. Leaves flat, fleshy. Flowers borne on preceding year's growth, yellow or reddish. Fruit conical, red, fleshy, Seeds small, roundish, hairy, white.

Includes about 11 species, distributed chiefly along the Pacific coast from Lower California to Guatemala.

Pereskiopsis Diguetii (Weber) Br. et R. = *Opuntia Diguetii* Weber. Central Mexico. Stem about 2 m. high, pale green, hairy. Leaves obovate, abruptly acuminate, 3 to 5 cm. long. Areoles large, with brown glochids, and with long hanging white hairs, later developing short brownish wool, with 1 or 2 spines, rarely more, up to 7 cm. long, black passing to greyish. Flower yellow.

Pereskiopsis Porteri (Brand.) Br. et R. = *Opuntia Porteri* Brand. = *O. Brandegeei* K. Sch. Mexico and Lower California. Stem up to 1 m. high, very spiny. Young stems spineless, or with 1 or 2 greenish or brownish spines. Areoles with numerous brown glochids. Leaves obovate, acute, 2 to 3 cm. long. Flower yellow, 4 cm. broad. Fruit fusiform, about 5 cm. long, orange red.

Pereskiopsis pititache (Weber) Br. et R. = *Opuntia pititache* Weber = *Pereskia pititache* Karw. Mexico. About 3 m. high, very spiny. Young stems slender, green. Leaves obovate-elongated, pale green, thin, about 4 cm. long. Areoles small, black, at first without glochids, but with white long hairs, and with 1 long spine. Areoles on older stems developing glochids, and 5 or 6 brown spines up to 3 cm. long.

Pereskiopsis aquosa (Weber) Br. et R. = *Opuntia aquosa* Weber. Mexico. Stem 1 to 2 m. high, bluish green, with cylindrical twigs 1½ to 2½ cm. thick. Leaves elliptical-elongated, 6 to 8 cm. long, and 2½ to 3 cm. broad, mostly reddish along the margin. Areoles round, at first with long white hair, later with short wool, and with 1 or 2 greyish spines, 3 cm. long. Flower yellow, reddish outside. Fruit yellowish green, pear-shaped, about 5 cm. long.

Pereskiopsis velutina Rose. Central Mexico. Stem 1 to 2 m. high, with short thick hairs when young. Leaves oval-elliptical or lanceolate, pointed at both ends, 2 to 6 cm. long, velvety. Areoles with long white hairs and short spines. Flower yellow, greenish or reddish outside. Ovary oblong, pubescent with leaf-like bracts.

Pereskiopsis spathulata (Weber) Br. et R. = *Opuntia spathulata* Weber = *Pereskia spathulata* Link. et Otto. Mexico. Habit the same as the preceding, with greyish green stems. Leaves fleshy, spathulate, 2½ to 5 cm. long. Areoles with whitish wool and with long white hairs when young, which soon drop off and are replaced with brown glochids, and with 1 or 2 (later up to 8) whitish or yellowish stiff spines, 2 to 3 cm. long. Flower red, fruit greenish.

QUIABENTIA Br. et R.

Tree-like or bushy, more or less straggling. Twigs slender, cylindrical, fleshy. Leaves mostly oval, flat and fleshy. Areoles large with whitish wool. Spines slender, numerous, often very small or like glochids. Flowers red, fully expanded and rotate, with a fusiform bracteate ovary. Seeds white, flat, disc-like, smooth, about ½ cm. broad. Includes 3 species.

Quiabentia Zehntneri Br. et R. = *Pereskia Zehntneri* Br. et R. Brazil. A bush 2 to 3 m. high. Leaves oval or roundish, acute, 2 to 4 cm. long. Spines numerous, small, very slender, whitish. Flower of a lively red. Fruit 6 to 7 cm. long and 1½ cm. thick. Flowers in October. The native name is *quiabent*.

Quiabentia Pflanzii Vaup. = *Pereskia Pflanzii* Vaup. Bolivia. A tree up to 15 m. high. Leaves oval, narrowed at the base, 4 cm. long and 2 cm. broad. Spines very short and slender. Flower pale red.

Quiabentia verticillata Vaup. = *Pereskia verticillata* Vaup. Bolivia. A shrub about 2 m. high. Leaves lanceolate-acute, 5 cm. long. Twigs about 1 cm. thick. Spines several, up to 7 cm. long. Flower pale red.

PTEROCACTUS K. Sch.

Low bushes, branching from the ground, with tuberous roots, and cylindrical succulent stems. Leaves very minute and scale-like, soon dropping off. Areoles with minute glochids, and short flexible hair-like spines. Flowers terminal, that is, at the end of the stem, like those of an Opuntia, with erect segments. Ovary with spines and glochids. Fruit dry, like a capsule, with large flat thin seeds, hard and unevenly winged.

Includes 6 species, all very interesting.

Pterocactus Kuntzei K. Sch .= *Opuntia tuberosa* Pfeiff. non Hort. = *P. tuberosus* Br. et R. Argentina and Patagonia. Plant with a large tuberous root, up to 8 cm. thick, deeply set in the ground, with numerous branches 3 to 40 cm. long, and 1 cm. thick, cylindrical, deep brownish green. Areoles very small and very close together, with whitish hair-like spines, mostly applied to the stem. Flower yellow, 2 to 3 cm broad. Fruit pear-shaped. Seed up to 1 cm. broad. This is the species more frequently met with in cultivation, grown on own roots in sandy soil, or grafted on species of *Opuntia*. Requires full sunshine, and a sandy soil with some leaf-mould, kept rather dry.

Pterocactus decipiens Gürke. Western Argentina. Differs from the preceding in growing taller, with thicker stems. The spines are brownish and longer. Flower larger, 4½ cm. broad, yellow inside, reddish brown outside. Wings of seed thicker. Rare in cultivation.

Pterocactus Valentinii Speg. Patagonia. Stems greener, or almost bluish green. The sterile branches are more erect and shorter, almost conical at the end, with white spines 1½ to 2½ cm. long, and glochids directed downwards. The flowering stems are mostly prostrate, also short, and 1½ to 2½ cm. thick. Flower about 2 cm. broad, reddish yellow. Vary rare in cultivation.

Pterocactus Hickenii Br. et R. Patagonia. Has short stems about 2 cm. thick, 3 to 10 cm. high, erect, arising from a thick rootstock, thickly covered with stiff straw-coloured spines, 2 to 3 cm. long. The flower is terminal, yellowish, 3 to 4 cm. across, with the petals fringed and somewhat crumpled.

Pterocactus Fisheri Br. et R. Patagonia. Has globular or oval joints or stems, 1 to 2 cm. thick, jointed one above the other, up to 10 or 15 cm. high, very warty, arising from a thick rootstock, with a few flexible yellow spines, 1 to 2 cm. long.

Pterocactus Arnoldianus Backbg. Patagonia. Similar to the preceding, but has black spines and a stouter habit of growth. Both these species are still very rare in cultivation.

TACINGA Br. et R.

(An anagram of *Caatinga*, the North Brazilian scrub country.)

Stems climbing and branching, cylindrical, slender, at first fleshy, later becoming woody. The young shoots are pointed, very slightly ribbed, hairy with minute abortive leaves which soon drop off. Areoles dark, with glossy white short glochids, which drop off easily. Spines 2 or 3, 2 to 3 mm. long, recurved, found only on young shoots. Flowers nocturnal; ovary oval-elongated, distinctly jointed to the side areoles on the upper part of the stems, spineless. Petals few, narrow, typically green, strongly reflexed or coiled back. There is a ring of hairs between the petals and the stamens. Stamens reunited together, forming a tube through which the pistil is protruded. Fruit oval-elongated, mostly hollow, with a few round white seeds having a hard aril.

Includes 2 species, mainly of botanical interest, natives of the *caatinga* or scrub country around Bahia (Brazil), both rare in cultivation.

Tacinga funalis Br. et R. Has greenish petals, and is the typical species.

Tacinga Zehntneri Backbg. Has shorter stems and twigs, and the petals are violet red. Possibly only a mere variety of the preceding.

MAIHUENIA Philippi

Low cespitose bushes, much branched and spreading, with cylindrical persistent leaves. Areoles woolly, without glochids, and mostly with 3 spines, the central one being longest. Flowers usually terminal, fully expanded or rotate, white, yellow or red. Stamens shorter than the petals. Ovary short, with leaf-like bracts persisting in the fruit, which is soft and juicy. Seeds with a thin shining black coat.

Includes at least 5 species, natives of Argentina, Patagonia and Chile, with the habit of a *Tephrocactus* or *Sphaeropuntia*.

Maihuenia Poeppigii Weber = *Peireskia Poeppigii* Salm-Dyck. Chile. Originally described as an *Opuntia*. Resistant to low temperatures, being covered with snow in winter on its native hills. Joints about 6 cm. long and 5 cm. thick, of oval shape, spiny all over. Leaves persistent, about ½ cm. long. Areoles whitish. Central spine 1½ to 2 cm. long; the two others are very short. Flower yellow, stigma with 10 green lobes. Fruit obovate, about 5 cm. long.

Maihuenia patagonica Speg. = *M. telhuelches* Speg. Patagonia. Same habit as the preceding. Joints cylindrical or conical, 2 to 8 cm. long and 1 to 2 cm. thick. Leaves about half as long as in the preceding species, and much less persistent. Central spine 2 to 4 cm. long, convex on the upper side, flat on the lower side; side spines ½ to 1 cm. long. Flower white inside, yellow outside.

Other species occasionally met with in cultivation are the following, natives of South Chile and Patagonia, the third being from Mendoza (Argentina):

Maihuenia Valentinii Speg. and *M. Philippi* Weber, with white flowers, and *M. brachydelphys* K. Sch. They are all resistant to cold, in their native country being mostly covered with snow all the winter

OPUNTIA Miller

(From *Opuntiani*, a people whose capital was the ancient Opus, near Phocis, in Greece, where *Opuntia vulgaris* Mill. had early become naturalized.)

This large but compact genus includes small and large bushes, or trees of considerable size, usually much branched. Stems jointed; the joints may be flat, cylindrical, clavate or globose, bearing areoles mostly woolly, with cylindrical leaves, spines and glochids or bundles of short stiff bristle-like spines, these glochids being always present on all the areoles, including those on the fruit. The leaves may be fugacious or deciduous, very rarely persistent. The spines may be roughened or barbed at the tip, or may be furnished with a loose membraneous sheath. The flowers are borne singly on the areoles, and have a spreading showy rotate corolla. Ovary with areoles bearing glochids, and sometimes also spines. Seeds large, discoid or margined, sometimes round. Fruit frequently edible. A number of species have the habit of developing new fruits or new joints from the areoles of the fruit. Most species are capable of developing new spines from the areoles on the old stems.

This genus now includes over 300 species, spread all over America, from Utah and Nebraska down to Patagonia.

Species of *Opuntia*, under the general term of *Cactus* or *Fig-Cactus* or *Indian Fig*, appeal most to the popular imagination. For a few a sandy soil is necessary, but the great majority will thrive in any soil, provided it is porous and well charged with calcareous matter. A good number of species are quite hardy in southern and central Europe, and most species which are purely tropical are also more or less hardy along the shores of the Mediterranean. A few species are spineless or almost spineless, but they are mostly well armed with spines, and sometimes, as in the case of *O. aoracantha*, the spines are over 10 cm. long, and as hard as iron. The barbed and sheathed spines of many North American species stick so fast to the skin at the least touch, that their removal is often painful, and sooner than leaving their hold, the joints or branches break off and remain attached to the skin, with no little alarm to the unwary victim, but fortunately hardly ever with any after effects. However, this formidable array of spines is less objectionable than the glochids or bundles of minute, very short, bristle-like spines, often almost transparent and invisible, which although incapable of inflicting serious injury, are a constant source of irritation, until they are removed, or washed off, or scraped off.

The stamens of most species of *Opuntia* possess to a remarkable degree, in full sunshine, the quality of *irritability*. When touched by an insect, or with the finger, they quickly respond to the stimulus, and close upon the stigma, to return to their normal expanded condition after the lapse of a few minutes.

Sub-Genus I. BRASILIOPUNTIA K. Schum. Tree-like, with a cylindrical main stem or leader, and lateral flat-jointed branches, which often fail to develop a leader when rooted separately. Ovaries compressed laterally, with a ring of thick hairs or staminodes next to the petals. Fruit large, hairy, with few seeds, mostly one-seeded.

Opuntia brasiliensis Haw. Brazil, Argentina, Paraguay and Bolivia. With a tree-like stem, up to 4 m. high, straight, cylindrical, slender, without joints, with spreading cylindrical side branches. Joints flat, thin, pale green easily dropping off. Spines few, 1 to 3 in each areole, 3 to 6 cm. long. Flower pale yellow, with hairs on the lower part of the inside of the petals and stamens. Fruit yellow, seeds small, woolly.

var. **minor** Hort. Berol. Plant smaller in all its parts.

Opuntia Bahiensis Br. et R. Brazil (Bahia). Is very similar, and grows up to 15 m. high. Lateral joints cylindrical, bearing terminal flat and thin joints, spineless, or with 1 or 2 slender spines. Fruit oblong, red, pulp red, seeds mostly 1 or 2, very hairy, 8 mm. broad.

Opuntia argentina Griseb. North Argentina. Up to 15 m. high. Terminal lateral joints flat, oblong, 5 to 12 cm. long, thin, pale green. Flowers greenish yellow. Fruit clavate, purplish violet, seeds lenticular, about 6 mm. broad.

Sub-Genus II. CONSOLEA Lem. Habit of *Platyopuntia*, with thick, disc-like or oval joints, growing from the lateral areoles of the main stem or leader, which continues growing, later on becoming cylindrical, the branching is therefore like a semaphore or a cross, hence the name of *Cruciformes*, often given to this group. The flower has a ring-shaped or bowl-shaped nectary at the base of the pistil.

Opuntia spinosissima Mill. = *Consolea spinosissima* Lem. = *O. ferox* Haw. = *O. cruciata* Hort. Jamaica. An erect shrub, 1 to 4 m. high, much branched, with joints borne mostly crosswise one over the other. Joints grass green, oblong or broadly linear, 6 to 12 cm. long, often longer, passing to greyish green, with closely set, white, round areoles, and with 1 cm. long tufts of yellow glochids, and very strongly armed with spines. Spines radiating, red when young; radial spines 5 or 6, later becoming more numerous, thin, white, about 1 cm. long; central spines 1 or 2, white or pale yellow, mostly directed upwards, 6 to 8 cm. long, red at the base. Flower 3 cm. broad, golden yellow, fading to reddish.

Opuntia moniliformis (L.) Haw. = *Cereus moniliformis* DC. = *Nopalea moniliformis* K. Sch. Haiti. A prostrate bush, with roundish or oval joints, often almost disc-like, 4 to 7 cm. long, and about 4 cm. broad, mostly arranged crosswise. Areoles with numerous yellow glochids. Spines often only one, sometimes 3 to 5, awl-shaped, spreading, yellowish to brown, 4 to 5 cm. long. Flower 8 or 9 cm. long, 3 cm. broad, with a long ovary, scaly and slightly warty. Perianth red; fruit red.

Opuntia macracantha Griseb. Cuba. Erect, up to 6 m. high, with a cylindrical stem thickly covered with long spines. Upper branches green, with many side joints from the marginal areoles, flat, oblong or ovate, with areoles 2 to 3 cm. apart, and many brown glochids. Spines 1 to 4, up to 15 cm. long, nearly white, thick, subulate, sometimes absent. Ovaries up to 3 cm. long, with many areoles and glochids; perianth orange yellow, 1 to 2 cm. long. A fine species, common in cultivation.

Opuntia Millspaughii Britton. Bahamas (Rock Island). A bush less than 1 m. high, with a cylindrical stem, branching at the top, bearing oblong elongated side joints, up to 40 cm. long, and 4 to 10 cm. broad, pale green. Areoles with short yellowish brown glochids. Spines on the stem up to 15 cm. long, those on the joints shorter and only on the marginal areoles, purple when young. Flowers crimson, 1 cm. broad. Fruit compressed, 2 cm. long, with areoles bearing spines 2 cm. long.

Opuntia Nashii Britton. Bahamas. An erect bush 1 to 4 m. high, dull green, with a cylindrical stem, flat at the top, with flat oblong side joints, often 30 cm. long and 8 cm. broad. Spines 2 to 5 on each areole, slender, greyish, 3 to 6 cm. long. Flowers red, 1½ cm. broad; ovary 3 cm. long, spiny.

Opuntia corallicola (Small) Werd. et Backbg. = *Consolea corallicola* Small. Florida. A low spreading bush. Joints elliptical, thin, up to 25 cm. long. Areoles with 5 to 9 spines, reddish passing to grey, up to 6 cm. long. Flower about 3 cm. long and 2 cm. broad, red. Fruit 4 to 5 cm. long, yellow, spiny.

Opuntia rubescens Salm-Dyck = *Consolea rubescens* Lem. West Indies. An erect branched shrub, 3 to 6 m. high, dark coppery green or reddish green, strongly armed in its native country, but in cultivation practically spineless. Joints oval or oval-elongated, up to 25 cm. long, and 3 to 6 cm. broad, with reddish prominences. Areoles yellowish passing to greyish or brownish, with short yellowish glochids, and in cultivation with 1 or 2 short white spines, often spineless. Flowers 5 cm. long, and 4 cm. broad, yellow; fruit reddish, subglobose, up to 8 cm. thick, seeds round, flat, up to 8 mm. broad. Very ornamental, and common in cultivation.

Opuntia bahamana Br. et R. Bahamas. A closely allied species, about 1½ m. high, dull green. Areoles spineless or bearing 1 to 4 short yellow spines. Flower about 6 cm. broad, dark rose. Rare in cultivation.

Sub-Genus III. Platyopuntia Weber. Joints more or less flat (*pads*), round, oval or elongated, with areoles on both sides and along the margin. Includes also the dwarf species from the high Andes, with small, almost globular joints or pads, like species of *Tephrocactus*, commonly known by the Indian name of *Airampo*.

Series A. Reductae. Low plants with small joints or pads.

1. *Pumilae*. Plant more or less downy or hairy, with cylindrical joints.

Opuntia pumila Rose. Mexico. Joints 6 to 20 cm. long, cylindrical, slightly flattened and warty, with whitish hairs. Areoles small, with 2 or more yellowish spines, up to 3 cm. long. Flower reddish outside, yellow inside, 1½ cm. long. Fruit round, 1½ cm. long, red.

Opuntia depauperata Br. et R. Venezuela (Caracas). Plant 10 to 20 cm. high, spreading. Joints dark green, cylindrical or slightly flattened, 3 to 12 cm. long, 2 to 3 cm. thick, slightly hairy. Spines 2 or 3, increasing to 6, reddish passing to brownish, 1 to 2½ cm. long. Glochids yellow, developing on old joints.

Opuntia pubescens Wendl. = *O. leptarthra* Weber. Central America to Mexico. A low prostrate bush. Joints almost cylindrical, 3 to 7 cm. long and about 1 cm. thick, slightly warty, deep green, usually hairy. Spines numerous, slender, brown passing to grey, about 1 cm. long. Flower yellow; fruit round, red, about 2½ cm. long.

Opuntia pascoensis Br. et R. Peru (Pasco). An erect bush, 30 cm. high. Joints cylindrical or slightly flattened, 3 to 12 cm. long, 1½ to 4 cm. thick, slightly hairy. Areoles with a dark spot, and with a semi-lunar furrow above them, and with long white hairs. Spines 4 to 8, or more, yellow, up to 2 cm. long.

Opuntia halophila Speg. Argentina. Joints oval or oval-cylindrical, somewhat flattened, 4 to 6 cm. long, and 2 to 3 cm. thick, greyish green, with numerous small low warts. Areoles small, somewhat hairy, with a small tuft of reddish brown glochids. Spines 9 to 14, greyish, up to 5 cm. long, rather thick, erect like a brush. Flowers borne on the side areoles of new joints, about 5 cm. long, whitish or pale pink, with whitish stamens and stigma with green lobes. Fruit warty, with a few spines on the upper areoles.

Opuntia albisetacens Backbg. Argentina. Plant low; joints glaucous green, cylindrical or somewhat flattened, up to 10 cm. long, and 1½ to 2½ cm. thick, covered with soft, bristle-like white spines, variously directed or curved, up to 5 cm. long. A new beautiful and rare species.

Opuntia Hoffmannii Helia Bravo. Mexico. Prostrate and much branched. Joints almost cylindric, 6 to 10 cm. long, and 2 cm. thick, dull green, with prominent warts and easily dropping off. Areoles few, with yellow glochids, and with 3 to 5 needle-like, yellowish spines, about 3 cm. long. Flower yellowish, fading to reddish. Fruit about 4½ cm. long, reddish, spiny.

2. *Divaricatae.* Joints broader and more flattened.

Opuntia triacantha Sweet. West Indian Islands. A spreading, much branched shrub, with oval-elongated joints 4 to 8 cm. long, pale green. Spines usually 3, white passing to yellowish, up to 4 cm. long. Flower 5 cm. broad, yellow fading to reddish. Fruit spineless, red.

Opuntia curassavica Mill. Curaçao and other islands off the coast of Venezuela. A spreading bush. Joints oval or elongated, flat but thick, pale green, 2 to 5 cm. long, with small areoles and long whitish hairs. Spines needle-like, 4 or more, about 2 cm. long, yellow passing to whitish. Flowers 5 cm. broad, yellow streaked red.

Opuntia repens Bello = *O. curassavica* Pfeiff. et Otto, non Mill. Porto Rico. A prostrate bush with long flattened joints, 5 to 6 cm. long and 2 to 3½ cm. thick, often furnished with white hairs. Areoles small, brown, with a few white hairs and numerous yellow glochids. Spines many, reddish passing to brown, up to 3½ cm. long. Flower yellow, fading to reddish, 4 cm. broad.

Opuntia Taylori Br. et R. Haiti. Prostrate and spreading. Joints narrow, oblong or linear, up to 12 cm. long and 1 to 2 cm. broad, smooth or hairy. Spines 3 to 6, needle-like, brownish passing to white, up to 4 cm. long. Glochids yellowish brown. Flowers small, yellow. Fruit pear-shaped, spineless.

Opuntia borinquensis Br. et R. Porto Rico (Cabo Rojo). Like *O. repens*, but has larger, broader and thinner joints, and the spines are longer.

Opuntia Drummondii Graham = *O. pes-corvi* Le Conte. Florida, Georgia, Carolina. Prostrate and spreading. Joints 6 to 12 cm. long and 3 to 6 cm. broad, somewhat elongated and irregular, pale green, more or less drooping, with brown areoles and pale yellow glochids. Spines 1 to 5, brownish or grey, up to 4 cm. long. Flower yellow, about 6 cm. broad. Fruit pear-shaped, red, about 3 cm. long.

Opuntia austrina Small = *O. Youngii* C.Z. Nelson. Southern Florida. Roots tuberous, 4 to 6 cm. thick. Plant mostly erect. Joints oblong or obovate, flat and thick, bright green, 5 to 12 cm. long.

Glochids yellowish. Spines 1 to 6, only on the upper areoles, mostly 2, pinkish to whitish. Flowers bright yellow, 6 to 7 cm. broad.

Opuntia Tracyi Britton. Georgia and Florida. Spreading, pale green, up to 20 cm. high. Joints oblong or linear, flat, 6 to 8 cm. long, 1½ to 2½ cm. broad; young joints almost cylindrical. Spines 1 to 4, greyish, dark at the tip, about 3 cm. long; glochids many, brownish. Flower 4 cm. broad, pure yellow.

Opuntia Darrahiana Weber. Bahamas. A bush up to 25 cm. high, much branched. Joints 7 to 8 cm. long and 4 to 5 cm. broad, green or glaucous green. Spines 6, up to 4 cm. long, white or greyish. Very rarely grown.

Opuntia pusilla Haw. = *O. foliosa* Salm-Dyck. West Indies. Usually prostrate. Joints narrow, slightly flattened, smooth, light green. Leaves 6 mm. long, soon dropping off. Areoles far apart. Spines 1 or 2, awl-shaped, brownish to yellowish. Flowers pale yellow.

Opuntia polyantha Haw. West Indian Islands. A low, much branched shrub, up to 1 m. high. Joints oval-elongated, flattened, yellowish green, 7 to 14 cm. long, with whitish areoles on low warts, and small awl-shaped reddish leaves which soon drop off. Glochids very numerous, yellowish brown. Spines 5 to 8, yellowish brown, 1 to 2 cm. long. Flowers 6 cm. broad, pale yellow, borne in great numbers.

3. *Airampoae*. Small, low plants. Joints small, roundish or flattened.

Opuntia inermis DC. = *O. stricta* Haw. Probably native of Cuba, Florida and Texas; naturalized in the Balearic Islands and southern France (*O. vulgaris balearica* Weber), as well as in Chile (*O. airampo* Phil.), and in Western Australia. The Indian name *airampo* originally given to this species by the Chileans, is now extended to all dwarf species of *Opuntia* growing on the high Andes. A low semi-prostrate bush, less than 1 m. high. Joints oval or oval-elongated, flattened, 8 to 15 cm. long, green or greyish green, rather thick. Areoles brownish, with short glochids. Spines 1 or 2, often absent, yellow, 1 to 4 cm. long. Fruit pear-shaped, 4 to 6 cm. long, red.

Opuntia Soehrensii Br. et R. = *Cactus ayrampo* Azara. Southern Peru, Bolivia, Argentina. Prostrate and spreading. Joints orbicular or oval, flattened, tuberculate, rather thin, 4 to 6 cm. long, pale green, often purplish, very spiny. Spines often as many as 8, slender, usually yellowish or brown, erect, up to 5 cm. long. Flowers pale yellow, or orange red, 3 cm. long. Fruit red, 3 cm. long, spineless.

Opuntia securigera Borg. Southern Argentina, Patagonia. Plant spreading and prostrate, much branched, up to 20 cm. high, forming broad cushions. Joints green or dull green, oval or somewhat conical, 6 to 8 cm. long and 4 to 6 cm. broad, the larger joints somewhat flattened on the upper and inner side, like an axe, covered with low warts, broad and rounded, bearing large round whitish areoles and yellowish brown glochids, deeply embedded. Radial spines 10 to 15, more numerous on older joints, bristle-like, white, $\frac{1}{2}$ to $1\frac{1}{2}$ cm. long. Central spines 1 to 3, also more numerous on older joints, glossy white, slender, flexible, 2 to 5 cm. long. Flower and fruit unknown. (For the Latin diagnosis of this species see first edition.)

Opuntia humilis Haw. Jamaica. A low plant hardly 10 cm. high, branching from the ground and rooting. Joints greyish green or slightly reddish, somewhat warty, obovate and thick, or almost cylindrical at the base, usually more or less flattened above, 2 to 4 cm. long, and $1\frac{1}{2}$ to $2\frac{1}{2}$ cm. broad above the middle, with small greyish areoles and a few small brown glochids. Spines only on the upper part of the joint, 1 to 3 on each areole, straight, slender, yellowish white, darker or brownish when new, 2 to 4 cm. long, along with 2 to 4 others much shorter, up to $\frac{1}{2}$ cm. long, brownish passing to white. Flowers yellow.

Opuntia Peckii Purp. Mexico. A low prostrate and spreading bush, with small roundish joints, densely spiny. Spines brown at the base, brownish or white towards the tip. Flowers large, pale yellow, darker at the base, reddish outside.

Opuntia microdisca Weber. Argentina. Very much branched and prostrate. Joints obovate or oblong, 4 to 8 cm. long, flattened or almost cylindric, greyish green, with purple leaves soon dropping off. Areoles large and closely set, white when young; glochids yellow. Spines 10 to 15, white or reddish, up to $2\frac{1}{2}$ cm. long. Flowers bright red, $2\frac{1}{2}$ cm. long, with purple filaments. Fruit top-shaped, small, red.

Opuntia quipa Weber. Eastern Brazil. Quite different from *O. inamoena*, with which it was often confused. Joints small, oval, some what flattened, thick, 3 to 4 cm. long, and about 2 cm. broad, dull green or reddish green, with prominent areoles usually spineless. Ovary slightly smaller than the joint, of oval shape; perianth almost funnel-shaped, reddish outside, yellowish or yellowish pink inside, with erect stamens forming a brush-like bundle.

Series B. PROSTRATAE. Low or prostrate species, more or less well armed, mostly hardy.

4. *Vulgares*. Low or prostrate, joints round or oval, with few spines.

Opuntia (L.) Karst. = *Cactus Opuntia* L. = *O. vulgaris* Mill. = *Cactus Opuntia* var. *nana* DC. North America, from Massachusetts to Virginia and to Ontario (Canada). Naturalized in southern Europe. Plant prostrate, with discoid or broadly obovate joints, thick, almost smooth, of a lively green, or purplish in winter, 5 to 10 cm. broad. Areoles greyish with few yellow glochids. Spines absent, or reduced to 1, on the upper areoles, yellow, up to 2 cm. long. Flower about 5 cm. broad, pale yellow, stigma with whitish lobes. Fruit oval, deep red, 3 cm. long.

Opuntia Rafinesquei Engelm. = *O. mesacantha* Raf. = *O. humifusa* Raf. = *O. caespitosa* Raf. Texas, New Mexico, Kentucky, Missouri, Kansas and Tennessee. A low prostrate and spreading shrub, with oval-elongated joints, thin and flat, 8 to 17 cm. long. Areoles far apart, glochids brown. Spines absent or borne only on the marginal areoles, 1 to 3 together, about 2 cm. long, white tipped dark, with 1 or 2 shorter spines, directed backwards. Flowers very numerous, about 8 cm. broad, sulphur yellow, reddish at the base of the petals. Fruit pear shaped, 4 or 5 cm. long, spineless. A variable species with many varieties and forms.

Opuntia grandiflora Engelm. = *O. Rafinesquei* var. *grandiflora* Engelm. Eastern Texas. Often considered as a variety of the preceding, with the same habit. Has spineless joints, 12 to 15 cm. long, and large flowers up to 12 cm. broad, yellow, red at the centre. Fruit edible, up to 6 cm. long, sweet and mildly acid.

Opuntia tortispina Engelm. = *O. cymochila* Engelm. = *O. Rafinesquei* var. *cymochila* Engelm. = *O. spirocentra* Hort. Wisconsin to South Dakota, Kansas, Texas, New Mexico, Colorado. Prostrate and spreading. Joints roundish to obovate, 15 to 20 cm. long. Spines 6 to 8, directed backwards, or upwards on the upper or marginal areoles, straight, often spirally twisted like a cord, 3 to 6 cm. long, yellow, white or brown. Flower sulphur yellow, about 7 cm. broad.

Opuntia eburnispina Small. Sandy coasts of Florida. Prostrate and spreading, with tuberous roots. Joints roundish or oval, rather thick, 6 to 13 cm. long, pale green. Spines thick, mostly 2 to 4, 1 to 2 cm. long, ivory white, tipped yellow, passing to dark grey, not twisted, greenish, when wet. Flower yellow, 4 to 5 cm. broad; fruit obovoid, up to 2 cm. long.

Opuntia macrorhiza Engelm. Central United States. A prostrate shrub with oval green joints 6 to 15 cm. long, with large areoles and prominent tufts of brown glochids. Spines several, but only on the upper areoles, 2 to 4 cm. long, yellowish white passing to ashy white. Flowers red. Develops large tuberous nodules, like small potatoes, on the roots underground, which will sprout into young plants if cut off and planted separately.

Opuntia stenochila Engelm. New Mexico. A prostrate shrub with obovoid joints, about 10 cm. long, rather thick; spines mostly 2, one of which up to 3 cm. long, often whitish or white; glochids brown. Flower yellow, 6 cm. long. Fruit pear-shaped, juicy.

Opuntia bella Br. et R. Colombia. Mostly erect, but low, up to 1 m. high. Joints oblong, thick, 10 to 16 cm. long, dull dark green. Areoles small, glochids brown. Spines 2 to 6, needle-like, up to 2 cm. long, white. Flowers sulphur yellow fading to orange red. Fruit small, greenish yellow. A very pretty species.

Opuntia prasina Speg. Argentina. A bush about 1½ m. high, much branched and straggling. Joints oval, up to 25 cm. long, glaucous green or coppery green, spineless or with very few spines. Flower about 5 cm. broad, orange yellow.

Opuntia atrovirens Speg. Uruguay (Corrientes). Like *O. prasina*,

(a) OPUNTIA CLAVARIOIDES CRISTATA

(b) OPUNTIA DIADEMATA (PAPYRACANTHA)

PLATE IV

(b) OPUNTIA AORACANTHA

(a) OPUNTIA MOELLERI

PLATE V

with dark green joints of about the same size, with few glochids and no spines, and with reddish or orange red flowers.

Opuntia Pollardii Br. et R. Mississippi. A prostrate shrub, with tuberous roots. Joints obovate, glaucous, bluish green when young, 5 to 16 cm. long. Glochids yellow, 2 to 3 cm. long. Upper and marginal areoles with one stiff stout spine, 2½ to 4 cm. long. Flowers yellow. Fruit red, with large seeds.

Opuntia Tuna (L.) Mill. = *Cactus Tuna* L. West Indies. A shrub up to about 1 m. high. Joints mostly small and discoid, 8 to 10 cm. long, sometimes obovate and up to 16 cm. long, brownish around the areoles. Areoles large, with yellow glochids; spines mostly 3 to 5 pale yellow, spreading. Flowers about 5 cm. broad; sepals yellowish striped red along the middle; petals yellow, slightly tinged with red. Fruit red, obovoid, about 3 cm. thick.

Opuntia decumbens Salm-Dyck. Mexico to Guatemala. A low shrub with spreading drooping branches. Joints broadly oval, about 12 to 15 cm. long and 8 to 10 cm. broad, dark green, minutely pubescent, reddish around the areoles. Glochids yellowish. Spines either absent, or only 1 or 2, up to 4 cm. long, yellow passing to white. Flower 5 cm. broad, pale yellow passing to reddish. Fruit deep red.

Opuntia depressa Rose. Mexico. A low and prostrate shrub. Joints obovate, glossy dark green, at first pubescent, 20 cm. long. Spines yellowish, 1 long and 2 or 3 short ones on each areole. Flower red; fruit small, globular.

Opuntia delicata Rose. Arizona. A small prostrate shrub. Joint ovate glaucous or bluish, thin, mostly 5 to 9 cm. long, with prominent areoles and brown glochids. Spines 1 or 2, slender and brownish, only on the upper areoles, 3 to 4 cm. long. Flowers yellow, 5 to 6 cm. broad; fruit oblong, spineless.

5. *Xerocarpae*. Plants low or prostrate, strongly armed; fruit only slightly juicy, more or less woody when ripe.

Opuntia fragilis (Nutt.) Haw. = *Cactus fragilis* Nuttal = *O. brachyarthra* Engelm. et Big. Central and Western United States and British Columbia. Plant low, prostrate and spreading. Joints roundish or oval or cylindrical, somewhat flattened at least on one side, 2 to 8 cm. long, smooth, whitish green. Areoles small, white. Spines 5 to 8, brownish to greyish, tipped darker, up to 3½ cm. long. Joints drop off at the least touch. Flowers rarely borne, 5 cm. broad, pale yellow. Fruit dry, spiny, about 2 cm. long. A common and invading species.

Opuntia arenaria Engelm. New Mexico and Texas, on sandy soils. A low bush, with a long and thick root. Joints 4 to 8 cm. long and 2 to 4 cm. broad, oval, with large brown areoles and numerous brown glochids. Spines 5 to 8, up to 4 cm. long. Flower yellow or red, 7 cm. broad, Fruit oval, 3 cm. long, dry, spiny. Very rare, even in its native habitat.

Opuntia trichophora (Engelm.) Br. et R. = *O. missouriensis trichophora* Engelm. New Mexico, Texas and Oklahoma. Prostrate and spreading; joints disc-like to obovate, 6 to 10 cm. broad, with closely set areoles. Spines numerous, unequal, up to 4 cm. long, needle-like, pale yellow or white, on old joints developing into long hair-like bristles up to 6 cm. long. Flowers pale yellow.

Opuntia hystricina Engelm. et Big. New Mexico to Arizona and Nevada. A spreading bush partly prostrate. Joints obovate or round, 8 to 20 cm. long. Areoles rather large and closely set. Spines numerous, pale brown passing to white, unequal, the longer ones 5 to 10 cm. long, stiff and somewhat flat, often reflexed. Glochids yellow. Flower 6 cm. broad, yellow; fruit more or less oblong, up to 3 cm. long, dry, spiny at the top.

Opuntia erinacea Engelm. California, Arizona, Utah and Nevada. A more or less erect bushy plant, up to 80 cm. high with oval or elongated joints, 8 to 15 cm. long, thick, flat or almost cylindrical, deep green, with closely set, small and somewhat prominent whitish areoles. Glochids few, small, yellow. Spines very numerous, spreading, slender, white or white tipped brown or brownish, about 5 cm. long, flexible, mostly directed upwards at the top. Flower 6 cm. broad, deep pink or yellow. Fruit very spiny.

var. **ursina** (Weber) = *O. rutila* Auct. non Nutt. This is the so-called *Grizzly Bear*, from the Mojave Desert, California. A beautiful variety with smaller joints (6 to 10 cm. long), and with more numerous and more slender, white or brownish, hair-like spines, up to 12 cm. long, exceptionally up to 25 cm. long.

Opuntia polyacantha Haw. = *O. missouriensis* DC. = *O. splendens* Pfeiff. From British Columbia and Alberta, Washington, Utah, to Arizona and Texas. An excessively variable species, quite hardy, with many varieties and forms in cultivation. Plant prostrate. Joints discoid or broadly oval, about 10 cm. broad, rather thin, pale green. Areoles numerous and close together, small, on low prominences, all spiny and with yellow glochids. Radial spines 5 to 10, whitish bristle-like, radiating. Central spines absent, or 1 to 5, up to 4 cm. long, dark brown, pale at the point. Spines on the lateral areoles mostly pointing upwards. Flower pale yellow, 5 cm. broad. Fruit dry, oblong, 2 cm. long, spiny.

The following are the best varieties or forms:

var. **albispina** Engelm. et Big. Spines all white.

var. **salmonea** Hort. Spath. Flower pale yellow, soon passing to reddish yellow, before fading.

var. **erythrostemma** Hort. Spath. Flower dark yellow: stamens red.

var. **subinermis** Engelm. Spines few and short.

var. **rufispina** Engelm. et Big. Spines reddish.

Opuntia Schweriniana K. Sch. Colorado. Same habit as the pre-

(b) OPUNTIA HERRFELDTII

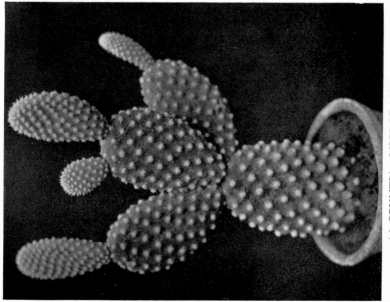

(a) OPUNTIA MICRODASYS
var. albispina

PLATE VI

PLATE VII

ceding. Joints about 5 cm. long and 3 cm. broad, slightly warty. Areoles with red glochids. Spines 7 to 10, at first whitish, passing to dark brown almost black, 1 to 1½ cm. long, straight, mostly directed upwards. Flower about 4 cm. broad, greenish yellow, yellowish red outside. Fruit spiny, dry.

Opuntia juniperina Br. et R. New Mexico. Same habit as *O. polyacantha*, but more erect. Joints obovate, 10 to 12 cm. long, broad and rounded at the top. Areoles small, farther apart, the upper ones bearing one stout spine, brown, 3 to 4 cm. long, and 1 or more shorter spines. Fruit 3 cm. long, oblong, spineless, dry.

Opuntia rhodantha K. Sch. = *O. utahensis* Purp. Nebraska, Colorado, Utah. An erect bush, 40 to 50 cm. high, spreading and sometimes prostrate. Joints oval, 7 to 15 cm. long, and 5 to 10 cm. broad, green passing to greyish, rather thick, with brownish areoles and brown glochids. Spines 2 to 4, with a few very short ones, the longest up to 4 cm. long, spreading, yellowish brown. Flower about 6 cm. broad, a lively carmine red, stamens red, stigma with 8 green lobes. Fruit spiny, dry. A beautiful and hardy species, free-flowering. Includes many varieties and forms, which may be classed under two subspecies.

(*a*) **pisciformis** (Spath.) More robust and almost tree-like, with narrower deep green joints, yellow spines. Flowers smaller, but very numerous.

(*b*) **xanthostemma** (K. Sch.). Colorado. Very pretty and perfectly hardy in temperate climates. Plant spreading and almost prostrate, with roundish or broadly oval joints, 6 to 10 cm. broad, of a lively green, with reddish brown warts. Glochids yellow or reddish brown. Spines 2 to 4, dark brown, 2 to 4 cm. long, often reflexed backwards. Flower carmine pink, with yellow stamens. Both often described as distinct species.

var. **Schumanmiana** Spath. = *fulgens* Spath. Flower of a deep carmine red. In the form *longispina* Hort. the spines are 5 to 8 cm. long.

Opuntia sphaerocarpa Engelm. et Big. New Mexico. A low spreading bush, with round joints, 6 to 7 cm. broad, rather thick and warty, pale green or purplish, areoles far apart, with yellow glochids. Spines 1 or 2, borne only on the upper and marginal areoles, brown passing to greyish, needle-like, up to 2 cm. long. Fruit small, spineless, dry.

Series C. DISCOIDEAE: Shrubs erect or tree-like, with medium sized to very large, oval or round, more or less disc-like joints.

6. *Pubescentes.* Joints with velvety hairs.

Opuntia basilaris Engelm. et Big. From northern Mexico and California to Nevada, Arizona and Utah. A bush about 1 m. high branching from the base. Joints oval, smooth or slightly pubescent broader above the middle, usually abrupt at the top, 10 to 20 cm. long bluish green or reddish green. Areoles numerous, brownish, with reddish brown glochids, and with one short spine, often absent. Flower 6 to 8 cm. broad, pale pink to carmine, showy. Fruit round,

F

dry, with a few large lenticular white seeds. A beautiful and popular species, resistant to low temperatures.

var. **ramosa** Parish. Joints thinner, branching from the top for 3 or 4 times.

var. **cordata** Hort. Joints thinner, branching only from the base, like the leaves of a cabbage, cordate at the top, of a beautiful bluish green.

var. **nana** Hort. Joints small and narrow, branching from the base, with small areoles very closely set and always spineless.

var. **albiflora** Weinb. Flower white.

There is also a cristate form with long, ribbon-like, thin joints.

Thrives well in a half-shaded place, in a loamy and sandy soil, with some calcareous matter. Should not be exposed to too much rain in winter.

Opuntia Treleasii Coulter. California. Very much like the preceding species, but lower, more spreading at the base, and often with branches of 2 to 4 erect joints. Joints obovate, about 15 cm. long, thick, pale bluish green, smooth. Areoles numerous, with dirty yellow glochids, usually spineless, rarely with a few short spines. Flowers pink. Fruit almost round, dry, with a few large seeds. Rare in cultivation.

Opuntia lubrica Griffiths. A very rare species from Mexico, grows taller and is more spreading. Joints obovate and almost orbicular, 12 to 15 cm. long, glossy grass-green, almost smooth. Areoles large, prominent, dark yellow; spines when present mostly 1 to 3, yellowish, 1 to 2½ cm. long. Fruit reddish, drying, with small seeds, thin-shelled.

Opuntia puberula Pfeiff. Mexico. An erect, spreading bush, up to 1 m. high. Joints broadly oval, numerous, yellowish green, covered with a very short velvety pubescence, 7 to 12 cm. long and 4 to 8 cm. broad, with large yellow areoles and prominent tufts of yellow glochids. Spines 3 to 8, spreading, 1 to 3 cm. long, yellowish, often absent. Flowers numerous, greenish yellow, about 4 cm. broad. Fruit round, red. The plant known under this name in cultivation and to which the above description applies is probably a natural hybrid of *O. microdasys*. The true *O. puberula* Pfeiff. is different, and the name is considered as a synonym of *O. decumbens* Salm-Dyck.

Opuntia microdasys (Lehm.) Pfeiffer. = *Cactus microdasys* Lehmann = *O. pulvinata* DC. Northern Mexico. An erect much branched bush, up to 1 m. high, very lovely and popular. Joints broadly oval, oval, or oval-elongated, of a pleasant yellowish green, with very short pubescence, 8 to 15 cm. long. Areoles thickly set, large, round, with a prominent rounded large tuft of golden yellow glochids, and rarely with 1 short yellow spine. Flower pale yellow, 4 cm. broad, petals often pointed reddish. Fruit round, red, with white pulp. Rather delicate as to temperature, being liable to suffer in severe winters on the southern shores of the Mediterranean.

var. **pallida** Hort. Joints as large as in the type or larger, with pale yellow areoles and glochids.

var. **gracilior** Hort. Joints smaller, more rounded, and thicker.

var. **minima** Hort. = *minor* Hort. Joints roundish or oval, 5 to 7 cm. long. Areoles and glochids of a deeper golden yellow. A very pretty variety, best grown grafted.

var. **albispina** Hort. Joints rather small, as in the variety *gracilior*, or even in the var. *minima*, and thinner. Areoles and glochids of a shining silvery white. A wonderful new variety from Mexico, easily grown. Requires warmth.

var. **monstrosa** Hort. Joints small, very elongated, of a paler green, with small and very thickly set areoles and pale yellow glochids. The joints have a marked tendency to grow indefinitely, becoming very elongated, often until the apex dries up. Best grown grafted on *O. ficus indica* or other strong species.

Opuntia rufida Engelm. = *O. microdasys* var. *rufida* K. Sch. Northern Mexico and Texas. An erect bush, about 50 cm. high. Joints like those of *O. microdasys* var. *minima* or var. *gracilior*, but of a dark greyish green, more elongated and slightly thicker. Areoles large, with brownish red or chocolate brown glochids. Spines absent. Flower yellow or orange yellow. A lovely and popular species.

Opuntia Herrfeldtii Kupper. Central Mexico (Queretaro). A beautiful recent introduction and fit companion of *O. microdasys*. Plant erect, bushy, up to 1 m. high, with a short stem. Joints discoid, or even broader than long, rarely somewhat oval, glaucous or greyish green, velvety, up to 15 cm. broad and 1 to 2 cm. thick. Areoles rather closely set, large, round, with prominent cushions of reddish brown glochids, spineless. Flower about 5 cm. broad, sulphur yellow. Fruit globular, 3 cm. thick, green, juicy. Requires warmth, but is easy to grow. No collection should be without it.

Opuntia macrocalyx Griffiths. Mexico (Saltillo). An erect and spreading bush, up to 1 m. high. Joints obovate, up to 22 cm. long and 9 cm. broad, greyish green, with velvety pubescence. Areoles large, roundish, rather closely set, yellowish brown; glochids numerous, short, reddish brown. Spines absent. Flower yellow, petals acuminate. Fruit oblong or almost cylindrical, about 7 cm. long, red, pulp greenish, with few small seeds. Rare in cultivation.

Opuntia velutina Weber = *O. Nelsonii* Rose. Southern Mexico. A tall shrub, 3 to 4 m. high. Joints broadly oval, 15 to 20 cm. long and 10 to 15 cm. broad below the middle, grass green, with a short velvety pubescence. Areoles white, with numerous yellow glochids, passing to brown. Spines 2 to 6, pale yellow, 3 to 5 cm. long. Flower yellow, 5 cm. broad. Fruit green, round, with numerous tufts of yellowish brown bristles.

Opuntia tomentosa Salm-Dyck = *O. Hernandezii* DC. Central

Mexico. Tree-like. Joints oval-elongated, broader above the middle, dark green, 10 to 20 cm. long, markedly velvety. Areoles far apart, with few pale yellow glochids. Spines usually absent, or sometimes 1 or 2 very short white ones. Flower fiery red, passing to dark red, about 5 cm. broad. Fruit oval, dark red, spineless.

Opuntia Wilcoxii Br. et R. Mexico (Sonora and Sinaloa). A tall bush, 1 to 2 m. high. Joints broadly oblong, up to 20 cm. long, dark green, minutely pubescent, more or less purplish around the areoles, which are far apart and furnished with long yellow glochids. Spines 1 to 3, the longest up to 5 cm. long, white or yellowish. Flowers yellow. Fruit pubescent, spineless, 4 cm. long.

Opuntia tomentella Berger. Guatemala. A tall bush about 2 m. high. Joints oval-elongated, broader above the middle, 20 to 30 cm. long and 9 to 15 cm. broad, pale green, very slightly pubescent. Areoles small, far apart, spineless or with one very short spine. Flower as in *O. tomentosa* but paler; fruit smaller.

Opuntia pycnantha Engelm. = *O. pycnacantha* K. Sch. Lower California. Mostly prostrate or very low. Joints oblong or orbicular, often 20 cm. long, slightly pubescent, very spiny. Areoles large and closely set, glochids yellow or brown, spines 8 to 12, yellow or brown, reflexed, 2 to 3 cm. long. Fruit globose, very spiny.

Opuntia leucotricha DC. = *O. leucacantha* Link. et Otto. Central Mexico. Tree-like, 3 to 4 m. high, freely branching. Joints oval or oval-elongated, up to 25 cm. long and 12 cm. broad, green, covered with very short greyish velvety hair. Areoles white, closely set, with yellow glochids, and with 1 to 3 white spines, short, and later increasing in number; and along with these there are numerous bristle-like or hair-like, white flexible spines, 5 to 8 cm. long, almost entirely covering the surface of the joint. Flower deep yellow, 6 to 8 cm. broad, with whitish stamens, deep red style and stigma with 6 green lobes. Fruit round, whitish or yellowish, aromatic, edible, sold in the markets of Mexico under the name of duraznillo. A beautiful and popular species, requiring warmth, but easy to grow.

var. **fulvispina** (Salm-Dyck). A form in which the long bristle-like spines are yellowish. There is also a pretty cristate form.

Opuntia Guilanchii Griffiths, from Mexico (Zacatecas), is probably only a variety of the preceding, with broader joints, devoid or almost devoid of bristle-like hairs, and with larger fruits.

Opuntia Ritteri Berger. Mexico (Zacatecas). Tree-like. Joints roundish to oval, rather large, pale green, with short velvety hairs. Areoles closely set, round, with yellowish spines 1 to 1½ cm. long, directed upwards. Flower large, pale red.

Opuntia comonduensis (Coulter) Br. et R. Lower California (Comondu). A spreading bush, about 20 cm. high. Joints obovate or roundish, 12 to 15 cm. long, softly pubescent, with large brown areoles and yellow glochids. Spines only on the upper areoles, mostly

1 or 2, but more numerous on old joints, thin, yellow, 3 to 5 cm. long. Flower yellow; fruit purple, 4 cm. long, spineless.

Opuntia Macdougaliana Rose. = *O. micrarthra* Griffiths. Southern Mexico. Tree-like, about 4 m. high. Joints oblong, about 30 cm. long and 8 to 10 cm. broad, softly pubescent. Areoles small; spines mostly 4, yellowish, passing to whitish, the longest up to 4 cm. long. Fruit globose, 5 cm. long, red, usually spineless.

Opuntia affinis Griffiths. Mexico (Oaxaca). An erect shrub, up to 2 m. high. Joints obovate, up to 35 cm. long and 13 cm. broad, densely pubescent and hairy. Areoles small, oval, white passing to grey, with pale yellow glochids. Spines on the upper areoles, 1 to 5, later on more numerous, up to 3 cm. long, flattened, angular, pale yellow, passing to white. Flowers small, 3 cm. broad, orange with a median red rib. Fruit small, globose, red.

Opuntia atropes Rose. Central Mexico. Is a nearly allied species with oblong joints 20 to 30 cm. long, deep green, softly pubescent. Areoles round, brownish, with long yellow glochids. Spines several, at first white or yellowish, passing to dark yellow, 3 to 6 cm. long, spreading. Flower reddish; fruit with large areoles and long glochids, almost spineless.

Opuntia durangensis Br. et R. Central Mexico. Tree-like. Joints broadly obovate, about 20 cm. long and 16 cm. broad, pale green, at first minutely pubescent,, later almost smooth. Areoles with brown glochids, and with 3 to 5 short spines, 1½ cm. long, yellow passing to brown. Flower yellow; fruit white or red, slightly spiny.

7. *Criniferae*. Areoles with fine woolly hair.

Opuntia crinifera Pfeiff. = *O. orbiculata* Salm-Dyck = *O. lanigera* Salm -Dyck = *O. senilis* Parm. Northern Mexico. A tall bush, about 2m. high. Joints oval or unequally oval, or roundish, 15 to 25 cm. long, and 10 to 15 cm. broad, usually glaucous or pale bluish green, thick, with large greyish areoles, and reddish yellow glochids. Spines about 6, straight, spreading or twisted, up to 4 cm. long, at first yellowish, soon passing to white or ash colour. There are also numerous curly white hairs, spreading all round the areole, mostly applied to and covering the surface of the joint. Flower large, yellow, reddish at the base, with yellow stamens, pink style and stigma with greenish lobes. Fruit red. A well-known species, deservedly popular.

Opuntia pilifera Weber. Mexico (Puebla). Tree-like, up to 4 m. high. Joints oblong or roundish, 12 to 20 cm. long, 7 to 12 cm. broad, broader above the middle, pale glaucous green or bluish green. Areoles whitish, with many curly white hairs, partly covering the joint; glochids brownish. Spines 3 to 5 or more, slender, whitish, 1 to 1½ cm. long. Flower large, red, with abundant hairs at the top of the ovary. Fruit red. Rather rare in cultivation.

Opuntia pailana Weingt. Mexico (Sierra de la Paila). About 1 m. high. Joints glaucous or bluish green, roundish or more often oblong or elongated, 8 to 14 cm. long, and 5 to 8 cm. broad. Areoles yellowish brown, with yellowish grey glochids and with brush-like tufts of many long milk-white hairs. Spines at first 3, later developing to 6 or more, acicular, 2 to 4 cm. long, at first white, passing to brownish, tipped darker. A very interesting and beautiful species. The white hairs are developed better in the shade or under glass. Frequently sold as *O. senilis*.

Opuntia Scheeri Weber. Mexico. Plant spreading and low, hardly more than 1 m. high. Joints oblong or roundish, 15 to 20 cm. long, pale greyish green or bluish green. Areoles closely set, yellowish brown, with yellowish brown glochids. Spines 8 to 12, slender, about 1 cm. long, golden yellow, associated with many long, pale yellow or yellow hairs, straight or curly, and spreading over the surface of the joint. Flower large, often 10 cm. broad, sulphur yellow, passing to reddish, with pink style and green lobes of stigma. Fruit globose, red. A very attractive species, requires warmth.

Opuntia hyptiacantha Weber. Mexico (Oaxaca). Tree-like, with joints 20 to 25 cm. long, oval or oval-elongated, green or greyish green, Areoles greyish, with few brown glochids. Spines 8 to 10, white. 1 to 2 cm. long, tortuous, with 2 or 3 central spines, which are slightly longer, deflexed and bent downwards. There are also 2 or 3, sometimes more, stiff, white, bristle-like hairs. Flower yellow or reddish. Fruit pale yellow.

8. *Myriacanthae*. Joints large, very spiny. Natives of the Galàpagos Islands.

Opuntia myriacantha Weber. Galàpagos Islands. (Charles Island and Albemarle). Tree-like and densely branched. Joints oval, pale green, up to 25 cm. long and 20 cm. broad, rather thin, with prominent woolly areoles about 1½ cm. apart, bearing golden yellow glochids ½ cm. long. Spines very numerous, up to 10 cm. long in their native country, needle-like, golden yellow passing to greyish. Flower up to 8 cm. long and 5 to 6 cm. broad, glossy yellow, with a pear-shaped, warty and spiny ovary; stamens and 9 lobed stigma whitish.

Opuntia galapageia Hensl. Galàpagos Islands. (James Island). Tree-like, 2 to 3 m. high, with a stem up to 20 cm. thick, very densely covered with spines. Joints up to 30 cm. long, oblong or elliptical, rather thick. Areoles with 3 to 4 spreading, flexible, bristle-like spines, later developing a brush-like bundle of the same spines. Flower small, 2 cm. broad, red, with woolly ovary. Style thick, stigma with 8 thick erect lobes. Fruit glossy red.

Opuntia Helleri K. Sch. Galàpagos Islands (Wenman Island). A prostrate and cespitose shrub, much branched. Joints oblong-elongated, acute at the top and base, up to 11 cm. long and 4 cm. broad, thin, smooth, covered with brown spines. Areoles round, small, yellow, with many short yellow glochids, not prickly. Spines about 20 about 1½ cm. long, yellowish brown, also not prickly. Flower about 3½ cm. broad, greenish yellow; stigma with 6 erect thick lobes.

A fourth species is **Opuntia insularis** Stewart.

9. *Indicae*. Joints large, with few spines or almost spineless. Fruits large, edible.

Opuntia Ficus-indica (L.) Mill. = *Cactus Ficus-indica* L. Tropical America, cultivated and naturalized in many countries. Tree-like, 3 to 5 m. high, with spreading branches. Joints oval or oval-elongated, 20 to 40 cm. long and 10 to 20 cm. broad, green or greyish green, almost smooth when young, quite smooth when fully developed. Areoles whitish, with short yellow glochids. Spines mostly absent, or 1 to 2, straight and awl-shaped, pale yellow. Flower about 6½ cm. long, with an elliptical spineless, warty ovary; corolla 4 to 5 cm. broad, canary yellow, with pale yellow stamens about half as long as the petals; stigma with 7 or 8 erect lobes. Fruit oval, 5 to 10 cm. long, or pear-shaped with a short green warty peduncle, white or white streaked yellow and red, or deep crimson, or yellow, or yellow streaked reddish, with pulp of the same colour, and with many areoles and yellow glochids, but no spines. As a fruit-bearing tree the following varieties are in cultivation.

var. **alba**. Fruits large, oval, white or white faintly streaked yellow or reddish.

var. **rubra**. Fruits oval or somewhat elongated and peduncled, crimson red.

var. **lutea**. Fruits oval, yellow. The sweetest.

var. **asperma**. Fruit oval, yellow, with a few abortive black seeds. A sub-variety (*asperma minor*), has smaller yellow fruits (5 to 6 cm. long), with very small abortive black seeds. The pulp is yellow.

var. **pyriformis**. Fruit pear-shaped and peduncled, large, 12 cm. long or more, yellow streaked reddish or violet. Pulp nankeen yellow. Seeds few.

var. **serotina**. Fruit oval, yellow, often shaded nankeen or reddish, flowering late and maturing very late (October—November).

Opuntia elongata Haw. Mexico. Tree-like, 2 to 3 m. high. Joints oval-elongated, 30 to 50 cm. long, and 9 to 15 cm. broad, dull green or greyish green, with brownish areoles and a few whitish glochids. Spines, when present, 1 to 3, white, 1½ to 2 cm. long. Flower about 8 cm. broad, pale yellow. Fruit club-shaped, 8 cm. long, greenish yellow, reddish on the sunny side, hardly eatable.

Opuntia lanceolata Haw. West Indies and South America. Closely allied to the preceding, possibly only a variety. Tree-like, 2 to 3 m. high, quick-growing, densely branched. Joints rhomboid or lanceolate, often irregular, but thick, 20 to 30 cm. long and 6 to 8 cm. broad, grassy green passing to dark greyish green, with oblong yellowish areoles and yellowish glochids. Spines 1 or 2, about 1 cm. long, easily dropping off, mostly absent, and only present on the upper joints. Flower 6½ cm. long, 5 cm. broad, outer petals green, inner petals sulphur yellow or chrome yellow. Fruit red, clavate, sweetish, with hard seeds.

Opuntia undulata Griffiths = *O. undosa* Griffiths. Mexico. Tree-like with spreading branches. Joints obovate, broadly rounded at top, up to 55 cm. long and 35 cm. broad, often scooped or wavy, glossy pale green, passing to dark glaucous green. Areoles greyish, far apart; glochids few, short, yellow. Spines often absent, mostly 1 or sometimes up to 5, white, about 1 cm. long. Fruit large, oval, about 10 cm. long, dull red, pulp streaked with red and orange, very sweet, with hard seeds. Cultivated as a fruit tree.

Opuntia decumana Haw. = *O. Labouretiana* Cons. = *O. gymnocarpa* Weber. Known only in cultivation. Native country doubtfully given as Tropical South America. Tree-like, 3 to 4 m. high. Joints oval or elliptical, 25 to 35 cm. long and 10 to 18 cm. broad, dull green, with a few white spines, 1½ to 2 cm. long. Flower 10 cm. broad, deep orange red. Fruit large, oval, red, spineless and with few glochids. *O. maxima* Mill. non Salm-Dyck, is doubtfully referred to this species.

Opuntia crassa Haw. = *O. glauca* Forbes. Mexico. A straggling bush up to 1 m. high. Joints oval or almost round, broad and bluntly rounded above, 7 to 12 cm. long, and 6 to 8 cm. broad, and 1½ to 2 cm. thick, smooth or very slightly pubescent, glaucous green or greyish green, thickly studded with large brown areoles, with broad and prominent tufts of glossy brownish yellow glochids. Spines 1 or 2, very short, white, usually absent in cultivation. A beautiful species with the general appearance of *O. microdasys* and often mistaken for it. Less liable to suffer from cold.

10. *Albispinosae*. Tree-like. Joints large, strong; areoles not woolly, but with more or less strong white spines.

Opuntia spinulifera Salm-Dyck. Mexico. Tree-like. Joints roundish or oval, 20 to 25 cm. long, dull green. Areoles small, of oval shape, white, with white glochids. Spines present only on the upper joints, 1 to 2 cm. long, yellowish. Flower yellow. **O. oligacantha** Salm-Dyck, from Mexico, is probably only a variety with bright green joints, round brownish areoles, brown glochids, and 1 to 3 white spines, up to 1¼ cm. long, usually absent. **O. candelabriformis** Martius, also from Mexico, is probably another variety, with more roundish and smaller and thicker joints, and with a few long white flexible spines intermixed with the others.

Opuntia streptacantha Lem. = *O. cardona* Weber. Mexico. Tree-like up to 5 m. high, with oval or elliptical or almost roundish joints, 20 to 30 cm. long, deep green, passing to light greyish green, rather thick. Areoles small, with yellowish glochids. Spines many, white, 1 to 3 cm. long, straight or twisted or bent, and reflexed. Flower large yellow. Fruit roundish, 5 cm. long, red, edible. Largely cultivated for its fruit in Mexico, which is sold under the name of *tuna cardona*, and extensively used for making preserves.

Opuntia amyclaea Tenore = *O. Ficus-indica* var. *amyclaea* Berger. First described from wild plants on Monte Pellegrino near Palermo (Sicily); native country unknown. Wrongly supposed to be the wild form of *O. Ficus-indica*. Joints oval-elongated, 30 to 40 cm. long, dark green passing to grey, with yellowish brown glochids, and 1 to 4 spines white or semi-transparent, straight, spreading, 3 to 4 cm. long. Flower yellow. Fruit yellowish red.

Opuntia lasiacantha Pfeiff. = *O. megacantha* var. *lasiacantha* Berger. Central Mexico. Tree-like. Joints obovate or oblong, 20 to 30 cm. long, with short red leaves and small areoles. Spines usually, 1 to 3, needle-like, white, 2 to 4 cm. long, spreading. Glochids numerous, long, dirty yellow or brown. Flowers large, yellow or deep orange, 6 to 8 cm. broad; ovary with long brown bristles, soon dropping off.

Opuntia megacantha Salm-Dyck = *O. Castillae* Griffiths. Mexico, where it is also much cultivated. A shrub about 2 m. high and spreading, Joints dull greyish green, passing to grey, oval or roundish, 28 cm. long, about 17 cm. broad, rather thin. Areoles small, whitish, but with brown wool when young. Glochids few, yellow. Spines 3 to 5, unequal, 1 or 2 being longer, up to 3 cm. long, white, and deflexed or geniculate. Flowers very numerous, golden yellow, 6 cm. broad. Fruit yellowish white, oval, with a yellowish pulp of a vinous taste. Grown as a fruit tree.

Opuntia inaequilateralis Berger. Origin unknown. A spreading, straggling shrub, 1 m. high. Joints irregularly oval, with unequal sides, up to 30 cm. long and 14 cm. broad, and 2 to 3 cm. thick, grass green, with small areoles and short brown glochids. Spines 4 to 7, of which one is central and up to 3 cm. long. All spines are white, and are more numerous on the upper areoles. Flower pale yellow, 6 cm. broad. Fruit roundish, yellowish green, about 5 cm. long, maturing in the second year, with an acid pulp. Doubtfully considered as native of Mexico.

Opuntia Eichlamii Rose. Guatemala. Tree-like, 5 to 6 m. high. Joints roundish or oval, broader above the middle, up to 20 cm. long and 15 cm. broad, greyish green, with brown glochids. Spines 4 to 6, up to 2 cm. long, spreading, the central one longer and somewhat flattened. Flower 3½ cm. long, carmine red; stigma with 8 to 11 pale green lobes. Fruit 4 cm. long.

Opuntia Deamii Rose. Guatemala. About 1 m. high, branched from the ground. Joints obovate or almost lanceolate, 25 to 30 cm. long, at first pale green, passing to dark green, with few small areoles. Spines 2 to 6, thick, 3 to 5 cm. long, yellowish passing to white, spreading. Flower 6 cm. broad, reddish. Fruit 6 cm. long, claret red.

Opuntia Dobbieana Br. et R. Ecuador. Tree-like, up to 4 m. high or often a low bush. Joints obovate or roundish, 10 to 25 cm. long, pale green, very spiny. Areoles small, closely set. Spines white, 5 to 12, needle-like or awl-shaped, 1 to 3 cm. long, associated with 2 to 4 reflexed hairs from the areole. Flower chocolate-coloured, 4 to 5 cm. broad, filaments and style pinkish, lobes of stigma green. Fruit 3 to 5 cm. long, red, juicy, at first spiny.

11. *Monacanthae*. Joints large, smooth and glossy. Areoles with one long spine, later with two or more.

Opuntia monacantha Haw. South Brazil, Uruguay, Paraguay and Argentina. Almost tree-like, 2 m. high, with a thick stem. Joints oval or oval-elongated, narrow at the point of insertion on the mother joint, 10 to 30 cm. long, often smaller, rather thin, glossy green. Areoles far apart, with 1 straight brown spine, 3 to 4 cm. long, sometimes with 2 or even 3 spines on the top joints. Flower about 8 cm. broad, deep yellow; outer petals reddish at the base. Fruit 7 cm. long, pear-shaped, red, spineless, proliferous. Sometimes miscalled *O. vulgaris* Mill, which is a very different species.

var. **variegata** Cels. A very pretty variety, with smaller joints, beautifully marbled with white or yellow, and often also with pink.

Opuntia Lemaireana Weber. Argentina. A closely allied species, perhaps a variety, of smaller size, with smaller joints, and smaller but much more numerous flowers.

Opuntia elata Link et Otto. Paraguay. A tall erect bush, with elongated green or deep green joints, smooth, 15 to 25 cm. long. Areoles far apart, margined dark brown, large, with whitish wool. Spines absent on new joints, or limited to 1, which is thick and 3 cm. long, more numerous on old joints. Flower orange yellow, with white stamens. Fruit pear-shaped, spineless, red.

Opuntia Delaetiana Weber. Paraguay and Northern Argentina. Often considered as a variety of the preceding, but is distinct. Plant more robust, with grass green joints, oblong, 25 cm. long, 8 cm. broad, at first spineless, with wavy margin. Areoles large, later bearing many brown glochids and 1 to 4 spines, straight or curved, pink passing to yellowish brown, up to 4 cm. long. Flowers numerous and large, orange yellow, very showy. Fruit elongated pear-shaped, 7 to 8 cm. long, red.

Opuntia Mieckleyi K. Sch. Paraguay. Similar to *O. elata*, with joints of the same shape, but smaller and narrower, and of a darker green, very thick. Areoles large, white. Spines absent, or reduced to one, awl-shaped, thick and whitish, about 3 cm. long. Flower orange red or brick-red, 6 cm. broad, with notched petals. Fruit pear-shaped, spineless, deep red.

Opuntia paraguayensis K. Sch. = *O. bonaerensis* Speg. Argentina and Paraguay. An erect, straggling bush. Joints unequal, oblong, often abrupt at the top, 19 to 21 cm. long, and 8 to 15 cm. broad, but often very narrow and almost cylindrical at the base. Areoles elliptical, yellowish, up to ½ cm. long, with a prominent tuft of yellow glochids. Spines absent. Flower about 8 cm. broad, deep yellow or orange, with brownish wool and glochids at the base of the outer petals. Fruit pear-shaped, about 7 cm. long, dull purple.

Opuntia grosseiana Weber. Paraguay. Closely allied to *O. elata*, with joints intermediate between that species and *O. anacantha*.

Opuntia anacantha Speg. Argentina. A low semi-prostrate shrub, with long lanceolate, thick, glossy, deep green joints, 15 to 40 cm. long. Areoles small, dark brown. Spines mostly absent. Flowers 5 to 6 cm. broad, very numerous, deep orange yellow, reddish outside. Fruit 3 cm. long, pear-shaped or oval, red, spineless.

Opuntia subsphaerocarpa Speg. Argentina. Almost tree-like, densely branched; joints large, oval, glossy green. Areoles with only 1 or 2 white spines, 1½ to 2½ cm. long, mostly absent. Flowers yellow. Fruit globose, red.

Opuntia Arechavaletai Speg. Argentina and Uruguay. A shrub 1 to 3 m. high, erect, much branched. Joints oblong or obovate, flattened, 25 to 30 cm. long, grass green. Areoles small, brown. Spines usually 1, sometimes 2 or 3, spreading, awl-shaped or flattened, white, up to 9 cm. long. Flowers yellow, with white stamens and style. Fruit pear-shaped, 7 cm. long, violet-purple.

Opuntia stenartha K. Sch. = *O. retrorsa* Speg. Paraguay. A prostrate and spreading shrub. Joints pale green, 8 to 25 cm. long, oval-elongated, very narrow, often not more than 2½ cm. at the middle, and also very thin (about ½ cm.). Areoles roundish to oval, with red glochids. Spines absent, or 1 to 5, awl-shaped, thick, honey-coloured, passing to black, up to 3 cm. long. Flower yellow, 3 cm. broad. Fruit pear-shaped, warty, red, about 2 cm. long.

Opuntia canina Speg. Argentina. Erect or decumbent, spreading; joints flat, 25 to 35 cm. long, narrowed at both ends, and about 4½ cm. broad, glossy green. Areoles on old joints with 1 to 3 spines, greyish white, 1½ to 3½ cm. long, reflexed. Flowers numerous, rather small, yellowish orange, 4 to 5 cm. broad, with yellow filaments and stigma with 5 lobes. Fruit obovoid, about 2½ cm. long, red, with white pulp. **O. kiska-loro** Speg., from Argentina, is very similar, but more prostrate and rooting, with longer spines, flower orange, with pale orange filaments; fruit 5 cm. long, deep violet-purple, pulp white.

Opuntia utkilio Speg. Northern Argentina. Prostrate and rooting at the joints, often with very long branches. Joints flat elliptic-elongated, 15 to 30 cm. long, 5 to 6 cm. broad, deep green; spines 2 to 5, later more numerous, the upper ones longer (3 to 4 cm.), all reflexed. Flowers small, yellowish. Fruit 3 cm. long, reddish violet, pulp of same colour, somewhat spiny.

Opuntia montevidensis Speg. Uruguay (Cerro de Montevideo). A cespitose shrub with erect branches, 30 to 50 cm. high. Joints 5 to 10 cm. long, obovate or elliptic, glossy green. Areoles small, with 4 to 6 spines, 3 longer and thicker, 2 very small and bristle-like, these last reflexed, the others erect or spreading, white, 2 to 3 cm. long. Flowers 4 to 5 cm. broad, orange; fruit clavate, about 4 cm. long, dark purple. Frequently grown in small pots for house decoration.

Opuntia aurantiaca Gill. = *O. extensa* Salm-Dyck. Argentina and Uruguay. Almost prostrate, and spreading. Joints dark green, or almost black, linear-lanceolate or almost cylindrical, 5 to 15 cm. long, and 1 to 2½ cm. thick. Spines 2 or 3, sometimes up to 6, brown or amber yellow, 1 to 3 cm. long, stiff, straight, awl-shaped. Areoles rather large, greyish, with short pale yellow glochids. Flower deep yellow or orange yellow, about 4 cm. broad. Fruit pear-shaped, 2 to 3 cm. long, deep red.

Opuntia discolor Br. et R. Argentina. Differs from the preceding by the dark brown areoles and brown glochids. The flower is deep yellow, 3 cm. broad; fruit very small, bright red. The spines are variegated, but mostly brown.

Opuntia fuscoatra Engelm. Eastern Texas. Prostrate. Joints orbicular or obovate, 5 to 8 cm. long. Areoles far apart, large, bearing 1 to 3 thick spines, yellow, passing to dark brown or nearly black. Glochids many, brown. Flower 7½ cm. broad, yellow, stigma with 5 lobes. Fruit red, 4 to 5 cm. long.

Opuntia macrarthra Gibbes. South Carolina. A low bush with prostrate or ascending branches, up to 1 m. high. Joints pale green, dull or somewhat shining, thick, oblong-elongated, narrowed at both ends, 10 to 25 cm. long and 4 to 8 cm. broad. Areoles very far apart, large, round, brownish, with pale brown glochids, often entirely spineless, or later developing 1 to 3 spines, 2 to 5 cm. long, stiff and thick, straw-coloured, blotched or zoned reddish. Fruit 4 to 6 cm. long, pear-shaped elongated, red.

Opuntia quimilo K. Sch. Northern Argentina. A much branched spreading shrub, up to 4 m. high, but in cultivation rarely more than 1 m. high. Joints large, elliptical or obovate, up to 50 cm. long and 25 cm. broad, often much smaller, 2 to 3 cm. thick, smooth, greyish green or glaucous. Areoles large and prominent, at first bearing only one long, stiff, spreading, white spine, 7 to 15 cm. long, straight or twisted, later developing 2 or 3 more, slightly shorter. Flower red, 7 cm. broad; fruit almost globose, 5 to 7 cm. long, greenish yellow. A very characteristic species.

Opuntia sulphurea G. Don. = *O. maculacantha* Först. = *O. pampeana* Speg. = *O. vulpina* Weber = *O. Tweediei* Hort. Argentina (Santiago). A low straggling bush, about 50 cm. high. Joints oval or elliptical, 10 to 20 cm. long, green or somewhat whitish or reddish, thick, with small areoles on broad irregular warts. Glochids yellowish red. Spines 2 to 8, spreading, straight or somewhat tortuous, awl-shaped, thick and very stiff, 3 to 10 cm. long, brownish red, passing to white or ash-colour, tipped darker, more or less zoned or blotched reddish brown. Flower large, sulphur yellow. A striking species, popular with growers.

12. *Elatiores.* Tree-like and erect. Joints large, very spiny.

Opuntia elatior Mill. = *O. nigricans* Haw. Panama to Venezuela.

About 5 m. high. Joints obovate or oval-elongated, 10 to 40 cm. long, rather thin, olive green. Areoles yellowish, passing to brownish. Spines 2 to 8, awl-shaped, 2 to 5 cm. long, very dark brown, spreading, reddish when young. Flower 5 cm. broad, yellow, variegated red or pink. Fruit pear-shaped, often spiny, red, with dark red pulp.

Opuntia Bergeriana Weber. Described from specimens at the Riviera: native country unknown. Tree-like, with spreading branches. Joints oval-elongated, pale green, passing to greyish green, 15 to 25 cm. long. Areoles greyish, with yellow glochids. Spines 2 or 3, awl-shaped, yellowish passing to grey, brown at the base, 2 to 4 cm. long. Flowers numerous, of a lively deep red, with dark pink stamens, white style and stigma with 6 green lobes. Fruit about 4 cm. long, pear-shaped, red.

Opuntia Schumannii Weber. Tropical South America. A bush 1 to 2 m. high, with large oval dull dark green joints, about 25 cm. long, irregular and warty along the margin, with few areoles. Spines spreading, brown, thick, about 4 cm. long. Flower yellowish red, with erect petals, slightly scented. Fruit oval, brownish red.

Opuntia Hanburyana Weber. Native country unknown. Described from specimens at La Mortola Gardens, Riviera. A hardy bushy plant, up to 1 m. high. Joints elongated, 20 to 30 cm. long, pale green, thin and narrow, with closely set brown areoles. Spines numerous, yellowish brown, up to 3 cm. long, spreading and bent. Flower small, yellow.

Opuntia brunnescens Br. et R. Argentina (Córdoba). Almost prostrate or up to 1 m. high, cespitose; joints oblong or roundish, 15 to 30 cm. long, smooth, dull green. Areoles prominent, with purplish blotches around them; spines 2 to 5, brownish, spreading or erect, thick, sometimes twisted, up to 4½ cm. long. Flower small, yellow; fruit small, pear-shaped. Flowers very freely, even on new joints.

Opuntia Boldinghii Br. et R. Venezuela, Trinidad. An erect, much branched bush, up to 2 m. high. Joints dull green or glaucous, easily dropping off, obovate, about 12 cm. long. Areoles large, prominent, brownish. Spines often absent or small and brownish, often 1 to 3 in each areole, awl-shaped, thick, brownish yellow, up to 4 cm. long. Flower pink, with pink filaments. Fruit pear-shaped, plump, spineless, 4 cm. long.

Opuntia distans Br. et R. Argentina (Catamarca). Tree-like, 3 to 4 m. high, densely branched. Joints obovate, 20 to 25 cm. long and 15 cm. broad, rather thick, smooth, bluish green passing to greyish green. Areoles large, few and far apart, roundish, with short glochids, but spineless. Flower 3 to 4 cm. broad, orange red.

Opuntia fuliginosa Griffiths. Central Mexico. Tree-like, about 4 m. high, much branched. Joints oblong or roundish, up to 30 cm. long, glossy green. Areoles far apart, with yellow or brown glochids. Spines few, rarely up to 6, yellowish brown or honey-coloured, about

3 cm. long. Flowers yellow, fading to red. Fruit pear-shaped, red, 3 to 4 cm. long.

Opuntia Soederstromiana Br. et R., from Eduador, and **O. zebrina** Small, from Florida, are two other species belonging to this series, but rarely grown.

13. *Dillenianae*. Bushy or tree-like; joints very spiny, with large areoles. Ovaries more or less clavate, without areoles on their lower part.

Opuntia Dillenii (Ker-Gawl.) Haw. = *Cactus Dillenii* Ker-Gawler = *O. horrida* Salm-Dyck. Coasts of Carolina, Florida, West Indies, Mexico and tropical South America: naturalized in India, China and Australia. A large, densely branched bush, up to 3 m. high, very spiny. Joints broadly obovate or elliptical or roundish, with an irregular and warty margin, more or less thick, green passing to greyish green, 20 to 25 cm. long. Areoles large, far apart, yellowish, with very numerous and long pale yellow glochids. Spines very variable: often absent on young joints, later developing up to 10 in number, especially on the upper and marginal areoles, straight or bent or tortuous, yellow or light brown, 1 to 3 cm. long, often up to 6 cm. long. Flower large, pale yellow. Fruit pear-shaped, about 7 cm. long, red. Long known in cultivation.

Opuntia Lindheimeri Engelm. = *O. texana* Griffiths. Louisiana, Texas, Mexico. Tree-like and spreading, 2 to 4 m. high. Joints discoid or broadly oval, up to 25 cm. long, greyish green, thin when young, and somewhat irregular at the margin. Areoles greyish, far apart, with very numerous and prominent yellow or brownish glochids. Spines at first 1 or 2, up to 6 cm. long, later increasing to 6 or 7, spreading, thick, pale yellow or straw-coloured. Flower yellow. Fruit plump, pear-shaped, 5 cm. long, deep violet red, with red pulp. There is a form with fiery red spines, described by Berger as *O. Winteriana*. A very beautiful and striking species, of quick growth.

Opuntia Beckeriana K. Sch. Probably Mexico. A low shrub. Joints oval, 8 to 10 cm. long, grass green. Areoles with numerous long yellowish brown glochids. Spines 2 to 6, straight, yellowish, zoned darker, passing to white, $\frac{1}{2}$ to 1 cm. long. Flower 7 to 8 cm. broad, dark yellow.

Opuntia chrysacantha Berger *Hort. Mortol.* Northern Arizona. Closely allied to *O. Lindheimeri*, with oval or roundish joints, grass green to olive green, with many yellow areoles and golden yellow spines. Flower yellow.

Opuntia procumbens Engelm. et Big. Arizona. A prostrate, bushy, much branched shrub, with large joints, discoid or unevenly oval, 18 to 28 cm. long, and 14 to 20 cm. broad, grass green. Areoles round, greyish, with prominent and thick yellow glochids, about 1 cm. long. Spines mostly 3, later increasing in number, spreading, awl-shaped, straight or curved, angular, pale yellow or straw-coloured, often reddish or brown at the base, up to $4\frac{1}{2}$ cm. long. Fruit red, juicy.

Opuntia laevis Coult. Arizona. An erect bush, 1 to 2 m. high. Joints obovate or elongated, 15 to 30 cm. long, pale green, thin at the upper margin. Areoles small and far apart, with prominent tufts of glochids and spines along the margin. Spines small, whitish, awl-shaped, 1 to 1½ cm. long, rarely more than 2 cm., except on the marginal areoles at the top. Flower yellow, about 7 cm. broad, with pale yellow stamens and style, and green stigma.

Opuntia linguiformis Griffiths. Southern Texas. Bushy, about 1 m. high. Joints elongated, broad at the base, tapering upwards, ovate-oblong or lanceolate, pale green or slightly glaucous. Areoles far apart, brown, with yellow glochids. Spines very slender, yellow, 2 to 4 on each areole, 1 to 2 cm. long. Flower about 7 cm. broad, yellow. Fruit reddish purple.

Opuntia tapona Engelm. Lower California. A low and spreading bush, about 50 cm. high. Joints roundish or obovate, glabrous, turgid, pale green, 20 to 25 cm. long. Areoles with brownish glochids. Spines 2 to 4, spreading or curved downwards, slender, yellow, one of them 5 to 7 cm. long. Fruit pear-shaped, 4 to 6 cm. long, dark purple, spineless.

Opuntia haematocarpa Berger. Native country unknown. Tree-like, 1 to 4 m. high. Joints about 20 cm. long, obovate, thin when young, pale green. Areoles far apart. Young joints with areoles bearing only one spine, about 1 cm. long, later developing 4 or 5, up to 4 cm. long. Flowers large and numerous, up to 10 cm. broad, golden yellow, orange red at the centre. Fruit violet red, with blood red pulp.

Opuntia aciculata Griffiths. Texas (Laredo). Bushy, about 1 m. high, but spreading. Joints obovate, rounded at top, dull dark green or glaucous, 12 to 20 cm. long, with large closely set areoles. Spines several, thin, needle-like, often reflexed, brownish tipped yellow, 3 to 5½ cm. long. Flower golden yellow 8 to 10 cm. broad. Fruit pear-shaped, purple.

Opuntia cantabrigiensis Lynch. = *O. cuija* Br. et R. Mexico. Described from specimen in the Cambridge Botanic Gardens, England. Bushy, 1 to 2 m. high. Joints discoid or ovobate, pale bluish green, 12 to 20 cm. long. Areoles large, brown, far apart, with many yellowish spreading glochids, 1 cm. long. Spines needle-like, 3 to 6 or more, yellow, reddish brown at the base, 1½ to 4 cm. long. Flower yellowish, with reddish centre; fruit globose, purple.

14. *Robustae*. Large bushes, with very large disc-like joints. Flowers yellow. Fruit roundish, deep red.

Opuntia robusta Wendl. = *O. flavicans* Lem. = *O. camuessa* Weber = *O. Larreyi* Weber = *O. gorda* Griffiths. Central Mexico. Tree-like and strong growing, and also very variable, the synonyms given in reality representing so many forms. Joints discoid or very slightly oval, or even broader than long, thick, up to 30 cm. broad, very smooth, greyish green and very glaucous, with a fine bluish white hue. Areoles brownish, the upper ones with 2 to 12 thick yellow spines, brown at the base, passing to white, up to 5 cm. long, but with only a few short spines in cultivation. Flower yellow, 7 cm. broad. Fruit globose, dark red, about 8 cm. long. A plant of remarkable beauty. The form *camuessa* Weber, is grown as a fruit tree in Mexico. The form *maxima* Hort. non Mill., has very large discoid joints of a beautiful bluish white colour, and is almost spineless.

Opuntia fusicaulis Griffiths. Known only in cultivation. Tree-like, up to 5 m. high. Joints oblong or elongated, 40 cm. long, glaucous or bluish green, spineless. Areoles small brown, often without glochids. Fruit greenish white.

Opuntia crystalenia Griffiths. Mexico. An erect bush, about 2½ m. high. Joints broadly obovate up to 25 cm. long, glaucous, bluish green. Glochids yellow. Spines 1 to 4, only on the upper areoles, white, spreading, up to 1½ cm. long. Flower yellow, stigma with 10 dark green lobes. Fruit almost globose, 4 cm. long.

15. *Phaeacanthae.* Low shrubby plants, with large discoid joints, well furnished with long spines, brown at the base. Flowers yellow. Fruit red, globose.

Opuntia phaeacantha Engelm. = *O. camanchica* Engelm. et Big. Mexico, Arizona, Texas. A very variable species, with many varieties and forms. Plant mostly prostrate or semi-prostrate. Joints discoid or broadly obovate, 7 to 15 cm. long, dull green or greyish green, rather thick, with areoles rather far apart, brownish. Glochids in large yellow or brown tufts. Spines 1 to 4, mostly reflexed downwards, brown, darker at the base, passing to greyish white, more numerous and more reflexed on the marginal areoles, 1 to 6 cm. long. Flower golden yellow, often reddish yellow at the centre. Fruit red, globose, about 3 cm. long. A pretty and resistant species, hardy even in comparatively cold climates the joints turning to a purplish brown colour in winter.

Sub-species **phaeacantha** = *O. phaeacantha* Engelm. The typical species has small, thick, rather bluish green joints, with dark brown spines, paler towards the tip. Flower yellow, 4 to 5 cm. long. Includes the forms: **brunnea** Engelm., **brunnea major** Engelm., and **mojavensis** (*O. mojavensis* Engelm.).

Sub-species **camanchica** = *O. camanchica* Engelm. et Big. Joints large and of a clearer green. Spines often longer, white or whitish, dirty yellow or brown at the base. Flower larger, 8 to 9 cm. long, varying from pale yellow to deep yellow, salmon, reddish or reddish brown. Includes many forms, the following being the best in cultivation.

albispina Hort. Spines white, brownish at the base; flower yellow.

longispina Hort. Spines up to 7 cm. long.

major Hort. Joints large, stamens pink.

gigantea Hort. Joints very large, at least 15 cm. broad.

minor Hort. Joints small, very spiny. Flower pale yellow.

(b) OPUNTIA PHAEACANTHA

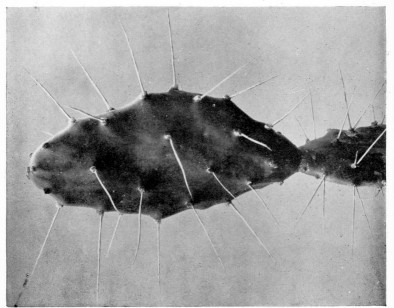

(a) OPUNTIA QUIMILO

PLATE VIII

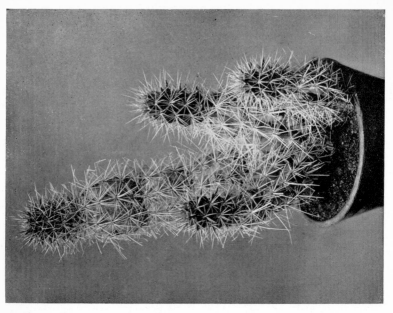

(b) GRUSONIA BRADTIANA

(a) NOPALEA DEJECTA

PLATE IX

pallida Hort. Flower yellowish white, greenish at the base.

rubra Hort. Flower reddish brown, stamens reddish yellow.

salmonea Hort. Spath. Flower brownish salmon.

Opuntia Covillei Br. et R. Southern California. A low bush; joints discoid or obovate, 10 to 20 cm. long, pale green, slightly glaucous, sometimes purplish. Areoles far apart. Spines several, up to 6 cm. long, white passing to brownish. Flower large, yellow.

Opuntia Vaseyi Br. et R. = *O. mesacantha Vaseyi* Coulter. Joints ovate, thick, 10 to 12 cm. long, pale green, slightly glaucous. Areoles brown, large. Spines 1 to 3, spreading, about 1½ cm. long, brown or greyish brown, whitish or yellowish at the tip. Flower deep salmon or red salmon. Fruit oblong, 4 to 5 cm. long, deep purple.

Opuntia Howeyi Purp. Mexico (Salinas). A semi-prostrate, spreading bush. Joints more or less roundish, of medium size, with round areoles and brown glochids. Spines stiff, greyish white, brown at the base, up to 2½ cm. long. Flower pale yellow, greenish at the base of the petals, which are margined reddish, stamens yellow, style yellowish, stigma pale green. Fruit globose, red, spiny.

Opuntia macrocentra Engelm. Texas, Arizona, Mexico. A bush about 1 m. high. Joints discoid or oblong, or broader than long, 10 to 20 cm. long, often bluish or purplish, 8 to 15 cm. broad. Areoles greyish, round or oval, with brown glochids. Spines 1 or 2, rarely more, straight or curved, the upper ones 4½ to 6½ cm. long, dark brown or almost black at the base, grey or dark grey at the tip. Flower 5 cm. long, yellow. Fruit pear-shaped, purple.

Opuntia Gosseliniana Weber. Sonora and Lower California. A bush about 1m. high, with spreading habit. Joints discoid or broader than long, 8 to 18 cm. broad, 1½ to 2½ cm. thick, light glaucous green, smooth, often purplish along the margin. Areoles large, yellowish, with prominent tufts of yellow or brownish glochids. Spines 1 to 5, slender, flexible, pale yellow or white, brownish at the base, 2 to 5 cm. long, the central one up to 10 cm. long, especially on the marginal areoles, at first reddish brown, or zoned reddish brown, passing to pale yellow or white on older joints. Flower yellow. Fruit red, globose. A beautiful species, well worthy of cultivation, still rare in collections.

Opuntia chlorotica Engelm. et Big. Sonora, California, Nevada and New Mexico. A tall bush 2½ m. high, much branched, with a straight cylindrical stem, very spiny. Joints obovate, pale bluish green, 12 to 20 cm. long, sometimes almost discoid, 12 to 16 cm. broad. Areoles large, round or oval, greyish, with yellow glochids up to 1 cm. long. Spines few in the lower areoles, 6 or more in the upper, 2 to 4 cm. long, brownish, slender, straight or reflexed. Flower about 5 cm. long and 7 cm. broad, yellow. Fruit pear-shaped, warty, with a deep navel, up to 3½ cm. long, often seedless.

Opuntia Palmeri Engelm. Utah. Is probably only a variety of the preceding, up to 1 m. high, with a more spreading habit. Joints large,

G

smooth, oblong, up to 25 cm. long and 20 cm. broad. Spines more numerous and shorter. Flower greenish yellow, margined reddish.

Opuntia santa-rita Rose. = *O. chlorotica santa-rita* Griffiths et Hare = *O. Shreveana* Nelson. South-eastern Arizona. A thick bush, ½ to 1½ m. high. Joints discoid, or broader than long, rarely oval, bluish green, but with deep purple about the areoles and margin, thin. Areoles 1½ cm. apart, round, bearing numerous chestnut brown glochids and occasionally a brown spine. Flowers deep yellow, 6 to 7 cm. broad; ovary oblong, purple. A very desirable species, similar to *O. Gosseliniana*, with joints of a deeper bluish green, but quite spineless, at least in cultivation.

Opuntia azurea Rose. Mexico (Zacatecas). Another lovely species, rather rare in collections. A low, compact, spreading bush, with a short stem. Joints discoid or obovate, 10 to 15 cm. long, pale bluish green, glaucous. Areoles 2 cm. apart, with numerous brown glochids. Spines only on the upper areoles, 1 to 3, dark brown, almost black, unequal, the longer ones 2 to 3 cm. long, thick, more or less reflexed. Flowers deep yellow, fading to pink, with whitish green filaments; lobes of stigma pale green. Fruit globose to ovoid, dull crimson, spineless.

Opuntia angustata Engelm. Arizona. Has oval-elongated and almost pointed joints, of a glaucous green, 13 to 22 cm. long and 6 to 9 cm. broad. Areoles oval, yellowish grey, with thin brown glochids. Spines 2 or 3, afterwards increasing in number, pale yellow or straw-coloured, brown at the base, 2 to 3½ cm. long, slender, straight, or twisted. Fruit pear-shaped.

Opuntia discata Griffiths. Arizona and Sonora. A spreading bush, 1½ m. high. Joints discoid or very broadly oval, about 22 cm. broad, pale bluish green and glaucous. Areoles brownish, rather far apart, with 2 to 5 or more grey spines, brown at the base, 2 to 3 cm. long, somewhat flattened. Flower 10 cm. broad, pale yellow, dark yellow at the centre. Fruit pear-shaped, about 7 cm. long, red. A striking species.

Opuntia atrispina Griffiths. Texas. A low and spreading bush. Joints nearly discoid, 10 to 15 cm. broad, pale green or slightly glaucous. Areoles with yellow glochids, passing to brown. Spines only on the upper areoles, 2 to 4, dark brown, almost black at the base, paler at the tip, spreading, flattened, short. Flower yellow. Fruit reddish purple.

Opuntia tardospina Griffiths. Eastern Texas. Low and spreading. Joints discoid or obovate, 16 to 24 cm. long, with large areoles far apart, with brown glochids. Spines 1 or 2, brown, only on the upper and marginal areoles, paler at the tip, 2 to 3 cm. long. Fruit red.

Opuntia Engelmannii Salm-Dyck. Mexico, New Mexico, Arizona, Texas. A spreading bush, or sometimes erect and up to 2 m. high. Joints oval-elongated or roundish, thick, pale green, 20 to 30 cm. long. Areoles rather large, whitish, with many brown glochids tipped yellow.

Spines 3 to 10, in the middle and upper areoles, white, reddish or brownish at the base, up to 5 cm. long, spreading, the longer ones often bent and flattened. Flower yellow, about 9 cm. broad. Fruit globose or oval, sometimes pear-shaped, about 4 cm. long. A variable species.

var. **cyclodes** Engelm. et Big. Joints discoid. Spines mostly only one, strong and longer.

var. **littoralis** Engelm. et Big. Joints dark green, about half as large as in the typical form, with more closely set areoles and yellow spines.

var. **occidentalis** Engelm. et Big. Spines all straight and entirely white, brown on young joints.

var. **dulcis** Coult. More prostrate, with smaller joints. Spines bent, often white. Fruit sweet. Seeds smaller.

Opuntia rastrera Weber. Mexico. Prostrate and creeping. Joints discoid to obovate, up to 20 cm. long. Areoles with yellow glochids. Spines several, white, dark at the base, up to 4 cm. long. Flower yellow. Fruit obovoid, purple, acid.

Opuntia strigil Engelm. (Often written *strigilis*). Texas. A bush about 60 cm. high. Joints discoid to obovate, 10 to 12 cm. long. Areoles prominent and closely set, with numerous yellow glochids. Spines 5 to 8, spreading or deflexed, red to reddish brown, paler at the tip, up to 2½ cm. long. Fruit globose, just over 1 cm. long, red.

Opuntia megarhiza Rose. Mexico. Roots long and thick; shrub with a low stem, much branched. Joints elongated, 20 to 30 cm. long, 13 cm. broad, thin. Spines 2 to 4, needle-like, brown, 1 to 2½ cm. long. Flower yellow, often shaded pink, 5 cm. broad.

Opuntia Ballii Rose. Western Texas. A low shrub, spreading, with roundish or obovate joints, 6 to 10 cm. long, rather thick, pale green, glaucous. Areoles with prominent brownish glochids. Spines 2 to 4, brownish, mostly erect, 4 to 7 cm. long. Fruit small, 2 cm. long, spineless.

Opuntia Pottsii Salm-Dyck = *O. filipendula* Engelm. Mexico, New Mexico, Texas. A prostrate shrub, about 30 cm. high, with tuberous nodules on the roots, which will sprout into young plants, if taken up and planted off separately. Joints roundish or broadly obovate, 5 to 12 cm. long, pale green or bluish green. Areoles large, whitish, round, with prominent tufts of yellow glochids. Spines 1 or 2, often absent, reddish passing to whitish, 2 to 4 cm. long, mostly reflexed downwards, often with 2 or more smaller spines. Flower of a lively red, 5 cm. broad. Fruit slender, spineless.

Opuntia tenuispina Engelm. Mexico, New Mexico, and Texas. Plant prostrate, up to 30 cm. high. Joints broadly obovate, narrow at the base, of a lively green. Areoles large, with numerous prominent brownish glochids, the upper and marginal ones bearing 1 to 3 slender spines, brown passing to white, 2 to 3 cm. long, or up to 5 cm. long on the marginal areoles. Flower large, yellow. Fruit oblong, 3½ cm. long.

Opuntia setispina Engelm. Mexico (Chihuahua). An erect bush, up to 1 m. high, with ascending branches. Joints roundish, small, about 5 cm. broad, glaucous, bluish green. Areoles round, with yellow glochids. Spines very slender, brownish yellow, 1 to 3, up to 3½ cm. long, with 3 to 7 others much shorter. Flower yellow; fruit purplish, about 4 cm. long.

Opuntia Mackensenii Rose. Texas. Plant low and prostrate or spreading, with thick tuberous roots. Joints discoid or obovate, 10 to 20 cm. long, deep green. Areoles small, with brown glochids. Spines 1 to 4, only on the upper areoles, usually brown at the base and white above, slender, somewhat flattened and tortuous, up to 5 cm. long. Flower yellow, reddish brown at the centre, stigma with 7 to 9 white lobes. Fruit 4 to 6 cm. long, rosy purple, spineless.

16. *Stenopetalae.* Fairly large plants. Joints large, greyish green, spiny. Flower small, with short narrow petals, and deeply sunk centre, unisexual, the pistil in the male flowers being abortive. Ovary thickly set with tubercles.

Opuntia stenopetala Engelm. Central Mexico. An erect or semi-prostrate shrub. Joints obovate, at first reddish, passing to pale green and then to greyish, 10 to 20 cm. long. Areoles brownish, rather far apart, with brown glochids. Spines 2 to 4, reddish brown, later almost black, passing to greyish, up to 5 cm. long, the longer ones reflexed. Flower 4 cm. broad, fiery red, stigma, with 8 or 9 yellow lobes. An almost dioecious species, the male plants bearing flowers with an abortive style.

Opuntia grandis Pfeiff. Mexico. A low shrub with very erect joints, greyish green or reddish, 12 to 18 cm. long, and 8 to 12 cm. broad. Areoles few, and rather far apart, with dark brown glochids. Spines 2, the upper one which is longer, is up to 3 cm. long, the lower one about 2½ cm. long, both brown or dark brown, passing to greyish. Flower small, reddish. Almost dioecious.

Opuntia glaucescens Salm-Dyck. Mexico. A low prostrate and spreading bush. Joints obovate, about 12 cm. long, reddish when young, passing to dull glaucous green, with small red leaves soon dropping off. Areoles greyish, glochids brown. Spines 2 to 4, white, up to 4 cm. long, developing late. Flower about 3 cm. broad, with yellowish red narrow petals, yellowish red stamens and red style. Almost dioecious.

17. *Parviflorae.* Joints medium-sized, more or less spiny. Flowers small, with long ovaries, having a deeply sunk navel or centre, and short and narrow petals, but hermaphrodite.

Opuntia inamoena K. Sch. Eastern Brazil. An almost prostrate, densely branched bush. Joints discoid or oblong, thick, 3½ to 9 cm. long and 2½ to 5 cm. broad, grass green, soon passing to bluish green or brownish green. Areoles small, with yellowish brown glochids easily dropping off. Spines usually absent. Flower small, brick-red, with orange filaments, yellow style and green lobes of stigma. Fruit globose, yellowish, about 3 cm. thick.

Opuntia quitensis Weber. Ecuador (Quito). About 1½ m. high, with oval-elongated, rather thick joints, 20 cm. long and 9 cm. broad, grass green when young, passing to greyish green. Areoles whitish, with yellow glochids, and with 1 to 3 straight, flexible, yellowish spines 1 to 4 cm. long. Flower 6 to 7 cm. long, with a small perianth about 2 cm. broad, and a long and warty ovary (about 5 cm.). Perianth fiery red, the inner petals being only 1 cm. long; stamens, style and 12-lobed stigma white. Fruit red.

Opuntia caracasana Salm-Dyck. Venezuela (Carácas). A straggling shrub, almost prostrate. Joints erect, of a lively glossy green, obovate-elongated, 15 cm. long and 6 cm. broad. Areoles whitish, with yellow glochids. Spines mostly deflexed, white or yellowish, ½ to 2 cm. long. Flower small, purplish red, pale pink outside, slightly scented. Fruit oval, whitish, with pink pulp.

Opuntia palmadora Br. et R. Brazil (Bahia). Usually erect, up to 3 m. high, but often low, with a definite stem, very spiny. Joints very thin and narrow, 10 to 15 cm. long, usually erect, very spiny. Areoles white. Spines 1 to 4 or more, yellow passing to white, up to 3 cm. long. Flower with erect petals, brick-red, orange filaments, creamy white style, and white lobes of stigma. Ovary top-shaped; fruit small.

Sub-Genus IV. CYLINDROPUNTIA Engelm. Joints cylindrical, or cylindrical under cultivation.

Group A. AUSTRO-CYLINDROPUNTIAE Backbg. South American species. Spines not furnished with sheaths.

1. *Verschaffeltianae.* Joints slender, bare, weakly tuberculate.

Opuntia Verschaffeltii Weber. North Bolivia. Stems cylindrical 10 to 15 cm. long and 1 to 1½ cm. thick; joints cylindrical or oval or globular, dull green, slightly warty or rough. Leaves ½ to 3 cm. long, cylindrical, persisting for a long time, often reddish. Areoles round, whitish, with small yellow glochids, and often with 1 to 3 white, slender, flexible, thread-like, spines, up to 6 cm. long. Flowers borne on old as well as on new joints, about 4 cm. broad, deep red, or blood red, or orange, very beautiful, lasting for several days. Stigma with 7 to 10 dark violet lobes. The plant has a low spreading habit, up to 30 cm. high, and the joints are often tinged reddish or purplish. Growth is slow. Often almost spineless.

var. **floribunda** Borg *n. var.* Stems and joints greenish purple, especially when young; leaves shorter, purplish green, persisting for a long time; areoles depressed, mostly with 1 to 3 bristle-like flexible spines, yellow passing to white. Stems mostly prostrate becoming erect when in flower. Flowers borne abundantly, glossy dark blood red, up to 5 cm. broad, with dark violet stigma. (Latin description given in the first edition).

Opuntia teres Cels. North Bolivia. Often considered as a synonym or a variety; is in reality a distinct species. Stems thicker and shorter, often oval or globular, grass green when young, not reddish or purplish. Leaves pale green, more fleshy and shorter, $\frac{1}{2}$ to 2 cm. long, less persistent. Areoles whitish yellow, with bundles of glassy white glochids, with about 5 radial glassy white spines 2 to 4 mm. long, and 1 or 2 pale brown central spines, 1 to 2 cm. long. Flowers unknown. Fruit yellowish green, tinted red, proliferous.

2. *Vestitae.* Stems slender, fleshy, but usually erect, furnished with hairs.

Opuntia vestita Salm-Dyck. Bolivia (La Paz). Stems mostly erect, or sprawling, up to 50 cm. long and 2 to 3 cm. thick, pale green, more or less irregular or warty and slightly branched. Leaves up to 1 cm. long, pale green, persisting for some time. Areoles round, yellowish, with many long white glochids, spines 4 to 8, up to 2 cm., long, stiff or flexible, awl-shaped, associated with many long white hairs, almost entirely covering the stem. Flower about 4 cm. broad, dark red, stigma with 4 red lobes. Fruit oval, woolly, red. Prefers half-shade. There is also a cristate form of remarkable beauty.

var. **major** Backbg. Stems thicker; leaves 4 to 5 cm. long, persisting for some time.

Opuntia Shaferi Br. et R. Northern Argentina. Stems erect, up to 30 cm. long, $2\frac{1}{2}$ to $3\frac{1}{2}$ cm. thick, indistinctly warty, Areoles round, white, with many whitish glochids. Leaves about $\frac{1}{2}$ cm. long, soon dropping off. Spines about 6, needle-like, brownish, 4 to 5 cm. long, associated with long white hairs. Fruit globose, 2 cm. thick, spineless. Rare in cultivation.

3. *Subulatae.* Stems thick, with jointed branches, long spines and large fleshy leaves.

Opuntia subulata Engelm. = *Pereskia subulata* Muehl. = *O. Segethii* Phil. Chile and Argentina. A shrub 2 to 4 m. high, strong-growing, well branched. Stems or joints cylindrical, green or dark green, with darker lines below the areoles, with broad flat rounded warts. Leaves half-cylindrical, up to 10 cm. long, awl-shaped or subulate, and somewhat curved upwards, pointed, very persistent. Glochids few, yellowish. Spines 1 or 2, rarely more, pale yellow, strong, straight, up to 8 cm. long. Flower red or reddish, large. Fruit large, oval-conical, green, often proliferous.

var. **minor.** Poselg. Plant smaller in all its parts.

Opuntia exaltata Berger. Ecuador, Peru, Bolivia. Very similar to *O. subulata*, but with more greyish stems and joints, much shorter leaves and brownish spines. Possibly only a distinct variety.

Opuntia cylindrica DC. Ecuador and Peru. Plant 1 to 2 m. high, with few branches. Branches or joints with continuous growth, cylindrical, 4 to 5 cm. thick, grass green, marked with lozenge-shaped, very flat warts, with cylindrical leaves 1 to 1½ cm. long, soon dropping off. Areoles whitish. Spines 2 or 3, some times up to 6, about 1 cm. long, whitish. Flowers red, borne only on old plants. Fruit oval-elongated, 4 cm. long, very warty.

var. **robustior** Hort. With thicker stems; more commonly cultivated.

There is also a good cristate form of the species, usually referred to as *minor*, and also of its variety, referred to as *major*.

Opuntia pachypus K. Sch. Peru. In habit like a *Cereus*. Stem erect, up to 1 m. high, slow-growing, solitary, or rarely branched in whorls, up to 8 cm. thick, with thickly set flat warts. Areoles large, round, whitish, with about 30 whitish spines, some very short, and a few up to 2 cm. long. Flower scarlet, about 7 cm. broad. Rather rare in cultivation.

Opuntia atroviridis Werd. et Backbg. Peru. A prostrate bush. Stems grass green to olive green or dark green, often oval or almost roundish, 3 to 3½ cm. thick, with small whitish areoles on low elongated warts. Glochids dark brown, ½ cm. long, associated with yellowish bristles about 2 cm. long. Spines 3 or more, unequal, up to 3 cm. long, awl-shaped, olive or greenish yellow or brownish. Leaves small, flat, obovate, about ½ cm. long, persisting for some time. Flower yellow.

4. *Miquelianae*. Short, thick joints, with prominent warts.

Opuntia Miquelii Monv. = *O. Gessei* Phil. = *O. pulverulenta* Pfeiff. = *O. rosea* Phil. = *O. carrigalensis* Phil.= *O. heteromorpha* Phil. = *O. rosiflora* K. Sch. Chile, province of Atacama. A spreading bush about 1 m. high, rather slow-growing. Stems or joints cylindrical, 6 to 20 cm. long, 3 to 6 cm. thick, green when young, passing to greyish glaucous green, with a powdery appearance, with prominent elongated warts as in *O. imbricata*, and with large areoles and brown glochids. Leaves cylindrical small, soon dropping off. Spines 6 to 12, up to 6 cm. long, white, passing to yellowish or greyish. Flower large, 6 cm. long, with petals 2 to 2½ cm. long, bright pink sometimes pale pink, with pink stamens and green stigma.

var. **heteromorpha** (Phil.). Has a pyramidal habit of growth, with small short thick joints; areoles with many bristle-like spines. Flower red.

var. **Gessei** (Phil.). Erect, profusely branched, bluish green, very powdery, with joints 10 to 12 cm. long, and 5 cm. thick, very warty, with white areoles, many short bristles, and spines up to 2 cm. long. Flower up to 10 cm. long and 4½ cm. broad, red, with a very warty ovary, furnished with scales and bristles.

5. *Salmianae*. Stems slender, smooth, not warty, much branched; branches with many oval or globose joints, easily dropping off at the least touch.

Opuntia Salmiana Parm. South Brazil, Paraguay and North Argentina. Plant up to 1 m. high, but rarely more than ½ m., with long, cylindrical, smooth stems, much branched, about 1 cm. in diameter and up to 25 cm. long, deep glaucous green, often reddish or purplish. Areoles very small, with many glochids, and with 3 to 5 yellowish spines, less than 1 cm. long. Flowers numerous, yellowish, passing to reddish. Fruit round, deep red, about 1 cm. thick, freely sprouting globose or oval joints at maturity.

Opuntia Spegazzinii Weber. = *O. albiflora* K. Sch. Western Argentina. Up to 1 m. high, very much branched. Branches cylindrical, up to 30 cm. long, 1 to 2 cm. thick, pale glaucous green, very smooth, with small areoles. Glochids numerous, but very short. Spines 2 to 5, less than 1 cm. long. Branches and joints dropping off at the least touch, particularly in autumn. Flowers small, white. Fruit round or oval, 1 cm. thick, deep red or bluish red, developing a number of small round or oval joints at maturity, which drop off and easily strike root.

Opuntia Schickendantzii Weber. Western Argentina. Plant about 1 m. high, usually much less in cultivation. Joints up to 20 cm. long, cylindrical or somewhat flattened, greyish green, 1½ to 2½ cm. thick, somewhat warty, with small whitish areoles, closely set, and whitish glochids. Spines 1 or 2, short and slender. Flower about 4 cm. broad, yellow. Fruit roundish or oval, small, about 1½ cm. long, with many prominent areoles, green or flushed red, often seedless, but freely proliferous.

6. *Etuberculatae*. Areoles very minute and very closely set.

Opuntia clavarioides Pfeiff. Chile. A very interesting and curious species, now frequent in collections. Plant low, bush-like, straggling. Joints greyish brown, smooth, cylindrical or terminating in a thickening like an inverted cone, often flat or concave at the top, or spreading almost fan-shaped, with great tendency at fasciation, with very small and closely set areoles, sometimes with short reddish leaves, and with 4 to 10 short white hair-like spines, arranged like a star. Flower rarely borne, about 5 cm. broad, pale greenish brown, with short white stamens, and stigma with 7 yellowish lobes. This is one of the very few species of *Opuntia* which require half-shade, and which suffer in full sunshine. It is best grown grafted on other species of *Opuntia*, such as *O. Ficus-indica*, or on species of *Cereus*, such as *Harrisia Jusbertii*. A very curious cristate form, called *Nigger's Hand*, is well known in cultivation.

Group B. Boreo-Cylindropuntia Backbg. Stems and joints cylindrical, with sheathed spines. North American species.

1. *Ramosissimae*. Shrubs with woody slender stems and many slender branches, with very low elongated tubercles or warts. Spines few, sheathed; fruit dry.

Opuntia ramosissima Engelm. = *O. tessellata* Engelm. Mexico,

California, Nevada, Arizona. A shrub up to 2 m. high, very much branched. Joints slender and almost woody, bluish green passing to ashy grey, 3 to 10 cm. long, and ½ to 1½ cm. thick, cylindrical, marked with 4 to 6 low, straight, indistinct angles, with oblong whitish areoles, each with a few glochids. Areoles often spineless, or with only one straight reddish spine, up to 6 cm. long, furnished with a yellowish sheath. Flower about 4 cm. broad, greenish yellow, borne in autumn on the side areoles. Fruit small, globose, warty, dry, spineless. There is also a pretty cristate form in cultivation.

Opuntia tesajo Engelm. Lower California. A low straggling bush, about ¼ m. high and about as broad, with slender joints, 3 to 7 cm. long, and only about ½ cm. thick, pale glaucous green, almost smooth. Areoles white, with dark brown glochids. Spines 2, dark brown, about ¼ cm. long, and on the upper areoles of the upper joints one central spine, up to 3 cm. long, whitish or greyish, with a yellowish sheath. Flower small, up to 2 cm. long, sulphur yellow, petals tipped reddish.

2. *Leptocaules*. Branches very slender, almost smoothly cylindrical, easily breaking off. Spines few. Fruit dry.

Opuntia leptocaulis DC. = *O. vaginata* Engelm. = *O. ramulifera* Salm Dyck. = *O. virgata* Lk. et Otto. Mexico, New Mexico, Texas, and Arizona. A bush 1 to 1½ m. high, densely branched. Joints up to 15 cm. long or longer, less than ½ cm. thick, almost woody, somewhat warty and furnished with short green scales when young. Glochids abundant, yellowish, in a prominent bundle. Spines 1 or 2, rarely 3, 2 to 5 cm. long, brown, in a reddish yellow sheath. Fruit 1 to 2 cm. long, red or yellow, spiny, sprouting. A variable species, common in cultivation.

The following varieties are recognized:

var. **brevispina** Engelm. Spines yellow, about ½ cm. long; often with very numerous and short joints. Free-flowering.

var. **longispina** Engelm. Spines 3½ to 5 cm. long. Glochids brown, and flowers brownish.

var. **vaginata** Engelm. Spines up to 4 cm. long, with loose straw-coloured sheaths. Glochids brown. Young joints pale grass green. Fruit with long spines.

var. **badia** Berger. Spines long and thick, with chestnut brown, sheaths.

var. **robustior** Berger. Joints thick, pale green, with short side joints. Spines long, pale yellow, with pale sheaths.

var. **pluriseta** Berger. Joints very slender, dark green. Areoles with several short spines and a few hairs.

Opuntia caribaea Br. et R. Haiti, Venezuela. A bushy plant about 1 m. high, with joints somewhat thicker than in the preceding species. Spines 1 to 3, 2 to 3 cm. long, with a thinner and darker sheath. Fruit red, up to 2 cm. long, bare or with short spines, mostly sterile.

Opuntia Kleiniae DC. = *O. Wrightii* Engelm. Texas, Mexico. An erect bush 1 to 1½ m. high, much branched. Joints about 10 cm. long and 1 cm. thick, with elongated warts and short thin scales. Areoles white, with yellowish glochids passing to brown. Only one spine, yellowish passing to brownish, up to 5 cm. long, with yellow sheath, often missing from the upper joints, sometimes associated with 2 to 4 smaller ones. Flower pale pink or pink, brownish outside.

Opuntia arbuscula Engelm. = *O. neoarbuscula* Griffiths. Arizona and Sonora. A much branched shrub, about 2 m. high. Joints about 8 cm. long and 6 to 7 mm. thick. Areoles large, round, white, with a long cluster of yellowish glochids. The joints have very prominent warts, and are easily broken off at the least touch. Spines 1 or 2, up to 4 cm. long, with a loose straw-coloured sheath. Flower yellow, about 3½ cm. broad. Fruit inversely conical or clavate, sprouting, usually with only one seed.

3. *Thurberianae*. Low shrubs with thicker stems and joints, markedly warty. Spines more numerous. Fruit dry.

Opuntia Thurberi Engelm. Mexico (Sonora). Tree-like, 2 to 4 m. high, much branched from the base. Joints up to 25 cm. long and about 1 cm. thick, with elongated warts, and short cylindrical leaves long persisting. Areoles round, brown, with very few glochids. Spines 3 to 5, 1 to 1½ cm. long, spreading dark yellow with brown sheaths. Flower about 5 cm. broad, brownish red. Fruit spineless and proliferous. **Opuntia tetracantha** Toumey, and **O. vivipara** Rose, are two species similar to *O. Thurberi*, and both are from Arizona.

Opuntia Davisii Engelm. et Big. Texas and New Mexico. A low, erect, spreading bush, about ½ m. high, abundantly furnished with yellow spines, much branched. Joints slender, 1 cm. thick and about 8 cm. long, with prominent warts. Areoles round, white, with straw-coloured glochids. Radial spines about 5, brownish, up to 1 cm. long: central spines 4 to 7, 2 to 3 cm. long, brownish, with a glossy satiny sheath. Flower up to 6 cm. broad, brownish or olive green outside, satiny pink inside, with dark red stamens and 4-lobed stigma, coloured violet. Fruit clavate, up to 3 cm. long, very warty and spiny.

Opuntia clavellina Engelm. Lower California. A straggling bush, up to 1 m. high. Upper joints slender, somewhat clavate, 5 to 10 cm. long, over 1 cm. thick, with prominent elongated warts. Spines 3 to 6, very long, the central one much longer and spreading, all furnished with straw-coloured or brown sheaths. Flowers yellow; fruit clavate, short, warty.

Opuntia viridiflora Br. et R. New Mexico. A bush 30 to 60 cm. high. Terminal joints 5 to 7 cm. long, 1½ to 2 cm. thick, easily breaking off, with prominent elongated warts. Areoles round, yellowish or greyish, with many short yellow glochids. Spines 5 to 7, up to 2 cm. long, with dark brown sheaths. Flowers small, green tinged with red. Fruit very warty, with deciduous bristles, not spiny.

Opuntia Whipplei Engelm. et Big. New Mexico and Arizona to southern Utah and Nevada. Plant bushy and straggling, 1 to 1½ m. high. Joints dull green, cylindrical or clavate, 5 to 30 cm. long, about 2 cm. thick, warty, becoming almost smooth with age. Areoles round, white, with few short glochids. Spines 6 to 10, 1 to 3 cm.' long, with white sheaths. Flowers numerous, red, 5 cm. broad. Fruit round, warty, yellow, not spiny.

var. **laevior** Engelm. et Big. Plant more spreading or prostrate. Spines fewer and shorter. Seeds smaller.

4. *Echinocarpae.* Low shrubs. Stems and joints fleshy and warty; the terminal joints at least 2 cm. thick. Spines more numerous, but short. Fruit dry and very spiny.

Opuntia echinocarpa Engelm. et Big. From Lower California to Nevada and Utah. Mostly prostrate and spreading, up to 1½ m. high, very much branched. Joints short and cylindrical, 6 to 7 cm. long and about 1½ cm. thick, with prominent elongated warts. Areoles whitish, with a few stiff yellow glochids. Radial spines 8 to 16, up to 2 cm. long, spreading outwards. Central spines 4, crosswise, up to 3 cm. long, whitish or straw-coloured with a darker sheath. Flower 4 cm. broad, greenish yellow.

var. **major** Engelm. = var. *robustior* Coult. More erect and taller. Joints often clavate, and up to 22 cm. long.

Opuntia acanthocarpa Engelm. et Big. Mexico, California, Arizona and Utah. Very much like the following, but grows taller, up to 2 m. high, with a tall cylindrical stem. Joints dull green, cylindrical, 8 to 15 cm. long and 2 cm. thick, warty, with slender reddish green leaves when young. Areoles round or oval, with whitish wool and very short glochids. Spines numerous, up to 25 or more; the central spines (1 to 8) being longer and thicker, up to 3 cm. long, with straw-coloured sheaths, passing to brownish. Flowers on the terminal joints, pink inside, coppery outside. Fruit globose or pear-shaped, about 2½ cm. thick, dry, warty, with many spines about 1 cm. long.

Opuntia Parryi Engelm. From California to Colorado. A low, spreading bush, very much branched from the base. Joints cylindrical or clavate, warty, usually 5 to 8 cm. long, sometimes up to 16 cm., and 2½ to 3 cm. thick. Areoles white, with stiff brownish glochids. Spines in 3 series: the outer 6 to 18, thin, stiff, spreading, bristle-like, up to 8 mm. long; the next 5 to 8, angular, spreading outwards, up to 11 mm. long; the inner 4, also angular and thicker, up to 3 cm. long. The smaller spines are whitish, the others are rough and greyish red, passing to grey. Flower 3½ cm. broad, greenish yellow. Fruit oval, 3 to 5 cm. long, very spiny.

var. **bernardina** (Engelm.) = *O. bernardina* Engelm. California (district of Bernardino). Plant more erect, less branched, less spiny and of a deeper green. Joints longer, up to 30 cm. Radial spines less numerous, all with pale yellow sheaths. Fruit smaller, less spiny.

Opuntia serpentina Engelm. = *O. californica* Coville. California and Lower California. Prostrate or erect, up to $1\frac{1}{2}$ m. high, with yellowish green, cylindrical, warty joints, 12 to 15 cm. long, and 2 to $2\frac{1}{2}$ cm. thick. Areoles closely set, white, with many whitish glochids. Spines 7 to 9, up to $1\frac{1}{2}$ cm. long, the lower ones being the longest and reflexed, white or reddish, with a white or brownish sheath. Flower 4 cm. broad, greenish yellow, the outer petals tinged red. Fruit hemispherical, with a deep cup-shaped navel, yellowish brown, dry, warty, very spiny, about $2\frac{1}{2}$ cm. long.

5. *Bigelowianae*. Very spiny shrubs. Stems and joints rather thick, with roundish or oval warts, and very spiny areoles. Fruit fleshy and spiny.

Opuntia Bigelowii Engelm. California, Nevada and Arizona. A shrub about 1 m. high, with erect branched stems. Joints light green, often almost globular, 5 cm. thick, or up to 15 cm. long, with prominent angular warts, very spiny. Areoles round, white, with yellow glochids. Spines very numerous, 6 to 10 radials, 1 to $1\frac{1}{2}$ cm. long, and 6 to 10 centrals, slightly longer, all furnished with pale yellow membraneous sheaths. Flower 4 cm. broad, purple. Fruit yellow, often without seeds, 2 cm. long, and freely sprouting into numerous shoots or other fruits.

Opuntia ciribe Engelm. Lower California. A low shrub, up to 1 m. high, much branched, with oval or slightly elongated dull green joints, about 3 cm. thick and 4 to 6 cm. long, with prominent round warts, and with 4 to 6 dark or black unsheathed radial spines, less than 1 cm. long, and about an equal number of central spines, up to $1\frac{1}{2}$ cm. long, thicker, and furnished with yellow sheaths. Flowers yellow; fruit very warty, spineless.

6. *Imbricatae*. Spiny shrubs, with thick jointed stems and branches, with prominent warts compressed laterally. Fruit globose, fleshy and spiny.

Opuntia Cholla Weber. Lower California. A tall shrub 1 to 3 m. high, usually much less in cultivation, branching from the base. Joints almost globose or oval or cylindrical and up to 25 cm. long, 4 to 5 cm. thick, dull green, very warty, but with rather low warts, with a brush-like bundle of yellow glochids on the areoles. Radial spines numerous, spreading, yellowish, about 1 cm. long. One central spine, $1\frac{1}{2}$ cm. long, with a loose yellowish brown sheath. Flower 3 to 4 cm. broad, deep pink. Fruit large, oval, warty, with few spines, with many small seeds, and generally with globular joints or other fruits sprouting from the areoles. *Cholla*, pronounced *shoyah*, is the local name.

Opuntia imbricata (Haw.) DC. = *O. rosea* DC. non Phil. = *O. arborescens* Engelm. From Central Mexico to Colorado. Tree-like, about 3 m. high, much branched, with a very warty and spiny stem. Joints cylindrical, 7 to 20 cm. long and 3 to 4 cm. thick, green passing to bluish green, with elongated prominent rounded warts and cylindrical leaves 1 to 2½ cm. long, quickly dropping off. Areoles large, yellowish white, with few short glochids. Spines numerous, 8 to 20 or more, whitish or yellowish, 1 to 3 cm. long, with a loose white membraneous sheath. Flowers numerous, 4 to 6 cm. broad, pink, deeper coloured at the base. Fruit roundish or almost hemispherical, with a deep navel, yellow, very warty, almost spineless. A well-known species, common in collections.

var. **Ruthei** Hort. Has shorter and thicker joints, more spiny, and flowers 8 to 9 cm. broad.

Opuntia versicolor Engelm. = *O. arborescens* var. *versicolor* E. Dams. Mexico and Arizona. A beautiful species, tree-like, 2 to 4 m. high, with joints 10 to 20 cm. long, 2 to 4 cm. thick, with prominent warts, dull green, often flushed purple, with cylindrical leaves 1 to 2½ cm. long, soon dropping off. Areoles and glochids reddish brown. Spines 5 to 12, up to 2½ cm. long, reddish brown, with a loose yellow sheath, often with a bluish or purplish sheen. Flowers about 5 cm. broad, variable in colour, greenish yellow, reddish, purple or brown. Fruit pear-shaped or clavate, 2 to 2½ cm. long, yellowish or reddish, almost dry, very warty.

Opuntia Lloydii Rose. Central Mexico. Is very similar, but more spreading. Joints 2 cm. thick, with oblong prominent warts. Leaves less than ½ cm. long. Spines fewer and on older joints. Flowers dull purple, 3 to 4 cm. broad. Fruit 3 cm. long, yellow or orange, only slightly warty. Often miscalled *O. lurida*.

Opuntia tunicata Lk. et Otto. = *O. furiosa* Wendl. Native of central Mexico, as well as of the region from Ecuador to northern Chile. Plant bushy, erect, about 50 cm. high, branched in whorls, entirely covered with long white-sheathed spines. Stems or joints 6 to 12 cm. long, and about 4 cm. thick, glaucous green, with prominent warts, large white areoles and pale yellow glochids. Spines 6 to 10, 4 to 5 cm. long, straight, stiff, pale yellow, barbed, enclosed in a loose papery white sheath, sticking fast into the skin as soon as they are touched. Flower yellowish green, about 5 cm. broad. Fruit round or pear-shaped, up to 3 cm. long, warty, whitish green, spiny. A beautiful and sun-loving species, but never was the name *furiosa* more richly deserved.

Opuntia Stapeliae DC. Mexico. A low, spreading plant, about 15 cm. high, with numerous erect stems or joints, more slender and shorter than in the preceding species, and also less warty and with shorter spines. Areoles small, round, whitish or yellowish, with numerous reddish glochids. Spines 3 to 5, very short, or up to 2½ cm. long, stiff, reddish, with white sheaths. Fruit pear-shaped, warty, reddish or reddish yellow, with few short spines. Is specifically distinct, although sometimes considered as a variety of the preceding. *O. Puelchana* Castellanos from Argentina (Pampa Central), is evidently the same as *O. tunicata*, which has found its way down there.

Opuntia molesta Brand. Lower California. A fit companion to *O. tunicata*, and just as troublesome to handle. A bush 1 to 2 m. high, with erect stems, slightly branched. Joints green, 2 to 4 cm. thick, and short, or of varying length up to 30 cm., with slightly prominent but long warts. Spines 6 to 10, about 1½ cm. long, with 1 to 3 central spines, 2 to 5 cm. long, with membraneous pale yellow sheaths. Flower 4½ cm. broad, purple red. Fruit oval, 2 to 2½ cm. long, soft and fleshy, warty, with few spines. **O. calmalliana** Coult., from Lower California (Calmalli), is very similar.

Opuntia pallida Rose, from Mexico (Hidalgo), is very much like *O. tunicata*, but has rose-coloured flowers and grows taller.

7. *Fulgidae*. Tall, erect, spiny shrubs, with thick jointed stems and branches, and with low broad warts.

Opuntia fulgida Engelm. Mexico and Arizona. Tree-like, up to 3 m. high, with a tall, thick, cylindrical, straight stem, thickly covered with spines, freely branched at the top. Joints 10 to 20 cm. long, and about 4 cm. thick, fleshy and easily breaking off, with prominent warts. Areoles small, with short white or yellowish glochids. Spines 10 or more, 2½ to 3½ cm. long, yellowish to brown, barbed and rough, with loose white sheaths. Flower about 3 cm. broad, with short petals, bright pink. Fruit oval or pear-shaped, green, warty, not spiny, freely sprouting into shoots or other fruits.

var. **mamillata** Coulter = *O. mamillata* Schott. Has shorter and more slender joints, fewer and shorter spines. Flowers yellowish red or yellow.

Opuntia spinosior Toumey = *O. Whipplei* var. *spinosior* Engelm. North Mexico, New Mexico and Arizona. Tree-like, 2 to 4 m. high. Joints dark green, 10 to 30 cm. long, and about 2 cm. thick, warty. Spines numerous, 8 to 12, later increasing in number up to 30, 1 to 1½ cm. long, with brown sheaths. Flower variable, white, yellow, reddish or purple.

Opuntia prolifera Engelm. Southern California and Lower California. A bushy plant 1 to 2 m. high, much branched. Joints dark green, 3 to 12 cm. long and about 4 cm. thick, with lozenge-shaped low warts, and yellowish glochids. Spines 6 to 12, brown, about 1 cm. long. Flower red, 3½ cm. broad and 5 cm. long. Fruit often sterile, freely proliferous.

Opuntia alcahes Weber. Lower California. A bush about 1 m. high, irregularly branched. Joints very pale green, 6 to 15 cm. long and 2 to 5 cm. thick, with low lozenge-shaped warts and yellow glochids. Spines 6 to 12, 2 to 3 cm. long, with white or straw-coloured sheaths. Flower 3 cm. long, yellowish green, margined reddish and reddish at the base. Fruit small, globose, yellowish, proliferous and often seedless.

Opuntia Burrageana Br. et R. Lower California. A low bush up to 1 m. high, with a stem 1 to 2 cm. thick, densely spiny. Joints cylindrical or slightly clavate, up to 15 cm. long, with closely set brown areoles and low rounded warts. Spines many, all alike, up to 2 cm. long, spreading, with bright yellow sheaths. Glochids short, pale yellow, often absent. Flower 3 to 4 cm. broad, brownish red, green at the base. Fruit globular, 2 cm. thick, warty, more or less dry, spiny, not proliferous.

Sub-Genus V. CLAVATOPUNTIA Frič = *Clavatae* (Berger) = *Engelmannia* Kunth. North American species, with short cylindrical stems and club-shaped joints, often almost oval or globose. Spines not furnished with sheaths.

Opuntia invicta Brand. Lower California. A thick-set, spreading bush, not more than 50 cm. high, with the habit of an *Echinocereus*. Joints dark green, mostly erect, 8 to 10 cm. long and about 7 cm. thick, with long but low warts. Areoles large, round, about 1 cm. apart, whitish with a few white glochids. Spines 18 or more, of which at least 10 are centrals, 4-angled or flat, curved, about 3 cm. long, at first red, or red below and white above, often tipped brown, later passing to grey. Flower yellow, about 5 cm. broad. Fruit roundish, with reddish spines. An interesting species, still rare in collections. Growth from seed is rather slow.

Opuntia clavata Engelm. New Mexico. Spreading and invading, but only up to 15 cm. high, with stems oval or conical or club-shaped 3 to 7 cm. long, and 2 to 3 cm. thick, with closely set areoles and numerous yellow glochids. Spines numerous, whitish; the radials about 10, needle-shaped, up to 1½ cm. long, the centrals 4 to 7, longer, one being very stiff and up to 3 cm. long or more. Flower yellow; fruit yellow, with abundant glochids, but no spines.

Opuntia Schottii Engelm. Mexico and Texas. A low, spreading bush, only about 20 cm. high, much branched. Joints erect, club-shaped, or oval, 4 to 7 cm. long, and not more than 2 cm. thick, very warty, with warts about 1½ cm. long. Areoles round, about ½ cm. broad, white with few white glochids. Radial spines 6 to 8, spreading, about 2 cm. long, needle-like, whitish. Central spines 4, crosswise, flat on the upper surface, up to 4 cm. long, dirty red, very rough. Flower yellow, 3 cm. broad.

Opuntia Stanlyi Engelm. = *O. Emoryi* Engelm. Mexico, New Mexico and Arizona. A low, spreading bush, about 35 cm. high, with joints of inverted oval-conical shape, or slightly elongated, 10 to 15 cm. long and about 6 cm. thick, with closely set elongated warts. Areoles about ½ cm. broad, white, with white glochids. Spines numerous spreading, whitish passing to reddish brown, straight, 3½ to 6 cm. long. Flower reddish brown outside, yellow and reddish inside, about 5 cm. broad. Fruit oval, yellow, 6 cm. long and 2½ cm. thick, very spiny.

Opuntia Kunzei Rose. Arizona. Very similar to the preceding. A low bush densely branched. Joints bluish green, very warty, with prominent elongated warts, 8 to 10 cm. long, cylindrical or club-shaped, 2 to 3 cm. thick. Leaves thin and acute, about 1 cm. long, quickly shed off. Areoles large, round or oval, with white wool and white glochids. Spines numerous, at first reddish, passing to whitish or greyish, up to 4 cm. long. Flower 4 to 5 cm. broad, pale reddish outside, pale yellow inside. Fruit pear-shaped, 2½ to 3 cm. long, yellowish, with prominent warts, white areoles, white glochids and a few short white spines.

Opuntia Moelleri Berger. Mexico (Coahuila). Very similar to *O. clavata*, and with the same habit. Stems usually shorter and more slender, with more prominent and elongated warts. Radial spines very numerous, but short and bristle-like. Central spines 5 or 6, thickened at the base, up to 1½ cm. long, ash-coloured, somewhat angular and rough.

Opuntia Parishii Orcutt = *O. Parryi* Hort. non Engelm. Southern California and Nevada. A low bush, creeping and rooting. Joints short, clavate, densely spiny, with short prominent warts. Spines at first reddish, passing to greyish and white; radial spines numerous and slender; central spines about 4, strongly angular and flattened, 2 to 4 cm. long. Fruit 5 cm. long, with large white areoles and yellow glochids, along with short spines. Closely related to *O. Kunzei*, but still very rare in collections.

Opuntia pulchella Engelm. Arizona and Nevada. A very pretty, low, spreading species, up to 20 cm. high. Joints cylindrical or clavate, slender, up to 6 cm. long, covered with low warts or knobs, and of a reddish colour. Areoles small, round, with yellow glochids. Radial spines 10 to 15, very short, Only one central spine, papery, reflexed downwards, up to 2½ cm. long. Flower of a beautiful purple, about 5 cm. broad. Fruit roundish or club-shaped, 2 cm. long, red, with white hair-like spines.

Opuntia dumetorum Berger. Mexico. About ½ m. high. Joints cylindrical or clavate, 5 to 6 cm. long, and 2 to 3 cm. thick, with low warts, often furnished with white hairs on the round white areoles. Spines numerous, yellowish brown, 1 to 1½ cm. long. Glochids white.

Opuntia agglomerata Berger. Mexico. A low spreading bush, with clavate or elongated joints, greyish green, rough and warty, with round white areoles, and pale yellow glochids. Radial spines about 6, whitish and very short; central spines few, yellowish, thickened at the base, 1 to 1½ cm. long.

Opuntia Grahamii Engelm. Mexico, New Mexico and Texas. A low, spreading bush, with clavate joints 3 to 4½ cm. long, and 1½ to 2 cm. thick, pale green, with prominent elongated warts. Areoles small, white, with numerous glochids, white passing to brown. Radial spines 4 to 6, up to 1 cm. long, spreading laterally, reddish when young, passing to whitish. Central spines 4 to 7, same colour, thicker and longer, some of them angular and rough, and up to 6 cm. long. Flower yellow; fruit oval 4½ cm. long and 2 cm. thick, thickly beset with glochids and short spines.

112

PLATE X

(b) ESPOSTOA LANATA
in flower

(a) CEREUS COERULESCENS

PLATE XI

Opuntia vilis Rose. Mexico (Zacatecas). Prostrate and spreading, with club-shaped or oval-globose joints, 4 to 5 cm. long, dull green or glaucous, irregular and warty. Spines numerous; the radials spreading, white, bristle-like, up to 1 cm. long; the centrals 3 or 4, reddish brown, tipped whitish, spreading, up to 3 cm. long. Flower blood red, stigma yellow. Fruit pale green, 2 to 2½ cm. thick, oval, warty, spiny. Seeds large, white.

Opuntia bulbispina Engelm. Mexico (Coahuila) and New Mexico. Plant low, spreading, cespitose, hardly 10 cm. high. Joints oval or clavate, 2 to 3 cm. long, very glaucous, warty, branching at the upper end. Radial spines white, 8 to 12, bristle-like, about ½ cm. long; central spines 4, stronger, up to 2 cm. long, reflexed, brown passing to whitish, bulbous at the base. The plant has a fleshy turnip-like root, and prefers a sandy soil, kept rather dry.

Sub-Genus VI Sphaeropuntia (*Tephrocactus* Lem.).

Low, spreading bushes, with spherical or oval joints, which do not become much elongated or cylindrical under cultivation, and are easily broken off. They are mostly of a dull glaucous or ashy green colour, hence the name *Tephrocactus = Ashy Cactus*, but some species have joints of a more or less lively green. The warts or tubercles are broad and low, and the glochids are often deeply embedded in the substance of the joint, and just showing at the surface. Their root system is weak, and growth is slow. *O. Turpinii* has white flowers, and so also has *O. aoracantha* and *O. glomerata* and its varieties, but in this last species the outer petals have often a violet dorsal band, fading off to white. In other species, as far as it is known, the flower is yellow. The fruit looks like a terminal joint, and is often about the same size, with a depressed navel, and has few seeds.

Series A. Elongatae. Growths somewhat elongated, often branching laterally.

1. *Floccosae.* Forming cushions. Joints roundish or clavate. Areoles developing hairs, or almost bare.

Opuntia floccosa Salm-Dyck = *O. Hempeliana* K. Sch. Peru and Bolivia. Stems sprawling and spreading, 5 to 10 cm. long and 3 to 4 cm. thick, glossy grass green with prominent warts and small thick leaves, lasting for a long time. Areoles large, white, with 1 to 3 yellow spines, up to 3 cm. long, straight and slender, with a few glassy glochids, and with many pure white, woolly, curly hairs, covering the plant. Flower yellow, 3 cm. broad. Fruit round, warty. A popular species delighting in full sunshine. Young plants are very much like seedlings of *Oreocereus Trollii*. A beautiful cristate form is also cultivated, usually grafted on *O. ficus-indica*.

var. **denudata** Weber, is an almost hairless form.

Opuntia lagopus K. Sch. South-western Peru and Bolivia, near Arequipa, uplands about 4000 m. high. Often catalogued as a yellow-

H

haired variety of *O. floccosa.* Same habit as the preceding, much branched, forming cushions and groups. Joints globose, or oval to cylindrical. often 10 to 12 cm. long, and 3 to 6 cm. thick, densely covered with pale yellow to brownish woolly hair, 1 to $1\frac{1}{2}$ cm. long. Leaves slender, acute, yellowish, 7 mm. long, soon dropping off. Spines 1 to 7, sharp, yellow to brown, up to 4 cm. long. The wool or hair is often in tufts, and may be creamy white to dark honey-coloured.

2. *Strobiliformes.* Joints like a fir-cone, or slightly cylindrical.

Opuntia strobiliformis Berger. Argentina. A very curious species, with an erect, much-branched habit. Joints oval-elongated, greyish green, with small prominent warts, very much resembling a pine-cone or a fir-cone. Areoles small, with few dark grey or brownish glochids, deeply embedded. Spines entirely absent, or reduced to 1 or 2 straight, brown spines. less than 1 cm. long, on the upper areoles. Grows well on own roots in full sunshine, but grows better grafted on *O. ficus-indica,* or other strong-growing species.

3. *Weberianae.* Globose or slightly cylindrical, practically leafless, warty, with long spines.

Opuntia Weberi Spegazzini. Argentina. Cespitose, spreading, but only up to 18 cm. high. Joints globose or oval-cylindrical, with warts arranged spirally, yellowish green, 2 to 6 cm. long. Spines 5 to 7, brown, 3 to 5 cm. long, erect, slender and flexible, the lower spines twisted or tortuous. Flowers small, solitary, rotate, yellow. Fruit dry, white, about 1 cm. thick. A very interesting species, now offered by dealers.

Series B. GLOBULARES. Joints spherical or slightly conical.

4. *Glomeratae.* Joints spherical or oval, usually with more or less long papery spines, particularly from the upper areoles.

Opuntia Turpinii Lem. = *O. glomerata* Haw. pro parte. Argentina. Plant low and spreading, hardly more than 10 cm. high, much branched, made up of globose or slightly oval joints, or slightly depressed, smooth, 2 to $3\frac{1}{2}$ cm. in diameter, green passing to dull ashy green. Areoles small, whitish, with small dark brown glochids deeply embedded, and with 1 to 3 white or whitish, flat, membraneous, papery spines on the upper areoles, 1 to 3 cm. long, and about 3 mm. broad, often longer and broader. Flower creamy white, or white, 3 to $3\frac{1}{2}$ cm. broad. Fruit dry, about $1\frac{1}{2}$ cm. thick, with a few round seeds, surrounded by a broad, star-like, corky ring. Commonly listed and sold as *O. diademata.* A form with only 1 or 2 white papery spines on each joint, or with none at all, is also in cultivation, to which the name *tonsa* may be given. Grows best in a sandy soil, in half-shade, but its growth is always very slow.

Opuntia diademata Lem. = *O. glomerata* Haw. pro parte = *O. papyracantha* Phil. Western Argentina. Joints oval, 5 to 8 cm. long and $3\frac{1}{2}$ to 6 cm. thick at the base, at first brownish green, passing to dull greyish green, with very low broad warts, on which are situated the large brownish areoles, with many reddish brown glochids, deeply embedded. Spines 1 to 4, papery, on the areoles near the top, 3 to 10 cm. long and 5 to 8 mm. broad, reddish brown along the margin, paler inside. Flower creamy white, 3 to 4 cm. broad, funnel-shaped, often with a pale violet band on the back of the petals. Fruit oval, dry, up to 5 cm. long. Seeds as in the preceding. A very interesting species, requiring the same treatment, but of quicker growth. If *O. Turpinii* is to be considered only as a variety of *O. diademata*, then Haworth's name *O. glomerata*, has a prior claim. The following varieties are in cultivation :

var. **calva** Weber. Habit more erect, joints greenish brown or reddish brown, much wrinkled especially in winter, entirely without spines.

var. **oligacantha** (Speg.) Hoss. Spines few (1 or 2), and only on the upper areoles.

var. **molinensis** (Speg.) Hoss. Habit more erect, joints oval-elongated, more or less pointed. Spines 3 to 5 on the upper areoles, and mostly erect and somewhat stiff, like parchment, few at the sides. A fast-growing variety.

var. **polyacantha** Hoss. Joints oval, large, greyish green or dark ashy green, with 1 to 4 long spines on all the areoles; spines reflexed and often tortuous.

var. **chionacantha** Hoss? Joints oval, large, dull green. Spines white or greyish, on the upper areoles.

Opuntia platyacantha Pfeiff. Chile and Patagonia. Plant low, prostrate and spreading. Joints oval or spherical or oval-elongated, 3 to 6 cm. long and 1½ to 2½ cm. thick, olive green or brownish green, almost smooth or with low warts, often associated with globose joints, less than 1 cm. thick. Areoles large, yellowish. Spines 5 to 7, the lowermost 2 or 3 being flat, flexible, leathery or papery, whitish or yellowish grey, or brown, up to 4 cm. long. Flower yellow. This and the two preceding species are often grafted on other species of *Opuntia* or on a *Trichocereus*, but thrive well on own roots in full sunshine. The following varieties are in cultivation:

var. **gracilior** Salm-Dyck. Joints smaller or more slender. Spines white.

var. **Monvillei** Salm-Dyck. Joints also more slender; spines brown.

var. **deflexispina** Salm-Dyck. All spines longer and reflexed, central spine strongly reflexed. This is the form commonly grown.

5. *Pentlandianae*. Joints conical, green or greenish, often developing smaller spherical joints.

Opuntia Pentlandii Salm-Dyck. Peru, Bolivia and Argentina. Plant spreading and forming cushions, 10 to 15 cm. high, but up to 1 m. broad. Joints green or grass green, oval or oval-elongated, usually 3 to 5 cm. long, sometimes almost twice as long, and 2 to 4 cm. thick, with broad low warts, or nearly smooth and somewhat reddish.

Areoles brownish, small, with yellow glochids. Spines 2 to 10, only on the upper areoles, and often absent, whitish, yellowish, or brownish, usually very short, occasionally up to 7 cm. long. Flower 2 to 3 cm. long, and 5 cm. broad, yellow or reddish yellow. **O. boliviana** Salm-Dyck, from the high Pampas of Bolivia, often considered as a synonym, has a more erect habit, with larger and more spherical joints of a pale greyish green, less spreading, with fewer spines or almost spineless.

Opuntia australis Weber. Patagonia. Plant prostrate and spreading. Joints oval or oval-elongated, with prominent warts, dark green or purplish, 6 to 8 cm. long and 1 to 2 cm. thick. Radial spines 10 to 15, spreading, white, very thin; central spines 2, longer ($2\frac{1}{2}$ to $3\frac{1}{2}$ cm.), dark brown or almost black, flat or papery, later passing to grey. Flower 3 cm. broad, pale yellow. The root is large and tuberous, 5 to 8 cm. long, 2 to 3 cm. thick, larger than the parts above ground. This is the southern-most species of Cactus so far known, extending down to the cold region of the Strait of Magellan.

Opuntia ignescens Vaupel. Peru and Chile. In groups up to 20 cm. high, Joints oval, fleshy, bluish green, 8 to 10 cm. long, 2 to 3 cm. thick. Upper areoles very spiny, the lower bare. Spines 6 to 15, erect, needle-like, yellow, 4 to 5 cm. long. Flower very showy, deep red; spines on the upper areoles of ovary 4 to 7 cm. long. Fruit red, 7 cm. long, warty, and spiny above. Seeds globular, $\frac{1}{2}$ cm. thick.

Opuntia campestris Br. et R. Peru. A straggling bush, up to 60 cm. high, but rarely more than 15 cm. high in cultivation, with branches and joints easily breaking off. Joints roundish or elliptical, 3 to 5 cm. long, warty when young, almost smooth when fully developed, of a dull dirty green or olive green. Areoles numerous, rather large, yellowish and prominent, with numerous yellow glochids. Spines mostly on the upper areoles, 5 to 10, up to 4 cm. long, needle-like, yellowish brown. Flower pale pink or pale yellow.

Opuntia unguispina Backbg. South Peru. A low, straggling bush. Joints spherical, 3 to 5 cm. thick, pale green passing to reddish brown. Areoles round, with yellowish white wool, on small warts, at first with a brush of 12 small spines directed backwards, afterwards developing about 18 claw-like spines, dark brown to greyish, up to $2\frac{1}{2}$ cm. long. Flowers 5 cm. across, glossy yellow.

Opuntia ignota Br. et R. Peru. A low, spreading plant, much branched. Joints oval, 2 to 3 cm. long, mostly purplish, well armed at the top. Areoles large, greyish, with a few yellow glochids. Spines on the upper areoles, 2 to 7, needle-like, brownish, the longer ones 4 to 5 cm. long.

Opuntia Alexanderi Br. et R. Argentina (La Rioja). Low, forming cushions. Joints globose, easily breaking off, greyish green, very warty, 2 to 3 cm. thick, covered with spines. Areoles small, round, closely set. Spines 4 to 12, flexible, white below, dark above, mostly tipped black, rough, up to 4 cm. long. Fruit red, dry, obovoid, 2 cm. long, with white weak spines on the upper areoles. Seeds white.

Opuntia Guerkei Schelle = *O. Schumannii* Speg. non Weber. Argentina. A prostrate, densely branched bush, with elliptical or oval joints, dark greyish green, 3 to 4 cm. long, and 2 to 2½ cm. thick. Areoles large and prominent, spineless, but with a brush-like bundle of yellow glochids.

6. *Aoracanthae.* Joints globular, often large, with very long, twisted, straight or angular spines.

Opuntia aoracantha Lem. Sometimes written *acracantha* Hort. = *O. formidabilis* Walton. Western Argentina. An erect or spreading bush, about 30 cm. high. Joints roundish or oval, 5 to 8 cm. long, very plump, greyish green or brownish green, with broad round flat warts, and easily breaking off if roughly handled. Areoles large, round, brown, with numerous chocolate-coloured glochids, deeply embedded. Spines 1 to 7, very stout, of iron hardness, brown or black, passing to greyish, angular, straight or tortuous or incurved, up to 13 cm. long. Flower white, 5 to 6 cm. broad. Fruit red, with low warts, dry. A very striking species, very properly named sword-spined or formidable. The root-system is weak, and growth is slow. Requires full sunshine, and very little water in autumn and winter.

7. *Nigrescentes.* Joints oval, small, more or less blackish green, often developing small spherical joints.

Opuntia nigrispina K. Sch. Re-discovered recently in Bolivia. Cespitose, low, about 10 cm. high, with oval or oval-elongated joints, 2 to 3½ cm. long, purplish black when young. Areoles with brown glochids, and with 2 to 5 spines, 1 or 2 of which are up to 2½ cm. long, straight, purplish black, rough, seen under a lens; the other spines smaller and of a paler hue.

8. *Rauppianae.* Spines soft, adpressed.

Opuntia Rauppiana K. Sch. Argentina (La Rioja). Joints oval, 7 cm. long and 4 cm. thick, green passing to greyish green or grey. Areoles large, round, yellowish, with pale yellow glochids. Spines 12 to 14, afterwards up to 20 or more, white, spreading or adpressed, soft, curly, up to 2 cm. long, hardly prickly. Very rare in cultivation.

Opuntia Weingartiana Backbg. A recent species from Argentina. Joints oval to oval-cylindrical, 10 to 15 cm. long, and 2 to 2½ cm. thick, warty. Areoles large, white, closely set, with yellowish glochids, and many reddish or red spines, rather soft, 2 to 5 cm. long, mostly directed downwards.

9. *Sphaericae.* Joints spherical, fairly large, branching, smooth, spiny.

Opuntia sphaerica Förster = *O. leucophaea* Phil. Peru to Chile. Has an erect bushy habit, but always low. Joints spherical or somewhat obovate, whitish glaucous green, with very low broad warts, branching regularly at or near the top, 3 to 5 cm. thick, easily breaking off.

Areoles large, yellowish brown, with deeply embedded brown glochids. Radial spines 8 to 12, white, flattened, radiating, straight or reflexed, of various lengths up to 5 cm. Central spines 3 or 4, greyish brown or ashy grey, very stiff, thick and angular, 4 to 7 cm. long, the longest reflexed downwards. A very desirable species, rare in collections, but of easy cultivation in full sunshine. Growth is slow.

Opuntia riojana Hosseus. Argentina (La Rioja). A low, slow-growing, erect plant, rare in collections. Joints perfectly, spherical, or very slightly oval, at first dull dark green, passing to dirty greyish green, almost perfectly smooth when full developed, $2\frac{1}{2}$ to $3\frac{1}{2}$ cm. thick. Areoles small, greyish, with whitish glochids. Spines only on the upper areoles, 4 to 10, straight, 1 to 2 cm. long, white with a dark blunt tip; sometimes almost awl-shaped and more or less flattened.

Opuntia Skottsbergii Br. et R. Argentina. Cespitose, with a thick fleshy root. Joints globular or oval, 3 cm. thick, very spiny. Areoles closely set, small, sometimes with long tufts of white wool, and with many long white glochids. Spines about 10, black, tipped yellow, 1 to 2 cm. long. Ovary spiny.

10. *Bruchianae*. Joints large, spherical, with strong bluish spines.

Opuntia Bruchii Speg. Argentina (Catamarca and Mazan). A much-branched bush about 50 cm. high. Joints oval, 7 to 9 cm. long, and 4 to $5\frac{1}{2}$ cm. thick, with low warts, at first green, passing to greyish. Areoles white, passing to brownish or grey, with few yellowish glochids. Spines only on the upper areoles, 12 to 14, spreading, 1 to 4 cm. long, white, passing to purplish, tipped bluish. The flower is stated to be deep blue, which would be a very extraordinary colour in Cacti.

11. *Kuehnrichianae*. Joints large, spherical or elongated, very spiny; forming extensive cushions.

Opuntia Kuehnrichiana Werd. et Backbg. Peru. Joints very large, oval or almost cylindrical, up to 12 cm. long, and $6\frac{1}{2}$ cm. thick, pale green, warty, dotted all over with minute white dots. Areoles rather closely set, white passing to greyish, with numerous glochids in prominent tufts. Spines 5 to 12, only on the upper areoles, ash-coloured, spreading or reflexed, the longest up to $3\frac{1}{2}$ cm. long; new joints with fewer spines. Leaves about $\frac{1}{2}$ cm. long, scale-like, soon dropping off.

var. **applanta** Werd. et Backbg. Joints smaller, roundish, somewhat flattened, 4 to 5 cm. thick, with more closely set areoles, with 1 to 3 milk white needle-like spines, developing on the top of new joints.

12. *Macrorhizae*. Joints small, spherical or oval, often developing very small spherical joints. Root large, much swollen.

Opuntia subterranea Fries. Argentina. A very curious species. The plant is quite small, consisting of a few joints above ground, but has a thick and long tap-root, out of proportion to the size of the plant, like a long irregular beet-root, about 5 cm. thick and 10 to 15 cm. long. The joints are few oval, about 3 cm. long, warty, brownish green, with whitish areoles, dark glochids, and 3 to 6 whitish flat, leathery spines, about 1 cm. long.

13. *Subnudae.* Joints oval, smooth and almost spineless.

Opuntia grata R.A.Phil. Chile (Santiago). Often confused with *O. ovata*, but quite distinct. A low spreading bush, with oval joints, pale brownish green, smooth, 3 to 4 cm. long and 2 cm. thick, with short yellowish glochids, and about 5 yellowish grey, straight or curved spines, up to 3 cm. long. Areoles white. Flower reddish yellow or reddish brown, about 4 cm. broad, stigma thick, with about 13 spreading pale yellow lobes.

Opuntia leonina Hge. et Schm. Chile. Possibly only a variety of the preceding. A much branched low bush, forming clumps up to 20 cm. high. Joints oval, sometimes almost spherical or cylindrical, 1 to 4 cm. long, 1 to 2 cm. thick, dirty green or brownish, later yellowish grey, with very low warts. Areoles small, yellow, with very small yellow glochids. Spines usually absent, or 1 to 3, very short, 2 to 3 mm. long, rarely up to 1½ cm., straight or curved.

Opuntia andicola Pfeiff. Western Argentina. Plant low, spreading, much branched, forming cushions. Joints oval, more or less pointed, 6 to 8 cm. long, dark green or brownish green or blackish. Glochids numerous, forming brush-like yellow tufts, up to 8 mm. long. Spines 3 to 5, of which 1 or 2 are flat, papery, white or reddish, up to 6 cm. long; the other spines, 1 to 3, are thin, cylindrical, white, reflexed at the tip.

var. **minor.** Hildm. Joints much smaller, 3 to 5 cm. long, brownish olive green; spines shorter.

Opuntia neuquensis Borg *n.sp.* Southern Argentina, near Neuquen. A low prostrate bush, 10 to 15 cm. high. Joints pale green or yellowish, oval-conical, 2 to 4 cm. long and 1 to 1½ cm. thick, almost smooth or with very low protuberances. Areoles small, white, with few very short pale yellow glochids. Radial spines 2 or 3, bristle-like, white, ½ to 1 cm. long, directed downwards. Usually only one central spine, rarely 2 or 3, white, flattened, flexible, 2 to 3 cm. long, yellowish or brownish at the tip. Flowers unknown.

(For the Latin diagnosis of this species see first edition.)

14. *Microsphaericae.* Joints very small, spherical or oval, sometimes spineless.

Opuntia Hickenii Br. et R. Patagonia. A low bushy plant, very densely branched, 10 to 15 cm. high. Joints oval, 2 to 4 cm. long and 1 to 2 cm. thick, smooth brownish green, with round yellowish areoles, bearing prominent tufts of yellow glochids. Spines 2 to 5, often absent, about 5 cm. long, white passing to dark brown, flexible or stiff. Flower yellow.

Opuntia Darwinii Hensl. Patagonia. Plant prostrate. Joints oval or almost spherical, smooth, olive-green, about 3 cm. long. Areoles large, with yellowish wool and yellowish glochids. Spines only on the upper areoles, 1 to 3 yellow or reddish yellow, 3 to 3½ cm. long, straight, later reflexed. Flower yellow. Fruit with large woolly areoles.

Opuntia Wetmorei Br. et R. Argentina (Mendoza). A low bush, forming extensive cushions. Joints 4 to 10 cm. long, globose to cylindrical, up to 2 cm. thick, dull green, purplish at the areoles, which are small, round, whitish or brownish, with short yellow glochids. Spines numerous, unequal, softish, white or straw-coloured or brownish, 3 or 4 lower ones hair-like and reflexed, the upper ones erect, flattened, 2 to 3½ cm. long. Fruit reddish purple, 3 cm. long, with white bristle-like spines on the upper areoles.

Opuntia tarapacana Phil. = *O. Rahmeri* Phil. Chile. A low cespitose bush, spreading. Joints ovoid, about 2 cm. long, by 1 cm. thick. Areoles with white wool. Spines only on the upper areoles, usually 3, straight, 1 to 1½ cm. long, white tipped yellow. Flower yellow, about 4 cm. broad, with an ovary 2 cm. long, but slender.

Opuntia Molfinoi (Speg) Werd. et Backbg. = *Maihueniopsis Molfino* Speg. Argentina, at elevations of about 3,500 m. A prostrate, densely branched bush. Joints roundish or oval, 1 to 1½ cm. long, with small whitish areoles and with prominent tufts of reddish glochids, and with one reddish grey spine on the upper areoles, 1½ to 2½ cm. long. Flower about 3 cm. long, greenish outside and sulphur yellow inside, with yellow stamens and stigma with 4 to 6 violet lobes.

15. *Ovatae*. Joints oval or obovate; forming cushions.

Opuntia ovata Pfeiff. Argentina. Spreading and forming cushions, 8 to 12 cm. high, much branched. Joints green or pale green, oval or oval-elongated, 4 to 7 cm. long, and 2 to 3 cm. thick, irregular, with low broad warts. Areoles large, pale yellow to brownish, with prominent brush-like tufts of stiff pale yellow glochids. Spines 5 to 9 awl-shaped, up to 1½ cm. long, yellowish passing to grey, often absent. Fruit half-elliptical with depressed navel, 1½ cm thick, dirty yellow, spiny.

Opuntia subinermis Backbg. Argentina? Low, densely branched, forming cushions, with sub-globular or oval joints, olive-green, with small areoles and tufts of yellow glochids, and with occasional spines only on the upper areoles.

Opuntia corrugata Salm-Dyck = *O. Parmentieri* Pfeiff. = *O. retrospinosa* Lem. = *O. eburnea* Lem. Northwestern Argentina. Plant low and spreading, about 10 cm. high. Joints greyish white, oval or elliptical, 2 to 4 cm. long, and 1½ to 2 cm. thick, wrinkled, but without warts. Areoles white, with yellowish brown glochids. Spines 6 to 8, about 1 cm. long, spreading, white, sometimes with 1 or 2 longer spines yellowish brown in the upper areoles. Flower reddish. Fruit round, red; seeds corky. A pretty, slow-growing species. In the variety *eburnea* (Lem.), growth is quicker, the joints are larger, whiter, more plump and never wrinkled.

Opuntia atacamensis Phil. Northern Chile (Atacama). A semierect, spreading bush, about 30 cm. high. Joints oval, about 3 cm. long and 1 to 1½ cm. thick, whitish green, with white woolly areoles, the lower ones with very short spines, the upper with 2 to 4 white radial spines, flat, ½ to 1½ cm. long, and 1 yellowish white central spine, erect, up to 2½ cm. long. Flower yellow. A very pretty species, of easy growth.

Opuntia leoncito Werd. et Backbg. Northern Chile. (Atacama), along with the preceding species. A much branched spreading bush, about 50 cm. high. Joints oval-elongated, about 4 cm. long, and 2 cm. thick. Areoles few and small, with yellow glochids. Spines present only on the upper areoles, 1 or 2, up to 4 cm. long, along with 1 or 2 smaller ones, yellowish brown, passing to whitish, flattish, like thick paper. Flowers 4 cm. broad, yellow.

Opuntia Russellii Br. et R. Argentina (Mendoza). A low bush, forming small clumps 10 to 20 cm. broad. Joints small, globose or obovoid, dull green or more or less purplish, 2 to 4 cm. long, very spiny at the top. Areoles small, at first with few glochids, later developing a tuft of yellowish glochids up to 2 cm. long. Spines 3 to 6 on the upper areoles, yellow, 2 to 3 cm. long, slightly flattened, with 1 or more shorter spines up to 1 cm. long. Fruit globose, 2 to 2½ cm. thick, spineless.

Opuntia hypogaea Werd. et Backbg. Argentina (Los Andes, at heights of 4,000 m.). A small bush, 10 to 15 cm. high, partly buried in the ground, with a thick woody root or stem, and many slender jointed branches. Joints small, oval, somewhat wrinkled and warty, up to 3 cm. long and 1½ cm. thick, often smaller or much smaller, greyish green, with yellowish areoles chiefly on the upper part, with numerous yellow glochids. Spines 1 to 5, 2 to 4 cm. long, flat, reflexed, stiff or leathery, whitish or greyish, tipped darker. A very interesting miniature species, to be grown in a sandy stony soil, in full sunshine.

The following are other new or rare species of Opuntia now in cultivation:

Cylindropuntia: **Opuntia setigera** Backbg., **O. haematacantha** Backbg., **O. humahuacana** Backbg.

Platyopuntia: **Opuntia aurea** Baxter, **O. boliviensis** Backbg., **O. Cedergreniana** Backbg., **O cordobensis** Speg., **O. Ireiss** Backbg., **O. nigra** Backbg.?, **O erectoclada** Backbg.

Sphaeropuntia: **Opuntia minuscula** Backbg., **O minuta** Backbg., **O. pseudorauppiana** Backbg., **O. rarissima** Backbg., **O. subsphaerica** Backbg., **O Wilkeana** Backbg.

NOPALEA Salm-Dyck

Nopal is the Mexican name for species of Opuntia.

Tall plants almost tree-like, with flattened joints and small fugacious leaves as in *Platyopuntia*, but with few glochids. Flowers red or pinkish, differing from those of an *Opuntia* by the segments of the perianth being erect, forming a sort of tube through which the stamens are protruded, being always longer than the petals. Includes 7 species, natives of Mexico and Guatemala. They require the same cultivation as an *Opuntia*, but in warmer conditions.

Nopalea coccinellifera (Mill.) Salm-Dyck = *Opuntia cochinelifera* Miller. Tropical Mexico. Almost tree-like, 3 to 4 m. high, with pale green joints, obovate-elongated, 8 to 25 cm. long and 5 to 12 cm. broad, smooth. Areoles far apart, with a few yellow glochids, passing to brownish. Spines absent, or few and small. Flower 6 to 7 cm. long, a lively red, with pink stamens, exserted like a brush beyond the petals. Stigma with 6 or 7 greenish lobes. Fruit elliptical, 5 cm. long, red. This is one of the species of *Nopalea* and *Opuntia* on which the cochineal scale-insect is reared.

Nopalea guatemalensis Rose. Guatemala. Tree-like, about 5 m. high, with bluish green obovate joints, 15 to 20 cm. long, and 8 to 10 cm. broad. Spines 5 to 8, at first reddish, soon passing to white, spreading, up to 3 cm. long. Flower red, about 6 cm. long.

Nopalea Auberi Salm-Syck = *Opuntia Auberi* Pfeiff. Mexico. A tree 8 to 9 m. high, with a thick round stem. Joints obovate, very elongated, thick and narrow, bluish green or greyish green, 20 to 30 cm. long, with prominent brown glochids, and spineless, or with 2 or 3 spines, 2 to 3 cm. long, white tipped brown. Flower pink.

Nopalea lutea Rose. Nicaragua, Guatemala, Honduras. Is very much like *N. guatemalensis*, but the joints are much narrower, and the spines are longer and yellow. The flower is red, 4 or 5 cm. long.

Nopalea dejecta Salm-Dyck = *Opuntia dejecta* Salm-Dyck. South Mexico to Nicaragua. A shrub 1 to 2 m. high, with a straggling and drooping habit. Joints green passing to greyish green, narrow, almost lanceolate, 8 to 25 cm. long, and 3 to 6 cm. broad, with white glochids. Spines 2 or more, at first reddish, soon passing to yellowish and greyish, up to 4 cm. long. Flower red. Fruit roundish or round, smooth, deep red, with many areoles.

var. **Guarnacciana** Hort. Joints marbled white.

Nopalea Karwinskiana (S.D.) K. Sch. = *Opuntia Karwinskiana* Salm-Dyck. Mexico. Tree-like with elongated joints, 15 to 20 cm. long and 5 to 8 cm. broad, pale green, often with a straggling and drooping habit, with many yellow glochids. Spines at first reddish, passing to yellowish and white, up to 4 cm. long, at first 1 to 3 in each areole, afterwards more numerous. Flowers large, 10 to 12 cm. long, red or pink, with yellow stamens.

Nopalea inaperta Schott. Mexico (Yucatan). Tree-like, up to 5 m. high, with a straggling habit, and with a very spiny stem. Joints obovate, 6 to 18 cm. long, and 4 to 8 cm. broad, pale green, somewhat warty on both sides and along the margin. Spines yellow, up to 2 cm. long, at first 3 to 6, afterwards more numerous. Flowers very small, red. Fruit small, red.

OPUNTIEAE

Grusonia F. Reichenbach

Joints cylindrical or oval-cylindrical, distinctly ribbed, with areoles along the ribs, bearing spines. Leaves small, soon dropping off. Flowers yellow, rotate. Includes only one species.

Grusonia Bradtiana Br. et R. = *Opuntia Bradtiana* K. Brand. = *Grusonia cereiformis* F. Reich. = *O. cereiformis* Weber. Mexico (Coahuila). A low bush up to 2 m. high, with elliptical-cylindrical joints, greyish green, with 8 to 9 ribs. Areoles 1 to 1½ cm. apart, large with whitish or greyish wool. Leaves small, soon shed off. Young growing joints have glochids, but are soon shed, only a few remaining at the top of the joint and on the ovary. Radial spines 12 or more, yellowish brown passing to milky white with a peculiar faint bluish tinge, the upper ones up to 2 cm. long. Central spines 4 or 5, one of which is cylindrical, directed upwards, up to 5 cm. long; the others are shorter and somewhat flattened. Flower 3 to 4 cm. broad, yellow; the ovary with white woolly areoles, bearing yellow glochids and long slender yellow spines.

A very attractive species, easily grown, requiring the same treatment as an *Opuntia*, with full sunshine and a warm and dry situation.

TRIBE III. CEREEAE

Stem very variable, succulent. Joints cylindrical or angular, elongated or globular. Petals united in a tube, which may be long and slender, or very short, so that they look almost distinct. Leaves absent. Seedlings globular or elongated, without cotyledons, or with cotyledons reduced to small prominences.

SUB-TRIBE I. CEREANAE

Stem cylindrical, ribbed or fluted, often columnar, erect or sprawling, branching, always well furnished with spines. Flowers always furnished with a tube, bell-shaped or funnel-shaped.

CEREUS Miller
(*Piptanthocereus* Berger)

Stems erect, sometimes prostrate or sprawling, branched, ribbed or angular. Areoles without long hairs, spines variable. Flowers generally large, nocturnal, trumpet-shaped or funnel-shaped, mostly white. Ovary and tube with few scales, but no areoles or spines, the withered flower dropping off from the fertilized ovary. Fruit large, red, sometimes yellow, eatable. Seeds black. This genus, as revised by Britton and Rose, now includes only about 26 species, the true *Cerei*. Formerly it included all the columnar or angular or cylindrical or trailing Cacti, now spread over the sub-tribes *Cereanae* and *Hylocereanae*, as well as certain genera of the sub-tribe *Echinocereanae*.

Cereus Hankeanus Weber. Northern Argentina. Stem columnar, 3 to 4 m. high, green passing to dark green, bluish green on new growths, about 8 cm. in diameter, with 4 or 5 wing-like ribs, $2\frac{1}{2}$ to 3 cm. deep, marked on the sides with curved S-like lines. The ribs are notched; in the notches are situated the areoles 2 to 3 cm. apart; each areole is about $\frac{1}{2}$ cm. broad, with greyish wool, with 4 stiff radial spines, yellowish brown, up to 1 cm. long, and 1 central spine up to 3 cm. long, thicker and horny. Flower 12 cm. long, green outside, the outer petals being brownish pink, and the inner white, pointed pale pink.

Cereus chalybaeus Otto. Argentina. Stem columnar, 3 m. high, sparingly branched, 5 to 10 cm. thick, at first of a beautiful deep blue or steel blue, passing to dark green, with 5 to 6 ribs hardly notched, up to 2 cm. deep, with prominent areoles, up to 2 cm. apart, furnished with brownish wool. Radial spines 7 to 9, the lowermost up to 14 mm. long. Central spines 3 or 4, slightly longer and thicker. All spines are straight and black. Flower up to 20 cm. long, the outer petals being red passing to reddish, the inner white and finely toothed. Fruit yellow. A lovely species deservedly popular. Thrives best in a half-shaded and airy situation. There is also a pretty cristate form known in cultivation as *C. Beysiegelii*.

Cereus coerulescens Salm-Dyck = *C. aethiopis* Haw. Argentina, along the Rio Negro. Stem erect, rarely branching, 3 to 4 cm. thick, at first deep blue passing to dark green, with 8 obtuse ribs bearing small prominences, with narrow furrows between the ribs. Areoles on the prominences, up to 1½ cm. apart, almost black. Radial spines 9 to 12, black, or the lower part white, ½ to 1½ cm. long. Central spines 4, black, thicker and up to 2 cm. long. Flower up to 20 cm. long, funnel-shaped. Ovary with narrow red-tipped scales: outer petals greenish, margined brownish, inner petals white or pale pink, toothed. A fine species, popular with growers.

var. **Landbeckii** K. Sch. Radial spines white.

var. **melanacantha** K. Sch. All spines larger, glossy black. Partilarly large (up to 5 cm. long) are the secondary central spines which develop on old stems.

Cereus azureus Parm. = *C. Seidelii* Lehm. Northern Argentina and southern Brazil. Stem erect, 1½ to 3 m. high, and 3 to 3½ cm. thick, slightly branched, bluish green passing to dark green, with a metallic sheen. Ribs 6 or 7, obtuse, swollen and slightly gibbose at the areoles, with deep and narrow furrows between them. Areoles about 1 cm. apart, round, brownish or greyish. Spines 8 to 16, black, awl-shaped, ½ to 1 cm. long, the central spines (2 to 4) being slightly longer. Flowers diurnal, large, 20 to 30 cm. long. Outer petals obtuse, reddish brown; the inner petals also obtuse and spathulate, white, finely toothed. Fruit oval, red, about 4 cm. long. Grows quickly and flowers freely. Prefers a sunny situation and a sandy soil. *C. Seidelii* Lehm., often considered as a synonym, is in reality a form with larger and more woolly areoles, and longer flowers.

Cereus caesius Salm-Dyck = *C. jamacaru caesius* Salm-Dyck = *C. cyaneus* Hort. Probably Brazilian, but known only in cultivation. Stem columnar, 4 to 5 m. high, 12 to 16 cm. thick, of a beautiful bluish green passing to dull green and greyish green, with 5 or 6 wing-like ribs, prominent and thin, slightly notched, with slight furrows on the sides. Areoles depressed in the notches, 4 to 6 cm. apart, at first woolly. Spines yellowish brown; the radials 7 or more, the centrals 5 to 7, stronger and longer, all spreading. Older areoles developing more spines, the centrals often more than 10 cm. long. Flower large, white; fruit unknown.

Cereus jamacaru DC. = *C. validus* Haw. South America. Stem columnar, up to 10 m. high, branched, 10 to 16 cm. thick, the main stem being sometimes 60 cm. in diameter at the base. New stems are bluish green, passing to dull green. Ribs 4 to 6, at first thin and deep, notched. Areoles in the notches, 2 to 4 cm. apart, large, greyish. Spines numerous, yellowish, of various lengths, the centrals up to 12 cm. or more. Flower 20 to 30 cm. long, green outside, outer petals obtuse margined brown, the inner white. Fruit purplish, oval, up to 12 cm. long. A cristate form is also in cultivation.

Cereus hexagonus (L.) Miller = *C. lepidotus* Salm-Dyck. South America. Columnar, up to 10 m. high, with many stems up to 14 cm. thick, bluish green passing to greyish green, covered with minute waxy scales. Ribs usually 4 or 5, wing-shaped, about 5 cm. deep, obtuse and notched. Areoles 2 to 4 cm. apart, broad, yellowish passing to greyish, at first with about 10 small spines, later developing spines of varying length, up to 6 cm. Flower about 14 cm. long; outer petals greenish, bordered red; inner petals lanceolate, white. Fruit oval, pale red.

Cereus Hildmannianus K. Sch. Eastern Brazil. Plant up to 5 m. high, much branched, with stems 10 to 12 cm. in diameter, at first bluish green passing to dull greyish green, with 5 or 6 wing-like narrow ribs, about 4 cm. deep, notched at intervals of 2 to 3 cm. Areoles brown passing to grey, almost spineless. Flower up to 24 cm. long, greenish outside, inner petals broad, obtuse, white, toothed. Lower down the stem old areoles are often strongly spined.

Cereus tetragonus Miller. Eastern Brazil. Plant 4 or 5 m. high, much branched, with erect branches, 9 to 10 cm. thick, dull green, with 4 or 5 wing-like ribs about 4 cm. deep, marked with lines laterally and slightly notched. Areoles large, 4 to 5 cm. apart, whitish. All spines brown or almost black, straight and awl-shaped or slightly curved; the radials about 6, up to 1 cm. long; 1 or 2 centrals slightly longer. Flower about 12 cm. long, the outer petals being reddish brown, the inner acutely pointed and red.

Cereus Forbesii Otto. Argentina (Tucuman and Catamarca). Often considered as a variety of *C. jamacaru* or *C. validus*, with the same habit of growth, but is otherwise quite distinct. Stem columnar, branched, 4 to 5 m. high, with erect branches, up to 12 cm. thick, making quick growth, at first bluish green, passing to dull green, with 4 to 7 (usually 6) wing-like ribs, 4 to 5 cm. deep, slightly notched, with large round areoles, yellowish to brownish, marked with side lines above and below the white areoles. These are $2\frac{1}{2}$ to 3 cm. apart, with 5 to 7 radial spines, awl-shaped, spreading outwards, 1 to 2 cm. long, yellowish or brownish, darker and almost black and bulbous at the base. Central spines 1 or 2, same colour and bulbous at the base, up to 5 cm. long. Flower about 25 cm. long, funnel-shaped; outer petals greenish, margined purplish brown, inner petals white.

var. **haematuricus** Weber. Stems with 6 or 7 ribs, very glaucous and bluish when young. Spines longer, dirty yellow or reddish, the central spine up to 9 cm. long.

var. **quadrangulus** Hildm. Stems with 4 or 5 ribs.

Cereus alacriportanus Pfeiff. = *C. paraguayensis* K. Sch. Uruguay, Paraguay and southern Brazil. A distinct species, although frequently considered as only a variety of *C. peruvianus*. Stem bluish green, passing to deep green, 2 to 3 m. high, slightly branched, with 5 wing-like ribs, rather thick, somewhat wavy and slightly notched. Areoles rather small, about 2 cm. apart, whitish, with 6 to 9 stiff, awl-shaped, spreading spines, up to 2½ cm. long, pale yellow, reddish at the base, passing to ash-grey. Flower up to 22 cm. long; outer petals obtuse, reddish; inner petals very pale creamy pink, toothed, obtuse and spathulate.

Cereus peruvianus Miller. South-eastern Brazil and northern Argentina. The name *peruvianus* is a misnomer, but has to be retained owing to the law of priority. Long known in cultivation. Plant erect or mostly erect, up to 10 m. high, much branched. Stem 10 to 20 cm. thick, at first bluish passing to dull green, obtuse and well furnished with brown wool and brown spines at the top. Ribs 5 to 8, thick and obtuse, about 2½ cm. deep, very slightly notched, with acute furrows between the ribs. Areoles round, brownish, about 2 cm. apart. Radial spines about 7, straight, spreading, brown, up to 1 cm. long; central spine only one, slightly longer, awl-shaped. The spines in the upper areoles are more numerous and longer. Flowers about 16 cm. long, brownish green outside, white inside, the outer petals being tipped reddish brown, and the inner entirely white, acute and toothed. There are also in cultivation a tall-growing and slender cristate form, named *monstruosa* DC., and a much thicker and dwarf cristate form named *monstruosa nana*, usually known as *Rock-Cactus*, and a third slender and dwarf cristate form known as *monstruosa minor* Hort. Resistant and of easy cultivation in a rich calcareous soil.

var. **longispinus** Hort. With 4 to 6 ribs. Areoles more thickly set, with straight, needle-shaped, yellowish brown spines of varying length, the centrals often up to 10 cm. long. There is also a cristate form of this variety.

Cereus obtusus Haw. Southern coastal region of Brazil. Stem erect or semi-prostrate, dark green, very slightly glaucous, with 3 to 5 thick obtuse ribs, about 2 cm. deep, slightly notched, with lines along the sides slanting down to the narrow furrows between the ribs. Areoles yellowish brown, variously distanced. Spines yellowish, 1 central and about 6 radials, up to 5 cm. long. Flower about 25 cm. long, outer petals very narrow, acute, greenish; inner petals white, toothed.

Cereus roseiflorus Spegazzini. Argentina. Tree-like, columnar; 4 to 5 m. high, slightly branched, of a lively green, with 6 ribs, 3½ cm. deep, straight and continuous. Areoles 2 to 2½ cm. apart, spineless when young, later developing 3 spines, up to 1 cm. long, almost conical, but not thickened at the base, dirty grey. Flowers freely borne near the tops of new joints, nocturnal, 20 cm. long. Ovary and tube furnished with scales, outer petals greenish, inner petals clear pink; stamens white, stigma with 5 or 6 creamy white lobes. Fruit oval, 6 to 7 cm. long, purplish or violet.

Cereus Dayamii Spegazzini. Argentina, in the forests of the southern Chaco. Plant erect or leaning on trees or rocks, up to 20 m. long, much branched. Stems 10 to 20 cm. thick, dull green, with 5 or 6 ribs, about 3 cm. deep, notched. Areoles with brownish wool .about 2 cm. apart. Spines 3 or 4, rarely more, reddish yellow passing to

127

reddish brown, up to 1 cm. long. Flower up to 25 cm. long, greenish outside, white inside. Often confused with *C. Hankeanus*.

Cereus stenogonus K. Sch. Argentina and Paraguay. Plant up to 8 m. high, much branched. Stems 6 to 9 cm. thick, at first bluish green, passing to pale glaucous green, with 4 or 5 ribs, deeply notched, very thin along the margin (about ½ cm. thick). Areoles in the notches, 2½ to 4 cm. apart. Spines usually 3, sometimes 4, spreading crosswise, conical, thick and bulbous at the base, black or black tipped yellow, up to ½ cm. long. Flower up to 22 cm. long, pink. Fruit oval, 10 cm. long, red, with red pulp.

Cereus xanthocarpus K. Sch. Paraguay. Plant up to 6 m. high, branched. Stems 6 to 9 cm. thick, bluish green passing to deep green, usually with 4 ribs, sometimes with 5. Ribs 3 cm. deep, wavy and rather thick, notched. Areoles yellowish or greyish, large, 2 to 3 cm. apart. Spines usually 4, rarely more, reddish yellow passing to reddish brown, straight, thick, needle-shaped, longer at the top of the stem, where they are up to 3 cm. long. Flower about 20 cm. long, pale yellowish green outside, pale pink or white inside. Fruit oval, yellow.

Cereus variabilis Pfeiff. = *C. pitahaya* DC. Brazil and Uruguay. Plant up to 4m. high, branched, with stems 6 to 9 cm. thick. Ribs 3 to 5, acute and notched, about 3 cm. deep, dull glaucous green. Areoles dark brown, passing to grey. Radial spines 5 to 7, awl-shaped, about 1½ cm. long, yellow passing to yellowish brown. Central spines 1 or 2, straight, slightly longer, same colour. Flower about 20 cm. long, brownish green outside, white inside, inner petals very much toothed. This variable species extends also into Central America, where it is known by the name of *Pitahaya*, and various forms are in cultivation, such as *trigonus*, *quadrangularis*, *prismatiformis*, *hexangularis*, *glaucus* etc. There are also two well known cristate forms, viz: *monstruosus* Hort. and *monstruosus glaucus* Hort. *C. Beysiegelii*, a beautiful cristate form of *C. chalybaeus*, is often referred to this species.

Cereus horridus Otto. South America. Not to be confused with *Acanthocereus horridus* Br. et R. Closely allied to *C. jamacaru*. Stem 4 to 6 m. high, branched, greyish green, with 4 acute ribs having broad furrows between them, and with deep lines on both sides above the areoles. These are about 2 cm. apart, round, large, prominent, with short black or greyish wool. Spines blackish passing to grey, thick, stiff, straight, spreading; the radials 10 to 12 in two series; the centrals 3, spreading, longer, 1 to 5 cm. Flower about 18 cm. long, funnel-shaped, with a cylindrical bluish green ovary, almost bare; a yellowish green tube with small brownish or reddish acute scales. The outer petals are obtuse, green flushed reddish; the next row are lanceolate, white on the inner side; the inner petals are white, lanceolate-acute, toothed.

Cereus pernambucensis Lem. = *C. formosus* Förster. Brazil and Uruguay, growing in large masses in the stony and sandy coastal districts. Closely allied to *C. variabilis*, and may be only a well-marked

(*a*) ESPOSTOA DAUTWITZII CRISTATA

(*b*) OREOCEREUS CELSIANUS
var. Bruennowii

PLATE XII

(b) CEPHALOCEREUS ALBISPINUS

(a) CEPHALOCEREUS SENILIS
var. longiseta

PLATE XIII

variety or a sub-species, with more slender stems, branching from the base, with pronounced joints separating one growth from the next, and therefore conical at the top, bluish green, often intensely glaucous, with 3 to 5 ribs more or less deeply notched. Areoles large, about 2 cm. apart, with brownish wool, and with 4 to 10 yellowish, needle-like, stiff spines, 2 to 3 cm. long. Flower as in *C. variabilis*.

Cereus argentinensis Br. et R. = *C. platygonus* Speg. non Otto. Argentina (Central Chaco). Stem erect, up to 12 m. high, much branched, with erect branches 10 to 15 cm. thick. Ribs 4 or 5, 4 to 5 cm. deep, thin, with broad furrows between them. Radial spines 5 to 8, brownish, 3 to 5 cm. long; central spines 1 or 2, up to 10 cm. long. Flower funnel-shaped, up to 22 cm. long; outer petals green, often tipped reddish, inner petals white. Fruit smooth. Closely allied to the preceding species.

Cereus repandus (L.) Miller non Haw. = *Cactus repandus* L. = *Cereus Hermannianus* Suringar. Tropical America, chiefly Curaçao. Tree-like, up to 10 m. high, much branched above ground, with more or less spreading branches curving upwards, greyish green, about 10 cm. thick, with 9 or 10 ribs, about 1 cm. high. Areoles small, 5 to 15 cm. apart, with many greyish, needle-like spines, up to 5 cm. long. Flowers funnel-shaped, nocturnal, 7 to 8 cm. long; tube slender, perianth green, about 3 cm. across, inner petals tipped white. Fruit 3 to 4 cm. long, oblong, red or white; seeds warty, dull black. Should not be confused with *Cereus repandus* Haw., which is a synonym for *Harrisia gracilis* (Mill.) Br. et R.

Cereus pachyrrhizus K. Sch. Paraguay. Stem erect, 2 to 3 m. high, with few branches and with tuberous roots. The stem is up to 10 cm. thick, obtuse and spiny at the top, yellowish green when young, brownish green later, with 6 acute and straight ribs, about 1 cm. thick, and 4 to 5 cm. deep. Areoles round, $2\frac{1}{2}$ to 3 cm. apart, with short greyish wool. Spines 10 to 13, stiff, awl-shaped, brownish, up to 3 cm. long, hardly distinguishable as radials or centrals. Should be kept dry in winter.

Other species in cultivation are: **Cereus lamprospermus** K. Sch., Paraguay, **C. margaritensis** Johow., Venezuela, and **C. grenadensis** Br. et R., Lesser Antilles.

MONVILLEA Br. et R.

Stems slender, long, more or less prostrate. Flowers nocturnal, of medium size, borne towards the tops of last year's growths, white, pinkish or yellow, with a slender tube, remaining attached to the ovary on fading. Fruit spineless, smooth, red, with black seeds. Includes 12 species, natives of South America.

Monvillea Cavendishii (Monv.) Br. et R. = *Cereus Cavendishii* Monv. South Brazil, north Argentina, Paraguay. Stem slender, 1 to $1\frac{1}{2}$ m. high, 2 to $2\frac{1}{2}$ cm. thick, with a conical top, dark green, with few branches, with 9 obtuse ribs, about 3 mm. high, somewhat warty.

129

I

Areoles less than 1 cm. apart, small, whitish or greyish. Radial spines 7 to 9, slender and flexible, at first pale yellow, passing to whitish or greyish, up to ½ cm. long. Central spines 1 to 4, up to 1½ cm. long, dark brown or black. Flower about 12 cm. long, and 10 cm. broad, with a few short brownish scales on the ovary and tube; outer petals fully expanded and reflexed, greenish white, inner petals white and expanded; stigma with about 12 lobes. Fruit round, smooth, red, 4 to 5 cm. thick. Free-flowering; full sunshine or half-shade.

Monvillea Paxtoniana (Monv.) Br. et R. = *Cereus Paxtonianus* Monv. South Brazil and north Argentina. Often described as a variety of the preceding, but really distinct, Stems thicker, 2½ to 3½ cm. thick, and about 1 m. high, with few branches, dark glossy green, with 9 ribs, more prominent and warty. Areoles about 1 cm. apart, large, white. Radial spines 7 to 9, at first very pale yellow, soon passing to milky white, erect, ½ to 1 cm. long. Central spines 1 to 4 or more, at first yellowish brown, passing to pale yellow or white, 1 to 1½ cm. long. Flower as in the preceding, but larger; much less free-flowering. Plant more robust.

Monvillea rhodoleucantha (K. Sch.) Berger = *Cereus rhodoleucanthus* K. Sch. Paraguay. Same habit as *M. Cavendishii*, but taller, rather more slender and more branched, often prostrate, with the same number of ribs. Areoles small, whitish passing to brownish, ½ to 1½ cm. apart. Radial spines 6 or 7, afterwards more numerous, erect, up to 1 cm. long, at first yellowish brown, passing to greyish with dark point. Central spines 1 to 3, same colour, up to 2 cm. long. Flower very pretty, about 13 cm. long, and 5 to 6 cm. broad. Ovary and tube with red scales, outer petals pink, the inner white, fully expanded. Stigma with 17 lobes. Fruit elliptical, 7 cm. long. Half-shade; of easy cultivation; very free-flowering.

Monvillea phatnosperma (K. Sch.) Br. et R. = *Cereus phatnospermus* K. Sch. Paraguay. Stem mostly prostrate, 1 to 2 m. long, pale green or brownish, about 2½ cm. thick, with 4 or 5 ribs, almost angular. Areoles 2 to 3 cm. apart, large, woolly. Spines awl-shaped, thick, brown passing to grey. Radial spines 5 or 6, spreading, up to 1½ cm. long: central spine only one or none, straight, thick and awl-shaped, up to 2½ cm. long. Flower 12 cm. long; outer petals narrow, brownish outside; inner petals slightly broader, white. Fruit elliptical, pointed, red, 7 cm. long. Seeds oval, glossy black, pitted.

Monvillea Spegazzinii (Weber) Br. et R. = *Cereus Spegazzinii* Weber = *C. marmoratus* Hort. Argentina. Stem stiff, erect or semi-prostrate, 1½ to 2 m. long, branched, 2 cm. thick, of a beautiful bluish green, marbled white, usually with 4 angles, rarely with 5. Areoles small, 2 to 4 cm. apart, on prominences along the angles. Radial spines 3 to 5, thick, conical, black, less than ½ cm. long. Central spine, when present, same shape and colour, up to 1½ cm. long. Flowers freely borne, and in 2 or more crops, in early summer, 11 to 12 cm. long, glaucous or greyish when in bud. Ovary smooth, tube almost smooth or with very small scales. Outer petals pale pink or reddish, linear, acute; inner petals obtuse, toothed, creamy white. Style and stigma white. Fruit roundish, almost angular, deep pink. Makes quick growth and is of easy cultivation.

Monvillea Anisitsii (K. Sch.) Berger = *Cereus Anisitsii* K. Sch. Paraguay. Probably only a variety of the preceding. Habit exactly similar, but the stems are more often with 5 angles and more rounded. Flowers larger, up to 19 cm. long and sweet-scented; outer petals of a deeper pink.

Monvillea saxicola (Morong) Berger = *Cereus saxicola* Morong. Argentina and Paraguay. Stem more or less erect, up to 1 m. high, of a glossy bluish green, without the bloom of the preceding species, 1½ to 3 cm. thick, with 6 to 9 ribs, low and rounded. Areoles about 1 cm. apart, yellowish passing to greyish. Radial spines slender, white, pointed black, up to ½ cm. long. One central spine, later 2 or 3, also slender and same colour, 1½ cm. long. Flower 12 cm. long; ovary and tube with short reddish scales; outer petals greenish white, brown-tipped, inner petals white with greenish midrib. Stamens short; stigma with 14 lobes.

Monvillea Brittoniana Werd. = *Cereus Brittonianus* Werd. = *Monvillea maritima* Br. et R. Ecuador. Stems bushy, up to 5 m. high, 5 to 8 cm. thick, with 4 to 6 warty ribs. Areoles 2 to 3 cm. apart. Radial spines about 8, short, greyish, tipped darker; central spines 1 or 2, longer and thicker, up to 6 cm. long. Flower about 6 cm. long, white. Fruit oblong, violet red.

Monvillea diffusa Br. et R. South Ecuador. A tall bush, much branched. Stems 4 to 5 cm. thick, with 8 or 9 narrow and high ribs. Areoles greyish, up to 3 cm. apart. Radial spines 6 to 10, needle-like, over 1 cm. long. Central spines 1 to 3, awl-shaped and curved or straight, greyish, tipped darker, 2 to 3 cm. long. Flower about 8 cm. long, white. Fruit roundish, 6 cm. thick, yellowish green, smooth. The comparatively thick stems and small flowers of these two species point to great affinity with the new genus *Haageocereus*.

Monvillea insularis (Hemsley) Br. et R. = *Cereus insularis* Hemsley. North Brazil (Island of St. Michael's Mount). Stem mostly trailing much branched, 2½ to 3 cm. thick, green, dotted. Ribs 6 to 8, straight, ½ cm. deep. Areoles greyish, ½ cm. apart. Spines 12 to 15, needle-like, brownish yellow passing to grey or dirty brown, up to 1 cm. long. Flowers yellow or yellowish, 12 to 15 cm. long: ovary and tube with small scales, but without hairs, bristles or spines; tube very slender, petals in several rows, stamens exserted, as also the star-like 13-lobed stigma.

Monvillea Lauterbachii (K. Sch.) = *Cereus Lauterbachii* K. Sch. Paraguay. Stem pale green, 1 to 2 m. high, mostly prostrate, 1½ to 2½ cm. thick, with 7 to 9 ribs, low, rather acute, warty. Areoles small, ½ to 1 cm. apart, greyish. Radial spines about 9, spreading, needle-like or flexible, ½ cm. long, yellowish passing to whitish. Central spines

3 to 5, up to $1\frac{1}{2}$ cm. long, needle-like, yellowish brown passing to yellowish white. Flowers white, freely borne in early summer. Full unshine and warmth.

Monvillea Smithiana (Rose) Werd. = *Pilocereus Smithianus* Rose = *Cephalocereus Smithianus* Br. et R. Venezuela (near Puerto Cabello). Rather quick-growing, branched. Stem dark glossy green, purplish at the growing top, up to 8 cm. thick, but usually thinner, with 8 rather low ribs, strongly crenate and notched. Areoles large, white, woolly, depressed in the notches. Radial and central spines alike, about 12 or more, the central one being the longest, 3 to 4 cm. at first reddish brown, passing to greyish white, tipped darker. Flowers nocturnal, 6 to 8 cm. long, sometimes up to 10 cm. long. Fruit oval, yellowish, with white pulp. Seeds small, dark brown.

ARTHROCEREUS Berger

Small plants mostly prostrate, typically with globular or elliptical joints, ribbed and spiny, or with clavate and spiny stems more or less erect. Flowers borne mostly on the sides of the terminal joints, small, but comparatively large for the size of the plant, nocturnal, with a long hairy tube and hairy ovary, and a funnel-shaped limb, white or pale pink. The root is thick, woody, turnip-shaped.

Includes 3 species, natives of Brazil.

Arthrocereus microsphaericus (K. Sch.) Berger = *Cereus microsphaericus* K. Sch. = *C. Damazioi* K. Sch. = *Monvillea Damazioi* Auct. Brazil (Minas Geraes, on sandy soils). Plant prostrate of a glossy green, much branched, consisting of globose or elliptical joints, as large as an olive, sometimes as large as a walnut, with 8 to 11 low rounded ribs. Areoles very small, brownish, 2 to 3 mm. apart. Spines erect, bristle-like, 2 to 4 mm. long, sometimes longer: the radials about 12, white, with about as many white bristles; the centrals 4 to 12, brown or reddish brown. Flowers 10 to 11 cm. long, deliciously scented, with a long slender hairy tube, and expanded funnel-shaped limb; the outer petals being green, linear and very acute, the inner also very acute, but broader and shorter, white. Stamens few, short, white; style long, stigma with 8 white lobes. Fruit globular.

A very pretty species to be grown in half-shade, in a mixture of equal parts of sand, leaf-mould, loam and limestone gravel or crushed old mortar. Thrives better when grafted on a *Cereus*.

The globular-jointed stem is the principal descriptive generic character of *Arthrocereus* (Jointed Cereus), as given by Berger. The two new species described hereunder, and included under this genus by Backeberg, have not this characteristic, and hardly differ from Monvillea, except in the hairy ovary and tube.

Arthrocereus Rondonianus Backbg. et Voll. Brazil, near Diamantinas, in the fissures of granitic rocks. Stem slender, cylindrical, half erect, bright pale green, up to 50 cm. long and $2\frac{1}{2}$ to 4 cm. thick, with 14 to 18 low rounded ribs. Areoles greyish, 5 to 10 mm. apart. Spines

40 to 50, needle-like, golden yellow, sometimes bristle-like, about
½ cm. long, with a few longer ones, up to 2 cm., and 1 or 2 central spines
up to 7 cm. long. Flowers lilac pink inside, outer petals pale lilac,
more double than in the preceding species, 8 to 10 cm. long. Tube
slender, with dark hairs and scales up to 2 mm. long, with a few bristles.
Stamens purple, shorter than the petals; stigma exserted, white.

Arthrocereus Campos-Portoi (Werd.) Backbg. = *Trichocereus
Campos-Portoi* Werd. Brazil, Sierra de Pietade (Bello Horizonte).
Stem semi-prostrate, bright green, branched and jointed. Joints cylindrical or clavate, up to 15 cm. long, and about 3 cm. thick, with about
12 low rounded ribs. Areoles closely set, about ½ cm. apart, at first
with yellowish grey wool. Spines and bristle-like spines 25 to 35,
white, up to 7 mm. long, and 1 or 2 central spines up to 4 cm. long.
All spines are somewhat brownish when young. Flowers 13 to 15 cm.
long, with a slender pale green tube, with scales and a few hairs. Outer
petals lanceolate, white, with a red brown band at the back, inner
petals white; stamens yellowish white, stigma white, not exserted.
Both these species grow well on own roots, in a more gritty soil, in
half-shade.

CEPHALOCEREUS (Pfeiff.) Br. et R.

This genus, as re-established by Britton and Rose, includes species
with tall erect columnar stems, often attaining large proportions.
Stem solitary or branched at the base, with branches rising parallel
to the main stem, or branched above ground at various heights, with
few or many ribs, very generally more or less woolly or hairy at the
areoles, especially at the top. Very often the flowering top of the stem
or the flowering areoles at the sides, develop an additional mass of
longer wool or hair, constituting a *cephalium* or rather *pseudocephalium*.
Flowers comparatively small, bell-shaped or funnel-shaped, or almost
tubular, more or less embedded in the mass of hair or wool of the
pseudocephalium, nocturnal, very rarely diurnal, with short petals
and many stamens arising from the sides of the tube. Pistil exserted.
Ovary and tube not scaly, or with only a few scales. Seeds black,
smooth or rugose.

Britton and Rose have included 48 species under this genus as
re-established by them. To these more than 20 others have been added
by Werdermann, Backeberg etc., mostly discovered recently in South
America. Most of the species were formerly included under *Pilocereus*
Lem., a very ill-defined genus which was made to include species of
little or no affinity, but is retained here as a sub-genus.

All species are of easy cultivation and very resistant. The soil
should be rather poor, gritty or gravelly, with garden loam, some
leaf-mould or old manure, and much calcareous matter, and should
be kept rather dry. A moist atmosphere is preferred, and nearly all
delight in full sunshine, and in the Mediterranean region, with little
or no protection in winter. Some of them are of slow growth, species
with thick stems particularly so. The flowers are inconspicuous and

usually are produced only on old and mature specimens, but the tall columnar shape of the stem, more or less ornamented with an abundant development of hair or wool, is always very interesting, and therefore this princely genus of Cactaceae is very much in request by all collectionists.

Sub-Genus I. EUCEPHALOCEREUS. Stem solitary, or branching from the base, or branching only when the apical growth is injured. When the injury occurs in quite young seedlings, from 1 to 12 new stems may develop simultaneously, and grow up vertically. The stem is usually many-ribbed, and the cephalium or pseudocephalium may be terminal or developed only on one side of the upper part of the stem. The fruit remains hidden in the woolly mass of the pseudocephalium, and emerges only at maturity.

Cephalocereus senilis (DC.) Pfeiff. = *Cereus senilis* DC. = *Pilocereus senilis* Lem. Mexico, States of Hidalgo and Guanajuato, growing in the fissures of slaty rocks. This is the "Old Man Cactus,"— deservedly popular, and always given pride of place in every collection, usually unbranched, but occasionally with several stems (up to 12) arising from the very base and directed vertically upwards. In its native country this species attains a height of 6 to 12 m. with a diameter of 30 to 40 cm. As the plant is of slow growth, such specimens must be more than 200 years old. The stem is at first light green, passing to grey with age. Young plants have 12 to 15 ribs, but in fine cultivated specimens over 1 m. in height, the number of ribs may be from 25 to 30 or more, with narrow furrows between them, the ribs being low and rounded. The areoles are large, round, closely set, on slightly prominent warts, with 1 to 5 slender yellow spines, 1 to 2 cm. long in young specimens, and up to 5 cm. long in older plants. From each areole, along with the spines, are developed from 20 to 30 white, hair-like soft bristles or "hairs", 6 to 12 cm. long, often growing in tufts or tresses. In aged specimens the lower part of the stem loses these hairs and only the spines remain, the thick development of hairs being retained only in the upper part, down to within 60 cm. from the top. The plant reaches flowering size when about 6 m. high, and then there is a thick fleecy development of hairs on one side of the top, or all around it, thus constituting the pseudocephalium. The flowers are nocturnal and are about 9 cm. long, and 6 cm. broad, partly hidden under the white hair, reddish externally, with white obtuse petals having a reddish midrib. The ovary is hairy, but devoid of spines. In the form *longiseta* the hair is longer (up to 20 cm.), and the stem thicker, even in young specimens, and the growth is slower. A curious cristate form is also cultivated, but is still rare in collections.

In newly imported specimens the hair is often matted together, very dirty, and almost greyish or brownish. These may be washed with soapy water, thoroughly but lightly because of the spines, and also in order not to damage the hair which is somewhat brittle, and then well rinsed to remove all traces of soap. They are then combed upwards to cause the hair to expand, and are planted after removing neatly with a clean cut all decayed and damaged roots. Until well established, the plants should be shaded off from direct sunshine and watered very sparingly. Instead of soap, *clensel* mixed with one or two parts of water, may be used to wash this and other species of Cacti, which of course, should be carefully rinsed in clear water before planting. If the plants happen to be very crooked, they may be somewhat straightened by tying firmly to a stout galvanized wire or to a stick, care being taken to loosen the ties gradually to prevent injury, as the plants are establishing themselves and becoming plump, after the curing and drying process to which they were subjected for safe travelling.

The root-system is remarkably weak, and too often imported plants have no sound roots at all, apart from the tap root, but they rarely fail to develop new roots and become fully established in a few months. This species is easily raised from seed, and with proper care the seedlings grow into nice well-shaped plants 8 cm. high or more, in about 4 years.

Cephalocereus Hoppenstedtii K. Sch. = *Pilocereus Hoppenstedtii* Weber = *P. lateralis* Weber. Southern Mexico. Stem columnar, solitary, unbranched, and without offsets at the base, fusiform in shape, in its native country attaining a height of 6 to 10 m. and a thickness of 20 to 30 cm. at the middle, and tapering at both extremities. Stem light ashy green, with about 16 ribs, low and narrow, with notches and warts. Areoles 5 to 7 mm. apart, small and bare, with a cluster of 10 to 15 soft white radial spines, spreading, the lower up to 1 cm. long. Central spines 5 to 10, thick, blunt and soft, up to 8 cm. long. At the growing top these central spines are yellowish white and directed upwards, afterwards passing to waxy white or milky white, and mostly directed downwards. There is also some development of whitish wool on the upper areoles. The flowers, borne only on old specimens, are about 7 cm. long, with the ovary and tube densely covered with yellowish wool, the outer petals being pink, or white-pointed pink, and the inner white or pale sulphur yellow. A very interesting species of slow growth, just as resistant and as easy of cultivation as the preceding, to which it is a worthy counterpart, and like it is easily propagated by seed. Both are often grafted on *Trichocereus macrogonus* to induce a quicker growth.

Cephalocereus polylophus (DC.) Br. et R. = *Cereus polylophus* DC. = *C. Nickelsii* Hort. = *Pilocereus polylophus* Salm-Dyck. Eastern Mexico. Stem thick, columnar, in its native country over 12 m. high and 30 to 35 cm. thick, at first grass green or deep green, later passing to dull green, with numerous ribs, up to 30 or more, not more than 1 cm. high, but sharp-angled. Areoles yellowish, round, about 1 cm. apart, with very short, yellowish white wool, and with yellow spines, tipped dark, all 1 to 2 cm. long; the radials 7 to 9, and 1 central, but on the flowering part of the stem the central spine is up to 7 cm. long, and there is also some development of yellow bristles. The flower is dark red, funnel-shaped, 4 to 5 cm. long, and 3 cm. broad, with red stamens, and scaly ovary and tube. An imposing species, resistant and of easy cultivation, growing well in full sunshine and also in half-shade. Growth is slow, but is popular on account of its thick many-fluted stem of a pleasant green.

Cephalocereus chrysacanthus (Orcutt) Br. et R. = *Cereus chrysacanthus* Orcutt = *Pilocereus chrysancathus* Weber. Mexico (Puebla and Oaxaca). A lovely species of fairly quick growth, with a columnar stem, branched from the base, rising to 3 or 4 m. 6 to 8 cm. thick, deep glossy green, with 10 to 12 acute ribs on which are closely set small round yellow areoles, with short golden yellow hairs and of about 12 golden yellow or brownish yellow spines, 1 to 2 cm. long. In some forms generally preferred for propagation and grafting, the hairy formation is more abundant on the upper part of the stem, even in young plants, and is of a lighter colour. The flowering stems are thickly covered with pale yellow hairs. The funnel-shaped nocturnal flower is about 8 cm. long and 5 cm. broad, deep pink, with ovary and tube abundantly covered with whitish or pale yellow hairs. Prefers full sunshine, and requires some protection in winter. Dislikes an excess of moisture, especially in autumn and winter, but is otherwise easy to grow.

Cephalocereus Guentheri Kupper. The Andes of Bolivia, Chuquisaca (Rio Grande). This is a recent species similar to the preceding, but of quicker and stronger growth. Stems up to 2 m. high, branching from the base, forming large groups. The stems are of a glaucous green colour, about 8 cm. thick, with 12 to 27 ribs, 1 cm. broad and 7 mm. high more or less rounded. Areoles small, round, closely set, with about 15 golden yellow, bristle-like spines 1 to 3 cm. long. Pseudocephalium on one side at the top of the stem, sometimes extending downwards along the stem for about 50 cm. with very thickly set areoles, each with 20 to 25 glossy brownish yellow bristles. Flowers bell-shaped, yellowish white inside. A very desirable species, perhaps even more attractive than the preceding, with the habit of a *Borzicactus*, resistant and of easy cultivation.

Cephalocereus aurisetus Werd. = *Pilocereus aurisetus* Werd. Brazil (Minas Geraes). Short columnar about 1 m. high, branched at the base. Stems 5 to 6 cm. thick, glaucous or bluish green. Ribs about 15, low. Areoles about 1 cm. apart, with greyish wool and white hairs 1 cm. long. Spines numerous, very slender and needle-like, 1½ to 2½ cm. long, yellowish grey tipped darker. The flowering part of the stem, about ½ m. or half its total length, is densely covered with the cephalium or pseudocephalium, consisting of golden yellow flexible bristles up to 5 cm. long. Flowers 4½ to 5 cm. long; ovary and tube green, segments of perianth 1 cm. long, oblong, pointed whitish. Stigma with 8 lobes, not longer than the stamens. A breautiful species of recent introduction, easily grown.

Cephalocereus polyanthus Werd. Brazil, Bahia (granitic, stony and sandy ground near Caeteté). Stem columnar, erect, freely branching from the base forming large groups, up to 1¼ m. high, glaucous green, 3½ to 5 cm. thick, covered with white wool and spines at the tip, with 15 to 20 low ribs. Areoles about 1 cm. apart, felted with white wool, especially at or near the flowering tops. Radial spines 20 to 30, needle-like, whitish or golden yellow, about 1 cm. long: central spines 3 to 7, up to 3 cm. long, golden yellow or pale brown or reddish. Flowers pale pink, only about 2 cm. long, with the tube bare on the outside, minutely scaly inside. Fruit small, about ½ cm. long, smooth, pink; seeds small, oval, glossy black. A pretty species, particularly the young seedlings and new shoots which are densely furnished with long white wool, like seedlings of *C. senilis*. Still rare in cultivation.

Cephalocereus Gounellei Weber in K. Sch. = *Pilocereus Gounellei* Weber. = *P. setosus* Gürke = *Cephalocereus Zehntneri* Br. et R. Brazil, States of Pernambuco and Bahia, in the dry inner districts. Stem 1 to 2 m. high, branching from the base and also above ground, up to 8 cm. thick, with thick whitish wool at the top, pale glaucous green, branches like those of a chandelier, 4 to 5 cm. thick, with 10 or 11 ribs slightly notched. Areoles large, round, 1 to 1½ cm. apart, with greyish wool and with whitish or yellowish silky hairs, 2 to 5 cm. long, more evident at the top. Radial spines 15 to 25, yellowish, spreading, needle-like and very sharp. Central spines 3 to 5, longer, spreading, honey yellow, rather thick, fading to white with age, 1½ to 3 cm. long, one of them being very strong, and often up to 10 cm. long. Flowering areoles with long bushy whitish or brownish hair. Flowers funnel-shaped, 7 to 9 cm. long, smooth outside, whitish: stigma with 15 to 18 lobes, shorter than the longest stamens. Fruit smooth, 3 to 6 cm. long and 2 to 4 cm. thick, reddish when ripe. Of fairly quick growth, often grafted on *Trichocereus Spachianus* or *T. macrogonus*. Large plants are still rare in cultivation.

Cephalocereus chrysostele (Vaup.) Werd. = *Cereus chrysostele* Vaupel. Brazil, State of Pernambuco. In habit very much like the preceding, but much taller. Stem erect, up to 5 m. high, often with short branches, and freely branching from the base, resulting in large clumps. Stems up to 9 cm. thick, deep coppery green, well furnished with yellow spines, with the top copiously covered with yellow spines or bristles. Ribs in young plants 12 to 18, increasing to 20-30 in older plants, straight, about ½ cm. high. Areoles thickly set, less than 1 cm. apart, woolly, yellow, and with a few yellowish white silky hairs 1 to 2 cm. long. Spines very numerous, about 30, not distinguishable between radials and centrals, golden yellow, later passing to brownish, slender, needle-like, 1 to 2 cm. long. The cephalium is developed along the side of the stem, towards the top, and always directed towards the west. It consists of closely set areoles with much white wool, with long golden yellow bristles, and with spines up to 5 cm. long. Flowers about 5 cm. long, oval or club-shaped, with smooth ovary and tube, olive green or yellowish petals. The stigma is included and has about 15 white lobes. Fruit olive green. round or depressed, 2½ to 3½ cm. thick.

CACTI

Cephalocereus Dybowskii (Gosselin) Br. et R. = *Cereus Dybowskii* Gosselin. Brazil and Bolivia. A most lovely species, with stems 2 to 4 m. high, and up to 8 cm. thick, erect, very even and cylindrical, freely branching from the base, with up to 26 low ribs, entirely covered with matted silky wool, greyish or yellowish white, concealing the radial spines, and becoming longer, more abundant and whiter on the flowering areoles, on the upper part of the stem facing the west. Radial spines numerous, needle-like. Central spines 2 or 3, spreading, yellowish, needle-like, 2 to 3 cm. long. Flowers about 4 cm. long, with white petals, Fruit round, bare, pink, up to 2½ cm. thick. Seeds black, rough. A very choice species, requiring full sunshine and warmth, and some shelter in winter. Makes quicker growth when grafted on a *Trichocereus*, but is also easy of cultivation on own roots.

Cephalocereus purpureus Gürke = *Cereus Goebelianus* Vaupel. Brazil, States of Bahia and Minas Geraes. Columnar, erect, up to 5 m. high and 12 cm. thick, rarely branching, pale green or glaucous, with up to 25 ribs, 1 cm. high, straight, obtuse, notched above the areoles, which are about ½ cm. apart. Radial spines 15 to 20 or more, up to 1½ cm. long. Central spines 4 to 6, often like the radials, spreading. one much longer, up to 5 cm. yellowish brown or dark brown, often curved upwards or inwards. Cephalium up to 12 cm. broad and up to 1 m. long, mostly on the western side of the top of the stem, with a compact mass of greyish wool and with reddish brown, sometimes almost black, curved bristles 2 cm. long. Flower 3½ cm. long, pale pink and smooth outside, whitish inside. Stigma with 8 yellowish lobes exserted beyond the stamens. Fruit top-shaped, 2 cm. long, purplish violet. Seeds warty, dull deep brown or black.

Cephalocereus Lehmannianus Werd. Brazil, State of Bahia, Columnar, 80 cm. to 2 m. high, copiously branching at the base and also above ground, 5 to 8 cm. thick, of a beautiful bluish colour, densely woolly and spiny at the top. Ribs up to 20, 5 to 8 mm. high; areoles closely set and woolly. Spines about 40, up to 2 cm. long, needle-like, whitish or yellowish. Cephalium mostly lateral at the top, 1½ to 4 cm. broad, and up to 50 cm. long, densely furnished with long greyish or rusty wool and hairs, up to 3 cm. long. Flowers 3½ cm. long, dark pink outside, white inside. Fruit pear-shaped, 2 to 2½ cm. long, smooth, purplish; seeds warty, dull black. A very desirable new species.

Cephalocereus fluminensis (Miquel) Br. et R. = *Cereus fluminensis* Miquel = *Cactus melocactus* Vellozo = *Pilocereus Vellozoi* Lem. = *Cephalocereus melocactus* K. Sch. Brazil, near Rio de Janeiro. Stem sprawling and decumbent, often coiled like a snake, branching from the base, 1 to 2 m. long, and up to 10 cm. thick, with 10 to 17 ribs, broad and rounded, and up to 1½ cm. high. Areoles with abundant white wool. Spines few and short, 4 to 7 radials and 1 central, pale yellow to greyish, softish, up to 3 cm. long. Cephalium 2 to 5 cm. broad and up to 1 m. long, furnished with white wool and yellow bristles. Flowers about 5½ cm. long, smooth or with a few minute scales on the tube; outer petals pale pink, inner petals pure white, shorter and more acute. Stamens white, stigma with about 11 white lobes, exserted beyond the petals. Fruit top-shaped, up to 2 cm. long, smooth purplish. A singular species, now offered by dealers.

Cephalocereus piauhyensis (Gürke) Br. et R. = *Cereus piauhyensis* Gürke = *Pilocereus piauhyensis* Werd. Brazil, States of Pernambuco, Piauhy and Bahia. Stem 5 to 10 m. high, erect, often very thick at the base, where it branches very freely. Ribs 12 to 16, acute, up to 1 cm. high. Areoles about 1 cm. apart, woolly; those at the top of the stem with greyish hair, which is more abundant and longer on the flowering areoles. Radial spines about 20, about 1 cm. long: central spines mostly 6, stronger, and up to 3 cm. long. All spines needle-like and yellowish brown. Flowers up to 4 cm. long, clavate when in bud. Inner petals white, pistil with about 10 stigmas, not exserted beyond the stamens. Fruit roundish, 4 to 5 cm. in diameter. Seeds oval, glossy black, minutely pitted. A fast-growing species with glaucous green stems, 5 to 8 cm. thick: thrives best in half-shade.

Cephalocereus Blossfeldiorum Werd. = *Cereus Blossfeldiorum* Werd. = *Thrixanthocereus Blossfeldiorum* Backbg. North Peru. Stem erect, branched from the base, about 5 cm. thick, with about 20 straight low ribs, bearing closely set and very woolly areoles, with short whitish hairs, more numerous and longer at the top. Pseudocephalium on one side, from the top down to 15-20 cm. with abundant tufts of greyish white hairs, 2 cm. long. Flowers immersed in the pseudocephalium, more or less funnel-shaped with a *hairy* tube and *hairy* scales, hence the new genus *Thrixanthocereus*.

Cephalocereus macrocephalus (Weber) Br. et R. = *Pilocereus macrocephalus* Weber. Mexico. A tall-growing columnar species with dull green stems 8 to 12 cm. in diameter, with numerous narrow ribs slightly rounded and notched, at first about 8, increasing to 12 or more. Areoles on prominences about 2 cm. apart, round, well furnished with yellowish brown wool. Radial spines about 8, yellowish brown, awl-shaped, the 3 upper ones about ½ cm. long, the lower ones up to 2 cm. long. One central spine 3 to 5 cm. long, same colour, thick and awl-shaped, bulbous and black at the base. The top of the flowering stems is densely covered with a pseudocephalium of yellowish wool, with whitish or yellowish brown spines and bristles. *Pilocereus tetetzo* Weber, is probably a synonym.

Cephalocereus cometes (Scheidw.) Br. et R. = *Pilocereus cometes* Scheidw. = *P. comatus* Scheidw. = *P. jubatus* Salm-Dyck = *P. flavicomus* Rümpl. Mexico, San Luis Potosi. A tall columnar species, with a stem 9 or 10 cm. thick, dull green or greyish green, branching from the base and above ground, with 9 to 15 prominent angular ribs. Areoles about 2 cm. apart, yellowish brown, with about 16 radial spines 1½ cm. long, pale yellow with a reddish or greyish point; and with 4 or 5 central spines, brownish yellow, about 2 cm. long. The growing tops of the stems have yellow spines and copious tufts of whitish or yellowish hairs, 2 to 3 cm. long, more abundant, longer and of a deeper yellow on the flowering side of the stem, like a mane, hence the name *jubatus*. An interesting species now becoming rare in collections.

Cephalocereus scoparius (Poselg). Br. et R. = *Pilocereus scoparius* Poselg. Mexico, near Vera Cruz. A tall columnar species, with thick dark green stems, with 12 to 25 rather prominent angular ribs, later on becoming less angular and almost flat. The areoles on the growing tops are somewhat oval and furnished with a few whitish hairs. Spines strong, dark brown passing to grey; the radials 5 to 7, about 1½ cm. long, and one central 2 to 3 cm. long. Both spines and hairs are more numerous and longer on the flowering tops of the stems. Flowers reddish, small, bell-shaped. Fruit small, round, red. Seeds rather large, glossy black.

Cephalocereus colombianus (Vaup.) Br. et R. = *Cereus colombianus* Vaupel = *Pilocereus colombianus* Rose. Colombia. Stem erect, branched from the base, 4 to 6 cm. thick, deep green, with 15 to 25 narrow low ribs. Areoles round, closely set, reddish brown, less than 1 cm. apart, with a few reddish yellow hairs about 1 cm. long, and a cluster of many reddish yellow or rusty-coloured spines, about 1½ cm. long, the central spines (1 to 4) being longer. Hairs more abundant at the top, and of a lighter shade. Flowers small, reddish.

Cephalocereus minensis Werd. Brazil (Minas Geraes). Stem erect, up to 2 m. high, branched from the base, 3 to 5 cm. thick, light green, spiny and woolly at the top. Ribs about 14, about ½ cm. high, with closely set areoles, at first woolly, afterwards bare. Spines about 30, needle-like, pale yellow passing to brown or almost black, ½ to 1 cm. long, very rarely up to 3 cm. long. Flowers about 5 cm. long; ovary and tube with a few small scales, each with a few short hairs in the axil. Stamens and style not exserted.

Cephalocereus Ulei K. Sch. = *C. robustus* Br. et R. = *Pilocereus Ulei* K. Sch. Brazil, near Rio de Janeiro and Cape Frio. A tall species up to 7 m. high, with a thick stem, much branched. Branches about 10 cm. thick, densely woolly at the top, with ribs like those of *C. Houlletii* Lem., 2 cm. high, acute and with deep furrows between them. Areoles large, very woolly and furnished with long silvery or greyish hairs. Radial spines about 10, spreading, thin, often curved, about 1½ cm. long, dark brown. Central spines 1 or 2, similar to the radials but longer, up to 2 cm. About 3 ribs near the top of the stem and branches are furnished with a pseudocephalium consisting of silvery wool or hairs 5 to 6 cm. long, from which spring the flowers. These are 4 to 5 cm. long, smooth outside, white inside. Stigma with 11 or 12 short lobes. Fruit globose depressed, up to 3 cm. thick, reddish, with carmine flesh. Seeds small, oval, black, pitted. Should not be confused with *Facheiroa* (*Cephalocereus*) *Ulei* Gürke.

Cephalocereus Lützelburgii (Vaup.) Br. et R. = *Cereus Lützelburgii* Vaupel = *Pilocereus Lützelburgii* Werd. Brazil (Bahia). An anomalous species, with a solitary unbranched stem, up to 1 m. high, at first globular, passing to oval elongated, later becoming bottle-shaped, more slender at the top. The stem is dark green, with whitish wool and honey-coloured spines at the top. Ribs 13 to 16, about 1½ cm. high; areoles about 1 cm. apart, with whitish wool, developing into curly white hairs, 1 to 2 cm. long, on the flowering areoles at the top. Radial spines 15 to 18, needle-like, up to 1½ cm. long, yellowish passing to grey. Central spines 4 or 5, of same colour, up to 3 cm. long, spreading. Flowers about 5 cm. long, glossy olive green, inner petals white. Stigma with 9 whitish lobes, not exserted. Fruit globose, depressed, about 3 cm. thick, Young roundish plants look like an Echinopsis, but when the slender top or neck is developed, the shape of the plant is reminiscent of a Chianti flask.

Sub-Genus 11. PILOCEREUS. Stem mostly with fewer ribs and of fairly quick growth, branching at the base or at various heights above ground. The growing fruits are not hidden in the woolly mass of the pseudocephalium. The flowers have shorter petals and a spreading or rotate shape, with a few scales and rarely with a few hairs. Established as a genus by Lemaire, it is so retained by most continental authors, although it hardly offers any difference of real generic value from *Cephalocereus*. Britton and Rose consider it as synonymous with *Cephalocereus*, and is is used here as a sub-genus or section.

Cephalocereus Palmeri (Rose) Br. et R. = *Pilocereus Palmeri* Rose = *P. Houlletii* Lem. = *Cereus Houlletii* Lem. Eastern Mexico, in warm valleys near Vera Cruz and Jalapa. Stem columnar and branched, rising up to 3 or 4 m. glaucous or bluish green, with 7 or 8 prominent but broad and rounded ribs. The areoles are large, round, very woolly, with abundant greyish white hairs. 2 to 4 cm. long, often matted together, much more abundant and longer on the flowering part or side of the stem, constituting a pseudocephalium, entirely hiding that side of the stem or the top. Spines yellow in young seedlings, dark brown or nearly black in grown-up plants, 7 to 12 radials about 1 cm. long and 1 or 2 centrals, thicker and up to 3 cm. long, longer on the flowering areoles. Flowers nocturnal, campanulate or funnel-shaped, about 8 cm. long, reddish green externally, pink or pale pink internally; ovary densely hairy. Fruit red, with red or crimson pulp, seeds black. Prefers half-shade, and a warm and moist atmosphere. It is a fast grower, strikes easily from cuttings, and is easy of cultivation. Next to *C. senilis*, it is perhaps the most popular species of *Cephalocereus*. More commonly propagated by means of imported cuttings, as seedlings make slow growth in the first three of four years. In the form *leucocephalus* Hort. (*Pilocereus leucocephalus* Berger), the wool or hair is almost pure white with a glossy sheen.

Very similar to the preceding, and perhaps identical, is **Cephalocereus Sartorianus** (Kupper) Br. et R. = *P. Houlletii* Lem. (pro parte), with stem more green, ribs usually 7, but may be 6 or 8, and more acute, areoles 1½ cm. apart, hair more whitish and shorter. Flowers smaller, yellowish pink. Native of eastern Mexico (Chihuahua) and also of Sonora.

Cephalocereus Maxonii (Vaup.) Br. et R. = *Cereus Maxonii* Vaupel. Guatemala. Is another closely allied species, differing chiefly on account of its light bluish green stem, branching at some distance above ground, the branches being more or less symmetrical and directed obliquely upwards. They are also more slender, with 6 to 8 ribs, with white hair 4 to 5 cm. long. Spines short and yellow, the central spine being only 1½ cm. long. Flowers smaller, only 4 cm. long.

Cephalocereus brasiliensis Br. et R. = *Pilocereus brasiliensis* Werd. Brazil, near Rio de Janeiro, along with *C. fluminensis*. Stem erect, 1 to 3 m. high, branched at or near the ground, very similar to *C. Palmeri*, but smaller in all its parts. The stem is more slender, somewhat fleshy and weak, bluish green passing to green, with 4 or 5 ribs, at first deep, but becoming almost flat on old stems. Areoles very thickly set, with white hairs. Radial spines very short, needle-like, spreading, brown; central spines 1 to 3, spreading, 1 to 2 cm. long, just showing above the hairs. Flowers about 5 cm. long; fruit roundish.

Cephalocereus lanuginosus (Rümpl.) Br. et R. = *Pilocereus lanuginosus* Rümpl. = *Cereus Consolei* Lem. Venezuela (Spanish Leeward Islands). Stems columnar, dark green, 4 to 6 cm. thick, with 8 or 9 acute and prominent ribs, woolly at the sides, the growing tops being well furnished with whitish wool, curled hair and brownish spines. Radial spines 9 to 12, brownish yellow or reddish brown ; central spines 1 to 3, about 3 cm. long. The flower is about 5 cm. long, half-immersed in the wool of the pseudocephalium, greenish outside, reddish inside. The variety *armatus* (*Cereus armatus* Otto), has central spines about twice as long. Usually grafted on a *Trichocereus*, but grows well on own roots. Growth is robust, but rather slow. Requires warmth and half-shade, and should be kept rather dry.

Cephalocereus Royenii (Rümpl.) Br. et R. = *Pilocereus Royenii* Rümpl. = *P. barbatus* Otto = *P. floccosus* Lem. West Indies (Island of Santa Cruz). Stem columnar erect, branched, bluish green, 4 to 8 cm. thick, with 6 to 10 acute ribs. The areoles are dark brown, with abundant white hairs, 1 to 2 cm. long, and with about 10 brownish red radial spines, 2 cm. long, very stiff and sharp, and 4 or 5 longer central spines. The flower is red, woolly and spiny on the outside. The form or variety to which the name *floccosus* properly belongs, has dark bluish green stems, more slender, with a denser formation of wool and longer spines on the flowering part of the stem. A beautiful species requiring warmth and sunshine; should be kept well sheltered and rather dry in winter. Is usually grafted, but grows just as well on own roots.

Cephalocereus nobilis (Haw.) Br. et R. = *Cereus nobilis* Haw. = *Pilocereus nobilis* Weber = *P. Haworthii* Cons. =*P. niger* Salm-Dyck. West Indies. Stem erect, branched above ground, 3 to 7 cm. thick, very dark green, with 5 to 7 ribs, prominent and rounded. Areoles large, yellow on the upper part of the stem, almost black downwards, 1½ to 2 cm. apart, with a few curled yellow or yellowish hairs 1 to 2 cm. long, and with many needle-like spines, reddish yellow when young, soon passing to yellow or yellowish brown. Radial spines about 9, 2 to 3 cm. long; central spines 1 to 4, longer. Flower 5 cm. long and 4 cm. broad, reddish green on the outside, red and pale pink inside. Fruit red or violet red. In the form *niger* (S.D.) the stem is very dark green, almost black, and very glossy, and this appears to be the typical form to which the specific name *nobilis* Haw., should be applied. A very lovely and fairly quick-growing species, easily grown.

The following are well-known forms listed by growers:

var. **Curtisii** (Salm-Dyck) = *Pilocereus Curtisii* Salm-Dyck. Stem taller and more robust, 5 to 6 cm. thick, with 8 or 9 ribs. Newer spines longer and more coloured. Central spines more stiff and up to 5 cm. long. The colour of the stem is almost grass green.

var. **nigricans** Hort. Stem dark green, about as thick as in the typical form, with 7 to 9 ribs. Lower areoles dark yellowish brown, upper areoles more copiously hairy, with longer hair, less curled.

There is also in cultivation a very attractive cristate form, fan-like, very dark glossy green, almost black, with short golden yellow spines.

Cephalocereus strictus (Rümpl.) Br. et R. = *Pilocereus strictus* Rümpl. West Indies. Very much like the preceding species, and may be only a variety. Stem 3 to 4 cm. thick, of quick growth and much branched, somewhat glaucous green, with 4 to 7 rounded ribs, usually freely branching above ground, and also sending up offshoots from the base. Areoles u.s., but more yellowish. Spines shorter, very thin, more yellow, those at the top being golden yellow. There is a scanty development of hair, but the flowering areoles are more woolly. Flowers freely borne, bell-shaped, 5 to 6 cm. long, greenish pink outside, very pale pink inside. Fruit globular depressed, 4 to 5 cm. in diameter, purplish green, flesh deep crimson; seeds small glossy black.

Cephalocereus leucocephalus (Poselg.) Br. er R. = *Pilocereus leucocephalus* Poselger = *P. Houlletii* Lem. pro parte. Mexico (Sonora and Chihuahua). Similar to *C. Sartorianus*, but quite distinct from the form *leucocephalus* (Berger) of *C. Palmeri*. Stems bluish when young, mostly with 12 ribs, rather slender. Spines 1 to 2 cm. long, honey yellow. Flowering areoles with abundant white wool or hair, up to 10 cm. long. Rare in cultivation.

Cephalocereus barbadensis (Berger) Br. et R. = *Pilocereus barbadensis* Berger. Barbadoes. Stem erect, green, branching from the base and also above ground, of fast growth, with 8 to 9 prominent rounded ribs, 4 to 6 cm. in diameter. Areoles about 1 cm. apart, yellowish brown. Spines numerous, spreading, needle-like and stiff, yellowish brown, 2 to 3 cm. long. radials and centrals alike, and all in the same areole of about equal length. Only the flowering areoles are furnished with whitish wool, about 1½ cm. long. Flowers pale red.

Cephalocereus perlucens (K. Sch.) Werd. = *Cereus perlucens* K. Sch. Brazil (Manaos). Stem erect, stiff, branched, 4 to 8 cm. thick, bluish green and glaucous, the growing tops furnished with curled whitish or brownish wool, and with short dark brown spines. Ribs 5 to 6, up to 6 mm. high, rounded, notched, bluish, with a violet tinge when young. Areoles about 1 cm. apart, round, with curled wool, later almost bare. Radial spines 8 to 10, spreading, dark brown, 1 to 2 cm. long, straight, needle-like. Central spines 1 or 2, slightly longer and thicker, dark brown almost black. Requires warmth and half-shade: growth is rather slow.

Cephalocereus Arrabidae (Lem.) Br. et R. = *Pilocereus Arrabidae* Lem. = *P. exerens* K. Sch. = *Cereus sublanatus* Salm-Dyck = *P. tilophorus* Lem. = *Pilocereus sublanatus* Hort. Brazil (Bahia and Pernambuco), on sandy wastes along the coast. A slender species with many stems and branches, up to 3 m. high, but often decumbent, 6 to 10 cm. thick, green or bluish green, with 6 to 8 rounded prominent ribs. Areoles closely set, brownish, with long white hairs, later almost bare. Spines brownish; the radials about 7, of which only 2 are up to 2 cm. long: central spines 1 or 2, thicker, darker with up to 4 cm. long. Flowers about 7 cm. long and 5 cm. broad, green on the outside, greenish white inside. The stem is sometimes glaucous and thicker, and to this form, frequent near Rio de Janeiro, the name *tilophorus* (Lem.) properly applies.

Cephalocereus albispinus (Rümpl.) Br. et R. = *Pilocereus albispinus* Rümpl. Venezuela (Island of Curaçao). Stem columnar, erect, stiff, deep green passing to greyish green, up to 10 cm. thick, with 8 to 12 low angular ribs. Areoles about 1 cm. apart, white or whitish, with short white hairs. Radial spines about 12, up to 1 cm. long, white tipped black: central spines 2 or 3, of the same colour, thicker and up to 4 cm. long. The new spines are red, but soon become white tipped black. The white hairs are longer and more abundant on the flowering areoles, but not more than $1\frac{1}{2}$ cm. long. The flower is pink outside, whitish inside. The fruit is oval, violet, with white pulp. A pretty species, well deserving of cultivation, but of rather slow growth.

var. **Weberi** Backbg. Has more slender and shorter spines, and reddish green fruits.

Cephalocereus Russellianus (Otto) Br. et R. = *Cereus Russellianus* Otto = *Pilocereus Russellianus* Rümpl. Colombia and Venezuela. An erect species with stiff stems, about 5 m. high, much branched, dull green or glaucous green, up to 10 cm. thick, with 6 or 7 angular ribs, rather irregular and rounded, furnished with large, round, woolly areoles of a brownish colour, 1 to $1\frac{1}{2}$ cm. apart. Spines at first red or dark red, afterwards dark brown, thick and stiff: the radials 6 to 10, up to 2 cm. long; the centrals 1 to 3, much longer and thicker, 4 to 5 cm. sometimes up to 10 cm. The top and upper areoles are well furnished with tufts of reddish brown hairs, 1 to 2 cm. long. The flowers are 7 to 9 cm. long, whitish. The fruit is oval, violet, with white pulp.

(b) OREOCEREUS TROLLII

(a) OREOCEREUS-CELSIANUS
var. fossulatus

PLATE XIV

(b) WILCOXIA SCHMOLLII

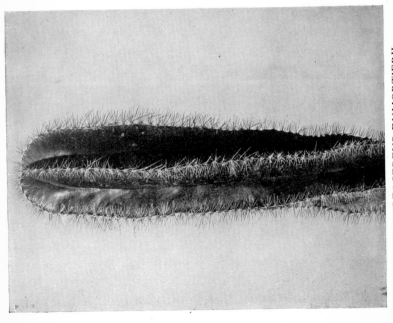

(a) LEMAIREOCEREUS DUMORTIERII

PLATE XV

Seeds rather large, dull black. A species of rather quick growth, requiring much warmth and full sunshine.

Cephalocereus remolinensis (Backbg.) = *Cereus remolinensis* Backbg. = *Pilocereus remolinensis* Backbg. Colombia (near Remolino, Magdalena). Stem erect and stiff, up to 12 m. high, much branched; branches 3 to 6 cm. thick, at first glossy green, passing to dull glaucous or greyish green, with 5 to 7 ribs having a V-shaped notch above the areoles. These are about 2 cm. apart, large, round, white, with white hairs when young, more abundant and longer on the flowering tops. Radial spines 7 to 13, up to 1½ cm. long; only one central spine, rarely up to 3 cm. long. All spines are very thin, dark brown or black, passing to grey or ash-coloured. Flowers 6 to 7 cm. long, petals creamy white, tipped pink or mauve. Fruit yellowish green, somewhat oval. Seeds rather large, dull black. Requires warmth and sunshine.

Cephalocereus hapalacanthus (Werd.) = *Pilocereus hapalacanthus* Werd. Brazil (Pernambuco). Columnar, up to 5 m. high, much branched from the base, with erect branches, clear green passing to greyish green, the tops furnished with yellowish spines and whitish wool. Ribs about 12, 1 to 1½ cm. high, lightly notched. Areoles about 1 cm. apart, woolly when young. Spines 15 to 20, all alike, thin and needle-like, flexible, about 1 cm. long, yellowish or brownish. Flowers about 6 cm. long, greenish outside, white inside, the 9 lobes of the stigma just exserted beyond the perianth. Fruit globose depressed, deep green, 3½ to 5 cm. thick.

Cephalocereus salvadorensis (Werd.) = *Pilocereus salvadorensis* Werd. Brazil (Bahia, along the coast at Sao Salvador). Columnar, up to 4 m. high, more or less branched, with greyish green branches up to 10 cm. thick, with a woolly and spiny top. Ribs 7 to 9, up to 2 cm. high; areoles 1 to 1½ cm. apart, the flowering areoles furnished with hair up to 1½ cm. long. Radial spines about 10, up to 1 cm. long, spreading, needle-like, yellowish, passing to brownish or greyish. Central spines 4, up to 2½ cm. long, needle-like, spreading crosswise, bulbous at the base, of same colour as the radials. Fruit globose depressed, 3½ to 5 cm. thick. Seeds oval, glossy black, pitted.

Cephalocereus euphorbioides (Haw.) Br. et R.=*Cereus euphorbioides* Haw. = *Cereus Olfersii* Otto = *Piliocereus euphorbioides* Rümpl. Brazil? Long known in cultivation. Stem columnar, erect, branched at the base and above ground, of rather fast growth, dull glaucous green, 6 to 9 cm. thick, with 8 very prominent and acute ribs. Areoles about 2 cm. apart, with short whitish wool: radial spines 4 to 9, white, flexible and blunt, 5 to 7 mm. long, dark-tipped; one central spine, 3 to 4 cm. long, thick and dark brown. Flowers numerous, borne on the growing top on areoles with some development of white wool, brownish pink outside, pale pink inside, about 8 cm. long and 7 cm. broad, funnel-shaped. Ovary slightly woolly and spinescent, with few scales, stamens white. Looks like an *Euphorbia*, hence its name. Prefers half-shade, but is otherwise of easy cultivation. Easily grown from seed produced on cultivated plants, and was originally introduced from Brazil, but its true home is unknown.

Cephalocereus phaeacanthus (Gürke) Br. et R. = *Cereus phaeacanthus* Gürke. Brazil (Bahia, on the stony wastes of the *Caatinga*). Stem up to 4 m. high, branched from the base, and mostly sprawling or decumbent, 2 to 5 cm. thick, with 8 to 10 ribs, low, grass green. Areoles ½ to 1 cm. apart, greyish white. Radial spines 10 to 12, spreading, up to 1 cm. long: central spines 1 to 3, up to 3 cm. long. All spines are needle-like, straight, very sharp, reddish yellow to dark brown or grey. Flower about 6 cm. long, almost closed, green outside: ovary and tube with a few broad scales; inner petals greenish white, the 8 lobed stigma not exserted beyond the petals. Fruit pear-shaped, 2 to 3 cm. long. There are a few reddish or yellowish brown hairs at the growing tops. A very pretty species, now fequently listed by growers; makes quick growth and prefers half-shade.

Cephalocereus Moritzianus (Otto) Br. et R. = *Cereus Moritzianus* Otto = *Pilocereus Moritzianus* Lem. et Cons. Venezuela and neighbouring Islands. An erect plant up to 10 m. high, with numerous branches of varying thickness, up to 10 cm., at first pale green and bluish, passing to greyish green, with 7 to 10 ribs, deeply notched. Areoles 1 to 1½ cm. apart, with white wool, afterwards bare; flowering areoles with long white hair. Spines 9 to 14, all alike, slender, straight, sharp, yellow or dark yellow. Flowers about 5 cm. long, white; fruit violet red, pulp white; seeds small glossy black.

Cephalocereus sergipensis (Werd.) = *Pilocereus sergipensis* Werd. Brazil (district of Sergipe del Rey). A very lovely new species, erect up to 3 m. high. Stem solitary or sparingly branched from the base. Growing tops 3½ to 4½ cm. thick, of a charming glaucous azure blue, covered with white wool and yelllow spines. Ribs 6, very rarely 7 or 8, about 1½ cm. high. Areoles about 1½ cm. apart, densely woolly and with silky white hairs. Radial spines 8 to 11, spreading horizontally, up to 1 cm. long, at first yellow passing to brownish: central spines 2 to 4, similar to the radials or slightly thicker. All spines are bulbous at the base. Fruit globose depressed, greenish or reddish. Seeds oval, glossy black, pitted. A striking species, makes fast growth and prefers full sunshine.

Cephalocereus glaucescens (Labouret) = *Pilocereus glaucescens* Labouret. Brazil (Bahia and Minas Geraes). Stem erect, up to 6 m. high, branched, not unlike the preceding as a seedling. Growing stems up to 10 cm. thick, glaucous pale blue, topped with white wool and short yellow spines, with 8 to 10 ribs, up to 1½ cm. high, later almost flat. Areoles about 1 cm. apart, with white hairs. Radial spines 13 to 18, needle-like, ½ to 1½ cm. long, yellowish white; central spines 5 to 7 up to 1½ cm. long, thicker, yellowish grey, thickened and brownish at the base. Flowers 6 to 7 cm. long, inner petals very short, white; tube greenish brown; stigma with 4 to 6 short whitish lobes. A fine species well worth growing. Growth is rather slow.

Cephalocereus glaucochrous (Werd.) = *Pilocereus glaucochrous*
Werd. Brazil (Bahia). Stem columnar, erect, sometimes sprawling
or decumbent, up to 4 m. long, mostly solitary, occasionally branching
from the base, 5 to 7 cm. thick, intensely glaucous or bluish. Ribs
5 to 9, slightly more than 1 cm. deep, notched or warty. Areoles whitish
or yellowish, 1½ cm. apart, with white hairs. Radial spines 9 to 12,
unequal, up to 2 cm. long, transparent straw-coloured, passing to
greyish; central spines 3 or 4, thicker, straw-coloured, sometimes up
to 5 cm. long. Flowers about 5 cm. long, glaucous and reddish outside,
whitish or pale pink inside. Fruit globose depressed, 3 to 5 cm. in
diameter, glaucous green or reddish. Seeds small, oval, glossy black,
pitted. A fast-growing species, requiring full sunshine, and a stony,
sandy soil.

Cephalocereus Bradei (Backbg. et Voll.) = *Pilocereus Bradei*
Backbg. et Voll. A rare species discovered by Dr. Brade, in Diamantinas, Brazil. Erect and branched, up to 2 m. high, and up to 8 cm.
thick, the growing tops of a very beautiful glaucous azure blue. Ribs
about 10, rounded, about 1 cm. deep, with narrow furrows between
them, and with transverse furrows between the areoles. These are
fairly large, about 2 cm. apart, with greyish wool. Radial spines about
6, about 1 cm. long, reddish brown: central spines 1 or 2, one of them
up to 2 cm. long, same colour. Flowering tops almost spineless;
flowers borne on one side of the stem, near the top, with some formation
of greyish wool. Flowers greenish white, about 7 cm. long including
tube about 4 cm. long, and 3 cm. broad.

Cephalocereus pentaedrophorus (Labouret) Br. et R. = *Cereus
pentaedrophorus* Labouret = *Pilocereus pentaedrophorus* Console.
Brazil (Pernambuco and Bahia). Columnar, up to 10 m. high, solitary
or branching from the base, erect, or reclined, bluish green, growing
tops 3 to 10 cm. thick. Ribs 4 to 6, rarely more, low, notched above
the areoles, which have only very short hairs. Spines unequal and
irregular, 5 to 12, at least one of them up to 4 cm. long, yellowish
passing to greyish brown. Flowering areoles almost hairless. Flowers
4 to 5 cm. long, often curved. Ovary and tube smooth and green. Fruit
globose depressed, 3 to 5 cm. in diameter, bluish green or reddish,
pulp purple violet.

Cephalocereus polygonus (Lam.) Br. et R. = *Cactus polygonus*
Lam. = *Cereus polygonus* DC. = *Pilocereus polygonus* K. Sch. =
Pilocereus tuberculatus Werd. Brazil (Pernambuco and Bahia). Stem
up to 4 m. high, branching regularly. Branches dark green, 2½ to 4 cm.
thick, with about 7 ribs notched into prominent tubercles or warts,
about 1 cm. high. Areoles large, brownish or greyish, but without
long hairs. Spines needle-like, flexible, dirty yellow; the radials
9 to 13, spreading up to 1½ cm. long; the centrals 4 to 7, thicker,
1 or 2 of them up to 4 cm. long. Flowers 5 or 6 cm. long, green outside,
white inside, style not exserted. Fruit globose depressed, 2 to 2½ cm.
in diameter.

Cephalocereus catingicola (Gürke) Br. et R. = *Cereus catingicola* Gürke = *Pilocereus catingicola* Werd. Brazil (Bahia, common in the stony ground of the Caatinga). Stem erect, much branched, up to 8 m. high; branches greyish green, 8 to 12 cm. thick, with 4 or 5 angular ribs 3 to 4 cm. high. Areoles 2 cm. apart, with a few greyish white hairs. Radial spines 8 to 12, spreading laterally, up to 1 cm. long: central spines 5 to 8, unequal, the longest up to 10 cm. long, very strong. All spines are awl-shaped, straight, yellowish or horny yellow. Flowers up to 8 cm. long, smooth and green outside, white inside; style not exserted, lobes of stigma white passing to reddish. Fruit globose depressed, 5 to 7 cm. thick, pulp red.

Cephalocereus cuyabensis (Backbg.) = *Pilocereus cuyabensis* Backbg. A rare species from Cuyaba, Central Brazil. Stem 1 to 2 m. high, erect, solitary or branched; branches greyish green, up to 6 cm. thick, very spiny and woolly at the top. Ribs 10 to 12, rounded, 8 mm. high. Areoles less than ½ cm. apart, with greyish wool. Spines about 15, radials and centrals hardly distinguishable, needle-like, yellowish brown, about 1 cm. long, but at least one of them 1½ to 2 cm. long. Flowers creamy white, borne all round the woolly top.

Cephalocereus oligolepis (Vaupel) = *Cereus oligolepis* Vaupel = *Pilocereus oligolepis* Werd. Brazil, British Guiana, Venezuela. Stem erect, up to 1 m. high, sparingly branched from the base, with 5 ribs over 1 cm. high, later almost flat. Areoles 1 cm. apart, with short wool and whitish hairs about 1 cm. long. Radial spines 8 to 10, spreading, thin, about ½ cm. long: one central spine, thicker and up to 2 cm. long. Flowers whitish, about 6 cm. long; ovary and tube with a few small scales; style whitish, stigma with 10 short lobes. Fruit globose depressed, about 3 cm. across. Seeds black, minutely pitted.

Cephalocereus rupicola (Werd.) = *Pilocereus rupicola* Werd. Brazil (District of Sergipe del Rey). Stem erect, up to 50 cm. high, scantily branched from the base, 3½ to 4 cm. thick, ashy green, with yellow spines and white hairs at the top. Ribs 9, about 1 cm. high. Areoles 1 cm. apart, densely woolly and with white hairs, later almost bare. Spines 18 to 21, all alike, up to 2 cm. long, needle-like, yellow passing to brown or black, bulbous at the base.

Cephalocereus arenicola (Werd.) = *Pilocereus arenicola* Werd. Brazil (North Bahia, on sandy soil). Stem erect, branched, up to 5 m. high. Branches about 7 cm. thick, ashy green, the tops covered with white hairs 2 to 3 cm. long. Ribs 5 to 7, about 1½ cm. deep. Areoles about 1 cm. apart, densely woolly, the flowering areoles at the top furnished with white or yellowish hairs. Radial spines 8 or 9, spreading outward, needle-like, pale yellow to dirty yellow, ½ to 1 cm. long; central spines 5 or 6, thicker, 1 to 1½ cm. long; all spines bulbous at the base. Fruit globose depressed; seeds oval, glossy black, pitted.

Cephalocereus Swartzii (Griseb.) Br. et R. = *Cereus Swartzii* Griseb. = *Pilocereus Swartzii* Griseb. Jamaica. A very beautiful and rare species, with a thick tall columnar stem, dark green, or brownish or almost black, without any hair formation, 2 to 7 m. high, often solitary, or branching above ground, with 10 ribs deeply notched between the areoles. Spines 8 to 10 or more, up to 2½ cm. long, spreading, thick, reddish brown, tipped silvery white. Flowers pinkish white to greenish yellow, borne near the top of the branches, surrounded with much white hair and long bristles, 5 to 6 cm. long. Fruit globose depressed, 3 cm. thick. Requires warmth and sunshine. Thrives better grafted on *Harrisia Jusbertii*.

Cephalocereus Backebergii (Weingt.) = *Cereus Backebergii* Weingt. = *Pilocereus Backebergii* Backbg. Venezuela, near Porto Cabello. Stem up to 5 m. high, well branched, 7 to 12 cm. thick, glossy pale green, glaucous at the top, with 9 to 15 ribs slightly notched. Areoles pale brown, with hanging silky white hairs. Radial spines 8 to 12, needle-like, rather thick, 1 to 1½ cm. long, horny yellow: one central spine, same colour, up to 5 cm. long. Flower yellowish green, whitish inside. Fruit much depressed, bluish violet, with red pulp. Seeds small, glossy black. One of the finest Venezuelan species; requires warmth.

Cephalocereus Fričii (Backbg.) = *Cereus Fričii* Backbg. *Pilocereus Fričii* Backbg. Venezuela, near Caracas and Porto Cabello. Stem tall, scantily branched. Branches dark green, with 6 to 8 ribs, deeply notched. Areoles densely woolly and with hanging hairs. Radial spines about 7, very stiff, 1½ to 2½ cm. long, the upper ones being the shortest. Central spines 1 to 3, up to 6 cm. long, very stiff. All spines horny yellow to dark reddish brown, spotted white. Flower greenish outside, white inside. Fruit oval, violet, with white pulp. Seeds rather large, dull black.

Cephalocereus atroviridis (Backbg.) = *Cereus atroviridis* Backbg. = *Pilocereus atroviridis* Backbg. Colombia, along the northern coast. Stem up to 12 m. high, much branched. Branches up to 20 cm. thick, dark green, with white hair at the top. Ribs 8 or more, notched, rounded. Areoles slightly woolly, with about 8 radial spines, ½ to 1 cm. long: central spines 3, one of which is up to 2 cm. long. All spines are white, tipped brown. Fruit oval, reddish green, with white pulp. Seeds rather large, dull black. A rare species even in its native country.

Cephalocereus claroviridis (Backbg.) = *Cereus claroviridis* Backbg. = *Pilocereus claroviridis* Backbg. Venezuela, near Caracas, on high ground. Erect and branched, pale green, somewhat bluish at the top, 6 to 8 cm. thick, with about 7 ribs, and areoles with white wool. Radial spines 10 to 12, thin, yellowish, unequal; central spines 1 to 3, also unequal, but slightly longer than the radials. Flower and fruit unknown Not unlike *C. Moritzianus*.

Cephalocereus Tweedyanus Br. et R. South Ecuador. Stem 5 to 6 m. high, with straight branches which are up to 10 cm. thick, greyish green, pale bluish at the top, with 7 to 9 ribs, 1 to 2 cm. high. Areoles about 2 cm. apart, greyish, with greyish white hairs 1 to 2 cm. long. Radial spines about 12, awl-shaped, dirty yellowish white tipped brown,

½ to 2 cm. long. Central spines mostly 4, often 1 to 3, crosswise, the laterals shorter, the upper one up to 4 cm. long, the lower up to 6 cm. long, awl-shaped and stiff. Flower 7 cm. long, on areoles with long white hairs. Fruit red.

Cephalocereus Robinii (Lem.) Br. et R. = *Pilocereus Robinii* Lem. Cuba. Up to 8 m. high, branching profusely just above the ground, forming a large crown. Branches 7 to 10 cm. thick, glaucous green passing to dull green, with 10 to 13 ribs. Areoles 1 to 1½ cm. apart, with short wool. Spines all alike, 15 to 20, needle-like, 1 to 2½ cm. long, yellow passing to grey. Flowers on closely set areoles, brownish green, 5 cm. long, with a few small scales on the ovary and tube, outer petals creamy white, inner petals white: style creamy white, exserted. Fruit globose depressed, 4 cm. thick, dark red; seeds glossy black, not pitted.

Cephalocereus Urbanianus (K. Sch.) Br. et R. = *Pilocereus Urbanianus* K. Sch. Island of Guadeloupe. Stem up to 4 m. high, 4 to 5 cm. thick, branching from the ground, with reddish brown spines at the top. Ribs 8 to 10, obtuse, 1 to 1½ cm. high, with narrow furrows between them. Areoles 1 cm. apart, more closely set on the flowering part of the stem, with whitish hairs 1 cm. long. Spines 10 to 13, all alike, spreading, flexible, up to 1½ cm. long, at first red or reddish, passing to ashy grey. Pseudocephalium on one side of the stem, with whitish hairs 2 cm. long. Flowers 6 cm. long, funnel-shaped.

Cephalocereus tehuacanus (Weingt.) = *Pilocereus tehuacanus* Weingt. Mexico (Tehuacan). Stem mostly solitary, pale green, deep bluish green at the top, with about 15 low ribs. Areoles 1 cm. apart, woolly, with whitish hairs. Spines about 25, all alike, needle-shaped, brown passing to grey, 1 to 2 cm. long.

Cephalocereus leucostele (Gürke) Br. et R. = *Cereus leucostele* Gürke = *Pilocereus leucostele* Werd. = *Stephanocereus leucostele* Berger. Brazil, in the stony Caatinga near Bahia. Stem columnar, about 3 m. high, often solitary, occasionally branching from the base and above ground, up to 10 cm. thick at the base, with 12 to 18 ribs, glaucous green. Areoles 1 to 1½ cm. apart, with wool 1 to 1½ cm. long, covering the stem. Radial spines up to 20, white passing to greyish or brownish, thin, needle-like, ½ to 1½ cm. long. Central spines 1 or 2, often 3 to 4 cm. long, whitish to golden yellow, very sharp. The growing branches are often not more than 4 cm. thick. The cephalium consists of a mass of white wool and golden yellow bristles at the top of the stem, the bristles passing to reddish brown forming a thick ring at the top of the stem, through which the stem continues its normal growth when it has done flowering. Flowers numerous, white, nocturnal, about 6 cm. long; ovary and tube yellowish. Stigma with 11 creamy lobes, exserted beyond the stamens. The fact that the cephalium is a crown-like structure at the top of the stem, through which the stem continues its growth to form again another cephalium at the following season has induced Berger to create the genus *Stephano-*

cereus for this species. This habit of flowering is exactly similar to that of the two species of *Arrojadoa* of Britton and Rose. This species makes quick growth and is of easy cultivation in full sunshine. Topped stems produce numerous offshoots suitable for propagation.

Sub-Genus III. ARROJADOA (Br. et R.). Stem slender, low and branched, often decumbent, with low narrow ribs, thickly studded with minute areoles. Cephalium or pseudocephalium developed every year at the top of the stem, and consists of a crown-like mass of wool and bristles, through which the stem continues its normal growth after it has done flowering, as in *C. leucostele.* Flowers small, diurnal, with an erect and almost tubular perianth of a red colour. Stamens and style included. Fruit a small berry, with small black seeds.

Cephalocereus rhodanthus (Gürke) Backbg. = *Cereus rhodanthus* Gürke = *Arrojadoa rhodantha* Br. et R. Brazil, in the underwood of the Caatinga in the States of Bahia, Pernambuco and Piauhy. Stem erect or decumbent or clambering, 40 cm. to 2 m. long, mostly branched from the ground, dark green, cylindrical, 2 to 5 cm. thick, with 10 to 12 low narrow ribs. Areoles about 1 cm. apart, with short wool. Radial spines about 20, needle-like, about 1 cm. long, yellowish to brownish: central spines 5 or 6, longer and thicker, up to 3 cm. long, dark brown; all spines passing to greyish. Cephalium formed at the top of last year's growth, and consists of a mass of wool 1½ to 2 cm. long, and of many reddish brown flexible bristles up to 3 cm. long. Flowers 3 to 3½ cm. long, funnel-shaped or almost tubular, fleshy, violet pink on the outside, with a smooth ovary and tube; inner petals about 4 mm. long, violet red: stamens, style and lobes of stigma whitish. Stigma with 10 lobes, not exserted. Fruit round, small, purple red. Thrives well on own roots in half-shade, in a gritty soil mixed with leaf-mould.

Cephalocereus penicillatus (Gürke) Backbg. = *Cereus penicillatus* Gürke = *Arrojadoa penicillata* Br. et R. Brazil, State of Bahia, in the drier localities of the Caatinga. Same habit as the preceding. Stem more slender, more branched, with 10 to 12 very low ribs. Areoles small, with greyish white wool. Radial spines 8 to 12, very short, thin and needle-like, applied to the stem: central spines 1 or 2, thicker and stiff, 1 to 3 cm. long, yellowish passing to brown, and finally greyish. Cephalium and flower as in the preceding species. Fruit round, small, up to 1 cm. thick, smooth, with the remains of the flower attached to it, glossy white, often flushed pink. Seeds very small, oval or pear-shaped, dull dark brown or black, minutely pitted.

The following species are hardly ever cultivated: **Cephalocereus Brooksianus** Br. et R., **C. Collinsii** Br. et R., **C. alensis** (Weber) Br. et R., **C. bahamensis** Britton, **C. Deeringii** Small, **C. fulvispinosus** (Haw.), **C. Gaumeri** Br. et R., **C. Hermentianus** (Lem. et Cons.), **C. Llanosii** (Werd.), **C. Millspaughii** Britton and **C. Purpusii** Br. et R.

It is not unlikely that other species are still awaiting discovery in the vast, unexplored regions of South America.

FACHEIROA Br. et R.

Columnar, with slender branched stems, with many spiny ribs. Flowers borne on a cephalium on one side of the stem. Ovary, tube and fruit, densely covered with scales, with many hairs in their axils. Includes one species.

Facheiroa Ulei (Gürke) Werd. = *Cephalocereus Ulei* Gürke, non K. Sch. = *Facheiroa publiflora* Br. et R. Brazil (State of Bahia). Columnar, erect, up to 5 m. high, very much branched. Branches 5 to 7 cm. thick, with 15 to 20 ribs, 6 to 8 mm. high, deeply notched above the areoles. These are 1 cm. apart, with greyish brown wool. Radial spines 10 to 15, spreading, 1 to $1\frac{1}{2}$ cm. long. Central spines 3 or 4, $1\frac{1}{2}$ to $2\frac{1}{2}$ cm. long. All spines are brown. Cephalium up to 20 cm. long, on one side of the top of the branches, consisting of a compact mass of reddish brown wool or hair, 3 to $4\frac{1}{2}$ cm. long. Flowers borne on the cephalium, 2 to 4 cm. broad; ovary and tube densely furnished with lanceolate brownish scales, with many hairs in their axils, about 1 cm. long. Petals white. Stigma with about 10 lobes. Fruit pear-shaped, about 4 cm. thick, with lanceolate scales, with or without a fringe of brownish hairs. Seeds, small, dull black, oval or kidney-shaped, minutely pitted.

Should not be confused with *Cephalocereus Ulei* K. Sch.

ESPOSTOA Br. et R.

Columnar species with many low and rounded ribs, hairy or woolly, with a pseudocephalium on the top of flowering stems. Flowers small, funnel-shaped, immersed in the wool of the pseudocephalium. Ovary scaly and tube hairy. Fruit a juicy edible berry. Seed very small, black, glossy. Includes 4 species, all very interesting and desirable.

Espostoa lanata (DC.) Br. et R. = *Cereus lanatus* DC. = *Pilocereus lanatus* H.B. et K. Native of Ecuador and Peru. Stem erect, green, about 1 m. high. branching at the top, 4 to 6 cm. thick, but up to 14 cm. when old, with many low rounded ribs, up to 20, with white roundish areoles about $\frac{1}{2}$ cm. apart, bearing about 12 glassy yellow, or yellowish white, or reddish short spines; 1 or 2 central spines up to 8 cm. long, and much silky white or pale yellow hair, 1 to 2 cm. long, entirely covering the stem, but not matted. Flower white; fruit oval, red. A beautiful species of slow growth, usually grafted on *Trichocereus Spachianus or T. macrogonus*, but thrives well on own roots. Requires warmth and thrives in half-shade as well as in full sunshine.

Espostoa Dautwitzii Haage jr. = *Pilocereus Dautwitzii* Haage jr. = *Cereus sericatus* (Backbg.) Werd. Native of Peru. Often considered as a variety of the preceding. Stem u.s. of a lighter green, ribs more numerous (26 to 30), and more acute. Areoles yellow, furnished with very silky pale yellow, or even golden yellow, hair, denser and longer at the top, but becoming lightly matted and veiling the stem lower down, less densely than in the preceding species, resulting in a fascinating transparent effect. Radial spines yellow, numerous, not longer than the hair; central spine one, reddish yellow, much longer. A very beautiful species, which should find a place in every collection. There is also an interesting and showy cristate form. Requires the same treatment as the preceding.

Espostoa melanostele Vaupel. = *Cephalocereus melanostele* Vaupel. = *Binghamia melanostele* Br. et R. = *Pseudoespostoa melanostele* Backbg. Peru (Chosica). May be only a variety of the preceding, but has darker green stems, branching from the base, hairless or almost hairless when young, with less numerous ribs, with short golden yellow spines, and tops of flowering stems with more woolly hair in tufts, and only slightly matted. Fruit roundish, reddish.

Espostoa Haagei Poselg. = *Pilocereus Haagei* Poselg. = *Pseudoespostoa Haagei* Backbg. Peru. Stem branching mostly at the base, like a Trichocereus, 5 to 6 cm. thick, dull green, with 20 to 30 low and narrow ribs, with spines u.s., but white or glassy. Stem thickly covered, not simply veiled, with matted white silky hairs, and similarly matted and denser at the top, resulting in a rounded woolly mass. Fruit round. On account of the round fruit, the stem branching mostly at the base, and the matted hair, Backeberg instituted the genus *Pseudoespostoa* to include these two species.

BROWNINGIA Br. et R.

Stem erect solitary, green, branching at the top, with 14 or more, low broad ribs, with narrow furrows between them. Areoles about $\frac{1}{2}$ cm. apart, rather large, round or oval, yellowish, with a cluster of 5 to 8 spreading radial spines, yellowish, brownish towards the tip, not more than 1 cm. long, and 1 to 3 central spines of same colour, about $1\frac{1}{2}$ cm. long. There is no development of hairs, but the flowering areoles are more spiny. Flower nocturnal, white, rather large and funnel-shaped. Ovary and tube scaly, without any hairs. Fruit yellow, seeds black and very hairy. Includes two species.

Browningia candelaris (Meyen) Br. et R. = *Cereus candelaris* Meyen. Native of Peru and Chile. This is the type of this aberrant genus, and to it the above description applies. A rare, rather slow-growing species, about 2 m. high, with sprawling or ascending branches 6 to 8 cm. thick, arising up the stem, above ground. Is usually grafted; prefers half-shade, but thrives well also in full sunshine.

Browningia microsperma (Werd. et Backbg.) = *Cereus microspermus* Werd. et Backbg. = *Gymnanthocereus microspermus* Backbg. North Peru. A species of uncertain affinity, described as a *Trichocereus* in the first edition of this work, but more probably it is a species of *Browningia*. Stem about $1\frac{1}{2}$ m. high, and 4 to 6 cm. thick, grass green, erect or semi-prostrate, with about 12 rounded ribs, $\frac{1}{2}$ cm. high. Areoles $\frac{1}{2}$ to 1 cm. apart, round, rather large, yellowish. Spines numerous, golden brownish yellow, reddish yellow or almost chestnut brown at the tip: radials 12 to 16, bristle-like, spreading, $\frac{1}{2}$ to 1 cm. long; centrals 3 to 5, up to $2\frac{1}{2}$ cm. long, sometimes longer. Flowers at or near the top of the stem, funnel-shaped, 3 to 4 cm. long; ovary and tube scaly, but without spines or hairs. Fruit green, roundish, 5 to 6 cm. thick, with the dried flower adhering to it; seeds small, dark brown or black, tuberculate. A very lovely species, on account of the emerald green stem and the beautiful colour of the spines. Of easy cultivation and quick growth.

OREOCEREUS Riccobono

Oreocereus or *Mountain Cereus*, was originally established by Riccobono for *O. Celsianus*, formerly included under the old and ill-defined genus *Pilocereus*, on account of the abundant hairy formation of that species. At present the genus *Oreocereus* includes five well-defined species, all natives of the eastern slopes of the Andes from Peru and Bolivia to Chile. They are plants of small or medium height, branching from the base, and often forming large groups. The areoles are large, furnished with long hairs, the flowering areoles being like the others, without a pseudocephalium. Flowers red or dark red, small, diurnal, with a narrow tube. Fruit small, round, scaly but spineless, dry; seeds small, dark or black.

These species require a warm, sunny and airy situation, and a well drained sandy and stony soil, rich in lime, and humus, and should be kept cool and dry in winter. They are very interesting, and no collection should be without them.

Oreocereus Celsianus (Lem). Riccobono=*Pilocereus Celsianus* Lem. Native of the eastern slopes of the Andes, in Peru, Bolivia and northern Chile. Stem erect, or mostly erect, over 1 m. high, branching from the base or a little above ground, 8 to 12 cm. thick, dark green or greyish green, with 9 to 17 rounded ribs, slightly notched, with large oval whitish woolly areoles, 1 to $1\frac{1}{2}$ cm. apart, bearing a cluster of slender, radiating, yellowish brown spines, 2 cm. long, and 1 to 4 longer and thicker central spines. From the areoles at the top, and for some distance down the stem, are developed long silky white hairs, 3 to 4 cm. long, often hiding the spines almost completely. Flowers borne, near the top, 7 to 9 cm. long, brownish red on the outside, paler inside, with the ovary and tube densely covered with hairs and bristles.

A lovely species, perfectly hardy in the Mediterranean region, of easy cultivation, whether grown on own roots or grafted, but of rather slow growth.

(a) var. **Bruennowii** K. Sch. = *Pilocereus Bruennowii* Haage jun. Rather a sub-species, having more slender stems, with 9 to 10 ribs, lively green, densely covered with matted brownish white woolly hairs. Central spines dark yellowish brown, 3 to 4 cm. long.

(b) var. **Williamsii** K. Sch. Stems densely woolly, with long white hairs, and shorter white wool, more or less matted. Spines white or very pale yellow, 1 to $1\frac{1}{2}$ cm. long.

Orecereus fossulatus (Lab.) Backbg. *O. Celsianus* var. *fossulatus* Lab. = *O. Celsianus* var. *faveolatus* Lab. With the preceding species in the Andes of Bolivia and Peru. Now recognized as a distinct species, with taller and stronger stems, of a dark green, with 9 to 14 rounded ribs, more deeply notched. Areoles larger, 2 to 3 cm. apart; spines longer and stouter, with the central and upper spines of a transparent honey yellow colour. Hairs not matted, fewer and longer. Flowers u.s., but larger and of a deeper red. Usually sold grafted on *Trichocereus macrogonus* etc., but grows well on own roots, in a mixture of sand crushed brick, garden loam and old leaf-mould in equal proportions, with some calcareous substance, and placed in full sunshine.

(a) var. **robustior** Hort. Stem thicker, of a darker green and of quicker growth. Areoles larger, often 1½ to 2 cm. long, and farther apart; spines stouter.

(b) var. **pilosior** Hort. Hairs more abundant, but shorter, and sometimes more or less matted around the stem. Top very hairy. Spines of a clearer yellow.

(c) var. **lanuginosior** Hort. Hairs more abundant, woolly, but rather short and more densely matted.

(d) var. **gracilior** Hort. Stem more slender, only 4 to 5 cm. thick, pale green, rarely with more than 9 ribs; areoles closer and smaller, and more woolly; hairs few but long, spines more slender.

(e) var. **spinis-aureis** Hort. Stem rather slender, with 9 to 12 ribs; areoles with few long silky white hairs, and long golden yellow spines.

Oreocereus Trollii (Kupper) = *Pilocereus Trollii* Kupper = *Cereus Trollii* Hort. Andes of Bolivia. A low-growing species, hardly reaching 1 m. in height, unbranched, but throwing up offshoots from the base. Stem 6 to 9 cm. thick, light green, notched, with about 9 ribs, which soon become obliterated, resulting in an almost round stem. Areoles large, oval, about 2 cm. apart, densely furnished with creamy white or light grey wool, which becomes matted around the stem. Spines at first reddish brown or reddish yellow, and afterwards waxy white, the radials about 7, 1½ to 2 cm. long, the centrals 1 to 3, much longer and stouter. Hairs abundantly produced, 3 to 5 cm. long, at first silky and creamy white, afterwards becoming woolly and dirty white, entirely covering the stem. Flowers very like *O. Celsianus*. Often written *Trollei;* synonym = Jrigoyenii.

To this species of comparatively recent introduction, has been given the appropriate name of "Old Man of the Andes." It grows readily from seed and is of easy cultivation.

Oreocereus Hendriksenianus Backbg. = *Pilocereus Hendriksenianus* Hort. This is another wonderful species recently introduced from the Andes of Bolivia and Peru. Differs from *O. Trollii* chiefly on account of its long glossy silky hairs, golden yellow or slightly reddish, passing to whitish. The stem is deep green, about 6 cm. thick, with 9 rounded ribs; areoles large, oval, about 2 cm. apart, with yellowish wool and long golden yellow or slightly reddish hairs 3 to 5 cm. long, turning to brownish or dirty white. Radial spines about 7, up to 2 cm. long, reddish; central spines 1 to 4, reddish passing to reddish brown, up to 5 cm. long. The stem makes rather quick growth, rising to 40 cm. or more, branching from the base or a little above ground.

Oreocereus Doelzianus (Backbg.) = *Morawetzia Doelziana* Backbg. Is another beautiful novelty recently discovered on the eastern slopes of the Andes in northern Peru. Stem erect, branched from the base or a little above ground, forming large groups, up to 1 m. high, 4 to 6 cm. in diameter, olive green to greyish green, with 9 or 10 rounded ribs, less than 1 cm. high, notched into rounded prominences on which are oval or roundish areoles 1½ to 2 cm. apart, with greyish silky hairs, 2 to 4 cm. long, more abundant and slightly longer on the flowering areoles at the top. Radial spines 10 or more, up to 1½ cm. long, needle-like, at first reddish passing to ashy grey. Central spines 4, crosswise, like the radials but stronger, the laterals up to 2 cm. long, the lower 2 to 3 cm. long, and the upper one, directed upwards, up to 4 cm. long. Flowers diurnal arising from a tuft of greyish wool at the top, with greyish hairs when in bud. Flower almost tubular, 4½ to 5 cm. long, usually regular, sometimes with the limb slightly irregular, with a scaly and hairy tube and retuse petals. Outer petals dark red, inner petals crimson red. Stamens many, slightly shorter than the petals, with crimson filaments and yellow anthers. Style as long as the petals, pale pink; stigma greenish with 12 or more lobes, forming a ball. This is evidently a species of Oreocereus, but chiefly on account of the partial irregularity of the limb, in early anthesis, not always present, the genus Morawetzia was created by Backeberg for this species.

STETSONIA Br. et R.

Tree-like, erect, much branched. Branches thick with prominent ribs. Spines strong and numerous. Flowers nocturnal, large, funnel-shaped. Ovary and tube scaly, without hairs or spines. Includes only one species.

Stetsonia coryne (Salm-Dyck) Br. et R. = *Cereus coryne* Salm-Dyck. North-western Argentina. A tree with a short thick stem, and a large crown of stems or branches, 5 to 8 m. high. Stems or branches 9 to 10 cm. thick, pale green passing to greyish green, with 8 or 9 prominent rounded ribs, with a V-shaped furrow above the areoles, which are oval, 1 cm. long, and 1 to 2 cm. apart, brownish. Radial spines 7 to 9, awl-shaped, spreading, up to 3 cm. long, yellowish brown or white when new, later passing to glossy black. Only one central spine, up to 8 cm. long, same colour, very straight. Flowers borne on the sides near the top, 15 cm. long, glossy greenish outside, white inside, with fully expanded and reflexed white petals in one series, somewhat twisted near the tip. Stamens very numerous, erect, greenish white; style thick with pale green stigma with numerous lobes. An attractive species of slow growth, usually grown from seed.

CEREEAE

JASMINOCEREUS Br. et R.

Tree-like, erect, with a much branched crown. Flowers brownish or yellowish, expanded, with a slender tube. Ovary and tube with small scales bearing tufts of whitish wool in their axils. Fruit slightly scaly; seed black, very small. Includes only one species.

Jasminocereus galapagensis (Weber) Br. et R. = *Cereus galapagensis* Weber. Ecuador (Galapagos Islands). Same characters as above. The flowers have a strong Jasmine-like perfume, hence the generic name. Rarely met with in cultivation.

ESCONTRIA Br. et R.

Another monotypic genus, consisting of tree-like plants, much branched. The stem is very short and very thick (up to 40 cm. in diameter), and the branches are up to 20 cm. thick, deep green, with 7 or 8 ribs, prominent, crenate and angled. Areoles elliptical, about 1 cm. long, with short greyish wool. Radial spines 10 to 15, stiff, awl-shaped and straight, spreading, up to 1 cm. long. Central spines 3 to 5, up to 5 cm. long, straight and thick, horny yellowish brown, with a darker tip. Flowers borne along the side, near the top of the stem, funnel-shaped, 3 or 4 cm. long, outer petals brownish yellow. inner petals pale yellow. Ovary covered with many translucent papery persistent scales, without hairs or spines in the axils, the persistent papery scales being characteristic of the genus. Stamens yellow, stigma with 8 to 10 lobes. Fruit round, scaly, brownish red, with violet pulp, edible, 3 cm. in diameter. Seeds black, rough, with flattened hilum. The only species known is:

Escontria chiotilla (Weber) Br. et R. = *Cereus chiotilla* Weber. Native of Mexico. The fruits are sold in Mexico, under the name of *chiotilla*. Until lately it was not known in cultivation, but now seeds are being offered in commerce. Cuttings strike root with difficulty, and is better grown from seed.

CORRYOCACTUS Br. et R.

Plants with the habit of *Trichocereus*. Stem erect, columnar, branching from the base, with prominent and very spiny ribs. Flowers large, broadly funnel-shaped, orange yellow or reddish, with stamens shorter than the petals. Includes three species, natives of South America.

Corryocactus brachypetalus (Vaup.) Br. et R. = *Cereus brachypetalus* Vaupel. South Peru. Plant 2 to 3 m. high, freely branching from the base. Stems 3 to 5 cm. thick, with 7 or 8 ribs, rather low. Areoles woolly, 2 cm. apart. Spines about 20, dark brown almost black, 1 cm. long, a few being up to 1½ cm. Flower broadly funnel-shaped, 4 to 6 cm. broad, deep orange, with broad petals.

Corryocactus brevistylus (K. Sch.) Br. et R. = *Cereus brevistylus* S. Kch. South Peru and North Chile. Same habit as the preceding, 2 to 3 m. high, but stems thicker, 4 to 6 cm. or more. Ribs 6 or 7, very prominent, with areoles 3 cm. apart, densely woolly. Spines about

15, dark brown, up to 2 cm. long. Flower broadly funnel-shaped, 7 to 8 cm. broad, yellow, sweet-scented.

Corryocactus melanotrichus (K. Sch.) Br. et R. = *Cereus melanotrichus* K. Sch. Bolivia, near La Paz. Same habit, 1 to 2 m. high, with more slender stems, with 7 or 8 ribs. Radial spines about 12, yellowish, 1½ cm. long, awl-shaped, about as long as the wool of the areoles. Central spines 1 to 3, straight, same colour, 3 to 5 cm. long. Flowers about 7 cm. broad, funnel-shaped, glossy pink. The areoles along the ribs have also long dark hairs.

PACHYCEREUS Br. et R.

This genus includes erect columnar species, with a definite trunk, branched, and often of majestic proportions, equalling or surpassing in size the celebrated Saguaro or *Carnegiea gigantea* of Arizona. They are all tall-growing species with a thick erect stem, more or less woody, branched at the base or above ground. Several species present a development of white or yellowish or brownish wool and bristles from the areoles on the top or flowering part of the stems, and therefore were included under the old genus *Pilocereus*. Those not having this woolly formation were included in the genus *Cereus*, under which names they are still often catalogued by dealers. The flowers are comparatively small, mostly diurnal, funnel-shaped or almost tubular, with a short tube and short petals. Stamens included. Ovary and tube covered with bracts and hairs or wool, and bristles. Fruit large, spiny. Seeds large and black. Includes ten species.

Pachycereus Pringlei (S. Wats.) Br. et R. = *Cereus Pringlei* S. Wats. Mexico and Lower California, massed in forests of considerable extent. Stems often exceeding 12 m. in height, with a diameter of over 1 m. at the base, branching at 50 cm. to 1 m. above ground, dark green. Ribs 10 to 16, prominent but rounded, closely studded with large oval areoles, with short greyish wool, with numerous spines, thick and stiff, about 3 cm. long, at first reddish to dark brown, afterwards almost ash-coloured, with 1 to 3 stronger and longer central spines. Flowers about 7 cm. long, almost bell-shaped; perianth greenish red outside, white inside. Fruit round, about 7 cm. in diameter, woolly, with yellowish spines or bristles. Prefers a sandy soil and full sunshine. Cuttings root with difficulty, but nice seedlings 20 to 40 cm. long, are frequently imported and sold cheaply.

Pachycereus pecten-aboriginum (Engelm.) Br. et R. = *Cereus pecten-aboriginum* Engelm. Mexico and Lower California. Stem up to 8 m. high, and 25 to 40 cm. in diameter at the base, usually branched at various levels above ground, deep green, with 10 to 12 acute ribs, usually purplish towards the top of the stem, with closely set greyish areoles, each with about 9 thick and stiff radial spines, about 3 cm. long, brownish or greyish, purple when young, and 1 or 2 central spines of about the same length. Flowers 5 to 7 cm. long, funnel-shaped, reddish outside, white inside. Fruit round, about 7 cm. in diameter, woolly, with yellowish spines. The specific name means *natives' comb*, who use or used for this purpose a bit of a rib with the spines on. It is a pretty plant well deserving of cultivation, and seedlings 15 to 30 cm. long, are frequently imported, but of course never grows to the size seen in its native country. Young plants are liable to suffer from a calcification of the base of the stem, and therefore should not be grown in a soil heavily charged with lime. Cuttings strike root with difficulty; growth is rather slow, and a sunny and warm situation is necessary.

Pachycereus chrysomallus (Hemsl.) Br. et R. = *Cereus chrysomallus* Hemsl. = *Pilocereus chrysomallus* Lem. = *Cephalocereus chrysomallus* K. Sch. = *Cereus militaris* Cels. non Salm-Dyck. Mexico. Stem freely branching from the base, 10 to 12 m. high, and 6 to 12 cm. thick, forming large groups, or branched above the base, forming a compact crown with vertical branches, very erect and stiff, light green, with 12 to 15 low ribs, on which are warts with large round or slightly oval areoles well furnished with wool, brownish yellow on new areoles, greyish on older ones. Areoles about 2 cm. apart, with 8 to 10 stiff radial spines up to 2 cm. long, brownish passing to greyish, and 1 to 3 central spines of same colour, about 3 cm. long. The flowering stems develop at the top masses of long wool of a yellowish brown colour, like a helmet, hence the specific name. The flowers are broadly bell-shaped, with a scaly ovary thickly furnished with brownish wool.

Pachycereus columna-trajani (Karw.) Br. et R. = *Pilocereus columna-trajani* Foerst = ? *P. tetetzo* Weber. Mexico (Provinces of Puebla and Oaxaca). A giant columnar species with stems up to 15 m. high, and 40 to 50 cm. in diameter at the base, branching from the ground, but sparingly. The colour is greyish green, with numerous ribs, low and acute. Areoles oval, with brown wool. Radial spines 8 to 10, very stiff and thick, 1 to 2½ cm. long, whitish, tipped dark. Central spines 1 to 3, much stronger and 4 to 5 cm. long, sometimes longer. The new spines, as well as the wool on the growing tops, are pinkish brown. Flowers are freely produced near the tops of aged plants; they are funnel-shaped, 6 cm. long, with a scaly and hairy ovary, reddish green outside, white inside. *Tetetzo* is the name given by the natives to this species and to *Cephalocereus macrocephalus*, both species being very similar when young. Growth is slow.

Pachycereus lepidanthus (Eichl.) Br. et R. = *Cereus lepidanthus* Eichl. Guatemala. Stems tall, slender, dull green, with 7 to 9 straight and low ribs, branching from the base or slightly above ground. Areoles round, large, with white wool, 1½ cm. apart. Radial spines about 10, almost flat on the ribs, 1 to 1½ cm. long, at first red tipped dark, passing to yellow and finally greyish. Central spines 1 to 3, on the upper part of the areole, 3 to 5 cm. long, angular, often thickened at the base, same colour as the radials but thicker. Flowers borne on the upper areoles, 7 cm. long, 2½ cm. across, with many thick fleshy scales on the tube, woolly in their axils. Petals in 3 series, fiery red, edged paler, and with a darker midrib. Stamens pale yellow, very numerous; style pink below and yellowish white above, stigma with 8 pale yellow lobes.

Pachycereus Orcuttii (K. Brand.) Br. et R. = *Cereus Orcuttii* K. Brandegee. Lower California. Stem erect and columnar, up to 3 m. high, and 15 cm. thick, with a woody core, branched, glossy green. Areoles round, 3 cm. apart, with short ashy grey wool. Radial spines 12 to 20, spreading, yellowish brown, the lower ones being twice as long as the upper, up to 7 cm. long. Central spines about 5, same colour, spreading, 7 cm. long or slightly longer. Flower 4 cm. long, lasting two days. Ovary thickly covered with short scales, with yellowish wool in their axils, and with 1 or more short bristles. Petals greenish brown, acute.

Other interesting species, rarely grown are: **Pachycereus grandis** (Haw.) Rose, and **P. ruficeps** (Weber) Br. et R., both from Mexico.

DENDROCEREUS Br. et R.

Created by Britton and Rose to include only one species **Dendrocereus nudiflorus** (Engelm.) Br. et R. = *Cereus nudiflorus* Engelm., native of Cuba. Tree-like in habit with a thick trunk, and many branches, upright or straggling. Branches or young stems with 3 to 5 ribs, prominent and acute. Areoles with many long spines. Flowers nocturnal, the withered flower dropping off from the ovary very shortly after fertilization. Petals white, shorter than the stamens. Ovary and tube with short spines. Fruit oval, greenish, smooth, with a very thick rind. Seeds brown, tuberculate. Rarely met with in cultivation, and is an essentially tropical species.

MACHAEROCEREUS Br. et R.

Plants bushy or prostrate, with thick stems, many-ribbed; ribs low and very spiny. Central spine flattened, stiff, dagger-like and very sharp (hence the generic name), directed downwards. Flowers tubular or funnel-shaped, diurnal. Ovary and lower part of tube furnished with many small scales and wool. Fruit round, with the dried flower persisting upon it, spiny, with red edible pulp. Seeds black. Includes two species.

Machaerocereus eruca (Brandegee) Br. et R. = *Cereus eruca* Brandegee. Lower California, on sandy beaches along the coast. Stem thick, 1 to 3 m. long, and 4 to 8 cm. thick, prostrate and creeping, like a huge caterpillar (*eruca* = caterpillar), rooting, with an ascending top, very spiny, sparingly branching. Ribs about 12, with large areoles 2 cm. apart. Spines about 20, greyish or whitish, the outer row awl-shaped and short, the inner row stronger. One central spine up to $3\frac{1}{2}$ cm. long, flattened, dagger-like, directed backwards, milky white. Flower 10 to 12 cm. long and 4 to 6 cm. broad, yellow or creamy yellow. Fruit 4 cm. long, spiny when young, losing the spines on maturing. A plant of uncouth and menacing aspect, but very interesting, and now frequently imported. Requires a sandy soil and a sunny situation. Cuttings strike root readily.

PLATE XVI

(b) TRICHOCEREUS CANDICANS

(a) HELIOCEREUS SPECIOSUS

PLATE XVII

CEREEAE

Machaerocereus gummosus (Engelm.) Br. et R. = *Cereus gummosus* Engelm. Lower California and adjoining islands. Stem erect, about 1 m. high and 4 to 6 cm. thick, sometimes branching from the ground, dark green or greyish green, with 8 ribs (rarely 9), obtuse and warty, with areoles 2 cm. apart. Radial spines 8 to 12, up to 1 cm. long; central spines 4 to 6, flattened, whitish, the lower one up to 4 cm. long, directed downwards. Flower 10 to 14 cm. long, purplish red, with a long narrow tube, the lower part of which, as well as the ovary, are furnished with many small scales, woolly and spiny. Fruit round, scarlet red, 6 to 8 cm. in diameter, spiny, with a red and acid pulp, but edible. The spines on the upper part of the stem are brown or almost black, lower down they are greyish or white.

BRACHYCEREUS Br. et R.

A monotypic genus established to include a rather aberrant species, **Brachycereus Thouarsii** (Weber) Br. et R. = *Cereus Thouarsii* Weber, native of the Galapagos Islands. Plant rather low, with regular erect branches, 3 to 5 cm. thick, with numerous low ribs and closely set areoles, each bearing a cushion of wool and small slender spines, not unlike *Binghamia multangularis*. Flowers yellow or yellowish, with a narrow tube and funnel-shaped limb, the segments of the perianth being longer than the stamens. Fruit spiny when young, later losing the spines, reddish violet when ripe, not unlike a large plum, with a white juicy pulp, somewhat acid, but edible. Seeds small, black.

LEPTOCEREUS Br. et R.

Plants shrubby or creeping. Stem with 3 to 8 ribs, acute and wavy, with needle-like spines. Flowers diurnal, small, campanulate. Fruit globular, spiny.

Eight species are included in this genus, natives of the West Indies, mainly of botanical interest, and therefore rarely met with in cultivation.

Leptocereus assurgens (C. Wright, Griseb.) Br. et R. = *Cereus assurgens* C. Wright. Cuba. A shrub 2 to 3 m. high. Stems about 3 cm. thick, with 4 very acute ribs or angles. Areoles brownish, 1 to 2½ cm. apart. Spines stiff, needle-like, brown, 2 to 8 cm. long. Flower 4 to 5 cm. long, bell-shaped, about 2½ cm. broad, pale red.

Leptocereus Weingartianus (Hartm.) Br. et R. = *Cereus Weingartianus* Hartm. Haiti. Plant tuberous-rooted; stems prostrate and creeping, 8 to 10 m. long, and 1 to 2 cm. thick, with 4 to 7 acute ribs. Spines yellowish brown, passing to greyish: radials about 12, spreading; centrals about 6, thickened at the base, 1 to 1½ cm. long. Flower bell-shaped, 4 cm. long, pale pink.

Leptocereus quadricostatus (Bello) Br. et R. = *Cereus quadricostatus* Bello. Porto Rico. A bushy dark green plant, much branched, with brownish wool at the top of the stems. Ribs 4, very acute, about 2 cm. high, wavy, the stems being 5 to 6 cm. thick. Areoles 1 to 3 cm. apart; brownish and woolly. Spines about 8 or 9, stiff, brown; the radials

L

about 7, up to 2 cm. long, one central spine somewhat longer and thicker. Flower 4 cm. long, bell-shaped, red, with a scaly woolly and spiny tube.

Leptocereus Maxonii Br. et R. Cuba. Stems 1 to 1½ m. high, branched, erect, or with recurved branches, with 5 to 7 thin ribs (mostly 6), concave. Areoles 1½ to 2 cm. apart. Spines about 20, needle-like, up to 3 cm. long, yellowish brown, passing to dark brown or whitish. Flowers 3 to 6 cm. long, bell-shaped, yellowish green; ovary densely covered with scales and yellowish spines.

Other West Indian species, all Cuban, belonging to this genus are: **Leptocereus arboreus** (Vaup.) Br. et R., **L. leonii** (Vaup.) Br. et R., **L. prostratus** Br. et R., and **L. Sylvestris** Br. et R.

EULYCHNIA R. A. Philippi

Shrubs with thick ascending stems, many-ribbed, very spiny. Flowers rather small, broadly bell-shaped, diurnal, white or pink. Ovary scaly. Fruit acid. Includes four species.

Eulychnia spinibarbis (Otto) Br. et R. = *Cereus spinibarbis* Otto. Chile. Often confused with *Trichocereus coquimbanus* K. Sch. = *Cereus nigripilis* Philippi. A shrub up to 4 m. high. Stems thick, with 12 to 13 ribs, narrow but prominent. Spines numerous and stiff, the radials up to 5 cm. long; the centrals up to 15 cm. long. The flowers are 5 to 6 cm. long, and about as broad, with a very short woolly tube and white petals, and a stigma with 24 long lobes. Fruit acid, round and woolly.

Eulychnia acida Philippi = *Cereus acidus* K. Sch. Chile. A tall-growing shrub, with thick stems with about 12 rounded ribs. Areoles 3 to 4 cm. apart, brown. Spines many and very long; the radials 3 to 5 cm. long, spreading; the centrals 1 to 4, up to 20 cm. long, very stiff, brown passing to greyish. Flowers as above, with pink petals. Fruit globular, woolly, greenish yellow, very juicy and sprightly acid.

Eulychnia castanea R. A. Philippi = *Cereus castaneus* K. Sch. Chile. A branched shrub, hanging down from the rocks on its native hills. Stems 5½ cm. thick with 9 ribs. Areoles with yellowish or greyish wool. Radial spines short, awl-shaped, unequal, up to 2 cm. long: one central spine up to 7 cm. long, brown. Flowers borne along the sides, about 4 cm. long, with a very short tube and 4 cm. across, white, petals acute. Ovary covered with dark brown spines, about 1 cm. long, and short reddish brown hairs, giving to the fruit the aspect of a chestnut.

Eulychnia iquiquensis (K. Sch.) Br. et R. = *Cereus iquiquensis* K. Sch. Chile (Iquique). Stem short, branching from the base, with erect or spreading branches, 2 to 7 m. high. Ribs 12 to 15, rounded, warty, with narrow furrows between them. Areoles closely set, with short white wool. Spines 12 to 15, some of them only about 1 cm. long, but 1 or 2 are up to 12 cm. long, very thick, directed outwards. Spines on flowering branches very numerous, but soft and hair-like or bristle-like. Flowers borne at the top, 6 to 7 cm. long, including the ovary which is covered with long silky white hairs. Petals short, white. Fruit round, 5 to 6 cm. thick, hairy, acid.

CEREEAE

LEMAIREOCEREUS Br. et R.

Plants mostly tall, with erect stems, branching from the base, sometimes also above ground. Areoles large, mostly with stout spines. Flowers mostly diurnal, small, sometimes fairly large, bell-shaped, or funnel-shaped, with short petals. Ovary and tube scaly and hairy, the areoles on the round fruit being well furnished with wool and with rather strong spines, which gradually fall off at maturity. Seeds black. Includes 23 species, most of which are of real ornamental value and are grown extensively.

Lemaireocereus Hollianus (Weber) Br. et R. = *Cereus Hollianus* Weber = *C. bavosus* Weber = *C. brachiatus* Gal. Mexico (Puebla). Stem columnar, 4 to 5 m. high, freely branching from the base, but with few branches above ground, greyish green, 5 to 6 cm. thick, with 8 to 10 angular ribs about ½ cm. high. Areoles 1 to 3 cm. apart, smallish, with white short hairs or wool, later passing to greyish. Radial spines 12, spreading, awl-shaped and very slender, up to 2 cm. long. Central spines 3 or 4, up to 10 cm. long, but remaining flexible. All spines are red at first, soon passing to black or grey. Flowers about 10 cm. long, white, borne at the top of the stems. Fruit oval, 8 to 9 cm. long, dark purple or red. Seeds glossy black. The native name is *baboso*, probably due to its foamy appearance.

Lemaireocereus Aragonii (Weber) Br. et R. = *Cereus Argonii* Weber. Costa Rica. A tall-growing species forming large clumps, often planted for hedges in its native country. Stems 3 to 6 m. high, freely branching from the base and above ground, branches very erect, dark green, about 12 cm. thick, with greyish stripes on new growth. Ribs 6 to 8, prominent, rounded, 3 cm. deep. Areoles large, 2 cm. apart at first with short brownish wool, passing to white. Spines greyish, at first about 8, afterwards very numerous, about 1 cm. long, and one stout central spine of the same colour, 2 to 3 cm. long. Flower 6 to 8 cm. long, funnel-shaped, reddish green outside, white inside. Ovary warty and spiny. Seeds large, glossy black.

Lemaireocereus laevigatus (Salm-Dyck) = *Cereus laevigatus* Salm-Dyck = *Lemaireocereus Eichlamii* Br. et A. Mexico. Columnar, erect, slightly branched, pale green, with about 10 straight rounded ribs, with narrow furrows between them. Areoles 1½ to 2 cm. apart, with greyish white wool, later bare. Radial spines 5, greyish white tipped black, 1 to 1½ cm. long, needle-like, the upper ones longer. One central spine, same colour, slightly thicker and longer. Flower 7 cm. long, 5 cm. broad, with toothed petals, outer petals pink. Ovary warty, with small scales and brownish hairs; tube with reddish green scales. Style white, stigma with pale pink lobes. Fruit large.

var **guatemalensis** Eichl. Guatemala. Stem grass green, very glossy when young.

Lemaireocereus pruinosus (Otto) Br. et R. = *Cereus pruinosus* Otto = *C. edulis* Weber. Central Mexico. A columnar species with few offshoots. Stem 10 to 12 cm. thick, dull green, bluish at the top, with 5 or 6 deep ribs, acute and with prominent knobs on which are situated the large areoles, which are 1 to 3 cm. apart, brownish or greyish. Radial spines 8 or 9, 1 to 2 cm. long, spreading, awl-shaped, at first reddish, afterwards passing to almost black, later becoming greyish with a dark point. Central spines 1 to 4, 3 to 4 cm. long, stronger and of the same colour. Flower funnel-shaped, about 9 cm. long, brownish green outside, white inside. The fruit is sold in the markets of Mexico. Grows well from seed, producing nice thick-stemmed plants in about 3 years.

Lemaireocereus griseus (Haw.) Br. et R. = *Cereus griseus* Haw. = *C. eburneus* Salm-Dyck. South America, Chile. A tall-growing, columnar species, branching from the base and above ground. Stem about 10 cm. thick, of a beautiful powdery grey, with 7 or 8 ribs, very prominent but obtuse, 3½ cm. deep. Areoles rather small, oval, on prominences along the ribs, 2 to 3 cm. apart, brownish or greyish. Radial spines about 10, about 1 cm. long, awl-shaped, greyish, dark tipped, the lower half reddish when young. Central spines 1 to 3, up to 2 cm. long, same colour. Flower 9 cm. long, with a scaly and spiny ovary and tube, yellowish green outside, white shaded pink inside. A pretty species, particularly when young. The large reddish fruit is eatable. Grown for its fruit.

Lemaireocereus chende (Goss.) Br. et R. = *Cereus chende* Gosselin = *C. del Moralii* Purpus. Mexico (Puebla and Oaxaca). A tall-growing species, freely branching, 4 to 5 m. high. Stems deep green, 6 to 10 cm. thick, with 7 to 9 ribs at first acute, afterwards rounded. Areoles 2 cm. apart. Radial spines up to 6, often only 1, greyish, 1 to 2½ cm. long; only one central spine, about as long or longer. Flowers small, 4 to 5 cm. long, funnel-shaped, outer petals very acute, pink with darker midrib, inner petals white with pale pink midrib. Ovary oval, scaly and furnished with brownish hairs. Fruit red, very spiny. A free-growing species, easily raised from seed. *Chende* is the native name.

Lemaireocereus chichipe (Goss.) Br. et R. = *Cereus chichipe* Gosselin = *C. mixtecensis* Purpus. Mexico (along with the preceding species). Freely branching from the base, 4 to 5 m. high. Stems 5 to 7 cm. thick, light green, with 11 or 12 acute ribs, 2 cm. deep. Areoles 1½ cm. apart. Radial spines 6 or 7, greyish, almost crimson red when young, ½ to 1 cm. long. One central spine, about 1½ cm. long. Flower very small, about 3 cm. long, funnel-shaped, outer petals striped brownish red, inner petals greenish yellow with reddish midrib. Young seedlings are thickly covered with a white powdery bloom. Growth rather slow. *Chichipe* is the local name.

Lemaireocereus stellatus (Pfeiff.) Br. et R. = *Cereus stellatus* Pfeiff. = *C. Dyckii* Mart. South Mexico. The fruit is sold in the markets of Mexico under the name of *Joconostle*, and is much relished. Stem columnar 1 to 3 m. high, branching from the base, dark dull green, 6 to 9 cm. thick, with at least 7 ribs, but generally 9 to 12, obtuse, low and rounded, notched. Areoles large, with whitish wool, and a V-shaped furrow above them. Radial spines 8 to 12, spreading star-like and recurved, up to 12 mm. long; central spines 4 or 5, up to 2½ cm. long. All spines are at first dark brown or black, afterwards ash-coloured. Flowers 5 to 6 cm. long, borne at the top of the stems, pale pink or pink, lasting for 2 or 3 days. A pretty species of easy growth.

Lemaireocereus Thurberi (Engelm.) Br. et R. = *Cereus Thurberi* Engelm. Arizona, Mexico and Lower California. Stem columnar, erect, 3 to 7 m. high, up to 15 cm. thick, branching from the base, dark green shaded purplish, afterwards greyish green, with 12 to 17 prominent and angular ribs, 1 to 2 cm. deep, bearing large black or dark brown areoles, 1 to 2 cm. apart, later passing to greyish brown. Spines at first glossy black, passing to brown and grey: the radials 7 to 9, about 1 cm. long, spreading and straight; centrals 1 to 3, thicker and 2 to 5 cm. long. Flowers borne at the tops, about 7 cm. long, funnel-shaped; ovary with small scales, and white and brown hairs, tube with green scales. Outer petals obtuse and reddish, inner petals pink with whitish margin. A very ornamental species, rather slow-growing. The fruit is edible.

var. **littoralis** K. Brand. Lower California, on sandy beaches. Plant more freely branching from the base. Stems more slender and tortuous.

Lemaireocereus deficiens (Otto) Br. et R. = *Cereus deficiens* Otto = *C. clavatus* Otto. Venezuela, where it is often planted for hedges. Columnar, erect, branching at the base, greyish green, 2 to 3 m. high, and 6 to 8 cm. thick. Ribs 7 to 9, broad and obtuse, notched, with large brownish or whitish areoles in the depressions, 2 to 3 cm. apart. Radial spines 7 or 8, 1 to 1½ cm. long; central spines 1 to 3, up to 3 cm. long. All spines are straight and slender, at first yellow, soon turning to brownish white with a dark point. Flower 5 to 6 cm. long, reddish externally, white internally. An attractive fast-growing species, requiring a sandy soil and full sunshine. Young seedlings are bluish green, very glaucous and mealy.

Lemaireocereus Weberi (Coult.) Br. et R. = *Cereus Weberi* Coult. = *C. candelabrum* Weber. Mexico (Puebla and Oaxaca). Stem columnar, very stiff, up to 10 m. high, with few offshoots from the base, but richly branched like a chandelier, about 10 cm. thick, dark glaucous green, almost bluish, with 8 to 10 prominent and obtuse ribs. Areoles large, elongated, 3 to 5 cm. apart, with short white wool. Radial spines about 9, depressed, 2 to 3 cm. long, yellowish white, passing to reddish and then to dark brown almost black, with a greyish central spine 5 to 7 cm. long, directed downwards. Flowers about 10 cm. long, white. Fruit large, round, about 6 cm. thick, covered with small scales with wool and spines in their axils.

Lemaireocereus marginatus (DC.) Berger = *Cereus marginatus* DC. = *C. gemmatus* Zucc. = *Pachycereus marginatus* Br. et R. Central and southern Mexico, where it is often planted in hedges. Stem columnar, erect and stiff, 3 to 7 m. high, branching from the base, and often also above ground, dark green or greyish green, 8 to 15 cm. thick, with 5 or 6 high broad and acute ribs. Areoles elongated, very close together, almost continuous or coalescing, with very short brown or greyish wool. Spines thick, awl-shaped, about 2 cm. long, 7 radials and 1 or 2 centrals, straight, at first reddish, soon passing to brown, the central up to $1\frac{1}{2}$ cm. long. Flowers almost bell-shaped, 4 to 5 cm. long, borne at the top of the stem, about 3 cm. broad, reddish externally, greenish white internally. This is a beautiful and fast-growing species. Requires full sunshine and warmth.

The form **gemmatus** (DC.) Zucc., is a smaller plant, $\frac{1}{2}$ to 1 m. high, with fewer offshoots, and with ribs very closely studded with oval white areoles, with hardly any spines.

The form **incrustatus** DC., is about the same size, but with oval areoles about $\frac{1}{2}$ cm. long, almost without wool, but furnished with spines, and especially with a long central spine, up to 2 cm. long. The form **gibbosus** Zucc. is also smaller, with an uneven stem more or less notched.

Lemaireocereus Cartwrightianus Br. et R. = *Armatocereus Cartwrightianus* Backbg. Ecuador and Peru. Stem 3 to 5 m. high, woody, much branched. Branches 8 to 15 cm. thick, 15 to 60 cm. long, with 7 or 8 ribs. Areoles large, brownish. Spines about 20, 1 to 2 cm. long, white, brown or black, on old stems up to 12 cm. long. Flower 7 to 8 cm. long, outer petals erect and reddish, inner petals small, white. Fruit round or oblong, 8 to 9 cm. long, red, with white pulp, spiny, but spineless at maturity. Makes fast growth, thrives better in half-shade.

Lemaireocereus Godingianus Br. et R. = *Armatocereus Godingianus* Backbg. Ecuador (Huigra). Tree-like, 3 to 10 m. high, with a woody trunk, much branched. Branches jointed, 6 to 9 cm. thick, bright green passing to greyish, with 7 to 11 ribs. Areoles small, with many needle-like spines 2 to 4 cm. long, brown passing to greyish. Flowers about 11 cm. long, white, with a fleshy tube 2 cm. long. Areoles on ovary and tube thickly set, with brown wool and yellow bristles; fruit oblong, 10 cm. long, with many yellow spines. Rare in cultivation.

Lemaireocereus Dumortieri (Salm-Dyck) Br. et R. = *Cereus Dumortieri* Salm-Dyck. Central Mexico, in the torrid valleys, along with *Cephalocereus senilis*. Stem columnar, or sometimes decumbent, 6 to 10 m. high, with numerous offshoots, 5 to $7\frac{1}{2}$ cm. thick, pale green or yellowish green. Ribs 5 or 6, very prominent and acute, about 2 cm. deep. Areoles about $\frac{1}{2}$ cm. apart, almost continuous, oval, yellowish. Radial spines 9 to 11, spreading, very slender, needle-like, yellowish white, about 1 cm. long; central spines 1 to 4, up to 3 cm. long, same colour, the lowermost directed upwards. Flowers borne along the sides, 5 cm. long, funnel-shaped. Ovary and tube scaly, hairy and furnished with bristles; the outer petals brownish red, the inner white. A beautiful and free-growing species, requiring warmth and full sunshine.

Lemaireocereus Beneckei (Ehrenb.) Berger = *Cereus Beneckei* Ehrenb. = *C. farinosus* Haage Jr. Central Mexico, on old lava formations. An erect, columnar species, 2 to 3 m. high. Stem 6 to 9 cm. thick, mostly unbranched and with few offshoots, entirely covered with a thick waxy white powdery bloom, more abundant at the top. Ribs 5 to 9, very obtuse, notched into knobs or warts on the growing tops. Areoles 2 to 5 cm. apart, round, at first white, passing to brownish, with about 5 stiff radial spines, up to 4 cm. long, at first blood red, soon passing to horny grey, and with one central spine of the same colour, and about as long, directed downwards. Flowers borne on the upper areoles, small, funnel-shaped, 4 cm. long, brownish outside, whitish inside. Ovary and tube furnished with scales, a few hairs and small yellowish bristles. A very beautiful and desirable species, rather free-growing and still rare in collections. Somewhat difficult to grow on own roots, requiring a soil rich in humus and very sandy and porous, much warmth and full sunshine, but thrives also well in half-shade. It is best grown grafted on *Harrisia Jusbertii*.

Lemaireocereus laetus (H.B.K.) Backbg. = *Cactus laetus* H.B.K. = *Cereus laetus* DC. = *Armatocereus laetus* Backbg. South Ecuador to central Peru. Tree-like, 4 to 5 m. high, with erect, columnar stems, freely branching from the base or a little above ground, bluish grey, markedly jointed, that is, with pronounced constrictions showing the growths of successive seasons. Ribs 4 to 8, broad and deep. Areoles 2 to 3 cm. apart. Spines 1 to 3, awl-shaped, sometimes up to 8 cm. long, at first brown, passing to grey. Flowers 7 to 8 cm. long, white, borne at or near the tops.

Lemaireocereus chlorocarpus (H.B.K.) Backbg. = *Cactus chlorocarpus* H.B.K. = *Cereus chlorocarpus* DC. = *Gymnanthocereus chlorocarpus* Backbg. Ecuador to North Peru. Tree-like 3 to 3½ m. high, branched above ground, dull green with minute dots. Ribs 9 or 10, about 2 cm. high, with narrow furrows between them. Areoles woolly, 2 cm. apart, the upper areoles often with a few hair-like pale yellow bristles. Radial spines about 9, up to 1 cm. long, straight, needle-like, grey. Central spines 3 or 4, sometimes only 1, up to 5 cm. long, awl-shaped, stiff, straight, same colour. Fruit green, with spinescent bristles.

Lemaireocereus Treleasei Br. et R. Mexico. Stem more or less erect and columnar, but often rather weak and sprawling, rarely branched, but throwing up offshoots from the base, glossy dark green, 4 to 6 cm. thick, with 8 or 9 ribs about 1 cm. high, obtuse and with narrow furrows between them. Areoles 1 to 1½ cm. apart, round, white. Radial spines 8 to 10, spreading star-like, slender, white with yellowish tip, the lower ones up to 1½ cm. long. Central spines 1 or 2, stouter and longer, up to 3 cm., ashy grey, yellow or horny tipped. Flowers pinkish, 4 to 5 cm. long; scales on ovary and tube with whitish bristles in their axils. Fruit red, 5 cm. thick, spineless at maturity: seeds dull black, rugose. Of easy cultivation, and of quick growth from seed.

CACTI

Lemaireocereus queretaroensis (Weber) Br. et R. = *Cereus quere-*
taroensis Weber. Mexico (Queretaro). Tree-like, about 6 m. high,
usually with a solitary trunk, 35 cm. thick and about 1 m. high, bearing
a much-branched crown 4 to 5 m. in diameter. Young stems and
branches dark glossy green, shaded violet or purplish like *L. Thurberi*,
with 6 or 7 ribs having narrow furrows between them, later more shallow
and almost cylindrical. Areoles about 2 cm. apart, depressed, with
dark brown wool. Radial spines 6 to 9, the lower ones up to 3 cm.
long, stout and awl-shaped, dark brown. Central spines 2 to 4,
stronger, up to 4 cm. long. Flowers borne freely at the top of the
branches, 10 to 12 cm. long. Ovary and tube with acute scales, with
wool and small spines in their axils. Perianth funnel-shaped, pale red.
Fruit a yellow or red berry, 2½ to 3 cm. long, spiny.

Other species, rare in cultivation, are the following: **Lemaireocereus
longispinus** Br. et R. from Guatemala, **L. hystrix** (Haw.) Br. et R. from
the West Indies and **L. montanus** Br. et R. from Mexico.

L. Mieckleyanus Weingt. = *Cereus Mieckleyanus* Weingt. is only
a rare monstrous form of *Lophocereus Schottii*, found in Sonora
(Mexico).

ERDISIA Br. et R.

Like *Eulychnia*, this is a genus of uncertain standing, and includes
only four species, natives of Peru and Chile. They are bushy plants,
with erect stems or branches, slender and much branched, many of the
stems being subterranean, as is the case with many species of *Echinocereus*. The ribs are few, bearing depressed areoles, well furnished with
spines. Flowers small, broadly campanulate; stamens much shorter
than the petals. Ovary warty, scaly and spiny. Fruit small, round,
spiny, with minute seeds. Rarely met with in cultivation.

Erdisia squarrosa (Vaup.) Br. et R. = *Cereus squarrosus* Vaupel.
Peru. This is the largest species with stems or branches 1 to 2 m. long,
1 to 3 cm. thick, with 5 to 8 ribs. Spines about 15, unequal, yellowish,
up to 4 cm. long. Flowers borne at the tip of the branches, about 4 cm.
long, and about as broad, pink to bright red. Fruit covered with
minute scales and areoles, with whitish wool and short spines.
E. Philippii (Regel et Schm.) Br. et R. = *Cereus Philippii* Reg. et Schm.
from Chile, is similar, but has shorter stems and branches, and more
slender. The flower is yellow, and the stamens are united in a tube.
E. Meyenii Br. et R. from Northern Chile (Arequipa) and **E. spiniflora**
(Philippi) Br. et R. from Chile (Santiago) have underground spineless
stems and clavate aerial branches, furnished with slender spines. This
last has purple flowers, the other has yellow flowers.

BERGEROCACTUS Br. et R.

Flowers small, yellow, fully expanded or rotate, with a very short
tube. Ovary with small scales, woolly and spiny. Includes only one
species.

CEREEAE

Bergerocactus Emoryi (Engelm.) Br. et R. = *Cereus Emoryi* Engelm. = *Echinocereus Emoryi* Rümpl. South California and Lower California. A bushy plant, low and spreading, with stems 3 to 6 cm. thick, and 20 to 60 cm. long, erect, or semi-prostrate, or ascending, freely suckering like an *Echinocereus*, pale green, with 15 to 25 low ribs, slightly warty, bearing areoles less than 1 cm. apart, with 10 to 30 golden yellow or yellowish brown, needle-like spines, the central spines (1 to 4) being longer and thicker and up to 4 cm. long. The flower is borne at the top of the stems, and is about 2 cm. broad, yellow, the ovary and very short tube being covered with minute scales, bearing wool and spines in their axils. Fruit round, 3 cm. thick, very spiny. Thrives well in a sunny situation, warm and rather dry. A sandy and light soil is the best. This is an aberrant species of uncertain connections, but very interesting and attractive.

LEOCEREUS Br. et R.

Bushy branched plants, less than 1 m. high. Stems slender, erect or decumbent, with numerous low ribs. Areoles very closely set, with spines, but not woolly. Flowers small, with a rather short tube. Ovary and tube thickly covered with scales, with long hairs and bristles in their axils. Fruit round, small; seeds black, dotted or tuberculate.

This small genus is closely related in habit, and also in its flowers, to the genus *Nyctocereus*, and includes four species natives of Brazil.

Leocereus melanurus (K. Sch.) Br. et R. = *Cereus melanurus* K. Sch. Brazil (Minas Geraes). Stems erect or ascending, cylindrical, 40 to 50 cm. long, and 3 cm. or more in thickness, mostly branching from the base, with 12 to 16 straight ribs, rounded, with deep narrow furrows between them. Areoles about $\frac{1}{2}$ cm. apart, round, whitish, passing to yellowish brown. Spines slender, about 20, ranging from 2 mm. to 5 cm. in length, these last being dark brown or black and spreading. Flowers borne near the top, 6 to 7 cm. long, funnel-shaped, white, outer petals linear-acute and greenish, the inner broader and obtuse. Ovary and short tube scaly and hairy. Fruit globular, 2 to 3 cm. thick, covered with brown wool, with the withered flower remaining attached. Seeds dark brown, tuberculate.

Leocereus Glaziovii (K. Sch.) Br. et R. = *Cereus Glaziovii* K. Sch. Brazil (Minas Geraes). Similar to the preceding in habit. Stems more slender ($1\frac{1}{2}$ to 2 cm. thick), with 12 straight, rounded ribs. Areoles small, elliptical, closely set. Spines more numerous (20 to 30) slender, dark brown, straight or curved, mostly less than $\frac{1}{2}$ cm. long, 1 to 3 being up to $2\frac{1}{2}$ cm. long. Flowers borne near the top of the stems, $7\frac{1}{2}$ to 8 cm. long, funnel-shaped, white, outer petals linear acuminate and greenish, the inner longer, lanceolate acute. Ovary and tube with small fleshy scales and wool. Fruit oval, pointed, 2 cm. long, and $\frac{1}{2}$ cm. thick, at first warty, smooth when ripe and without the remains of the withered flower. Seeds dark brown, minutely tuberculate.

169

CACTI

Leocereus bahiensis Br. et R. Brazil (Bahia). Stem erect or ascending, slightly branched, up to 2 m. long, 1 to 1½ cm. thick, with 12 to 14 low ribs. Areoles round, whitish, closely set. Spines very numerous, spreading, needle-like, yellow, very short, the spines in the middle of the areole being much longer, up to 3 cm. Flowers about 4 cm. long. Ovary and tube scaly, with wool and bristles, outer petals greenish, the inner white. Fruit about 1 cm. thick.

Leocereus paulensis Speg. Brazil (State of Sao Paulo). Stem erect mostly solitary, up to 1 m. high, 2 to 3 cm. thick, with 13 to 15 ribs, about ½ cm. deep. Areoles closely set, about ½ cm. apart, dirty white or greyish. Radial spines about 11, greyish yellow, bristle-like: one central spine, up to 3½ cm. long, mostly curved upwards. Flowers at the top of the stem, 6 to 7 cm. long. Ovary and tube scaly, with long greyish wool and bristles in the axils of the scales. Inner petals purplish violet, with white stamens and purple anthers. Stigma with 11 or 12 whitish or pinkish lobes.

WILCOXIA Br. et R.

Plants with tuberous roots, and with slender and weak stems, with few and low ribs. Flowers diurnal, comparatively large, funnel-shaped or bell-shaped, red or purple, with the ovary and tube densely covered with bristles and hairs. Seeds black, with a prominent aril. Includes 5 species, natives of Texas, Mexico and California.

Wilcoxia Poselgeri (Lem.) Br. et R. = *Echinocereus Poselgeri* Lem. = *Cereus Poselgeri* Coult. = *C. tuberosus* Poselg. = *Echinocereus tuberosus* Rümpl. Southern Texas and Mexico (Coahuila). Roots thickened, tuber-like, 5 to 8, each 1½ to 7 cm. long, and 2 or 3 cm. thick. Stems 30 to 60 cm. long, 1 to 1½ cm. thick, cylindrical, dark green, with 8 low ribs; areoles very close together, very small, woolly. Radial spines whitish or greyish, applied to the stem star-like, slender, hair-like, only about 2 mm. long; one central spine, straight directed upwards, thickened at the base, about ½ cm. long, white or grey or black. Flowers 4 to 5 cm. long, borne near the top of the stems or on the sides, lasting in bloom for 4 or 5 days, funnel-shaped, pink, with reddish scales as well as bristles and whitish hairs on the ovary and tube, the inner petals being narrow, pointed, toothed, with a darker pink midrib. Stamens pink; stigma with 8 green lobes. Fruit oval, green.

Wilcoxia Schmollii Weingt. Mexico. Often catalogued as *Echinocereus tuberosus senilis* Hort. A new species differing from the preceding on account of its shorter and usually thicker stems, more profusely branched, with 8 to 10 low ribs, entirely hidden under a mass of whitish or greyish hairs, silky and spreading, ½ to 1½ cm. long. Spines as in the preceding species. Flowers also as in the preceding, purplish red or violet red, with the ovary and tube densely covered with the same silky hairs, as well as with scales and bristles, the outer petals being greenish purple with a darker midrib.

Wilcoxia viperina (Weber) Br. et R. = *Cereus viperinus* Weber. Mexico. Stems long and trailing, 1 to 3 m. long, very uniformly cylindrical and smooth, 8 mm. to 1½ cm. thick, covered with short and applied hairs, giving to the stems a reddish brown appearance. Ribs 8, low, with very closely set areoles, each with about 8 very short applied spines. Flower red, 3 to 5 cm. long; ovary with numerous dark brown or black short spines.

Wilcoxia striata (Brand.) Br. et R. = *Cereus striatus* Brand. = *C. Diguetii* Weber. Lower California and adjoining islands. Stem about 1 m. long, very slender, only about ½ cm. thick, rarely up to 8 mm. thick, sprawling, new stems being bluish green, soon passing to greyish, with 8 or 9 very low ribs, with straight narrow furrows between them, giving to the stem a striated appearance. Areoles ½ to 1 cm. apart, with 9 or 10 very short and slender spines, applied to the stem, brown or black. Flowers borne along the sides of the new stems, about 10 cm. long, purplish red; ovary and tube with long wool and bristle-like spines. Fruit 3 to 4 cm. long, red, with red pulp. Grows on the sand dunes of the coast, and has parsnip-like tuberous roots, up to 40 cm. long.

Wilcoxia papillosa Br. et R. Mexico (Sinaloa). Not to be confused with *Echinocereus papillosus* A. Linke, native of Texas. Stems slender, with few branches, 30 to 50 cm. long, up to ½ cm. thick. Areoles small, with white wool, 1 to 3 cm. apart. Spines in clusters of 6 to 8, 1 to 3 mm. long, yellowish brown. Flowers scarlet, 4 to 5 cm. long. Ovary and tube with small scales, those on the top of the tube woolly and with several brown bristles. Root parsnip-like, 4 to 7 cm. long, with many rootlets. This species is not in cultivation.

PENIOCEREUS Br. et R.

Plant with long and thick turnip-like, fleshy roots, and with many slender stems, usually with 4 or 5 angles, with very closely set minute areoles and minute spines. Flowers white, comparatively large, nocturnal, closing by day, and blooming again the following night, with long and slender tubes, scaly, with abundant hairs in the axils of the upper scales, and with spines in the axils of the scales on the lower part of the tube and on the ovary. Fruit oval, spiny, scarlet, with black seeds. Includes two species.

Peniocereus Greggii (Engelm.) Br. et R. = *Cereus Greggii* Engelm. Northern Mexico and Arizona. Root very thick and long, sometimes up to 60 cm. in diameter, and up to 50 kilograms in weight. Stems erect, 2 to 2½ cm. thick, and 30 cm. to 3 m. long, of a dark greyish green, almost black, with short white hairs on the growing top. Ribs 4 or 5, rarely 3 or 6, angular, the edges closely set with small prominences on which are situated the elliptical woolly areoles. Spines 7 to 11, very short and conical, only about 2 mm. long. Flowers borne along the sides, erect, 15 to 20 cm. long; the ovary and the slender tube furnished with scales and bristle-like spines, the upper scales on the tube being very hairy. Petals white, fully expanded; stigma with 10 lobes. The flower is strongly perfumed, and opens two nights in succession. Easily grown on own roots, and is also grown from seed. Makes quick growth when grafted.

Peniocereus Johnstonii (Berger) Br. et R. = *Cereus Johnstonii* Berger. On the sand dunes of the southern part of Lower California. Differs from the preceding chiefly owing to the absence of hairs on the growing top of stems, and the longer spines. Like the preceding, requires full sunshine in an open situation and a light soil made of a mixture of sand and leaf-mould, with a little loam. The generic name is a reference to the *poor* and stunted development of the plant, as compared to the opulence of its root.

NYCTOCEREUS Br. et R.

Includes a few species which differ but little from the true Cerei. The stems are slender, at first erect and afterwards trailing, without aerial roots, sparingly branched. Ribs numerous but low, with closely set small areoles, each with 10 or more very slender spines. Flowers large or medium, nocturnal, borne along the sides of the stem, sometimes terminal, the growing stem finishing in a flower, white or rosy white. Tube furnished with short bracts and with clusters of short spines. The fruit is red, and the seeds are black. Natives of Mexico and Central America.

Nyctocereus serpentinus (DC.) Br. et R. = *Cereus serpentinus* DC. Mexico. This is the species most commonly met with in cultivation. Stems very elongated, often reaching 5 or 6 m. in length, 3 to 4 cm. thick, dull green, with 12 ribs or more. Areoles about 1 cm. apart, with clusters of spines of about the same size, about 2 cm. long, at first purplish, passing to yellowish or white. Flowers 15 to 20 cm. long, of a pale rose colour, the inner petals being white. All petals rather narrow, but fully expanded. Fruit red, covered with deciduous spines, 4 cm. long. Seeds large, about ½ cm. long, black. Freely flowering, sweet-scented, and of the easiest cultivation.

var. **splendens** (DC.) = *albispinus* Weingt. Stem glossy green. Spines soft, white, new spines white.

var. **ambiguus** (DC.) = *Cereus ambiguus* DC. Stem thicker, more erect; spines yellow or pale yellow. Flower 20 cm. long, of a deeper rose on the outer petals.

var. **strictior** Först. Stems thinner, spines yellowish, outer petals yellowish brown.

Nyctocereus Hirschtianus (K. Sch.) Br. et R. = *Cereus Hirschtianus* K. Sch. Nicaragua. Stems much shorter and more slender, 2 to 2½ cm. thick, with about 10 low but sharp ribs; spines pale yellow, 1 to 1½ cm. long. Flowers freely borne in August or earlier, about 10 cm. long, fully expanded, with a scaly tube; outer petals pale carmine, inner petals very pale rose or white, all petals very narrow.

Nyctocereus guatemalensis (Vaup.) Br. et R. = *Cereus guatemalensis* Vaupel. = *C. nyctago* Berger. Guatemala. Stems mostly erect, 3 to 6 cm. thick, with 8 to 12 ribs, low and somewhat rounded. Areoles bearing clusters of about 10 yellowish and softish spines, 3 to 4 cm. long. Flowers 15 to 20 cm. long, pale carmine red or yellowish red outside, white inside. Fruit spiny, about 2 cm. long.

Nyctocereus Neumannii (K. Sch.) Br. et R., from Nicaragua, and **Nyctocereus oaxacensis** Br. et R., from Mexico (Oaxaca), are not known in cultivation.

ACANTHOCEREUS (Engelm.) Br. et R.

Shrubby plants, sometimes almost tree-like. Stems erect at first, or almost prostrate later on, with many branches, and usually with 3 ribs or angles, sometimes with 4 or 5, exceptionally up to 7, mostly thin and very spiny. Joints of various thickness, newly developing joints often have more ribs, and spines of a different type. Flowers nocturnal, large, with a long tube, and a spiny ovary; petals numerous, the outer ones green, the inner white, fully expanded. Stamens erect and shorter than the petals. Fruit red, mostly spiny, with red pulp. Seeds black.

Includes about 12 species.

Acanthocereus albicaulis Br. et R. Brazil (Bahia). Stem slender, 1 to 3 cm. thick, sparingly branched, at first erect, afterwards sprawling, with 3 or 4 very acute ribs or angles, of a peculiar greyish green or bluish ashy grey, very glaucous. Areoles with brown wool. Spines 2 to 6, needle-like, more or less thick, bulbous at the base, brownish, 2 to 5 cm. long, but all equal on the same areole. Flower and fruit unknown. A very rare and interesting species, now obtainable from dealers.

Acanthocereus brasiliensis Br. et R. Brazil (Bahia). Stem weak, at first erect, afterwards sprawling or prostrate, 3 to 5 cm. thick, branching from the base, tender green, more or less glossy. Ribs mostly 5, or up to 7, about 1 to 1½ cm. deep, very acute, slightly notched. Areoles 4 or 5 cm. apart, whitish or greyish brown. Spines varying in number from about 9 to 20 or more, needle-like, ½ to 2 or 3 cm. long, radials and centrals alike, white or greyish yellow, tipped darker, to greyish brown or almost black. Flowers up to 15 cm. long: ovary with whitish or brownish areoles, with 4 to 10 yellowish brown spines up to 2 cm. long; tube very slender, with scales woolly in their axils. Fruit round, about 8 cm. thick, warty, green, covered with spines easily dropping off, pulp greenish white. Seeds few, small oval, brownish. Common at Bahia, but rare in cultivation.

Acanthocereus horribilis Berger. = *A. horridus* Br. et R. Guatemala. Not to be confused with *Cereus horridus Otto*, from South Brazil and Argentina. Stem mostly erect, branches up to 10 cm. thick, with 3 broad wing-like ribs, with crenate margins. Radial spines 1 to 6, about 1 cm. long, spreading. Central spines 1 or 2, very thick, up to

8 cm. long, brown or black, passing to grey. Flower 20 cm. long, outer petals greenish or brownish, inner petals white. Ovary with small scales, slightly woolly, almost spineless.

Acanthocereus acutangulus (Otto) Br. et R. = *Cereus acutangulus* Otto. Native country doubtfully given as Mexico. Stem erect or semi-prostrate, 4 cm. thick, with 4 acute ribs (sometimes 3), crenate, with areoles about 1 cm. apart, with an arched furrow on each side of the rib below the areole. Radial spines 4 to 6, very short. Central spine only one, about 1½ cm. long, awl-shaped. Often considered as a variety of the following.

Acanthocereus baxaniensis (Karw.) = *Cereus baxaniensis* Karw. = *C. ramosus* Karw. = *C. principis* Salm-Dyck. Mexico and Cuba, Similar to the preceding, but with thicker stems of a deep dull green. Ribs usually 4, broad and wing-like. Radial spines brownish, 5 or more, about 1½ cm. long; central spines 1 to 3, yellowish brown, up to 3 cm. long, thick and straight. Flowers freely borne on the sides near the top, large, about 20 cm. long, brownish green outside, white inside, with a spiny ovary. A well-known and distinct species, but often confused with the following.

Acanthocereus pentagonus (L.) Br et R. = *Cereus pentagonus* L. non Haw. = *Cactus pentagonus* L. Florida, Louisiana, West Indies and South America. Stems usually erect, mostly 5-ribbed, rarely with 3 or 4 angles, dark green, 6 to 7 cm. in diameter. Ribs broad and wing-like, deeply crenate. Areoles greyish, 2½ to 3 cm. apart. Radial spines 6 to 8, awl-shaped, spreading, up to 1 cm. long. Central spines 1, rarely 2 or 3, thick, awl-shaped, somewhat thickened at the base, 3½ to 5 cm. long, brown or yellowish brown, passing to greyish, the radials being of the same colour. Flower 18 to 21 cm. long, with spiny ovary and spinescent tube; outer petals brownish green, the next row green, and the inner white; stamens white, stigma with 15 yellowish white lobes. Fruit roundish or ovoid, deep red, 4 cm. long, with long spines; pulp juicy, red.

Acanthocereus colombianus Br. et R. Colombia. Plant erect, 2 to 3 m. high. Joints 3-ribbed, 9 cm. thick, branching dichotomously, with large areoles 5 cm. apart. Radial spines less than ½ cm. long; 1 or 2 central spines, very strong, 4 to 6 cm. long. Flower about 25 cm. long, white, with a thick tube and a broad throat.

Other species very rarely cultivated, are: **Acanthocereus floridanus** Small, Florida, **A. occidentalis** Br. et R., and **A. subinermis** Br. et R. Mexico, **A. thalassinus** Otto, and **A. horribarbis** Otto, Brazil.

This genus seems to be rather ill-defined, both as to the generic characters and to the number of species.

HELIOCEREUS Berger

Stems slender, weak, trailing or bushy, soft-fleshed, Ribs or angles 3 or 4 (rarely up to 6 or 7), very prominent and acute. Flowers diurnal, funnel-shaped. large, mostly red, strongly perfumed. Ovary furnished with spines of bristles, Includes 7 species, all very beautiful and desirable flowering Cacti, of easy cultivation and propagation, in a soil made of sand, grit and leaf-mould, requiring warmth, and thriving well in half-shade, and also in full sunshine.

Heliocereus speciosus (Cav.) Br. et R. = *Cactus speciosus* Cavanilles = *Cereus speciosus* K. Sch. = *C. speciosissimus* DC. Central Mexico. Plant erect or trailing ot hanging, freely branching. Stems up to 1 m. long, with 4 angles, the growing top dark red or reddish, passing to dark green; the angles or ribs are acute, of uneven width, about 1 or 2 cm. broad, unevenly toothed or serrated. Areoles 1 to 3 cm. apart, large, woolly. Spines 5 to 8, afterwards more numerous, soft, yellowish, passing to whitish or brownish, awl-shaped, 1 to 1½ cm. long. Flower 12 to 15 cm. long, with a green tube about 8 cm. long, furnished with red scales and bristles. Inner petals green at the base, spathulate, obtuse, of a glossy carmine with a lovely steel blue sheen. Ovary warty, furnished with scales, wool and bristles. Stamens green below and red above; style longer than the stamens, stigma with 8 or 9 yellow lobes. This species crossed with species of *Ephiphyllum* (*Phyllocactus*) has given origin to most of the beautiful modern varieties of *Phyllocactus*.

Heliocereus amecamensis (Heese-Weingt.) Br. et R. = *Cereus amecaensis* Heese. Mexico (Amecameca). The white counterpart of the preceding species, and possibly a local mutation or sport, perpetuated in cultivation. Stems pale green, and their growing tops green. Flowers entirely white. The rest as in *H. speciosus*. A remarkable and very beautiful white variety.

Heliocereus Schrankii (Zucc). Br. et R. = *Cereus Schrankii* Zucc. Mexico (Zimapan). Stems dull green, the growing tops being of a lively red, with 3 or 4 angles or wings, 2 to 3 cm. broad, serrated. Areoles 1½ to 2 cm. apart, with whitish wool. Spines 7 or more, about 1 cm. long, white passing to yellowish, the upper 3 being thicker, and the lower 3 darker. Flower 14 cm. long, with a short green tube, limb funnel-shaped, 8 to 9 cm. broad, the inner segments being acute, scarlet red or blood red, with a shining bluish carmine red spot at the base. Ovary angular and warty, scaly, woolly and spinescent. Stamens many, white, bluish carmine at the middle of the filament. Style thick, longer than the stamens, white towards the base, deep carmine above; lobes of stigma red, tipped yellow.

Heliocereus cinnabarinus (Eichl.) Br. et R. = *Cereus cinnabarinus* Eichl. Guatemala. Stems with 3 angles, 2 to 3 cm. thick, dark green, mostly erect and fleshy, much branched, with acute and somewhat serrated angles. Growing stems green, or slightly reddish. Spines few, less than 1 cm. long, needle-like, spreading, yellowish brown, often associated with a few bristles. Flower 8 to 9 cm. long, and 4 to 5 cm. broad. Ovary warty, with scales with wool and yellowish white bristles in their axils. Segments of perianth in two rows, lanceolate; those in the outer row greenish, the innner ones being of a glossy cinnabar red. Stamens whitish, with purplish anthers, passing to pink; style white below, pink above, longer than the flower, stigma whitish. Fruit globose, greenish white, with pink pulp.

Heliocereus elegantissimus (Berger) Br. et R. = *Cereus elegantissimus* Berger = *C. coccineus* Salm-Dyck, non Engelm. Mexico. Stems mostly hanging from the fissure of rocks, about 3 cm. thick, with 3 to 4 obtuse angles, growing tops brownish. Angles somewhat serrate, bearing areoles 1 to 4 cm. apart, somewhat woolly. Spines 6 or more, about ½ cm. long, slender, yellowish brown, passing to grey. Flower up to 13 cm. long, with a long angular green or brown tube, somewhat curved, and an angular and warty ovary, with scales and short wool, and with yellow bristles up to 7 mm. long. Outer segments of perianth greenish, the inner lanceolate, red flushed carmine, green at the base. Stamens few, white below, carmine above; style as long as the stamens and of the same colour, stigma with 8 white lobes.

Heliocereus superbus (Ehrbg.) Berger = *Cereus superbus* Ehrbg. Central Mexico. Sometimes considered as a natural sport of *H. speciosus*. Differs from *H. speciosus* owing to its thicker stems with 7 angles or ribs, the growing tops being of a lively red. Spines small, slender, numerous, less than 1 cm. long. A very beautiful species or variety, with flowers as large as those of *H. speciosus*, but of a glossy cinnabar red.

Heliocereus serratus Weingt. = *Cereus serratus* Weingt. Guatemala. Stems thick and erect, rather short, with 4 angles, rarely with 3 angles, dull deep green. Angles serrated, with stiff needle-like yellowish or brownish spines, less than 1 cm. long. Flowers of a beautiful purplish red colour.

All these species of "Sun Cactus" flower better in full sunshine, and require warmth. They thrive well on own roots in a mixture of sand, leaf-mould, some loam and crushed bricks added, with a little crushed charcoal and some old cow manure. Grafted on *Cereus Hassleri* or on *Selenicereus Macdonaldiae*, they grow into quite fine specimens and flower profusely.

TRICHOCEREUS Riccobono

Stem columnar and erect, typically branched from the base, but sometimes branching also slightly above ground, in time often forming quite large clumps. Usually with many ribs, more or less thickly set with areoles, usually very spiny, but without development of permanent hairs. The stems are not jointed except where branching, growth being continuous. The areoles on the top of growing stems are often furnished with short whitish or yellowish hairs, which soon drop off, but flowering areoles very generally develop a large tuft of hair or wool, whitish or brownish, which is persistant, and through which emerges the flower bud. Flowers large and showy, nocturnal, funnel-shaped, mostly white, often highly perfumed. Ovary and tube scaly, with abundant long dark hairs in the axils of the scales, but without spines or bristles. The

(b) BORZICACTUS AURIVILLUS

(a) HARRISIA TORTUOSA

PLATE XVIII

PLATE XIX

generic name is in reference to the marked development of hairs on the flower bud and in the axils of the scales.

A very interesting genus, exclusively South American, now comprising over 30 species, mostly bearing superb flowers.

Trichocereus pasacana (Weber) Br. et R. = *Cereus pasacana* Weber = *Pilocereus pasacana* Rümpl. North-western Argentina and Bolivia. A giant species, with stems 1 to 5 m. high and 30 to 50 cm. in diameter, mostly solitary, sometimes branching from the base, but in cultivation rarely more than 20 cm. thick. The colour is light dull green, with 15 to 35 ribs, broad, low and rounded, with rusty brown areoles, furnished with numerous thick, stiff spines, awl-shaped, 4 to 8 cm. long, varying in colour from a pale brown to dark reddish brown or tan. Flowering tops develop long bristles on the upper areoles, the bristles being white in the form with dark brown spines, hence the name *albicephala* given to it. The flower, borne on the sides of the stem from the upper areoles, is about 10 cm. long; ovary and tube with scales and brownish hairs. The fruit called *pasacana* by the natives, is roundish, greenish, about 3 cm. thick, and is edible. A resistant species of rather slow growth, delighting in full sunshine, and is usually grown from seed, on own roots.

Trichocereus cephalopasacana Backbg. North Argentina, Bolivia. Very similar to *T. pasacana*, but the plant is usually smaller and more branched. Areoles at the top of the flowering stems, and for some distance down, thickly covered with bristle-like hairs, not unlike a true cephalium.

Trichocereus cephalomacrostibas Backbg. Peru, south-western mountains. Stems erect, up to 2 m. high, branching from the base, pale green passing to greyish, up to 12 cm. thick, with about 10 obtuse ribs, 2 cm. broad and 1 cm. high. Areoles large, closely set, yellowish white passing to greyish. Outer radial spines very small, up to 4 mm. long; inner radials 3 to 5, thick, spreading, up to 3 cm. long; one central spine very thick, up to 7 cm. long, directed outwards or downwards, often twisted. Flower large, white; fruit somewhat oval, reddish or orange yellow.

Trichocereus Bertramianus Backbg. North Bolivia, near Mine Comanche. Stem solitary, or with one or two branches arising from the base, up to 1½ m. high, and up to 25 cm. thick, pale green, club-shaped above. Ribs about 20, rounded, 1 to 2 cm. high. Areoles thickly set, about 3 mm. apart, the flowering areoles at the top of the stem having much yellowish white wool. Radial spines about 12, of varying length, up to 2½ cm. long, spreading laterally and downwards: central spines 4, up to 7 cm. long, one of them directed downwards. All spines pale straw-coloured, sometimes reddish at the base. Flowers borne at the top of the stem, 10 to 12 cm. long, yellowish white, very scaly and hairy on the outside. Fruit round, hairy.

Trichocereus poco (Hort.) = *Pilocereus poco* Hort = *Cephalocereus poco* Hort. Uplands of Peru and Bolivia. *Poco*, often written *pocco*,

M

is the name given to this species by the natives. Stem mostly solitary, rarely branching from the base, up to 1 m. high, and up to 20 cm. thick, olive green, passing to dull green or greyish. Ribs many, up to 24, rounded and prominent at the top, with deep furrows between them, low and flat lower down the stem. Areoles large, oval, yellow, with yellowish wool, 3 to 4 cm. apart. Spines many and long, covering the top of the plant and all round the stem: the radials 12 to 18, radiating, curved laterally, up to 4 cm. long, horny yellow, passing to whitish; central spines 6 to 9, reddish brown, passing to horny yellow, darker at the tip, straight or curved upwards, up to 7 cm. long. Flowers borne at the top, on full grown specimens, dark red. Young globular plants are very similar to *Eriosyce korethroides*, and possibly both species are identical. A resistant species of easy cultivation in full sunshine, but growth is slow.

Trichocereus Werdermannianus Backbg.   Uplands of Bolivia. A species of gigantic size, with a thick pale green stem, passing to greyish, often 60 cm. thick at the base, branching above ground into huge tree-like specimens. Shoots erect, up to 16 cm. thick, at first with 6 ribs, afterwards with 12 or more. Areoles white, closely set. Spines straw-yellow, 8 radials and 1 central, this last much thicker and longer, awl-shaped, darker at the base. Flowers funnel-shaped, large, white. A resistant species, now obtainable as seedlings. Growth is slow at first.

Trichocereus Terscheckii (Parm.) Backbg. = *Cereus Terscheckii* Parm.   Northern Argentina, where it is known by the local name of *Cardon grande*, often growing along with *T. pasacana*. A magnificent plant up to 12 m. high, with a strong stem, branching from the base or above ground, with many branches 10 to 20 cm. thick, of a pale dull green, with 8 to 14 rounded ribs, with narrow furrows between them. Areoles large, yellowish brown, 2 to 3 cm. apart. Spines 8 to 15, very strong, awl-shaped, mostly straight, yellowish, up to 10 cm. long. Flowers freely borne, at or near the top of grown up stems, white, about 20 cm. long. Makes fairly quick growth.

Trichocereus lamprochlorus (Lem.) Br. et R. = *Cereus lamprochlorus* Lem. = *Echinopsis lamprochlora* Weber. Northern Argentina. Stem erect, 50 cm. to 1 m. high, freely branching from the base, glossy grass green, 6 to 8 cm. thick, with 10 to 15 ribs, slightly notched below the areoles, which are to 1 to 1½ cm. apart. Spines golden yellow, passing to yellowish brown. Radial spines about 12, up to 1 cm. long; central spines mostly 4, up to 2 cm. long. Flowers borne at the top of the stem from a large tuft of brownish wool, very beautiful, about 24 cm. long; ovary and tube scaly and furnished with greyish wool, the outer petals being reddish, the inner white. A fast growing and robust species, and is also an excellent stock for grafting.

Trichocereus Spachianus (Lem.) Riccobono = *Cereus Spachianus* Lem. Western Argentina. A popular and beautiful species, largely used as stock for grafting. Stem up to 1½ m. high, and 4 to 6 cm. thick, very freely branching from the base, bright light green, with 10 to 15 obtuse and rounded ribs. Areoles about 1 cm. apart, at first yellowish, passing to grey. Spines at first yellow, passing to brown; the radials about 8, bristle-like, up to 1 cm. long; the centrals 1 or 2, slightly longer and thicker. Flowers very freely produced on old plants, around the top of the stems, about 20 cm. long; ovary and tube scaly and with dark hairs, outside petals greenish, the inner white, blooming at night and remaining in bloom well into the morning. The soil should not be overcharged with lime.

Trichocereus thelegonus (Weber) Br. et R. = *Cereus thelegonus* Weber. North-western Argentina. Stem rather weak, erect or sprawling, solitary or branching from the base, up to 1½ m. high, and 5 to 8 cm. thick, dark green or somewhat glaucous, with about 12 broad flat ribs, with deep very narrow furrows between them. Areoles round, brown, about 1 cm. apart. Spines at first transparent yellow, afterwards brownish or grey; the radials about 6, spreading, straight, 1 to 2 cm. long; only one central spine, straight, up to 4 cm. long. Flowers very beautiful, fully expanded, about 20 cm. long, borne on the sides at the upper part of the stem, the flowering areoles being furnished with a big tuft of dark grey wool. Ovary and tube with scales and long dark brown wool, outer petals greenish, the inner white. Fruit red at maturity. Grows quickly and flowers freely.

Trichocereus tephracanthus (Lab.) Br. et R. = *Cereus tephrancanthus* Lab. Bolivia. Stem up to 1½ m. high, erect, deep green, 5 to 6 cm. thick, with 8 broad rounded ribs, branching from the base, but very sparingly. Areoles large, white, passing to grey. Radial spines about 7, thick and stiff, whitish, brownish at the base, up to 1 cm. long; central spine only one, longer and brownish, later passing to ashy grey. Flowers about 18 cm. long, borne along the upper part of the stem, funnel-shaped; outer petals green margined brown, inner petals greenish white. Grows rather slowly, and flowers sparingly.

var. **boliviensis** Weber. Has yellow spines and whiter flowers.

Trichocereus chiloensis (Colla) Br. et R. = *Cereus chiloensis* Colla. Chile. A very variable species. Stem erect, columnar, sparingly branching from the base, often exceeding 3 m. in height, but of slow growth, 6 to 12 cm. thick, dull green. Ribs 10 to 15, rounded, notched and furrowed above the areoles, which are large, round, with whitish wool, and 2 to 2½ cm. apart. Spines at first brownish yellow, afterwards ashy grey. Radial spines 8 to 12, thick, awl-shaped, up to 4 cm. long, spreading; central spines 1 to 4, stronger, 5 or 6 cm. long, sometimes up to 12 cm. long. Flowers borne along the side of the upper part of the stem, 15 cm. long: ovary and tube scaly and with brownish or dark hairs, outer petals greenish margined reddish or brown, inner petals white.

var. **panhoplites** K. Sch. = *Cereus panhopleatus* Monv. Young spines almost black, central spine very long.

var. **eburneus** K. Sch. Spines white, radials and central very long, the central sometimes 12 cm. long. Flowers pink or shaded pink.

var. **pycnacanthus** K. Sch. Spines very short and thick, 3 to 4 cm. long.

var. **polygonus** Salm-Dyck. Ribs more numerous, 12 to 17, but low. Growth robust and rather fast.

var. **Funkii** K. Sch. = *Cereus Funkii* K. Sch. Spines smaller, areoles more closely set, stem light green.

var. **Zizkaanus** K. Sch. = *Cereus Zizkaanus* Hort. Spines small; central spine slender, very long, directed upwards.

var. **quisco** Weber = *Cereus quisco* Remy. Stem thick, dark green, central spines very long, black tipped.

var. **spinosissimus** Hort. Radial spines about 12, central spines 3 or 4, all long, slender, brownish or greyish, directed upwards.

Quisco is the name given by the natives to this variable species, which is found all over Chile, from Bolivia to Patagonia.

Trichocereus macrogonus (Salm-Dyck) Br. et R. = *Cereus macrogonus* Salm-Dyck. Argentina and Bolivia. Stem columnar and stiff, 2 to 3 m. high and 5 to 9 cm. thick, bluish green, particularly so the young stems, with 6 to 9 (usually 8) prominent, very rounded ribs, with narrow furrows between them. Areoles 1½ to 2 cm. apart, greyish. Radial spines 6 to 9, spreading, straight, needle-like, brown, up to 2 cm. long. Central spines 1 to 3, thicker, spreading out horizontally, light brown or yellowish brown, sometimes up to 5 cm. long, but usually up to 3 cm. long, and brownish. Flowers large and showy, about 18 cm. long; ovary and tube scaly and with brown hairs, outer petals greenish white, inner petals white. The flowers are borne 2 to 4 or more together, at or near the top of the stem, and bloom together. A species of quick growth and robust habit, affording an excellent stock for grafting *Echinocacti*, *Echinopsis*, *Cephalocerei*, etc. A cristate form is commonly cultivated.

Trichocereus fascicularis (Meyen) Br. et R. = *Cereus fascicularis* Meyen. Southern Peru and northern Chile. Stem erect, freely branching from the base, resulting in large clumps, varying in thickness from 4 to 6 cm. with 16 low, rounded ribs, the general colour being pale green. Areoles thickly set, brown. Spines very numerous, yellowish passing to brown. Radial spines spreading, needle-shaped, 1 cm. long. Central spine mostly one, awl-shaped, strong and greyish, up to 4 cm. long. Flowers about 10 cm. long, freely produced at the top, reddish outside, greenish white with brownish margin inside. Rather rare in cultivation, of slow growth, but resistant to low temperatures.

Trichocereus coquimbanus (K. Sch.) Br. et R. = *Cereus coquimbanus* K. Sch. = *C. breviflorus* K. Sch. Along the coast of central Chile. Stem stiff, erect, about 1 m. high and 7 to 8 cm. thick, pale green, with about 12 ribs, rounded, with deep furrows between them, and irregularly notched. Areoles large, 1 cm. long and 2 cm. apart, with brownish wool. Radial spines about 25, spreading, curved, hair-like, at first yellowish brown passing to black. Central spines about 4, the upper one being up to 7 cm. long. Flower about 12 cm. long, ovary, tube and outer petals densely covered with black hairs, inner petals very acute and white. Prefers a moist sandy soil and full sunshine.

var. **nigripilis** R.A. Phil. = *Cereus nigripilis* R.A. Phil. Stem more slender, 4 to 7 cm. thick, of a deeper shining green, at first erect, afterwards sprawling, with large oval areoles, furnished with abundant blackish wool, on prominences between two notches. Central spines slightly shorter. Flowers more hairy.

Trichocereus Bridgesii (Salm-Dyck) Br. et R. = *Cereus Bridgesii* Salm-Dyck. Bolivia, where it is often planted in hedges. Stem erect or partly prostrate, 1 to 5 m. high, greyish green or glaucous, 5 to 10 cm. thick, freely branching from the base, with 4 to 8 broad and obtuse ribs (usually 6), with narrow furrows between them. Areoles small, 2 cm. apart, with yellow wool. Spines 2 to 6, straight, dark yellow passing to brown, the longest up to 10 cm. long, and directed upwards. Flowers borne at the top, about 18 cm. long; ovary, tube and outer petals with dark hairs; outer petals greenish brown, inner petals white. The flowers exhale a strong perfume of Jasmine, and often last well into the day. Requires a substantial soil and full sunshine.

var. **brevispinus** K. Sch. Ribs 7 or 8. Spines very small.

var. **longispinus** Hort. Ribs 4 or 5. Central spines very long.

var. **lageniformis** (Först.) K. Sch. Stems more or less club-shaped, with 6 or 7 ribs; spines numerous, but short.

Trichocereus Schickendantzii (Weber) Br. et R. = *Echinopsis Schickendantzii* Weber. North-western Argentina. Stem erect very freely branching from the base, 50 to 75 cm. high, and 5 to 7 cm. thick, shining dark green, with about 16 ribs obtuse and rounded, ½ cm. deep. Areoles yellowish white passing to brown, less than 1 cm. apart. Spines yellow, passing to yellowish brown and grey, ½ to 1 cm. long; the radials about 10, very slender; the centrals 1 to 4, thicker. Flowers very large and beautiful, about 22 cm. long, freely borne at the top of the stems, with a long tube furnished with scales and black hairs, petals white. The flowers last in bloom for 2 or 3 days, and exhale a delicious perfume. The plant is of fast growth, is very easily propagated, and affords an excellent grafting stock.

Trichocereus strigosus (Salm-Dyck) Br. et R. = *Cereus strigosus* Salm-Dyck. North-western Argentina. Stem erect, stiff, pale green passing to greyish green, often more than 1 m. high, 5 to 7 cm. thick, with 12 to 18 low, obtuse ribs, more or less rounded. The species branches freely from the base, and also for some distance above ground. Areoles small, round, less than 1 cm. apart, at first whitish, passing to grey. Spines numerous, of variable length and colour, whitish, yellowish, yellowish red or red to dark red, with darker points. Radial spines about 15, up to 1½ cm. long; central spines 4, thicker, and 2½ to 5 cm. long. Old spines are yellowish brown or reddish brown, passing finally to greyish. Flowers borne at the sides of old stems, near the top, about 18 cm. long; ovary and tube scaly and with abundant dark rusty brown hairs; outer petals narrow, white, brownish at the back, reflexed; inner petals in 5 rows, broad, white, of a delicate satiny texture, spreading or recurved. A very refined flower, in some forms scentless, in others exhaling a strong perfume of Magnolia. This species is popular on account of its coloured spines, and is of fairly quick growth and easy cultivation, but flowers sparingly. The flower bud comes out of a tuft of golden brown hairs.

var. **intricatus** Weber = *Cereus intricatus* Salm-Dyck. Stems often tortuous. Spines long, crimson and tipped dark when young.

var. **longispinus** Hort. Spines very long, almost blood red when young.

var. **variegatus** Hort. Spines yellowish or reddish yellow, tipped brown, when young.

Trichocereus auricolor Backbg. Peru? Stem pale green, mostly tortuous, erect or sprawling, up to 1½ m. high and up to 6 cm. thick, freely branching from the base or just above ground. Ribs 16 to 24, rounded, prominent near the top of the stem. Areoles large, round, or slightly oval, with short yellowish wool, ½ to 1½ cm. apart. Radial spines 12 or more, straight, needle-like, ½ to 1½ cm. long, the lower ones being the longest, golden yellow. Central spines 1 or 2, stiff, straight and needle-like, directed upwards, later directed outwards or downwards, up to 3 cm. long, golden yellow, darker towards the base, slightly bulbous.

Trichocereus huascha (Weber) Br. et R. = *Cereus huascha* Weber. Western Argentina. Stem erect, 30 to 90 cm. high, and 5 to 8 cm. thick, light green, with 12 to 18 ribs, low, obtuse and rounded, branching freely from the base. Areoles whitish, about ½ cm. apart. Spines numerous, needle-like, yellowish passing to brown, about 1½ cm. long. Central spines 4 to 6, same colour but stronger, and up to 6 cm. long. Flowers yellow, borne along the sides of the stem, 7 to 10 cm. long, funnel-shaped, with brownish hairs on the ovary and tube.

var. **rubriflorus** Weber = *Cereus andalgalensis* Weber. Stems more slender, yellowish green, with 12 ribs. Spines shorter. Flowers red.

var. **flavispinus** Hort. A thick-stemmed variety, with golden yellow spines.

Trichocereus candicans (Gill.) Br. et R. = *Cereus candicans* Gill. = *Echinopsis candicans* Weber. North-western Argentina. Stem erect, up to 1 m. high, and 6 to 16 cm. thick, freely branching from the base, resulting in large clumps, clear glossy green on top, dull green lower down, with 9 to 11 ribs, broad and rounded. Areoles 1½ to 2 cm. apart, large with whitish wool. Radial spines 10 to 14, spreading, clear yellow or whitish, up to 4 cm. long. Central spines 1 to 4, thicker, yellow, darker towards the tip, straight or tortuous, up to 10 cm. long. Flowers borne along the sides near the top, very large and beautiful, up to 25 cm. long, with long brownish hairs on ovary and tube, petals white, arranged funnel-shaped, very sweet-scented. Fruit large, round, red, with glossy black seeds. A very interesting cristate form is also grown.

var. **robustior** Salm-Dyck. Stem 14 to 16 cm. thick and even more; spines very thick, with central spines 5 to 6 cm. long.

var. **gladiatus** K. Sch. = *Cereus gladiatus* Lem. Areoles very large, central spines brownish yellow, twisted and thick, up to 10 cm. long.

var. **Linckii** K. Sch. Stem more slender, 6 or 7 cm. thick, with 9 or 10 ribs, of a paler green. Spines golden yellow, the centrals up to 6 cm. long.

var. **Courantii** K. Sch. Stem slender, ribs closer together, spines yellow, shorter.

Trichocereus purpureopilosus (Weingt.) Backbg. = *Cereus purpureopilosus* Weingt. Argentina. Nearly allied to *T. Schickendantzii*. Stem about 1 m. high, glossy dark green, with about 12 obtuse low ribs. Areoles very closely set ($\frac{1}{2}$ to 1 cm. apart), whitish. Radial spines about 20, slender, straight, pale yellow, about $\frac{1}{2}$ cm. long. Central spines 4, same size or slightly longer, red at the base, almost transparent, yellow towards the tip. Flower 21 cm. long, petals white, issuing near the top of the stem, from a large tuft of purplish dark hairs. Ovary and tube scaly and with dense reddish brown or purplish hairs; outer petals purplish green, inner petals white. Delights in full sunshine and a substantial soil. Easily propagated by means of offsets freely produced around the base of the stem.

Trichocereus Pachanoi (Werd.) Br. et R. = *Cereus Pachanoi* Werd. South Ecuador and north Peru, where it is known under the name of San Pedro. Stem up to 6 m. high, erect, with many vertical branches around the base and up the stem, dark green, growing stems bluish green, with 6 to 8 broad ribs. Spines 3 to 7, up to 2 cm. long, yellow or brown, often practically spineless. Flowers borne at the top of the stems, 20 cm. long, sweet-scented, white, with ovary and tube covered with scales and long brown hairs. A beautiful and imposing species, still rare in collections. It is an excellent grafting stock for other Cacti.

Trichocereus deserticolus (Werd.) Backbg. = *Cereus deserticolus* Werd. Chile. Stem branching from the base or above ground, 1 to 1$\frac{1}{2}$ m. high, dull green, with 8 to 10 acute ribs about 2 cm. deep. Areoles 1$\frac{1}{2}$ cm. apart, dark brown. Radial spines 15 to 25, up to 1$\frac{1}{2}$ cm. long, very thin and often curved, dark brown passing to grey. Centrals 1 to 3, up to 12 cm. long, straight, same colour. Flower 7 to 8 cm. long, white; ovary and tube with dark hairs. Closely allied to *T. coquimbanus*.

Trichocereus cuscoensis Br. et R. Peru. Stem 4 to 6 m. high, very similar to that of *T. macrogonus*, branching freely from the base, pale green or bluish green passing to dull green, with 7 or 8 prominent rounded ribs. Areoles brownish, 1 to 1$\frac{1}{2}$ cm. apart, with about 12 spines, strong and straight, brownish passing to grey, the centrals up to 7 cm. long. Flower about 14 cm. long, white. Ovary and tube very scaly and hairy.

Trichocereus peruvianus Br. et R. = *Cereus Rosei* Werd. Peru. Plant 2 to 4 m. high, much branched, with stems 6 to 10 cm. thick, erect or prostrate, bluish green passing to green or dull greyish green, with 6 to 8 ribs, and brownish areoles about $2\frac{1}{2}$ cm. apart. Spines about 10, brownish, up to 4 cm. long. Flowers 22 to 25 cm. long, white, sweet-scented. The name *Rosei* was given by Werdermann to distinguish it from *Cereus* (*Piptanthocereus*) *peruvianus*. Very similar to *T. macrogonus*, but usually more slender and often prostrate.

Trichocereus uyupampensis Backbg. and **T. Vollianus** Backbg. are two other new species from Bolivia.

BINGHAMIA (Br. et R.)
(*Seticereus* Backbg.)

This genus has been and is still the theme of considerable discussion. It was established by Britton and Rose, who included under it two species, viz: *B. melanostele*, now *Espostoa melanostele*, and *B. acrantha*, now *Haageocereus acranthus*. It was also used by others to include *Cereus multangularis*, *C. icosagonus* or *aurivillus*, etc. and for these Backeberg has proposed a new genus, *Seticereus*. As however, *Binghamia* has been long in common use, it is better to retain it under a modified form, as synonymous with *Seticereus*. Eight species are here included under this genus.

Plants with the habit of *Trichocereus*, but smaller and lower. Stems erect or semi-prostrate, rather slender, branching from the base, somewhat hairy, the hairs being more numerous, straight or curly, at the top of flowering stems. Flowers small, red or orange, somewhat zygomorphic.

Binghamia multangularis (Haw.) Br. et R. = *Cereus multangularis* Haw. Peru. Stem cylindrical, erect, up to 60 cm. high, 4 to 6 cm. thick, pale green, branching from the base, with 14 to 18 low ribs, obtuse and slightly notched. Areoles very numerous, up to 8 mm. apart, small with whitish wool. Spines often over 40, up to $1\frac{1}{2}$ cm. long, bristle-like and flexible, at first pale brown, passing to yellowish, spreading, covering the stem; the central spines being often up to 2 cm. long, horny yellow, passing to greyish. Flowers borne on the sides near the top, about 11 cm. long; ovary warty and scaly, with white hairs and a bundle of bristle-like spines in the axils of the scales. Limb funnel-shaped, about 8 cm. across; tube with many areoles bearing white wool and 10 to 12 very thin yellowish brown spines; the segments of the perianth are orange red.

var. **limensis** (Salm-Dyck) = *Cereus limensis* Salm-Dyck. A plant of stronger growth. Spines more reddish. Central spine absent.

var. **rufispina** Haw. Stem dark green, of same size as in the typical form: spines red when young, passing to pale reddish brown. Central spine as the radials.

var. **pallidior** Haw. Stem pale yellowish green. Areoles white; spines amber yellow, intermixed with white hairs.

Binghamia laredensis (Backbg.) = *Cereus laredensis* Backbg. Bolivia (near Laredo). A remarkable new species, with an erect stem 4 to 5 cm. thick, branching from the base and fast-growing, densely covered with slender, bristle-like spines, 1 to 3 cm. long, of a pretty orange yellow colour when young, passing to yellowish, whitish or greyish. The flowers are red. The grown-up plant looks like a specimen of *Haageocereus pacalaensis*, but more slender and with shorter spines.

Binghamia icosagona (DC.) = *Cereus icosagonus* DC. = *Cereus isogonus* K. Sch. = *Borzicactus icosagonus* Br. et R. This species from the hills of Ecuador is considered identical with *Cereus aurivillus* K. Sch. = *Borzicactus aurivillus* Br. et R. = *Seticereus icosagonus* Backbg., from the Andes of Peru. It is an erect species, 1½ m. high when old, but rarely more than 50 cm. high in cultivation, light green, 3 to 4 cm. thick, with 16 to 20 narrow and rounded ribs, with areoles of oval shape and rather large, ½ to 1 cm. apart, yellowish white. Spines very numerous, 30 or more, about 1½ cm. long, clear yellow, central spines golden yellow, 6 to 8, up to 2 cm. long, stronger and longer than the radials, yellowish brown or horny yellow. Flowers 7 to 8 cm. long, red or orange red, with white and brownish hairs on the outside, with yellowish red midrib on the inner petals. Stamens and style white, stigma green. A lovely species of easy cultivation, usually grafted on *Trichocereus Spachianus*, but thrives very well on own roots.

Binghamia Humboldtii (H.B.K.) = *Cereus Humboldtii* H.B.K. = *Borzicactus Humboldtii* Br. et R. = *Cereus plagiostoma* Vaupel. = *Seticereus Humboldtii* Backbg. Peru, on high hilly ground. Closely allied to the preceding. Stem upright, about 70 cm. high, 3 to 5 cm. thick, dull green with white dots, with 12 to 13 ribs up to 1 cm. deep, notched between the areoles which are 1 to 1½ cm. apart, small, with yellowish wool. Radial spines up to 25, spreading straight, stiff, needle-like, about 1 cm. long. Central spines 4 to 7, slightly longer. All spines on new growth are clear brown or brown, often reddish, later passing to greyish. Flowering stems with many hairs, straight or curly, at the top, whitish. Flower about 5 cm. long, varying from pale pink to crimson, somewhat zygomorphic. Very free-flowering.

Binghamia acanthura (Vaup.) = *Cereus acanthurus* Vaupel = *Borzicactus* Backbg. = *Seticereus* Backbg. Peru, on high hilly ground. Stem green, semi-prostrate, up to 30 cm. long, branching from the base, 4 to 6 cm. thick, with 15 to 19 low straight gibbose ribs. Areoles very closely set, brownish. Radial and central spines hardly distinguishable, very numerous, very short, slender, bristle-like, yellowish, the central spines being thicker and up to 1½ cm. long. Flower about 5 cm. long, scarlet red.

var. **ferox** Backbg. Has longer spines.

Binghamia eriotricha (Werd. et Backbg.) = *Cereus eriotrichus* Werd. et Backbg. = *Borzicactus* Werd. et Backbg. = *Loxanthocereus*

Werd. et Backbg. = *Seticereus* Backbg. Peru on the mountains at Matucana. This new species has a semi-prostrate stem,, up to 40 cm. long, about 4 cm. thick, branching from the base, pale greyish green, with abundant white hairs at the top. Ribs 15 or 16, straight, rounded, about ½ cm. deep. Areoles rather large, roundish or slightly oval, white, 1 cm. apart. Radial spines about 15, spreading, less than 1 cm. long. Central spines 3 to 6, slightly longer. All spines yellowish white, passing to greyish, the central spines being darker and tipped black or dark. Flower red. Fruit yellowish green.

Two other new species viz: **Seticereus ferrugineus** Backbg. and **S. oehmeanus** Backbg., both from Peru, may be included under Binghamia.

BORZICACTUS Riccobono

Stems partly erect, or weak and decumbent, or prostrate, with many ribs more or less closely studded with areoles. Flowers small, orange or scarlet, diurnal, with a short tube and spreading perianth, often more or less zygomorphic. Stamens as long as the perianth or slightly longer. Fruit round, small.

This genus, originally created by Riccobono for *B. Ventimigliae*, has been extended to include about nine species.

Borzicactus ventimigliae Riccobono. Probably native of Ecuador; originally raised from seed received from Ecuador, at the gardens of La Mortola, Ventimiglia. Stem mostly erect, rarely branched, but throwing up offshoots from the base when old, deep green, about 2 m. high, 4 to 6 cm. thick, with 8 to 10 broad low ribs, deeply notched transversely like an inverted A between the areoles, which are 2 to 3 cm. apart, oval, with short brown wool. Spines brownish yellow, the radials about 6, and 1½ to 2½ cm. long, the centrals 1 or 2, up to 4 cm. long. Flowers 5 to 6 cm. long, regular, funnel-shaped, pale red, outer petals dark red. Rather fast-growing, delighting in full sunshine.

Borzicactus sepium (DC.) Br. et R. = *Cereus sepium* DC. Ecuador. Stem light green, about 1¼ m. high, mostly erect, 4 to 5 cm. thick, sending up offshoots from the base, but rarely branching, with 8 to 11 low broad ribs, with a transverse notch between the areoles, which are small, oval, 1½ to 2 cm. apart, brown, afterwards grey. Radial spines 8 to 10, up to 1 cm. long, brownish; central spines 1, rarely 2, up to 2 cm. long. Flower about 4 cm. long, u.s., outer petals red, inner pink. Stamens red, style reddish, stigma green. Fruit small, round, red, eatable. Fairly fast-growing, flowers even on young specimens. Closely allied to the preceding.

var. **Roezlii** (Fred. Haage), also referred to as a *Lemaireocereus*, has thicker stems of a deeper green, more erect, almost columnar, with 6 to 9 ribs. Flowers pale red.

Borzicactus Faustianus Backbg. A recent species from the Andes of Peru. A fast-growing species, with a grass green stem, erect or prostrate, 4 to 5 cm. thick. Ribs 12, narrow and prominent, or acute, with large oval areoles, about ½ cm. apart, furnished with short brownish yellow wool. Spines very numerous 30 or more, 1 to 1½ cm.

long, the lower spines being bristle-like and pale yellow, the upper ones stronger, yellow or bronze yellow. Flower red, u.s. Stems branched from the base, about 1 m. long, usually sprawling when longer than 15 cm. This is another lovely species well deserving of cultivation.

Borzicactus tominensis (Weingt.) Br. et R. = *Cereus tominensis* Weingt. Andes of Bolivia. Stem erect, light powdery green, up to 1½ m. high, and 5 to 8 cm. thick, with 10 to 12 ribs, broad and low, with narrow transverse notches between the areoles, which are 1 to 2 cm. apart, and are oval in shape, with short yellowish wool. Spines yellowish white, soft; the radials about 6, from 1 to 2 cm. long; the centrals 1 or 2, up to 5 cm. long. Flowers red, about 8 cm. long. Stems branching from the base. Growth rather slow, but thrives well on own roots and requires full sunshine. Rather rare in cultivation.

Borzicactus platinospinus Werd. et Backbg. = *Cereus platinospinus* Werd. et Backbg. Peru, near Arequipa. Stem erect or semi-prostrate, up to 50 cm. long, and about 5 cm. thick, branching from the base, dull green, very thickly covered with spines and hairy at the top, with about 13 ribs, ½ cm. deep, and strongly notched between the areoles, which are greyish. Spines on new growth whitish, tipped brown or black. Radial spines up to 13, spreading, stiff, needle-like, up to 1½ cm. long, greyish white, tipped dark. Central spines 2 to 4, awl-shaped, very stiff, platinum grey, the lowermost up to 6 cm. long. Flower scarlet, about 6 cm. long.

Borzicactus Morleyanus Br. et R. Ecuador. Stem up to 1 m. high, erect or prostrate, branching from the base, 3 to 6 cm. thick, dark green, with 11 to 16 low narrow ribs, with a V-shaped notch above the areoles, which are ½ to 1 cm. apart. Spines about 20, unequal, slender, soft but sharp, brownish, up to 2½ cm. long. Flowers zygomorphic, carmine, with a slender tube: stamens violet above, stigma creamy white. Fruit roundish, about 2 cm. thick, yellowish green.

Borzicactus Websterianus Backbg. Ecuador. Stem erect, branched from the base, pale green, up to 10 cm. thick, with about 14 ribs, narrow at the top, broad below, low, with a V-shaped groove above the areoles. Spines golden yellow, radiating, about 20 radials and 4 centrals, 6 to 12 mm. long, one of the centrals much thicker and up to 5 cm. long. Flowers carmine, distinctly zygomorphic.

var. **rufispinus** Backbg. Stem dark green; spines dark reddish brown.

Borzicactus Fieldianus Br. et R. Peru (Huaraz). Stems 3 to 6 m. long, erect or semi-prostrate, branching mostly from the base, with only 6 or 7 broad ribs, 1 to 2 cm. high, notched between the areoles, which are large, round, with a transverse furrow above them. Spines 6 to 10, white, awl-shaped, unequal, 1 or 2 of them about 5 cm. long. Flowers borne at the top of the stems, 6 to 7 cm. long, with a cylindrical tube and short spreading limb, red. Ovary and scales of tube hairy. Fruit globular or ovoid, 2 cm. thick.

Borzicactus jajoianus Backbg. is another species of recent introduction, similar to *B. Sepium*.

CACTI

HARRISIA Br. et R.

Stems at first erect, tall-growing, but rather slender and weak, and soon become prostrate or sprawling, branched, with 5 to 11 broad rounded ribs. Spines variable, but usually long. Flowers rather large, with a long tube, nocturnal, mostly white, borne near the tops of the stems, of the preceding year's growth. Fruit round, large, naked, red or yellow. Seeds large, black. Includes about 19 species, many of which are favourites in cultivation.

Harrisia eriophora (Pfeiff.) Br. et R. = *Cereus eriophorus* Pfeiff. Cuba. Stem pale green, 4 cm. thick, and over 3 m. high, with 8 or 9 ribs, rounded and close together, with narrow furrows between them, with gibbosities on which are situated the areoles, which are 2 to 4 cm. apart, elongated, whitish. Spines 6 to 9, spreading, brownish, with a darker point and up to 4 cm. long. Flowers about 18 cm. long, with a greenish tube, petals reddish outside, white inside. Requires much warmth and sunshine.

Harrisia gracilis (Mill.) Br. et R. = *Cereus gracilis* Mill. Jamaica. Another warmth-loving species, originally described by Miller in 1768, described again by Haworth in 1812, under the name of *Cereus repandus* Haw., and again in 1819 under the name of *Cereus subrepandus* Haw., this last being probably a mere form. Should not be confused with *Cereus repandus* Mill. Stems up to 7 m. long, dark green, slender, about 3½ cm. thick, sprawling, with 9 to 11 ribs, closely set, broad and gibbose, with whitish areoles about 2 cm. apart. Spines 10 to 16, up to 2½ cm. long, white, tipped black. Flowers issuing from tufts of white hairs on the upper areoles, about 20 cm. long. Ovary and tube with scales and few hairs; outer petals brownish, inner petals white. Fruit round, about 4 cm. thick, yellow. There is a pretty cristate variety in cultivation. A purely tropical species, very free-flowering, but more delicate than the preceding.

Harrisia Bonplandii (Parm.) Br. et R. = *Cereus Bonplandii* Parm. = *Eriocereus Bonplandii* Riccobono. Brazil, Argentina and Paraguay. Stem about 3 m. long, and 3 to 6 cm. thick, bluish green passing to greyish, with 4 to 6 ribs (sometimes only 3), with low, broad furrows between them. Areoles 1½ to 3 cm. apart, greyish. Spines 3 to 5 or more, grey, up to 4 cm. long. Flower large and showy, up to 25 cm. long, with a scaly and hairy ovary, the outer petals brownish green, the inner white. Fruit round, 5 to 6 cm. thick, red, warty and scaly, but without hairs.

Harrisia Jusbertii (Reb.) Br. et R. = *Cereus Jusbertii* Reb. = *Eriocereus Jusbertii* Berger. Argentina or Paraguay. Possibly a variety or a natural hybrid of the preceding, and is often referred to as *Harrisia Bonplandii* var. *brevispina* Hort. Stem mostly erect, slightly branched, dark green, 4 to 6 cm. thick, with 5 or 6 ribs, with broad and shallow furrows or grooves between them. Areoles 2 cm. apart, yellowish passing to grey. Radial spines about 7, thick, conical, but very short, not more than ½ cm. long, dark brown, almost black. Central spines of the same shape and colour, and slightly longer. Flowers about 18 cm. long, freely borne, outer petals brownish green, inner petals white. Very frequently used as stock for grafting.

Harrisia pomanensis (Weber) Br. et R. = *Cereus pomanensis* Weber = *Eriocereus pomanensis* Berger. North-western Argentina. Stem mostly erect, bluish green passing to greyish, with 3 to 6 ribs, obtuse and rounded. Areoles about 2 cm. apart, brownish. Radial spines 6 to 8, about 1 cm. long, awl-shaped, whitish or greyish, tipped black. Central spines 1, rarely 2, up to 2 cm. long, same shape and colour. Flower about 16 cm. long, white, outer petals greenish.

var. **Grossei** Weingt. Stem pale green, with 3 or 4 ribs, more slender. Flowers more freely, and has longer spines.

Harrisia Martinii (Lab.) Br. et R. = *Cereus Martinii* Lab. = *Cereus monacanthus* Cels. non Lem. = *Eriocereus Martinii* Riccobono. Argentina. Stems about 2 m. long, sprawling, branched, green passing to greyish green, 3 to 5 cm. thick, with 4 or 5 low broad, gibbose ribs. Areoles on the gibbosities, 3 to 3½ cm. apart, greyish. Radial spines 5 to 7, very short. Central spines 1, rarely 2 or 3, pale brown tipped darker, up to 3 cm. long, straight and stiff. Flowers freely produced throughout the summer, about 20 cm. long, outer petals pale green with reddish tips, inner petals white. Fruit red, round, warty, spiny.

Harrisia perviridis Weingt. = *Cereus perviridis* Weingt. Argentina. Similar to the preceding, with more slender stems and also much longer, of a grass green colour, with a shorter central spine. The flower is as large or larger, with narrower petals, of same colour.

Harrisia Regelii Weingt. = *Cereus Regelii* Weingt. = *Cereus regalis* Hort. Argentina? Similar to *H. Martinii*, with thicker stem, and 2 to 4 central spines, which are also longer. The flowers are of the same size or larger; the outer petals are pale pink and the inner white, sweet-scented. The fruit is smaller, more warty, bright red. Very free-flowering, often flowering again in autumn. Possibly these two species are in reality only well-marked varieties of *H. Martinii*.

Harrisia Guelichii (Speg.) Br. et R. = *Cereus Guelichii* Speg. = *Eriocereus Guelichii* Berger. Argentina. Stem slender, 2 to 4 cm. thick, very long and sprawling, branched, pale green, with 3 or 4 prominent ribs, with flat and shallow grooves between them. Areoles at first white, passing to grey, 2 to 6 cm. apart. Spines reddish when young, passing to ashy grey, tipped dark or black. Radials 4 or 5, about ½ cm. long. Central spine only one, much thicker, and up to 2½ cm. long. Flowers up to 25 cm. long, greenish outside, white inside, with large scales on the ovary and tube, but with very few hairs. Fruit round, red, scaly, spineless. A fast-growing and free-flowering species. Rather liable to suffer from cold, and dislikes a soil containing an excess of soluble lime. Is best grown in a mixture of sand and leaf-mould.

Harrisia tortuosa (Forb.) Br. et R. = *Cereus tortuosus* Forb. = *Eriocereus tortuosus* Riccobono = *Cereus atropurpureus* Haage.

Argentina. Stem about 1 m. long, branched, erect or sprawling, 3 to 4 cm. thick, dark purplish green, with 5 to 7 ribs more or less arranged spirally. The ribs are broad, rounded, gibbose, with narrow furrows between them. Areoles greyish, about 2 cm. apart. Radial spines about 8, spreading, stout, up to 2 cm. long, at first reddish brown, passing to brown and greyish. Central spines 1 to 3, same colour, thicker and up to 4 cm. long. Flowers borne freely, about 16 cm. long. Ovary warty, with reddish green scales, whitish hairs and small spines. Outer petals brownish green, the inner white. Fruit large, round, red, warty and spiny.

Cereus Arendtii Hildm. et Mathss., from Uruguay, is probably only a variety of *Harrisia tortuosa*, with more numerous and longer spines.

Harrisia adscendens (Gürke) Br. et R. = *Cereus adscendens* Gürke = *Eriocereus adscendens* Berger. Brazil (Bahia). Stem erect or partly sprawling, up to 2 m. long, pale glaucous green, 2½ to 5 cm. thick, with 7 to 10 ribs, low, rounded, with long gibbosities on which are situated the large greyish areoles, 4 to 5 cm. apart. Spines about 10, stout, 2 to 4 cm. long, at first reddish brown, passing to brown and grey, tipped dark, spreading. Flowers about 25 cm. long, greenish outside, white inside; ovary and tube scaly and spiny, with yellowish brown hairs. Grows fast and flowers freely.

Harrisia platygona (Otto) Br. et R. = *Cereus platygonus* Otto = *Eriocereus platygonus* Riccobono. Argentina? Stem slender about 2 cm. thick, much branched, with 6 to 8 low rounded ribs, with narrow furrows between them. Areoles small, on prominences, less than 1 cm. apart. Spines about 14, radiating, at first golden brown, passing to grey, bristle-like, about 1 cm. long. Only one central spine, slightly longer. Flowers about 12 cm. long, outer petals green outside, brownish inside, inner petals white.

Other species occasionally cultivated, are.

Harrisia Fernowii Britton, from Cuba.

H. fragrans Small, from Louisiana and Florida.

H. portoricensis Britton, from the West Indies.

H. Earlei Br. et R. from the West Indies.

H. Brookii Britton, from the West Indies

HAAGEOCEREUS Backbg.

The genus *Haageocereus* was created by Backeberg for *Haageocereus decumbens*, a plant from the dry Pacific regions of Peru. According to Backeberg, the genus is characterised by the night-blooming flowers being larger than those of *Borzicactus*, borne near the top of the stem, with a slender tube 8 to 12 cm. long, and with a broad limb, regular, and fully expanded. The tube has small scales and a few hairs. The inner segments of the perianth are greenish white, creamy, or mostly pink. The fruit is roundish or oval, 3 to 4 cm. long, with a few scales and hairs, but no spines, green or pinkish, with the remains of the withered flower attached to it. The seeds are black.

The genus was afterwards extended by Backeberg to include also other species, all Peruvian plants of the Pacific Andes, growing in a very dry soil, but capable of resisting damp, thus proving that the region was formerly much less dry than at present.

Haageocereus decumbens (Vaup.) Backbg. = *Cereus decumbens* Vaupel = *Borzicactus decumbens* Br. et R. Peru. Stem dull green, semi-prostrate or prostrate, up to 50 cm. long, and 4 to 6 cm. thick, branching from the base, with about 20 low ribs, notched between the areoles, which are ½ cm. apart, small, yellowish, woolly. Radial spines very numerous, bristle-like, snowy white passing to greyish, up to ½ cm. long. Central spines 2 to 5, black or dark brown, 2 of which are stronger and up to 4 cm. long, mostly directed upwards. Flowers white, nocturnal, 7 cm. long, sweet-scented. Fruit pink, roundish, as large as a pigeon's egg, smooth or with a few hairy scales. Seeds small, black, rather dull.

Haageocereus pacalaensis Backbg. A comparatively new species from the same Pacific region of Peru. Has thick clustering stems, mostly erect and tall, 5 to 6 cm. thick, with about 15 straight ribs, slightly notched, with closely set oval areoles and amber-coloured spines. The flowers are about as large as those of the preceding species, of a lively pink and fully expanded.

Haageocereus acranthus (Vaup.) Werd. et Backbg. = *Cereus acranthus* Vaupel = *Binghamia acrantha* Br. et R. From the same region of Peru, near Chosica. Has thick clustering stems, with a stiff erect habit of growth, rather tall, but not so thick as in the preceding species, with 10 to 14 low ribs, rather thick, and slightly notched near the top. Areoles closely set, oval, large, with many radial yellow spines and 1 or 2 central spines up to 2 cm. long, very thick and awl-shaped, yellowish brown, passing to greyish. The flowers are borne at the top of the stems, greenish white or pale pink, 6 to 8 cm. long; stamens exserted beyond the throat of the flower.

Haageocereus australis Backbg. Desert regions of southern Peru. Plant up to 1 m. high, branched, with joints up to 2½ cm. long, and 6 cm. thick, dark green, usually clavate at the top. Ribs about 14, low; areoles about ½ cm. apart, at first yellowish white. Spines ashy grey; about 20 radials up to 8 mm. long, slender; central spines 8 to 12 up to 4½ cm. long, 1 or 2 of them being longer than the others, thicker and darker at the tip. Flower white, about 7 cm. long. Fruit large, pink when ripe.

Haageocereus Olowinskianus Backbg. = *Cereus Olowinskianus* Backbg. Central Peru. Stems erect, up to 1 m. high and about 7 cm. thick, grass green, with about 13 ribs, broad and low. Areoles oval, about 11 mm. apart, with a V-shaped groove above them, at first yellowish white. Spines pale yellow, passing to brown and grey; radial spines 30 or more, stiff and up to 1 cm. long; central spines 10 to 12, thicker and slightly longer, but 1 or 2 of them up to 6 cm. long and directed downwards. Flowers white, about 8 cm. long.

Haageocereus versicolor Backbg. = *Cereus versicolor* Werd. et Backbg. From the same region of Peru, where it grows in association with *Neoraimondia macrostibas*. This new species is one of the most beautiful *Cerei*, with stiff erect stems up to 1½ m. high, and up to 8 cm. thick, growing in clumps branching from the base. The stems are light green, with about 12 ribs, low and obtuse. Areoles rather close together, and somewhat hairy, with numerous radial spines (up to 30), straight, about ½ cm. long, and 1 or 2 central spines, up to 4 cm. long, mostly directed downwards. All spines are yellow, prettily variegated with reddish brown zones, sometimes entirely purplish or rusty red. Flower about 11 cm. long: tube slender, with white hairs. The fruit is roundish, about 3 cm. across, yellow, somewhat hairy. The seeds are small, dull black.

var. **lasiacanthus** Werd. et Backbg. Central spines shorter and more spreading; radial spines more slender and bristle-like.

var. **xanthacanthus** Werd. et Backbg. Stem more erect, with fewer ribs (10 to 12), less prominent and more notched. Central spines up to 2½ cm. long, lighter yellow.

var. **humifusus** Werd. et Backbg. Stems prostrate, grass green, with about 12 low ribs. Areoles smaller, with fewer radial spines. Central spines up to 3 cm. long, more slender, yellow with a dark point.

To the above species the characters of the genus *Haageocereus* apply more distinctly. To the same genus Backeberg also referred *Binghamia chosicensis* Werd. et Backbg. = *Cereus chosicensis* Backbg., which is very similar to, and probably identical with, *Pseudoespostoa melanostele* Backbg. = *Binghamia melanostele* Br. et R. = *Cereus melanostele* Vaup., from Peru (Chosica, along the road Lima-Oroya), *Cereus rigidissimus* Backbg., and *Cereus pseudomelanostele* Backbg., all natives of the same Peruvian region. This last species is now frequently offered by dealers, and a brief description is given hereunder:

Haageocereus pseudomelanostele Werd. et Backbg. = *Cereus pseudomelanostele* Backbg. = *Binghamia pseudomelanostele* Werd. et Backbg. Peru, near Cajamarquilla, on the Lima-Oroya road. Stems about 1 m. high, freely branching from the base, more or less club-shaped. Ribs 18 to 22 or more. Areoles woolly, with numerous whitish or golden yellow bristle-like spines, associated with curly bristles of the same colour. Central spines 1 or more, golden yellow to greyish yellow, up to 8 cm. long. Flower 4 to 5 cm. long, greenish white.

The characters of *Haageocereus* are still rather obscure, and it is not clear whether to accept it as a distinct genus, or as a sub-genus of *Borzicactus* and a term of passage from *Binghamia* and *Harrisia* to *Borzicactus*. However, all the species are very desirable and of easy cultivation.

(*a*) SELENICEREUS GRANDIFLORUS

(*b*) SELENICEREUS JALAPENSIS
PLATE XX

(b) APOROCACTUS FLAGELLIFORMIS

(a) MEDIOCACTUS LINDMANNII

PLATE XXI

CEREEAE

CLEISTOCACTUS Lemaire

Stems mostly slender, erect or decumbent, throwing up offshoots from the base, or branched, with numerous ribs more or less rounded, bearing round areoles, usually small and closely set. Flowers small, with a long narrow tube, recurved, sometimes almost straight, with the perianth tube-like and almost closed, through which just protrude the stamens. Ovary and tube scaly and hairy. Fruit a small round berry with black seeds. The colour of the flowers is usually scarlet or orange. Includes 14 species.

The species are all South American, and all deservedly popular, of fast growth and of easy cultivation, requiring warmth, full sunshine, and frequent watering when in bloom. They are easily propagated by seed, cuttings of the topped stems or offshoots.

Cleistocactus Baumannii Lem. = *Cereus Baumannii* Lem. Western Argentina, Uruguay and Paraguay. Stem stiff, mostly erect, 3 to 4 cm. thick, and up to 1 m. high, with about 14 ribs, studded with yellow or yellowish brown areoles, bearing numerous yellowish or yellowish brown. spines, the upper spines directed upwards being stronger and up to 4 cm. long. Flowers cropping up throughout the summer, from areoles which have developed a small tuft of white wool. They are orange scarlet, 6 to 7 cm. long, curved, scaly and hairy at the tip, with crimson stamens just exserted and close to the upper lip of the perianth. Fruit a small round berry.

var. **flavispinus** Hort. Stem more slender, 2 to 3 cm. thick. Areoles yellow and all spines pale yellow, 1 to 3 from each areole directed upwards, and up to 4 cm. long.

Cleistocactus colubrinus Lem. = *Cereus colubrinus* Otto = *C. Baumannii colubrinus* K. Sch. Native of the same countries as the preceding. Has thick stems (4 to 5 cm.) of a darker green, with dark brown areoles, with longer and darker spines, almost black. The flowers are slightly larger, scarlet or dark scarlet, but not so freely borne. The stems are sometimes sprawling. Often classed as a variety of *C. Baumannii*.

var. **Grossei** Hort. From Paraguay. Has yellow spines and pink flowers.

var. **flavispinus** Salm-Dyck. Has pale yellow areoles, and long pale yellow spines. Flowers scarlet.

Cleistocactus smaragdiflorus (Weber) Speg. = *Cereus smaragdiflorus* Weber. Argentina, Uruguay and Paraguay. Sometimes classed as a variety of *C. Baumannii*, but is certainly quite distinct. Stems 4 to 6 cm. thick, stiff and erect, often over 2 m. high, later more or less decumbent. Areoles yellow to yellowish brown, closely set. Spines numerous, yellowish brown to dark brown, the upper spines up to 3 cm. long, but slender and flexible. Flowers $3\frac{1}{2}$ to 5 cm. long, tubular, straight or very slightly recurved, reddish yellow or scarlet, the tips of the tiny petals being of an emerald green, contrasting vividly with the colour of the tube.

N

var. **flavispinus** Borg. *n. var.* Spines yellow, passing to pale yellow or almost white. Growth very robust.

Cleistocactus anguinus (Gurke) Br. et R. = *Cereus anguinus* Gürke. Paraguay. A fast-growing species with long slender trailing stems, 2 to 3 cm. thick, and about 2 m. long. Stem dark green with about 12 ribs. Areoles black, spines pale yellow or white. The flowers are curved as in *C. Baumannii*, of a lively cinnabar red. but more slender, 5 to 6 cm. long, produced continuously in late spring and summer.

Cleistocactus serpens (H.B.K.) Backbg. = *Cactus serpens* H.B.K. = *Cereus serpens* DC. North Peru, near Huancabamba. Stem slender, branching from the base, prostrate and trailing. Ribs 10 or 11, at first prominent and warty, later low and almost flat. Areoles ½ to 1 cm. apart, with greyish wool. Radial spines 10 to 15, spreading upwards, about ½ cm. long. One central spine, up to 3 cm. long. New spines are pale yellow to brown, later grey. Flowers about 5 cm. long, tubular, almost straight, pink or pale pink.

Cleistocactus aureispinus Frič = *Cereus aureispinus* Frič. Boundary Argentina-Bolivia. Stems 3 to 4 cm. thick, freely branching from the base, at first erect, afterwards sprawling, up to 60 cm. long, with many slender flexible needle-like spines 2 to 4 cm. long, directed outwards, yellow to pale yellow or almost creamy white. Ribs many, narrow and rounded. Flowers about 4 cm. long, tubular, slightly recurved, pale orange yellow.

Cleistocactus Herzogianus Backbg. Central Bolivia (Quebradas), at a height of 2,500 m. Stem up to 2 m. high, erect and branched from the base, and often also above ground, about 5 cm. thick, greyish green, somewhat glaucous, with about 11 rounded ribs, prominent and notched into tubercles, on which are round yellowish or greyish areoles. Radial spines about 8, up to 6 mm. long, pale yellow. Only one central spine, directed outwards, up to 2 cm. long, same colour, often absent. Flowers about 3 cm. long, tubular, straight, borne on the sides of the stem near the top, scaly and hairy, yellowish red, with the tip of the petals recurved and bright red. Style greenish,slightly exserted beyond the petals. Fruit small, round, red; seeds small, glossy black.

Cleistocactus Buchtienii Backbg. Possibly a variety of the preceding, with stiff erect stems, about 1½ m. high, freely branching from the base, about 4 cm. thick, with closely set brownish areoles, and many reddish spines, slender and spreading 1½ to 2½ cm. long.

Cleistocactus Strausii (Vaup.) Backbg. = *Cereus Strausii* Vaupel = *Pilocereus Strausii* Heese = *Borzicactus Strausii* Berger. A most lovely species from the hills of Bolivia. Stems slender, erect, up to 1 m. high, sending up offshoots from the base, but rarely branching unless topped, entirely covered with delicate white spines. The stem is light green, with about 25 narrow low ribs. Areoles small, about ½ cm. apart, with whitish wool, with 30 or more hair-like, straight, white bristles, about 1½ cm. long, and about 4 pale yellow spines, 2 to 4 cm.

long. Flowers borne sparingly along the sides of old stems, red, 8 to 9 cm. long, only slightly curved, scaly and hairy at the tip, where the expanded petals assume a carmine or violet carmine hue, with pale red stamens. A variety in which the 4 central spines are of a glassy white, and only slightly longer than the bristle-like radials is frequent in cultivation, and a very pretty cristate form is also met with. Popular with all growers, particularly so the charming variety with glassy white spines.

var. **Fricii** Doerfler. Stems thickly furnished with straight long white hairs at the top.

var. **jujuyensis** Frič. The 4 central spines are brown. It is the form found growing at Jujuy (Argentina).

Cleistocactus nivosus *sp. nov.* Imported from the Bolivian Andes, along with a snow white variety of *C. Strausii*, and sold out as such, now turns out to be a very distinct species. Stem shorter than that of *C. Strausii*, up to 50 cm. high, 4 to 6 cm. thick, but more rigid, branching from the base, entirely covered with white bristle-like spines and snowy white hairs down to the base. Ribs about 26, straight, obtuse. Areoles rather large, ½ cm. apart, with whitish or greyish wool. Radial spines many, bristle-like, ½ to 1 cm. long, spreading over the ribs, glassy white, later greyish, with many soft long hairs, up to 2 cm. long, and 1 or 2 central spines, one over the other, 2 to 3 cm. long, with 1 to 3 others much smaller, spreading out, transparent yellow and slender. Flowers borne in late spring, on the upper part of the stem. Flower 7 to 8 cm. long, perfectly straight, about twice as long as that of *C. Strausii*, the colour is strawberry red or cochineal red, the tube being 1 cm. thick, with linear scales densely covered with white silky hairs; outer petals greenish purple violet, inner petals just shorter, ovate, obtuse, purple violet. Stamens as long as the inner petals, purplish violet, in a thick bundle around the style, with purplish anthers. Style thick, purplish, exserted for about 1 cm. beyond the inner petals; stigma with about 12 greenish purple lobes. Ovary roundish, 13 mm. thick, with many hair-like spinescent bristles at the base, scaly and densely covered with long silky white hairs.

The following is the Latin diagnosis of the new species:

Cleistocactus nivosus sp. nov. *A basi ramosus, rigidus, ad 50 cm. elatus, 4 ad 6 cm. validus; spinis radialibus plurimis, adpressis, albidis, setaceis ½ ad 1 cm. longis, et niveis capillis ad 2 cm. longis prorsus indutus; costis circiter 26, rectis, obtusis; areolis grandiusculis, 5 mm. remotis; una aut duabus spinis centralibus, superimpositis, aureis, pellucidis, 2-3 cm. longis, porrectis, tenuioribus, 1-3 spinis exiguis additis; flore 7-8 cm. longo, tubo crassitudinis 1 cm., recto, coccineo, squamis linearibus dense pilosis; sepalis externis ovatis, obtusis, purpureo-violaceis virescentibus, petalis vix brevioribus purpureo-violaceis; staminibus ad petalis longis, purpureo-violaceis, antheribus purpurinis; stylo crassiore purpurino ad 1 cm. ultra flore exserto, lobis stygmatis ad 12, purpurino-virescentibus; ovario globoso, squamuloso, dense piloso, basi* *setis albidis spinescentibus ad 1½ cm. longis, et capillis sericeis praedita.*

Cleistocactus areolatus (Muehl.) Br. et R. = *Cereus areolatus* Muehlenpf. Bolivian Andes. Stems glaucous green, erect or semi-prostrate, branching from the base, of rather slow growth and often jointed, 30 to 50 cm. long, 3 to 4 cm. thick, with 12 low ribs. Areoles yellowish brown passing to greyish. Spines about 12, yellowish white, needle-like, short, with one central spine of the same colour, 2 to 3 cm. Flowers 4 to 5 cm. long, recurved, of a lively pinkish red. Now rather rare in cultivation.

Cleistocactus tupizensis Vaupel = *Cereus tupizensis* Vaup. Tupiza (Bolivia). Stems slender, branching from the base, mostly erect, with 10 to 12 ribs, and 2 to 3 m. high, and 2½ to 3½ cm. thick. Areoles large oval, with 15 to 20 sharp and awl-shaped, but short radial spines and 2 central spines about 4 cm. long. All spines reddish brown. Flower tubular, recurved, zygomorphic, 8 cm. long, salmon-pink.

Cleistocactus Morawetzianus Backbg. Ravines of Central Peru. Stems up to 2 m. high, erect, with a sturdy habit of growth, 5 to 6 cm. thick, branching from the base, greyish green. Ribs 14 to 16, rounded, low, with a V-shaped furrow above the areoles. Spines many, but short, golden yellow or pale yellow, passing to whitish or greyish, 1 to 3 of them up to 2 cm. long. Flowers about 5½ cm. long, tubular, slightly curved, constricted above the ovary, greenish white or white or honey coloured. The only known species with white flowers.

Cereus parviflorus K. Sch. from the Bolivian Andes, and **C. hyalacanthus** K. Sch., from Jujuy (Argentina), are obviously species of Cleistocactus, but apparently they have disappeared from cultivation.

CARNEGIEA Br. et R.
(*Lepidocereus* Engelmann)

This genus, created by Britton and Rose in honour of Carnegie, the well-known American philanthropist, includes only one species, **Carnegiea gigantea** (Engelm.) Br. et R. = *Cereus giganteus* Engelm. = *Lepidocereus giganteus* Engelm. = *Pilocereus giganteus* Lem., the celebrated *Sahuaro* or *Saguaro* of Arizona, south-eastern California and Sonora in Mexico.

The following generic characters may be taken also as those of the species. Stem columnar, very tall and thick, dark green, branched rather sparingly at some distance above ground, the branches being erect and parallel to the main stem, which may be up to 14 m. high, with 1 to 8 or more branches. Ribs 12 to 24, obtuse. Areoles 2 to 2½ cm. apart, with brown wool. Spines numerous, brown passing to greyish, with darker tip, awl-shaped, thick and stiff, bulbous at the base: the radials spreading, up to 2 cm. long; the centrals 3 to 6, thicker and longer, up to 8 cm. long. Flowers produced near the top of mature specimens, the flowering areoles being furnished with more numerous needle-like spines. The flower is about 12 cm. long, and about as broad, with a scaly ovary, and a short slightly scaly tube, greenish outside with a few whitish hairs, white inside, the petals being obtuse and the inner ones shorter. Stamens very numerous, with yellow anthers, and only about three-fourths the length of the petals. Pistil thick, creamy white, stigma with about 15 lobes. Fruit, a berry, 6 to 9 cm. long, red, spiny at the base, with red pulp, eatable. Seeds small, of a shining black colour.

Flowers in May-June, the flowers remaining in bloom for 4 to 9 hours. Grows slowly, a plant 1 m. high being about 30 years old, afterwards growth is quicker; but the huge specimens at Arizona and Sonora, with a stem about 12 m. high and 50 cm. thick at the base, must be over 200 years old. The fruit is relished by the natives. In conformity with the rules of priority the generic name should be *Lepidocereus* Engelmann.

RATHBUNIA Br. et R.

Bushes with straggling stems, more or less slender, with 4 to 8 ribs, mostly irregular. Central spine awl-shaped. Flower tubular, and funnel-shaped at the limb, diurnal, red; limb regular or somewhat irregular, with the stamens in a brush-like bundle, longer than the perianth. Fruit at first spiny, smooth towards maturity, with the dried flower persisting upon it. Seeds black, pitted. Includes 4 species, natives of hot and dry regions in Mexico.

Rathbunia alamosensis (Coult.) Br. et R. = *Cereus alamosensis* Coulter. Mexico (Alamos-Sonora). A bush 2 to 4 m. high. Stem erect branching above and from the base, up to 8 cm. thick, deep green, with 58 irregular obtuse ribs, deeply indented or crenate. Radial spines about 12, whitish, spreading. Central spines 1 to 4, spreading, same colour, thicker and longer, up to 5 cm. Flower 4 to 10 cm. long, terracotta red, with a more or less irregular limb and rather short segments of perianth. Ovary scaly, with a little wool and small spines, which drop off at maturity. Growth vigorous and quick.

Rathbunia Kerberi (K. Sch.) Br. et R. = *Cereus Kerberi* K. Sch. Mexico (Pacific side of Colima volcano.) A bush 1 to 2 m. high, with erect branched stems. Ribs 4, straight, deeply indented or crenate, obtuse. Areoles round or elliptical, greyish brown. Spines up to 16, stiff, spreading, awl-shaped; central spines 1 to 4, 3 to 5 cm. long. Flowers borne on the side near the top, up to 12 cm. long. Ovary ovoid, warty, with small red scales, brownish wool and bristles; tube funnel-shaped and somewhat tubular, with small reddish scales, and limb irregular or zygomorphic, about 4 cm. across, pink, the outer petals being lanceolate and narrow, the inner broader. Stamens longer than the petals, red, with purple anthers: style red, with a 5-lobed stigma.

Rathbunia sonorensis (Runge) Br. et R. = *Cereus sonorensis* Runge = *C. Simonii* Hildm. Mexico (Sonora). A low bush about 60 cm. high, much branched. Stems softish and weak, dull pale green, 2 to 3 cm. thick, often sprawling and pendulous, somewhat tinged reddish, very uneven in diameter, 2 to 5 cm. thick. Ribs 4 to 7, spiral or straight, blunt, uneven and irregular, deeply indented. Areoles small, white, ½ to 1 cm. apart. Spines slender, hair-like and flexible, yellowish passing to white; radials very short, centrals 2 to 5, up to 2 cm. long, mostly curved or twisted. Flower funnel-shaped, 8 to 9 cm. long, and about 5 cm. broad, almost regular, of a glossy carmine red.

Rathbunia pseudosonorensis (Runge) Berger = *Cereus pseudosonorensis* Runge. Mexico, same region as the preceding, to which it is similar but with longer and thicker stems, more erect. Flower regular, with shorter segments of perianth, of a glossy scarlet red.

ZEHNTNERELLA Br. et R.

Stems erect or prostrate, up to 60 cm. long, branching from the base, the branches being 20 to 30 cm. long, with many ribs. Areoles small, with many short spines. Flowers white, quite small, with many long hairs inside the throat. Tube short, both ovary and tube being covered with small scales, with white hairs in their axils. Fruit small, globose, with very small brown or black seeds. Includes one species, chiefly of botanical interest. **Zehntnerella squamulosa** (Gürke) Br. et R. = *Cereus squamulosus* Gürke non Salm-Dyck = *C. squamosus* Gürke = *Leocereus squamosus* (Gürke) Werd. Brazil (Bahia and Piauhy). Should not be confused with *Rhipsalis squamulosa* = *Cereus squamulosus* Salm-Dyck = *Lepismium commune* Pfeiff., a humble species of triangular-stemmed *Rhipsalis*, common in cultivation.

LOPHOCEREUS (Berger) Br. et R.

Stems erect, columnar, mostly unbranched, but sending up offshoots from the base, with few ribs and short thick spines, without any development of hairs. Flowering stems develop tufts of long hair-like bristles from the upper flowering areoles, and each one of these areoles produce simultaneously or successively several flowers.

There is only one species.

Lophocereus Schottii (Engelm.) Br. et R. = *Cereus Schottii* Engelm. = *Pilocereus Schottii* Lem. Sonora, Arizona and Lower California. Stems dull green, erect, branching from the base, about 6 cm. thick. and 1 to 5 m. high, with 5 to 7 (occasionally 9) broad, acute ribs. Areoles large, with short whitish wool, about 1 cm. apart, with 4 to 7 thick conical spines, less than 1 cm. long, of a dark colour, almost black, afterwards becoming greyish. The central part of the growing top of the stem is often of a violet or purplish colour. Flowering stems have larger areoles, with a tuft of about 20 greyish brown bristles, not spinescent, and about 6 cm. long, the tufts at the top of the stem forming a sort of crest, to which the name of the genus is due. Flowers nocturnal, 3 to 4 cm. long, with a short tube, greenish outside, red inside, with white stamens. Fruit round, red. Growth is slow, but is otherwise easy of cultivation, thriving well in half-shade or in full sunshine.

var. **australis** K. Brand. More slender stems, usually with 6 ribs.

var. **Sargentianus** Orc. = *Pilocereus Sargentianus* Orc. Has longer spines (1 to 2 cm.), and smaller flowers.

var. **Gatesii** M. Jones. Has slender stems and rounded ribs.

There is in cultivation a monstrous form of peculiar appearance, with irregular ribs and spineless areoles on prominent warts. Another monstrosity, recently introduced from Sonora (Mexico), has slender stems, slightly purplish green, with irregular but smooth ribs, and very small spineless areoles. To this last the name of *Cereus* (*Lemaireocereus*) *Mieckleyanus* Weingt. has been given, under the impression that it was a distinct species, and is still sold under that name.

Myrtillocactus Console

A small genus of large shrubs reaching a height of 3 or 4 m. with a short thick stem and thick erect branches, very stiff, 8 to 10 cm. thick, very smooth, with 6 to 8 ribs or angles. Flowers produced several together from the same areole, small, diurnal with a spineless ovary. Fruit a small, fleshy, olive-shaped or globular berry, edible, with minute black seeds.

This genus includes five species, natives of Mexico, California, and Guatemala. They thrive well in the open in the Mediterranean region, growing into imposing specimens when planted in large pots or in the open ground, but do not flower unless very old.

Myrtillocactus geometrizans (Mart.) Console = *Cereus geometrizans* Martius = *C. pugionifer* Mart. non Lem. Central Mexico to Guatemala, where it is extensively used for planting as hedges, hence the specific name. Stems and branches of a beautiful bluish green; the main stem is short, branching at about 30 cm. from the ground. Branches mostly erect, 6-ribbed; ribs acute and very smooth. Areoles large, 1½ to 3 cm. apart, very slightly woolly. Radial spines 5, spreading, 2 to 10 mm. long, the upper two being shorter. One central spine, sword-shaped, 2 to 2½ cm. long. All spines very dark or black. Flowers in a cluster of 5 to 9 from each of the upper areoles, small, diurnal, with a short tube and one row of spreading white petals. The fruit is a small round- ish berry, smooth, blue, like the fruit of the Blueberry or Whortleberry (*Vaccinium myrtillus*), hence the generic name. The fruit is regularly gathered and sold in the country towns of Mexico, under the name of *garambullos*.

Myrtillocactus pugionifer (Lem.) Berger = *Cereus pugionifer* Lem. Limited to Mexico, where it is commonly planted in hedges, as the preceding species, of which it is often considered as a variety. Differs chiefly on account of its much larger central spine and also the radials. These are 5 to 15 mm. long or longer, and the central up to 8 cm. long, sword-shaped, very thick, with a rhomboid section, black, becoming greyish with age.

Myrtillocactus cochal (Orc.) Br. et R. = *Cereus cochal* Orc. Lower California. The young stems and branches are less intensely bluish, with 6 to 8 ribs, with broad shallow furrows between them. Central spine 2 to 5 cm. long, broad and rhomboid at the base, for the rest slender and very acute, often arcuate. This also is often considered as a variety of *M. geometrizans*.

Myrtillocactus Schenckii (Purp.) Br. et R. = *Cereus Schenckii* Purpus. A distinct species with dark green stems up to 10 cm. thick, with 7 or 8 ribs, branching into a compact crown, about 30 cm. above the base. Areoles not woolly, with 5 to 7 slender radial spines, and one brownish central spine up to 5 cm. long. The ribs are very acute, and the flowers are small, brownish outside, white or creamy yellow inside. The fruit is small, round, red. This species is as hardy as *M. geometrizans*, but far less common in cultivation.

Myrtillocactus Eichlamii Br. et R. Guatemala. Stems or branches deep green, or somewhat glaucous, up to 10 cm. thick, with 6 obtuse angles. Areoles large, round, 2 cm. apart, with 6 radial spines thickened at the base, and with one central spine, longer than the radials. There is some greyish wool on the flowering areoles. The flower buds are dark purple, and the flowers are small, greenish outside, creamy white inside, with a delicate fragrance. Fruit small, globular, about 6 mm. thick, red. Very rare in cultivation.

NEORAIMONDIA Br. et R.

Tree-like, with a thick stem, branched almost from the base, with few ribs. Areoles furnished with many long spines. Flowering areoles more or less thickly covered with brown wool. Flowers small, almost tubular or trumpet-shaped, with a broad tube and short petals. Fruit globose, its areoles having short brown wool and short spines. The seeds are dull black. Includes one species.

Neoraimondia macrostibas (K. Sch.) Br. et R. = *Cereus macrostibas* K. Sch. Central and northern Peru, southern Ecuador. A large shrub or tree, branching just above the base, with erect, vertical branches 10 to 15 cm. thick, with 5 to 8 very straight ribs, prominent and acute, with broad concave furrows between them. Areoles large, 3 to 5 cm. apart, the flowering areoles with an abundant growth of brownish wool, resembling a cephalium. Flowers white, only 3 to 4 cm. long, borne along the sides near the top, trumpet-shaped, with a short expanded tube. Fruit red. This large shrub is 3 to 4 m. high.

var. **gigantea** Werd. Tree-like, up to 7 m. high, branching profusely about ½ m. above ground. Stems or branches much thicker, up to 25 cm. in diameter or more. Spines also much longer, up to 15 cm. Peru.

var. **roseiflora** Werd. Flowers pink. Peru (Chosica).

NEOABBOTTIA Br. et R.

Another monotypic genus created to include: **Neabbottia paniculata** (Lamk.) Br. et R. = *Cereus paniculatus* Lamk. Native of the West Indies. This is a tree-like plant, with stout-ribbed branches, very spiny, with the upper areoles covered with a woolly growth like a cephalium, and flowering year after year. The flowers are small, whitish, with a narrow spiny tube and spiny ovary.

CEREEAE

Sub-Tribe II Hylocereanae

Mostly epiphytic plants, often of large growth, or plants with semi-epiphytic habit, with long trailing stems, climbing by means of aerial roots. Stems angular, or cylindrical and fluted, with small spines, branching freely. Flowers large, often very large and beautiful, mostly night-flowering, commonly with a long tube, and with an ovary covered with areoles and spines.

Hylocereus, Br. et R.

Plants of epiphytic or semi-epiphytic habit, with high climbing stems, three-angled or winged, adhering to trees, walls or other support by means of numerous aerial roots. Areoles in notches along the ribs or angles, far apart. Spines short and small, or inconspicuous. Flowers nocturnal, very large, with red or purplish or greenish sepals, and with white petals. Ovary and tube scaly; stamens numerous, white, shorter than the perianth. Fruit large, spineless or almost spineless, covered with numerous leaf-like bracts or scales.

There are about 18 species, all natives of the *wooded* warm regions of the West Indies, Central America, Mexico and Equatorial America, and were formerly all included under *Cereus*. *Hylocereus* means Wood-Cereus. They all require or prefer half-shade, in a very warm and sheltered situation, and liberal watering during summer. They are all much branched, with distinctly jointed stems.

Hylocereus undatus (Haw.) Br. et R. = *Cereus undatus* Haw. = *C. triangularis* Auct. non Haw. = *C. tricostatus* Goss. This species is very commonly met with in cultivation, being known to most gardeners by the name of *Cereus triangularis*, and is often used as stock for *Zygocactus*, *Epiphyllum*, *Rhipsalis*, etc. Stems deep green, much branched, with numerous branches or joints of all sizes, often reaching 4 or 5 m. in height. The stems or joints are triangular, 5 to 6 cm. in diameter, and very much elongated, 50 cm. or more; or they may be shorter, the angles prolonged into wings, which may also be more or less wavy, with a total diameter of 10 to 12 cm. Spines very short and thick, at first brown or black, and afterwards ash-coloured. Flowers very large, up to 30 cm. long, freely produced in August-September, greenish yellow with purplish outside, the inner petals being broad and white. The fruit is oval, about 10 cm. long, red, with broad scales. The pulp is white, of good flavour.

Hylocereus Lemairei (Hook.) Br. et R. = *Cereus Lemairei* Hooker. West Indies. Tall-growing, afterwards decumbent or trailing. Stems dull dark green, with a neat triangular section and rounded angles, 4 to 7 cm. thick. Areoles far apart, with 2 very short brownish spines, directed downwards. Flowers about 17 cm. long, the outer petals yellowish green tipped reddish, the inner petals white suffused reddish or pink. A beautiful and interesting species, easily grown in a porous soil with the addition of old leaf-mould. Being mostly epiphytic, all species of *Hylocereus* will thrive all the better in a soil containing a good percentage of leaf-mould, or of old cow-manure.

Hylocereus stenopterus (Weber) Br. et R. = *Cereus stenopterus* Weber. Costa Rica. Stems erect or trailing, light green, 4 cm. thick, 3-ribbed. Areoles on prominences along the ribs, with 1 to 3 small spines. Flowers nocturnal, very beautiful, about 12 cm. long, of a deep violet red colour, with short stamens and thick pistil. Very free-flowering, requiring half-shade and a high temperature during the growing season.

Hylocereus extensus (Salm-Dyck) Br. et R. = *Cereus extensus* Salm-Dyck. Lesser Antilles and Trinidad. Stems very elongated, triangular, about 3 cm. in diameter, often much less, with rounded angles. Areoles about 2 cm. apart, with 2 or 3 very short and thick spines. Flowers diurnal, sweet-scented, about 15 cm. long, with a tube 8 cm. long, with green scales. Outer petals yellowish green and purplish, inner petals white flushed pink, all petals very long and acuminate.

Hylocereus Napoleonis (Graham) Br. et R. = *Cereus Napoleonis* Graham = *C. triangularis* Haw. var. *Napoleonis* Graham. Often considered also as a variety of *H. extensus*. West Indies. Stems yellowish green, or marbled yellow, three-angled, often very elongated, with rounded angles and areoles bearing clusters of short, stiff, brownish spines. Flowers very large, produced in midsummer, diurnal, scented; tube about 15 cm. long, with pale pink scales; outer petals greenish yellow, well expanded, inner petals broad, white, forming a broad conical cup.

Hylocereus trigonus (Haw.) Br. et R. = *Cereus trigonus* Haw. West Indies. Stems with elongated joints, straggling, 2 to 3 cm. thick, very rampant, up to 10 m. high, deep green, three-angled. Areoles with about 8 stiff spines, $\frac{1}{2}$ to 1 cm. long, dark brown, with a few bristles. Flowers large, white. Fruit pear-shaped, with only a few scales. There is a variety with joints marbled green, yellow and white.

Hylocereus triangularis (Haw.) Br. et R. = *Cereus triangularis* Haw. non Auct. Jamaica. Stems or joints three-angled, 3 to 4 cm. broad, with almost straight ribs. Areoles on prominences along the ribs, which are very acute. Spines 6 to 8, needle-shaped, those on the lower areoles being more numerous, shorter and spreading. Flowers white, 20 cm. long.

Hylocereus monacanthus (Lem.) Br. et R. = *Cereus monacanthus* Lemaire. Colombia and Panama. Joints triangular, green, with rounded angles. Areoles about 3 cm. apart, bearing 1 or 2 small spines of a conical shape. Flower about 28 cm. long; outer petals greenish yellow, inner petals white, flushed pink at the base.

Hylocereus Ocamponis (Salm-Dyck) Br. et R. = *Cereus Ocamponis* Salm-Dyck. Mexico. Has a more erect habit, with fewer aerial roots, rising to a height of 2 to 3 m. Joints 15 to 30 cm. long, and 5 to 8 cm. in diameter, of a dull glaucous green colour, with thick fleshy wings, each bordered with a broad rust-coloured band along their whole length. Spines several about 2 cm. long, yellow to dirty white.

Flowers very much like those of *H. undatus*, scales red on the outside. The flower is about 30 cm. long: the outer petals are glossy pale yellow, lanceolate; the inner petals are broader, acuminate, satiny white; stamens pale yellow, style yellowish, very thick, stigma with 22 sulphur yellow lobes.

Hylocereus Purpusii (Weingt.) Br. et R. = *Cereus Purpusii* Weingt. Western Mexico. Stems 1 to 2 m. high, mostly erect, green, but entirely covered with a glaucous bluish bloom. Joints bluntly triangular, often quadrangular with a thick horny margin. Spines small, brownish, in clusters of 3 to 6, 1 to 2 cm. long. Flowers fairly large, very beautiful, with red sepals and rose-coloured petals, fading to almost white. Flowers in August-September, but very sparingly, except on old plants. Grows best in a mixture of sand and leaf-mould. Requires much warmth.

Hylocereus costaricensis (Berger) Br. et R. = *Cereus costaricensis* (Berger) = *C. trigonus costaricensis* Weber. Costa Rica. Stems mostly erect; joints very thick, up to 10 cm. in diameter, triangular, with angles often folded, with areoles on prominences along the margin, which is not horny. The colour is at first green, soon turning to glaucous green, more or less intense, and finally passing to greyish green. Spines 1 or 2, short and thick. Flower very large, 30 cm. long or more, strongly perfumed, outer petals red, the inner white. Fruit pear-shaped, large, red, edible.

Hylocereus polyrhizus (Weber) Br. et R. = *Cereus polyrhizus* Weber. Panama and Colombia. Joints mostly triangular, often with 4 or 5 angles, 3 to 4 cm. thick, at first green, soon turning to greyish white, afterwards passing to dull green, with straight angles and rounded margins, with many aerial roots descending from the stems and reaching the ground. Spines brownish, 2 to 4, less than ½ cm. long, thick, associated with a few bristles. Flowers 25 to 30 cm. long, strongly perfumed. Ovary and tube with red scales, outer petals reddish, the inner white.

Hylocereus guatemalensis (Berger) Br. et R. = *Cereus guatemalensis* Berger = *C trigonus guatemalensis* Eichlam. Guatemala and San Salvador. Joints 2 to 7 cm. thick, mostly triangular, strongly glaucous, greyish or bluish. Ribs acutely angular, with a horny border. Spines conical, 2 to 4, brown, less than ½ cm. long. Flower very large, up to 30 cm. long, strongly scented, the outer petals being pink, and the inner white. Fruit 6 to 7 cm. long, ovoid, scaly red dotted white, pulp red, edible.

Hylocereus venezuelensis Br. et R. Venezuela (near Valencia). Similar to *H. polyrhizus*. Joints mostly triangular, often quadrangular, 3 to 4 cm. thick, deep bluish green, passing to dull green. Spines 2 to 4, short, brown, almost black. Flower smaller than that of *H. polyrhizus*, but of the same form and colour, and strongly perfumed.

Hylocereus bronxensis Br. et R. Native country unknown. The plant is similar to *H. Ocamponis*, with dull greyish green joints, thick and 3-angled, 3 to 4 cm. broad; ribs very wavy, with brown horny margins.

Areoles 2 to 3 cm. apart. Spines about 10, needle-like, 6 mm. long, brownish. Flowers 25 cm. long, white, outer segments broad, obtuse and almost retuse; inner segments narrower, obtuse, apiculate or retuse; scales on ovary greenish, broad.

Hylocereus cubensis Br. et R. Cuba (Province of Habana). Stems slender, much elongated, 3-angled, dull green, 2 to 4 cm. thick, with straight ribs or angles, later becoming horny along the margins. Spines 3 to 5, conical, black, 2 to 3 mm. long. Flowers about 20 cm. long, white; ovary with large leafy scales. Fruit oval, reddish, 10 cm. long.

Hylocereus antiguensis Br. et R. Antigua. A tall, high-climbing species, dark dull green. Joints 3-angled, sometimes 4-angled, 2 to 4 cm. thick, with straight plain margins. Areoles 2½ to 3½ cm. apart, with 2 to 4 spines about 6 mm. long, and 2 to 5 small, bristle-like spines. Flowers 14 cm. long; outer petals linear greenish white, inner petals broader, white or yellowish white. Ovary and tube with linear acute scales.

Hylocereus calcaratus (Weber) Br. et R. = *Cereus calcaratus* Weber. From Costa Rica. A tall-climbing plant, with long 3-winged joints, 4 to 6 cm. broad, of a lively green, the margin of the wings or ribs cut into prominent rounded lobes just below the areoles, which are small, and spineless, but with 2 to 4 short white bristles.

It is known that only three or four species of *Hylocereus* are commonly met with in cultivation. Perhaps this is due to the fact that they require much warmth to develop their flowers. But they are all of easy cultivation, in a mixture of loam, sand or gravel and leaf-mould, with the addition of some old manure, and although their stems may not be very interesting, they fully compensate by the magnificence of their flowers. Plants of flowering size, if placed in the shade of tall trees in April-May, in a sheltered and warm situation, will flower better than under glass, during the summer.

SELENICEREUS (Berger) Br. et R.

Stems slender, branched, trailing and climbing, mostly with aerial roots. Areoles with bundles of small, short, or needle-like spines, occasionally almost spineless. Flowers very large and showy, nocturnal, white or partly coloured, with a long tube, often somewhat curved. Stamens very numerous, in two series, shorter than the petals. Ovary and tube hairy and spiny. Fruit large, red or reddish, losing the spines at maturity. Includes more than 25 species, natives of Texas, Mexico, West Indies and down to Argentina.

The "Moon" Cerei are deservedly popular, the size and beauty of the flowers more than compensating for the comparative insignificance of the stem. Their flowers are the finest and largest of all the Cactaceae. They are night-flowering, or mostly so, the flowers expanding in all their glory towards sunset, in some cases saturating the air around them with their fragrance, and wither off at sunrise, hence the popular designation of "Queen of the Night" or "King of the Night" bestowed on some species. They are particularly beautiful when seen by artificial light. The flower buds generally make their appearance in May, as soon as the plants start growing after the winter rest, the flowering period commencing at the close of May, and continuing in June and July, or later.

Selenicereus grandiflorus (Mill.) Br. et R. = *Cereus grandiflorus* Miller. West Indies. No collection of Cacti should be without this marvel of the Vegetable Kingdom, to which properly belongs the title of "Queen of the Night." Stems 2 to 3 cm. thick, trailing or climbing up to 5 m. or more, branched, light greyish green, often becoming pinkish or purplish with age, with 5 to 7 ribs, rarely up to 8. Areoles 1 to 1½ cm. apart, with whitish yellow wool, the new areoles on growing stems being also furnished with yellowish or tawny hairs, which disappear as the stems are maturing. Spines 7 to 11, needle-like, about ½ cm. long, yellowish, afterwards grey and white at the tip. The flower buds are developed on stems one or two years old, and appear towards the end of May or in June, and bloom in June or July. They are thickly furnished with short yellow spines and fawn-coloured hairs. The ovary is spiny and hairy, and so also is the tube, which is 10 to 15 cm. long, and often curved. In the typical form both sepals and petals are strongly incurved, forming a large globular cup 10 to 15 cm. long, the total length of the flower being 22 to 30 cm. The sepals are narrow, yellowish brown or nankeen-coloured on the outside, and a lighter yellow inside. The petals are broad, and pure white. The stamens and anthers are yellowish, and the style is whitish, with a greenish yellow many-lobed stigma. The fruit is globose, yellowish streaked red, about 8 cm. long, with brownish wool and yellowish spines. The flowers expand at sunset and fade off in the morning, emitting all the time a powerful vanilla-like perfume.

Like all its congeners, it is easily propagated by cuttings, throughout the summer, and grows well in a mixture of leaf-mould, garden loam, crushed brick, sifted mortar, rubbish or sand, with some calcareous matter, and is suitable for trailing along the wall of a shed or greenhouse. It is liable to suffer from cold or frosty weather, even in the mild winters of the Mediterranean region, and therefore requires some shelter, in order to be in a condition to flower properly with the advent of warm weather. As soon as the flower buds appear, the plant also starts growing, and continues in growth throughout the summer and early autumn, requiring frequent watering during this period, and is also greatly benefited by syringing or spraying. A large plant may produce dozens of blooms.

There are numerous varieties, several of which may be really distinct species, with altogether different characters. The best known are the following:

var. **barbadensis** Weingt., has long needle-like yellow spines, and few hairs on the growing stems. The flower is very large, with sepals more reddish-coloured and partly reflexed.

var. **affinis** Salm-Dyck = *Cereus albisetus* Monv. Probably a distinct species, with shorter stems, 7-ribbed, branching freely from the base. Hairs on growing stems whitish.

var. **ophites** Lem. Stems usually more slender ($1\frac{1}{2}$ to $2\frac{1}{2}$ cm. thick), less trailing, deep greyish green, usually with 6 ribs, but may have only 4, or even 8, or more. The growing tips are purplish and the more thickly studded areoles have very short dark brown wool. The spines are radiating, very short, thick and whitish. Probably a distinct species.

var. **Uranos** Hort., has pale yellowish green stems, with long yellow spines later turning to grey. Sepals and petals more spreading, very numerous and narrow.

var. **mexicanus** Hort. A robust and fast growing variety. Stems light green, 3 to 4 cm. thick, usually 5-ribbed, with clusters of radiating slender dirty white spines, 2 cm. long. Growing stems have a few fawn-coloured hairs on the areoles. Flower large, with spreading or partly recurved sepals and cup-shaped petals. Looks like a hybrid between *S. grandiflorus* and *S. pteranthus*. Has a very penetrating perfume.

var. **irradians** Lem. Resembles var. *barbadensis*, with deep green, slender stems $1\frac{1}{2}$ to 2 cm. thick, usually with 6 ribs, small whitish areoles and tufts of radiating slender, softish, white spines, about $\frac{1}{2}$ cm. long. Growth rather slow. Flowers as in the typical form, but smaller, with petals more expanded.

var. **callianthus** (Rümpl.) = *major* Hort. Probably a natural hybrid of *S. grandiflorus* with *S. pteranthus*. Stems very like those of *S. pteranthus*, but more slender. Flower very large, outer petals or sepals slightly incurved, greenish red, narrow, inner petals white, also narrow; exhales the same perfume as the typical *grandiflorus*.

var. **Tellii** Hort. Stems very slender, about 1 cm. thick, with 4 ribs, rarely 5, deep green. Areoles brownish; spines small, brownish. Flowers as in the typical form, but smaller.

Selenicereus jalapensis (Vaup.) Br. et R. = *Cereus jalapensis* Vaupel = *Selenicereus Pringlei* Rose. Eastern Mexico (near Jalapa). Stem light, glaucous green, much branched, 1 to $1\frac{1}{2}$ m. long, and about 3 cm. thick, with few aerial roots. Ribs 6 or 7, at first acute, soon becoming rounded and almost flat; new growth with a few white hairs at the tip. Areoles 1 to 2 cm. apart, with a few whitish bristles and with 6 or 7 radiating spines, at first yellow, soon passing to white, $\frac{1}{2}$ to 1 cm. long. Flowers about 20 cm. long, with brownish hairs on the ovary and tube; sepals very narrow, white tinted purplish, inner petals white, shorter and very acuminate.

Selenicereus paradisiacus (Vaupl.) Br. et R. = *Cereus paradisiacus* Vaupel = *C. Urbanianus* Gürke. Haiti. Stem $1\frac{1}{2}$ to 4 cm. thick, at first clear green, afterwards dull green, slightly glaucous or reddish, with 5 or 6 ribs, rarely with 4 ribs, acute on young stems. Spines in a spreading cluster, needle-like, about 1 cm. long, straw-coloured, brownish on old stems. Young stems with white hairs at the tip, and with 1 or 2 brownish bristles on each areole. Flower perfumed, up to 30 cm. long; ovary ribbed, scaly, slightly spiny and with whitish hairs. Sepals spreading, narrow, brownish green outside, tipped reddish, green inside; petals broader, cup-shaped, acute, yellowish white. Stamens and style greenish yellow, stigma yellow. Growth is rather fast, with few aerial roots; the stem is 1½ to 3 m. long, well-branched.

Selenicereus pteranthus (Lk. et Otto) Br. et R. = *Cereus pteranthus* Lk. et Otto = *C. nycticalus* Lk. = *C. Peanii* Beguin. Native of Mexico, but grown all over Central America. A magnificent species aptly called "King of the Night" or "Princess of the Night." Stems stiff, 2 to 4½ cm. thick, dull glaucous green, usually flushed purple, with 4 or 5 angles, but may have 6 angles or more, branched, trailing and freely rooting, but rarely more than 3 m. long, often becoming cylindrical with age. Areoles with short white wool, and with very short thick and stiff spines, less than ½ cm. long. The growing stems are purplish, with short white wool and a few white hairs on the areoles. The flower buds develop late in May or in June, on old stems, and are very woolly, with white hairs. The flowers bloom in June or July. They have a hairy ovary and tube, with long white hairs and short slender spines. The sepals are very narrow and long, purplish yellow on the outside, lighter coloured on the inside, expanding horizontally and recurving. The petals are broad, pointed, creamy white or white, forming a broad or funnel-shaped cup. The stamens are very numerous and white, shorter than the petals; the style is as long as the stamens, white, with a many-lobed yellowish stigma. Fruit round, reddish, 6 to 7 cm. thick, hairy and spiny. When expanded the flower is at least 30 cm. across, and about as long. It is practically scentless. The species is free-flowering and more hardy than *S. grandiflorus*.

Selenicereus coniflorus (Weingt.) Br. et R. = *Cereus coniflorus* Weingt. = *C. nycticalus* var. *armatus* K. Sch. Eastern Mexico (near Vera Cruz). A quick grower and a long trailer reaching a length of about 6 m. with many aerial roots. Stems light glaucous green, often shaded reddish or purplish, with 4 to 6 ribs or angles, with small white areoles, on which are 3 to 6 stiff needle-like yellow spines, 2 to 3 cm. long. Flowers freely produced, the buds appearing late in May or early in June, covered with whitish hairs, and develop quickly, blooming in June or early in July. The ovary and tube are hairy, and have short yellow spines. The sepals or outer petals are long and narrow, brownish purple on the outside, reddish or yellowish inside, and become reflexed when fully expanded. The broad white petals in 4 rows form a broad conical cup, with numerous white stamens shorter than the petals or just as long; the thick white style has a greenish many-lobed stigma. The outer petals are so recurved that they touch the tube, and the flower has therefore a globular radiating appearance, about 25 cm. across, and about as long or longer, with a tube often curved. The flower has a peculiar fragrance, weak very close to the flower, becoming quite powerful and almost over-powering at a distance.

Selenicereus Macdonaldiae (Hook.) Br. et R. = *Cereus Macdonaldiae* Hooker = *C. Donati* Hort. Uruguay and Argentina. A quick-growing species, much branched and long-stemmed, trailing and rooting, attaining a length of about 8 m. Stem dark glossy green, often shaded dark purplish, with 5 to 6 or 7 ribs, well marked and prominent, with brownish areoles situated on prominences along the ribs. Spines few, very short, brown. The flower-buds are freely produced, and appear late in May, enveloped in long dark rusty brown wool. The flowers expand in June and July, and are very similar to those of *S. pteranthus*, and just as large or larger, with the same absence of appreciable fragrance. The ovary and tube have rusty brown hairs and short brownish spines. The sepals are reddish purple or orange purple, partly reflexed. Petals white or creamy white, broad, more or less toothed and acutely pointed. Stamens and style white, shorter than the petals, with a many-lobed yellowish stigma. The flowers are often 35 cm. long, and are the largest of all Cactaceae.

Selenicereus Grusonianus (Weingt.) Berger. = *Cereus Grusonianus* Weingt. Mexico. A free-growing and free-flowering species, and worthy companion of the preceding. Stems very long, dark green, with many aerial roots. Ribs 6 or more, narrow and low. Areoles brownish, small, on more pointed protuberances than in the preceding species, with greyish wool, and with 3 or 4 conical spines about 2 mm. long, the lower one being reddish brown, the others yellowish white, tipped brown, with 1 or more white bristles. The flowers are about as large as those of *S. Macdonaldiae*, but more refined, and with even more numerous petals, and devoid of fragrance. A desirable species, but rarely listed in the catalogues of dealers.

Selenicereus Vaupelii (Weingt.) Br. et R. = *Cereus Vaupelii* Weingart. Haiti. Stems greyish green, rather slender 1½ to 2 cm. thick, 2 to 3 m. long, much branched, growing stems furnished with greyish hairy scales. Ribs 5, narrow, low. Areoles small, round, with greyish wool, about 2 cm. apart. Spines very small, about ½ cm. long, greyish; radial spines 2 to 5, often absent, central spines 1 or 2, with a few hairs and bristles. Flower-bud with greyish wool. Flower about 25 cm. long; ovary and tube with a few scales, spiny, with greyish hairs. Sepals very narrow, reddish green outside, yellow inside, recurved. Petals broad, white, erect. Stamens white, style pale yellow, stigma with 14 yellow lobes. The flower has a delightful vanilla-like fragrance. Growth is rather slow, but free-flowering.

Selenicereus Boeckmannii (Otto) Br. et R. = *Cereus Boeckmannii* Otto. Cuba. A very distinct species, although sometimes considered as a hybrid of *S. grandiflorus* and *S. pteranthus*. Stem light green, about 2 cm. thick and 1½ to 2 m. long, branched, with 5 to 7 ribs, more or less low and rounded, with many aerial roots. Areoles with greyish wool, about 1½ cm. apart; 3 or 4 radial spines, greyish, only

(a) APOROCACTUS FLAGRIFORMIS

(b) CHAMAECEREUS SILVESTRII

PLATE XXII

(b) APOROCACTUS MALLISONII

(a) APOROCACTUS MARTIANUS

PLATE XXIII

1 mm. long, but stiff; 1 central spine, brown, stronger, and about 2 mm. long. Flower about 30 cm. long and 20 cm. across. Ovary and tube with small scales, short wool, rather long brown hair, and small brown spines. Sepals very narrow, spreading, greenish brown outside, yellow inside, with reddish tip; inner sepals dark yellow outside, lemon yellow inside; petals lanceolate, white. Stamens and style yellowish green, stigma pale yellow, many-lobed. A very refined and beautiful flower, richly perfumed. The plant is of fairly quick growth, resistant, and free-flowering.

Selenicereus Kunthianus (Otto) Br. et R. = *Cereus Kunthianus* Otto Central America, probably Honduras. Stem very much like that of *S. Macdonaldiae*, but not so rampant, green, with 7 to 10 ribs, about 2 cm. thick. Areoles with brownish wool, and 4 brown very small but stiff radial spines, and 1 central spine often absent. Flower about 24 cm. long, with a vanilla fragrance. Ovary and tube with small scales, white bristle-like spines, and white or greyish pink hairs. Sepals very numerous and narrow, the outer reddish green, the inner light reddish brown; petals very acuminate, white. Stamens and style greenish yellow.

Selenicereus Rothii (Weingt.) Berger = *Cereus Rothii* Weingart. Paraguay. Similar to *S. Macdonaldiae*, but only $1\frac{1}{2}$ to 2 m. long, much branched, old stems cylindrical and thickened, young stems tender green, with 5 or 6 ribs, with pronounced warts. Areoles on the warts, 1 to $1\frac{1}{2}$ cm. apart, with 4 or 5 spines spreading crosswise, 3 to 5 mm. long. Flower 25 cm. long, weakly perfumed; the outer sepals reddish green, the inner yellow; petals white or creamy white.

Selenicereus radicans (DC.) Berger = *Cereus radicans* DC. Native country unknown. Stem pale glossy green, $1\frac{1}{2}$ cm. thick, somewhat rigid, but breaking off very easily. Ribs mostly 5, sometimes 3 or 4, at first very acute, afterwards low and almost flat, old stems being cylindrical, and the ribs marked out by vertical lines. Prominences well marked on young stems, on which are the areoles, $1\frac{1}{2}$ cm. apart. Radial spines 3 to 5, conical, at first red, passing to grey, 3 to 4 mm. long. One central spine, slightly longer, often absent. Aerial roots many. Flower about 32 cm. long. Ovary warty and scaly, with brown hairs and bundles of spines; tube dull green, narrow, similarly furnished with hairy and spiny scales. Sepals reddish outside, yellow inside; petals white. Stamens and style white, stigma with 16 yellow lobes.

Selenicereus hondurensis (K. Sch.) Br. et R. = *Cereus hondurensis* K. Sch. Honduras. Stems very long, deep green, 20 to 22 mm. thick, very uniform in thickness, with 7 to 10 ribs, narrow and low. Areoles small, with dark brown wool, and on growing stems, with curly dark hairs about $1\frac{1}{2}$ cm. long, and also with a few white bristles. Spines yellowish brown, about 7 radials becoming white with age, stiff and less than $\frac{1}{2}$ cm. long, and 1 central, stronger and slightly longer. Flower about 23 cm. long, and 15 to 18 cm. broad. Sepals reddish green or yellowish green; petals white or yellowish white. Ovary and

209

O

tube scaly and spiny, and densely covered with greyish or brownish white hairs.

Selenicereus Maxonii Rose = *Cereus Roseanus* Vaupel. Cuba (Eastern Province). An epiphytic species, living on the trunks of Palm trees. Stems slender, greyish green, with 5 or 6 ribs. Areoles very small. Spines very short, yellowish, associated with a few white bristles on the growing tips of stems. Flower 20 cm. long. Ovary and tube scaly, with very short spines and bristles, and with white wool and hair. Outer petals greenish, brownish or pale pink on the outer side; inner petals broader, white. Style thick, creamy white.

Selenicereus brevispinus (Berger) Br. et R. = *Cereus brevispinus* Berger. Cuba. Stems very long, light green, with 8 to 10 ribs. Areoles small, with brown wool, on prominences along the ribs, and with many white hairs on growing stems. Radial spines about 8, very short and conical, brown. Central spines 3 or 4, slightly longer and curved. Flower about 25 cm. long. Ovary and tube scaly and spiny, with white hairs. Sepals narrow, dark brown outside, brownish green inside; petals very broad and white.

Selenicereus spinulosus (DC.) Br. et R. = *Cereus spinulosus* DC. Mexico. Stems very long, green, rigid, with many aerial roots, trailing or climbing, with 5 ribs, at first very acute. Areoles 1 to $1\frac{1}{2}$ cm. apart, reddish brown on slight prominences. Spines about 8, stiff, less than $\frac{1}{2}$ cm. long, yellowish brown. Flower about 15 cm. long; ovary and tube scaly, with reddish brown hairs and yellowish bristles and spines. Sepals spreading, star-like, greenish yellow, reddish at the base; petals narrow, white, with white stamens and style, and yellow stigma.

Selenicereus Nelsonii (Weingt.) = *Cereus Nelsonii* Weingt. Mexico. Stem pale green, often purplish, $1\frac{1}{2}$ to 2 cm. thick, up to 3 m. long, branched, with few aerial roots, mostly with 6 narrow ribs, acute, margined purplish. Areoles 1 to 2 cm. apart, round, whitish. Spines needle-like, radiating, pale yellow: the radials about 10, paler, slender, up to 1 cm. long; the centrals 1 to 4, longer and thicker. Flower-buds borne mostly at or near the tips of the stems, with whitish hairs and bristles. Ovary roundish, with many white areoles, short scales, hairy and with long softish white or yellowish spines. Tube about 12 cm. long, with purplish scales and hairs and bristles; sepals very narrow, greenish white, slightly reddish on the outside; petals lanceolate, acuminate, 10 cm. long, pure white, the total length of the flower being about 25 cm. Stamens many, white; style white, much exserted beyond the stamens, and as long as the petals, with a many-lobed, brush-like stigma. The flower is markedly fragrant.

Selenicereus inermis (Otto) Br. et R. = *Cereus inermis* Otto. Colombia and Venezuela. Stems very long, glossy light green, with few aerial roots, 1 to $2\frac{1}{2}$ cm. thick, with 3 to 5 ribs or angles. Areoles distant (4 to 5 cm.), with a few bristles, but no spines. Flower about 15 cm. long: ovary and tube scaly and slightly spinescent, but without hairs. Sepals greenish yellow, reddish at the base. Petals white, also reddish at the base, with a thick reddish style and yellowish green stigma. Flower scentless. Grows fast, but flowers sparingly.

Selenicereus Wercklei (Weber) Br. et R. = *Cereus Wercklei* Weber. Costa Rica (near Miravalles). A species growing epiphytically on trees or hanging down from ledges of arid rocks. Stem much branched, cylindrical, green, about 1 cm. thick, rarely up to 1½ cm., with about 12 straight and low ribs, spineless, with the habit of a *Rhipsalis*. Flower large, white, nocturnal. Fruit about as large as a hen's egg, round, yellow, very spiny, with white pulp.

Selenicereus vagans (Brand.) Br. et R. = *Cereus vagans* Brand. = *C. longicaudatus* Weber. Mexico. Stems vigorous, deep green 1 to 1½ cm. thick, rambling and rooting, with 5 or 6 ribs, acute, later low and flattened. Areoles brownish, on protuberances; spines brown, thick, up to 4 mm. long. Flowers diurnal, very freely borne at the top of the stems, 15 cm. long; tube 9 cm. long, slightly curved, brownish; sepals linear, brownish or greenish white, 6 cm. long; petals white, of same length, with short acuminate tips, toothed above. Stamens white, often green at the base; style slender, greenish below, creamy above; stigma with 12 lobes.

Selenicereus Donkelaeri (Salm-Dyck) Br. et R. = *Cereus Donkelaeri* Salm-Dyck. Mexico (Yucatan). An epiphytic species growing mostly on trees in dense forests, among Orchids. Stems very long, dark green, with 6 to 8 ribs, but only about 1 cm. thick. Areoles minute, white. Spines very small, bristle-like, whitish or greyish, spreading over and covering the ribs. One or more central spines, brownish, about 2 mm. long. Growing stems tipped with white hairs. Flower about 18 cm. long: sepals reddish outside, white inside; petals white. Stamens and style white, greenish at the base. Should be grown in leaf-mould, with the addition of crushed bricks and some sharp sand, but also thrives well in a mixutre of leaf-mould, garden loam and sand. Keep in half-shade.

Selenicereus Murrillii Br. et R. Mexico (near Colima). Has very slender stems, about 8 mm. thick, but 6 m. long or more, of quick growth with many aerial roots. The stems are dark green, with 7 or 8 low ribs more or less purplish, as also the tips of growing stems. Areoles 1 to 2 cm. apart, small, with white wool: spines 5 or 6, minute, the 2 lower ones longer and reflexed, 1 to 2 cm. long, the other spines conical, greenish or black. Flower nocturnal, 15 cm. long: tube purplish green, with minute scales. Sepals greenish yellow, the outer ones purplish on the back, spreading, linear to linear-lanceolate; petals white, cup-shaped, broadly spathulate: stamens and style creamy white, stigma with 9 creamy lobes. Rare in cultivation.

Selenicereus hallensis Weingt. = *Cereus hallensis* Weingt. Colombia. Stem trailing and rooting, branched, about 3 m. long, pale green, usually with 5 or 6 acute ribs or angles. Areoles on small prominences,

2 to 3 cm. apart, small, brownish. Spines often absent, or 2 to 6, brownish yellow, slender, 1 to 3 up to 1 cm. long, the others quite small. Flowers borne in June, large and very beautiful, 30 cm. long and 28 cm. broad, spreading. Tube scaly, hairy and spinescent, mahogany red or brownish red: outer sepals fully expanded or recurved, mahogany red; the next three rows ochre yellow, erect or spreading; petals in three rows, white, forming a cup. Stamens many, yellowish, much shorter than the pistil, which is thick, creamy yellow, as long as the inner petals; stigma with about 16 more or less twisted lobes. The flower exhales a Vanilla-like perfume, from sunset until it fades in the morning.

Selenicereus hamatus (Scheidw.) Br. et R. = *Cereus hamatus* Scheidw. = *C. rostratus* Lem. Southern and eastern Mexico, and the Lesser Antilles. Stems very vigorous and very long, reaching 12 m. or more, often growing 2 m. or more in one season, glossy grass green, with few aerial roots, well branched, mostly with 4 angles, sometimes with 3 or 5, with hooked or beak-like prominences along the ribs, very pronounced, about 1 cm. long, and 4 to 5 cm. apart, with small round brown areoles above them. Spines 5 or 6, whitish, soft, bristle-like, about ½ cm. long; and 1 to 3 central or lower spines, stronger and brownish. Flowers borne sparingly, but appearing at intervals throughout the summer until October, varying in size, 25 to 40 cm. long, and 20 to 30 cm. across. Ovary covered with slender white spines and dark or black hairs: tube light green, purplish towards the top, with short green retuse scales, with a tuft of long black hairs in the axils; upper scales longer, in 3 series, the uppermost tipped purple. Outer sepals in 2 series, narrow, reddish purple outside, chrome yellow inside; inner sepals in 2 series, broader and acutely pointed, greenish yellow outside, chrome yellow inside. Petals in 3 series forming a cup, pure white, very broad, retuse. Stamens very numerous, creamy white; anthers yellow. Style very thick, creamy white, longer than the stamens, stigma with 15 to 18 lobes. The flower is strongly scented, with an aromatic fragrance.

In addition to a few natural hybrids, there is now in commerce quite a large number of beautiful horticultural hybrids, the result of crosses between *S. grandiflorus* and its varieties, and other species, notably *S. pteranthus*, *S. coniflorus*, *S. Grusonianus*, *S. paradisiacus* and *S. Macdonaldiae*, and also with species of *Heliocereus*. As these hybrids are mostly unnamed, they are known simply as *S. grandiflorus hybr.* It would greatly assist the collectionist if a selection of these hybrids were given a fancy name, to distinguish them from each other, as in the case of hybrids of *Epiphyllum* (*Phyllocactus*), provided that no misleading Latin names are used.

One of the first hybrids of horticultural origin, and one of the most beautiful, is *Cereus Maynardii* Paxton (better written *Maynardae*, being dedicated to the Viscountess Maynard), a cross of *S. grandiflorus* with *Heliocereus speciosus*, described as a red "Queen of the Night." Another red-flowering hybrid is *Cereus fulgidus* a cross of *S. grandi-*

florus with *H. speciosissimus*. Other crosses between species of *Selenicereus* have resulted in the production of flowers as large as the largest, of greater beauty of form and of more vivid colours.

WILMATTEA Br. et R.

A monotypic genus established to include the aberrant species **Wilmattea viridiflora** (Vaup.) Br. et R. = *Cereus minutiflorus* Vaupel, an epiphytic climbing plant of the forests of Guatemala and Honduras, with dark green, slender, triangular, rooting stems or joints, with straight angles. Areoles 2 to 4 cm. apart, with 1 to 3 small spines. Flowers nocturnal, small, about 5 cm. long, sweet-scented, with a very short tube and small ovary, with triangular reddish scales, slightly hairy and with 1 or 2 bristles at the axils; outer petals reddish, the inner narrower, very acute and white.

DEAMIA Br. et R.

Another monotypic genus established for the very curious species **Deamia testudo** (Karw.) Br. et R. = *Cereus testudo* Karw. = *C. pentapterus* Otto = *C. miravallensis* Weber = *C. pterogonus* Lem. Southern Mexico to Colombia. Stems or joints up to 25cm. long, very variable in shape, and therefore described as so many different species, with 3 to 8 wings or angles, with aerial roots, climbing and trailing. The joints are often closely applied flat to trunks of trees or other support, and may be 18 to 20 cm. broad, humped up in the middle, not unlike the carapace or shield of a tortoise, hence its name of Tortoise Cactus. Other joints are smaller, with 2 side wings and 3 lower central wings, or they may be almost straight and triangular, with bristle-like spines. Flowers diurnal, up to 28 cm. long, white, with many stamens. Ovary and tube covered with very small scales, with brown hairs, spines and bristles. Fruit red, very spiny. An interesting plant of strange appearance, now rarely met with in cultivation. Requires much warmth and a moist atmosphere, and also a suitable support for its stems.

MEDIOCACTUS Br. et R.

Epiphytic plants with long triangular stems with aerial roots. Areoles with short bristle-like spines. Flowers large, white, nocturnal. Ovary warty and scaly, with wool and bristle-like spines in the areoles. Fruit roundish or ovoid, red, spiny. Includes two species.

Mediocactus setaceus (Salm-Dyck) = *Cereus setaceus* Salm-Dyck in DC. = *Mediocactus coccineus* (Salm-Dyck) Br. et R. (*Cereus coccineus* Salm-Dyck in DC is identical with, or a variety of *Heliocereus Schrankii*, and therefore that specific name has nothing to do with *Mediocactus*). Brazil and Argentina. Stem mostly erect, up to 80 cm. long, freely branching from the base, less freely above, pale green, triangular, sometimes commencing with 4 or 5 angles, straight and acute, somewhat obtuse above. Areoles irregular, 1 to 3 cm.

apart, with 2 to 4 conical spines 1 to 3 mm. long, at first reddish passing to brown, and 8 to 10 white soft long bristles. Flower about 25 cm. long; ovary and tube with small scales, few hairs and 1 or 2 short spines. Outer petals narrow, green; inner petals spathulate, toothed, typically white, yellowish at the base. Stamens and style yellowish: stigma with 16 yellowish lobes. Fruit ovoid, red, spiny, spines 1 to 2 cm. long.

The following, described as species, are probably mere varieties of the preceding.

Cereus Hassleri K. Sch. Paraguay. Stems thicker (up to 3½ cm.), and more erect. Flower about 20 cm. long, yellowish white, with very slender stamens. Ovary and tube spiny. Fruit with shorter spines. Stems pale green, of strong growth, with obtuse angles.

Cereus Lindmannii Weber = *C. Lindbergianus* . Paraguay. Stems dark green, erect or semi-prostrate, freely branching, 2 to 3 cm. in diameter, 3-angled, rarely 4-angled, angles very acute when young. Flower about 20 cm. long, white.

A hybrid between this variety or species and *Heliocereus speciosus*, with the growing joints or stems coloured crimson red, and bearing wonderful diurnal flowers of an intense crimson violet, 20 cm. broad, is often sold as *Cereus Lindmannii*.

Mediocactus megalanthus (K. Sch.) Br. et R. = *Cereus megalanthus* K. Sch. Eastern Peru, and possibly Colombia and Bolivia. An epiphytic bush with long hanging branches, rooting freely, 3-angled, often only 1½ cm. thick, with straight or slightly wavy angles. Spines 1 to 3, yellowish, 2 to 3 mm. long, with several white bristles on young growth. Flowers very large, 38 cm. long, white; petals 11 cm. long and 3½ cm. broad; stamens and lobes of stigma numerous.

WEBEROCEREUS Br. et R.

Epiphytic plants with very slender, trailing stems, cylindrical or with 3 to 5 angles, occasionally flat and therefore with two angles, usually with aerial roots. Areoles small, with wool and slender spines. Flowers white or pink, nocturnal. Ovary warty and furnished with bristles, these extending to the lower part of the tube, the upper part being scaly. Fruit spineless, but with hair on the areoles. Includes three species, denizens of the half-shaded forests in warm and moist districts of Costa Rica and Panama.

Weberocereus tunilla (Weber) Br. et R. = *Cereus tunilla* Weber. Costa Rica. Stems ½ to 1½ cm. thick, mostly 4-angled, sometimes 3- or 5-angled, occasionally flat. The growing stems are almost cylindrical, pale green, reddish at the top, with minute areoles 1 to 6 cm. apart. Spines about 8, less than 1 cm. long, yellow passing to brown, later dropping off. Flower 5 to 6 cm. long. Ovary with prominent warts, and a few yellow bristles. Outer petals narrow, obtuse and brownish, inner petals broader, longer, pale pink.

Weberocereus Biolleyi (Weber) Br. et R. = *Cereus Biolleyi* Weber.

Costa Rica. Stems very long and slender, ½ to 1 cm. thick, cylindrical or irregularly angled. Areoles far apart, occasionally with 1 to 3 slender spines. Flower 3 to 5 cm. long. Ovary warty and with few bristles, the lower part of the tube also with bristles, with scales on the upper part. Outer petals fleshy and deep pink, inner petals longer, pale pink.

Weberocereus panamensis (Berger) Br. et R. = *Cereus panamensis* Berger. Panama. A curious species with very slender stems, with 3 angles, very much like a *Rhipsalis*. The flower is small, white.

WERCKLEOCEREUS Br. et R.

Stems or joints triangular, with aerial roots. Areoles with short, slender, soft spines. Flowers short, funnel-shaped, with numerous stamens. Ovary and tube densely furnished with areoles bearing black wool and black spines. Fruit globose, spinescent. Epiphytic trailing and climbing plants, inhabiting the warm and moist forests of Central America. They are purely tropical and, like those of the preceding genus, must have the shelter of a temperate house or hothouse throughout the year, especially in winter, and a very porous soil consisting of leaf-mould, sharp sand and crushed bricks, with a little crushed charcoal.

Werckleocereus Tonduzii (Weber) Br. et R. = *Cereus Tonduzii* Weber. Costa Rica. Stems slender, pale green, with 3 angles, rarely with 4, the angles more or less rounded and toothed. Areoles small, far apart, with short weak spines. Flower broadly funnel-shaped, 8 cm. long and 6 cm. broad. Ovary and tube with black wool and spreading black spines: outer petals long, brownish pink, inner petals about as long, flesh-coloured or creamy yellow. Stigma green. Fruit yellow, spiny, white-fleshed.

Werckleocereus glaber (Eichl.) Br. et R. = *Cereus glaber* Eichlam. Guatemala. This is the other species belonging to this genus, and like the preceding very free-flowering. Stems 2 to 2½ cm. thick, triangular, or rather with a T-shaped section, at first pale greyish green, with toothed angles. Areoles 3 to 5 cm. apart, small, with brownish wool. Spines mostly 1, rarely 2, very short. Flower about 10 cm. long. Areoles on ovary and tube with brown wool, and with 8 spreading yellowish or dark brown short spines: outer petals greenish or brownish, lanceolate, inner petals lanceolate-obtuse, white.

STROPHOCACTUS Br. et R.

Includes only one species: **Strophocactus Wittii** (K. Sch.) Br. et R. = *Cereus Wittii* K. Sch. An epiphytic twining plant of the upper Amazon, Brazil, in the periodically inundated forests at Manaos. Stem very long, jointed and branched, flat and leaf-like, broad, very rarely 3-winged, closely sticking to, and twining around the branches of trees, by means of short roots. Spines short needle-like, yellow, on closely set areoles along the toothed wings of the stem. Flower funnel-shaped, about 23 cm. long, nocturnal, large, with the ovary and long tube spinous and hairy, the outer petals being narrow and pale pink; the inner shorter, snow white. Fruit ovoid, spinescent; seeds angular, black.

These last six genera, *Wilmattea, Deamia, Mediocactus, Weberocereus, Werckleocereus* and *Strophocactus*, are closely allied to *Selenicereus*, and certain continental writers have suggested to unite them with *Selenicereus*. Far from an improvement, this arrangement would reduce the generic value of *Selenicereus* to a vanishing point.

APOROCACTUS Lemaire

Includes a few species with slender, creeping, branched stems, hanging from the stems and thick branches of trees, or from ledges of rock, with aerial roots. Flowers rather small, diurnal, red, slightly irregular or zygomorphic, with stamens longer than the petals. Fruit a small globose red berry, with long soft bristles. Seeds very small, reddish brown. Natives of Mexico and Central America.

Aporocactus flagelliformis (Mill.) Lem. = *Cereus flagelliformis* Miller. Mexico. This is the best known species and most popular. Stems $1\frac{1}{2}$ to 2 cm. thick, and up to 2 m. long, glossy green when young, afterwards greyish, creeping or hanging, with 10 to 14 slightly prominent ribs, closely studded with minute areoles, at first white, afterwards greyish, on which are situated radiating clusters of 15 to 20 spines, about $\frac{1}{2}$ cm. long, reddish when young on the growing stem, afterwards pale yellow, golden yellow or brownish. Flowers borne profusely along the stems in April and May, about 8 cm. long, zygomorphic, crimson pink, lasting for one week or more. May be grown on own roots in hanging baskets, in mixture of leaf-mould, sand and some loamy earth, but is more commonly grafted, especially on *Selenicereus Macdonaldiae* $\frac{1}{2}$ to 1 m. high, and the stems trailed on an umbrella-like wire support. Delights in full sun, and should be liberally watered during the summer. A cristate form is also in cultivation. Several fine varieties are met with.

Aporocactus flagriformis (Zucc.) Lem. = *Cereus flagriformis* Zuccarini. Mexico. Very similar to the preceding, with the same habit of growth and same requirements, but the stems have fewer ribs (7 to 10), with areoles farther apart, and clearer yellow spines; the stems are often slightly thicker. Areoles yellowish, with 6 to 8 pale yellow or brownish spines, and with 2 or more central spines, stronger and up to 1 cm. long. Flowers borne u.s., 8 to 9 cm. long, crimson red, tending to scarlet, the inner petals passing to pink along the margins.

Aporocactus leptophis (DC.) Br. et R. = *Cereus leptophis* DC. Mexico. Stems about 1 cm. thick, dark green, with 7 to 8 ribs. Areoles white, with 9 to 14 radial spines, at first violet on the growing stems, passing to yellowish, about $\frac{1}{2}$ cm. long, and soft. Flowers 4 to 5 cm. long, and 5 cm. broad, slightly zygomorphic; outer petals a lively red, inner petals paler, with a violet midrib. Stamens pale pink.

Aporocactus Martianus (Zucc.) Br. et R. = *Cereus Martianus* Zucc. Mexico (State of Oaxaca). Stems mostly erect or sprawling, up to 1½ m. long, and 2 cm. thick, or slightly more, dull glaucous green, with 8 low ribs. Areoles on prominences about 1 cm. apart. Radial spines about 8, about ½ cm. long, yellowish brown, darker at the base: central spines 3 or 4, stronger and darker. Flower 10 cm. long, or slightly longer, and 6 cm. broad, with an almost straight tube, and almost regular flowers; outer petals brownish red on the outside, the others scarlet red with a narrow violet margin. Stamens whitish, as long as the petals, A very beautiful species, rather free-flowering, now becoming rare in collections.

Aporocactus Conzattii (Berger) Br. et R. = *Cereus Conzattii* Berger. Mexico (State of Oaxaca). Is similar to the preceding, but the flowers are smaller and more numerous and the inner petals are not long acuminate as those of *A. Martianus*. Stems 1 to 2½ cm. thick, less erect, more creeping or hanging; spines more numerous, light brown, up to 1 cm. long. The flowers keep in bloom for two days.

Aporocactus Moenninghoffii Fischer = *Cereus Moenninghoffii* Fischer. Is supposed to be a hybrid between *A. flagriformis* and *A. Martianus*, this last being the female parent. Some of its stems are like those of *A. Martianus* and others like those of *A. flagriformis*. The flowers are like those of *A. Martianus*, carmine red, with darker midribs, the inner petals being almost violet with red midribs.

Aporocactus Mallisonii Hort. = *Cereus nothus* Wendl., is a large-flowered hybrid obtained in England, between *A. flagelliformis* and *Heliocereus speciosus* with large fiery red flowers, freely produced. May be grafted like *A. flagelliformis*, of which it has the habit, but will do well grown on own roots.

Sub-Tribe III Echinocereanae

Stems various, roundish or oval, or elongated, branching mostly from the base, erect or prostrate, often growing into large clumps, but never tall, with ribs or with warts on low ribs. Areoles more or less woolly, with spines. Flowers large or fairly large, usually highly coloured, borne as usual over the areoles. The new shoots or branches often springing or bursting through the tissues.

Echinocereus Engelmann

Formerly included under *Cereus*, the genus *Echinocereus* is a very natural one, and is made up of a considerable number of distinct, but closely allied species. The stem is usually cespitose, of varying thickness, rarely more than 40 cm. long, and from 2 cm. or less to 8 cm. or more in diameter, soft and very fleshy, erect or sprawling or hanging, and very spiny. Flowers mostly large and showy, of various shades of pink, red and purple, rarely yellow, borne on the sides of the stems in May-July, opening by day and lasting in bloom for several days; with a globose spiny ovary, and short spiny tube, the petals being expanded, funnel-shaped or bell-shaped. The lobes of the stigma are green. A peculiarity of the genus is that the shoots and buds are formed deeply within the stem, and grow out by breaking through the epidermis, but flower buds develop on the areoles as usual. This large genus includes about 78 species, and fresh additions are frequently made. They are North American, and mostly Mexican, extending as far north as Wyoming and Utah.

Very generally species of *Echinocereus* are of the easiest cultivation, thriving well in full sunshine and in exposed situations, and are fairly resistant to cold weather, often forming large clumps. They should be watered liberally in summer, when they are growing freely, but should be kept rather dry in winter, plants in pots being watered just enough to prevent the roots from drying completely. The soil should be moderately rich, and definitely calcareous, but a few of them prefer a sandy soil. They are easily multiplied by cuttings, or by division of the clumps, or by seed, or by grafting, and are justly popular, especially with beginners.

The following classification has no systematic meaning, and is solely meant to facilitate identification.

A. *Stems low, globular or oval.*
(a) *Stems spineless or with short spines.*

Echinocereus Knippelianus Liebe. Mexico. Stem 5 cm. thick, globular or oval, deep dark green, with 5 ribs or angles, separated by broad furrows. Areoles small, at first spineless, later developing 1 to 3 bristle-like, white, recurved spines, up to 1½ cm. long. Flowers funnel-shaped, about 4 cm. long, dark brown outside, carmine violet inside, with very acute petals. Stigma with 6 to 7 lobes.

Echinocereus subinermis Salm-Dyck. Mexico. Stem at first globular, passing to oval or cylindrical, branching, at first pale bluish green, passing to green, 8 to 9 cm. thick, with 5 to 8 ribs, with narrow furrows between them. Areoles small, slightly woolly. Spines yellowish, not more than ½ cm. long, 8 radials and 1 central. Upper areoles almost spineless. Flower about 8 cm. long, funnel-shaped; outer petals brownish outside, yellow inside, with reddish midrib, inner petals yellow. Stigma with 10 lobes.

Echinocereus pulchellus K. Sch. = *Echinocactus pulchellus* Mart. Mexico. Stem top-shaped, branching from the base, 4 to 5 cm. thick, bluish green passing to dull or greyish green, with 11 to 13 low ribs, slightly notched into tubercles about ½ cm. apart, bearing small areoles. Spines yellowish passing to grey, 3 or 4, spreading, the lowest up to 1 cm. long. Flower funnel-shaped, 4 cm. long, dark green outside, pale pink or pink inside, with acute toothed petals. Stigma with 8 or 9 lobes. Free-flowering.

Echinocereus amoenus Först. = *Echinopsis amoena* Dietr. Mexico. Often considered as a variety of the preceding, but is different. Stem top-shaped, stronger, 6 to 7 cm. thick, becoming elongated with age, branching from the base, with 10 to 14 ribs of a more lively green and more prominent. Areoles with 7 small spines, the lowest up to 1 cm. long. Flowers of a lively pink colour, the outer petals with a broad green midrib outside. Very free-flowering.

(b) *Stems spiny*.

Echinocereus Weinbergii Weingt. Mexico. Stem greyish green, about 12 cm. thick, at first globular, passing to oval-elongated, with white wool at the top, branching sparingly from the base, with 15 acute ribs, bearing areoles of oval shape about 8 mm. apart, with about 10 short and thick radial spines, white reddish at the base and dark at the tip, the longest only about 1 cm. long. No central spine. Flowers borne at the top, funnel-shaped, 5 cm. long, of a lively pink colour, with narrow acute petals. A beautiful species, still rare in cultivation. There is a form with spines entirely white, = *albispinus* Hort.

Echinocereus coccineus Engelm. = *E. phoeniceus* Rümpl. New Mexico and Arizona, as far as Utah and Colorado. Stem dark green, globular, very slowly becoming elongated, 5 to 7 cm. thick, with 8 to 11 ribs, slightly notched. Areoles elliptical, 1 to 2 cm. apart, with about 9 bristle-like radial spines, yellowish white, 1 to 2 cm. long; and 2 to 4 central spines, up to 3 cm. long, yellow with reddish brown tip. Flower funnel-shaped, about 6 cm. long, fiery scarlet, with narrow blunt petals, yellowish at the base. Stamens white below and red above. Stigma with 7 or 8 lobes. Becomes very much shrivelled in winter, but is resistant to cold.

var. **inermis** K. Sch. Colorado. Is a smaller form, almost spineless.

Echinocereus conoideus Engelm. et Big. Texas and California. Often considered as a variety or subspecies of the preceding, from which it differs by its very long and thick central spines. The flower is also larger, fiery red, with a strongly angular ovary.

Echinocereus paucispinus (Engelm.) Rümpl. = *Cereus paucispinus* Engelm. Texas, New Mexico and Colorado. Stems oval, passing to cylindrical, 8 to 22 cm. long, and about 6 cm. thick, erect or semi-prostrate, pale green, with 5 to 8 warty ribs, with narrow furrows between them. Areoles round, whitish, 1 to 2 cm. apart, with 3 to 6 radial spines, which may be straight or curved or tortuous, $1\frac{1}{2}$ to 2 cm. long, thickened at the base, the upper ones reddish or brown, the lower pale brown. Only one central spine, up to $3\frac{1}{2}$ cm. long, angular, almost black, often absent. Flower funnel-shaped, 5 cm. long, outer petals brownish red, inner petals linear, blunt, dark scarlet, yellowish at the base. Stigma with 7 lobes. The following varieties are often considered as distinct species.

var. **triglochidiatus** K. Sch. = *Cereus triglochidiatus* Engelm. Radial spines 3 to 6, mostly 3, strong angular, straight or bent, up to $2\frac{1}{2}$ cm. long, all ashy grey.

var. **hexaedrus** K. Sch. = *E. hexaedrus* (Eng. et Big.) Rümpl. Radial spines 5 to 7, straight more slender, yellowish red, up to 3 cm. long. Central spine strong and angular, same length, sometimes absent.

var. **gonacanthus** K. Sch. = *E. gonacanthus* (Engelm. et Big.) Lem. Radial spines 8, very thick, angular and long, the upper one as long as the central, up to 7 cm. long, yellow tipped dark. Centrals sometimes 2, one of them up to 8 cm. long.

B. *Stems stiff, erect, oval-cylindrical.*

(a) *Spines small, spreading star-like.*

Echinocereus dasyacanthus Engelm. Mexico, New Mexico and Texas. Stem branching from the base, cylindrical, 5 to 7 cm. thick, and rarely more than 20 cm. high, erect and stiff, with about 18 straight ribs. Areoles roundish, closely set, about ½ cm. apart, with about 20 radial spines, greyish, reddish when young, spreading, about 1 cm. long. Central spines 3 to 7, slightly longer. Flowers large, up to 10 cm. long, borne at the top of the stem, funnel-shaped, glossy canary yellow, the outer petals with a reddish midrib. Free-flowering.

Echinocereus rubescens Dams. Mexico. Stem freely cespitose, up to 25 cm. long, and 5 to 6 cm. thick, stiff and erect, with 12 to 14 ribs. Areoles thickly set, oval, with whitish wool and with 12 to 14 spreading, awl-shaped radial spines, about ½ cm. long, at first ruby red passing to grey, tipped reddish. Central spines 1 or 2, short. Flower large, beautiful, greenish yellow. Often classed as a variety of the preceding. Not to be mistaken for *E. rubescens* Hort. which is a variety of *E. caespitosus.*

Echinocereus ctenoides Engelm. Texas and California. Very much like *E. dasyacanthus*, with similar flowers. Ribs disposed spirally, and spines disposed in alternate zones of grey and reddish around the stem. Radials fewer, disposed star-like. Centrals also fewer and shorter.

Echinocereus pectinatus Engelm. = *Cereus pectinatus* Engelm. = *Echinocactus pectinatus* Scheidw. Central Mexico. A popular and free-flowering species of easy cultivation, similar to *E. dasyacanthus.* Stem roundish, or oval-elongated, or cylindrical, up to 20 cm. high, and about 6 cm. thick, branching from the base, and sometimes also above ground, with about 20 obtuse ribs. Areoles oval, thickly set, with short white hairs when young. Radial spines about 25, spreading star-like or comb-like, up to 9 mm. long, white, pinkish when young. Central spines 2 to 6, very short. Flower 6 to 8 cm. long, with white hairs and spines outside, lively pink inside.

Echinocereus caespitosus Engelm. = *Cereus caespitosus* Engelm. = *Echinocactus Reichenbachii* Terscheck. = *Echinocereus Reichenbachii* Haage Jr. Texas and northern Mexico. Often considered as a variety or subspecies of the preceding. Stem oval or cylindrical, stiff and erect, with about 16 straight ribs, freely cespitose, up to 20 cm. high, and about 6 cm. thick. Areoles oval, thickly set. Radial spines numerous (20 to 30), in two series, comb-like, yellowish passing to whitish, dark tipped. Central spines 1 or 2, small, often missing. Flower 6 to 7 cm. long, well expanded, lively pink. A resistant species, very free-flowering. A cristate form is also cultivated.

var. **adustus** Engelm. Mexico. Often described as a distinct species. Stem more slender, with fewer ribs, sparingly cespitose. Spines dark reddish brown towards the tip. The form *castaneus* Engelm. has chocolate brown spines.

var. **armatus** Poselg. = *Echinocereus spinosus* Coulter. Has longer radial spines, yellow, reddish towards the tip; central spines short and yellow.

var. **chrysacanthus** K. Sch. Stem more slender. Spines yellow, passing to yellowish white.

var. **rubescens** Hort. Spines tipped reddish.

var. **rufispinus** K. Sch. Stem thick, up to 9 cm., flowers large, deep pink. Spines longer, awl-shaped, reddish.

var. **Reichenbachii** Terscheck = var. *candicans* Hort. Identical with the type, but has white spines.

var. **tamaulipensis** Frič. Mexico (Tamaulipas). Spines very numerous, white; stem thick; flowers very large, of a beautiful pink. A very desirable variety.

Echinocereus rigidissimus Rose = *E. pectinatus* var. *rigidissimus* Engelm. Mexico and Arizona. This is the popular "Rainbow Cactus." Stem stiff and erect, slightly cespitose, 6 to 9 cm. thick, and up to 30 cm. high, with a rounded top or slightly depressed, with 16 to 23 ribs, straight and obtuse. Areoles elongated, with 16 to 20 radial spines, spreading comb-like, very stiff, up to $1\frac{1}{2}$ cm. long, whitish or very pale pink, or reddish, or brownish, in alternate zones on the stem, hence the name of Rainbow Cactus. Flowers pink, 6 to 7 cm. long, with whitish hairs and spines outside.

(b) *Spines longer and more stiff.*

Echinocereus viridiflorus Engelm. New Mexico, Wyoming and South Dakota. Stem globular to oval, sometimes elongated or almost cylindrical, freely branching from the base, $2\frac{1}{2}$ to $4\frac{1}{2}$ cm. thick, dark green, with about 13 low obtuse ribs and elongated areoles. Spines white or brown or parti-coloured mostly arranged in zones of the same colour. Radials about 15, stiff, up to 1 cm. long. Centrals 2 or 3 , up to 2 cm. long, often absent. Flowers borne on the areoles at the sides, up to $2\frac{1}{2}$ cm. long, green, with a darker midrib. A variable and free-flowering species, with many varieties.

Echinocereus chloranthus Engelm. = *Cereus chloranthus* Engelm. Mexico, Texas and New Mexico. Stem oval or cylindrical, about 6 cm. thick, and up to 20 cm. long, erect, slightly branching from the base, dull green, with 15 to 18 ribs, well furnished with spines at the top. Areoles round, white. Radial spines 12 to 20, stiff, straight, spreading, white, often tipped red, 1 cm. long. Central spines 3 to 5, up to $2\frac{1}{2}$ cm. long, white or reddish. Flowers borne along the sides of the stem, about 3 cm. long, yellowish green, with narrow acute petals.

Echinocereus Roemeri (Engelm.) Rümpl. = *Cereus Roemeri* Engelm. = *E. octacanthus* Br. et R. Texas. Stem oval or almost cylindrical, up to 15 cm. high, and 6 to 8 cm. thick, pale green, freely branching from the base, with 7 to 11 ribs, irregular and warty, with narrow furrows between them. Areoles round white. Radial spines about 8, brownish passing to white, spreading, up to 2½ cm. long. One central spine, thicker and longer, bulbous at the base, same colour. Flower up to 5 cm. long, funnel-shaped, inner petals obtuse, carmine red, lasting for several days. Free-flowering.

Echinocereus Roetteri (Engelm.) Rümpl. = *Cereus Roetteri* Engelm. = *E. Kunzei* Gürke. Mexico, New Mexico, Texas. Stem erect, up to 15 cm. high, and about 6 cm. thick, of a lively green, well furnished with brown spines and whitish wool at the top, slowly branching from the base, with 10 to 13 straight ribs, notched. Areoles round, white, Radial spines 6 to 10, awl-shaped, bulbous at the base, reddish brown passing to white, up to 1 cm. long. Central spines 2 to 5, thicker and longer, bulbous at the base, reddish brown to brown. Flowers borne on the side areoles, about 6 cm. long, greenish brown outside, violet purple inside, with retuse petals.

Echinocereus Hildmannii Arendt. Texas. Stem cylindrical, bluish green, branching from the base, with 12 to 13 acute and warty ribs. Areoles oval, brown. Radial spines variable, spreading, about 1 cm. long, white tipped brown; central spines about 4, about as long. Flowers borne near or at the top, 12 cm. long, 5 cm. broad; petals greenish on the outside, with a brown midrib; orange yellow inside, fading to pale yellow along the margin.

Echinocereus stramineus (Engelm.) Rümpl. = *Cereus stramineus* Engelm. Mexico, New Mexico and Texas. Stem erect and stiff, pale green, up to 25 cm. high, and about 6 cm. thick, with 10 to 13 acute ribs, slightly warty or notched, with deep furrows between them, thickly covered at the top with long straw-coloured spines, passing to white. Areoles small, round, white, 1 to 2½ cm. apart. Radial spines about 10, spreading, up to 3 cm. long; central spines 3 or 4, up to 9 cm. long. Stem very freely suckering and branching from the base, and often also above ground. Flowers rather sparingly borne on the side areoles, 9 to 12 cm. long, funnel-shaped, purple, with long blunt-toothed petals. Stigma with 10 to 13 lobes. Prefers a very calcareous soil.

var. **major** Hort. Stems thicker and spines longer.

C. *Stems more or less stiff, erect, cylindrical. Spines stiff, mostly white.*

Echinocereus cinerascens (DC.) Rümpl. = *Cereus cinerascens* DC. = *C. Deppei* Otto. Central Mexico. Stem erect or partly sprawling, but stiff, pale green, up to 20 cm. long, and 4 to 5 cm. thick, very freely branching from the base, with 6 to 8 blunt prominent ribs, slightly warty, with narrow furrows between them. Areoles yellowish or white, round. Spines white, straight, slender, reddish and thickened at the base; the radials 8 to 10, spreading, up to 2 cm. long; the centrals 1 to 4, about the same length. Flowers freely borne on the side areoles, large, 7 cm. long, funnel-shaped, brown violet outside, violet red inside, with toothed and pointed petals, and a woolly and spiny ovary and tube. Stigma with 11 lobes.

Echinocereus cirrhifer (Lab.) Rümpl. = *Cereus cirrhifer* Labouret. Mexico. Very similar to the preceding in habit. Stems with 5 or 7 rather acute and slightly warty ribs. Areoles with 10 pure white, slender, pliable radial spines, spreading, up to 4 cm. long, and 4 central spines yellowish or brownish, about as long. All spines are thickened at the base. Flowers as in the preceding, but of a livelier purplish red. A variable species.

Echinocereus glycimorphus (Först.) Rümpl. = *Cereus glycimorphus* Först. Central Mexico. Freely suckering and branching from the base. Stem erect or semi-prostrate, up to 25 cm. long, and 4 cm. thick, pale green passing to dull green, with 6 to 7 acute ribs, notched and warty. Areoles round, yellowish, about 2 cm. apart, with 8 or 9 white awl-shaped radial spines, up to 1½ cm. long. Central spine only one, thicker and slightly longer and, like the uppermost radial spine, of a brownish colour. Flower campanulate, 6 to 8 cm. long, brownish outside, purplish red inside, with narrow acute toothed petals.

Echinocereus Ehrenbergii Rümpl. Mexico. Stem erect or almost prostrate, about 15 cm. long and 2½ cm. thick, green or greyish green, freely suckering and branching from the base, with 6 straight ribs, slightly notched and warty. Areoles small, round, white, about 2 cm. apart, with 8 to 10 stiff, very slender spines, up to 1½ cm. long, glassy white or yellowish white, and one central spine of the same colour, up to 2½ cm. long. Flower 7 cm. long, funnel-shaped, purplish red to violet red, with pointed toothed petals. A beautiful cristate form is also in cultivation.

Echinocereus enneacanthus Engelm. Mexico, Texas and New Mexico. Stem mostly erect, up to 20 cm. long, and 3½ to 5 cm. thick, rather soft, pale green, or dark green, freely sprouting from the base, with 8 to 10 warty ribs, and white or whitish round areoles about 1 cm. apart. Radial spines 8 or 9, spreading, bulbous at the base, up to 1½ cm. long, white. Central spines 1 to 3, stronger, and slightly brownish, up to 4 cm. long. Flower 5 to 6 cm. long, fully expanded, lively red. A cristate form is also cultivated.

var. **carnosus** K. Sch. = *E. carnosus* Rümpl. Stems thicker and softer, radial spines longer.

var. **major** Hort. Stem thicker, flower larger.

Echinocereus leonensis Mathsson. Mexico. Stem erect, rather stiff, up to 25 cm. long, and 4 to 5 cm. thick, pale green with 6 or 7 ribs, straight and acute, with white roundish areoles 1½ cm. apart, with about 8 awl-shaped, white, stiff radial spines up to 1½ cm. long, and one straight central spine up to 3 cm. long. Flower 8 cm. long, with blunt toothed petals, purplish red, with darker midrib. A beautiful species, freely branching from the base, and free-flowering.

Echinocereus Baileyi Rose. Oklahoma. A very desirable species, still rather rare in collections. Stem erect, cylindrical, 10 cm. high and 4 to 5 cm. thick, with about 15 narrow acute ribs. Areoles elongated, whitish. Radial spines 16, spreading, needle-shaped, white or yellowish, 2 to 3 cm. long. Central spine absent. Flowers 6 cm. long, funnel-shaped, pale pink. Branches freely from the base, and is free-flowering.

Echinocereus Brandegeei K. Sch. Lower California. Stem stiff, mostly erect, up to 35 cm. long and 4 to 5 cm. thick, dull green, cylindrical, with indistinct ribs almost entirely superseded by warts, on which are situated the roundish, white to brownish areoles. Radial spines about 12, spreading, needle-like, 2 to 3 cm. long, at first yellow, reddish at the base, passing to greyish. Central spines 1 to 4, the lowermost flattened, up to 8 cm. long, directed downwards, white or yellowish white. Flower red. A characteristic species, freely sprouting from the base, and suckering.

Echinocereus acifer (Salm-Dyck) Lem. = *Cereus acifer* Salm-Dyck. Mexico. Stem erect, up to 20 cm. high, and 4 to 5 cm. thick, grass green, stiff, freely branching from the base, with about 10 ribs, slightly warty. Areoles round, white, $\frac{1}{2}$ to 1 cm. apart, with about 9 radial spines, spreading, up to $1\frac{1}{2}$ cm. long, the upper ones brownish, the others white passing to grey. Central spines 1 to 4, spreading, up to $2\frac{1}{2}$ cm. long, brown. Flower 9 or 10 cm. long, funnel-shaped, 6 or 7 cm. broad, scarlet red, with blunt petals. Stigma with 9 or 10 lobes. A very variable species.

var. **durangensis** K. Sch. = *E. durangensis* Poselg. Has smaller flowers, and stigma with fewer lobes.

var. **trichacanthus** K. Sch. Spines more slender and shorter; flower larger, scarlet red, with red stamens.

var. **diversispinus** K. Sch. Central spines longer, mostly 1 or 2, directed upwards; flower small, red.

Echinocereus Engelmannii (Parry) Rümpl. = *Cereus Engelmannii* Parry. Mexico, California, Arizona, Nevada and Utah. Stems mostly erect, stiff, freely branching from the base and close together, 10 to 25 cm. high, and 4 to 6 cm. thick, pale green, thickly covered with long, stiff spines of various colours; with 11 to 14 low and obtuse ribs, with narrow furrows between them. The areoles are large, round, about 1 cm. apart, with about 12 awl-shaped, angular, spreading and partly reflexed radial spines, 1 cm. long, white, sometimes tipped brown when young. Central spines 4 or more, thick and angular, or flattened, spreading, somewhat bulbous at the base, yellowish, brownish at the base and at the tip, or zoned yellow and brown, passing to greyish white with age. Flower 5 to 8 cm. long, and about as broad, spreading, purplish red, with retuse toothed petals. A resistant and attractive species of rather slow growth. Requires a sandy soil.

var. **chrysocentrus** Engelm. et Big. The 3 upper central spines are 6 to 8 cm. long, golden yellow, the lower ones white and curved.

(a) ECHINOCEREUS PULCHELLUS

(b) ECHINOCEREUS GLYCIMORPHUS

PLATE XXIV

(b) ECHINOCEREUS BAILEYII

(a) ECHINOCEREUS COCCINEUS

PLATE XXV

var. **variegatus** Engelm. et Big. Central spines mostly curved, the upper ones black, the next horny yellow, the lower white, 4 to 5 cm. long.

Other forms are: *albispinus* Cels., *fulvispinus* Cels., *Pfersdorffii* Heyder, *robustior* Hildm., and *versicolor*.

D. *Stems stiff, erect. Spines numerous, long, soft, hair-like.*

Echinocereus De Laetii Gürke. Mexico, Province of Coahuila, on hilly ground, in arid calcareous or sandy soil. A beautiful and popular species of easy cultivation. Stem stiff, mostly erect, 10 to 25 cm. high, pale green or yellowish green, freely sprouting or suckering from the base, with 20 to 24 straight ribs, entirely covered with long white hairs. Areoles large, round, 1 cm. apart. Radial spines numerous (18 to 36), straight, yellowish white, stiff, up to 1 cm. long. Central spines about 5, bristle-like or needle-like, bulbous at the base, straight or tortuous, yellowish tipped reddish, 2 to 3 cm. long. From the areoles proceed also numerous white or greyish hairs 6 to 10 cm. long, rather stiff and rough, but tortuous, entirely covering the stem, like those of *Cephalocereus senilis*, but of rougher texture. Flowers borne on the side areoles, about 7 cm. long, of a lively pink; stigma with 11 or 12 lobes.

This very attractive species, commonly known as the "Lesser Old Man Cactus," thrives well in a very sunny situation, in a stony calcareous and sandy soil, and should be abundantly watered in summer. It soon sends up numerous suckers, resulting in a nice group of several stems in about three years.

Echinocereus longisetus (Engelm.) Rümpl. = *Cereus longisetus* Engelm. Mexico (Coahuila). A pretty species long lost sight of, but recently rediscovered and brought under cultivation. Has erect stems, 10 to 20 cm. long, and 4 or 5 cm. thick, with few ribs, and small round white areoles, without hairs, but with 9 to 14 radial spines, white, up to 1 cm. long, and with 3 or 4 white, very slender, very long and flexible central spines, directed upwards. Freely branching from the base. Flower red.

Echinocereus barcena Reb. Central Mexico. Stem stiff, erect, 10 to 20 cm. long, branching from the base, deep grass green, with 8 or 9 low ribs, slightly warty, at first acute. Areoles about 1 cm. apart. Radial spines about 7, $\frac{1}{2}$ to 1 cm. long, white. Central spine only one, at first yellowish, passing to white, up to 2 cm. long, soft and flexible. Flowers red. Rather scarce in cultivation.

E. *Stem mostly erect, softish, short, oval to oval-cylindrical.*

Echinocereus Fendleri (Engelm.) Rümpl. = *Cereus Fendleri* Engelm. Mexico, Texas, Arizona and Utah. Stem 10 to 15 cm. high and 5 to 6 cm. thick, with 9 to 12 ribs, slightly warty, dull green. Areoles 1 to 1½ cm. apart, with very variable spines. Radials about 8, spreading 1 to 2 cm. long, straight or curved. Only one central spine, awl-shaped, thickened at the base and up to 4½ cm. long. The spines may be pale yellow, or brownish, or dark brown almost black. Flower broadly

P

funnel-shaped, about 8 cm. long, purplish violet, with long spathulate deeply toothed petals. Stigma with 10 to 15 lobes. Freely flowering, and branching from the base, but growth is rather slow.

Echinocereus pacificus (Engelm.) Br. et R. = *Cereus pacificus* Engelm. Lower California. Stems 15 to 25 cm. long, 5 to 6 cm. thick, freely branching from the base and forming large clumps, with 10 to 12 obtuse ribs. Spines grey flushed reddish, the radials about 12, ½ to 1 cm. long, the centrals 4 or 5, up to 2½ cm. long. Flowers 3 cm. long, deep red, with yellowish brown wool and reddish brown spines on the ovary and tube.

Echinocereus Rosei Wooton and Standley. Mexico, New Mexico, Texas. Stems 10 to 20 cm. high, and 5 to 8 cm. thick, forming large clumps, with 8 to 11 obtuse ribs. Areoles closely set. Spines reddish passing to greyish; the radials about 10 spreading; the central 4, up to 6 cm. long. Flowers 4 to 6 cm. long, scarlet, with the inner petals broad and obtuse. Ovary and tube with brownish or yellowish spines and short hairs.

Echinocereus luteus Br. et R. Western Mexico. Stem mostly solitary, rarely branching near the base, short and thick, rarely more than 10 cm. long, bluish green, with 8 or 9 thin ribs, prominent and rounded. Areoles 1 cm. apart. Spines small, the radials 6 to 8, 2 to 8 mm. long; one central spine slightly longer. Flowers 7 cm. long, pale yellow, sweet-scented, outer petals streaked red.

Echinocereus perbellus Br. et R. Texas. A beautiful species, often sold as *E. caespitosus*. Stem 5 to 10 cm. high, slowly clustering, with 15 low ribs. Areoles elongated, very closely set. Spines all radials, 12 to 15, spreading, about ½ cm. long, pale brown or reddish, white below. Flowers purple, 4 to 6 cm. long, with broad acuminate petals.

Echinocereus scopulorum Br. et R. Mexico. Stem usually solitary, 10 to 40 cm. long, and 6 or 7 cm. thick, with about 14 low ribs, entirely covered with short coloured spines. Areoles closely set. Spines brownish or pinkish with dark tips, later passing to grey, about ½ cm. long: the radials many, spreading, the centrals 3 to 6, like the radials. Flowers large, 9 cm. broad, borne at the sides near the top, pink or purplish rose, paler outside, sweet-scented.

Echinocereus sciurus (K. Brand.) Br. et R. = *Cereus sciurus* K. Brand. Lower California, near San José del Cabo. Stem mostly erect, up to 20 cm. high, green, and 3½ to 5 cm. thick, covered with rather short bristle-like, pale yellow spines. Ribs 12 to 17, low, notched into low warts. Areoles at first woolly, afterwards almost bare, with 15 to 18 pale yellow slender spines, at first tipped red, afterwards tipped brown, up to 1 cm. long, spreading. Central spines about 4 shorter and thicker, same colour. Flowers borne near the top, very large and beautiful, 9 cm. long, and up to 12 cm. across, fully expanded, rosy violet. The flowering tops of the stems are often curved, like a squirrel's tail.

Echinocereus Fitchii Br. et R. Texas. Stem erect, 10 to 15 cm. high, and 6 to 8 cm. thick, dull green, slowly branching from the base, with 12 to 14 low ribs, spiral towards the top, straight below, with small yellowish areoles, less than 1 cm. apart, furnished with numerous yellowish spines, straight or curved, about 1 cm. long, pinkish-brown when young. Flower with a long spiny and hairy ovary, funnel-shaped, about 9 cm. across, violet red, with abruptly acuminate petals, partly reflexed. Very free-flowering; flowers borne at the top, even on young plants, but growth is slow.

Echinocereus maritimus (Jones) K. Sch. = *Cereus maritimus* Jones. Lower California. Stems roundish or cylindrical, 5 to 15 cm. long, and 2 to 2½ cm. thick, lively green passing to greyish, very freely branching from the base and also above ground, with 8 to 10 straight ribs. Areoles 1 to 2½ cm. apart, with 9 to 10 radial spines, straight, yellowish white passing to grey, the upper ones being up to 2½ cm. long. Central spines 1 to 4, angular, thicker, of the same colour, and up to 3½ cm. long. Flowers borne at the top of the stems, about 4 cm. long, pale yellow.

Echinocereus mojavensis (Engelm.) Rümpl. = *Cereus mojavensis* Engelm. California, Nevada, Arizona and Utah. Stems 5 to 20 cm. long, and about 5 cm. thick, pale green, very freely suckering and branching from the base. Ribs 8 to 12, with prominent warts. Areoles round, white passing to grey, 1 cm. apart. Spines at first reddish, passing to white, and to grey on the lower areoles. Radial spines straight, stiff, spreading, about 10 in number, up to 5 cm. long. Central spine only one, 3 to 5 cm. long. Flower about 7 cm. long, carmine red, with blunt toothed petals.

F. *Stems long, cylindrical, soft, mostly sprawling.*

Echinocereus dubius (Engelm.) Rümpl. = *Cereus dubius* Engelm. Sandy wastes of south-eastern Texas. Stems yellowish green, soft, very fleshy and semi-prostrate, 10 to 20 cm. long, and 4 to 6 cm. thick, freely branching from the base, with 7 to 9 broad, rounded ribs, slightly warty, with round yellowish or greyish areoles, 1 to 1½ cm. apart. Radial spines 5 to 8, straight, spreading, yellowish passing to greyish, 1 to 3 cm. long. Central spines 1 to 4, thickened at the base, straight or slightly curved, 4 to 7 cm. long, same colour as the radials. Flower about 6 cm. long, with spiny ovary, and short scaly tube with a few whitish short spines. Limb funnel-shaped, with obtuse pink petals. Stigma with 8 to 12 lobes. A common species in cultivation.

Echinocereus conglomeratus (Först) Maths. = *Cereus conglomeratus* Först. Mexico. In habit the same as the preceding, but with stems more erect, pale green, with 11 to 13 ribs, rather narrow and more warty, with white spines passing to greyish. Radial spines 9 or 10, spreading, up to 2½ cm. long. Central spines 1 to 4, soft and flexible, somewhat curved, up to 4 cm. long. Flower 7 cm. long, fully expanded, of a beautiful purple, with broad petals and with long tortuous spines on the ovary and tube. A form with thicker stems (*robustior* Hort.) is also cultivated.

Echinocereus Merkeri Hildm. Mexico. Stems up to 40 cm. long, and 12 to 15 cm. thick, erect or semi-prostrate, pale green passing to greyish or brownish, with 8 or 9 ribs, rounded and with prominent warts. Areoles whitish, passing to grey, 2 cm. apart, with 6 to 9 radial spines, spreading, thickened at the base, glassy white, up to 5 cm. long, and 1 or 2 central spines of same colour and about the same length. Flower 6 cm. long, purplish red, with long blunt petals.

Echinocereus Hempelii Fobe. Mexico, on sandy soil. Stem almost erect, 15 to 20 cm. long, and about 6 cm. thick, branching from the base, dark green, with 8 to 10 ribs, notched into warts. Areoles round, white. Radial spines 5 or 6, straight, spreading, about 1 cm. long, white with a brown point. No central spines. Flower 6 cm. long, fully expanded, reddish violet, with long, obtuse toothed petals. Stamens green, stigma with 8 or 9 lobes.

Echinocereus polyacanthus Engelm. Mexico. Stems freely branching from the base, dark green, 10 to 25 cm. long, and about 6 cm. thick, mostly erect, with about 10 ribs. Areoles 1 to 1½ cm. apart, with 8 to 12 spreading radial spines about 2 cm. long, at first reddish, afterwards white, tipped dark. Central spines 3 or 4, bulbous, spreading, up to 5 cm. long, but usually 3 cm. long, horny yellow to brownish. Flowers 6 cm. long, funnel-shaped, with the inner petals obtuse, blood red or pink. Ovary with white or reddish bristles; stigma with 8 or 9 lobes. A beautiful and variable species.

var. **Galtieri** (Reb.) = *Echinocereus Galtieri* Reb. Spines pure white.

var. **nigrispinus** Hort. Stem thicker; spines longer, black above, whitish below.

var. **rufispinus** Hort. Stem longer and almost prostrate. Spines at first reddish brown, passing to dull brown.

var. **longispinus** Hort. Spines longer.

Echinocereus Berlandieri (Engelm.) Rümpl. = *Cereus Berlandieri* Engelm. Mexico. Stems 6 to 10 cm. long, dull green, sprawling, 1½ to 2 cm. thick, very freely branching and suckering, with 5 or 6 spiral ribs, notched into warts, with brownish small round areoles. Radial spines 6 to 8, spreading, straight, up to 1 cm. long, at first yellowish brown, passing to white. One central spine, yellowish brown, up to 2 cm. long. Flowers 6 to 8 cm. long, fully expanded and rotate, of a lively pink, with one row of narrow obtuse petals, slightly toothed. Stigma with 7 to 10 lobes.

Echinocereus Viereckii Werd. = *E. Scheeri* Hort. (non Rümpl.). Mexico. Stems 20 to 30 cm. long, and about 4 cm. thick, semi-prostrate, yellowish green, freely branching from the base, with 7 or 8 acute, straight ribs, 1 cm. deep, very slightly warty. Areoles about 1 cm. apart, round, small, yellowish passing to brown. Radial spines 8 to 10, up to 1 cm. long, spreading, bristle-like, whitish, the middle upper one very small and brown. Central spines 3 or 4, straight, spreading

(b) ECHINOCEREUS FITCHII

(a) ECHINOCEREUS SCIURUS

PLATE XXVI

PLATE XXVII

crosswise, bulbous, needle-like, yellow passing to grey, up to 4 cm. long. Flower large, well expanded, pink.

Echinocereus Scheeri Rümpl. (non Hort.). Mexico. Stem erect or semi-prostrate, 10 to 22 cm. long, and $2\frac{1}{2}$ to 3 cm. thick, glossy dark green, branching from the base, with about 8 low ribs, with small warts. Areoles yellowish, with 7 to 9 radial spines, $\frac{1}{2}$ to 1 cm. long, spreading, white, yellow at the base. Central spines 3, brown, tipped red, up to 1 cm. long. Flower about 12 cm. long, funnel-shaped, of a beautiful pink. Stigma with 10 lobes. Free-flowering. Growth rather slow.

Echinocereus procumbens (Engelm.) Rümpl. = *Cereus procumbens* Engelm. Mexico. Stems mostly prostrate, freely branching from the base, about 15 cm. long, and 2 cm. thick, green or dark green, with 4 or 5 ribs, mostly arranged spirally, notched into low warts. Areoles whitish, $\frac{1}{2}$ to 1 cm. apart, with 4 to 8 awl-shaped, radial spines, about $\frac{1}{2}$ cm. long, at first brownish, passing to white, tipped brown. Only one central spine, often absent, brownish, $1\frac{1}{2}$ cm. long. Flower about 8 cm. across and 10 cm. long, broadly funnel-shaped, violet red, whitish or yellowish at the base, with abruptly acuminate petals, more or less toothed. Stigma with 10 to 14 lobes. Very freely growing and flowering.

var. **longispinus** Hort. Radial spines $1\frac{1}{2}$ to 2 cm. long; central spine up to 3 cm. long.

Echinocereus Salm-Dyckianus Scheer. Mexico. Stem somewhat stiff, semi-prostrate, 15 to 20 cm. long, and 2 to $2\frac{1}{2}$ cm. thick, dark green, very freely branching from the base, with 7 to 9 ribs, straight or spiral, slightly warty. Areoles closely set, yellowish passing to brownish. Radial spines 8 or 9, yellowish, tipped red, less than 1 cm. long; only one central spine, awl-shaped, red passing to yellowish, up to $1\frac{1}{2}$ cm. long. Flowers about 10 cm. long, narrowly funnel-shaped, yellowish red. Stigma with 10 to 12 lobes. A lovely species, fast-growing.

var. **gracilior** Hort. Stem more slender, deep green; flower more spreading, orange red.

Echinocereus pentalophus (DC.) Rümpl.. = *Cereus pentalophus* DC. = *C. pentalophus* var. *leptacanthus* Salm-Dyck = *E. leptacanthus* K. Sch. Mexico. Stem about 12 cm. long, and about 2 cm. thick, pale green, mostly sprawling, with 5 warty ribs, often arranged spirally. Areoles closely set, whitish. Radial spines 3 to 5, whitish or yellowish, passing to grey, up to 2 cm. long. No central spine. Flower about 10 cm. long, fully expanded, almost rotate, lilac or pink, with narrow, blunt, toothed inner petals, Stigma with 10 to 13 lobes.

Echinocereus Blanckii (Poselg.) Palmer = *Cereus Blanckii* Poselg. Often written *Blankii*, by mistake. Stems up to 35 cm. long, and about 3 cm. thick, at first erect, later sprawling, dark green, with 5 or 6 warty ribs, and brownish areoles. Radial spines about 9, spreading, white, up to 2 cm. long, the uppermost much smaller and black. Central spines also glossy black, the others white or partly black passing to white, and up to 3 cm. long. Flower about 9 cm. long, broadly funnel-shaped, violet, with broad blunt petals. Stigma with 9 to 11 lobes. A beautiful species, branching and suckering freely, resistant and free-flowering.

Echinocereus Poselgerianus A. Linke. Mexico. Stem up to 30 cm. long, and 3 to 5 cm. thick, pale green, passing to dull green, with 6 or 7 notched and warty ribs, somewhat acute. Areoles small, round, whitish, with 8 or 9 radial spines up to 1 cm. long, white tipped yellow, the uppermost one reddish and very small. Central spines 1 to 3, brownish, up to 2 cm. long. Flower about 9 cm. long, funnel-shaped, reddish violet, with narrow blunt petals. Stigma with 12 to 14 lobes.

Echinocereus Leeanus (Hook.) Lem. in Först. = *Cereus Leeanus* Hooker. Mexico. Stem mostly erect, up to 30 cm. long, and 7 to 9 cm. thick, grass green passing to dull green, freely branching from the base, with 12 to 14 straight low ribs, slightly warty, with narrow furrows between them. Areoles round, white, about 1 cm. apart. Radial spines 10 to 14, very slender, up to 1½ cm. long, at first reddish brown, passing to greyish. Central spines 2 or 3, same colour, up to 2½ cm. long. Flower 7 cm. long, fully expanded, dark carmine, with petals abruptly acuminate. Stigma with 8 or 9 lobes. Considered synonymous with *E. pleiogonus* Rümpl.

var. **multicostatus** K. Sch. = *E. multicostatus* Rümpl. Central spines 1 or 2, red. Petals almost obtuse.

Echinocereus papillosus A. Linke. Texas. Stems up to 24 cm. long, and about 2½ cm. thick, sprawling, branching and suckering from the base, pale green, with 7 to 9 ribs, notched into prominent warts about 1 cm. high. Areoles yellowish. Radial spines about 7, up to 1 cm. long, white passing to brownish. One central spine, bright yellow, brownish at the base, about 2 cm. long. Flower yellow, reddish at the base of the petals, which are lanceolate. Stigma with 9 lobes. Rather rare in cultivation; shrinks very much in winter. Usually grafted.

var. **rubescens** Hildm. New spines pink to ruby red, passing to brownish.

Echinocereus ochoterrenae Ortega. Mexico. Stems up to 10 cm. long, and 4 to 7 cm. thick, green or purplish green, erect or prostrate, branching from the base, with 10 or 11 ribs, prominent and slightly notched. Areoles about 1 cm. apart, whitish, later passing to brown, with 8 to 9 radial spines, reddish yellow passing to brown, ½ to 1 cm. long. Central spines 1 to 4, about 1 cm. long, same colour but darker, when only one is present it is up to 2 cm. long. Flower 7 cm. long, canary yellow. Stigma with 8 to 11 lobes.

Echinocereus pensilis (K. Brand.) Purpus = *Cereus pensilis* K. Brand. Lower California. Stem prostrate or hanging, branching from the base, 30 to 40 cm. long, and 2½ to 4 cm. thick, with 8 to 10 ribs, notched into low warts. Areoles about 2 cm. apart. Radial spines 8, and central spine 1, all 1 to 2 cm. long, slender, bulbous at the base, yellow, passing to reddish or brown. Flower about 6 cm. long, of a lively red.

Echinocereus mamillatus (Engelm.) Br. et R. = *Cereus mamillatus* Engelm. Lower California. Stem cespitose, prostrate or ascending, cylindrical, 20 to 30 cm. long, 3½ to 6 cm. thick, with 20 to 30 ribs, deeply notched. Radial spines 10 to 25, needle-like, ½ to 1 cm. long; central spines 3 or 4, much thicker and 1 to 2½ cm. long. All spines pinkish passing to white. Very rare in cultivation.

The following are other species rare in cultivation: **Echinocereus huitcholensis** Weber, **E. chlorophthalmus** Br. et R., **E. sarissophorus** Br. et R., natives of Mexico; **E. Runyonii** Orcutt, from Texas and California; **E. Sandersii** Orcutt, from California; **E. neo-mexicanus** Stand., from New Mexico; **E. arizonicus** Rose and **E. Boyce-Thompsonii** Orcutt, from Arizona; and **E. grandis** Br. et R., **E. Standleyi** Br. et R. and **E. Barthelowianus** Br. et R., from Lower California.

CHAMAECEREUS Br. et R.

Low, mostly prostrate, much branched, with small cylindrical stems, with low ribs. Flowers small, funnel-shaped, red, diurnal. Fruit small, round and dry, hairy or woolly. Includes one species.

Chamaecereus Silvestrii (Speg.) Br. et R. = *Cereus Silvestrii* Spegazzini. Western Argentina. A miniature plant, with many short stems, very much branched. The longer stems mostly prostrate, light green, 1½ to 2½ cm. thick, rarely more than 15 cm. long, with 8 to 10 obscure ribs, closely studded with areoles bearing 10 to 15 radiating, white, bristle-like spines, about 2 mm. long. Flowers borne profusely in May-July, 5 to 7 cm. long, of a beautiful scarlet, with a scaly and hairy ovary. Outer petals acute, the inner shorter and more obtuse. Stamens shorter than the petals, red, pistil greenish or yellowish. Requires full sunshine and frequent watering during the growing period. The joints or stems drop off at the least touch, and soon strike root. Is easily grown on own roots, and also makes pretty plants when grafted on an *Opuntia* or a *Cereus*.

var. **elongata**. Stems more slender, 1 to 1½ cm. thick, and often up to 20 cm. long or more.

var. **lutea** Hort. Stems etiolated and entirely yellow, or occasionally streaked green.

var. **cristata** Hort. A form with thickened and cristate stems, almost as free-flowering as the type.

var. **crassicaulis cristata** Backbg. Shoots at first normal, but thicker, later becoming fasciated and half-monstrous. Flowers freely; the flowers are larger, compressed or partly fasciated, and set good seed, the normal plant being self-sterile. Should be grown on own roots.

Quite recently there were offered by dealers a number of hybrids with species of *Lobivia* etc., to which misleading specific Latin names have been given.

Frič had proposed the transfer of a species of *Lobivia*, viz: *Lobivia grandiflora* Br. et R., from Argentina, as a second species of *Chamaecereus*, under the name of *Ch. grandiflorus* (Br. et R.) Frič, but the suggestion appears to be hardly acceptable.

AUSTROCACTUS Br. et R.

Low plants bearing warty ribs, and hooked central spines. Flower diurnal, pinkish yellow, borne on the top areoles. Tube and ovary very spiny, fruit spiny, with flattened seeds. Stigma red, many-lobed.

Includes one species, possibly two, natives of Patagonia and Argentina.

Austrocactus Bertinii (Cels.) Br. et R. = *Cereus Bertinii* Cels. = *Echinocactus Bertinii* Berger. Patagonia. Stem ovoid or cylindrical, about 6 cm. high, and 3 to $3\frac{1}{2}$ cm. thick, branching from the base, green passing to deep green, with 10 to 12 tuberculate low ribs, rounded. Areoles less than 1 cm. apart, sparingly furnished with yellowish wool, passing to white. Radial spines 10 to 15, less than 1 cm. long, straight, glassy, needle-like. Central spines 4, darker, up to 3 cm. long, strongly hooked at the end. Flowers about 6 cm. long and 10 cm. broad, brownish red outside, pinkish yellow inside, with the stamens in two bundles. Style red, stigma with 16 red lobes. Very rare in cultivation.

Austrocactus Dusenii (Weber) Backbg. = *Cereus Dusenii* Weber. = *Echinocactus intertextus* Phil, non Engelm. = *E. Coxii* K. Sch. = *Malacocarpus patagonicus* Br. et R. In the plain at the foot of the Andes in the north-west of Patagonia, and in South Argentina, at Chubut near General Roca (Rio Negro). In accordance with the rules of priority this name should be altered to *Austrocactus Coxii* (K. Sch.). Stem dark green, mostly solitary, ovoid to cylindrical, 6 to 10 cm. long, and up to 60 cm. long, when very old, and 3 to 5 cm. thick, with 8 to 12 broad and prominent ribs notched into conical warts about 7 mm. high. Areoles round or oval, with white wool. Radial spines 6 to 10, up to 1 cm. long, purple red when young, passing to white. Central spines 1 to 4, thicker, longer, hooked at the tip, dark brown or black. Flower $3\frac{1}{2}$ cm. long and about as broad, whitish pink, with pointed petals. Stigma dark purple. May be a variety of subspecies of the preceding.

REBUTIA K. Sch.

Small plants, more or less globose, resembling a *Mammillaria*, not ribbed, but with spirally arranged tubercles or warts, and small spines, usually branching freely around the base. Flowers small, diurnal funnel-shaped, with a slender tube, lasting for several days, closing in the evening, and opening again in the morning, for several days in succession, ranging in colour from deep red, to red, pink, salmon, yellowish red or orange, and violet, borne on the areoles around the stem or at its base. Fruit a small berry, with persistent withered scales, spineless. Seeds black, minute.

The number of species has been greatly increased since the recent discoveries in South America, which is their home. Originally 5, they now number over 35 species, and fresh additions are frequently being made. The plants do not offer any great diversity of form, and are not very attractive, but they are of simple cultivation, whether grown on own roots or grafted, and they flower profusely, the flowers though small, being of exquisite beauty, for which reason they are popular and greatly in demand.

Sub-genus *Eurebutia*: *Flowers more or less bright red; pistil free.*

Rebutia minuscula (Weber) K. Sch. = *Echinopsis minuscula* Weber = *Echinocactus minusculus* Weber. North-west Argentina. Stem globular, depressed at the top, grass green or pale green, 4 cm. broad, and 2 to 2½ cm. high, branching around the base. Tubercles or warts spirally arranged in about 20 rows, round or almost hexagonal. Spines 20 to 25, very small and weak, whitish or yellowish, with a central spine 2 to 3 mm. long. Flowers freely borne around the base of the stem, throughout spring and summer, up to 4 cm. long, funnel-shaped, 2 cm. broad, with a slender tube, lasting for several days. Ovary round, reddish, with a few reddish scales, tube likewise scaly as well as somewhat hairy. Segments of perianth about 15, obtuse, of a beautiful lively red, yellowish at the base, with yellow stamens, and stigma with 4 or 5 white lobes. A well known species of easy cultivation, thriving well in half-shade or in full sunshine.

var. **multiflora** Frič. Stem pale green, somewhat glaucous. Flowers profusely several times in late spring and summer.

A cristate form, just as free-flowering, is also cultivated.

Rebutia senilis Backbg. North Argentina (North Salta). Stem globular, depressed, pale green, about 7 cm. high and the same across, with spirally arranged tubercles. Spines bristle-like, glassy white, 35 to 40, up to 3 cm. long. Flowers borne around the base, clear carmine red, funnel-shaped, 5 cm. long and 4 cm. broad; ovary pale red.

var. **aurescens** Backbg. Top covered with yellowish bristles.

var. **Stuemeriana** Backbg. Flower larger, yellowish red, with more or less yellowish throat. = *R. Stuemeriana* Backbg.

var. **lilacino-rosea** Backbg. Flower lilac pink.

var. **elegans** Backbg. Spines shorter.

var. **cana** Backbg. Spines dull white.

Rebutia violaciflora Backbg. North Argentina (Salta), on mountain sides 3000 m. above sea level. Stem globular, depressed at the top, about 5 cm. thick, olive-green, with 20 to 25 rows of tubercles spirally arranged, close together, 5 to 7 mm. high, bearing oval areoles with yellowish or greyish wool. The plant sprouts abundantly around the base, forming groups. Radial spines 15 or more, yellowish to whitish, ½ to 1 cm. long, spreading; central spines 5 to 10 or more, longer and thicker, at first glassy white, passing to honey yellow, bulbous and reddish at the base. Flowers very numerous, borne at the sides of the stem in May-June, funnel-shaped, about $3\frac{1}{2}$ cm. long. Ovary reddish with a few brownish scales; tube slender, also scaly; outer petals short and narrow, inner petals in three rows, lanceolate, retuse, fully expanded, a lovely deep lilac rose. Stamens many, white. Style longer than the stamens, but shorter than the petals, white or pale pink; stigma with 5 or 6 white recurved lobes.

var. **luteispina** Backbg. All spines yellow.

Rebutia xanthocarpa Backbg. North Argentina (Salta). Stem globular, 5 cm. thick, sprouting around the base, pale green, covered with white, glassy, bristle-like spines, very slender, about $\frac{1}{2}$ cm. long. Flowers small, up to 2 cm. long. Differs from *R. senilis* on account of the smaller flowers and shorter bristles. The flowers are campanulate, red, with yellow ovaries and fruits.

var. **citricarpa** (Frič) Backbg. = *R. citricarpa* Frič. Ovary greenish.

var. **coerulescens** Backbg. = *R. dasyphrissa* Werd. Flowers bluish red : ovary yellowish.

var. **salmonea** (Frič) Backbg. = *R. salmonea* Frič. Flowers and ovaries pale red.

Rebutia Haagei Frič et Schelle. Probably identical with *Lobivia neo-Haageana* Backbg. North Argentina, on mountain sides 4,500 m. above sea level. A small plant, freely clustering from the base, globose or almost cylindrical, dull green, or reddish brown. Tubercles in 10 spiral rows, about 6 mm. apart, with minute whitish or brownish areoles. Spines all radial, 4 to 12, spreading, bristle-like but stiff and straight, 3 to 7 mm. long. Flowers borne about the middle of the stem or towards the base, $3\frac{1}{2}$ cm. long, clear pink.

Rebutia chrysacantha Backbg. North Argentina. Plant globular to short cylindric, sprouting around the base, dull green, with spirally-arranged prominent tubercles, bearing stiff bristle-like spines, about 2 cm. long, golden yellow. Flower pink.

Rebutia Steinbachii Werd. Bolivia, on mountain sides, 2,500 to 3,000 m. above sea level. Stem grass green, freely sprouting around the base, forming cushions. Tubercles long, in irregular rows. Central spines 1 to 3, radials 6 to 8, all whitish passing to dark brown, up to 6 mm. long, needle-like. Spines on imported plants are more numerous and longer. Flowers borne at about the middle of the stem, $3\frac{1}{2}$ cm. long, very slender, with scarlet red petals.

Sub-genus *Aylostera* Speg. *Pistil united to the tube; flowers mostly dark red.*

Rebutia pseudominuscula (Speg.) Br. et R. = *Echinopsis pseudominuscula* Speg. = *Aylostera pseudominuscula* Speg. Described by Spegazzini as the type of a new genus (*Aylostera*), owing to the fact that the pistil is continuous with the tube of the flower. North Argentina (Salta) about 3,000 m. above sea level. Stem somewhat cylindrical, freely branching from the base, forming groups, with a thick rootstock, dark green, flushed reddish, about 8 cm. high, and 3 to 4 cm. thick, with about 14 spirally arranged rows of tubercles. Areoles oval, almost bare. Spines yellowish white, brown at the base and tip, bristly and slender; radials 7 to 10, 4 cm. long, 1 to 4 centrals, about as long. Flowers up to 3 cm. long, fiery red, fully expanded with a slender tube, somewhat hairy, borne on the sides of the stem. Pistil and stamens white, united with the tube. Fruit small, red, covered with bristles.

Rebutia Fiebrigii (Gürke) Br. et R. = *Echinocactus Fiebrigii* Gürke. Bolivia, up to 3,600 m. above sea level. A beautiful and free-flowering species. Stem globose or elongated, depressed at the top, about 6 cm. broad, glossy green. Tubercles about ½ cm. high, in about 18 rows, more or less spiral. Areoles rather large, whitish, with 30 to 40 bristle-like, white spines, 2 to 5 of which are centrals, up to 2 cm. long, tipped brownish. Flowers borne at the sides, 3½ cm. long. Ovary and tube scaly, with a few hairs and bristles. The inner petals are obtuse, of a lively yellowish red, with white stamens; style and 6-lobed stigma pale yellow.

Rebutia spinosissima Backbg. North Argentina (Salta). Stem pale green, globular, about 4 cm. thick, more or less depressed at the top, abundantly sprouting around the base. Areoles with white hairs, on spirally arranged tubercles, very closely set. Radial spines numerous, bristle-like, whitish, up to 1 cm. long; central spines 5 or 6, thicker horny yellow, tipped brown, passing to whitish. Flowers borne at the sides of the stem, about 4 cm. long and 3 cm. broad, pale minium red, with a somewhat hairy yellowish green tube.

var. **brunispina** Backbg. Central spines brown.

Rebutia deminuta (Weber) Berger = *Echinopsis deminuta* Weber = *Echinocactus deminutus* Gürke. Argentina. Stem globular, freely branching around the base, 5 to 6 cm. high. Tubercles in 11 to 13 rows, more or less spiral. Spines 10 to 12, white tipped brown, or entirely brown, about ½ cm. long. Flowers borne very freely around the stem, 3 cm. long. Scales of ovary with white bristles. Petals deep orange red, stamens pink, stigma white, with 8 lobes.

Rebutia pseudodeminuta Backbg. North Argentina (Salta), about 2,500 m. above sea level. Stem grass green globular, 5 to 6 cm. thick, depressed at the top, freely clustering around the base; areoles small, on prominent tubercles. Radial spines 11, one erect and very small, the others spreading, 3 to 7 mm. long; central spines 2 or 3, slender, the uppermost up to 13 mm. long; all spines glassy white, more or less tipped brown. Flowers arising from the base and sides, funnel-shaped, about 3 cm. broad, golden yellow or red, dusted golden yellow. Pistil and stamens whitish, continuous with the tube. Fruit round, small, with many bristles. Seeds minute, dull black. Backeberg mentions three varieties: *grandiflora*, *Schneideriana* and *Schumanniana*.

Rebutia Spegazziniana Backbg. North Argentina (Salta), on rocky mountain sides. Stem cylindrical, about 10 cm. high, and 3 to 4 cm.

thick, pale green, freely sprouting around the base, forming groups. Tubercles about 4 mm. high, arranged spirally. Areoles only slightly woolly. Radial spines about 14, whitish, up to 4 mm. long, spreading and almost applied to the stem. Central spines usually 2, one above the other, only 2 mm. long, yellowish tipped brown. Flowers borne around the base, dark red, inner petals incurved, outer petals spreading. Style white. Ovary and fruit well furnished with bristles. Seeds dull black.

var. **atroviridis** Backbg. Stem deep green; flower dark blood red.

The following are other species recently introduced to cultivation: **Rebutia allegraiana, R. cabratai, R. Einsteinii, R. gracilis, R. grandiflora, R. Kuntheana, R. Kupperiana, R. Marsoneri, R. Maresii, R. melanea, R. Petersainii, R. rubispina.**

MEDIOLOBIVIA Backbg.

This small genus, recently instituted by Backeberg to include a few new species discovered in Argentina in 1932, differs from *Rebutia* proper chiefly on account of the larger flowers not unlike those of a *Lobivia*, but always smaller. They are usually cespitose, with globular stems, and ribs divided into low tubercles arranged spirally. The presence of ribs, however indistinct, is also important, as in *Rebutia* proper there is no trace of ribs. The flowers are fairly large, yellow or orange yellow, with a slender scaly and hairy tube. The seeds are also larger than those of *Rebutia*. Notwithstanding these differences, the characters of *Rebutia* are predominant, and therefore it would be more convenient to consider *Mediolobivia* as the third sub-genus of *Rebutia*, although it is here described separately.

The species included by Backeberg under his new genus are the following:

Mediolobivia aureiflora Backbg. = *Rebutia aureiflora* Backbg. North Argentina (Salta), about 2,800 m. above sea level. Stem globular or almost cylindrical, 4 cm. thick, dark green often flushed reddish, freely cespitose, with ribs spirally arranged and deeply broken up into prominent warts, 6 mm. high. Radial spines 15 to 20, bristle-like, whitish or brownish white; central spines 3 or 4, same colour, but longer, up to 1 cm. long. Flowers freely borne around the stem, 4 cm. across, golden yellow, with a white throat; petals in two series. Tube with acute reddish green scales. Fruit globose, covered with bristles; seeds dull brownish black. A very desirable species, of easy cultivation, whether grafted or grown on own roots.

var. **longiseta** Backbg. Flower fiery orange red; spines and bristles about twice as long, of a rusty colour.

var. **lilacinostoma** Backbg. Flower with lilac throat.

var. **albi-longiseta** Backbg. Bristles twice as long, white.

Mediolobivia elegans Backbg. = *Rebutia elegans* Backbg. North Argentina (Salta), up to 3,000 m. above sea level. Stem pale green,

(b) ECHINOCEREUS BLANCKII

(a) ECHINOCEREUS SALM-DYCKIANUS

PLATE XXVIII

(a) ECHINOCEREUS DE LAETII

(b) ECHINOPSIS EYRIESII

PLATE XXIX

cespitose, globular, about 4 cm. thick, with spirally arranged ribs cut into warts, bearing areoles with yellowish white hairs. Radial spines about 14, bristle-like, yellowish white, very slender, about 3 mm. long; central spines 3 or 4, at first darker, about ½ cm. long. Flowers 4 cm. across, borne on the stem and near the top, funnel-shaped, bright yellow, with a slender tube, furnished with scales and fine hairs. Fruit reddish, scaly and bristly.

var. **gracilis** Backbg. Stem more slender.

Mediolobivia Duursmaiana Backbg. North Argentina (Salta), up to 3,000 m. above sea level. Stem clustering, globular or oval, 4 to 5 cm. thick, deep green, often overlaid dark purplish red, with 16 or more ribs, cut into plump and prominent tubercles, arranged spirally. Areoles ½ cm. apart, at first with yellowish white hairs. Radial spines about 10, slender, bristle-like, white; one central spine or bristle, spreading, white tipped yellowish, 3 mm. long. Flowers borne around the stem, funnel-shaped, about 4 cm. long, with a very slender tube, orange yellow with a white throat. Ovary and tube scaly and hairy. Fruit reddish brown; seeds dull brownish black.

Mediolobivia Boedekeriana Backbg. = *Rebutia Boedekeriana* Backbg. North Argentina (Salta), up to 2,800 m. above sea level. Stem freely clustering, greyish green or yellowish green, globular, 2½ to 3 cm. thick, with about 14 ribs, cut into globular warts, 3 mm. broad. Radial spines bristle-like, 11 or 12, up to ½ cm. long, white spreading; only one central spine, shorter. Flower large, 5 cm. broad, fully expanded, clear orange, with a white throat. Ovary and tube scaly and hairy.

The following are other large-flowered species, recently discovered in the same region, and originally described by Backeberg under *Rebutia*, have now been transferred by the same author to this genus or sub-genus:

Mediolobivia Blossfeldii, M. Haageana, M. Hartlingiana, M. nidulans, M. Reichii, M. rubelliflora and **M. Waltheriana.**

LOBIVIA Br. et. R.

(An anagram of Bolivia, the home of most of the species)

Plant globular or almost cylindrical, single or in clusters, with definite ribs, more or less acute and spiny. Flowers diurnal, rather large, funnel-shaped or bell-shaped, with a short wide tube, mostly red, sometimes yellow or white. Ovary and tube scaly and hairy. Fruit small, globular.

This genus originally included 20 species, now increased to about 70, and probably the number of species will be further increased, when the results of recent explorations in South America are better known. They are of easy cultivation, whether on own roots or grafted, mostly requiring half-shade in the open, with some shelter from cold and too much rain in winter. Some of them are free-flowering, the flowers closing at night, and opening again in the morning for several days in succession, and are remarkable for the beauty of their various shades of red or yellow. All species do well in a porous soil, rather rich, made up of a mixture of loam, leaf-mould, crushed bricks or gravel, with some crushed old mortar or other calcareous matter added, and kept rather dry and cool in winter. The old species were formerly known as *Echinopsis* or *Echinocactus*.

Besides many beautiful natural varieties, a large number of horticultural hybrids between various species of *Lobivia*, as well as between species of *Lobivia* and species of *Rebutia* and *Chamaecereus*, have been raised, chiefly by Frič of Prague, and quite recently are being offered to the trade. Many of these hybrids display even finer shades of colour, and are often more free-flowering than their parents, but it is regrettable that they are being listed in trade catalogues under Latin names, or names with a Latin declension, which is sure to mislead the buyers and to result in chaos and disappointment, particularly in the case of beginners.

Sub-genus I. PYGMAEOLOBIVIA. Plants of small size, with the habit of *Rebutia*, but with much larger flowers. Stem distinctly ribbed, with acute ribs spirally arranged and deeply notched into warts compressed laterally. Ovary and tube scaly and hairy.

Series 1. *Rebutioides*.

Lobivia rebutioides Backbg. North Argentina (Salta), on mountain sides, up to 3,000 m. above sea level. Plant densely and broadly cespitose, with a large rootstock. Stems globular or oval, dull bluish green, about 1½ cm. thick. Ribs 12 to 14, straight, acute, with areoles on prominences closely set. Radial spines 8 or 9, bristle-like, glassy white, 1½ to 2 mm. long, one of them longer, directed upwards. No central spines. Flowers about 4 cm. long, funnel-shaped, of a lively red. Tube scaly and hairy. Fruit small, round, hairy.

var. **multiflora** Backbg. Very free-flowering.

var. **citriniflora** Backbg. Flowers lemon yellow, or pale yellow.

var. **Baudysiana** Jajo.

Lobivia Nealeana Backbg. Plant small, cylindrical, mostly solitary, up to 7 cm. high, and about 3 cm. thick, becoming bare and reddish brown at the base. Ribs about 14, low, pale green, 2 mm. high, 3 mm. broad. Areoles small, almost bare. Radial spines 7 to 9, up to 4 mm. long, very thin, reddish and thickened at the base. Flowers beautiful and comparatively large, 5 cm. long and 6 cm. across, bright red, with a metallic sheen, broadly expanded, with grey hairs when in bud. Fruit oval, green, with grey hairs. A wonderful flower on a poor plant.

Lobivia pseudocachensis Backbg. North Argentina (Salta), in grassy uplands at elevations of 2,500 m. Plant globular, slightly depressed at the top, tender green, cespitose, about 6 cm. thick, with a turnip-like tap root, with 12 to 14 or more, slightly rounded ribs. Areoles small, ½ to 1 cm. apart. Radial spines about 10, thin, rusty yellow, recurved laterally on the ribs, ½ to 1 cm. long. One central spine, darker and almost black, slightly longer, curved upwards. Flower funnel-shaped, 6 cm. long and about as broad, bright dark red, with a scaly and hairy tube. Style green or purplish. Fruit small, hairy, with dark brown small and dull seeds.

Lobivia euanthema Backbg. Bolivia, at elevations of 3,500 m. Plant small, forming cushions of small extent, with a thick tap root. Stem dull green, globose-elongated or oval, up to 5 cm. high and 3 cm. thick. Ribs vertical, low, with low warts, up to 3 mm. broad. Areoles with about 12 glassy white bristles, reddish at the base, the upper two up to 1 cm. long. Flower 4 cm. long, and about as broad, outer petals carmine red, or with a darker central broad band, the next row yellowish red and the inner reddish.

Lobivia sublimiflora Backbg. North Argentina (Salta) at about 3,000 m. elevation. Plant cespitose, with a long turnip-like root. Stems globose or oval, tender green to reddish, about 2 cm. thick. Ribs about 12, straight or vertical, low, about 3 mm. broad, slightly warty. Radial spines about 10, bristly, very thin, white, 2 to 3 mm. long, spreading laterally and applied to the stem. One central spine, erect, slightly longer. Flowers broadly funnel-shaped, about 6 cm. broad, and the same across, fully expanded, pale crimson, with a pink throat, and green stigmas. Tube greyish and hairy. Fruit small, hairy.

Other species belonging to this series are: **Lobivia albispina** Backbg., and **L. spiralisepala** Jajo.

Series 2. *Pygmaeae.*

Lobivia pygmaea (R. E. Fries) Backbg. = *Echinopsis pygmaea* R. E. Fries = *Rebutia pygmaea* Br. et R. Bolivia and north-western Argentina. A very small plant, sparingly cespitose. Stem ovoid to ovoid -cylindrical, 1 to 3 cm. long, and 1 to 2 cm. thick, with a thick tap root, with 8 to 12 spiral ribs, cut into small tubercles. Radial spines 9 to 11, short, whitish, 2 to 3 mm. long, applied to the stem. No central spines. Flowers borne on the sides, 2 to 2½ cm. long, purplish pink. Ovary and tube scaly and hairy.

Lobivia neo-Haageana Backbg. = *Rebutia Haagei* Frič = *Echino-cactus Haagei* Hort. North Argentina. A cespitose plant, forming small groups, with long tuberous roots. Stems 6 to 8 cm. high, and 3 to 4 cm. thick, bluish green, often tinged reddish on the tubercles, with 10 to 11 ribs, slightly spiral, cut into warts. Areoles oval, 4 mm. apart, brownish, bearing 10 to 12 bristle-like, glassy white spines, reddish at the base, up to 3 mm. long, applied to the stem. Flowers borne along the sides of the stem, numerous, about 4 cm. long and the same across, rotate, pale salmon to deep salmon. Looks very much like a *Rebutia.*

Lobivia Steinmannii (Solms.) Br. et R. = *Echinocactus Steinmannii* Solms-Laubach. = *Rebutia Steinmannii* Br. et R. Bolivia, on high mountains. Plant slightly cespitose; stem oval, about 2 cm. high and 1 to 1½ cm. thick, with a thick and long tap-root. Ribs 10 to 12, spiral, cut into warts. Spines about 8, whitish or brownish, up to 1 cm. long.

Flowers borne on the sides of the stem, bell-shaped, pink to dark red, outer petals acuminate, inner petals rounded. Now offered by dealers.

Other species of this series are: **Lobivia atrovirens** Backbg., **L. digitiformis** Backbg., **L. Einsteinii** Backbg., **L. eucalyptana** Backbg., **L. Nicolai** Frič, **L. oruensis** Backbg., **P. pilifera** Frič, **L. Peterseimii** Frič.

Sub-genus II. EULOBIVIA. Includes the true species of *Lobivia*, the species belonging to the former sub-genus *Pygmaeolobivia* representing rather terms of passage from *Rebutia* to *Lobivia*, in the same way as *Mediolobivia*. Species of this sub-genus are rather large plants, mostly cespitose, bearing large flowers of great beauty. Some species are almost as free-flowering as species of *Rebutia*, others are far less free with their flowers, but all of them are worth growing. Species of *Eulobivia* have rather thick stems, globular, or short-cylindric, or cylindrical, usually well armed with spines, with well-marked ribs, more or less acute, notched into flat hatchet-like warts, with the areoles depressed in the notches. The great diversity of form of the numerous species, the varying shape and wide range of colour of the flowers, are good evidence that *Lobivia*, like *Rebutia* and *Echinopsis*, are plants of comparatively recent origin, and that their evolution is still in full activity.

Series 1. *Famatimenses*.

Lobivia famatimensis (Speg.) Werd. = *Echinocactus famatimensis* Spegazzini. North Argentina (La Rioja). A small species, solitary or cespitose. Stem oval or elongated, up to 15 cm. long, 4 to 5 cm. thick, with about 20 low ribs, somewhat irregular and warty, with many whitish or yellowish short spines, covering the stem. Flowers borne freely on the upper part of the stem, 4 cm. long; ovary and tube scaly and with whitish or greyish hairs. The colour of the flower varies from yellowish white to deep red. A most beautiful species, with numerous varieties. The typical form is pure yellow.

var. **albiflora** Hort. Flower white or very pale yellow.

var. **aurantiaca** Backbg. Flower golden orange.

var. **densispina** Backbg. Spines more numerous and short, yellow or dirty yellow. Flower large, yellow.

var. **longispina** Backbg. Spines 1 to 2 cm. long.

var. **oligacantha** Backbg. Spines long, but few.

var. **haematantha** Werd. Flowers blood red.

var. **rosiflora** Backbg. Flowers large, pink.

var. **carneopurpurea** Backbg. = *scoparia* Hort. Flower pale purple.

var. **setosa** Werd. Spines long, softish, greyish brown. Flower yellowish white or yellow.

Lobivia Drijveriana Backbg. North Argentina (Salta), on uplands at 3,800 m. above sea level. Plant mostly solitary, deeply embedded in the ground, greyish green, with a thick and long turnip-like root. Stem 3 to 8 cm. thick, with low straight ribs. Radial spines 10 to 12,

(b) REBUTIA HAAGEI

(a) REBUTIA SENILIS

PLATE XXX

(b) REBUTIA PSEUDODEMINUTA

(a) REBUTIA FIEBRIGII

PLATE XXXI

spreading star-like or applied to the stem, bristle-like, whitish. Central spines 1 to 4, developing with age, thick, straight, whitish to dark brown, up to 2 cm. long, directed outwards or downwards, sometimes slightly curved downwards. Flowers bell-shaped, pale yellow, with a green style. Seeds dull dark brown.

var. **aurantiaca** Backbg. Flower orange, style purple.

var. **nobilis** Backbg. Flower dark orange, style pale purple.

Sub-species: **astranthema** Backbg. North Argentina (Salta) near Cachi, on stony ground. Plant cespitose, greyish green, with globular or short-cylindric stems, about 3 cm. thick, with about 16 low narrow ribs, notched above the areoles, which are small and oval. Radial spines about 12, pectinate, ½ cm. long, yellowish grey. Sometimes there is one central spine 8 mm. long, yellowish brown, slightly curved. Flowers 5½ cm. across, fully expanded and star-like, with narrow retuse petals, bright yellow. Fruit small, hairy. Seeds small, dark brown.

Lobivia Janseniana Backbg. North Argentina (Salta), at elevations of 3,500 m. Plant mostly solitary, 7 to 20 cm. high and 5 to 8 cm. thick, dull greyish green, with a long tuberous root. Ribs 11 to 14, straight, about ½ cm. broad and 2 to 3 mm. high, rounded below, rather acute at the top, slightly notched. Areoles with yellowish white wool, slightly depressed, small. Spines about 10, black, about 1 cm. long, reddish at the base when young; later about 4 other spines are developed, slightly longer and thicker. Flowers borne at the sides, near the top, broadly funnel-shaped, 4 cm. long and 6 cm. across, golden yellow, reddish at the throat.

var. **leucantha** Backbg. Stem pale green; spines brownish or greyish; flower mostly pale yellow.

Lobivia breviflora Backbg. Argentina (North Salta) at elevations of 3,000 m. Stem spherical, depressed, glossy greyish green, 6 to 8 cm thick, slightly cespitose. Ribs about 24, 3 to 6 mm. wide, rounded deeply notched, bearing oval-elongated areoles, with white wool. Spines more or less pectinate and recurved, all similar, about 25, up to 13 mm. long, brownish passing to grey, the central ones thicker. Flowers fiery red, funnel-shaped, about 3 cm. broad, with a short tube. The plant looks like *Echinopsis hamatacantha*.

Lobivia Shaferi Br. et R. Argentina. Stem cylindrical, 7 to 15 cm. high, and 2½ to 4 cm. thick, densely spiny and with closely set areoles. Ribs 10, very low and obtuse. Radial spines 10 to 15, 1 cm. long, needle-like; central spines 3 to 5, up to 3 cm. long. Flowers borne on the sides, funnel-shaped, 4 to 6 cm. long, pale yellow; ovary and tube scaly and with white hairs.

Lobivia Staffenii Frič = *Andena Staffenii* Frič. Bolivian Andes. Stem solitary, oval or short-cylindric, 5 to 8 cm. high, 3 to 4 cm. thick, with 14 to 16 ribs, straight or slightly spiral, acute, slightly notched. Areoles closely set, with about 12 radial spines, whitish or greyish, ½ cm. long, and 1 to 4 central spines, same colour, up to 1½ cm. long, mostly directed downwards. Flower borne at the sides near the top, about 4 cm. long, 5 cm. broad, funnel-shaped, pale yellow.

var. **lagunilla** Frič. Plant smaller, flower smaller, often coppery yellow or orange red.

Lobivia cachensis (Speg.) Br. et R. = *Echinopsis cachensis* Spegazzini. Argentina (Salta, near Cachi), at heights of 2,500 m. Stem oval or elgonated, 9 cm. high, and 6½ cm. thick, solitary or slightly clustering, with about 19 ribs, ½ cm. high. Spines softish, greyish tipped yellowish: the radials 7 to 20, 4 to 5 mm. long; central spines 4, 1 or 2 of them longer and hooked. Flowers 6 to 7 cm. long; inner petals linear-lanceolate, red; stamens dark purple, style yellowish, stigma with 10 yellowish white lobes.

Lobivia grandiflora Br. et R. Argentina. Stem globose or oval, 15 to 20 cm. high and 7½ to 10 cm. thick, mostly solitary, with about 14 acute ribs; areoles about 1 cm. apart in notches, with about 15 slender, awl-shaped spines, yellowish, about 1 cm. long. Flower funnel-shaped, large and showy, 10 cm. long, with narrow acuminate petals 4 to 5 cm. long, of a lively pink: ovary and tube with narrow scales, slightly hairy.

Series 2. *Haageanae.*

Lobivia Haageana Backbg. Boundary between Bolivia and Argentina, at elevations up to 3,800 m. Plant cespitose, up to 30 cm. high, dull greyish green, with about 12 ribs, acute, ¾ cm. broad. Areoles large, oval, 2 cm. apart, with white wool. Radial spines about 10, spreading laterally, yellowish, up to 2 cm. long. Central spines 3 to 4, up to 7 cm. long, at first black, passing to greyish yellow. Flowers up to 7 cm. long, with grey wool when in bud, bell-shaped or funnel-shaped, bright yellow. Stamens red, style yellow. Fruit oval, hairy; seeds dull black. Very free-flowering.

var. **albihepatica** Backbg. Flower yellowish white, with the throat reddish ochre yellow.

var. **chrysantha** Backbg. Flower a delicate yellowish pink, throat flushed reddish.

Lobivia chrysantha Werd. Argentina, boundary with Bolivia, at high elevations. Stem solitary, globular, dull greyish green, often irregular, with about 13 acute ribs, about 6 mm. high. Areoles 1½ cm. apart, with greyish wool when young. Spines 5 to 8 all radial, reddish and tipped dark when young, later greyish, spreading, thin, stiff, straight, awl-shaped, up to 2 cm. long. Flower about 5 cm. long, with golden yellow petals, purplish red at the throat, very sweet-scented. Ovary and tube with scales and brownish hairs. Stigma with 9 purple lobes.

Lobivia pampana Br. et R. Southern Peru. Stem globular, 5 to 7 cm. thick more or less cespitose, with 17 to 21 more or less wavy ribs. Areoles far apart, very spiny, but in cultivated plants almost spineless. Spines 5 to 20, needle-like, often curved, up to 5 cm. long. Flowers

5½ to 6 cm. long, red, with acute to acuminate petals. Ovary with ovate scales, acuminate, with long white hairs.

Lobivia Hossei Werd. Argentina (Cordoba and Los Andes). Similar to *L. chrysantha*, but more cylindrical. Radial spines 7 to 8, centrals 1 to 3, up to 3 cm. long. Flower about 6 cm. long, yellowish orange, often tinged reddish outside, slightly perfumed. Stigma with 10 to 12 pale green lobes.

Lobivia rubescens Backbg. Boundary Bolivia-Argentina. Stem globular to short cylindric, about 5 cm. thick, dull green, covered with reddish or purplish slender spines, densely cespitose. Ribs 20 to 24, very acute, slightly notched. Areoles small up to 1 cm. apart, with about 10 slender radial spines, bristle-like, spreading, almost applied to the stem, 5 to 8 mm. long, reddish or purplish; central spines 1 to 4, longer and thicker, one directed downwards up to 1½ cm. long. Flowers freely borne on the sides of the stem, funnel-shaped, 5 cm. long and about as broad; outer petals lanceolate, inner petals spathulate and retuse, glossy yellow with purple throat.

Series 3. *Tegelerianae.*

Lobivia Tegeleriana Backbg. Bolivia? Mostly solitary or slightly cespitose. Stem globular or oval, 4 to 5½ cm. thick, glossy dark green, with about 14 ribs, prominent and acute, notched into flat hatchet-like warts, with round whitish depressed areoles. Radial spines 7 or 8, slender, straight, bristle-like, whitish, spreading. Central spines 1 to 4, thicker, 1½ to 2 cm. long, dark or black, mostly directed upwards. Flowers borne at the sides, 4 to 5 cm. long, and about as broad, with spreading obtuse petals, pink or pale orange red. Three varieties are recognized: *Eckardiana, Medingiana* and *Plominiana.*

Series 4. *Cinnabarinae.*

Lobivia cinnabarina (Lab.) Br. et R. = *Echinopsis cinnabarina* Lab. Bolivia. Stem at first globular and depressed, 10 to 15 cm. broad, glossy dark green, later short cylindric, slowly cespitose, with 18 to 21 spirally arranged, acute ribs, about 1 cm. high, with notches for the round slightly woolly areoles. Radial spines 8 to 10, spreading, up to 1½ cm. long: central spines 2 or 3, slightly thicker; all more or less curved, at first pale brown, passing to dark brown and grey. Flowers borne on the middle or the upper part of the stem, funnel-shaped, 6 to 7 cm. long and about 8 cm. broad, with spathulate toothed petals, scarlet to carmine red. Stamens dark red; stigma with 8 dark green lobes. A charming species; the flowers remain in bloom for 2 days.

Another species belonging to this series is **Lobivia brevifolia** Backbg.

Series 5. *Pentlandianae.*

Lobivia Pentlandii (Salm-Dyck) Br. et R. = *Echinopsis Pentlandii* Salm-Dyck. Slopes of the Andes in Bolivia and Peru. Stem globular or almost cylindrical, dark green, abundantly branching into large clumps, with 12 to 15 prominent and acute ribs, with depressions about 2 cm. apart, for the areoles, which are rather large, whitish passing to brownish. Radial spines 7 to 12, brownish, 1 to 3 cm. long, spreading, straight or curved. Only one central spine, directed outwards, straight or curved upwards, 3 to 4 cm. long, longer in certain varieties. Flowers borne on the sides of the stems 5 to 6 cm. long, and 4 to 5 cm. broad, funnel-shaped, orange red to carmine, with obtuse petals. Ovary and tube with short triangular scales, hairy and spiny. Stamens green at the base, yellow above; pistil green, stigma with 6 to 8 yellowish lobes. Fruit globular 1 to 2 cm. thick, green, scaly and hairy, with the flavour of strawberry or pineapple. This is the best known species of *Lobivia*, and includes many varieties all well deserving of cultivation. They are easy to grow, but do not always flower readily.

var. **achatina** Hort. Stem slender, dark green. Flower red.

var. **albiflora** Hort. Fl. very pale yellow, almost white.

var. **Cavendishii** Hildm. Stem slender; fl. pale red.

var. **cinnabarina** Hort. Fl. carmine red.

var. **Colmari** Neub. Very narrow furrows, between the ribs; areoles deeply sunk; spines yellowish brown, flower orange red.

var. **elegans** Hildm. Spines long, pale yellowish brown.

var. **ferox** Hort. With long curved spines.

var. **gracilispina** Lem. Spines more numerous, but shorter and more slender.

var. **longispina** Rümpl. Stem thicker, pale green; spines dark brown, 4 to 6 cm. long. Fl. large, carmine.

var. **luteola** Hort. With glossy yellow spines.

var. **Maximiliana** Heyder = *tricolor* Hort. = *Echinopsis Maximiliana* Heyder. Stem more elongated, pale green; spines longer. Fl. dark red outside, yellow inside, pointed carmine.

var. **ochroleuca** R. Mey. Spines straw-coloured. Flower yellow or reddish yellow.

var. **Pfersdorffii** Hort. Stem thicker, with long spines.

var. **pyracantha** Lem. Probably a distinct species. Ribs lower, spines smaller and more numerous, fiery red when young. Flower orange red.

var. **radians** Lem. Plant smaller, spines and flower smaller.

var. **rosea** Hort. Flower pink.

var. **Scheeri** Salm-Dyck. Petals more pointed, pale cinnabar red, with darker midrib.

var. **vitellina** Hildm. Stem pale green. Spines few and short. Flower red.

Lobivia caespitosa (Purp.) Br. et R. = *Echinopsis caespitosa* Purpus. Bolivia. Stem cylindrical, about 4 cm. thick, spineless at the top, freely sprouting at the base and sides, with 10 to 12 straight ribs, acute and notched. Areoles 1 to 1½ cm. apart, round, with about 12 radial spines, brown, 1 to 2 cm. long, and one central spine, curved, up to 5 cm. long. Flowers borne on the sides of the stem, 6 to 8 cm.

long, and 4 to 6 cm. broad, reddish yellow outside, carmine inside, with a reddish blotch at the base. Ovary and tube scaly, with wool and hair in the axils of the scales. Upper part of stamens reddish, and upper part of style yellowish, stigma with 8 whitish lobes.

Lobivia mistiensis Werd. et Backbg. South Peru (Arequipa, near the volcano Misti). Stem mostly solitary, globular or almost conical, with 25 to 30 narrow acute ribs, about ½ cm. high, with closely set areoles, furnished with greyish white wool when young. Spines 7 to 9, all radial, spreading, mostly curved upwards, up to 5 cm. long, the lower ones shorter, greyish, darker at the tip. The stem is about 8 cm. high and 4 to 5 cm. thick. The new spines are dark red soon passing to brown and later to grey. Flowers pink, at least 6 cm. long; outer petals narrow, spreading, inner petals of a clear pink, with a darker central band.

Lobivia Claeysiana Backbg. A rare species from southern Bolivia (Tupiza) at elevations of 2,800 m. Stem solitary, more or less globular, up to 12 cm. across, dull greyish green, with 16 ribs at first acute and thickened at the areoles, which are at first round, later elongated, with yellowish white wool. Radial spines, horny yellow, darker at the tip, often reddish at the base, spreading, up to 22 mm. long; one central spine, more or less curved upwards, same colour, up to 5 cm. long. Flower 5½ cm. broad and 4½ cm. long, pale yellow, darker outside, greenish near the tube. Stigma with 13 green lobes.

Lobivia Wrightiana Backbg. Central Peru. Stem solitary, rarely cespitose, more or less clavate or short-cylindric, dark greyish green. Ribs 16 or 17, slightly spiral, low, slightly notched, with round white areoles. Radial spines about 10, soft, spreading over the rib, 5 to 7 mm. long. Usually one central spine, up to 7 cm. long, more or less compressed and curved upwards or laterally. Flower funnel-shaped, pale lilac pink.

Lobivia Higginsiana Backbg. Bolivia, high mountains around Lake Titicaca. Solitary or slightly cespitose, globular, depressed at the top, greyish green, up to 10 cm. thick. Ribs about 16, very acute, notched into hatchet-like warts. Areoles round, about 2 cm. apart. Radial spines about 10, greyish, variously curved and twisted, from 6 mm. to 4½ cm. long. One central spine up to 7½ cm. long, curved upwards, often twisted. Flowers funnel-shaped, about 6 cm. long, reddish outside, yellowish red within. Stigma with 8 green lobes.

Lobivia Wegheiana Backbg. Bolivia, at elevations up to 4,500 m., where it is rare, but widely distributed. Plant solitary, with a thick and long tap root; stem about 5 cm. thick, more or less globular and depressed at the top, thickly covered with long spines, greyish green; with about 20 ribs, 6 mm. high, very acute, notched into hatchet-like tubercles. Areoles round, about 1 cm. apart, with greyish wool. Radial spines 7 or 8, directed laterally, at first dark brown, passing to grey, 1 to 3 cm. long. One central spine same colour, up to 4 cm. long, directed upwards. Flowers 6 cm. long, funnel-shaped, pale violet outside, almost white inside (like those of *Echinopsis violacea*); tube scaly and hairy. Stigma with 9 green lobes. Fruit hairy, seeds dull dark grey.

Lobivia korethroides Werd. North Argentina (Los Andes). At first described as a species of *Echinocactus*. Stem solitary, globular or ovoid, up to 30 cm. in circumference, pale green, spiny at the top when young, with yellowish or dark brown spines, almost spineless at the top when adult. Ribs 16 to 20 or more, narrow and acute at the top, 4 to 8 mm. high. Areoles 1½ to 2 cm. apart, with whitish or yellowish wool when young. Radial spines 12 to 30, whitish or yellowish, tipped dark, mostly straight and needle-like, up to 3 cm. long. Central spines about 4, reddish yellow to brown or zoned, somewhat longer. Flowers borne near the top 6 to 7 cm. long, funnel-shaped, pale red to deep red. Ovary and tube with scales and long brown hairs.

Lobivia saltensis (Speg.) Br. et R. = *Echinopsis saltensis* Spegazzini. Argentina (Salta to Tucuman). Stem at first solitary, later densely cespitose, pale green, glossy, globular to oval, with 17 or 18 ribs, low, obtuse, notched. Radial spines 12 to 14, 4 to 6 mm. long; central spines 1 to 4, thicker, straight, about 1 cm. long. Flowers borne on the sides of the stem, 4 cm. long, funnel-shaped, with short obtuse petals, about 1 cm. long, red.

Lobivia oreopogon Spegazzini = *Echinopsis oreopogon* Werd. Argentina (Mendoza). Stem solitary, 20 cm. high and about 30 cm. broad, olive green, flattened at the top with 18 to 20 notched ribs, 2½ cm. high. Areoles large, greyish, 2 to 2½ cm. apart. Spines slender, flexible, reddish or yellowish, passing to grey: the radials 10 to 15, the centrals 1 to 5, all alike, 5 to 7 cm. long. Flowers borne near the top, 9 to 10 cm. long. Ovary and tube with acute scales and long greyish hairs; petals narrow, spathulate-lanceolate, golden yellow. Rare in cultivation.

Lobivia varians Backbg. Northern Argentina (Salta). Stem globular to oval, 5 to 6 cm. across, the lower part naked and tuber-like, dull greyish green, with about 14 spiral ribs, notched into closely set, more or less conical warts, bearing round areoles 5 to 8 mm. apart, with a brush-like bundle of stiff erect spines, mostly directed upwards, up to 3 cm. long, with 3 or 4 central spines stronger and longer. Flowers borne around the top, small, funnel-shaped, 3 to 3½ cm. long, bright red, with golden yellow throat.

var. **crocea** Backbg. Flower saffron yellow.

Other species belonging to this series are: **Lobivia boliviensis** Br. et R., with beautiful orange yellow flowers, **L. Bruchii** Br. et R., **L. grandis** Br. et R. and **L. andalgalensis** Br. et R.

Series 6. *Hertrichianae*.

Lobivia Hertrichiana Backbg. South-east Peru. Plant solitary or cespitose, about 10 cm. thick, globular, glossy light green, with about 11 ribs 1 cm. broad, deeply notched above the areoles, which are round, with white wool. Radial spines 6 to 8, yellowish brown, spreading, up to 1½ cm. long. One central spine, straw-coloured, curved upwards, up to 2½ cm. long. Flower rather large, spreading and rotate, 6 cm. long and 7 cm. broad, fiery scarlet. Fruit round, small, hairy.

Lobivia corbula (Herrera) Br. et R. = *Mammillaria corbula* Herrera. North-western shore of Lake Titicaca. Stem cespitose, more or less globular, depressed at the top, pale green, with 12 to 18 acute ribs, deeply notched into prominent hatchet-like warts. Areoles round, with white wool. Radials 7 to 12, up to 5 cm. long, horny yellow. Sometimes there is one central spine, curved upwards. Flower about 3 cm. long, with a short tube; petals spreading, the outer recurved; outer petals carmine scarlet, inner petals shorter and broader, lemon yellow or orange.

Lobivia potosina Werd. Bolivia (Potosi). Plant usually solitary, almost globular, lively green, about 8 cm. thick. Ribs about 13, very prominent and acute, up to 2 cm. high. Areoles few but large, 4 to 5 cm. apart, with short light brown wool when young. Spines 9 to 13, of which 1 to 4 are centrals, at first whitish or rust-colour, with darker point, passing to greyish brown, up to 4 cm. long, very stiff, thickened at the base, curved upwards, mostly hooked at the tip. Flowers borne at the side of the stem, 6 cm. long, 8 cm. across, broadly funnel-shaped, with lanceolate pointed petals, pink or crimson red.

Lobivia longispina Br. et R. North Argentina. Stem globular to cylindrical, 10 cm. thick, and up to 25 cm. high. Ribs 25 or more, deeply notched. Spines at first brown, passing to grey; the radials 8 to 10, the centrals 1 to 4, these last up to 8 cm. long, straight or curved. Flower 4 cm. long, white.

Other species under this series are: **Lobivia allegraiana** Backbg., **L. Binghamiana** Backbg. and its var. **robustiflora** Backbg., and **L. incaica** Backbg.

Series 7. *Lateritiae*.

Lobivia lateritia (Gürke) Br. et R. = *Echinopsis lateritia* Gürke. Bolivia (La Paz). Stem globular or somewhat elongated, about 7 cm. high and 6 cm. thick, greyish green, with about 16 to 18 ribs, straight or slightly spiral, about 1 cm. high and 1 cm. broad. Areoles sunken, in notches, 2 to 3 cm. apart, round, at first with yellowish or greyish wool. Radial spines about 10, up to 2 cm. long, more or less curved, with 1 or 2 central spines, spreading and longer, brown with darker zones, thickened at the base. Flower funnel-shaped, 4 to 5 cm. long, 4 cm. broad, with obtuse toothed petals, brick red to carmine red, with a green tube, scaly, with dark grey or black hairs in the axils of the scales. Stamens red, in 3 bundles, pistil green, stigma with 8 to 9 lobes.

Lobivia Backebergii (Werd.) Backbg. = *Echinopsis Backebergii* Werd. Bolivia (La Paz, at altitudes of 3,600 m. above sea level). Stem solitary or cespitose, globular or oval, pale green, 4 to 5 cm. thick, with about 15 ribs, acute and notched, more or less arranged spirally. Areoles 1 to 1½ cm. apart, somewhat woolly when young. Spines all radial, 3 to 7, spreading, brown or dark brown passing to grey, slender, variously curved, $\frac{1}{2}$ to 5 cm. long, almost hooked at the end. Flower borne on the upper part of the stem, $4\frac{1}{2}$ cm. long, inner petals carmine with bluish sheen. Ovary and tube with scales and brown or white hairs. Stigma with 8 lobes.

Lobivia leucorhodon Backbg. Bolivia, Highlands of La Paz. Stem oval or conical, 8 to 10 cm. long, 5 to 6 cm. thick, with the lower part rough and tuberlike, cespitose around the base, deep green. Ribs about 21, straight and thin, notched into flat acute tubercles, about 1 cm. long, with sunken areoles between them. Top of stem bare. Radial spines about 7, yellowish, reflexed laterally, $\frac{1}{2}$ to 1 cm. long; one central spine, horny yellow, about 2 cm. long, mostly curved upwards. Flowers borne on the sides of the stem, about 4 cm. long, funnel-shaped, with a green tube, scaly and hairy, somewhat compressed, and a spreading and rotate limb, with short blunt petals, pale lilac, with a white throat.

Lobivia Schneideriana Backbg. Northern Bolivia, at altitudes of 3,800 m. Stem solitary, later slightly cespitose, short cylindric, corky at the base, with a short bluish green top, about 5 cm. thick. Ribs 14 to 18, acute, deeply notched, with round woolly areoles. Spines 8 or 9, spreading, horny yellow, 4 to 12 mm. long; sometimes one central spine up to 4 cm. long, same colour tipped darker, curved upwards. Flower funnel-shaped 5 to 6 cm. long, and about as broad, dirty white, often coppery yellow or pale pink.

Lobivia Jajoiana Backbg. = *Andena Greggeri* Frič. Northern Argentina (Salta), at altitudes of 3,000 m. Solitary or slightly cespitose with the habit of Echinopsis, tender green, globular at the top, later short-cylindric, 5 to 6 cm. thick. Ribs 20 or more, acute, deeply notched into sharp-edged tubercles, with sunken large round or oval areoles. Radial spines about 10, whitish or very pale reddish, up to 1 cm. long. One central spine up to 2 cm. long, but thinner than the radials, dark brown or black. Flowers funnel-shaped, 6 cm. long, 5 cm. across, dark claret, tinged bluish. Fruit small, round, hairy.

var. **Fleischeriana** Backbg. All spines longer, 4 of the radials stiffer, the upper ones sometimes hooked. Central spine very thin, up to 5 cm. long. All spines more vividly coloured.

Lobivia Schreiteri Castellanos = *Echinopsis Schreiteri* Werd. Northern Argentina (Tucuman, Portezuelo de la Cienaga). A rare small plant deeply embedded in the ground, sprouting around the base and forming groups about 30 cm. across. Each stem is globular, dark green, $1\frac{1}{2}$ to $3\frac{1}{2}$ cm. thick, new growths lively green, with 9 to 14 ribs, more or less spirally arranged and cut into low pyramidal tubercles, bearing small white areoles. Radial spines 6 to 8, very slender, curved, whitish, up to $1\frac{1}{2}$ cm. long. Only one central spine, often absent, very short, curved upwards, up to 2 cm. long. Flowers borne at the sides about $3\frac{1}{2}$ cm. long, and as broad, greenish outside, with scales and hairs, inner petals purple red.

Lobivia polycephala Backbg. Bolivia, boundary with Argentina. Stem globular to oval, about 6 cm. thick, freely cespitose, forming large clumps, dull green, with about 16 acute ribs, notched into hatchet-like warts 5 to 8 mm. high. Areoles round, about 1½ cm. apart, with whitish wool passing to grey. Radial spines 8 to 10, star-like, spreading and recurved, 1 to 1½ cm. long, brownish to greyish. One central spine, often absent, variously curved. Flowers borne near the top of the stem, about 4 cm. long, 4½ to 5 cm. across, rotate, with rounded spathulate petals, fiery red. Ovary and short tube scaly and woolly.

The following are other species belonging to this series: **Lobivia (Andena) Dragai** Frič, **L. (Andena) Kuhnrichii** Frič, **L. Hermanniana** Backbg., **L. Marsoneri** Backbg., and **L. nigrispina** Backbg.

Sub-genus III. *Pseudoechinopsis.*

Lobivia aurea (Br. et R.) Backbg. = *Echinopsis aurea* Br. et R. Western Argentina (Cordoba). Stem globular or elongated, 5 to 10 cm. high, 4 to 6 cm. thick, freely sprouting at the base and sides, dark green, with 14 or 15 prominent and acute ribs, with deep furrows between them. Areoles about 1 cm. apart, brownish. Radial spines 8 to 10, spreading; central spines 4, thicker and somewhat flattened, 2 to 3 cm. long, brownish or black below, yellowish towards the tip. Flowers freely borne on the sides, below the middle of the stem, 9 cm. long and 8 cm. broad, with a slender funnel-shaped tube, somewhat curved, greenish white, with scales reddish at the base, and with white and black hairs. Petals in 3 whorls, glossy lemon yellow, abruptly acute. Style green, very short; stigma creamy white. A lovely species, resistant and easy to grow, requiring full sunshine and a rather dry soil.

var. **elegans** Backbg. Outer petals very narrow, recurved, glossy yellowish white; inner petals narrower than in the type, glossy lemon yellow; all petals acuminate.

var. **grandiflora** Backbg. Flower slightly larger.

var. **robustior** Backbg. Plant more robust, less freely sprouting, deep green.

Lobivia cylindrica Backbg. From the same region as the preceding, to which it is nearly allied. Has a cylindrical stem, up to 15 cm. high, deep green, with black spines and large yellow flowers.

ECHINOPSIS Zuccarini

Stem globular or cylindrical, sometimes columnar, solitary or clustered, with prominent acute ribs, continuous or notched. Flowers borne on the sides of the stem, with a long or very long tube, and spreading limb, mostly white. Ovary and tube scaly and woolly or hairy. Stamens very numerous, inserted within the throat or on the tube, collected in a bunch around the style, which is mostly longer; stigma with spreading lobes. Fruit a fleshy hairy berry, mostly oval and green, at maturity splitting on one side. Seeds very small, minutely pitted. Includes at least 36 species, all natives of South America.

Many species formerly included under this genus are now classified under *Lobivia* and *Rebutia*. The genus may not offer the great diversity of form and spines seen in *Echinocactus* and allied genera, but this drawback is amply compensated by the freely borne flowers, mostly diurnal, always large and of exquisite beauty, and often deliciously fragrant. The cultivation is of the easiest; any porous soil moderately rich, with about one-third old cow manure or leaf-mould is good for them, and with very few exceptions they delight in full sunshine, with frequent watering in summer. They are also fairly resistant to low temperatures, and although they require more warmth than *Lobivia* and *Rebutia*, at least in the Mediterranean region, they need no other shelter in winter, beyond a sunny wall. Their propagation by offsets is most easy, and often the offsets are already rooted before they are separated from the mother plant. Propagation by seed is also satis-factory, although at first growth is rather slow. Natural varieties, as well as natural hybrids and forms, are numerous, and these are often given specific Latin names, and catalogued as distinct species. The number of horticultural hybrids is also large, and lately many new and beautiful forms have been raised.

Sub-Genus I. PSEUDOLOBIVIA. Flowers mostly whitish or white. Stem spherical, or slightly elongated or flat, mostly solitary, rarely cespitose, usually strongly armed with spines, often with hooked or curved central spines. Tube of flower mostly short.

Echinopsis Ducis Paulii Först. = *Lobivia Ducis Paulii* Br. et R. Argentina. Stem solitary, more or less columnar, dull dark green passing to ashy green, 6 to 7 cm. thick, with 18 to 21 ribs, acute and low, notched. Areoles about 1½ cm. apart, oval, with 6 to 8 spreading radial spines, slender and more or less strongly curved, up to 2 cm. long, at first purplish brown, passing to reddish grey. Central spines 2 to 4, same colour, but longer and much thicker, awl-shaped, more curved upwards, thickened at the base. Flowers about 8 cm. long, white.

Echinopsis Klimpeliana Weidl. et Werd. = *Lobivia Klimpeliana* (Werd.) Berger. Argentina. Stem globular, depressed or flat at the top, dark green, about 10 cm. thick, with about 19 straight ribs, 1 cm. high, acute, notched. Areoles about 2 cm. apart, oval, yellowish brown, passing to brown. Spines straight or partly curved, awl-shaped, brown-ish or black, passing to greyish; the radials 6 to 10, and 2 centrals up to 4 cm. long. Flowers borne at the sides, funnel-shaped, about 4 cm. long, white; ovary and tube with scales and whitish hairs. Stamens white, style short, stigma with 12 yellowish lobes.

Echinopsis chionantha Speg. = *Lobivia chionantha* (Speg.) Br. et R. Argentina. Very similar to the preceding. Stem more slender and of a paler green, with fewer ribs. Flowers larger, white, faintly scented, lasting three days.

Echinopsis spiniflora (K. Sch.) Berger = *Echinocactus spiniflorus* K. Sch. Argentina. Stem globular or elongated, dark green, up to 60 cm. high and 15 cm. thick, very spiny at the top, with 17 to 22 acute ribs, slightly notched. Areoles less than 1 cm. apart, roundish, whitish or greyish. Spines straight, needle-like 10 to 20, reddish brown **or**

yellowish, passing to whitish, reddish at the base and at the tip, about 2 cm. long; central spines 1 to 3, slightly thicker. Flower funnel-shaped, 4 cm. long and 4 cm. broad, pink, woolly outside and with yellow spinescent scales. Style short, stigma with 19 lobes. On account of the spinescent scales of the calyx, this species, as well as *E. Klimpeliana* and *E. violacea*, which have similar spinescent scales, have been grouped together by Backeberg under a special sub-genus, *Acanthocalycium*.

Echinopsis Kratochviliana Backbg. Northern Argentina (Salta). Stem globular, dull green, with a bare depressed top, often flushed reddish. Ribs about 17, narrow, acute, ½ cm. high. Radial spines about 10, greyish white, up to 7 mm. long. Central spines 1 or 2, mostly curved and hooked, 1½ cm. long. Flowers short, 5 cm. long; tube short, with black hairs; outer petals short and narrow, inner petals broader, greenish outside, creamy white inside.

Echinopsis leucorhodantha Backbg. Northern Argentina (Salta). Stem globular to short-cylindric, dark green. Ribs about 20, narrow, acute, slightly warty, 3 to 4 mm. high. Radial spines 9, yellow passing to grey, about 1 cm. long. Central spines 1 or 2, yellow, tipped darker, 1 cm. long, one often curved upwards. Flowers 13 cm. long, brownish white outside, white and pale pink inside; very beautiful and sweet-scented.

Echinopsis nigra Backbg. Argentina (North Jujuy), at elevations up to 3,000 m. Stem globular or oval, bluish green, with about 20 very acute ribs, deeply notched into flat hatchet-like tubercles, with large, elliptical areoles, very far apart. Spines numerous and irregular, very long, at first dark brown to black, passing to grey. The stem is 10 to 15 cm. thick, entirely covered with spines. Radial spines 12 to 14, radiating and curved over the stem, up to 4 cm. long. One central spine directed upwards 4 cm. long, another directed downwards up to 7 cm. long and usually curved or hooked; and 2 or more others, 7 cm. long, curved and directed irregularly. Flowers borne on the sides of the stem, about 10 cm. long, with a thick tube, reddish green outside, white inside. Fruit ovoid, green, hairy.

Echinopsis hamatacantha Backbg. Argentina. Stem globular, flattened and depressed at the top, solitary, or rarely cespitose, 10 to 15 cm. thick, dark dull green or reddish green. Ribs about 15, prominent, rounded, 1 cm. high, notched. Areoles about 1 cm. apart, roundish or oval, large, depressed, with yellowish wool. Radial spines about 14, awl-shaped, up to 1 cm. long, spreading or pectinate, straight or recurved, yellow or reddish towards the tip. Central spines 1 to 4, erect, 1 cm. long, more reddish, hooked at the tip. Flower white, with a short tube, 6 to 8 cm. long.

Echinopsis violacea Werd. Argentina (Cordoba). Plant solitary, globular to cylindrical, up to 20 cm. high, and 12 to 13 cm. thick, pale green, with abundant yellowish or yellow spines at the top, with about

15 ribs, acute, 1 to 1½ cm. high, notched, at the areoles. These are 1½ to 2 cm. apart, round, whitish when young, rather large, with about 12 spines, strong, straight, needle-like, more or less spreading, yellow, tipped dark yellow, up to 3 cm. long. Central spines 3 or 4, developing later, yellow tipped brown, up to 4 cm. long. Flowers borne freely at or near the top, erect, about 7½ cm. long, trumpet-shaped. Ovary and tube with pointed spinescent scales and whitish hair or wool; the inner petals of a tender violet colour, hairy at the throat. A free-growing and free flowering species of recent introduction.

Echinopsis polyancistra Backbg. Northern Argentina (Salta), at elevations of 2,500 m. Stem very small, globular, flat, up to 6 cm. thick, mostly solitary, very variable, with 17 to 30 ribs, 4 mm. wide and 3 mm. high, narrow, slightly rounded and warty, pale green or green. Spines numerous, bristly, spreading laterally and applied to the stem; central spines 1 to 4, straight, up to 12 mm. long, often curved or hooked, irregularly disposed, often quite short. Flowers up to 10 cm. long, funnel-shaped, with a very slender tube, often only 4 mm. thick. Petals white. Flowers sweet-scented. A lovely species, the smallest known, but very rare.

Echinopsis obrepanda (Salm-Dyck) K. Sch. = *Echinocactus obrepandus* Salm-Dyck = *Echinopsis Misleyi* Lab. = *E. cristata* Salm-Dyck. Bolivia. Stem globular, rarely sprouting, glossy dark green, not spiny at the top, with 17 or 18 acute ribs, deeply notched. Areoles 1½ to 2 cm. apart, inserted in the notches, greyish brown. Spines dark brown, paler towards the base; the radials 9 to 11, rather curved, the lower ones short, the others up to 3 cm. long; centrals 1 to 3, the lower one up to 4 cm. long. Flowers borne at the top, 18 to 20 cm. long, and about 18 cm. broad, with a pale green tube, warty and scaly, the scales being triangular and margined reddish, with dark brown hair in the axils. Outer petals brownish or reddish green, the inner oval-elongated, minutely toothed, white. Stamens pale yellow or white. Stigma with 12 lobes.

Echinopsis ancistrophora Spegazzini. Argentina, high mountains between Tucuman and Salta. Stem solitary, more or less globular, 5 to 8 cm. thick, glossy green, with 15 or 16 thick ribs, 1 cm. high, slightly notched. Radial spines 3 to 7, slender, ½ to 1½ cm. long, directed backwards: one central spine, curved or hooked, 1 to 2 cm. long. Flowers 12 to 16 cm. long: outer petals linear, acuminate, green; inner petals oblong, acute, white, Ovary and tube with woolly scales.

Echinopsis Spegazziniana Br. et R. Argentina (near Mendoza). Stem solitary, slender, dull green, about 30 cm. high, and 9 cm. thick, with 12 to 14 ribs slightly notched. Radial spines 7 or 8, straight, awl-shaped, brown. One central spine, much longer than the radials, 2 cm. long, a little curved, mostly directed downwards. Flowers borne on the sides of the stem, 15 to 17 cm. long, petals many, short, broad, white. Ovary and tube with small scales, very hairy. Long known, now again in cultivation.

Other species belonging to this sub-genus are: **Echinopsis Ritteri** Böd. and **E. hamatispina** Werd. = *Lobivia Graulichii* Frič.

Sub-Genus II. EUECHINOPSIS. These are the true *Echinopsis*, bearing large flowers with a long tube, white to pale pink, or pink, or pale lilac pink, often sweet-scented, opening at sunset and lasting for at least two days, if not scorched by the sun. The stem is thick, cespitose, with prominent straight ribs, often cereoid, reaching a height of 50 cm. to 1 m. Ovary and tube scaly and hairy, but not spinescent.

Echinopsis Eyriesii Zucc. = *Echinocactus Eyriesii* Turpin. Uruguay, Southern Brazil and Argentina. Stem globular, later elongated and almost cylindrical, 12 to 15 cm. thick, dark green, abundantly sprouting, with 11 to 18 straight ribs, prominent and acute, with deep furrows between them, about 2 cm. deep. Areoles round, greyish, up to $3\frac{1}{2}$ cm. apart. Spines about 14, short, conical, dark brown, up to $\frac{1}{2}$ cm. long. Flowers borne on the sides, 17 to 25 cm. long, 10 to 12 cm. broad, funnel-shaped or trumpet-shaped, with a long pale green tube. Ovary and tube furnished with lanceolate curved scales, and grey or brown curly hair. Inner petals white, pointed and toothed. Stamens greenish white, style green, stigma with 12 or 13 pale green lobes. The following are varieties or hybrids.

E. Duvalii Hort. Flower with obtuse petals.

E. Pudantii Pfersd. A small form, with closer areoles, whitish slender spines, and 4 to 6 darker central spines.

E. grandiflora R. Mey. A beautiful variety, with very acute ribs, and large dark pink flowers.

E. Shelhasei Zucc. Has more acute ribs, and areoles with yellowish brown wool.

E. Eyriesii Tettaui Rümpl. Is a cross with *E. tubiflora*.

E. Eyr. Wilkensii Hort. and *E. Eyr. Lagemannii* Dietr. are two hybrids with *E. oxygona*. *E. Lagemannii* has long yellowish brown spines (2 to 4 cm.).

Other forms in cultivation are: var. **E. Mulleri** Hort., **E. nigerrima** Hort., **E. Quehlii** Hort., **E. undulata** Hort., as well as var. **major** Hort., **rosea** Hort., **inermis** Hort., etc. There are also in cultivation cristate forms of *E. Eyriesii* (type) as well as of *E. Pudantii* and other varieties. A most beautiful variety, with rather long pale brown spines, is *E. Eyriesii triumphans fl. pleno* Jacobi, with 7 whorls of pink petals.

Echinopsis oxygona (Link) Zucc. = *Echinocactus oxygonus* Link. Southern Brazil, Uruguay and Argentina. Stem at first globular or almost conical, later cylindrical, 20 to 30 cm. high, and up to 20 cm. in diameter, green passing to greyish green, sprouting along the sides above the ground. Ribs 13 to 15, acute, very even, with large areoles 2 to $2\frac{1}{2}$ cm. apart, furnished with short wool. Spines spreading, awl-shaped, $1\frac{1}{2}$ to 2 cm. long, all equal, at first whitish tipped brown, passing to pale brown; the radials 12 to 16 (on young areoles 6 to 8), the centrals 5 to 7, of which 1 to 3 are slightly longer. Flower up to

25 cm. long, and 10 to 12 cm. broad. Ovary with scales and grey wool; tube glossy green; outer petals very acute, brownish red, the inner spathulate abruptly pointed, externally dark pink to carmine red, internally white flushed pink. Stamens and pistil white, stigma with 10 to 12 lobes.

var. **inermis** Jacobi. Has very short black spines.

Echinopsis multiplex (Pfeiff.) Zucc. = *Cereus multiplex* Pfeiff Southern Brazil. Stem globular, pale green or yellowish green, 15 cm. high, sprouting freely from the base and sides. Ribs 12 to 14, straight, acute, with deep sharp furrows between them; areoles woolly, 2 cm. apart. Spines thick, awl-shaped, brown tipped darker: the radials 8 to 9, spreading, up to 2 cm. long; the centrals 2 to 5, darker, up to 4 cm. long. Flower 18 to 20 cm. long, and 12 to 15 cm. broad; ovary and tube scaly and with greyish wool, the tube being reddish above; outer petals lanceolate, acute, pink; the inner spathulate, abruptly pointed, flesh-coloured, pink at the point. The flower is very fragrant. Stamens and style white, stigma with 8 to 10 lobes. Fruit ovoid, almost dry. Very free-flowering. Often listed as *E. Mulleri* Hort.

var. **floribunda** Hort. Free-flowering all the summer.

var. **picta** Hort. = *variegata* Hort. Petals spotted yellow.

var. **rosea** Hort. Inner petals pale carmine.

There are also various cristate forms: *cristata, cossa, cristata major* (strong-spined) and *cristata minor* (small-spined).

Echinopsis turbinata (Pfeiff.) Zucc. = *Cereus turbinatus* Pfeiff. = *Echinopsis gemmata* K. Sch. South Brazil and Argentina. Stem globular or conical, later cylindrical or club-shaped, dark green, sprouting at the base or low down the sides; with 13 or 14 ribs, straight or spirally arranged, notched. Areoles 1 cm. apart, with yellowish white wool, passing to greyish. Radial spines 10 to 12, about $\frac{1}{2}$ cm. long, spreading, yellowish brown, passing to horny brown. Central spines about 6, very short (2 mm.), black or dark brown, stiff. Flower 15 to 17 cm. long, 7 to 8 cm. broad, funnel-shaped, with a green tube furnished with acute scales and long greyish hair. Outer petals narrow, acute, dark green; inner petals spathulate-lanceolate, hairy at the tip, white with a greenish midrib on the dorsal side. Style white, stamens white, half as long as the petals, stigma with 11 to 13 lobes. The flower has a strong perfume of Jasmine.

Echinopsis Decaisneana Lem., often considered as a distinct species, is a very sweet-scented variety, with large flowers of a beautiful pale red.

Echinopsis falcata Rümpl. is another form with a lively pink midrib on the dorsal side of the inner petals.

The variety *picta* Hort. has the stem spotted yellow and var. *rosea* Hort. has a pale pink flower. There is also a cristate form in cultivation.

Echinopsis tubiflora (Pfeiff.) Zucc. = *Cereus tubiflorus* Pfeiff. = *Echinopsis Zuccarinii* Pfeiff. Argentina and Southern Brazil. Stem globular, later cylindrical, up to 75 cm. high, and 12 to 15 cm. thick, dark green, sprouting along the sides and at the top, with 11 to 12 straight and acute ribs, irregularly notched, with deep acute furrows between them. Areoles about 2 cm. apart, with whitish wool, passing to grey or black. Radial spines many, yellowish tipped brown, up to $2\frac{1}{2}$ cm. long; central spines 3 or 4, thicker, the lower one up to $3\frac{1}{2}$ cm. long. Flower about 24 cm. long and 10 cm. broad, with scales and dark or black hairs on the ovary and tube; outer petals lanceolate, green, tipped brown; inner petals spathulate, acute, white with a green midrib on the dorsal side. Stamens and style white, stigma with 9 to 11 lobes.

var. **nigrispina** Monv. Has short black spines.

var. **grandiflora** Hort. Flowers larger.

var. **paraguayensis** R. Mey. Often considered as a distinct species. Has long spines and is very freely sprouting. Includes several very beautiful forms.

var. **Graessneriana** Hort. Stem globular, glossy dark green, with very prominent and acute ribs. Petals flushed pink.

Echinopsis Poselgeri R. Mey. and its varieties **brevispina** and **longispina** Hildm., are large-flowering hybrids with *E. leucantha;* and **E. Rohlandii** Först is a long-spined and large pink-flowered hybrid with *E. oxygona.* **E. Droegeana** Berger is another hybrid with *E. oxygona,* and has the outer petals pink and the inner white.

There are also various cristate forms of this species and its varieties.

Echinopsis Meyeri Heese. Paraguay. Closely allied to the preceding species. Stem globular, solitary or sparingly sprouting, pale green, up to 12 cm. thick with 14 to 15 acute ribs, somewhat spiral, with greyish areoles on prominences usually of a dark reddish colour. Radial spines 7 or 8, thick and awl-shaped, 2 to 3 cm. long, thickened at the base, and reddish brown at the tip, zoned yellowish grey at the middle; central spines 3 or more, same colour, slightly longer. Flower 15 to 20 cm. long, and about 12 cm. broad, blooming very irregularly, the outer petals brownish green, tipped brown, the inner petals greenish white or whitish. Style yellowish, stamens white, stigma with 8 to 10 lobes.

Echinopsis leucantha Walp. = *E. salpingophora* Lem. = *E. yacutulana* Weber. Western Argentina. Stem globular, later oval or elongated, greyish green, about 12 cm. thick, with long spines at the top, sprouting very sparingly, with about 14 obtuse ribs, slightly notched, 1 to $1\frac{1}{2}$ cm. high, with narrow furrows between them. Areoles 1 to $1\frac{1}{2}$ cm. apart, with yellowish white wool; radial spines about 10, more or less tortuous, up to $2\frac{1}{2}$ cm. long, yellowish brown; only one central spine, thick, brown, curved upwards, 5 to 10 cm. long. Flowers borne near the top, up to 20 cm. long, with a long woolly tube, and nearly erect limb, the outer petals being brownish green and the inner white, more or less pointed reddish. Stigma with 12 yellow lobes. Fruit a fleshy deep red berry. The flower has the fragrance of violets.

var. **brasiliensis** Speg. Has shorter radials and smaller flowers.

var. **aurea** Hort. Stem yellow or marbled yellow.

Echinopsis campylacantha R. Mey. non Pfeiff. = *E. salpingophora* Preinr. non Lem. Western Argentina. Stem globular, later almost columnar, dark green, with 12 to 14 straight ribs. Areoles yellowish with 7 or 8 radial spines, 2 to 3 cm. long, spreading, straight, pale brown, tipped darker; only one central spine, 4 to 5 cm. long, curved upwards, thick and dark brown, passing to greyish. Flowers borne at the sides of the stem, 15 to 17 cm. long, up to 6 cm. broad; tube with brown acute scales and brownish wool; outer petals brownish green, the inner obtuse and fully expanded, white, flushed pink, slightly perfumed. Stigma with 12 to 15 erect green lobes.

Echinopsis rhodotricha K. Sch. North-east Argentina and Paraguay. Stem oval or cylindrical, 30 to 80 cm. high, and up to 14 cm. thick, sprouting from the base and forming groups, dull green, with brown spines and yellowish wool at the top. Ribs 8 to 13, straight, prominent; areoles 2 to 3 cm. apart, yellowish passing to greyish. Spines yellowish brown, tipped black, passing to pale horny brown; the radials 4 to 7, spreading, thick, curved, up to 2 cm. long; only one central, often absent, up to 3½ cm. long, curved upwards, brown, zoned darker. Flowers borne on the sides, about 15 cm. long, and 8 cm. broad, white, with a slender tube curved upwards, with scales and reddish hairs. Stamens and style white, stigma with 11 green lobes. Fruit oval, 4½ cm. long. A beautiful and free flowering species.

var. **argentinensis** R. Mey. Stem dark greyish green, globular or oval, Radial spines 7, dark reddish, up to 2½ cm. long; central spine strongly curved upwards.

var. **robusta** R. Mey. Stem globular, large, with 16 ribs. Radial spines 9 or 10, brown with a darker point, 1½ cm. long; central spine up to 2½ cm. long, dark brown. Flower larger.

Echinopsis Huottii Lab. = *E. apiculata* Lke. Bolivia. Stem cylindrical, dark green, up to 35 cm. high and about 8 cm. thick, sprouting at the sides, with 9 to 11 straight ribs, obtuse or rounded, about 1 cm. high. Areoles 1½ to 2 cm. apart, greyish. Spines pale brown, tipped dark; the radials about 10, spreading, needle-like, up to 2 cm. long; the centrals 1 to 4, straight, directed horizontally, up to 4 cm. long. Flowers borne near the top, up to 20 cm. long, and 12 cm. broad. Ovary and tube dull green, with scales and greyish hair. Outer petals lanceolate, white or pale pink, with greenish midrib, inner petals spathulate-acute, white. Stamens white, style green, stigma with 14 green lobes.

Echinopsis calochlora K. Sch. Brazil (Corumba). Stem globular or oval, 6 to 9 cm. thick, deep glossy green with about 12 acute ribs, lightly notched. Areoles whitish or greyish, with 14 to 22, slender straight, radial spines, ½ to 1 cm. long, yellowish passing to brownish. Central spines thicker and of a darker colour. Flower about 16 cm.

(b) LOBIVIA FAMATIMENSIS

(a) LOBIVIA CINNABARINA

PLATE XXXII

(b) LOBIVIA LATERITIA

(a) LOBIVIA POTOSINA

PLATE XXXIII

long, and 10 cm. broad, with white spreading petals; tube slender, hairy, yellowish green. Stamens white, style yellow, stigma with 9 green lobes. A beautiful and free-flowering species, now again obtainable in commerce, chiefly seedlings, offsets being scarce.

Echinopsis albiflora K. Sch. Argentina. Stem globular, about 10 cm. thick, bluish green, passing to greyish green, sprouting at or near the base, 10 or 11 acute ribs, lightly notched. Areoles standing on the prominences of the notches, 1 to 1½ cm. apart, with about 15 spines, all alike, straight or curved, 1½ to 2 cm. long, at first reddish brown, passing to greyish, tipped dark, the inner spines being shorter. Flowers borne on the sides, about 20 cm. long, and 16 cm. broad; tube slender, furnished with scales and greyish hairs. Outer petals linear, acute, bluish green, inner petals pure white. Stamens white, style pale green, stigma greenish with 13 lobes. This is another species recently reintroduced.

Echinopsis cordobensis Spegazzini. Argentina (Cordoba). Stem solitary, large 40 to 50 cm. high, and about 35 cm. thick, dull green, somewhat glaucous, with 13 ribs, straight, acute, not notched. Radial spines 8 to 10, 1 to 2 cm. long; central spines 1 to 3, the lower one 3 to 5 cm. long, bulbous at the base; all spines straight, dark passing to grey. Flowers 20 to 22 cm. long: ovary and tube with hairy scales; inner petals acute white, flower scentless. Fruit globose, 2½ cm. long, yellowish red. Rare at its native home.

Echinopsis Shaferi Br. et R. Argentina (Tucuman). This is another great rarity. Stem solitary, columnar, up to 1½ m. high, erect, 16 to 18 cm. thick, dark green, with 10 to 12 ribs, 2 cm. high. Areoles closely set, not more than 1 cm. apart. Radial spines 6 to 9, slender, awl-shaped, brownish passing to greyish, 1½ to 3½ cm. long, straight. One central spine, up to 10 cm. long, somewhat curved, directed upwards. Flower 20 cm. long, white, with a slender funnel-shaped tube, scaly and hairy, style and stamens pale green. Fruit ovoid, 3 cm. long, brick-red. The growing top is covered with a mass of brown wool. This is the tallest known species of *Echinopsis*.

Echinopsis intricatissima Spegazzini. Argentina (Mendoza). Stem solitary, oval or almost conical, 20 cm. high, with 16 ribs. Spines pink, passing to greyish : the radials 8 to 13, 3 to 4 cm. long; central spines 4 to 6, 6 to 8 cm. long, the lower ones up to 10 cm. long. Flowers 20 to 22 cm. long, inner petals lanceolate, white. Fruit ovoid, 3 cm. long. A cristate form is also cultivated.

Echinopsis valida Monv. = *Cereus validissimus* Weber. Paraguay. Stem columnar, up to 1 m. high and 20 cm. thick, dull greyish green, with 10 to 14 obtuse ribs, very slightly notched. Areoles yellowish, up to 3 cm. apart. Spines yellowish brown, tipped dark, passing to grey: the radials 7 or 8, spreading, up to 2 cm. long; only one central, straight, thick, markedly bulbous at the base, more so than the radials, 3½ to 4 cm. long. Flowers borne on the sides and near the top, 10 cm. long, and 6 to 8 cm. broad, white; ovary and tube scaly and with dark hairs; stamens, style and the 10-lobed stigma white.

var. **Forbesii** A. Dietr., with only 3 or 4 radial spines, central spine often absent.

var. **gigantea** R. Mey. Stem pale greyish green, with 8 to 11 ribs. Areoles with reddish yellow wool; radial spines 5 to 10, light brown, curved upwards.

Echinopsis Bridgesii Salm-Dyck = *E. Salmiana* Weber. Bolivia (La Paz). Stem cylindrical, up to 30 cm. high, and 7 to 8 cm. thick, glossy dark green, passing to greyish green, sprouting from the base, with 11 to 14 broad and obtuse ribs, deeply notched. Areoles in the notches, about 2 cm. apart, large, brownish, with about 10 radial spines, straight, up to 1 cm. long, and 4 central spines, spreading crosswise, up to 2 cm. long, brown to greyish, like the radials. Flower 18 cm. long, white, similar to that of *E. Huottii*; ovary and slender tube furnished with scales and grey or black hairs. The stem is often club-shaped.

Echinopsis Fiebrigii Gürke. Bolivia. Stem globular, 15 to 18 cm. thick, spineless at the top, greyish green. Ribs 18 to 24, obtuse, irregular, about $1\frac{1}{2}$ cm. high. Areoles in notches, 3 to 4 cm. apart, yellowish grey. Spines at first pale yellow, passing to brownish, often zoned, finally greyish, thick and stiff; the radials 8 to 10, 1 to $2\frac{1}{2}$ cm. long; only one central spine, curved upwards, up to $3\frac{1}{2}$ cm. long. Flowers borne on the sides, 17 to 19 cm. long, and about 9 cm. across, with a slender tube having many narrow pale green scales and pale brown or white hairs 2 cm. long. Outer petals narrow, pale green; the inner elongated, obtuse, pure white, curved inwards. Stamens and style pale green, stigma with 11 green lobes. A beautiful species, free-growing and free-flowering; the flowers are slightly perfumed.

Echinopsis formosa (Pfeiff.) Jacobi = *Echinocactus formosus* Pfeiff. = *Cereus Gilliesii* Weber. Argentina (Mendoza). Stem solitary, never sprouting unless made to do so artificially, globular, later oval or even columnar, up to 50 cm. high, and 15 to 17 cm. thick, pale greyish green, rounded at the top, the upper areoles well furnished with whitish or yellowish wool, and with many long spines, reddish when young. Ribs 15 to 22 or more, straight, rounded, up to 2 cm. high, slightly notched. Areoles 2 cm. apart, oval, more than $\frac{1}{2}$ cm. long, with short yellowish or whitish wool. Radial spines 11 to 13, sometimes less, the longest up to 4 cm. long, awl-shaped, straight or curved, thick, white with reddish point. Central spines 6 to 8, pale reddish or flesh-coloured, dark at the tip, up to 7 cm. long. Flowers borne along the sides, near the top, about 8 cm. long, funnel-shaped, 7 to 8 cm. across: ovary scaly and woolly; tube short, with short hairs. Inner petals glossy golden yellow. Stamens and style white. An attractive species and easy to grow. Seedlings make quick growth and are now easily obtainable.

var. **spinosior** Salm-Dyck. Spines more numerous and longer.

var. **crassispina** Monv. Spines thicker and more rigid.

var. **rubrispina** Monv. Spines bright red or blood red.

var. **laevior** Monv. Has fewer spines.

Echinopsis albispinosa K. Sch. Bolivia and Paraguay. Stem globular, later oval or columnar, sprouting from the base, olive green, very spiny at the top, 6 to 10 cm. thick, with 10 to 12 ribs, straight, somewhat rounded, prominent, about 1 cm. high. Areoles yellowish white, large, round, ½ to 1 cm. apart. Radial spines about 12, white or tipped yellow, the laterals up to 2 cm. long, straight or slightly curved. Central spines 1 to 4, dark reddish brown or black below, yellowish towards the point, the lowermost directed downwards, up to 4 cm. long. Flowers freely borne on the sides, 19 cm. long and, 12 cm. broad ; ovary and tube with scales and greyish wool; outer petals bluish green, the inner white. Stamens white, style yellowish or greenish white, stigma with 13 lobes. A very beautiful and quick growing species.

Echinopsis Silvestrii Spegazzini. Argentina. Stem globular, large, about 15 cm. thick, often short-cylindric, greyish green, depressed at the top. Ribs 20 or more, rather acute and narrow. Areoles white, round, 1 to 1½ cm. apart. Spines yellowish white in young plants, in grown-up plants yellow passing to grey, the centrals curved downwards. Flowers very large, 25 cm. or more in length, and 12 to 15 cm. broad, with spreading white petals. One of the largest flowering species, flowering even when young. Usually propagated by seed, offsets being scarce.

The following are other species of recent introduction: **Echinopsis Dehrenbergii** Frič, from Paraguay, **E. mirabilis** Speg., **E. Baldiana** Speg., **E. minuana** Speg., **E. tucucamensis** Backbg. and **E. Smrziana** Backbg. from Argentina.

Sub-Tribe IV   Echinocactanae

Stem globular or elongated, always distinctly ribbed. Flowers borne singly, and always on the new areoles at the top of the plant or at its centre, rather small with a short tube, more or less funnel-shaped. Fruit also small, dry and opening by a pore at the base, or somewhat juicy with septifragous dehiscence, or marcescent. Seeds black or brown. Seedling with a very fleshy hypocotyl; cotyledons reduced to mere traces.

Denmoza Br. et R.
An anagram of Mendoza, Argentina.

Stem globular to cylindrical, with many undulating ribs. Spines uneven, many, reddish, curved or tortuous. Flowers tubular, somewhat irregular, small, red, with wool in the throat, and with short petals erect or closed on the stamens, which protrude along with the style. Ovary and tube scaly and woolly. Fruit globular, dry, splitting on one side when ripe; seeds pitted, black.

This aberrant genus, of obscure affinity, includes only two species.

Denmoza rhodacantha (Weber) Br. et R. = *Cereus rhodacanthus* Weber = *Echinopsis rhodacantha* Salm-Dyck = *Cleistocactus rhodacanthus* Lem. = *Echinocactus coccineus* Otto. Argentina (Mendoza). Stem globular, later more or less cylindrical, very sparingly sprouting at the base, dull dark green, 9 to 16 cm. thick, with about 15 acute ribs, straight, but more or less wavy, with deep narrow furrows between them, and with large oval greyish areoles on slight prominences, 2 to 2½ cm. apart. Spines at first yellowish red or blood red, passing definitely to a rusty red, and grey when old; all equal, up to 3 cm. long, thick, awl-shaped, curved backwards and upwards; the radials 8 to 10; only one central, or absent. Flower 7 cm. long, on the top of the stem; petals 1 cm. long, red, closed together, through which is exserted the brush-like mass of red stamens with red anthers, red style and stigma with 8 deep red lobes.

An interesting species of easy cultivation. Seedlings develop fairly quickly, and offsets are also occasionally produced. Grafted on *Trichocereus macrogonus* or on *T. Spachianus* soon makes good growth.

Denmoza erythrocephala (K. Sch.) Berger = *Pilocereus erythrocephalus* K. Sch. Argentina (Mendoza). Stem always solitary, at first globular, 15 to 30 cm. thick, becoming cylindrical with age and reaching a height of 1½ m. with 20 to 30 ribs, somewhat low and rounded, with deep narrow furrows between them. Spines very numerous, 30 or more; the inner ones straight or variously curved, very stiff, fuchsine red when young, passing to rusty red or reddish brown, and finally to grey; the outer spines are slender and whitish, and flexible or almost hair-like. Flower 7½ cm. long: as in the preceding species.

Both Spegazzini, and Britton and Rose, were of opinion that this second species represented the old stage of the first, but it is certainly a distinct species as seedlings are altogether different, and young plants show all the characters of the species to which they belong. Both species are very interesting and attractive, particularly the second one with its highly coloured and ornamented top.

ARIOCARPUS Scheidweiler
(*Anhalonium* Lemaire)

Plants with a long beet-like tap-root, low, round, flat-topped and spineless, with tubercles more or less triangular and prismatic, terminating mostly in a callosity. Areoles small, situated in the middle of the tubercle or towards the tip, sometimes in a groove, with a woolly growth, and perhaps with one small spine. Flowers diurnal, lasting for more than one day, fully expanded, borne on the areoles in the centre of the plant, with a short tube immersed in the woolly formation of the areoles, white, yellowish, pink or purplish. Fruit, a smooth berry, elliptical, later drying; seeds black, retained for a long time in the dried berry amid the wool of the areoles.

Includes 7 species.

(b) ECHINOPSIS VIOLACEA

(a) LOBIVIA DENSISPINA

PLATE XXXIV

(b) ECHINOPSIS LEUCANTHA

(a) ECHINOPSIS OBREPANDA

PLATE XXXV

Ariocarpus retusus Scheidw. = *Anhalonium retusum* Salm-Dyck = *Anhalonium prismaticum* Lem. Mexico (on porphyric formations at Potosi). Tubercles spreading, shortly triangular-pyramidal, with the upper surface flat or slightly convex, intensely glaucous, 1½ to 2½ cm. long, terminating in a horny point or callosity, up to 3 mm. long. Flower about 4 cm. long, pale pink or flesh-coloured, with spreading petals, narrow, obtuse, hairy or toothed at the top. Stamens about half as long as the petals, stigma with 6 to 8 white lobes.

Thrives well in cultivation; like other species of this genus, requiring full sunshine, open air, and a porous sandy and stony soil with some leaf-mould. Should be grown in rather deep pots, and kept dry, especially in winter.

Ariocarpus trigonus K. Sch. = *Anhalonium trigonum* Weber. Mexico (Nuovo Leon, Tamaulipas). Tubercles more numerous and much more erect, 3½ to 5 cm. long, and 2 to 2½ cm. broad at the base, greyish green, acutely triangular with a flat upper surface, and a very acute keel, horny along the angles and at the tip, with the areole situated near the tip. Flowers numerous, from the woolly axils at the centre, 5 cm. broad, yellowish, with white stamens and stigma with 8 to 10 white lobes.

Ariocarpus scapharostrus Boedeker. Mexico (Nuevo Leon). Plant solitary, with stem up to 9 cm. thick, with triangular tubercles up to 5 cm. long, dull greyish green, with an oval callosity at the tip, on the upper surface. The tubercles have acute angles with grey membraneous margins. There are no areoles on the tubercles. Flower of a lively purplish. In its native country grown on barren stony ground, under a broiling sun.

Ariocarpus furfuraceus Thompson. = *Mammillaria furfuracea* S. Watson. Mexico (Coahuila). Tubercles very numerous, triangular, acutely pointed, small, close together, forming a sort of mosaic, pale glaucous green, with minute whitish or rust-coloured scales. Flowers 2½ to 3 cm. long, and 4 to 5 cm. across, white or very pale pink, the outer petals with a brownish green dorsal nerve; the inner petals linear, obtuse, toothed at the top, up to 1 cm. broad. Stamens short, white, with golden yellow anthers; style longer than the stamens, stigma with 12 white spreading lobes. The rust-coloured scales on the tubercles of this singular plant, give it a dry and lifeless appearance, but the newly formed tubercles at the centre are deep green, and keep so for a long time.

var. **rostratus** Berger. Tip of tubercles sharper and more beak-like; the aeroles at first more woolly, with 2 to 4 very small, horny yellow spines 1 to 1½ mm. long.

Ariocarpus fissuratus K. Sch. = *Anhalonium fissuratum* Engelm. = *Mammillaria fissurata* Engelm. = *Roseocactus fissuratus* Berger. South-west Texas and Mexico (Coahuila). Known to the colonists as "living rock". Stem solitary, or sprouting from the base and forming clumps, globular, flattened, woolly at the base, 10 to 15 cm. broad.

Tubercles 2 to 3 cm. broad at the base, greyish, triangular, with the upper surface fissured and warty, and with two furrows, one along each margin, and also with a central furrow woolly at the base, finishing in an areole. Flowers borne at the centre, 3 to 4 cm. broad of a beautiful pink with a darker midrib. Stamens and style white, stigma with 5 to 9 lobes. Fruit oval, pale green. Seeds black, rough.

Ariocarpus Lloydii Rose = *Roseocactus Lloydii* Berger. Central Mexico. Often considered as a mere variety of the preceding, from which it differs by its larger size, and by the upper surface of the tubercles being rhomboidal and not triangular, more flattened, with the central furrow often coalescing with the laterals. Flowers purplish red.

Ariocarpus Kotschubeyanus (Lem.) K. Sch. = *Anhalonium Kotschubeyanum* Lem. = *Ariocarpus sulcatus* K. Sch. = *Anhalonium sulcatum* Salm-Dyck. = *Anhalonium fissipedum* Monv. = *Roseocactus Kotschoubeyanus* Berger. Central Mexico. Plant sprouting from the base, forming groups. Stem 3 to 5 cm. broad, its top being almost level with the ground. Upper surface of tubercles dark green, triangular, 7 to 8 mm. broad, very even, with a median woolly furrow. Flowers 2½ to 3 cm. broad, outer petals obtuse and brownish, inner petals lanceolate, pink or carmine red. Stamens and style white, stigma with 5 lobes. As in the preceding species, the flowers issue from the woolly centre of the plant.

The genus *Roseocactus* was created by Berger, in honour of Dr. J. N. Rose, co-author with Dr. N. L. Britton of "The Cactaceae," to include the last three species, owing mainly to the presence of the median woolly furrow on the upper surface of the tubercles.

ENCEPHALOCARPUS Berger

Established by Berger in 1928, to include one species, **Encephalocarpus strobiliformis** (Werd.) Berger = *Ariocarpus strobiliformis* Werdermann. Native of Mexico (Tamaulipas). The genus differs from *Ariocarpus* chiefly owing to the presence of very numerous incurved scale-like or bract-like tubercles, keeled at the back, imbricated, and closely applied on each other, resulting in a globular scaly stem very much like the cone or *strobilum* of a Conifer, or the pineapple-like inflorescence of *Encephalartos* (*Cycadaceae*).

In this species, the only one included in the genus, the stem is almost perfectly globular, 4 to 6 cm. across, the tubercles or scales being greyish green, keeled on the dorsal side, finishing in a point with a small oval areole on the inner side, with minute spines and wool. The axils of the tubercles are woolly, and from those of the new tubercles at the top are borne the flowers, which are 3 to 3½ cm. broad, the outer petals being narrow, greenish and fringed, and the inner petals of a lively violet pink, broader, fringed or toothed at the top. Stamens few, half as long as the petals, yellow; style yellowish and longer, stigma yellowish, with 3 to 5 short lobes. The stem is entirely above ground and is cespitose, forming small groups. Same cultivation as *Ariocarpus*.

NEOGOMESIA Castenada

Plant low, simple, with a thick fusiform root. Tubercles few, spreading, resembling the leaves of an Agave, cartilaginous, rosulate, the outer tubercles being much longer than the inner, 2 to 4 cm. long, rugose, greyish green, about 6 mm. wide, acute or mucronate, flat or slightly convex, or slightly carinate on the lower surface, bearing a roundish areole on the upper surface about 1 cm. below the apex, 3 to 4 mm. in diameter, with abundant greyish wool, and without spines, or with 1 to 3 very short whitish spines.

Flowers borne in November or December, 1 to 2 on each plant, pink, large, funnel-shaped, with a long tube, produced on the nascent areole of new tubercles, with yellow filaments and stigma with 5 white lobes. Fruit red, clavate; seeds black, tuberculate, with a broad hilum.

A distinct genus, nearly allied to Ariocarpus.

The only species is:

Neogomesia agavioides Castaneda. Discovered and described by M. Castaneda, in Mexico, in the state of Tamaulipas, on gravelly hills near Tula. A small plant of botanical interest.

OBREGONIA Frič

Includes only the following species:

Obregonia Denegrii Frič. Mexico (Tamaulipas). Plant with a thick tap root, occasionally sprouting into small groups. Stem globular, flattened at the top, but not depressed, greyish green or dark green, 8 to 12 cm. across. Tubercles leaf-like, spirally arranged, thick and stiff, 2 to 2½ cm. broad at the base, and 1 to 1½ cm. long, flat on the upper surface, and strongly keeled on the under surface, without any spines or woolly formation when fully developed. Areoles at the tip of the tubercles, small, at first slightly woolly, and with 2 to 4 bristle-like spines which soon drop off. Flowers borne at the centre, white, short, funnel-shaped, 3 to 4 cm. broad; ovary and tube bare, but there are a few short scale-like outer petals. Fruit white, juicy, with the dried flower attached to it. Seeds large, black. An interesting species of easy cultivation in full sunshine.

LOPHOPHORA Coulter

Plants with a long and thick tap root, round, spineless, rising only a few centimetres above ground, solitary or sprouting, with broad flat ribs, bearing a series of low tubercles with areoles, each with a tuft of matted hairs, from which the generic name is taken. Flowers diurnal, remaining in bloom for 2 or 3 days, white, or pink, or pale yellow, borne on the central areoles. Fruit elongated, red; seeds few, black, tuberculate.

Includes 3 species, natives of Mexico and Texas.

Lophophora Williamsii (Lem.) Coulter = *Echinocactus Williamsii* Lem. = *Anhalonium Williamsii* Rümpl. Central and northern Mexico and southern Texas. Stem at first solitary, afterwards freely sprouting

CACTI

laterally, resulting in groups of 9 to 50 or more, rising only 4 or 5 cm. above ground. The stem is globular, flattened and depressed above, very glaucous, 5 to 8 cm. in diameter, with 5 to 13 broad flattened ribs, separated by narrow furrows. Along the middle of the ribs there is a row of low tubercles 1½ to 2 cm. apart, bearing a rather large areole on which there is a prominent tuft of white or whitish matted wool or hair. The flowers are borne on the newly-formed areoles in the centre of the plant, and are 2½ cm. broad, pink or pale pink or almost white, with a darker midrib. Stamens and style white, stigma with 3 to 7 reddish or yellowish lobes. The fruit mostly matures in the following year. The plant has a tendency to become much shrivelled and quite soft in winter, but soon recovers in spring. It is resistant and of easy cultivation, delighting in full sunshine.

This is the famous *mescal* or *peyotle* of the ancient Mexicans, who used to cut off the top of the plant and eat it at their festivals, an evil practice which is now prohibited by law. The plant has powerful exhilarating, and afterwards narcotic, properties, similar to those of Indian Hemp or Hashish, in this case due to three alkaloids, viz.: *mescaline*, *lophophorine* and *anhalonine*. The term *mescal* means a mushroom, and the dried tops of the plant strung into chaplets or garlands, used to be sold as mescal in the Mexican markets, and as botanical travellers were in search of a fungus and not of a Cactus, it was a long time before it was ascertained that the so-called *mescal buttons* were the dried tops of this Cactus.

Lophophora Lewinii (Henn.) Thompson = *Echinocactus Lewinii* Henn. = *E. Williamsii var. Lewinii* K. Sch. = *Anhalonium Lewinii* Henn. Mexico. Often considered as a variety of the preceding. Differs chiefly on account of the plant being larger, with more numerous and more pronounced but narrower ribs, with more prominent tubercles and larger tufts of wool. The flowers are pale pink or very pale yellow, with far less tendency to sprout.

Lophophora Ziegleri Werd. Mexico. Still very rare in cultivation. Stem mostly solitary, very glaucous and very smooth, with about 8 ribs just marked out by lines or slight furrows. Tubercles very low, with small tufts of white or whitish matted wool. The stem is more rounded, and hardly depressed at the centre, and the flowers are pale yellow. There is in cultivation a very interesting cristate form of *L. Williamsii*, grown on own roots or grafted.

AZTEKIUM Boedeker

A monotypic genus created by Boedeker in 1929, to include a new species described as an *Echinocactus* by the same author, the year before.

Aztekium Ritteri Boedeker = *Echinocactus Ritteri* Boedeker Mexico (Nuevo Leon, on dry stony hills). Stem globular, depressed about 5 cm. thick, sprouting at the base and sides forming small groups, with 9 to 11 ribs, somewhat spiral, about 1 cm. high and 8 mm. broad, more or less acute, olive green, with minute areoles very closely set, with short whitish hairs, with horizontal narrow furrows passing from the areoles all round the rib, and with notches above and below each areole. Spines 1 to 4, glassy white, flattened, papery, curled, up to 4 mm. long, later dropping off. Flowers borne at the centre from the new areoles, funnel-shaped, 1 cm. long and 8 mm. broad; outer petals smaller, white with a reddish band, inner petals white; stigma yellowish with 4 lobes. Fruit small, pink. Of easy cultivation in a porous sandy and stony soil and in full sunshine.

The very even horizontal furrows across the ribs and stems remind one of the designs on the sculptures of the aboriginal Azteks, hence the generic name.

COPIAPOA Br. et R.
(From Copiapo, a province of Chile.)

Plant globular or somewhat conical, with a dense development of wool at the top, on which the flowers are borne. Flowers yellow, or with the outer petals reddish, immersed in the wool, campanulate or broadly, funnel-shaped. Lobes of stigma yellow. Fruit small, smooth, with green scales at the top. Seeds large, black, smooth and glossy. Includes 9 species, all natives of Chile.

Copiapoa coquimbana (Karw.) Br. et R. = *Echinocactus coquimbanus* Karw. Chile (Coquimbo). Stem globular or conical, up to 12 cm. thick, pale green, with 10 to 17 warty ribs, with areoles on the prominences, about 2 cm. apart, large, roundish and woolly. Radial spines 8 to 10, straight or curved downwards; central spines 1 or 2, thicker and longer, $1\frac{1}{2}$ to $2\frac{1}{2}$ cm. long. All spines are black, passing to grey. Flowers bell-shaped, 3 cm. long, almost hidden among the mass of wool at the top; outer petals green or reddish green, the inner broader and obtuse, clear yellow. Tube very short; stamens, style and stigma yellow. Usually solitary in cultivation, but in its native home abundantly sprouting from the base, forming large groups.

Copiapoa gigantea Backbg. Chile (Pampa Antofagasta). Plant globular to columnar, up to 1 m. high and 20 cm. thick, olive green, branching from the base and forming groups, very spiny at the top, where it is furnished with reddish or yellowish brown wool. Ribs almost straight, 14 to 22, thickened at the areoles, which are about $1\frac{1}{2}$ cm. apart, brownish or black. Spines all equal, 1 to 2 cm. long, horny yellow tipped darker, spreading, straight or slightly curved, 7 radials and 1 or 2 centrals. Flowers yellow.

Copiapoa cinerascens (Salm-Dyck) Br. et R. = *Echinocactus cinerascens* Salm-Dyck = *E. ambiguus* Hildm. Chile. Globular to cylindrical, pale green, with dense yellowish white wool at the top, 10 to 12 cm. thick, with about 20 acute ribs, $1\frac{1}{2}$ to 2 cm. high, thickened at the areoles, which are 2 cm. apart, and large. Spines at first brown, passing to black and finally to grey: the radials about 8, about 1 cm. long; one central spine, straight and slightly thicker and longer. Flowers yellow, with the inner petals lanceolate and toothed.

Copiapoa marginata (Salm-Dyck) Br. et R. = *Echinocactus marginatus* Salm-Dyck = *E. streptocaulon* Hooker = *E. columnaris* Pfeiff. Chile. At first globular, later cylindrical, up to 40 cm. high, and about 11 cm. thick, pale green passing to dull green, with a mass of yellow wool at the top, with 12 to 15 straight ribs, somewhat rounded, only slightly warty, about 1 cm. high. Areoles about 1 cm. apart, round or roundish, large, woolly. Spines at first dark yellow, tipped brown, passing to grey: the radials 7 to 9, up to 2 cm. long; 1 or 2 centrals, straight and thick, up to 2½ cm. long. Flowers about 2 cm. long, almost hidden among the wool at the top, bell-shaped, canary yellow, outer petals oblong, the inner lanceolate, toothed. Stamens, style and the 10- to 12-lobed stigma yellow.

Copiapoa echinoides (Lem.) Br. et R. = *Echinocactus echinoides* Lem. Northern Chile. Stem mostly solitary, rarely sprouting, globular or conical, dull green, about 13 cm. high and 10 cm. thick, with a thick cap of whitish or yellowish wool, and with 10 straight, prominent ribs, rather obtuse and 1½ cm. high. Areoles large, round or oval, 1 to 2 cm. apart, brownish. Spines brownish passing to grey: the radials 5 to 7, thick, mostly curved and spreading outwards, about 2 cm. long; only one central spine, straight, up to 3 cm. long. Flower 4 cm. long, 3 cm. broad, bell-shaped; outer petals oblong, obtuse, greenish yellow; inner petals lanceolate, acute, toothed, canary yellow. Stamens, style and the 10-lobed stigma pale yellow. A variable species.

Copiapoa taltalensis Werdermann = *Echinocactus taltalensis* Werd. Chile (Taltal, Sierra Esmeralda). Stem solitary, or sprouting very sparingly, more or less globular or elongated, 5 to 15 cm. tall, and 5 to 10 cm. thick, with silky brownish wool and spines at the top. Ribs 15 or 16, notched into warts. Areoles brownish passing to grey. Spines slender, awl-shaped, spreading, often almost curved, about 4 cm. long, the central one up to 5 cm. long. Flowers borne at the top, about 2½ cm. long, with a short scaly tube, but without wool or bristles; petals yellow, stigma with 9 to 13 lobes.

Copiapoa cinerea (Phil.) Br. et R. = *Echinocactus cinereus* Philippi. Chile (Taltal). Stem cylindrical, about 6 cm. thick and up to 1 m. high, at first solitary, later sprouting and forming groups. Stem chalky white, with fibrous roots above ground, and with about 18 low, broad and rounded ribs, almost straight. Areoles very closely set, 3 or 4 mm. apart, with a little greyish white wool, more abundant on the top areoles, where it is ashy grey. Spines at first 5 or 6, later reduced to only one, erect, black. At first all spines are paler at the base, up to 2 cm. long, but a few are quite short. Flower up to 2½ cm. long, yellow, fruit yellowish pink; seeds glossy black.

Copiapoa Malletiana (Lem.) Br. et R. = *Echinocactus Malletianus* Lem. Chile. Stem mostly solitary, globular to oval-elongated, 5½ to 7½ cm. thick, greyish green, with 10 acute straight ribs, with small depressed areoles, white passing to greyish. Radial spines 4 to 6, about 4 cm. long, very stiff, at first brownish, passing to darker, almost black. One central spine, same colour, thicker and longer. Flower campanulate, about 4 cm. long, and 3 cm. broad: outer petals yellow, tipped brown, inner petals narrower, canary yellow. Stamens, style and stigma pale yellow or yellow. Top of stem very woolly and spiny.

Copiapoa megarhiza Br. et R. Chile (near Copiapo). Plant with a large fleshy root, 7 to 8 cm. thick and often 25 cm. long. Stem solitary, or rarely sprouting, globular to cylindrical, 4 to 9 cm. thick and up to 26 cm. long, dull green to almost white, with about 13 low ribs, with long white wool at the top of the stem. Spines about 12, yellow passing to grey, rather thick, about $1\frac{1}{2}$ cm. long. Flowers yellow, $2\frac{1}{2}$ cm. long. Fruit green, less than 1 cm. long, with 5 green scales at the top.

PEDIOCACTUS Br. et R.

Plant solitary or sprouting and forming groups, with a globular stem, somewhat flattened and with definite ribs spirally arranged, on which are numerous tubercles like those of a *Mammillaria*. Flowers small, pink, fully expanded. Ovary scaly near the top. Fruit greenish, drying and splitting on one side. Seeds dull black, keeled, rough.

Includes only one species.

Pediocactus Simpsonii (Engelm.) Br. et R. = *Echinocactus Simpsonii* Engelm. = *Mammillaria Simpsonii* Marcus E. Jones = *M. Purpusii* K. Sch. Kansas, New Mexico, Nevada, Washington, Idaho and Montana. Stem 12 cm. high and up to 15 cm. broad, with very numerous warts or tubercles like a *Mammillaria*, but inserted on spiral ribs, the warts bearing areoles about 4 mm. broad, at first well furnished with white wool. Central spines 5 to 7, brown or reddish brown, white at the base, the radial spines being more numerous (15 to 20), spreading, white, more slender and slightly shorter (1 to 2 cm.). Flower pink, bell-shaped, broadly expanded up to 2 cm. long, the outer petals being obtuse, and the inner more numerous, linear, acute. Stamens deep yellow, style and 4- to 7-lobed stigma yellowish green.

var. **minor** Engelm. Plant smaller in all its parts.

var. **robustior** Coult. Plant larger, with larger tubercles. Radial spines up to $2\frac{1}{2}$ cm. long, central spines 1 to 3 cm. long.

TOUMEYA Br. et R.

Includes only one species: **Toumeya papyracantha** (Engelm.) Br. et R. = *Echinocactus papyracanthus* Engelm., native of New Mexico. It is a small plant, oval or short-cylindric, $4\frac{1}{2}$ cm. high, and 3 to $3\frac{1}{2}$ cm. thick, at first solitary, later freely cespitose, with 8 to 13 spiral ribs, cut into prominent tubercles like a *Mammillaria*. Spines thin, flat, papery, flexible, glossy white; the radials about 8, spreading, less than $\frac{1}{2}$ cm. long; the central 3 or 4, curved, 1 to 2 cm. long, the lower one curved downwards, slightly longer and broader. Flowers borne at the top, about 2 cm. long. Ovary scaly; tube very short and scaly; limb funnel-shaped, petals linear, acute, silky white. Stamens about half as long as the petals, stigma with 5 or 6 white spreading lobes.

Both this and the preceding species are unaccountably rare in collections.

CACTI

EPITHELANTHA Weber

Includes only one species, as hereunder:

Epithelantha micromeris (Engelm.) Weber = *Mammillaria micromeris* Engelm. North Mexico and western Texas, on calcareous hills. Plant solitary or cespitose and forming small groups: stem globular, up to 6 cm. high, covered with small tubercles, very closely set together in spiral rows, each tubercle bearing a tuft of about 20 very small white spines, these tufts entirely covering the plant. Flowers borne at the tip of the new tubercles at the top or centre of the plant, amongst thick hairs or hairs thickened at the tip. Flowers very small, white or pale pink, with few petals, often not more than five, with mostly ten stamens. Fruit small, club-shaped, red, maturing the following year. Seeds few black. The fact that the flowers are borne on the areoles at the tip of the tubercles at once separates this plant from the genus *Mammillaria*, in which the flowers are borne in the axils between the tubercles.

var. **Greggii** Engelm. Grows larger in size, with longer tubercles. There are also forms with a well developed central spine on the tubercles, as well as a very pretty cristate form.

The plant and its variety are of slow growth. A rich calcareous soil, and much sun and warmth are necessary. Should be kept dry in winter.

NEOPORTERIA Br. et R.

Flowers funnel-shaped, pink or red, from the areoles on the top of the plant. Ovary and fruit scaly. Scales on the ovary and tube with bristles and long hairs, which persist on the fruit. Lobes of stigma creamy to reddish. Fruit small, round and dry, rising above its base at maturity. Seeds brown, with minute warts. Includes about 14 species, all South American, natives of Chile.

Neoporteria nidus (Soehrens) Br. et R. = *Echinocactus nidus* Soehrens. North Chile. Stem solitary, at first globular or oval, later almost cylindrical, 5 to 9 cm. thick, entirely surrounded and covered with long curved spines, greyish green, with 16 to 18 ribs, acute and deeply notched. Areoles closely set, small, elongated, with dark wool and about 30 spines; the outer spines being slender, hair-like, white, spreading and curved, 1 to 2 cm. long; the inner spines (6 to 8) being thicker, more tortuous and curved, and 2 to 3 cm. long, 1 or 2 being directed upwards and incurved, and up to 5 cm. long, but always rather soft and of a greyish or yellowish white colour. The flower is 4 cm. long, reddish, with narrow and acute petals.

A very interesting species, now frequently imported, but rather difficult to deal with. Requires a very porous and sandy soil, moderately rich, with some old leaf-mould, and should be kept in full sunshine, and rather dry even in the growing season. Grows and thrives better if grafted.

var. **senilis** (Phil.) = *Echinocactus senilis* Phil. North Chile. Often considered as indentical with the preceding, and sometimes as a

(b) ECHINOPSIS CALOCHLORA

(a) ECHINOPSIS CAMPYLACANTHA

PLATE XXXVI

(b) ECHINOPSIS FORMOSA

(a) ECHINOPSIS BRIDGESII

PLATE XXXVII

distinct species, is really a well-marked variety. Has the same habit of growth, but the spines are all white, the central spines being at first creamy white, passing to pure white, turning to ashy white with age, and are more slender and shorter and more tortuous and twisted

Neoporteria occulta (Phil.) Br. et R. = *Echinocactus occultus* Phil. Chile (Copiapo and Antofagasta). Stem single, globular or oval, 5 to 8 cm. high, flat at the top, dirty brownish green, with 14 obtuse ribs, much notched into protuberances on which are the elongated woolly areoles 1½ cm. apart. Spines 1 to 10, or absent, erect, all similar but unequal. 1 to 4 cm. long. Flower funnel-shaped, yellow, the outer petals with a reddish median nerve.

Neoporteria ebenacantha (Monv.) Berger = *Echinocactus ebenacanthus* Monv. = *E. fuscus* Muehlpf. = *E. humilis* Först = *E. Hankeanus* Först = *Neoporteria fusca* Br. et R. Chile. Stem single, globular or oval, sometimes pointed at the top, with wool and ebony-black spines. The stem is dark green passing to greyish, and up to 10 cm. thick, with 12 to 13 prominent obtuse ribs, notched into prominences about 1 cm. apart, bearing large oval areoles with yellowish wool. Spines all at first black, later whitish or greyish at their lower part; the radials 5 to 7, the centrals about 4, about 3 cm. long, curved upwards. Flowers borne at the centre, 3 to 4 cm. long, the outer petals being brownish, the inner yellowish and acutely pointed. Stamens yellowish, stigma with 10 to 12 lobes. Rather rare in cultivation, but thrives well and is easily grown from seed.

Neoporteria nigricans (Dietr.) Br. et R. = *Echinocactus nigricans* Dietr. Chile. Stem solitary, oval-cylindrical, dark green passing to greyish green, 5 to 6 cm. thick, with whitish wool and black spines at the top, and with 15 ribs notched into oval warts on which are oval areoles. Radial spines 8 to 9, spreading and somewhat curved, less than 1 cm. long; central spines 1 or 2, straight or curved, thick, 1 to 1½ cm. long. All spines are at first glossy black, the centrals passing to dull black and the radials to greyish. Flowers borne at the centre, funnel-shaped, 5 cm. long; outer petals olive green with a darker median nerve, inner petals lanceolate, pale yellow. Stamens white, stigma 9-lobed. *Echinocactus cupreatus* Poselg., is probably a variety with a dark bronze green stem, and fewer spines of a dark browinsh or black colour, paler at the base.

Neoporteria Jussieui (Monv.) Br. et R. = *Echinocactus Jussieui* Monv. Chile. Stem u.s. dark green or almost black, at the top spineless and only slightly woolly, with 16 acute ribs, notched into rounded prominences, with oval areoles about 1 cm. apart, yellowish to greyish. Spines at first white, later horny yellow; the radials 7 to 14, the centrals 1 or 2 thicker and up to 2½ cm. long. Flower u.s. up to 4 cm. long, pale pink, petals with a dark median nerve. Stamens green, stigma with 6 reddish lobes.

Neoporteria acutissima (Otto et Dietr.) Berger = *Echinocactus*

acutissimus Otto et Dietr. Chile (near Valparaiso). Stem at first globular, later oval, over 10 cm. high, and about 8 cm. thick, pale green passing to grey, very spiny at the top, continuing its growth until it is about 1 m. long and falls prostrate on the ground. Ribs about 20, rather closely set and 1 cm. high, notched into prominent tubercles, bearing areoles 1 cm. apart, large, at first with yellowish wool. Spines very numerous and acute, at first dirty yellow, passing to brown or dark brown, with their lower part whitish; the radials about 24, awl-shaped; the centrals 4 or 5, thicker and slightly longer, up to 3 cm. long. Flower 4 to 5 cm. long, broadly funnel-shaped, with a short yellowish tube and linear acute pink petals. Stamens and style white, stigma with 8 yellowish lobes. A cristate form is also cultivated.

Neoporteria subgibbosa (Haw.) Br. et R. = *Echinocactus subgibbosus* Haworth = *Chilenia subgibbosa* Backbg. Chile, same region as the preceding. Very similar to *N. acutissima*. Stem globular to short-cylindrical, dark olive green, 8 to 12 cm. high and 6 to 8 cm. thick. Ribs 14 to 16, with less prominent tubercles, bearing roundish woolly areoles. Spines less numerous and shorter, at first yellowish, passing to dark grey or brown. Flowers u.s.

Neoporteria exsculpta (Otto) = *Echinocactus exsculptus* Otto = *E. interruptus* Otto. Chile, slopes of the Andes near Valparaiso. Stem globular, later columnar, up to 30 cm. high, and up to 10 cm. thick, pale green passing to greyish green, with the top covered with dark golden yellow or brownish spines. Ribs about 20, straight or somewhat spiral, divided into prominent tubercles about 1 cm. high, bearing oval areoles about 1 cm. apart, with yellowish wool passing to greyish. Radial spines about 18, bristle-like, white or pale yellow, with 1 or 2 thicker ones up to 12 mm. long. Central spines 4 to 7, stiff, straight, awl-shaped, up to 2 cm. long, dark golden yellow, later almost transparent. Flowers borne at the top, 5 cm. long; ovary scaly and hairy; tube short, scaly, green, pink at the top, funnel-shaped; petals lanceolate, pink; stamens white, about half as long as the petals; style white, stigma with 6 yellow lobes.

Neoporteria Odieri (Lem.) Berger = *Echinocactus Odieri* Lem. Chile (Copiapo). Stem solitary, globular or oval, dark brown, about 5 cm. thick, later columnar and up to 20 cm. high, with many ribs spirally arranged, notched into small low prominences, bearing small oval areoles almost bare. Spines all radial, 6 to 9, greyish brown passing to grey, up to ½ cm. long. Flower up to 5 cm. long, funnel-shaped; outer petals narrow, dirty green, dark red at the tip; inner petals broader, white, pink on the dorsal side, with darker median nerve. Style red, stigma with 14 pale pink lobes.

var. **Mebbesii** Hildm. More easily sprouting at the base, and has stiffer and more spreading spines.

Neoporteria Pepiniana (Lem.) Br. et R. = *Echinocactus Pepinianus* Lem. = *E. echinoides* var *Pepiniana* Lab. Chile. Stem solitary, columnar, rounded at the top, with abundant yellowish wool and stiff spines, pale green, passing to dull green, up to 20 cm. high, and 9 to 10 cm. thick; with 12 straight ribs, acute and about 1 cm. high, notched into warts, with round woolly areoles 1½ to 2 cm. apart. Radial spines 7, spreading, stiff, straight or slightly curved, dark yellow passing to grey, up to 2 cm. long; only one central spine, slightly thicker and longer.

Neoporteria napina (R.A. Phil.) = *Echinocactus napinus* R.A. Phil. = *E. mitis* R.A. Phil. = *Malacocarpus napinus* Br. et R. = *Notocactus napinus* Berger. Chile (Huasco). Plant small, with a long and thick tap root, like a turnip, on which the stem is inserted by a narrow neck. Stem globular or conical or flat at the top, dark reddish grey or dark brownish green, 3 to 9 cm. high, and 2½ to 5 cm. thick, with about 14 spiral ribs deeply cut into round prominences or warts, about 8 mm. in diameter, bearing small areoles very slightly woolly, with 3 to 9 spreading spines, black or dark brown, not more than 3 mm. long. Flower 3 to 3½ cm. long, funnel-shaped, yellow. Ovary and tube furnished with white wool and bristles. Stigma with 8 to 13 reddish lobes. A characteristic species requiring a sandy soil, loose and moderately rich, kept rather dry and in half-shade. It is usually grafted. *E. mitis* Phil. is probably a form of smaller size, with oval warts and longer radial spines, from the same district.

Neoporteria Reichei (K. Sch.) = *Echinocactus Reichei* K. Sch. = *Malacocarpus* Br. et R. = *Notocactus* Berger. Chile. Stem globular, usually sprouting freely all round the stem and top, 5 to 7 cm. thick, greyish green, with 30 to 40 low ribs, straight or spiral, entirely notched into round low warts, ½ cm. broad, on which are small oval areoles, at first with some white wool and with 7 to 9 spines, whitish and curved, about 3 mm. long. Flower broadly funnel-shaped, 2½ to 3½ cm. long; ovary and the very short tube furnished with white wool and bristles; outer petals lanceolate, sulphur yellow, with a reddish dorsal median nerve, inner petals yellow. Style red, stigma with 10 to 12 pale pink lobes.

Neoporteria villosa (Monv.) Berger = *Cactus villosus* Monv. = *Echinocactus villosus* Lab. = *Bridgesia villosa* Backbg. = *Chileniopsis villosa* Backbg. Chile. Stem solitary, globular, later cylindrical, up to 12 cm. high, and 4 to 8 cm. thick, greyish green passing to dark reddish or almost black, woolly and spiny at the top, with 13 to 15 straight ribs, notched into somewhat elongated warts directed downwards. Areoles about 1 cm. apart, round or oval, with white wool. Radial spines 12 to 16, yellowish, tipped dark, 1 to 2 cm. long, slender and hair like, directed upwards. Central spines about 4, thicker and darker up to 3 cm. long. Flowers small but numerous, 2 cm. long, funnel-shaped; ovary and tube scaly but not woolly; petals lanceolate, white at the base, pink or carmine red above. Stamens and style white, stigma 8-lobed.

var. **nigra** Hort. Stem very dark, spines longer.

var. **polyraphis** (Pfeiff.), written also *polyrhaphis* and *polygraphis* = *Echinocactus polyraphis* Pfeiff. = *Bridgesia polyraphis* Backbg. Has an olive green stem, more numerous bristle-like radial spines, and about 7 golden brown central spines.

CHILENIA Backbg.

Proposed by Backeberg in 1935, for *Echinocactus (Neoporteria) chilensis*, and immediately extended for other species. The flowers are pink or carmine red, often developing in pairs, one on each side, from the same areole, with the inner petals erect. Ovary, tube and fruit almost bare, but for a few small scales and a few hairs. The frequent development of flower buds in pairs from the same areole, although one of the buds is often abortive, seems to offer sufficient ground for separating this genus from *Neoporteria*, although the plants are very similar in habit and other characters. Includes at least 3 species.

Chilenia chilensis (Hildm.) Backbg. = *Echinocactus chilensis* Hildm. = *Neoporteria chilensis* Br. et R. Chile (western slopes of the Andes). Stem at first globular, later cylindrical, up to 25 cm. long, and about 9 cm. thick, green, with 20 straight ribs slightly notched. Areoles oval, whitish passing to greyish or brownish. Radial spines about 20, slender, yellow or whitish, about 1 cm. long; central spines 6 to 8, yellow passing to brownish, whitish at the base, darker at the tip, thicker and up to 2 cm. long. Flowers funnel-shaped, about 5 cm. long, with numerous lanceolate, finely toothed petals of a lively carmine red, with a darker median nerve. Stamens white, and lobes of stigma yellow.

var. **confinis** Hildm. Central spines shorter and yellow.

Chilenia nigrihorrida Backbg. Chile, western slopes of the Andes, south of Coquimbo. Stem globular-depressed, bluish green to dull grey green, up to 10 cm. broad and 6 cm. high, with 16 to 18 straight ribs, thickened to about 7 mm. at the areoles, but narrow and acute between them. Areoles large, oval, about 7 mm. apart, with short wool. Radial spines about 16, spreading laterally, up to 1½ cm. long, often twisted irregularly. Central spines 6 to 7, thick, erect, awl-shaped, up to 3 cm. long. All spines are dirty silvery grey, turning to jet black when wet. Flowers about 4 cm. long with narrow acute petals, carmine red, white inside. Fruit reddish green.

Chilenia castaneoides (Cels.) Backbg. = *Echinocactus castaneoides* Cels. Chile. Stem mostly solitary, globular or oval or short-cylindric, up to 15 cm. high and 5 to 8 cm. thick, pale green, passing to greyish green and grey, rather flat at the top. with short whitish wool. Ribs about 14, straight, notched. Areoles elliptical, about 9 mm. long, at first well covered with whitish wool, later almost bare. Radial spines up to 20, spreading, straight or slightly curved, white, up to 2 cm. long. Central spines 6 or 7, thicker and up to 3 cm. long, pale chestnut brown or honey yellow, very acute, passing to grey. Flowers borne at the top, 3 cm. long, funnel-shaped, ovary scaly and hairy. Outer petals very narrow, pink; the next row lanceolate acute, carmine red, white

(a) DENMOZA ERYTHROCEPHALA

(b) CHILENIA CHILENSIS

PLATE XXXVIII

(*a*) DENMOZA RHODACANTHA

(*b*) ARIOCARPUS LLOYDII
PLATE XXXIX

inside; the inner row pale pink, shorter, white inside. Stamens white, style white, stigma with 8 reddish lobes.

Other species or varieties now included under this genus are: **Chilenia densispina** Backbg. and **C. heteracantha** Backbg., both natives of Chile.

AREQUIPA Br. et R.

A small genus, consisting of plants with a globular or short-cylindric many-ribbed stem, single or sprouting from the base. The flowers are borne at the top of the plant, with a slender tube furnished with acute scales and white wool. Stamens in two bundles, protruding beyond the petals. The ribs are warty, with many spines, and the flowers are scarlet and somewhat irregular. Includes three species, natives of Peru and Chile.

Arequipa leucotricha (Phil.) Br. et R. = *Echinocactus leucotrichus* Philippi = *E. Rettigii* Quehl = *Echinopsis Hempeliana* Gürke. South Peru (Arequipa). Stem globular, later elongated or cylindrical, up to 60 cm. long, and then mostly prostrate, greyish green, about 10 cm. thick, with abundant pale yellow wool at the top. Ribs about 20, straight, obtuse, notched into tubercles about 1 cm. broad and ½ cm. high, 1 to 1½ cm. apart, bearing round or oval areoles, rather large, furnished with pale yellow wool. Spines 12 to 16: the radials (8 to 12) pale yellow, up to 3 cm. long, curved; the centrals 3 or 4, also curved upwards, up to 4½ cm. long, at first deep yellow or orange red, tipped brown. Flowers 7½ cm. long, and 3 to 3½ cm. broad; the petals being lanceolate-acute, cinnabar red or carmine red. Stamens carmine red, style pale red above, stigma with 6 yellow lobes. Formerly rare in cultivation, now frequently offered by dealers. Full sun, and a sandy stony soil kept rather dry.

Arequipa clavata (Soehrens) Br. et R. = *Echinocactus clavatus* Soehrens. Chile. Stem at first globular, later columnar or club-shaped, greyish green, up to 1½ m. high, erect, and at its upper part up to 20 cm. thick, entirely covered with long spines, straight or curved, and with greyish silky wool on the new areoles at the top. Ribs about 10, straight, somewhat acute, notched into prominent warts, on which are elliptical areoles, 1½ cm. long, and 2 to 2½ cm. apart. Radial spines 4 to 6, very thick, straight or curved, spreading outwards, up to 3 cm. long; only one central spine, directed outwards or downwards, often curved. Flowers borne at the top, almost cylindrical, with an elongated ovary, furnished with triangular acute scales and with whitish wool in their axils; tube likewise scaly and woolly. Petals 1½ cm. long, red. Rare in cultivation.

Arequipa Weingartiana Backbg. Peru. A new species with short thick stems. Ribs 14 to 16, acute. Areoles large, oval-elongated, with 8 to 15 thick spines, more or less tortuous, 1 to 2 cm. long. The flowers, freely borne at the top, are red and similar to those of the other species, but the habit of the plant is very different.

273

S

CACTI

OROYA Br. et R.

Stem globular, flattened or depressed at the top, single or sprouting at the base, with many low ribs, bearing elongated linear areoles with pectinate spines. Flowers borne on the new central areoles, small, pink to glowing red. Includes only one species, found at Oroya near Lima, Peru.

Oroya peruviana (K. Sch.) Br. et R. = *Echinocactus peruvianus* K. Sc. Central Peru, near Lima, at elevations of about 4000 m., in gravelly soil, often deeply embedded, with its top just showing above the ground. Stem globular, flat and depressed at the top, dark dull green, with 12 to 23 low rounded ribs. When fully developed the stem is 7 to 9 cm. high and about 14 cm. in diameter, usually with several offsets round its base. The ribs are slightly notched into obtuse elongated warts on which are the linear areoles up to 2½ cm. apart and about 1 cm. long, yellowish to brown. Spines brownish yellow to brown, darker at the base, 1 to 2 cm. long, the radials 14 to 18, the lower ones very short, arranged in one series around the areole, spreading and recurved towards the stem very evenly, like a comb; central spines, when present, 2 to 5. Flowers many, borne on the central areoles, bell-shaped or funnel-shaped, 1½ to 2½ cm. long, with a few scales and hairs on the ovary and tube; petals erect, recurved at the tip, pale pink, yellowish at the base, intensely red at the tip; stamens pale yellow, style reddish, lobes of stigma pale yellow, very short. Fruit clavate, reddish brown, bare. Seeds 2 mm. long, cap-shaped, black, minutely pitted.

A very beautiful and interesting species, of easy cultivation in a sandy and gravelly soil, in full sunshine. A form with yellowish spines and another with reddish spines are listed by dealers under the name of *neoperuviana*.

MATUCANA Br. et R.

Another monotypic genus, consisting of a plant with a solitary globular stem, later cylindrical, with many low broad ribs slightly notched. Areoles small, oval, closely set together, densely woolly when young. Spines numerous, thin needle-like. Flowers borne at the centre, red, funnel-shaped, with a slender tube.

Matucana Haynei (Otto) Br. et R. = *Echinocactus Haynei* Otto. Often written *Haynii*. Peru, close to the village of Matucana in central Peru, at elevations of about 2,600 m. Stem globular to cylindrical, up to 60 cm. high, and up to 10 cm. thick, always solitary, grass green, entirely covered with white spines, with 25 to 30 low warty ribs. Areoles thickly set, oval, bulging out on the warts, densely furnished with yellow wool, which later drops off. Spines numerous, 30 or more, stiff, slender, needle-like, white passing to grey, dark at the tip, up to 3½ cm. long, spreading out irregularly, the middle ones being longer and darker. Flowers borne at the top, 6 to 8 cm. long, with a few scales on the ovary and the slender tube, but no hairs, about 6 cm. broad, deep red on the outside, orange red margined violet inside. Stamens pink, stigma with 4 yellowish lobes.

Easily grown, but rather shy blooming.

HAMATOCACTUS Br. et R.

Plants globular or elongated; ribs rounded or acute, more or less spiral. Areoles circular and woolly; central spines long, cylindrical or half-cylindrical, and at least one of them is sharply hooked at the tip. Flowers funnel-shaped or almost tube-like. Fruit small, round or oval, red or reddish; seeds black, warty. Includes three species.

Hamatocactus setispinus (Engelm.) Br. et R. = *Echinocactus setispinus* Engelm. Northern Mexico and southern Texas. Stem globular or short-cylindric, grass green, 8 to 12 cm. thick, sprouting from the base and sides when old, with 13 rather narrow and acute ribs, notched and warty, with areoles situated on the warts, about 1 cm. apart, furnished with short white wool. Radial spines 12 to 15, spreading, needle-like, white or brown, up to 4 cm. long; central spines 1 to 3, longer and thicker, mostly white, hooked at the tip. Flowers borne on the top, up to 7 cm. long, funnel-shaped; ovary and tube scaly; outer petals greenish yellow, edged reddish; inner petals lanceolate-acute, yellow, reddish at the base. Stamens and style yellow, stigma with 5 to 8 yellow lobes. Fruit round or oval, with a few scales, red, almost dry, splitting at the base. Of easy cultivation in full sunshine, in a porous stony calcareous soil, moderately rich. Makes quick growth.

var. **Cachetianus** (Monv.) K. Sch. = *Echinocactus Cachetianus* Monv. A well-marked variety or subspecies. Stem more cylindrical, with more acute ribs. Spines white and more slender, central spine longer.

var. **hamatus** Engelm. = *Echinocactus hamatus* Muehlenpf. Stem oval, thick, spines longer, central spines brown, strongly hooked.

var. **mierensis** K. Sch. Plant smaller, spines yellow.

var. **Orcutti** K. Sch. Stem cylindrical, central spine very long, yellow, spreading horizontally.

Hamatocactus hamatacanthus (Muehlpf.) = *Echinocactus hamatacanthus* Muehlpf. = *E. longi-hamatus* Gal. = *Ferocactus longihamatus* Br. et R. = *Brittonia Davisii* Houghton. Northern Mexico, southern Texas and New Mexico. Stem globular or elongated, more fleshy than in the preceding species, up to 60 cm. high, dark green, 10 to 15 cm. thick, with about 13 high ribs, rounded and notched into round warts 2 to 3 cm. apart, bearing large roundish or oval areoles, at first with yellowish white wool. Spines at first ruby red, passing to yellowish or whitish; the radials 8 to 12, spreading, needle-like, 5 to 7 cm. long; the centrals 4, semicylindrical, that is, flat on the upper surface, round on the lower, the upper 3 spines being erect, straight and slightly hooked at the tip, the lower one up to 12 cm. long, strongly hooked downwards at the tip. Flowers funnel-shaped, 7 cm. broad, with the ovary and tube scaly; outer petals brownish green, the inner narrower, toothed, glossy yellow, red at the base, and reddish on the dorsal side. Stamens, style and 15- to 18-lobed stigma yellow. Fruit oval, up to 5 cm. long, green. A free-growing and flowering species, rightly appreciated by collectionists. *Echinocactus Treculianus* Lab. is probably a synonym.

var. **crassispina** Engelm. Spines thicker, radials more numerous, all more or less angular and flat on the upper side.

var. **gracilispina** Engelm. Spines more slender and more numerous, up to 20, including the 4 centrals.

var. **brevispina** Engelm. Spines more numerous and more slender; central spines almost cylindrical, and hardly longer than the radials.

var. **sinuata** *Weber*. Plant smaller, radials more slender and often hooked, the 4 centrals slender and hooked, the lowermost very long.

Hamatocactus uncinatus (Gal.) = *Echinocactus uncinatus* Gal. = *Ferocactus uncinatus* Br. et R. = *E. ancylacanthus* Monv. From western Texas to central Mexico. Stem solitary, oval, or short-cylindric, 10 to 20 cm. high, and 5 to 7 cm. thick, dull dark green, well furnished with long hooked spines, with 9 to 13 straight, thick, obtuse, ribs, notched into prominent warts or tubercles, with a gibbosity at their base, bearing oval areoles with whitish wool. Radial spines 7 or 8, the upper ones straight, the lower ones hooked and spreading; central spines 1 to 4, up to 12 cm. long, cylindrical, or flat on the upper surface, erect, hooked at the tip. All spines are at first red, later reddish brown to creamy white, often zoned. Flowers 2 to 2½ cm. long, ovary and tube with acute scales; petals numerous, erect, linear, dark reddish brown, toothed, edged with a membraneous pale pink border. Stamens yellowish red, stigma with 10 pale pink lobes. Fruit oval, about 2 cm. long, reddish, covered with whitish scales.

var. **Wrightii** Engelm. Spines longer and more markedly red, retaining the colour for a long time.

Grows well from seed, reaching flowering size in about 3 years. In winter is liable to shrivel too much, if left too dry.

STROMBOCACTUS Br. et R.

Plants low, more or less flat, with or without spines, with spiral ribs, notched into rhomboid and more or less flat tubercles. Flowers whitish, small, borne on the top or centre of the plant. Ovary and fruit with few scales; seeds very small. Includes 4 species.

Strombocactus disciformis (K. Sch.) Br. et R. = *Mammillaria disciformis* DC. = *Echinocactus disciformis* K. Sch. = *E. turbiniformis* Pfeiffer. Central Mexico (Hidalgo). Plant occasionally sprouting at the base; stem round, much flattened, almost disc-like, 5 to 7 cm. broad, grey or greyish green, with a few spines at the centre, with 12 to 18 spiral ribs, cut into flat rhomboid tubercles, 1 to 1½ cm. broad, raised at the centre, each bearing a whitish areoles, with 1 to 4 bristle-like spines up to 1½ cm. long, which drop off with age. Flowers white, ovary with pointed reddish scales, petals lanceolate, reflexed, the outer with a reddish dorsal median nerve, the others white, yellowish at the base. Stamens about half as long as the petals, white or yellow, as also the 8 to 10 lobes of the stigma. Fruit brownish, about 7 mm. long, dry.

A curious plant, not difficult to grow in a porous calcareous soil, with some leaf-mould. Requires warmth and sunshine.

Strombocactus Schmiedickeanus Boedeker = *Echinocactus Schmiedickeanus* Boedeker. Mexico (Tamaulipas). A diminutive plant, with an oval stem, somewhat flat at the top, greyish green, solitary or sprouting into small groups, 5 to 6 cm. long, and 2 to 3 cm. thick, with long incurved spines at the top. Ribs 10 to 12, spiral, cut into four-angled pyramidal depressed warts, about ½ cm. broad, bearing roundish white areoles, woolly, but later bare, with 1 to 4 spines (mostly 3) up to 2½ cm. long and rather thick, curved inwards on the top of the plant, the upper spine being flat or grooved, white, blunt, passing to greyish, black at the tip. Flowers borne at the centre, funnel-shaped, about 2 cm. broad, pale pink, with a violet median nerve on the inner petals and brownish on the outer petals; petals lanceolate-acute. Stamens and style pink, stigma with 4 whitish lobes.

Strombocactus macrochele Werd. et Backbg. Mexico (San Luis Potosi). Stem solitary, globular, flattened or depressed, up to 3 cm. high and 4 cm. thick, its top almost level with the ground, and covered with white wool and long grey spines, its ribs cut into warts, small, but large in proportion to the size of the stem, which is dull greyish green. Warts scale-like, with elongated areoles, furnished with white wool when young, and bearing 3 to 5 (mostly 4) spines up to 4 cm. long, curved inwards like hooks, flat and flexible, papery in texture, at first yellowish, dark at the tip, passing to dark grey. Flowers white. A very small species, like the preceding.

Strombocactus lophophorides Werd. et Backbg. Mexico. A new species somewhat larger than either of the preceding two, but smaller than *S. disciformis*. Plant solitary, dull greyish green, 4 to 5 cm. thick, and 3 to 4 cm. high, embedded in the soil, flattened at the top, with a thick root, and with about 12 ribs, cut into lozenge-shaped warts, bearing small areoles with whitish wool at the top, and with 3 to 5 short spines, about ½ cm. long, yellowish passing to greyish. Flowers borne at the top or centre, white, comparatively large, fully expanded, 4 to 5 cm. broad.

LEUCHTENBERGIA Hooker

This genus was created by Hooker in 1848, in honour of the Prince Leuchtenberg, Eugene de Beauharnais, and includes only the following species.

Leuchtenbergia principis Hook. Central and northern Mexico. A very characteristic plant with a long parsnip-like root and a thick fleshy stem, becoming somewhat woody with age; usually solitary, sometimes branched dichotomously, occasionally sprouting from adventitious buds at the base of the stem. It has very long, acutely triangular, greyish green tubercles, 10 to 12 cm. long, arranged more or less spirally, with the angles sometimes reddish. Areoles rather large, with greyish wool, at the tip of the tubercles, bearing angular papery spines, the radials 8 to 14, up to 5 cm. long, the centrals 1 or 2, thicker and up to 10 cm. long, with a few brown bristles hidden in the wool of the areole. Flower borne at the tip of new tubercles, from the inner side of the areole, and is funnel-shaped, fully expanded, 5 to 6 cm. across, of a pure glossy yellow, the outer petals being reddish brown, and the inner lanceolate-acute, finely toothed. The ovary is globular or oval, with a few broad scales; the stamens, style and the 10- to 14-lobed stigma are yellow. Fruit dry, scaly, splitting at the base. Seeds round, dark brown, with minute warts. The plant is up to 50 cm. high.

A very interesting species, of easy cultivation, requiring full sunshine and warmth, and to be kept rather dry. The pots should be deep to accommodate the long tapering root, and the soil must be very porous, with sand, leaf-mould, some garden loam, some calcareous matter and crushed bricks or stone chips. Is easily grown from seed, the seedlings reaching flowering size in 4 or 5 years. As a curiosity, it may be propagated by planting the tubercles in sand, leaving the tip exposed, the young plant sprouting from the areole.

STENOCACTUS K. Sch.
(*Echinofossulocactus* Br. et R.)

Stenocactus, established as a sub-genus by Dr. K. Schumann in 1898, is a very convenient name, describing the principal characteristic of these plants, viz.: their very thin ribs. Drs. Britton and Rose (1924-26) exhumed the very uncouth name *Echinofossulocactus*, used by Lawrence in 1841, who included under this name species of widely different relationship, and therefore Lawrence's genus cannot be considered as a botanical entity. No doubt, Britton and Rose, in reviving the generic name, have amended it to suit the circumstances, so that it is an entirely new entity. However, according to the laws of priority, Schumann's genus *Stenocactus* should have had due preference, and it was accordingly revived by the late Dr. Alwin Berger. The difficulty of using the generic name *Echinofossulocactus* is shared by others. In fact, in 1923—that is before the publication of "The Cactaceae" by Britton and Rose—Spegazzini had also suggested the name *Brittonrosea* for this genus, but again the laws of prioity are a bar to its use.

The genus *Stenocactus* includes rather small plants, with numerous or very numerous thin ribs, often wavy. Areoles on each rib far apart; spines not hooked, usually flattened and papery. Flowers small, pink or greenish pink or greenish yellow, with a short tube and mostly erect limb or only partly expanded. Fruit with papery scales. Seeds black, with broad hilum. Includes at least 32 recognized species, several of which are evidently intermediate forms or natural hybrids. They are natives of Mexico.

Stenocactus coptonogonus (Lem.) Berger = *Echinocactus coptonogonus* Lem. Mexico. This is the only species with broad ribs. Stem globular, rather flat at the top, greyish green, 5 to 10 cm. high and 8 to 11 cm. thick, with 10 to 14 broad and very acute ribs, about 1½ cm. high, deeply notched, with areoles in the notches, 2 to 3 cm. apart, elongated at first woolly. Spines 3 to 5, curved upwards, up to 3½ cm. long, angular and soft, the lowermost cylindrical up to 1½ cm. long. All spines are red at first, passing to horny yellow and finally to greyish. Flowers numerous borne at or near the top, 3 cm. long, and 4 cm. broad, with linear acute petals, whitish with a pink median line. Stamens yellow or reddish, style violet, stigma with 7 to 9 white lobes.

Stenocactus Lloydii (Br. et R.) Berger = *Echinofossulocactus Lloydii* Br. et R. = *Echinocactus Gasseri* Hort. Mexico (Zacatecas). Stem globular, 12 to 14 cm. thick, covered with spines on the sides and top; with very numerous thin ribs, markedly wavy or crisp, with greyish wool on the areoles. Radial spines 10 to 15, white, needle-like, spreading up to 1½ cm. long; central spines 3, much thicker, pale brown, curved upwards, the upper one papery, the other two shorter and thicker. Flower small, very pale pink, the outer petals with a green median nerve, the inner narrower and acute.

Stenocactus hastatus (Hopff.) Berger = *Echinocactus hastatus* Hopff. Mexico. Stem pale green, broadly globular, with about 35 acute wavy ribs. Areoles with white wool. Radial spines 5 or 6, the upper one flat but stiff, yellow, up to 3 cm. long. Central spine only one, straight, flat, stiff, up to 4 cm. long. Flower yellowish white.

Stenocactus tetraxiphus (Otto) Berger = *Echinocactus tetraxiphus* Otto. Mexico (Hidalgo). Stem globular to cylindrical, pale green, about 15 cm. high and up to 10 cm. thick, very abundantly covered with spines at the sides and top. Ribs 30 or more, very thin and wavy, with whitish wool on the areoles. Radial spines 16 to 18, whitish, needle-like, the lowermost up to 1½ cm. long; central spines 4, flattened, the upper one up to 4 cm. long, mostly curved and directed upwards, dark yellow passing to brown, often zoned. Flowers 3 to 5 cm. broad, petals white with a red median nerve, and red at the throat.

Stenocactus multicostatus (Hildm.) Berger = *Echinocactus multicostatus* Hildm. Eastern Mexico. Stem globular, depressed, 6 to 10 cm. broad, grass green. Ribs 80 to 120, very thin, closely pleated together, wavy, each with two areoles, which are round and furnished with white wool. Spines 6 to 9, the 3 upper ones 4 to 8 cm. long, sometimes much less (½ to 1 cm.), upright or spreading, yellowish passing to greyish, thin, flexible and papery, almost angular, the lower ones smaller ½ to 1½ cm. long. Flower 2½ cm. long, whitish, outer petals lanceolate-acute, the inner often obtuse; ovary with very thin, broad and acute scales.

A very interesting species, varying considerably in size, and in the length of the spines, which are sometimes very long, and sometimes almost absent or reduced to 2 to 5, hardly ½ cm. long.

Stenocactus zacatecasensis (Br. et R.) Berger = *Echinofossulocactus zacatecasensis* Br. et R. Mexico (Zacatecas). Globular, pale green, 8 to 10 cm. broad, with about 55 ribs, very thin and wavy, and areoles at first with white wool. Radial spines about 10, spreading, needle-like, white, up to 1 cm. long; central spines 3, brownish, the middle one the longest, flattened, erect, 3 to 4 cm. long, the two others awl-shaped. Flowers 3 to 4 cm. broad, with linear whitish petals tipped pink.

var. **brevispina** Hort. Spines very short.

var. **longispina** Hort. Central spine over 4 cm. long.

Stenocactus Wippermannii (Muehlpf.) Berger = *Echinocactus Wippermannii* Muehlpf. Mexico. Stem globular, dull green, about 8 cm. thick and 6 cm. high, flat at the top and somewhat woolly, with 40 to 50 thin wavy ribs. Areoles round, with white wool. Radial spines 18 to 20, white, curved and brownish at the base, spreading, thin, up to 2 cm. long: central spines 3 or 4, the upper one flattened, erect, up to 3 cm. long, the others spreading, not flattened and shorter. All central spines are reddish brown, tipped dark, later becoming zoned or ringed. Flower dirty yellow, funnel-shaped, about 1½ cm. long, with a dark median nerve on the dorsal side of the petals. *Echinocactus acifer* Hopff. and *E. spinosus* Wegener are considered as synonyms.

Stenocactus lancifer (Dietrich) Berger = *Echinocactus lancifer* (Dietrich) = *E. Dietrichii* Heynhold. Mexico. Stem globular to ovoid, depressed at the top. Ribs numerous, wavy, thickly pleated and very thin. Areoles 2 or 3 on each rib, woolly when young. Spines white or greyish, tipped white or brownish, about 8, some of them broad and flat. Flowers rather large, pale pink, with fully expanded linear oblong obtuse petals.

Stenocactus Boedekerianus Berger = *Echinocactus Boedekerianus* Berger. Mexico (Zacatecas). Globular, flattened at the top, 6 to 7 cm. broad, 5 to 6 cm. high, dull dark green, with spines and white wool at the top. Ribs about 40, thin and wavy. Areoles roundish, 2½ cm. apart. Radial spines about 20, spreading, straight or curved, slender, needle-like, white, up to 1 cm. long. Central spines 6 to 9, bulbous at the base, up to 2½ cm. long, yellowish or brownish, tipped reddish brown, needle-like curved upwards.

Stenocactus pentacanthus (Lem.) Berger = *Echinocactus pentacanthus* Lem. = *E. biceras* Jacobi. Mexico. Globular, flattened and covered with spines at the top, greyish green, about 7 cm. thick. Ribs 30 to 40, closely pleated together, thin, acute and wavy. Areoles 1½ to 2 cm. apart, round, with greyish wool. Spines 5, the upper 3 up to 5 cm. long, spreading, curved upwards, somewhat flattened, stiff, greyish brown, later becoming ringed, the two laterals being angular; the lower two spines of the same colour, and also strongly curved, are only up to 1 cm. long. Flowers about 2 cm. long, surrounded by the spines at the top, funnel-shaped; petals linear, pale yellow, with a violet or purplish midrib.

Stenocactus heteracanthus (Muehlepf.) Berger = *Echinocactus heteracanthus* Muehlepf. Mexico. Closely allied to *S. tetraxiphus*. Globular, dull green, 7 to 8 cm. thick, well protected with spines all round, with 40 to 50 thin, wavy, closely pleated ribs. Areoles about 2 cm. apart along their ribs, and almost bare. Radial spines 10 to 13, spreading star-like, 6 to 7 mm. long, white, yellowish at the base. Central spines 4, the upper one dagger-shaped, flat, erect or incurved, 1½ cm. long, greyish, tipped dark brown, the others angular or cylindrical, about 1 cm. long. All central spines are at first reddish brown.

Stenocactus anfractuosus (Mart.) Berger = *Echinocactus anfractuosus* Mart. Mexico (Hidalgo). Stem solitary, elongated or cylindrical, 7 to 8 cm. thick, and 12 to 15 cm. high, dark bluish green, with at least 30 thin wavy ribs, with oval areoles at first with white wool, later bare. Radial spines 7, the upper 3 flat, dark brown, up to 2½ cm. long, the lower 4 cylindrical, shorter, almost glassy white. One central spine, yellowish brown, up to 2 cm. long.

Stenocactus tricuspidatus (Scheidw.) Berger = *Echinocactus tricuspidatus* Scheidw. = *E. phyllanthus* var. *tricuspidatus* Först. = *E. Melmsianus* Wegener. Mexico. Solitary, globular to short-cylindric, 5 to 7 cm. thick and up to 12 cm. high, pale green to dark green. Ribs 25 to 30, thin and wavy. Areoles small, round or oval, at first with whitish wool, later bare. Spines 9 to 11, the upper 3 leaf-like, equal, or the uppermost a little longer, up to 1 cm. long, at first ruby red, passing to horny brown, tipped darker; the other spines awl-shaped, spreading, cylindrical, glassy white, 5 to 7 mm. long, all equal. Flowers numerous, borne at the centre, small, about 1½ cm. long, funnel-shaped, yellowish green, the outer petals with a brown midrib.

Stenocactus oligacanthus (Salm-Dyck) Berger = *Echinocactus oligacanthus* Salm-Dyck = *E. brachycentrus* var. *oligacantha* Först. Mexico. A robust species, solitary globular to cylindrical, pale green, with white floccose wool at the top, up to 20 cm. high, and up to 15 cm. thick. Ribs about 35, very thin and wavy. Areoles oval, 2 to 3 cm. apart, at first with much snow white wool, later bare. Spines mostly 5, all alike, awl-shaped, reddish yellow when new, passing to amber yellow, tipped darker, the lowermost up to 2½ cm. long.

Stenocactus lamellosus (Dietr.) Berger = *Echinocactus lamellosus* Dietrich. Mexico (Hidalgo). One of the prettiest species, common in cultivation. Stem bluish green, globular, later cylindrical, up to 12 cm. high, and 6 to 8 cm. thick, with about 35 ribs, thin and irregularly wavy. Areoles small, at first with whitish wool. Radial spines 5, flat, the upper ones up to 2 cm. long; only one central spine, flat, straight or slightly curved inwards. 3 to 4 cm. long. All spines white, tipped brown. Flowers about 4 cm. long, not fully expanded; the scales on the ovary are red margined white, and abruptly acute; the petals are linear, acute, narrow, pale pink outside, carmine red inside. Stamens red, style white, stigma with 5 to 8 yellow lobes.

Stenocactus crispatus (DC.) Berger = *Echinocactus crispatus*

DC. = *E. undulatus* Dietr. = *E. flexispinus* Salm-Dyck, non Engelm. Mexico (Hidalgo). Stem globular, later cylindrical, bluish green to greyish, about 8 cm. high, and 7 or 8 cm. thick, with 26 to 35 ribs, acute, thin, very regularly wavy. Areoles 3 to 4 cm. apart, oval, at first with whitish wool, later bare. Radial spines 7 or 8, the upper ones up to 2 cm. long, flattened, horny greyish yellow, straight or slightly curved, the lower ones about half as long and white. Only one central spine, stiff and straight, cylindrical, 2 cm. long, brown, paler at the base and darker at the tip. Flowers about 3½ cm. long, not fully expanded; outer petals oval, white with a broad median violet brown stripe and with a violet edge; the other petals acute, violet, with a carmine red median band. Stamens white, style pale pink, stigma with 8 or 9 creamy lobes.

Stenocactus arrigens (Link et Otto) Berger = *Echinocactus arrigens* Link et Otto = *E. sphaerocephalus* Muehlpf. = *E. xiphacanthus* Miq. = *E. ensifer* Lem. = *E. arrectus* Otto. Mexico. Stem globular, rounded at the top, bluish greeen, with 30 or more ribs, acute and wavy. Spines 5 to 7, the uppermost flattened, curved, yellowish white with a brown tip, and about 2 cm. long, the next pair flat and slightly shorter, yellowish grey, the others cylindrical, shorter and curved backwards. There is no central spine. Flowers up to 2½ cm. long, not fully expanded; petals white with a red median band. Stamens pink, style white, stigma with 6 or 7 yellow lobes.

Stenocactus obvallatus (DC.) Berger = *Echinocactus obvallatus* DC. Mexico (Hidalgo). Differs from the preceding, to which it is very similar, owing to the areoles being closer together (2 cm. apart). Radial spines 7 or 8, the upper one linear, flattened, up to 1 cm. long, the laterals longer, and the lower ones less than 1 cm. long. Only one central spine, straight or slightly curved. The spines are at first red, passing to brown. Flower 2 cm. long, funnel-shaped, more expanded; petals lanceolate obtuse, abruptly acuminate, pale pink, with a purplish red median band. Stamens white, so also the style; stigma with 9 yellow lobes.

Stenocactus gladiatus (Salm-Dyck) Berger = *Echinocactus gladiatus* Salm-Dyck. Mexico. Stem pale green, oval or cylindrical, 6 to 14 cm. high and about 6 cm. thick. Ribs 26 to 30, very acute and thin, uniformly wavy. Areoles in notches 4 to 5 cm. apart, round or elliptical, rather large, at first with whitish wool. Radial spines 4 or 5, spreading crosswise, stiff, erect, somewhat curved, pale yellow to brownish, about 1 cm. long. Only one central spine, thick and stiff, up to 4 cm. long, straight or curved, dirty yellow, finally greyish. Flowers about 2 cm. long, funnel-shaped, the outer petals greenish with a yellowish margin; the inner lanceolate-acute, often toothed, clear sulphur yellow. Stamens, style and 6- or 7-lobed stigma yellow.

Stenocactus phyllacanthus (Mart.) Berger = *Echinocactus phyllacanthus* Mart. Mexico (Hidalgo). Stem globular, somewhat depressed, dark green, the top covered with spines, about 8 cm. high. Ribs 30 or more, thin and wavy; areoles 2½ to 3 cm. apart, round or oval, at first with white wool. Spines about 8, the upper ones flattened, lanceolate, keeled, 4 to 8 cm. long, erect, at first red, passing to brown, often ringed; the other spines spreading, awl-shaped and more slender. Flowers 1½ cm. long, short funnel-shaped; petals yellowish or white; with a reddish median nerve. Stamens and style white, stigma with 5 or 6 yellowish lobes.

Stenocactus violaciflorus (Quehl)Berger = *Echinocactus violaciflorus* Quehl. Mexico (Zacatecas). Stem globular or elongated, 8 to 10 cm. thick, dull bluish green. Ribs about 35, wavy and thin, with round areoles about 2 cm. apart, at first with greyish wool. Spines 7, the upper one linear-lanceolate, flattened, up to 3 cm. long, and ½ cm. broad, curved upwards, keeled and ringed, at first yellowish tipped brown, later greyish; the other spines spreading, shorter and thicker, the lowermost pair about 1 cm. long. Flowers 2½ cm. long, petals white with a violet median band. Stamens and style violet, stigma with 9 yellowish lobes.

Stenocactus dichroacanthus (Mart.) Berger = *Echinocactus dichroacanthus* Mart. Mexico (Hidalgo, near Zimapań). Stem oval or almost cylindrical, pale green, with about 32 acute, thin, wavy ribs. Areoles 2 to 4 cm. apart, round, at first with whitish wool. Spines about 6, somewhat flattened, straight, ringed, at first ruby red, passing to dark red, the lower ones yellowish white, the longest spines up to 2 cm. long. The plant is up to 20 cm. high, and about 8 cm. thick.

Stenocactus grandicornis (Lem.) Berger = *Echinocactus grandicornis* Lem. Mexico. Stem oval or almost cylindrical, 10 to 12 cm. high, bluish green, spiny at the top, with about 35 acute and wavy ribs. Areoles oval, rather large and regularly arranged, about ½ cm. long, at first with yellowish white wool. Radial spines 8, the lowermost about 1 cm. long, the upper ones shorter, straight or slightly curved, whitish passing to greyish. Central spines 3, very strong and broad, up to 5 cm. long, the upper one straight, the laterals curved symmetrically like horns; the central spines are at first yellow and dark purplish at the tip, passing to greyish. Flower 3 cm. long, funnel-shaped, the outer petals greenish white, the inner white with a brown central band. Stamens and style white, stigma with 6 yellow lobes.

Stenocactus Vaupelianus Werd. et Backbg. = *Echinocactus Vaupelianus* Werd. Mexico. Stem solitary, globular to oval, 9 cm. high and 7 to 9 cm. thick, dull green, with white wool and white or dark spines at the top. Ribs 30 to 40, very thin, wavy, 5 to 8 mm. high. Areoles 1½ to 2 cm. apart, at first well furnished with white wool. Radial spines 12 to 25, radiating, needle-like, transparent white, often tipped dark, straight, 1 to 1½ cm. long. Central spines 1 or 2, up to 7 cm. long, awl-shaped or somewhat flattened, acute, straight or incurved, brownish black, passing to reddish brown. Flowers 2 cm. long, petals creamy yellow with a dark median band. A beautiful new species, to be grown in a dry sandy soil.

Stenocactus albatus (Dietrich) = *Echinocactus albatus* Dietrich. Mexico. This is a very lovely species, and probably the most popular. Stem single, like all other species very rarely sprouting from the base or sides, globular and depressed at the top, becoming oval or almost cylindrical with age; bluish green, with much white wool and long spines at the top. Ribs very numerous, acute, thin, uniformly wavy and pleated together, notched at the areoles, which are rather large and 1½ to 2 cm. apart, at first with abundant white wool, the stem being from 6 to 12 cm. in diameter. Radial spines about 10, bristle-like and partly erect, about 1 cm. long. Central spines 4, much thicker and longer, the upper most up to 4½ cm. long, erect, straight or curved inwards, flattened and sabre-shaped, the others are about half as long, and of similar shape. All spines are yellowish white. Flowers about 2 cm. long, funnel-shaped, with lanceolate-acute petals, pure white. Stamens and style white, stigma with 7 yellowish lobes.

Stenocactus confusus (Br. et R.). Mexico. Stem single, pale green, ovoid or elongated, 6 to 15 cm. high and 6 to 8 cm. thick, with 25 to 30 thin, low, wavy ribs. Areoles 2 to 3 cm. apart, at first woolly, afterwards bare. Spines awl-shaped, all yellow: radial spines 4 or 5, slightly flattened, 7 to 10 mm. long; central spine only one, spreading, up to 4 cm. long. Flowers purplish, 4 cm. broad, with oblong acute petals.

Recently the following new species from the same region (Mexico) have been described under the generic name of *Echinofossulocactus*, and are now offered by dealers for cultivation: **Stenocactus Bravoiae** Tiegel, **S. carneus** Tiegel, **S. densispinus** Tiegel, **S. ochoterrenaus** Tiegel, **S. rectispinus** Tiegel, **S. sphacelatus** Tiegel and **S. Rosasianus** Helia Bravo.

FEROCACTUS Br. et R.

Stem globular or cylindrical, often quite large, with thick and prominent ribs, very well armed with spines, which are long, thick and stiff, the central one often hooked. There is an extra-nuptial nectary on the upper or inner side of the areoles. Flowers fairly large, bell-shaped, red, violet or yellow, borne on the upper or inner part of the young areoles at or near the centre. Ovary and tube with many scales, but without wool in their axils. Fruit oblong, dry, splitting or dehiscing by a basal pore. Seeds black, pitted.

Includes about 34 species, many of which are of imposing proportions, and all of them deserving of cultivation. *Ferocactus* means ferocious Cactus, a good descriptive name and well justified by the fierce aspect of the armament of spines of most species. They are natives of Mexico, Texas, California and Arizona.

Ferocactus acanthodes (Lem.) Br. et R. = *Echinocactus acanthodes* Lem. = *E. cylindraceus* Engelm. = *E. Lecontei* Hort. non Engelm. Southern California. Plant solitary, or rarely sprouting from the base. Stem oval, oval-cylindrical or columnar, up to 3 m. high and up to 80 cm. thick, glaucous green, with 13 to 23 broad, obtuse ribs, slightly wavy, entirely covered with long curved spines. In cultivation it is rarely more than 1 m. high and 35 cm. thick at the base. Areoles in depressions along the ribs 1½ to 2 cm. apart, oval, about 1 cm. long, at first with short yellowish wool, later greyish or naked. Spines white, yellowish, reddish or red. Radial spines 9 to 13, up to 4½ cm. long, curved, of various colours or zoned, mostly cylindrical, very sharp. Central spines 4, the upper and the lower being angular or flattened, up to 12 cm. long, all being spreading and strongly curved, but not hooked at the tip. Flowers yellow or orange, up to 5 cm. long, lobes of stigma about 14, yellow, long. Fruit roundish to oblong, about 2 cm. thick. Seeds large. An attractive species, with its long curved spines, variously coloured. Like all species of Ferocactus, requires full sunshine and warmth, and a moderately rich soil, porous and perfectly drained, consisting of garden loam, leaf-mould or old cow manure, gravel or stone chippings or crushed bricks, with much old mortar or hard limestone gravel, and should be kept rather dry.

Ferocactus Lecontei (Engelm.) Br. et R. = *Echinocactus Lecontei* Engelm. Northern Mexico, Lower California, Arizona. Stem globular or oval, in old age cylindrical, up to 2 m. high and about 80 cm. thick, dark green passing to greyish green, with 13 to 24 ribs, acute and straight, up to 3 cm. high. Areoles 2 to 3 cm. apart, large, elliptical, and up to 2 cm. long, with short yellowish wool passing to brownish. Spines flattened, curved and flexible. One central spine not hooked at the tip, up to 5 cm. long, ringed like a file. Flowers yellow, 4 cm. long. Seeds smaller.

Ferocactus Wislizeni (Engelm.) Br. et R. = *Echinocactus Wislizeni* Engelm. = *E. Emoryi* Engelm. (pro parte). = *E. arizonicus* Kunze. Texas, Sonora and Arizona. Stem at first globular, depressed at the top, later oval, in old age cylindrical and over 2 m. high, and 80 cm. to 1 m. thick, dark green passing to greyish green. Ribs 15 to 25, up to 3 cm. high, rather acute, with large oval areoles about 2 cm. long and 2 to 3 cm. apart, at first with yellowish wool passing to brown or grey, finally bare. Radial spines about 20, whitish or yellowish, bristle-like or awl-shaped, up to 5 cm. long. Central spines 4, longer, very thick, flat, strongly hooked at the tip, all ringed transversely, at first yellowish or reddish, passing to reddish brown. Flowers 5 to 6 cm. long, bell-shaped or funnel-shaped, with a green tube. Ovary and tube furnished with kidney-shaped scales. Outer petals green; the inner longer, reddish yellow, acute. Stamens, style and 18- to 20-lobed stigma yellow. Fruit oblong, yellow, scaly, 4 to 5 cm. long. Thrives well in cultivation and like *F. acanthodes* and *F. rectispinus* may attain quite a large size.

Ferocactus horridus Br. et R. Lower California. Similar to *F. Wislizeni*, but more strongly armed. Stem globular, or becoming elongated, 30 to 40 cm. thick, with 13 broad, obtuse ribs, 2 cm. high. Areoles large, oval, 1½ to 2½ cm. apart. Radial spines 8 to 12, slender, white, spreading, 3 to 4 cm. long; central spines 6 to 8, reddish, very strong, spreading outward, straight, 5 to 7 cm. long, one of them up to 12 cm. long, flattened, strongly hooked. Very rare in cultivation. Possibly another form of *E. Emoryi* Engelm.

Ferocactus rectispinus Br. et R. = *Echinocactus Emoryi rectispinus* Engelm. Lower California. One of the largest species, in its native country reaching a height of over 2 m. with a diameter of over 60 cm. Now not rare in cultivation. Stem dark green, or dark greyish green globular to cylindrical, with 13 to 24 obtuse ribs, rather wavy, straight along the sides and spiral at the top, where they are also more acute. Areoles on prominences of the ribs, 3 to 4 cm. apart, large, about 3 cm. long, roundish to oval, later elliptical or linear, with short whitish wool, passing to greyish. Radial bristles 10, flat, ringed, white, about 2½ cm. long. Radial spines 7 to 9, awl-shaped, somewhat angular, straight or curved, white or reddish, ringed, 3 to 6 cm. long. Central spine only one, flat, erect, straight, or slightly curved towards the tip, very thick and stiff, reddish brown, but like the radials red when young, strongly ringed, up to 13 cm. long. Flower large, yellow, 6 to 7 cm. long, the inner petals lanceolate-acute, toothed, the outer petals being lanceolate-obtuse, flushed reddish brown. Stamens half as long as the petals, stigma with 18 to 20 purple-red lobes.

Ferocactus chrysacanthus (Orc.) Br. et R. = *Echinocactus chrysacanthus* Orcutt. = *E. Emoryi chrysacanthus* Hort. Lower California. A species of smaller size, about 1 m. high, and 30 to 40 cm. in diameter. Stem dull greyish green, with 13 to 20 ribs, as above, with protuberances on which are roundish or oval areoles, large, 2 to 3 cm. apart, with whitish wool when young, passing to brownish or almost naked. Radial spines 4 to 6, slender, white; other spines 4 to 10, mostly curved at the tip, and angular or flattened, the longest 5 to 7 cm. long, at first all red, soon passing to yellow or brownish yellow. Rather delicate in cultivation.

var. **rubrispina** Haage jr. A rare form with red spines.

Ferocactus peninsulae (Weber) Br. et R. = *Echinocactus peninsulae* Weber. Southern part of Lower California. Stem globular, somewhat depressed at the top, later cylindrical, up to 2½ m. high, and 30 to 50 cm. thick at the base, dark glaucous green, passing to greyish green, with about 18 thick ribs, straight, bearing large roundish areoles 2 to 4 cm. apart, with brownish wool. Spines at first red, tipped yellow: the radials about 11, spreading, flattened, soft, straight, white, the lower ones being thicker up to 3 cm. long; the centrals 5 to 7 or 8, the outer, ones being spreading, cylindrical, ringed, very acute and straight, reddish brown or dark reddish grey, 3 to 5 cm. long, and a central one directed outwards, of the same colour, flat, about ½ cm. broad, ringed, 6 to 7 cm. long, strongly hooked at the tip. Flowers about 4 cm. long, funnel-shaped; outer petals brownish violet; inner petals narrower, violet, toothed, with a carmine red median band. Stamens purplish red, stigma with 12 to 15 reddish yellow lobes.

Ferocactus Orcuttii (Engelm.) Br. et R. = *Echinocactus Orcuttii*

Engelm. Lower California (Palm Valley). Stem at first globular, later columnar, up to 1 m. high and 30 cm. thick, round at the top, light green passing to dark green, branching at the base and forming groups. Ribs 13 to 22, obtuse, rounded, about 2 cm. high, straight below, spiral at the top. Areoles large, oval, 1½ cm. long, and 3½ to 4 cm. apart, with greyish wool. Radial spines about 12, spreading, cylindrical, stiff, straight, ringed, the lower ones thicker, shorter and hooked, 1 to 2 cm. long. Central spines about 7, the lower ones thicker, angular, up to 3 cm. long, the upper 3 being shorter and directed upwards. The radials are at first whitish and the centrals dirty yellow, later all become horny grey. Flower 4 cm. long, bell-shaped; the inner petals are carmine red, edged greenish yellow. Rare in cultivation. There is also a cristate form.

Ferocactus Stainesii (Hook.) Br. et R. = *Echinocactus pilosus* Galeotti = *E. pilifer* Lem. = *E. Stainesii* Hooker. The original *Echinocactus Stainesii* Hook. (written incorrectly *Steinsii* by Salm-Dyck and others), was only a variety or form of *E. pilosus* Gal., and this name should have precedence. Mexico (San Luis Potosi). Stem at first globular, pale green, with a rounded top, later cylindrical, up to 1½ m. high, and 25 to 30 cm. thick, sprouting at the base when old. Ribs 15 to 20, straight, acute, notched into rounded warts, about 4 cm. high. Areoles elliptical, 3 to 4 cm. apart, and about 1 cm. long with short yellowish wool passing to greyish. Radial spines 4 to 6, awl-shaped, stiff, straight or slightly curved, up to 2 cm. long, mixed with many long white bristles, soft and hair-like, 2 to 3 cm. long. Central spines 4, crosswise, yellowish, thicker and more curved, 3 to 4 cm. long. All spines are ringed transversely, and at first of a lively red or ruby red, retaining this colour for a long time, afterwards yellowish passing to greyish. Flowers 4 cm. long, bell-shaped, orange-red. A popular species, very frequently grown on account of its ruby red spines, and its resistance under adverse conditions. There is also a form with violet flowers.

var. **flavispinus** Hort. Spines at first pale red, passing to yellow. Flowers yellow.

Ferocactus Pringlei (Rose) Br. et R. = *Echinocactus Pringlei* Rose = *E. pilosus* var. *Pringlei* Coult. Central Mexico. One of the largest species, up to 3 m. high and about 50 cm. thick. Not unlike the preceding, branching from the base and forming groups. Ribs 16 to 18, with large areoles thickly set, oval or confluent together, with short yellowish wool and long hair-like, straw-coloured bristles. Spines as above, red, thick, very stiff, ringed, straight or curved, but not hooked. Flowers 4 or 4½ cm. long, bell-shaped, red or orange red outside, yellow inside. Rare in cultivation.

Ferocactus Covillei Br. et R. = *Echinocactus Covillei* Berger = *E. Emoryi* Engelm. (pro parte). Northern Sonora and southern Arizona. Stem bluish green, passing to greyish green, up to 1½ m. high and up to 60 cm. thick. Ribs up to 32, thick, obtuse, deeply notched into prominences along the sides, thinner and somewhat spiral at the centre, with large oval areoles 3 to 4 cm. apart, with short brownish wool. Spines red or white, ringed; the radials 5 to 8, awl-shaped, straight or curved backwards, 3 to 6 cm. long; one central spine mostly flat and hooked, 5 to 8 cm. long. Flowers reddish or tipped yellow, or entirely yellow, 6 to 7 cm. long, with the inner petals linear-acute, often serrate. Fruit oblong, 5 cm. long, scaly; seeds 2 mm. long. Very exceptionally sprouting from the base. Similar to *F. rectispinus*, but in this species the central spine is longer, always very straight and erect, and never curved, although often slightly hooked at the tip.

The original species, *Echinocactus Emoryi* Engelm (1848), has been divided into 4 or more species, but it is not unlikely that a further study of this princely genus of Cacti, may bring about a revival of the name as the typical species, reducing the others to the status of well-marked varieties.

Ferocactus nobilis (L.) Br. et R. = *Cactus nobilis* L. = *C. recurvus* Miller = *Echinocactus recurvus* Link et Otto = *E. spiralis* Karw. = *E. curvicornis* Miq. Mexico. Stem solitary, globular, usually greyish green, up to 25 cm. high, and 20 cm. thick, more or less rounded at the top, with 10 to 14 prominent and acute ribs, up to 3 cm. high, straight, notched. Areoles 2 to 4 cm. apart, round, with short greyish wool. Radial spines 8, reddish, awl-shaped, thick and stiff, 2½ cm. long. Only one central spine, flattened on the upper surface, very strong, 4 to 5 cm. long, strongly hooked at the tip, of the same colour. When young the smaller spines are yellowish, the others of a lively red. Flowers 5 cm. long, bell-shaped; ovary and the outer petals with many brown scales, edged with white hairs; the inner petals pink red with a darker midrib. Stamens and style purplish, stigma with 19 yellowish lobes. More commonly known as *Ferocactus recurvus*.

var. **spiralis** (Karw.) K. Sch. = *E. spiralis* Karw. Ribs more or less straight at the sides, spiral at the centre.

A beautiful species, now frequently imported, and also easily raised from seed. At first slow to establish itself, but afterwards makes good growth. Should be well matured at the close of summer, and allowed to shrivel a little.

Ferocactus latispinus (Haw.) Br. et R. = *Cactus latispinus* Haw. = *Echinocactus corniger* DC. = *E. latispinus* Hemsl. Eastern and central Mexico, up to 3,000 m. above the sea. A well-known and very popular species, frequently imported and also easily raised from seed. Stem half-globular or broadly globular, flattened and depressed at the top, greyish green, 25 to 30 cm. high, with 8 to 14 ribs when young, up to 21 when adult, rather narrow and acute, 1½ to 2½ cm. high, notched, bearing in the notches large roundish areoles, up to 4 cm. apart, with short greyish wool. Radial spines 6 to 12, spreading, 2 to 2½ cm. long, white or red, ringed. Central spines 4, ringed, much stronger, and more highly coloured, red when young, passing to reddish, erect or directed outwards, up to 3½ cm. long, the lower one being strongly hooked at

(b) ARIOCARPUS TRIGONUS

(a) ARIOCARPUS RETUSUS

PLATE XL

(b) EPITHELANTHA MICROMERIS

(a) ENCEPHALOCARPUS STROBILIFORMIS

PLATE XLI

the tip, longer, flattened, up to 7 mm. broad, very much like that of the preceding species. Flowers 3½ cm. long, with brown scales, edged with short white hairs on the outside; inner petals very acute, whitish or reddish, toothed; stigma with 10 to 12 lobes. Fruit oblong, very scaly, 2 cm. long. Frequently the flowers are mauve to deep violet blue, with a red stigma.

var. **flavispinus** Haage jr. Spines longer and narrower, yellow or yellowish red.

var. **latispinus** Hort. Often confused with the type, has the central hooked spine broader, 7 to 8 mm., and rather short.

Ferocactus Fordii (Orc.) Br. et R. = *Echinocactus Fordii* Orcutt. Lower California, where it grows up to 40 cm. high. Stem globular, with a slight depression at the centre, greyish green, with about 21 ribs, acute and slightly notched. Areoles 2 cm. apart, with greyish wool. Radial spines about 15, needle-like, white, spreading; central spines 4, ringed, the longest one erect, spreading outwards, flat, hooked at the tip, up to 4 cm. long. Flowers 4 cm. long, pink, with the inner petals linear-acute. Stamens pink, style and lobes of stigma whitish or yellowish. An interesting and beautiful species, resistant, and grows well from seed.

Ferocactus crassihamatus (Weber) Br. et R. = *Echinocactus crassihamatus* Weber = *E. Mathssonii* Berger. Mexico (Queretaro). Stem 10 to 15 cm. thick, dull bluish green, with 13 prominent and obtuse ribs, notched into plump and prominent tubercles on which are large round areoles, about 3 cm. apart, furnished with white wool and with a woolly furrow on the upper part of the tubercle. Radial spines 7 to 11, up to 3 cm. long, very stiff and acute, yellowish to reddish, paler at the tip, the lower three spines being hooked downwards at the tip. Central spine 1 or more, 4 to 6 cm. long, somewhat flat towards the base, hooked laterally at the tip, red or yellow, semi-diaphanous, paler at the tip. Flowers borne at the centre, from the furrow at the upper end of the areole, 2½ to 3 cm. long, funnel-shaped, petals violet, edged white, greenish red on the tube. Stamens and style reddish, stigma white. A beautiful species, very resistant and easily grown in half-shade.

Ferocactus Rostii Br. et R. = *Echinocactus Rostii* Berger. Texas and California, where it grows up to 3 m. high. It is similar to *F. acanthodes*, but the stem is thinner and the spines are more curved. The ribs are low, 16 to 22, with areoles closer together, large, furnished with white wool and with many spines. Central spines 3 or 4, yellow or reddish, strongly curved in all directions, but not hooked. Stem sometimes branching from the base forming groups. Radial spines 6 to 9, and radial bristles 2 to 8, white or yellowish. Flowers dark yellow; fruit red.

Ferocactus macrodiscus (Mart.) Br. et R. = *Echinocactus macrodiscus* Mart. = *E. campylacanthus* Scheidw. Mexico (San Luis Potosi), up to 3,000 m. above sea level. Stem semi-globular or strongly depressed

289

T

at the top, 20 to 25 cm. broad, pale green, with 16 to 21 acute ribs, about 2 cm. high, notched, with areoles in the notches $1\frac{1}{2}$ to 3 cm. apart. New areoles with abundant pale yellowish wool. Radial spines 6 to 8, spreading, curved symmetrically, reddish yellow or blood red, 2 cm. long; the centrals 4, thicker and more strongly curved, the lowermost curved upwards, up to $3\frac{1}{2}$ cm. long. Flower funnel-shaped, 5 cm. long, the inner petals slightly longer than the outer, glossy carmine red, linear-lanceolate, minutely fringed and with a darker median line or band.

var. **multiflorus** R. Mey. Spines tawny yellow. More free-flowering.

Ferocactus californicus (Monv.) = *Echinocactus californicus* Monv. Lower California. Not unlike *Ferocactus rectispinus*, but smaller. Stem globular to short-cylindric, bluish green, with 15 to 20 straight, obtuse, notched ribs. Areoles large, oval, with short greyish wool. Radial spines 5 to 9, straight, stiff, awl-shaped, up to 4 cm. long, more or less ringed. Central spines 4, the upper 3 straight, erect and thick, the lower one up to 6 cm. long, strongly ringed, curved at the tip, more dark-coloured. All spines are at first reddish or yellowish, passing to maroon. Flower 6 cm. long, funnel-shaped, reddish yellow; stamens deep red. **Ferocactus gracilis** Gates, from the same district, is probably a more slender variety, with white radials, and red or reddish brown centrals.

Ferocactus haematacanthus (Monv.) Br. et R. = *Echinocactus haematacanthus* Monv. = *E. Gerardii* Weber. = *E. electracanthus haematacanthus* Salm-Dyck. Central Mexico. Stem solitary, sometimes sprouting from the base, globular to short columnar, up to 50 cm. high and 30 cm. thick, rounded and woolly at the top, grass green, with 12 to 20 straight, broad ribs, notched. Spines blood red, tipped yellow; 6 radials, stiff, straight, awl-shaped; 4 centrals, thicker and stronger, up to 6 cm. long, the lower one curved downwards. Flowers 6 cm. long, purplish red. Fruit oblong, 3 cm. long, purple, with roundish purple scales edged white.

Ferocactus Diguetii (Weber) Br. et R. = *Echinocactus Diguetii* Weber. Lower California (Islands of the Gulf of California). One of the largest species. Stem elongated or cylindrical, up to 4 m. high and 80 cm. thick, rounded at the top and very spiny. Ribs about 34, straight and acute, later almost flat down the stem. Areoles $1\frac{1}{2}$ cm. apart, oval, about 1 cm. long, with yellowish red wool when young. Spines 6 or 7, almost all alike, slender, needle-like, not ringed, the central one also straight or slightly curved, but not hooked, reddish yellow passing to greyish yellow, 6 to 7 cm. long. Flowers up to 7 cm. long, funnel-shaped, outer petals oval, obtuse, reddish brown; the inner lanceolate, yellow. Ovary and tube with many crescent-like scales, but without hairs or bristles. Stem mostly solitary.

Ferocactus melocactiformis (DC.) Br. et R. = *Echinocactus melocactiformis* DC. = *E. electracanthus* Lem. = *E. oxypterus* Zucc. = *E. Coulteri* G. Don. Eastern Mexico. Plant usually solitary in cultivation, but sprouting at the base in its native country. Stem globular, somewhat flattened at the top, 30 to 60 cm. high, and 20 to 30 cm. thick, becoming elongated with age, pale green passing to bluish green or greyish, with few ribs when young, and with up to 25 ribs when adult. Ribs acute, up to 2 cm. high, with oval areoles 2 to 4 cm. apart, at first with short yellowish wool, later greyish on prominences into which the ribs are notched. Radial spines about 8, up to 4 cm. long, straight or slightly curved, cylindrical, slightly ringed, at first pale yellow, passing to horny yellow, often reddish or greyish at the tip. Central spines 1 to 4, mostly 3, straight like the others, but thicker and up to 6 cm. long. Flower funnel-shaped, 3½ cm. long, pale yellow, reddish outside, stigma with 6 green lobes. A popular species, and easily grown from seed, but growth is slow at first.

Ferocactus rafaelensis (Purpus) Br. et R. = *Echinocactus rafaelensis* Purpus. Mexico (San Luis Potosi, Minas de San Rafael). Not unlike *F. melocactiformis* in habit of growth, but smaller. Stem broadly globular, later elongated, rather flat and spiny at the top, bluish green, with 14 to 22 acute ribs, 2 to 3 cm. high, and slightly wavy. Areoles large, oval, with whitish wool, passing to brown or grey. Radial spines about 8, star-like, mostly recurved, 3 to 4 cm. long, awl-shaped, ringed, very stiff and acute, at first reddish, passing to whitish yellow or dirty yellow or brownish, finally greyish. One central spine, straight, ringed, directed downwards, often angular, thicker, 5 to 7 cm. long, same colour, but darker towards the tip. Flowers yellow.

Ferocactus santa-maria (Rose) Br. et R. = *Echinocactus santa-maria* Rose. Lower California (Santa Maria Bay). Stem mostly solitary, up to about 60 cm. high, very strongly armed. Ribs about 14. Outer spines several, thread-like. Central spines in two series; all straight, awl-shaped, somewhat flattened, ringed, greyish; the central spine longer, flattened, thicker and dagger-like, directed upwards, somewhat curved at the tip. Flowers 6 to 7 cm. long. Fruit 3 to 4 cm. long, with round scales; seeds 2 mm. long, minutely reticulated.

Ferocactus alamosanus Br. et R. = *Echinocactus alamosanus* Br. et R. Mexico (Southern Sonora, Alamos Mount). Stem usually solitary, rarely clustering, globular, somewhat flattened at the top, green, 30 cm. thick, later becoming elongated to about 50 cm. Ribs about 20, narrow. Spines all yellow, about 8 radials, 3 to 4 cm. long, spreading. One central spine, erect or spreading outwards, somewhat flattened laterally, very straight, about 6 cm. long. Flower clear yellow.

Ferocactus tortulospinus Gates. Lower California. Stem globular or conical, later cylindrical, up to 60 cm. high, dull greyish green, with 16 to 20 ribs, rather acute. Areoles large, with brown wool, 3 or 4 cm. apart. Radial spines about 10, awl-shaped, spreading, reddish to brownish, 3 to 4 cm. long. Centrals 4 or 5, flattened, ringed, 5 to 6 cm. long, 1 or 2 being longer, up to 8 cm., erect, spreading, twisted, curved, slightly hooked at the tip, of a beautiful pink when young, passing to reddish.

Ferocactus Townsendianus Br. et R. Lower California. Plant of medium growth, with a globular stem, later short-cylindrical, grass green passing to greyish green, with broad obtuse ribs, deeply notched. Areoles on the prominences between the notches, about 3 cm. apart, large, with greyish wool. Radial spines about 8, spreading, brown, passing to greyish, about 3 cm. long. Centrals 5, slightly flattened, ringed, brown, hooked at the tip. Flower 5 to 6 cm. long, outer petals reddish edged yellow, inner petals pink with broad greenish yellow margins. Stamens and style dark pink, stigma with pale greenish lobes.

Ferocactus coloratus Gates. Lower California. Similar to the preceding in habit, the radial spines being thicker and ringed, the 5 centrals being thicker and longer, 6 to 7 cm., and hooked at the tip. All spines are of a beautiful crimson when young, passing to reddish or mahogany.

Ferocactus robustus (Link et Otto) Br. et R. = *Echinocactus robustus* Link et Otto, non Karw. = *E. agglomeratus* Karw. = *E. Galeottii* Scheidw. Mexico (Puebla). Stem freely sprouting from the base, forming large clumps; globular or oval, 10 to 20 cm. thick, dark glossy green, with 8 acute ribs. Areoles round, $1\frac{1}{2}$ to $3\frac{1}{2}$ cm. apart, with 10 to 14 radial spines, bristle-like, yellowish, and 4 to 6 central spines, often somewhat flattened, up to 6 cm. long, straight, brownish yellow at the base. Flowers yellow, funnel-shaped, about 4 cm. long, inner petals lanceolate, narrow, golden yellow, stigma with 10 reddish lobes. Fruit ovoid, about 2 cm. long, covered with green round scales. Grows quickly from seed, and is also easily propagated by means of the branches or sprouts borne abundantly around the base and up the stem.

Ferocactus echidne (DC.) Br. et R. = *Echinocactus echidne* DC. (often written *echidna*) = *E. gilvus* Dietr. = *E. dolichacanthus* Lem. = *E. dolichocentrus* Salm-Dyck. Mexico (Hidalgo). Stem mostly solitary, globular, in its native country sprouting around the base and with 20 heads or more, pale green, passing to greyish green, up to 20 cm. high, with about 14 ribs, acute and straight or slightly wavy. Areoles 2 to 3 cm. apart, elliptical or broadly linear, with greyish wool. Radial spines 7 or 8, at first amber yellow, passing to greyish, slightly curved. Only one central spine, thicker and longer, up to 4 cm., straight or slightly recurved downwards. Flowers 3 cm. long, outer petals oval, greenish yellow; inner petals lanceolate, toothed, glossy yellow; stamens, style and 10-lobed stigma yellow.

Ferocactus glaucescens (DC.) Br. et R. = *Echinocactus glaucescens* DC. Central Mexico. Stem mostly solitary, but often sprouting around the base, globular, becoming slightly elongated with age, 20 to 40 cm. high and about 20 cm. thick, in the typical form pale greyish green and intensely glaucous, with 11 to 15 acute ribs, 2 to $3\frac{1}{2}$ cm. high. Areoles oval or elongated, about 1 cm. long and 1 cm. apart, with yellow wool, later almost bare. Radial spines 6, spreading, erect, awl-shaped, ringed, amber yellow, 3 to 4 cm. long; only one central spine, or absent, about the same length and colour. Flower funnel-shaped, 3 to 3½ cm. long, petals glossy yellow, lanceolate, finely toothed or ciliated. Stamens style and 12- to 15-lobed stigma yellow. The flowers last in bloom for over one week. A very attractive species of easy cultivation; grows quickly from seed.

var. **Pfeifferi** (Zucc.) = *Echinocactus Pfeifferi* Zucc. Stem far less glaucous and more greyish green or dull green; spines mostly honey-coloured passing to greyish.

Ferocactus viridescens (Torr. and Gray) Br. et R. = *Echinocactus viridescens* Torrey et Gray = *E. Californicus* Hort. non Monv. Southern California. Stem single, or occasionally sprouting at the base, globular, depressed at the top, later becoming elongated, 25 to 40 cm. high and 25 to 35 cm. thick, glossy dark green, with 13 to 21 broad and obtuse ribs 1 to 2 cm. high, slightly notched at the areoles, which are 1½ to 2½ cm. apart, roundish or oval, with short whitish wool, later almost bare. Radial spines 9 to 20, spreading, awl-shaped, ringed, straight or slightly curved, about 2 cm. long, at first red, passing to greenish red. Central spines 4, crosswise, thicker and longer, straight or curved sideways, up to 3½ cm. long, same colour as the radials. Flowers about 4 cm. long, green or yellowish green; tube and ovary with oblong obtuse scales; petals linear, obtuse, toothed, greenish yellow with a brown median band. Stamens and style yellowish or greenish, stigma with 12 to 15 lobes. Fruit roundish, up to 2 cm. long, scaly, bluish green.

Ferocactus flavovirens (Scheidw.) Br. et R. = *Echinocactus flavo-virens* Scheidw. = *E. poliocentrus* Lem. Mexico (Tehuacan). Stem at first solitary, afterwards freely sprouting from the base, globular to short-columnar, grass green, yellowish green at the top and centre, 30 to 40 cm. high, bearing round or oval areoles, greyish, up to 2 cm. apart. Radial spines about 14, spreading, up to 2 cm. long; central spines 4, the lower 5 to 8 cm. long. All spines are awl-shaped, stiff, ringed, at first red, passing to brown and grey, often dirty yellow or straw-coloured. Flowers reddish yellow, funnel-shaped, 3 to 4 cm. long, with linear-lanceolate ciliated petals.

Ferocactus Johnsonii (Parry) Br. et R. = *Echinocactus Johnsonii* Parry. Western Utah and southern Nevada. Stem mostly solitary oval to short-columnar, 10 to 30 cm. high, and 8 to 10 cm. broad, olive green or dull green, very spiny all round and at the top. Ribs 17 to 21, acute, low, straight, notched above the areoles; these are 2 to 3 cm. apart, oval, hardly woolly. Radial spines 10 to 14, spreading, straight, slender, mostly white, the lower 3 to 4 red or reddish grey, up to 3½ cm. long. Central spines 8 to 10, in two series, all red, straight, awl-shaped, spreading, 4 of them being thicker and longer than the others, spreading outwards crosswise, up to 5 cm. long. The young spines are of a lovely crimson red. Flowers borne at the top, 5 to 6½ cm. long, funnel-shaped, with a scaly ovary, petals pale red to carmine. Seeds minutely pitted.

CACTI

var. **octocentra** Coult. Has 8 shorter central spines, bulbous at the base, curved upwards, red above. Flower smaller.

Ferocactus Johnstonianus (Turner) Br. et R. = *Echinocactus Johnstonianus* Turner. A very rare species from Lower California (Island Angel de la Guarda). Stem solitary, globular to short-cylindric, up to 35 cm. thick and up to 60 cm. high. Ribs 24 to 31, acute, wavy along the margin. Areoles oval and closely set. Spines about 20, awl-shaped, all alike, slightly recurved outwards, not hooked, about 7 cm. long, golden yellow passing to brownish. Flowers about 5 cm. long, ovary and tube with round scales, petals red above, deep yellow below: stigma pale pink, with 8 to 13 lobes. Fruit roundish, about 2½ cm. long. Closely allied to *F. Diguetii*.

ECHINOMASTUS Br. et R.

Plants of small size; stem usually solitary, globular or short cylindrical, with low ribs more or less arranged spirally, notched into warts more or less prominent, bearing woolly areoles, with numerous straight needle-like spines. Flowers purple, borne on the new areoles at the centre. Fruit small, dry, scaly. Seeds large, black. Includes 7 species, natives of Mexico, Texas and Arizona, all furnished with beautiful spines.

They are resistant species, requiring warmth and full sunshine, but thriving well in any good porous soil, rich in lime and in leaf-mould. They are free-flowering, producing several crops of very attractive flowers throughout the summer, and should be kept rather dry in winter.

Echinomastus erectocentrus (Coult.) Br. et R. = *Echinocactus erectocentrus* Coult. South-east Arizona. Stem globular, bluish green, 4½ to 9 cm. thick, with 21 acute ribs, notched into rounded warts, on which are elongated areoles. Radial spines 14 to 18, spreading, comb-like and curved on the stem, white tipped dark, about 1 cm. long. Only one central spine, erect or curved inwards, up to 1½ cm. long, at first red, later white, dark or black towards the tip. Flowers reddish purple, 3 to 5 cm. long; stigma with 8 red lobes. Ovary with a few dry scales.

Echinomastus Macdowellii (Reb.) Br. et R. = *Echinocactus Macdowellii* Reb. Northern Mexico. A most beautiful species, with a pale green stem, solitary, globular or elongated, 8 to 15 cm. high, 7 to 8 cm. thick, entirely covered with long white spines. Ribs 20 to 25, low, entirely notched into conical rhomboid warts, about ½ cm. high, bearing areoles abundantly furnished with white wool. Radial spines 15 to 20, white or transparent white, 1½ to 2 cm. long, spreading and slightly curved. Central spines 3 or 4, straw-coloured, passing to white, straight, directed upwards, 3 to 6 cm. long, Flowers 5 cm. long, of a lively pink, very showy.

Echinomastus unguispinus (Engelm.) Br. et R. = *Echinocactus unguispinus* Engelm. = *E. Trollietii* Reb. Central Mexico (Chihuahua).

Stem globular or conical, 10 to 12 cm. high and 7 cm. thick, pale bluish green, covered with black and white spines. Ribs 21, notched into low warts, bearing round areoles, at first with white wool. Radial spines about 25, spreading, white, tipped dark, the upper ones up to 2 cm. long. Central spines 4 to 8, 3 to 4 cm. long, thick, curved upwards and inwards, at first reddish, soon passing to black, later bluish grey. Flowers 2½ cm. long, tube short, scaly; outer petals lanceolate, the inner obtuse, reddish. Stigma with 8 to 15 lobes.

Echinomastus durangensis (Runge) Br. et R. = *Echinocactus durangensis* Runge. Mexico (Durango). Stem oval, about 8 cm. high and 7 cm. thick, solitary, with 18 ribs cut into rhomboid warts about 8 mm. high, bearing oval areoles, at first with whitish wool. Radial spines about 30, mostly curved upwards, the lower 1½ cm. long, the upper up to 3 cm. long, dark greyish, almost black. Central spines 4, the upper 3 as long as the longest radials, strongly curved upwards, bluish black, the lower one short. Flowers purplish. The plant is often twice as large in its native home.

Echinomastus intertextus (Engelm.) Br. et R. = *Echinocactus intertextus* Engelm. Texas, Mexico, New Mexico and Arizona. Stem grass green, oval, occasionally sprouting at the base, rounded at the top, entirely covered with spines, about 9 cm. high and 7 cm. thick, with 13 ribs divided into rhomboid warts, bearing areoles at first with abundant short white wool. Radial spines 16 to 25, spreading outwards or curved upwards, very stiff and sharp, the longest up to 1½ cm. long, white, or reddish white at the base. Central spines 4, like the radials, up to 2 cm. long. Flowers 2 cm. long, petals dark red with whitish margin, inner petals purplish red; stigma with 7 or 8 purple lobes.

Echinomastus dasyacanthus (Engelm.) Br. et R. = *E. intertextus* var. *dasyacantha* Engelm. South-west Texas. Originally described as a variety of the preceding. Has longer spines, at first purplish red, passing to bluish grey, the outer ones longer and thinner, curved upwards, closely covering the top. The plant is also larger and stronger.

Echinomastus Krausei (Hildm.) Berger = *Echinocactus Krausei* Hildm. Arizona. Stem conical-cylindrical, up to 20 cm. high, and 12 cm. thick, glaucous green, with 21 to 23 ribs, more or less spiral, notched into warts about 1 cm. high, 1 to 1½ cm. apart, bearing oval areoles at first with white wool. Radial spines 14 to 20, spreading outwards, the upper row spreading like a comb, very sharp, white, brown at the tip and at the base, up to 3 cm. long; central spines 2 or 4, the lower ones the longest, up to 4 cm. long, brown. Flower 3½ to 4 cm. long, funnel-shaped; outer petals brownish green, the inner glossy pink, white at the base; stigma with about 10 short dark purple lobes.

GYMNOCALYCIUM Pfeiffer

Plants solitary or cespitose, with many well-marked ribs, straight or spiral, notched into warts or tubercles, with a more or less pronounced protuberance or "chin" below the areoles, which are only slightly woolly. Spines various. Flowers borne on the upper areoles near the centre, mostly large and diurnal, white or pink, rarely yellow, with a short or long tube, furnished with broad obtuse scales, naked at their axils (hence the generic name), that is without spines, bristles or hairs. Fruit oblong, mostly red, with brown cap-shaped, warty seeds.

Includes about 50 species, many of which are very free-flowering, even when quite young, and others are remarkable for their beauty of form. This genus is typically South American, replacing the genera *Ferocactus* and *Echinocactus* proper, of North America. Their cultivation is easy, in any moderately rich and porous soil, and they are not too liable to suffer from excess of moisture, but must be kept somewhat dry in winter, and most of them are fairly resistant to low temperatures.

Gymnocalycium denudatum (Lk. et Otto) Pfeiff. = *Echinocactus denudatus* Link et Otto. Southern Brazil, Uruguay, Paraguay, Argentina. Stem broadly globular, deep green, 5 to 10 cm. high, and up to 15 cm. thick, with 5 to 8 very broad and obtuse ribs, only slightly notched, with a "chin" or "rostrum" below the areoles hardly pronounced. Areoles roundish, slightly woolly, 1 to 2 cm. apart. Spines 5 to 8, awl-shaped, curved laterally or upwards, yellowish, about 1 cm. long. Central spine absent. Flower 5 to 7 cm. long, with a thin ovary and tube; outer petals obtuse, green, margined white, the middle one white or pale pink, with a green dorsal band, the inner ones white, acute and toothed. Stamens white, half as long as the tube; stigma with 6 to 8 pale yellow lobes. Known as the *Spider Cactus*, on account of the shape and position of the spines. The typical form, with 5 broad smooth ribs and large white flowers was recently rediscovered. Very variable.

var. **Bruennowii** Haage jr. With 12 ribs.

var. **paraguayense** Haage jr. Has more prominent ribs.

var. **roseiflorum** Hildm. Inner petals pink.

There are also various natural hybrids with *G. multiflorum*.

Gymnocalycium Anisitsii (K. Sch.) Br. et R. = *Echinocactus Anisitsii* K. Sch. Paraguay. Often considered as a variety of the preceding. Stem sometimes sprouting at the base, globular when young, 7 to 10 cm. broad, later short cylindrical, with 8 to 11 ribs, straight, somewhat acute, of a fresh green, cut into warts with a slight chin below the areoles, which are elliptical, 1 to 2 cm. apart. Spines 5 to 7, more or less angular, variously curved, slightly thickened at the base, white, the upper one up to 6 cm. long, the others slightly shorter. Flowers very numerous and last for several days, funnel-shaped, 4 cm. broad. Ovary and tube with oval scales. Outer petals more elongated, acute, but not toothed, white. Stamens, style and 7-lobed stigma white. Fruit fusiform, 2½ cm. long, red.

Gymnocalycium Fleischerianum Jajó = *G. denudatum* var. *Anisitsii* Hort. non K. Sch. Paraguay. Stem globular, glossy bright green, depressed at the top, with 8 rounded ribs, up to 2½ cm. broad, smooth, without chin or prominence below the areoles, which are round, large, with thick brownish white wool. Spines about 20, yellowish white or brown, passing to grey, up to 2½ cm. long, awl-shaped or bristle-like, radiating, variously curved or straight, with a central spine like the radials. Flowers funnel-shaped, white, inner petals glossy pink.

Gymnocalycium Sutterianium (Schick.) Berger = *Echinocactus Sutterianus* Schick. Argentina. Broadly globular, flat and spineless at the top, dull green. Ribs 10, warty; warts or chins long. Areoles at first with whitish wool. Spines mostly 5, ashy grey, the upper two spreading and curved backwards, the next two curved laterally, up to 1½ cm. long, the lower spine curved upwards. Flower large, pale pink, with darker dorsal band on the petals; ovary and tube longer than the petals. Possibly a variety or hybrid of *G. denudatum*.

Gymnocalycium megalothelos (K. Sch.) Br. et R. = *Echinocactus megalothelos* K. Sch. Paraguay. Stem sprouting from the base, broadly globular and flat, about 16 cm. broad, becoming short-columnar with age, pale green passing to dark green, with 9 to 12 broad thick ribs, with narrow furrows between them, notched, with a broad chin below the areoles, which are elongated and slightly woolly. Spines 7 to 10, directed outwards, curved asymmetrically, yellow passing to horny grey, 1½ cm. long. Flowers said to be reddish white.

Gymnocalycium Bodenbenderianum (Hoss.) Berger = *Echinocactus Bodenbenderianum* Hosseus. Argentina (Cordoba). Stem flat and disc-like, about 8 cm. broad, brownish or greyish green, spineless at the centre, but with numerous prominent warts. Ribs 11 to 14, low, broad, cut into notches about 6 mm. apart. Warts 5-sided at the base, with a prominent nose-like hump below the areoles, which are roundish and at first with greyish or sooty wool. Spines 3 to 5, all radials, stiff, awl-shaped, curved backwards, at first almost black, passing to greyish brown, the laterals sickle-like, 1 cm. long, the middle one reflexed on the wart. Flowers white, flushed pink, with a brownish median band, with bluish ovary and tube, longer than the petals. Very free-flowering.

Gymnocalycium stellatum Speg.? *G. occultum* Frič. Argentina (Cordoba). Very similar to the preceding and to the following. Stem brownish and flat. Flowers more expanded, with a more slender tube, and more narrow outer petals. Fruit larger and longer, fusiform, and with a powdery bloom.

Gymnocalycium Quehlianum (F. Haage Jr.) Berger = *Echinocactus Quehlianus* F. Haage Jr. Argentina (Cordoba). Stem flattened, 4 cm. high, and up to 15 cm. broad, flat at the top, bluish green, with 8 to 13 ribs, with prominent chin-like warts below the areoles, which are roundish, with short grey wool. Spines mostly 5, all radials, curved upwards and laterally, ½ to 1 cm. long, diaphanous yellow. Flowers 5 to 6 cm. long, with a slender and long tube; petals obtuse, the outer greenish edged reddish, the inner pure white, red at the base; ovary and tube with broad roundish scales. Stamens red below, yellow above, longer than the style, which is thick and white; stigma with 16 yellow lobes. Very free-flowering. Closely allied to the following.

Gymnocalycium platense (Speg.) Br. et R. = *Echinocactus platensis* Spegazzini. Argentina. Stem almost globular, 6 to 8 cm. broad, and 8 to 10 cm. high, greyish green, depressed at the top, with 12 to 14 ribs divided into obtuse warts 5-angled at the base, with a prominent chin about ½ cm. high, below the areoles, which are elongated and furnished with short greyish wool. Spines mostly 7, all radials, spreading outwards, curved, the lowermost one up to 1½ cm. long, white, reddish at the base, curved upwards; the other spines shorter. Flower greyish green or bluish green outside, white inside, with a long slender tube. A beautiful and variable species, free-growing and free-flowering, closely related to the following.

Gymnocalycium capillense (Schick.) Backbg. = *Echinocactus capillensis* Schick. Argentina. A rare new species, intermediate between the preceding and the following. Stem broadly globular, up to 8 cm. across, and about as high, dull bluish green, freely sprouting around the base forming large clumps, with about 13 ribs, very broad and later becoming almost flat, with broad chin-like warts below the depressed or deeply sunk areoles, which are round and about 1 cm. apart. Spines mostly 5, all radials, up to 12 mm. long, yellowish white, awl-shaped, curved over the warts. Flowers large, up to 7 cm. long and 5 cm. broad, pale pink. Fruit somewhat calvate, powdery bluish green. Looks like a large specimen of *G. platense*.

Gymnocalycium Sigelianum (Schick.) Berger = *Echinocactus Sigelianus* Schick. Argentina. Broadly globular, 5 to 7 cm. thick, spineless at the top, greyish brown or greenish brown, with 10 low ribs. Areoles about 1 cm. apart, with a slightly raised wart below them, and at first with whitish wool. Spines 3, the two laterals about 1 cm. long, straight or slightly curved, the lower one slightly longer, curved upwards; all spines are stiff and dark, passing to a lighter colour, tipped darker.

Gymnocalycium gibbosum (Haw.) Pfeiff. = *Cactus gibbosus* Haw. = *Echinocactus gibbosus* DC. Argentina and Patagonia. A variable species. At first globular, passing to cylindrical, up to 25 cm. high, and 8 cm. thick, dark bluish green, later sooty or brownish green, almost spineless at the top. Ribs 12 to 19, straight, notched, rounded, with a prominent chin below the areoles, which are round, with greyish wool, 1½ to 2 cm. apart. Radial spines 7 to 10, spreading outwards, pale brown, straight or slightly curved, up to 3½ cm. long. Central spines similar, 1 or 2, or absent. Flower about 6 cm. long, white to reddish, inner petals lanceolate. Stamens and style white, stigma with 12 yellowish lobes. A well-known and popular species.

var. **caespitosum** Hort. Freely sprouting around the base and sides, forming groups.

var. **ferox** Lab. More slender, with the prominences or warts almost 4-angled. Spines more numerous, 2¼ cm. long, slightly curved, flexible, yellow, and red at the base when young.

var. **leucacanthum** K. Sch. Ribs 19; spines reddish white at the base.

var. **Schlumbergeri** K. Sch. Like var. *ferox*, but with low warts; spines straight, stiff (not flexible), pink red, passing to horny yellow.

var. **nobilis** K. Sch. Plant thicker, with more pronounced protuber- ances, larger areoles, with up to 25 radial spines and 6 centrals; all spines straight, white, ruby red at the base, flexible, up to $3\frac{1}{2}$ cm. long.

var. **leonensis** Hildm. Plant slender and with fewer ribs.

var. **nigrum** Backbg. Stem blackish green, spines pitch black.

Gymnocalycium hyptiacanthum (Lem.) Br. et R. = *Echinocactus hyptiacanthus* Lem. = *E. Leeanum* Hook. Uruguay. Broadly globular, flat at the top, dull green to brownish green, 5 to 8 cm. broad, with 9 to 11 broad and obtuse ribs, divided into 6-sided warts, rather low and prolonged downwards. Areoles about 1 cm. apart, elongated, slightly woolly. Radial spines 5 to 9, curved and spreading laterally, whitish, brown at the base, later greyish. Only one central spine, some- times absent, straight or curved upwards, short; the lowermost radial is about $1\frac{1}{2}$ cm. long, strongly curved downwards over the wart. Flower $4\frac{1}{2}$ to 5 cm. long; ovary with kidney-shaped scales, tube long and with similar scales. Outer petals oblong, green with brown dorsal band, inner petals narrow, acute, yellowish white. Free-flowering.

Gymnocalycium Spegazzini Br. et R. = *Echinocactus loricatus* Speg. = *G. loricatum* Speg. Argentina. Stem globose-depressed to short-cylindric, up to 14 cm. high, and 6 to 8 cm. broad, dark dull green, with 10 to 13 broad flat ribs, with low warts below the areoles. These are round, brownish, typically bearing 5 strong, awl-shaped, recurved spines, at first yellowish, passing to brown and grey, up to $3\frac{1}{2}$ cm. long; the upper 2 directed laterally on either side, the lower 3 directed downwards. Flowers borne at the centre, about 4 cm. broad, white, with rounded petals; tube rather short.

var. **major** Backbg. Much larger; up to 22 cm. high and 20 cm. across, bright bluish green, with 9 claw-like spines. At Salta (Argen- tina) about 3,000 m. above sea level.

Gymnocalycium multiflorum (Hook.) Br. et R. = *Echinocactus multiflorus* Hooker=*E. Ourselvianus* Monv. Southern Brazil, Uruguay, Paraguay, Argentina. Stem broadly globular, glaucous bluish green, 9 cm. high, and 12 to 15 cm. broad, with 10 to 15 ribs with deep narrow furrows between them, cut into prominent warts up to $1\frac{1}{2}$ cm. long, prolonged into a chin-like rostrum below. Areoles elliptical, about 1 cm. long, woolly. Spines 7 to 10, all radials, thick, awl-shaped, some- what flattened, sharp, radiating comb-like, the middle lower one up to 3 cm. long, yellowish or slightly pinkish, bluish or reddish at the base, the upper one very small. Flowers 4 cm. long, funnel-shaped, tube rather short, ovary and tube covered with semi-circular scales. Outer petals green, brownish towards the tip, the next row are pink with a green and brown median nerve, the inner row are whitish pink and toothed. Stigma with 8 to 10 yellow lobes. Extensively spread in its native habitat, and very variable.

var. **albispinum** K. Sch. Spines reddish at the base, pure white above, thick and strongly curved.

var. **parisiense** K. Sch. Spines red at the base, white above, stronger and more numerous, strongly curved.

var. **hybopleurum** K. Sch. Stem shorter, ribs thicker and more plump, with prominent warts. Spines fewer. Flower white, speckled red at the base, rather smaller.

The species and its varieties are very free-flowering and of easy cultivation, preferring half-shade.

Gymnocalycium brachyanthum (Gürke) Br. et R. = *Echinocactus brachyanthus* Gürke. Northern Argentina. Broadly globular and flattened, 18 cm. broad, 7 to 9 cm. high, dull green, with about 22 ribs, divided into warts with 5 or 6 sides, and with a prominent chin below the elongated areole. Radial spines 5 to 7, spreading and curved on each side, awl-shaped, sharp, 1 to 2½ cm. long, pale yellow, later greyish. Central spine mostly absent. Flower funnel-shaped, 6 cm. long, with a short tube, and broad roundish scales, margined by a transparent membrane, on both ovary and tube. Outer petals greenish brown, edged pale pink, inner petals white or pale pink. Stigma with 12 yellow lobes. Rare in cultivation; requires half-shade.

Gymnocalycium Stuckertii (Speg.) Br. et R. = *Echinocactus Stuckertii* Speg. Northern Argentina. Broadly globular, 4 cm. high, and 6 to 7 cm. broad, dark green, flattened and spineless at the top, with 9 to 11 ribs cut into warts, with a pronounced chin below the areoles, which are 1 to 1½ cm. apart, elongated, with 7 to 9 radial spines, spreading and slightly curved laterally, the lowermost curved upwards, 1 to 2½ cm. long, greyish tipped brown, with minute powdery scales. Flowers 4 cm. long, with a short tube, greenish outside, inner petals spathulate acute, white or pale pink. Stigma with 12 white lobes.

Gymnocalycium ochoterenai Backbg. Northern Argentina. Stem globular depressed, flat at the top, dull olive green, with brownish warts, 6 to 10 cm. broad, and up to 5 cm. high, with about 16 ribs, rounded, later becoming almost flat, deeply notched above the areoles, and with a short chin below them. Areoles round, slightly woolly. Spines 3 to 5, all radials, curved laterally and downwards, horny yellow passing to yellowish white, tipped darker, 1 to 2 cm. long. Flowers about 3½ cm. long, with a short tube, white, pale pink at the throat.

var. **cinereum** Backbg. Stem ashy grey, almost powdery. Spines 4 or 5, blackish.

Gymnocalycium castellanosii Backbg. Northern Argentina. Stem solitary, globular, elongated, velvety bluish green, up to 15 cm. high, and 10 cm. thick, with 10 to 12 broad, flattened ribs, with low rounded or angular warts below the areoles, which are large, roundish or oval, woolly, white, about 2 cm. apart. Spines all white, tipped dark, up to 2½ cm. long, straight or slightly curved, spreading, 5 to 7 radials and one central, this last often absent. Flowers 4½ cm. broad, bell-shaped, whitish, flushed pink. Fruit more or less roundish, green, with powdery bloom.

Gymnocalycium prolifer Backbg. Argentina (Cordoba). Stem bright green, globular depressed, up to 6 cm. thick, freely sprouting at the base and sides. Ribs 9 to 11, low, rounded, deeply notched, with a prominent chin-like wart below the areoles, which are large, round or roundish, with abundant whitish yellow wool, afterwards almost bare. Spines about 9, all radials, up to 1 cm. long, yellow passing to whitish, strongly curved over the rib. Flowers large, funnel-shaped, 6 to 7 cm. long, and up to 5½ cm. broad, whitish or brownish white, or flushed pink, red in the throat. Stamens and style yellowish white. Fruit small, oval, bluish green, scaly.

Gymnocalycium Saglionis (Cels.) Br. et R. = *Echinocactus Saglionis* Cels. = *E. hybogonus* Salm-Dyck. Argentina (Tucuman). Stem broadly globular, slightly flattened, mostly solitary, spiny at the top, dark dull green or bluish green, of large size, up to 30 cm. broad, with 10 to 30 ribs divided into large rounded prominences, 4- or 5-sided with a chin below the areoles very slightly pronounced. Areoles 2 to 4 cm. apart, large, elliptical, woolly. Spines dark brown to black, somewhat reddish, passing to greyish and then to ashy white. Radial spines 7 to 12, spreading outwards and curved laterally, 2½ to 4 cm. long; central spines mostly 3, one above the other, somewhat shorter, almost straight or slightly curved upwards. Flowers 3½ cm. long, broadly funnel-shaped, with a short tube, green outside, white or pale pink inside, with spathulate, pointed, toothed petals. Ovary and tube with semicircular scales. Stamens and style pale red, stigma with 12 to 14 yellow lobes. A beautiful and distinct species, fast-growing, requiring half-shade.

var. **luteispinum** Hort. Spines yellow or brownish yellow.

Gymnocalycium Schickendantzii (Weber) Br. et R. = *Echinocactus Schickendantzii* Weber. North-west Argentina. Plant similar to *G. Saglionis*, broadly globular, somewhat flattened and spiny at the top. Ribs 7 to 16, cut into broad, obtuse 5-sided warts, with a slightly prominent chin below the areoles, which are elongated and with short wool. Spines 6 or 7, all radial, slightly flattened, reddish grey or horny grey, recurved laterally or downwards, about 3 cm. long. Flowers about 5 cm. long, funnel-shaped; outer petals broadly spathulate, green or reddish, the inner longer, obtuse, white or reddish. Stamens white, in 2 groups, one inserted at the base, and the other at the throat. Style white, stigma with 12 yellowish lobes.

var. **De Laetii** K. Sch. = *Echinocactus De Laetii* K. Sch. Is a variety with more rounded warts, shorter spines and longer flowers, reddish when in bud.

Gymnocalycium Monvillei (Lem) Pfeiff. = *Echinocactus Monvillei* Lem. Paraguay and Argentina. Stem broadly globular, yellowish green, 20 to 30 cm. broad, and up to 10 cm. high, with 13 to 17 ribs, deeply cut into 5- or 6-sided warts, 2 cm. high, with a pronounced conical chin. Areoles elongated, with yellow wool. Spines 7 to 13, all radial, awl-shaped, pale yellow, red at the base, 4 to 6 cm. long, symmetrically arranged and slightly curved upwards. Flower 8 cm. long, white or pale pink; ovary and tube with green scales edged brown; outer petals obtuse, tipped brown and with a green dorsal band, inner petals spathulate. Stamens, style and stigma white.

Gymnocalycium Kurtzianum (Gürke) Br. et R. = *Echinocactus Kurtzianus* Gürke. Argentina (Cordoba). Stem broadly globular, pale green, 10 to 15 cm. broad, depressed and spiny at the top, with 10 to 18 broad ribs cut into broad warts, with deep furrows between them, slightly prominent with a conical chin below the areoles, which are 2 to 3 cm. apart, elongated, with yellowish white wool. Radial spines 8, spreading, curved backwards, thick, brown, $2\frac{1}{2}$ to 4 cm. long; only one central spine. Flower large, petals acute, white, red at the base, the outer with a greenish dorsal band, which is reddish on the inner petals. Stamens yellow, style greenish yellow, stigma with 14 pale yellow lobes.

Gymnocalycium Damsii (K. Sch.) Br. et R. = *Echinocactus Damsii* K. Sch. Northern Paraguay. Globular, somewhat flattened at the top, green, with 10 to 12 straight ribs, broad, notched into low warts, with slight protuberances below the areoles, which are roundish, $1\frac{1}{2}$ cm. apart. Spines 6 to 8, up to 12 mm. long, white, tipped brown, passing to grey, spreading and slightly curved upwards. Flowers about 6 cm. long, with a slender green tube, having obtuse scales edged white; outer petals lanceolate-acute, green, edged reddish; inner petals pure white. Stamens, style, and stigma white. Fruit elongated, red.

Gymnocalycium Mostii (Gürke) Br. et R. = *Echinocactus Mostii* Gürke. Argentina (Cordoba). Stem deep green, 6 to 7 cm. high and 12 to 13 cm. broad, spineless and depressed at the top. Ribs 11 to 14, broad and obtuse, deeply notched into warts with a prominent roundish chin. Radial spines 7, curved backwards, $\frac{1}{2}$ to $2\frac{1}{2}$ cm. long; one straight central spine. Flower bell-shaped, with a very short tube, clear red, 7 to 8 cm. across.

Gymnocalycium mazanense Backbg. = *Echinocactus mazanensis* Backbg. Argentina (near Mazan). Stem globular, depressed at the top, dull green, 7 to 10 cm. across, with 14 to 18 straight, broad rounded ribs, with narrow furrows between them, notched into warts $1\frac{1}{2}$ to 2 cm. apart, with a rounded chin below the areoles, which are large, oval, and woolly. Spines 9 to 12, of which 1 to 3 are central, all alike, stiff, awl-shaped, 2 to $3\frac{1}{2}$ cm. long, spreading, mostly recurved unevenly, brownish passing to greyish. Flowers borne at the centre, pale pink or pink, about 4 cm. across, with spathulate rounded petals; tube very short, furnished with greenish or brownish rounded scales.

Gymnocalycium Hossei (Fr. A. Haage jr.) Berger = *Echinocactus Hossei* Fr. A. Haage jr. Argentina (Cordoba). Similar to *G. Schickendantzii*. Stem globular, somewhat flattened and slightly depressed at the centre, dark greenish brown, spineless at the top. Ribs 13, broad, flat, divided into angular warts, with prominent angular chins below the areoles, which are oval, 1 to 1½ cm. apart, slightly furnished with greyish wool. Spines about 7, spreading and almost curved backwards, stiff, awl-shaped or somewhat flattened, brown, passing to greyish, tipped darker, the lower ones up to 1½ cm. long, the last one about as long and curved upwards. Flower with a short tube, funnel-shaped, and with clear pink petals.

Gymnocalycium Mihanovichii (Frič et Gürke) Br. et R. = *Echinocactus Mihanovichii* Frič et Gürke. Paraguay. A small plant broadly globular, 3 to 5 cm. broad, greyish green, flushed reddish, bare at the top, with 8 ribs broadly triangular, with deep furrows between them, cut into low warts. Areoles small, 1 cm. apart. Spines all radials 5 or 6, greyish yellow, curved, 1 cm. long. Flower 4 to 5 cm. long, with a slender tube covered with broad scales: outer petals obtuse, deep red; the inner also obtuse greenish white or yellowish white. Stamens in two groups, yellowish white, style thick, greenish, lobes of stigma yellowish.

Gymnocalycium Joossenianum (Böd) Br. et R. = *Echinocactus Joossenianus* Böd. Northern Argentina, Paraguay. Broadly globular, about 8 cm. across, dull green, slightly depressed and spiny at the top, with 9 to 11 straight ribs, divided into warts, with the chin-like process hardly marked. Areoles elongated, 2 cm. apart, with white wool. Spines 6 to 9, all radial, up to 2½ cm. long, irregularly spreading, the lower one shorter, curved upwards, yellowish passing to greyish, tipped brown. Flower 4 to 5 cm. long funnel-shaped: outer petals green and reddish, edged white; inner petals lanceolate, lilac. The flower-bud is carmine pink. Stamens white, style and lobes of stigma yellowish.

Gymnocalycium lafaldense Vaupel = *Echinocactus lafaldensis* Berger = *G. Bruchii* Backbg. Argentina (Cordoba). A small plant, freely sprouting around the base, forming large clumps. Stem globular, 2½ to 3½ cm. across, dark green, spiny at the top, with 12 low ribs divided into roundish warts, with hardly the trace of a chin-like process below the areoles, which are closely set, elongated, with some white wool. Spines slender, bristle-like, white, brown at the base; 12 to 15 radials, spreading, about ½ cm. long, curved; one central spine, straight and darker, often absent. Flower about 3 cm. long, with a short tube, with few scales: outer petals obtuse, greenish brown; the inner acute, pale violet pink, with darker midrib. Stamens white, style and 8-lobed stigma yellow. Free-flowering.

Gymnocalycium Netrelianum (Monv.) Br. et R. = *Echinocactus Netrelianus* Monv. Argentina. A small globular plant, dark green, freely sprouting from the base, with 14 rounded ribs, cut into rounded warts with low chin-like protuberances above which are the areoles. Spines all radials, 5 to 8, bristle-like, brownish, about 1 cm. long. Flower funnel-shaped, 4½ cm. long, with a short tube; outer petals pale greenish; inner petals lemon yellow, reddish at the tip. Requires half-shade, like the preceding and the following.

Gymnocalycium Guerkeanum (Heese) Br. et R. = *Echinocactus Guerkeanus* Heese. Bolivia. Another small, low plant, deep green, with 9 obtuse ribs, with a pronounced chin below the areoles, which are roundish, 1 cm. apart, with 5 curved yellowish spines, about 1 cm. long, the lower one curved upwards. Flower funnel-shaped, 5 cm. long, yellow.

Gymnocalycium leptanthum Speg. Argentina. A small globular plant, somewhat flattened, dark green, with 9 to 12 ribs, cut into roundish warts, with a slight prominence below the areoles, which are round, with white wool. Spines all radial, 7 to 9, whitish, bristle-like, curved over the wart all round, about 1 cm. long. Flower 5 cm. long, with a long tube covered with semicircular light-coloured scales. Petals white.

Gymnocalycium Andreae (Böd.) Werd. et Backbg. = *Echinocactus Andreae* Böd. Argentina (Cordoba). Stem globular, slightly flattened, dark green, or bluish green, 4½ cm. broad, freely sprouting around the base, with about 8 flat ribs, divided into roundish flat warts, with hardly any formation of chin below the areoles, which are whitish. Radial spines about 7, spreading horizontally, slender, needle-like, slightly curved, white, less than 1 cm. long. Central spines 1 to 3, like the radials, but dark brown and curved upwards. Flower 3 cm. long, funnel-shaped, sulphur yellow. Free-flowering.

Gymnocalycium brachypetalum Speg. = *Echinocactus brachypetalus* (Speg.) Werd. Argentina (Rio Negro). Stem almost cylindrical, 8 to 10 cm. long, and 6 to 7 cm. thick, dark bluish green, with about 13 ribs, divided into warts. Areoles elongated, with ashy white wool. Spines 5 to 7, all radial, spreading, acute, yellow passing to grey, ½ to 2½ cm. long. Flower about 5½ cm. long; inner petals white.

Gymnocalycium Pflanzii (Vaup.) Werd. et Backbg. = *Echinocactus Pflanzii* Vaupel. Bolivia. Very similar to *G. Saglionis*, but with fewer spines, and the flower buds are longer and more pointed. Flower about 4 cm. long, inner petals red, edged violet, with a violet blotch at the base.

Gymnocalycium nigriareolatum Backbg. Northern Argentina (near Mazan). Stem solitary, globular, about 15 cm. thick, pale green, with about 10 ribs, broad, bearing low acute warts. Areoles more or less oval, 6 mm. long, at first with thick white wool, afterwards passing to black. Radial spines about 7, very pale pink, slightly curved: one central spine, slightly longer, curved upwards, up to 3 cm. long. Flowers white, bell-shaped, half-opened, with a green throat. Fruit round; seeds dull black.

Gymnocalycium oenanthemum Backbg. Argentina (Mendoza).

(b) NEOPORTERIA NIDUS

(a) LOPHOPHORA WILLIAMSII

PLATE XLII

(b) NEOPORTERIA ACUTISSIMA

(a) NEOPORTERIA JUSSIEUI

PLATE XLIII

Stem solitary, globular, dull pale green, about 8 cm. thick, with about 11 ribs, 2 cm. broad, with sharp-angled warts above the areoles, from which they are separated by a sharp deep furrow. Areoles oval, with yellowish wool. Radial spines 5, up to 1½ cm. long, reddish, slightly curved. There is no central spine. Flowers large, up to 5 cm. long, funnel-shaped, petals pale claret red, or pale coppery red; tube with pink-edged scales. Fruit pale green, slightly powdery.

Gymnocalycium Venturianum (Frič) Backbg. = *Echinocactus Venturianus* Frič. = *G. Venturi* Hort. Uruguay (near Montevideo). Stem solitary, globular, somewhat depressed at the top, pale bluish green, about 5 cm. thick, with 9 broad rounded ribs, with small round areoles, having chin-like warts below them. Radial spines 5, yellowish, 6 to 7 mm. long, 1 pointing downwards, the others laterally. There is no central spine. Flowers small, funnel-shaped, about 4 cm. long, bright carmine, with greenish red outer petals; tube slender and scaly. Fruit small, oval. Stamens and style yellow. This plant looks like a *Rebutia*.

Other species in cultivation are:

Gymnocalycium euchlorum Backbg., **G. melanocarpum** Arech., **G. nidulans** Backbg., **G. uruguayense** Arech., **G. Weissianum** Backbg., and **G. Valnicekianum** Jajó.

ECHINOCACTUS (Link et Otto) Br. et R.

Stem globular or cylindrical, often very large, with prominent ribs, usually straight and continuous. Areoles large, very woolly at the top, the flowers being often deeply embedded in the wool. Spines numerous and strong, mostly straight. Flowers borne on the new areoles at the centre, comparatively small or medium size, yellow, rarely reddish, with small petals, the outer ones often with spinescent point. Ovary densely woolly and scaly, the scales continuing on the tube. Fruit scaly and woolly. Seeds black, smooth, glossy, with a minute hilum.

As amended by Britton and Rose, this genus now contains only a few species, about 9, exclusively North American, inhabiting Mexico, Texas and California.

Echinocactus Grusonii Hildm. Central Mexico. A most beautiful species, very well known as "golden barrel" or "golden ball," rarely sprouting from the base, globular, and somewhat flattened at the top, 40 to 80 cm. in diameter, when old up to over 1 m. high, with 20 to 27 acute and rather thin ribs, of a glossy lively green, with white or yellowish wool and very spiny at the top. In very young plants the ribs are divided into conical warts, almost like a *Mammillaria*, but later they are straight and continuous. Areoles large, 1 to 2 cm. apart, at first with yellowish wool, passing to whitish and later to greyish. Spines awl-shaped, at first golden yellow or even reddish, afterwards paler and almost white, diaphanous, minutely ringed; the radials 8 to 10, up to 3 cm. long; central spines 3 to 5, almost crosswise, thicker and slightly curved, up to 5 cm. long. Flowers 4 to 6 cm. long, tube with long pointed scales; outer petals brownish on the outer side and acutely pointed, yellow inside; the inner petals are shorter, narrower, pointed, of a glossy yellow. Stamens many, yellow, style with its 12-lobed stigma yellow. The dried flower remains attached to the fruit. Delights in a calcareous and stony soil, moderately rich, and requires half-shade during the hot days of summer, being liable to scorchings in a too powerful sun. Grows well in cultivation, and magnificent specimens are often paraded at shows. Seedlings reach a diameter of 9 to 10 cm. in about 4 years.

Echinocactus ingens (Zuccarini)=*E. minax* Lem. Mexico (Hidalgo). Stem globular, depressed, or elongated when old, up to 1½ m. high and up to 1¼ m. across, greenish grey or almost reddish, very woolly at the top. Ribs 5 to 8 when young, much more numerous (up to 55) when adult, broad, rounded, straight, more or less divided into broad rounded warts. Areoles 2½ to 3 cm. apart, with abundant yellowish wool. Spines brown, straight, 2 to 3 cm. long, very stiff: 8 radials, and 1 central slightly longer, all ringed. Flowers 3 cm. long and 4 to 5 cm. broad, borne at the top of adult plants, reddish yellow outside, canary yellow inside, very glossy, with toothed petals. Stamens and style yellow; stigma with 8 reddish lobes. Growth is slow.

Like all the following species requires full sunshine and warmth, and a calcareous and stony soil, moderately rich, and should be kept almost dry in winter.

Echinocactus Visnaga Hooker = *E. ingens* var. *Visnaga* K. Sch. Mexico (San Louis Potosi). Plant larger, and when adult more elongated, 2 to 3 m. high, 70 cm. to 1 m. across, greyish green, with abundant tawny wool at the top. Ribs up to 40, narrow and high, with roundish or elongated areoles on thickened parts of the ribs. Spines 4, directed crosswise, pale brown, ringed, the upper one the thickest and longest, up to 5 cm. long, directed upwards. Flowers 7 to 8 cm. across, with spathulate toothed petals, glossy yellow. Stamens, style and 8-lobed stigma yellow.

var. **helophorus** K. Sch. Ribs very obtuse, deeply notched into rounded warts.

var. **subinermis** K. Sch. Ribs obtuse, straight and continuous. Spines reduced to 1 or 2, short and slender.

var. **aulacogonus** Lem. = *Echinocactus aulacogonus* Lem. Ribs obtuse, with deep furrows between the areoles, which are very elongated and with yellow wool.

Echinocactus grandis Rose. Mexico (Puebla). Plant very large, 1 to 2 m. high and 60 cm. to 1 m. across, very woolly at the top. Ribs 40 or more, rather thin, more or less blotched or splashed purplish. Areoles far apart on young plants, very close together on adult plants. Spines very strong, awl-shaped, yellow, passing to reddish brown; 5 to 6 radials, 3 to 4 cm. long; one central directed upwards, 4 to 5 cm. long. Flowers numerous, yellow, 4 to 5 cm. long; ovary thickly woolly;

outer petals acutely pointed and ciliated; inner petals linear, obtuse, toothed.

Echinocactus Palmeri Rose = *E. saltillensis* Poselg. (pro parte) = *E. ingens* var. *saltillensis* K. Sch. Northern Mexico (Coahuila to Zacatecas). Plant 1 to 2 m. high, and 40 to 50 cm. across, when adult; with 12 to 26 ribs, broad and obtuse, slightly notched, more or less splashed purplish. Radial spines 4 to 6; centrals 4, crosswise, straight, the lowermost somewhat flattened, the laterals shorter and thinner, and the upper one erect, 6 to 8 cm. long. All spines yellow to yellowish brown, the central thickened and brown at the base. Flowers somewhat smaller than those of the preceding species, with fringed petals.

Echinocactus polycephalus Engelm. et Big. South California, Sonora, Arizona, Nevada and Utah. Stem globular or elongated, up to 80 cm. high and 25 cm. thick, at first solitary, later abundantly sprouting from the base, resulting in large clumps, green, woolly and spiny at the top and all round, called "niggerheads" by the colonists. Ribs 13 to 21; areoles up to 3 cm. apart, at first with white wool. Radial spines 4 to 8, almost flattened, 2 to 5 cm. long; central spines 4, stronger, ringed, 3 to 9 cm. long, all more or less curved, but not hooked, yellowish or pinkish passing to brown or reddish brown. Flowers yellow, 5 to 6 cm. long. Fruit woolly, with spinescent scales. A quick-growing species, not common in cultivation.

var. **Parryi** Engelm. = *Echinocactus Parryi* Engelm. Mexico (Sonora). Possibly a distinct species. Stem globular or slightly depressed, 16 to 25 cm. high and 21 to 30 cm. thick, mostly solitary, with about 13 acute ribs. Areoles oval, about 1 cm. long, at first with abundant whitish wool. Radial spines 8 to 11, straight or slightly curved, up to 3 cm. long; central spines 4, the lowermost up to 5 cm. long, curved downwards. All spines are white or whitish.

Echinocactus xeranthemoides Coulter = *E. polycephalus* var. *xeranthemoides* Coult. Arizona and Utah. Like *E. polycephalus*, but smaller and more freely sprouting around the base. Ribs fewer and more spiny, the lower central spine flattened, broad and straight.

Echinocactus horizonthalonius Lem. = *E. horizontalis* Hort. = *E. equitans* Scheidw. = *E. laticostatus* Engelm. et Bigel. Northern Mexico, New Mexico, Texas and Arizona. Stem solitary, globular, much flattened, greyish or bluish green, up to 25 cm. high and 30 to 40 cm. across, with 7 to 13 ribs, mostly 8, broad and obtuse, with deep narrow furrows between them. Areoles woolly, 1 to 2 cm. apart, roundish or oval, or almost heart-shaped. Radial spines 6 to 9, stiff and thick, sometimes flattened, ringed, straight or curved, or strongly curved back on the ribs, at first yellowish, reddish or brown at the base, later greyish, 2 to 4 cm. long. One central spine, often absent, longer and thicker. Flowers 5 to 7 cm. long, with a short and broad tube; ovary very woolly and with spinescent scales like the tube. Outer petals brownish pink, spinescent at the tip; inner petals spathulate, obtuse, toothed, of a showy pink. Thrives well in cultivation, and is free-flowering even when young.

var. **curvispina** Salm-Dyck. Spines more curved, the lower one flattened.

var. **Moelleri** Haage jr. Plant smaller; spines more slender; more free-flowering.

Echinocactus platyacanthus Link et Otto. Mexico. Is a distinct species, although sometimes considered as a mere form of *E. ingens*. It has a broadly globular stem, solitary, flattened and somewhat depressed at the top, greyish green, with yellowish wool passing to greyish. Ribs many, obtuse or round. Spines greyish brown, central spines flattened and ringed. The plant is smaller than *E. ingens*, but may be 70 cm. thick.

HOMALOCEPHALA Br. et R.

Plants globular, depressed, with prominent, acute ribs and strong, ringed spines. Flowers large, pink, with deeply fringed petals, borne on the central areoles. Ovary very scaly, with much white wool in the axils of the scales, both scales and wool dropping off in the mature round scarlet fruit. Seeds black, smooth, kidney-shaped.

Includes only one species.

Homalocephala texensis (Hopff.) Br et R. = *Echinocactus texensis* Hopff. = *E. Courantianus* Lem. = *E. Lindheimeri* Engelm. = *E. platycephalus* Muehlenpf. = *E. laciniatus* Berlandier. Texas, New Mexico and northern Mexico. Stem globular, much flattened, 10 to 15 cm. high, and up to 30 cm. broad, dark greyish green, depressed and woolly at the centre, with 13 to 27 prominent, and acute ribs, with areoles far apart, woolly and somewhat depressed. Radial spines mostly 6, sometimes 7, reddish, a little flattened, thick, ringed, spreading or strongly reflexed backwards, 1 to 2 cm. long, the two laterals up to 4 cm. long. One central spine, like the others, stronger and reflexed downwards on the rib. Flower bell-shaped, 5 to 6 cm. long, and as broad. Ovary and tube with narrow acute scales, with much white wool in the axils. Outer petals linear-acute, fringed; the inner broadly lanceolate, deeply fringed and ciliated, satiny pink, tipped brown, and red at the base. Stamens yellow, red at the base, style white, stigma with 11 red lobes. The flower has a delightful fragrance, and lasts for about 4 days, closing at night and reopening in the morning. A very beautiful and free-flowering species, of easy cultivation in full sunshine. Very common in Texas, where it is despised by the farmers as a troublesome weed! The plant is usually solitary, and rarely throws up any offsets, but grows well from seed, although at first growth is rather slow.

ASTROPHYTUM Lemaire

Species of *Astrophytum*, or "Star Cacti", were formerly included in the genus *Echinocactus*. They have a globular stem, with 4 to 8 ribs, usually very pronounced and acute, more or less covered with very small star-like hairs or scales, closely applied to the epidermis. Flowers borne on the areoles at or near the top, fairly large, diurnal, funnel-shaped, with spreading petals, yellow or yellow with reddish centres. Fruit of the size and shape of a small olive, greenish yellow or reddish, woolly and spiny, with septifragous dehiscence when ripe. Seeds boat-shaped, with depressed hilum, black or brown, glossy.

There are four species, all Mexican, and numerous varieties, all requiring a porous sandy and stony soil, rich in lime, with some leaf-mould or old cow manure, and should be kept more or less dry in winter, but make good growth in summer if placed in full sunshine and frequently watered. They are resistant to adverse conditions of soil and climate, and are of easy cultivation. They never, or very rarely, produce any offsets, and are exclusively raised from seed, or by importations from their native country. Sometimes seedlings have two or more heads, which grow together on a single stem. In planting, it is important not to cover too much with soil the globular part of the stem, as this may cause the plant to rot.

Astrophytum asterias (Zucc.) Lem. = *Echinocactus asterias* Zuccarini. Mexico (Tamaulipas). Has a flat, dome-shaped body, 5 to 8 cm. in diameter, with 8 straight deep grooves, dividing the body into 8 broad, rounded, flat ribs or segments, along each of which there is a row of small white woolly areoles, but no spines. The flowers are 3 cm. long, and 3 to 4 cm. across, yellow, reddish at the centre. Fruit a small, olive-shaped berry, covered with woolly and spinescent scales. Seeds few, black or reddish black. Thrives well on own roots, and is often grafted on columnar Cacti. Seedlings reach flowering size in 3 or 4 years. There are no natural varieties, but numerous hybrids have been raised by crossing with other species of *Astrophytum*.

Astrophytum myriostigma (Salm-Dyck) Lem. = *Echinocactus myriostigma* Salm-Dyck. Hilly wastes in central Mexico, at about 2,500 m. above the sea. Stem globular, or slightly depressed at the centre or becoming elongated with age, 10 to 20 cm. in diameter, with 4 to 8 (normally 5) very pronounced ribs, acute in some forms, more or less rounded in others, with a row of woolly brownish areoles along each rib, but no spines. The whole body is densely dotted with minute white star-like scales or hairs, which give it a greyish white, stone-like appearance, completely hiding the green colour. Flowers fairly large, 4 to 6 cm. long and as broad, cropping up repeatedly throughout the summer and autumn, satiny yellow, or yellow with a reddish blotch at the base, borne on the areoles at or near the top. Fruit as in the preceding species, but larger; seeds more numerous, large, glossy black, boat-shaped, with turned-in margins.

A most lovely species of striking appearance, deservedly popular and of easy cultivation, delighting in full sunshine. There are numerous varieties, as many as 25 being frequently listed by dealers, but they may be reduced to the following.

var. **quadricostata** Moeller = *tetragona* Hort. This is the well-known Parson's Cap, with 4 straight, broad, rounded ribs and globular body. Flowers clear glossy yellow, usually smaller.

var. **coahuilensis** Moeller. Coahuila (Mexico). Often described as a subspecies. A desirable variety with 5 straight broad ribs, less rounded and more angular than in the preceding variety. The body is also more conical, with a slightly raised centre, and is even more densely covered with white or greyish starry scales somewhat soft to the touch and almost velvety, giving the plant a dirty white appearance, more like a sculpture in stone. Flowers large, yellow, with a central reddish blotch. Fruit more fleshy, purplish.

var. **potosina** Moeller. San Louis Potosi (Mexico). Often described as a subspecies. Body broad, somewhat depressed at the centre; ribs straight, acute, sometimes rounded, 5 or more, less densely covered with white scales, and therefore greenish grey. Flowers smaller, yellow or clear yellow, usually without the reddish blotch at the centre. In some forms the body is almost green, with few scales (form: *nudus* Hort.), or elongated and columnar (form: *columnaris* Hort.).

var. **tulensis** Hort. Tula-Tamaulipas (Mexico). Another pretty variety, very variable, usually 5-ribbed, but may have as many as 8, or even up to 10 ribs. These ribs are straight on the sides of the body, but are very acute and never rounded, and are always spiral or twisted like a screw at the centre. Flowers large, yellow, usually blotched with red at the base.

There are also numerous varieties with short spines, which are evidently natural hybrids with *A. ornatum*.

Astrophytum capricorne (Dietr.) Br. et R. = *Echinocactus capricornis* A. Dietrich = *Maierocactus capricornis* Rost. Northern Mexico. Stem 10 to 20 cm. high, and about 10 cm. in diameter, at first globular and afterwards ovoid or elongated, with about 8 acute and deep ribs, more or less studded all over with white star-like scales, with large brownish woolly areoles along the ribs, with a variable number of long reddish or black or ash-coloured, angular, twisted and recurved spines, 3 to 10 cm. long. Flowers borne on the areoles at or near the top, large, 6 to 7 cm. long, widely expanded; outer petals reddish with spinescent tip; inner petals lemon yellow, with an orange red blotch at the base; sweet-scented and cropping up repeatedly throughout the summer; stamens, style and 7- to 10-lobed stigma yellow; remaining in bloom for 3 or 4 days. Fruits and seeds as in the preceding species.

An interesting species of easy cultivation, but is less resistant than the preceding, and dislikes any excess of moisture. It is also less easily raised from seed.

var. **majus** Hort. = *crassispinum* Moeller. Plant larger in all its parts, with angular or flattened and thickened ashy-grey spines, mostly twisted and curved upwards. Flower yellow, without orange red blotch.

var. **niveum** Hort. A new variety. Plant large, with strong ashy grey spines, curved upwards as in the preceding variety. Body entirely covered with snowy white scales, like a good specimen of *A. ornatum* var. *Mibellii.* = *A. capricorne* var. *niveum* Kays.

var. **minus** Runge et Quehl. Plant smaller, 10 to 12 cm. high and 4 to 6 cm. thick, pale green, fairly well studded with white scales. Spines more numerous, but shorter and less angular, mostly twisted and recurved in all directions, black or blackish. Flowers smaller.

var. **senile** Frič. Plant larger, up to 35 cm. high and 15 cm. thick, tender green, far less studded with white scales or with only a few. Areoles farther apart. Spines 15 to 20, almost cylindrical, twisted and curved irregularly in all directions, covering the stem, black when young, passing to ashy grey with age.

var. **aureum** Moeller (Sierra de la Paila, Coahuila). Like the preceding, but with more abundant white scales; the younger spines in the upper areoles are yellow, passing to blackish and later to ashy grey.

Astrophytum ornatum (DC.) Weber. = *Echinocactus ornatus* DC. Mexico (Hidalgo and Queretaro). Stem more cylindrical, up to 30 or 35 cm. high, and 12 to 15 cm. thick, but at first globular, more or less studded with star-like silvery scales, mostly disposed in bands around the stem. Ribs 8, acute, high, straight or somewhat spiral. Spines 5 to 11, awl-shaped, mostly straight, very sharp, amber yellow passing to brown, 3 to 4 cm. long. Flowers 7 to 9 cm. broad, of a beautiful clear yellow, ovary and tube with narrow scales; inner petals broadly spathulate, obtuse, toothed. Fruit and seeds u.s., but the fruit is less fleshy and at maturity breaks open star-like. Very free flowering. This species is often considered as a natural hybrid between *A. myriosstigma* and an *Echinocactus*. It is resistant and of easy cultivation. Seedlings make quick growth.

var. **Mirbellii** K. Sch. A most lovely form with golden yellow spines, and body entirely covered with scales of a shining silvery white.

var. **glabrescens** Weber. Body very sparingly furnished with white scales. Spines yellow or brownish. Areoles with very short wool or almost bare.

ERIOSYCE Philippi

Plant large, short-columnar, with many ribs and very spiny. Flowers bell-shaped; ovary and tube with acute scales and white wool; petals red, short and narrow. Fruit dry, spiny. Seeds large, dull black, pitted.

Includes three species.

Eriosyce ceratites Otto = *Echinocactus ceratites* Otto (also written *ceratistes* and *ceratitis*). = *E. sandillon* Remy = *Eriosyce sandillon* Philippi. Chile, on the Andes at Coquimbo and Aconcagua. Stem solitary, at first globular, later elongated up to 1 m. high and up to 30 cm. or more in thickness, with abundant white wool and yellow spines at the top. Ribs about 35, thick, somewhat notched, 2 to 3 cm. high, with large oval areoles up to 2 cm. long, 2½ to 4 cm. apart, with much white wool. Spines 18 to 40, awl-shaped, mostly straight, thickened at the base, 2½ to 3½ cm. long, dirty yellow, passing to brownish. Flowers 4 cm. long, borne on the side areoles near the centre, bell-shaped, not fully expanded, about 3 cm. across; petals small, lanceolate, carmine red. Stamens many, yellow; style thick, deeply divided into the many pale red lobes of the stigma.

Eriosyce korethroides Werd. = *Echinocactus korethroides* Werd. = *Echinopsis korethroides* Werd. Northern Argentina (Los Andes). Solitary, globular to short-cylindric, up to 30 cm. across, in its native home pale green, somewhat glossy, flat and somewhat depressed at the top, covered with yellowish or dark brown spines. Ribs 12 to 20 or more, more or less arranged spirally, narrow and acute at the top, less than 1 cm. high. Areoles large, oval, 1½ to 2 cm. apart, with whitish to dirty yellowish wool. Radial spines 12 to 20, whitish or yellowish, needle-like, spreading horizontally, mostly straight, up to 3 cm. long. Central spines 4 or more, yellowish brown or reddish brown, zoned, and somewhat flattened. Flowers borne on the areoles near the top, 6 to 7 cm. long, pale red. Ovary and tube scaly and with long brown hairs.

Eriosyce aurata (Pfeiff.) Backbg. = *Echinocactus auratus* Pfeiff. = *Echinopsis aurata* Salm-Dyck. Chile, mountains north-east of Santiago. Very much like *Echinocactus Grusonii* in appearance, and grows to nearly the same size, depressed at the top and very spiny, with about 28 straight ribs, rather acute. Areoles 2½ cm. apart, woolly, at first rosy white passing to dark grey. Radial spines 12, up to 3 cm. long, slightly curved and compressed, golden yellow to grey: central spines 1 or 2, awl-shaped, same colour and about as long. Flowers unknown.

MALACOCARPUS Salm-Dyck

Plants globular or short-cylindrical, felted at the top. Ribs continuous or notched into warts, spiny. Flowers yellow, stigma with red lobes. Ovary with scales, with wool and sometimes also with bristles in their axils. Fruit soft (hence the name of the genus), pink or reddish, round or oval, immersed in wool, and with scales woolly in their axils, and with a few bristles at the top, with the remains of the flower still attached. Seeds cap-shaped, brown or black, with a broad base and a white scar.

Most species delight in full sunshine and are also fairly resistant to low temperatures. Their flowers last for several days and are attractive, although the plants themselves do not offer a great diversity of form. Many species formerly included under this genus by Britton and Rose are now more correctly classified under *Notocactus* and *Pyrrhocactus*. At present the genus includes only about 12 species, all South American.

Malacocarpus Sellowii (Link et Otto) K. Sch.=*Echinocactus Sellowii* Link et Otto = *Malacocarpus tephracanthus* K. Sch. Southern Brazil, Uruguay, Argentina. Stem globular or slightly depressed, dark green or light greyish green, woolly at the top, up to 15 cm. across, with 16 to 18 acute ribs having deep narrow furrows between them, slightly notched above the areoles, which are roundish, 1 to 1½ cm. apart, with white wool when young. Radial spines 5 to 7, the upper 2 or 4 shorter, the lower 3 stronger and up to 2¼ cm. long. Only one central spine, often absent, straight or curved downwards, up to 2 cm. long. All spines are honey-yellow, passing to greyish. Flowers borne on the new areoles at the centre, 4 to 4½ cm. long, and about as broad; inner petals spathulate, abruptly acuminate, toothed, canary yellow. Stamens yellow, style reddish, stigma with 8 red lobes. Berry pink. Includes the following well marked varieties:

var. **Courantii** Gürke = *Echinocactus Courantii* Lem. Stem glossy dark green, with 19 to 21 ribs, thickened above the areoles. Central spine present. Flower larger, pale yellow. Lobes of stigma dark red.

var. **macracanthus** Arech = *E. macracanthus* Arech. Pale green, with 12 to 14 ribs. All spines stronger, the radials almost curved, up to 3 cm. long. There is a central spine. Flower large, pale yellow.

var. **macrogonus** Arech = *E. macrogonus* Arech. Dark green, broader and more flattened, up to 20 cm. across. Ribs 12 to 21, high and broad. Radial spines 9, the lower 3 longer. Central spine absent.

var. **tetracanthus** Lem. = *E. tetracanthus* Lem. Dark green, much flattened, up to 20 cm. across. Ribs 21 to 26, acute, thickened above the areoles. Radial spines 4, crosswise, up to 1 cm. long, the lower 3 slightly curved, and often tipped brown. Flower smaller.

var. **Martinii** K. Sch. = *E. Martinii* Cels. Stem grey green, small, with 12 ribs, thickened above the areoles. Radial spines 4 or 5, the lower 3 long. Central spine absent. Very free-flowering.

var. **turbinatus** Arech. Dark green, cake-like, very flat at the top, with 12 to 20 ribs. Radial spines 5 to 10; central spine absent.

Malacocarpus corynodes Salm-Dyck = *Echinocactus corynodes* Otto = *E. acutangulus* Zucc. Southern Brazil, Uruguay and Argentina. Stem globular to cylindrical, up to 20 cm. high and 10 cm. thick, dark green, woolly at the top, with 13 to 16 acute ribs, notched, thickened at the areoles, which are 1 to 2 cm. apart, round, at first with white wool. Radial spines 7 to 12, awl-shaped, dark yellow or yellow, zoned darker, the lower 3 up to 2 cm. long. One central spine slightly longer, often absent. Flower funnel-shaped, about 5 cm. across: outer petals linear-lanceolate, greenish yellow; inner petals lanceolate, acuminate, toothed, canary yellow. Style and stamens yellow, stigma with 10 red lobes. Fruit oblong, sooty red.

Malacocarpus Kovaricii Frič = *Echinocactus Kovaričii* Frič. Uruguay. Like the preceding, but with a dark green, flattened stem. Ribs 16, very acute; areoles depressed in notches, with white wool when young. Spines about 10, reddish brown, the lower 3 stronger. One central spine, longer than the radials.

Malacocarpus leucocarpus Arech. = *Echinocactus leucocarpus*

Arech. Argentina. Another new species, like the preceding. Differs from *M. corynodes*, owing to the bluish grey colour of the stem. Flowers with more numerous petals, and the fruit is of a characteristic white colour.

Malacocarpus erinaceus (Lem.) Rumpl. = *Echinocactus erinaceus* Lem. Southern Brazil, Uruguay and Argentina. Stem globular to short cylindrical, dark green, 15 cm. thick, woolly at the top. Ribs 15 to 20, more or less arranged spirally, obtuse, notched, with areoles in the depressions, 1 to 1½ cm. apart, round, with abundant white wool when young. Radial spines 6 to 8, the upper ones shorter, up to 1 cm. long, the lower ones twice as long, dark brown, later greyish; central spine only one, 2 to 2½ cm. long, curved downwards, of the same colour. Flower funnel-shaped, about 4 cm. long, and 7 cm. across: outer petals lanceolate and green; the inner spathulate, toothed, canary yellow. Stamens yellow, style reddish, stigma with 8 red lobes.

Malacocarpus Arechavaletai (K. Sch.) Berger = *Echinocactus Arechavaletai* K. Sch. Uruguay, on granitic rocks at Maldonado. Stem globular, dark green, up to 8 cm. thick, woolly and spiny at the top, with 16 to 18 notched ribs, rather low and rounded, with areoles on the warts between the notches, 1 cm. apart, round, with abundant white wool when young. Radial spines 9, spreading, white, red at the base, tipped black, all alike. Central spines sometimes 2 or 3, but mostly only one, thick, 2 cm. long, straight, directed backwards, same colour but darker, passing to greyish. Flower funnel-shaped, 3 to 4 cm. long and 5 cm. across, golden yellow. Petals spathulate, obtuse. Stigma with 8 red lobes. Ovary and tube with pale green scales, pale brown hairs and a few bristles. In cultivation, young plants have usually glossy black spines.

Malacocarpus Langsdorffii (Link et Otto) Br. et R. = *Echinocactus Langsdorffii* Link et Otto = *Malacocarpus acutatus* Salm-Dyck. Southern Brazil. Stem globular or slightly elongated, 10 cm. across, with abundant white wool at the top, dull green, with about 17 obtuse, notched ribs, with areoles 1 cm. apart. Spines 7, 6 radials and 1 central, at first erect, later directed downwards, 2½ cm. long. Flower small, yellow, 2¼ cm. across, with about 20 petals abruptly acute.

Malacocarpus Fricii (Arech.) Berger = *Echinocactus Fričii* Arech. Uruguay. Globular, depressed at the top, 4 cm. high and 6 cm. across, glossy pale green, with 20 acute ribs, wavy, about 1 cm. high. Areoles round, 3 or 4 on each rib, with white wool. Spines 6 or 7, all alike, curved, flexible, brownish. Flower 3 cm. long, immersed in the wool at the top of the stem; tube short, with white wool; petals spathulate, yellow.

Malacocarpus pauciareolatus (Arech.) Berger = *Echinocactus pauciareolatus* Arech. Uruguay, on granitic ground near Maldonado. Stem globular and flattened, 10 to 12 cm. thick, with 15 to 21 acute ribs, thickened at the areoles, which are round and very woolly when young. There are only two areoles on each rib. Spines 4, stiff, awl-shaped, 3 directed downwards, and the fourth, smaller and often absent, directed upwards. Later, 1 or 2 other small spines may develop on each side of the upper one. Flowers with the ovary and tube immersed in the wool at the top, about 5 cm. broad, golden yellow, the outer petals reddish on the dorsal side, the inner spathulate.

Malacocarpus Vorwerkianus (Werd.) Backbg. = *Echinocactus Vorwerkianus* Werd. Colombia, near Bogota. Stem globular, much flattened, almost hemispherical, glossy pale green, 4 to 5 cm. high and 7 to 9 cm. across, with greyish or ashy wool on the top areoles. Ribs about 20, arranged somewhat spirally, acute and less than 1 cm. high, notched or thickened into round warts, about 2 cm. apart, on the upper side of which are situated the roundish areoles, which are large, with greyish white wool when young, later almost bare. Radial spines 5 or 6, dirty yellowish white, curved on the wart, usually less than 1 cm. long. In adult plants there is usually a central spine, like the radials, curved upwards. Flower about 3 cm. broad, pale yellow, dorsal side of outer petals reddish yellow. Fruit glossy deep pink or purplish red. Seeds dull black, warty.

NOTOCACTUS K. Sch.

Ribs many, low, notched into low warts tipped with areoles. Flowers fairly large, or small, diurnal, lasting for several days, yellow to orange scarlet, stigma mostly red. Ovary scaly, with wool or hair and bristles in the axils of the scales. Fruit dry, hence the generic name. Formerly included under *Malacocarpus* by Britton and Rose. They are beautiful plants, deservedly popular. The genus includes 25 species, all South American.

A. *Stem with few or no spines and hairs at the top. Flowers large.*

Notocactus concinnus (Monv.) Berger = *Echinocactus concinnus* Monv. Southern Brazil, Uruguay. Stem broadly globular, about 6 cm. high, and 10 cm. across, glossy green, slightly depressed and warty at the top, with about 18 ribs notched into warts, with areoles about ½ cm. apart, in the notches, small, with short white wool. Radial spines pale yellow, 10 to 12, bristle-like, 5 to 7 mm. long; central spines 4, crosswise, yellowish or reddish brown, the lower one about 1½ cm. long, thickened at the base. Flowers at the top, 7 cm. long, funnel-shaped, ovary and tube with scales, with long white wool and brown bristles in their axils; outer petals spathulate-acute, reddish with darker dorsal band, the inner petals satiny canary yellow, very showy. Outer stamens yellow, the inner red at the base; stigma with 10 red lobes. Flowers very freely, even when quite young. Requires full sunshine. A pretty cristate form is frequent in cultivation.

Notocactus Velenowskyi Speg. Argentina. A most beautiful species, recently discovered, of fast growth and with showy flowers, requiring full sunshine. Stem broadly globular, 7 to 8 cm. high, and 10 to 15 cm. across, glossy grass green, depressed and spineless at the top. Ribs about 20 or more, 1 cm. high, cut into warts with a prominent conical chin below the areoles. These are round, with abundant white wool when young. Radial spines 9 to 12, $\frac{1}{2}$ to $1\frac{1}{2}$ cm. long, yellow, tipped reddish, straight or irregularly curved; centrals 1 to 4, the lowermost up to $2\frac{1}{2}$ cm. long, slightly curved and directed downwards, the others shorter and directed upwards; all centrals bulbous and red at the base, for the rest yellowish white, often tipped reddish. Flowers funnel-shaped, with a short tube, 5 to 6 cm. broad, glossy golden yellow, with a red stigma. Ovary and tube covered with short hairs and bristles.

Notocactus Ottonis (Link et Otto) Berger = *Echinocactus Ottonis* Link et Otto. Southern Brazil, Uruguay, Paraguay and Argentina. Stem solitary or sprouting from the base, globular or elongated, flattened at the top, of a lively green, 5 to 11 cm. across, with a few spines and wool at the top. Ribs 10 to 13, straight, broad and obtuse, often definitely spiral, more or less notched. Areoles depressed, about 1 cm. apart, roundish with short wool. Radial spines 10 to 18, spreading, slender, yellow, straight or curved; central spines 3 or 4, seldom absent, stronger, brown or reddish, pale at the tip, up to $2\frac{1}{2}$ cm. long. Flower funnel-shaped, 4 to 6 cm. long, and at least as broad, lasting for 3 or 4 days; ovary and tube with greyish or brownish wool and with a few brown bristles in the axils of the scales; outer petals lanceolate, somewhat reddish on the dorsal side; inner petals spathulate, toothed, deep glossy yellow. Stamens yellow, often red at the base, style pale yellow, stigma with 14 dark red lobes. The stem often sprouts freely around the base. This is a beautiful free-flowering species, well known in our collections.

The following varieties are also in cultivation:

var. **tenuispinus** K. Sch. Spines more slender, paler, the centrals reddish brown, 2 to 3 cm. long.

var. **tortuosus** K. Sch. Ribs more spiral and more deeply notched. Radial spines longer, irregularly spreading, brown when young, passing to greyish. Flower smaller.

var. **multiflorus** Hort. Very free-flowering.

var. **paraguayensis** Haage jr. Ribs more acute, spines more markedly red.

var. **uruguayensis** Arech. Plant stronger, with 11 broad, rounded ribs. Areoles farther apart.

var. **Linkii** (Lehm.) = *Echinocactus Linkii* Lehm. Radials thin, short, reflexed on the stem. Central spine longer, curved. Flower smaller, with obtuse petals. Stigma with 8 to 10 red lobes.

var. **brasiliensis** Haage jr. Radials erect, yellowish brown. Central spine shorter, straight, brownish. Petals spathulate, emarginate and almost heart-shaped. Stigma with 11 red lobes.

Notocactus pampeanus (Speg.) Berger = *Echinocactus pampeanus* Spegazzini. Uruguay and Argentina. Stem dark green, at first globular, afterwards elongated, up to 10 cm. high, and 5 or 6 cm. across, broadly depressed and spineless at the top, with white wool, with pronounced chin-like warts below the areoles. Ribs 21, straight. Radial spines 7 to 10, yellow, tipped darker, spreading, very acute, 1 cm. long. Central spine 1 only, rarely 2, thicker, stiff, almost curved, furrowed on the under surface, horny yellow, reddish at the base. Flower 3 cm. long, and 4 to 5 cm. broad: ovary roundish, covered with scales, with abundant dirty yellow wool and stiff brownish bristles in the axils; the inner petals are oval, abruptly acute, toothed, yellow.

Notocactus mammulosus (Lem.) Berger = *Echinocactus mammulosus* Lem. Uruguay and Argentina. Stem as in *N. pampeanus*, green or dark green, depressed and spineless at the top. Ribs 18 to 20, low, deeply notched, with the warts prolonged into a chin-like protuberance below the areoles, which are deeply set, woolly, about ½ cm. apart. Radial spines 10 to 13, very thin, less than ½ cm. long, yellowish, brown at the base and tip; central spines 2, stronger, awl-shaped, very acute, yellow, tipped darker, 1 to 1½ cm. long, one directed upwards, the other downwards. Flowers borne at the centre, about 4 cm. long, ovary and tube with white wool and brown or black bristles; outer petals yellow with a red midrib, the inner spathulate, obtuse, toothed, canary yellow, darker at the throat. Stigma with 9 purplish red lobes. Full sunshine.

Notocactus submammulosus (Lem.) Berger = *Echinocactus submammulosus* Lem. Uruguay and Argentina. Stem light green, with 13 ribs, notched as above. Spines stronger; radials 6, only one central, reflexed upwards, 2 cm. long. The rest as in the preceding species.

Notocactus rubriflorus Frič. Is a rare new species, recently discovered in Argentina. It is the only species with red flowers in this section.

B. *Stem with hairs and bristle-like spines at the top. Flower mostly small.*

Notocactus scopa (Link et Otto) Berger = *Echinocactus scopa* Link et Otto. Southern Brazil and Uruguay. A lovely species, deservedly popular. Stem globular, later elongated, pale green, entirely covered with white softish spines, up to 12 cm. high, and 4 to 6 cm. thick, occasionally sprouting from the base. Ribs 30 to 35, low, obtuse, notched into small warts. Areoles close together, about ½ cm. apart, with short white wool when young. Radial spines up to 40, very slender, just over ½ cm. long, at first snow white and softish. Central spines 3 to 4, stronger and longer, brown or dark brown. Flowers borne at the centre, 4 cm. long. Ovary with greenish scales, brown wool and dark brown bristles; petals acute, toothed, canary yellow; stigma with 10 to 12 red lobes.

var. **candida** Hort. Central spines white, tipped slightly pink when young. There is also a much appreciated cristate form of this variety.

var. **ruberrima** Hort. Central spines crimson red. A very attractive variety. A rare cristate form of this variety is occasionally met with.

Both the species and its varieties thrive well in full sunshine, requiring half-shade only during the hottest period of summer. The soil should be fairly rich, and freely watered during the growing season, but must be kept dry or almost dry in winter.

Notocactus Haselbergii (F. Haage) Berger = *Echinocactus Haselbergii* F. Haage. Southern Brazil. Another lovely species of small size, Stem globular or short-cylindrical, flat at the top and slightly depressed at the centre, entirely covered with slender and softish white spines, pale yellow at the top. The stem is up to 12 cm. high and 5 to 10 cm. across, often semi-prostrate, with 30 or more low ribs, divided into low round warts, 5 to 7 mm. apart. Areoles small with white wool. Radial spines 20 or more, needle-like, spreading more or less obliquely at first yellowish, passing to white, up to 1 cm. long. Central spines 3 to 5, mostly 4, slightly longer, up to 2 cm. at first golden yellow passing to yellowish. Flowers on the top areoles, 1½ cm. long, and about 1 cm. across, outer petals red, inner petals fiery red, or deep orange red, lasting for one week or more. Ovary round, with scales, with white wool and bristles in their axils. Style yellow, stigma with 6 dark yellow lobes. The plant is of easy cultivation in half-shade, occasionally sprouting from the base. Seedlings develop slowly, and are mostly grafted on *Trichocereus Spachianus*, and then they thrive better and are more free-flowering. Sometimes the plant is more robust, with flowers about twice as large, with the outer petals deep crimson, the inner scarlet orange. To this form the name *major* may be given.

Notocactus Leninghausii (K. Sch.) Berger = *Echinocactus Leninghausii* K. Sch. Southern Brazil. Stem oval-elongated or cylindrical, up to 1 m. high and up to 10 cm. thick, mostly tortuous, pale green, covered at or near the top with whitish wool and with long hair-like golden yellow spines, with about 30 low obtuse ribs, slightly notched. Areoles close together, round, with whitish wool when young. Radial spines up to 15, about ½ cm. long, slender and bristle-like, pale yellow; central spines 3 or 4, up to 4 cm. long, bristle-like or hair-like, golden yellow, arched backwards. Flowers borne at the top, near the centre, 4 cm. long, and 5 cm. across, on old stems: the outer petals greenish, the next yellow tipped green, the inner glossy yellow, toothed. Ovary and tube with scales, hairs and brownish bristles. Stamens very numerous, whitish yellow, as also the style; stigma with 9 to 14 pale yellow lobes. A beautiful and popular species, of easy growth in half-shade, to be kept rather dry at all times. The plant only flowers when it reaches a certain height, and then sprouts are also freely developed around the base and up the stem, resulting in nice groups. Small plants are very pretty. Grows very well on own roots, and it is often grafted, but growth is always slow. The flowers last for several days.

Notocactus muricatus (Otto) Berger = *Echinocactus muricatus* Otto. Southern Brazil and Uruguay. Stem globular or elongated, 8 to 15 cm. high, and 7 to 10 cm. thick, pale green, with up to 20 ribs, low, broad and obtuse, notched, with areoles in the depressions about ½ cm. apart, well furnished with white wool. Spines 15 or more, bristle-like, about ½ cm. long, spreading laterally, slightly curved, brown. Central spines 3 or 4, slightly longer and darker. Flower about 3½ cm. long: ovary and tube with scales, white wool and black bristles; petals lanceolate, pale yellow, stigma with 9 to 11 purplish red lobes. There is also a variety with longer spines. Requires full sunshine.

Notocactus floricomus (Arech.) Berger = *Echinocactus floricomus* Arech. Uruguay. Stem broadly globular, later elongated, up to 18 cm. high and up to 13 cm. across, with 20 ribs, notched into chin-like conical warts. Areoles 3 mm. apart, with white wool. Spines 20 or more, spreading, unequal, whitish or greyish, red at the base: central spines 4 or 5, stronger, 2 to 2½ cm. long, the central one straight and erect, the others radiating. Flowers numerous, around the top, 5½ to 6 cm. long, petals yellow, spathulate, toothed. Ovary and tube with scales, white wool and dark grey bristles. Stigma with 8 dark red lobes. Fruit oval, greenish, covered with white wool. Growth is rather slow. A very free-flowering species, requiring half-shade.

C. *Stem with few hairs at the top, but with rather stiff long spines. Flower small.*

Notocactus Graessneri (K. Sch.) Berger = *Echinocactus Graessneri* K. Sch. Southern Brazil. Stem globular, flattened and depressed at the top, 6 to 10 cm. high, and about as much across, pale green, entirely covered with short golden yellow spines. Ribs 50 to 60, low, arranged spirally, cut into very small warts, very close together, bearing small round areoles with yellow wool. Spines very numerous, in bundles: the radials needle-like, pale glassy yellow, up to 2 cm. long; the centrals 5 or 6, thicker and of a deeper yellow. Flowers at the top, around the centre, about 2 cm. long. Ovary and tube with scales, with white wool and yellow bristles in their axils; petals greenish yellow, stigma with 7 or 8 lobes. Requires half-shade. It is often grafted, but makes quick growth also on own roots.

Notocactus Schumannianus (Nicolai) Berger = *Echinocactus Schumannianus* Nicolai. Northern Argentina and Paraguay. Stem globular, later cylindrical and procumbent, up to 1 m. long, and about 12 cm. thick, pale green, passing to dark green, and finally almost corky, with white wool and spines at the top. Ribs about 30, low, acute, notched. Areoles small, round, less than 1 cm. apart. Spines 4 to 7, bristle-like, slightly curved backwards, reddish brown when young, passing to grey, the lowermost up to 5 cm. long, easily dropping off. Flowers borne at the top, 4 to 5 cm. long, and about the same across, funnel-shaped; petals spathulate, narrow, with few teeth, narrow, yellow. Stigma with 12 to 14 yellow lobes. Berry at first fleshy, pale yellow. Seeds many brown. Requires half-shade.

var. **nigrispinus** F. Haage jr. Ribs about 20; spines 9 or 10, arched backwards, at first reddish, passing to dull silver grey. Flower 3½ cm. long. Paraguay.

Notocactus Grossei (K. Sch.) Berger = *Echinocactus Grossei* K. Sch. Paraguay. Stem at first globular, later cylindrical and procumbent, up to 1.7 m. long, with 16 or more ribs, broad and obtuse, notched. Areoles in the notches, small, round, about 2 cm. apart, with short greyish wool. Spines 3 to 7 (mostly 4), spreading, variously curved, reddish yellow when young, passing to brown and greyish, the lower-most up to 4 cm. long. Flowers many, funnel-shaped, 4 cm. long, yellow, outer petals lanceolate, the inner spathulate and toothed.

Notocactus apricus (Arech.) Berger = *Echinocactus apricus* Arech. Uruguay, on sandy and grassy land, in exposed situations and full sunshine. Plant sprouting around the base and forming groups. Stem globular 3 to 5 cm. across, pale green, covered with reddish yellow spines, with 15 to 20 low ribs, slightly notched. Areoles round, 3 to 4 cm. apart, woolly when young. Radial spines 18 to 20, bristle-like, yellowish grey, curved; central spines 4, larger, red at the base, yellow above, the lowermost curved upwards, up to 3 cm. long. Flowers fairly large, 8 cm. long, with a thick tube 2 to 3 cm. long, clad with white wool and red bristles; petals yellow, the outer reddish on the dorsal side, the inner obtuse and toothed. Outer stamens yellow, the inner red. Stigma with 13 red lobes. Fruit oval, woolly, dark red.

Notocactus tabularis (Cels.) Berger = *Echinocactus tabularis* Cels. Uruguay and Southern Brazil. Stem globular or elongated, bluish green, 4½ to 8 cm. thick, with 16 to 23 low, obtuse ribs, notched, straight or oblique. Areoles about ½ cm. apart on the tip of the warts, small, with white wool. Radial spines 16 to 18, needle-like, spreading, glassy, up to 1 cm. long: central spines 4, crosswise, slightly curved backwards, white, tipped brown, slightly longer. Flower 6 cm. long, with wool and bristles on the ovary and tube; petals linear, glossy yellow, carmine red at the throat. Stamens, style, 12 to 13 lobed stigma, carmine red. A beautiful free-growing and free-flowering species, which thrives best in half-shade.

PYRRHOCACTUS Berger

Ribs notched; areoles large, with many subulate stiff spines. Ovary scaly, with white wool and sometimes with bristles in the axils of the scales. Flowers reddish yellow, hence the generic name, which means "flame-coloured Cactus." All species were formerly included by Britton and Rose under *Malacocarpus*. They are interesting species, remarkable for their formidable armament of numerous and strong spines.

Pyrrhocactus Strausianus (K. Sch.) Berger = *Echinocactus Strausianus* K. Sch. Western Argentina. Stem solitary, globular to oval, greyish green, up to 16 cm. high, and 9 cm. thick, with 13 prominent ribs, slightly spiral, thick, obtuse, notched into rounded warts, bearing elliptical areoles 1½ cm. long, at first with yellowish or greyish wool. Spines 9 to 20, not distinguishable in radials and centrals, all thick and awl-shaped or subulate, and very sharp, reddish brown, the 4 inner spines being thicker and slightly longer, up to 3 cm. long. Flower small, 1½ cm. long; outer petals brownish; the inner more numerous, linear-lanceolate, acute, salmon pink; scales of ovary and tube with

(a) HAMATOCACTUS HAMATACANTHUS (b) STENOCACTUS COPTONOGONUS

PLATE XLIV

(b) ECHINOCACTUS INGENS

(a) FEROCACTUS LATISPINUS

PLATE XLV

white wool and a few bristle-like spines. Stamens and style white, stigma with 12 creamy white lobes.

Pyrrhocactus tuberisulcatus (Jac.) Berger = *Echinocactus tuberisulcatus* Jac. = *E. Soehrensii* K. Sch. = *Cactus horridus* Colla. Chile (near Valparaiso). Stem solitary, broadly globular, much flattened, but not depressed at the centre, pale green, entirely covered with strong brown or grey spines. Ribs 16 to 20, about 2 cm. high, straight, notched into large prominent obtuse warts, with a pronounced chin below the areoles. These are 2 to 3 cm. apart, large, elliptical, 1½ cm. long; but are quite small, very woolly and spineless when young. Radial spines 10 to 12, at first few, developing to this number in the second or third year. Central spines 4 or 5, stronger and longer, up to 2½ cm. long. All spines are very stiff, awl-shaped, straight or slightly curved, at first brown or dark brown, zoned darker, passing to grey. Flowers 4½ cm. long, very numerous, borne at the top, 2 or 3 in the same areole, funnel-shaped; petals brownish yellow with a red median band. The scales of the ovary and tube have a little whitish wool, and a few bristles in their axils. Stamens and style are yellow above, reddish below; stigma with 13 reddish lobes collected in a globular mass. A beautiful species, now frequently grown.

Pyrrhocactus Kunzei (Först.) Berger = *Echinocactus Kunzei* Först. = *E. supertextus* Pfeiff. Chile, at high altitudes. Stem broadly globular, flattened, and somewhat depressed at the centre, entirely covered with stiff yellow or dark grey spines, at first pale green, passing to ashy green. Ribs 16 to 21, about 1 cm. high, divided into rounded warts, compressed laterally, with a well marked chin below the areoles. These are less than 1½ cm. apart, elliptical, about ½ cm. long, with short whitish wool. Radial spines 9 to 12, the middle pair, the longest, up to 2 cm. long; central spines mostly 4, stronger, the upper one up to 2½ cm. long. Almost all spines are more or less curved upwards, yellow, tipped dark, when young, passing to yellowish brown and later to greyish. Flowers numerous, bell-shaped, 5½ to 6 cm. long, brick red. Ovary and tube with wool and dark brown bristles in the axils of the scales. Stamens yellow, stigma with 8 to 12 yellow lobes.

Pyrrhocactus curvispinus (Bert.) Berger = *Cactus curvispinus* Bert. = *Echinocactus curvispinus* Remy. Chile (south of Constitucion). Stem globular or elongated, about 16 cm. thick, greyish green, with few spines at the top. Ribs 16, up to 3 cm. high, thick and obtuse, divided into elongated rounded warts, with a chin-like prominence below the areoles. These are elliptical, 2 to 3 cm. apart, and up to 1½ cm. long, with short whitish wool. Spines 14 to 18, awl-shaped or subulate, stiff, the middle one curved upwards, the lower pair up to 3 cm. long, at first yellow or yellowish grey, tipped darker, later greyish. Flowers many, 5 to 6 cm. long, funnel-shaped. The small acute scales on the ovary and tube have whitish wool and small bristles in their axils. Petals yellowish with a median brownish band, the inner petals obtuse. Stamens, style and the 10-lobed stigma yellow.

W

Pyrrhocactus Froelichianus (K. Sch.) Berger = *Echinocactus Froelichianus* K. Sch. Chile. Stem globular or short-columnar, pale green, up to 15 cm. high, and 16 to 17 cm. thick, slightly depressed and almost spineless at the top. Ribs 16, straight or almost spiral, rounded, about 3 cm. high, divided into large rounded warts, with a very slight chin-like process below the areoles. These are 2 to 3 cm. apart, elliptical or linear, 1½ cm. long, with yellowish white wool. Spines up to 17, straight or slightly curved, awl-shaped, the lowest pair the longest, 3 cm. long, more or less curved upwards. All spines are yellow or yellowish grey when young, passing to grey. Flowers numerous, 5½ to 6½ cm. long, with a green globose ovary, covered with small oval acute scales, with wool and a few bristles in their axils. Tube short, petals expanded, oblong, yellow, pointed pink; the inner petals are spathulate, obtuse, minutely toothed, brownish outside, glossy yellow inside. Nearly allied to the preceding, and often considered as a mere variety.

Pyrrhocactus centeterius (Lehm.) Berger = *Echinocactus centeterius* Lehm. = *E. pachycentrus* Lehm. = *E. hybocentrus* Lehm. = *E. mamillarioides* Hook. Chile, and the Argentinian Andes. Stem globular, dark green, 10 to 15 cm. thick, with about 15 ribs, almost spiral, notched into round warts with a pronounced chin below the areoles. These are 1 to 1½ cm. apart, elliptical, hardly woolly. Radial spines 10 to 12, awl-shaped, but slender, spreading, variously curved. Central spines 4, crosswise, stronger, thickened, at the base, blackish curved. Flowers many, funnel-shaped, 3 to 4 cm. long, outer petals lanceolate-acute, greenish yellow, with a median brown band; the inner petals yellow, with a reddish yellow median band. Stamens reddish, style and 8- to 10-lobed stigma yellow.

var. **pachycentrus** (Lehm.) Salm-Dyck = *E. pachycentrus* Lehm. Warts much more prominent, with the chin-like process about twice as long; central spines longer.

Pyrrhocactus umadeave (Frič) Werd. et Backbg. = *Friesia umadeave* Frič. = *Echinocactus umadeave* Werd. North Argentina (Salta and Jujuy), up to 3,000 m. above sea level. Stem solitary or branching from the base, more or less globular, dull green, in its native country up to 40 cm. high and 25 cm. thick; middling specimens in cultivation are 10 to 12 cm. across, the top covered with a mass of long spines. Ribs 18 to 27, 1 cm. high, slightly notched into low warts. Areoles large, with whitish wool. Spines 30 to 35, radials and centrals alike, fewer in young specimens, awl-shaped, stiff, whitish or light brownish pink, tipped darker, 3 to 4 cm. long, all more or less curved upwards. Flowers on the new areoles at the centre, 3 to 3½ cm. long. Ovary and tube scaly, with whitish wool and a few pale yellow bristles in the axils of the scales. Flower yellow, outer petals mostly reddish yellow on the dorsal side.

This singular plant lives on sandy and barren ground at 2,500 to 3,000 m. above the sea, and is therefore resistant to low temperatures.

Should be planted in sand or very sandy soil and should not be watered, but only slightly sprayed now and then. It has a long and thick tap root, requiring the use of long pots, and should be placed in an exposed situation and in full sunshine. It is rather difficult to deal with on own roots, and is usually grafted on thick-stemmed Cerei, such as *Trichocereus macrogonus* and *T. Pachanoi*.

Austrocactus Bertinii Br. et R. = *Cereus Bertinii* Cels., was included under this genus by its author, Dr. Alwin Berger, but this species, native of Patagonia, appears to have little relationship with the species of *Pyrrhocactus* above described.

PARODIA Spegazzini

(*Hickenia* Br. et R.; *Microspermia* Frič; *Islaya* Backbg.)

Small plants with globular or elongated stems, very spiny, solitary or sprouting from the base. Ribs well marked, straight or spiral, with small low tubercles. Spines straight, or one of the centrals hooked at the tip. Usually with abundant white wool and bristles in the axils of the small scales of the ovary. Areoles on the top of the tubercles, with white wool, especially at the top or centre of the plant. Includes at least 28 species.

(*a*) *Rectispinae. Spines not hooked.*

Parodia islayensis (Förster) = *Echinocactus islayensis* Förster = *Malacocarpus islayensis* Rose = *Islaya islayensis* Backbg. Peru, sandy wastes at the foot of the Andes. Globular or short-cylindric, depressed, about 18 cm. high, deep greyish green. Ribs numerous, low, more or less spirally arranged, notched into tubercles. Radial spines 15 to 20, diaphanous yellowish grey. Central spines 4 to 7, straight and up to 1½ cm. long, brownish yellow, passing to greyish. Flowers borne on the new areoles at the centre, 1½ to 2 cm. long: ovary and tube scaly, woolly, and furnished with reddish bristles. Petals yellow.

Parodia minor (Backbg.) = *Islaya minor* Backbg. Peru, same district as the preceding. Plant smaller, globular, depressed, with about 17 acute ribs, 6 mm. high. Areoles woolly at first, 3 mm. apart. Radial spines about 20, stiff, thin, black at first, passing to grey, up to 6 mm. long. Central spines 4, arranged crosswise, black passing to silvery grey, longer and thicker. Flowers arising from the yellowish wool at the top of the plant, about 2 cm. broad, golden yellow.

For this and the preceding species Backeberg has instituted the genus *Islaya*, owing to the fact that in both species "the fruit is globular, like that of a Notocactus, hollow inside, and bears the seeds arranged in a ring."

Parodia Faustiana Backbg. North Argentina (Salta). Plant solitary, globular, 5 to 6 cm. thick, pale green. Ribs about 16, cut into low tubercles. Radial spines about 20, very slender, glassy white, spreading laterally, about 1 cm. long; central spines 4, about 2½ cm. long, brown, thick and stiff. Flowers scarlet outside, golden yellow inside.

var. **tenuispina** Backbg. Central spines very slender; flowers blood red outside.

Parodia chrysacanthion (K. Sch.) Speg. = *Echinocactus chrysacanthion* K. Sch. Argentina. Stem single or sprouting, globular to short-columnar, 5 to 6 cm. high and 5 cm. thick, pale green, with 24 or more ribs arranged spirally, and entirely made up of small conical warts, ½ cm. long and ½ cm. apart, tipped with a small areole with yellow wool. Spines numerous, 30 to 40; the outer very slender and bristle-like, the lower less than ½ cm. long, whitish yellow, spreading; the inner thicker and longer, golden yellow passing to golden brown, very glossy, about 2 cm. long. Flowers at the top around the centre, on the upper side of the areoles, less than 2 cm. long, funnel-shaped, golden yellow; tube and outer petals, as well as the ovary, covered with golden yellow wool and bristles or spines; the inner petals spathulate, obtuse or abruptly acute. Berry oval, small, with minute seeds. Stamens, style and the 6- to 8-lobed stigma yellow. Requires half-shade. A pretty and interesting miniature species.

Parodia microthele Backbg. North Argentina. Stem roundish or oval, about 5 cm. thick, grass green, with small tubercles, arranged spirally. Spines very slender, all straight, numerous, 4 to 8 mm. long, white, with a few yellow or brownish ones among them. Flowers about 2 cm. across, orange red. Very free-flowering; closely allied to *P. microsperma*.

Parodia nivosa Frič = *Microspermia nivosa* Frič. Argentina. Stem globular or short-cylindric, 4 to 5 cm. thick, depressed at the top, grass green, covered with abundant snow-white wool at the top. Ribs 16 to 20, arranged spirally, cut into round conical tubercles 3 mm. long, bearing round areoles, comparatively large, with much white wool, especially when young. All spines are straight. Radial spines 15 to 20, 2 to 4 mm. long, white, bristle-like. Central spines 3 to 5, up to 1½ cm. long, at first reddish yellow, soon passing to white. Flowers fiery scarlet. Full sunshine. A charming miniature plant, closely allied to *P. microsperma*.

(*b*) Uncinatae. *At least one of the central spines hooked.*

Parodia microsperma (Weber) Speg. = *Echinocactus microspermus* Weber = *Hickenia microsperma* Br. et R. = *Microspermia microsperma* Frič. Argentina (high, dry mountainous regions in various provinces). Stem sprouting freely from the base, globular, light green, 5 to 10 cm. thick, somewhat elongated when old, very spiny. Ribs many, arranged spirally, divided into low conical warts, 2 to 3 mm. apart, bearing small woolly areoles. Radial spines 10 to 20, spreading, glassy white, about ½ cm. long. Central spines 3 or 4, up to 2 cm. long, reddish brown, the lowermost hooked at the tip. Flowers several, borne at the centre, funnel-shaped, 3½ to 5 cm. across, with a short tube; outer petals pale red with a darker midrib, inner petals orange yellow. A very pretty species, well worthy of cultivation. The seeds are very minute, brown and smooth, with a white corky scar, and the fruit is small, round, thin-walled. Thrives best in half-shade, and is easily propagated by offsets.

var. **macrancistra** K. Sch. The hooked spines are twice as long and thick; petals pointed brown. Flowers freely even when young.

var. **elegans** Hort. More woolly; spines more slender and paler.

var. **brunispina** Hort. Central spines darker brown.

var. **rigidissima** Hort. Radial spines thicker; central spines thicker and stiffer.

Parodia Maassii (Heese) Berger = *Echinocactus Maassii* Heese. = *Malacocarpus Maassii* Br. et R. Bolivia and northern Argentina. Stem globular or elongated, 5 to 15 cm. thick, pale green, with some white wool and yellowish or brownish spines at the top. Ribs 13 to 21, arranged spirally, obtuse, $\frac{1}{2}$ to 1 cm. high, divided into roundish or compressed warts with a chin-like process on the lower side. Areoles on the top of the warts, round, almost bare when old, about $\frac{1}{2}$ cm. apart. Radial spines 7 to 15, spreading outwards, $\frac{1}{2}$ to 1 cm. long, bristle-like, straight or sometimes 1 or 2 curved, honey yellow, later almost white. Central spines 4, stronger and longer, bulbous at the base, curved downwards or hooked, the lower one the strongest and longest, 3 to 4 cm. long, directed downwards, always strongly hooked at the tip, pale brown, passing to honey yellow. Flower large, like that of *P. microsperma*. Ovary very woolly; the short tube has long white hairs and also brown bristles in the axils of the scales. Petals linear-lanceolate, brick red. Stigma with yellow lobes. Thrives best in half-shade. Will do well on own roots, but grows better and faster when grafted.

Parodia brasiliensis (Werd.) Speg. = *Echinocactus brasiliensis* Werd. Brazil (Santos). Stem solitary or sprouting around the base, globular, 3 to 4 cm. across, grass green. Ribs about 15, cut into conical warts, bearing small areoles with short brownish wool. Radial spines 8 to 10, very thin, spreading on the stem, about $\frac{1}{2}$ cm. long, whitish or yellowish; one central spine about 1 cm. long, curved backwards, brown, with its tip hooked backwards. Flowers borne at the centre, about $2\frac{1}{2}$ cm. long, scaly, woolly and with brown bristles on the outside; inner petals whitish or very pale pink. Half-shade.

Parodia amambayensis Werd. et Backbg. = *Echinocactus amambayensis* Werd. et Backbg. = *Parodia paraguayensis* Speg. Paraguay (Sierra de Amambay). Solitary or forming groups; stem globular, 3 to $4\frac{1}{2}$ cm. across, partly embedded in the ground, greyish brown, with 8 to 12 ribs, lightly notched into warts. Areoles 3 to 5 on each rib, lightly woolly when young. Radial spines 5, curved backwards, up to 1 cm. long. One central spine, stronger, $1\frac{1}{2}$ to 2 cm. long, hooked at the tip. All spines are at first ash grey, passing to horny yellow. Flowers 2 to $2\frac{1}{2}$ cm. long, with scales, reddish brown wool and bristles on the outer side. Inner petals golden yellow.

Parodia schwebsiana Werd. et Backbg. = *Echinocactus Schweb-*

sianus Werd. et Backbg. Bolivia. Similar to *P. Maassii,* but smaller, solitary or forming groups. Stem globular, somewhat flat at the top, pale glossy green, 5 to 6 cm. high, with white wool at the top. Ribs 13 to 20, 4 mm. high, lightly notched into warts, with areoles about ½ cm. apart, with much white wool when young. Radial spines about 10, spreading laterally, up to 1 cm. long, yellowish or brownish, later greyish white, rather thick and needle-like. One central spine up to 2 cm. long, thick, brownish curved backwards, often hooked at the tip. Flowers 3 to 4 cm. long; ovary and tube with scales, with white hairs and a few brown bristles in their axils; inner petals wine red or rusty red.

Parodia Stuemeri Werd. et Backbg. = *Echinocactus Stuemeri* Werd. et Backbg. North Argentina (Salta). Plant solitary or forming groups when old. Stem globular, up to 10 cm. thick, pale grass green, with whitish or brownish wool at the top, along with dark brown spines. Ribs about 20, low, cut into conical warts, with areoles 1 cm. apart, with whitish or greyish brown wool when young. Radial spines 25, needle-like, spreading laterally, many almost curved, white 1 to 2 cm. long. Central spines mostly 4, the lower one the longest and often hooked at the tip, all the four stiff and needle-like, about 2 cm. long, brown tipped darker. Flowers about 4 cm. long; ovary and tube scaly, with reddish brown wool and a brown bristle or two, about 1 cm. long. Petals clear golden yellow, pale orange with brown at the tip.

var. **tilcarensis** Werd. et Backbg. North Argentina, at Tilcara. Spines fewer. Flowers 3 cm. long, clear orange red.

Parodia carminata Backbg. North Argentina (Salta). Stem roundish or oval, about 5 cm. thick, bluish green. Ribs 10 to 12, spiral, cut into roundish tubercles. Radial spines about 18, slender, white, up to 8 mm. long. Central spines 4, arranged crosswise, dark brown or black, up to 2 cm. long, the lowest one hooked, sometimes all straight. Flowers 2½ cm. long, and as broad, glossy carmine to dull orange.

Parodia rubricentra Backbg. North Argentina (Salta). Stem spherical, 7 to 8 cm. thick. Ribs about 16, spirally arranged, cut into broad tubercles, 1 cm. apart. Radial spines many, white, bristle-like, spreading, longer than the centrals, flexible, up to 1 cm. long, usually 3 to 5, only slightly curved, yellowish red, later passing to white or grey, pink at the centre, one of them sometimes hooked. Flower small, pale coppery red.

Parodia erythrantha Speg. North Argentina. Stem spherical, grass green, about 5 cm. thick, with small tubercles, spirally arranged in about 16 rows. Areoles at first very woolly. Radial spines about 20, very slender and short, spreading laterally. Central spines 4, up to 1 cm. long, slender, white at the base like the radials, but reddish above, one of them hooked. Flowers freely borne, about 2½ cm. broad, red, stigma white.

Parodia aureispina Backbg. Argentina. Globular, small, covered with golden spines. Ribs spiral, cut into small warts. Radial spines about 40, short, thin, bristle-like, white. Central spines 6, longer, up to 2 cm., golden yellow, thickened at the base, one of them hooked at the tip. Flowers borne at the top, golden yellow, 3 cm. across; tube with white hairs. A rare and very pretty species from the province of Salta, perfectly hardy.

Parodia aureicentra Backbg. Argentina (Salta). Stem globular to short-cylindric, glossy lively green, solitary or forming groups, 4 to 6 cm. thick. Ribs 13 to 16, slightly spiral, broad and obtuse, cut into prominent tubercles 5 mm. high, bearing large round areoles, 1 cm. apart, thickly furnished with yellowish white wool, more abundant at the top of the plant. Radial spines 16 to 22, white, bristle-like, spreading, up to 1 cm. long. Central spines mostly 4, golden yellow, the upper one straight up to $1\frac{1}{2}$ cm. long, the other three up to $2\frac{1}{2}$ cm. long, hooked at the tip. Flowers yellow. Another rare and charming species, of quick growth.

Parodia gigantea Frič. Argentina (Salta). Stem at first globular, later much elongated or cylindrical, up to 30 cm. high, and 5 to 6 cm. thick, solitary or forming groups, pale glaucous green, with 13 to 18 ribs, very spiral, obtuse, but narrow and closely set, about $\frac{1}{2}$ cm. high, notched into round tubercles, tipped with a large round areole, at first with much yellowish grey wool, later almost bare. Radial spines many, white, bristle-like, passing to yellow up to $\frac{1}{2}$ cm. long. Central spines 4 or 5, golden yellow, the upper 1 or 2 straight, about $\frac{1}{2}$ cm. long, the other 3 up to 1 cm. long, hooked at the tip. Flowers yellow

Parodia setifer Backbg. Argentina, from the high hills of Salta. Plant small, globular, depressed, dark green, with 18 narrow ribs, 6 mm. high. Radial spines about 20, white, up to 8 mm. long. Central spines 3 or 4, pale pink, passing to black, one of them hooked. Flowers whitish, $3\frac{1}{2}$ cm. across, borne at the top.

var. **nigricentra** Backbg. Central spines glossy black.

var. **orthorachis** Backbg. All spines almost straight.

Parodia mutabilis Backbg. Argentina, on high hills at Salta, like the preceding, at elevations of 2,800 m. Globular, glaucous green, about 8 cm. thick, with white wool at the top. Ribs indistinct or cut into warts, with large woolly areoles. Radial spines about 50, very thin and bristle-like, white. Central spines mostly 4, arranged crosswise, white to orange, tipped darker, one of them hooked at the tip. Flowers borne at the top, golden yellow, sometimes with a red throat, 5 cm. across, lasting for several days. A variable and beautiful species.

var. **carneospina** Backbg. Central spines pale pink.

var. **elegans** Backbg. Central spines glossy black.

var. **ferruginea** Backbg. Central spines rusty red.

Parodia sanguiniflora (Frič) Backbg. = *Microspermia sanguiniflora* Frič. Argentina (Salta, at elevations of 2,000 m.). Stem solitary, globular, depressed, tender green, woolly at the top. Ribs spirally arranged, cut into conical warts, bearing areoles 6 mm. apart, at first very woolly.

Radial spines about 15, bristle-like, white, radiating, 6 to 8 mm. long.
Central spines 4, arranged crosswise, brownish, the lowest hooked at
the tip and up to 2 cm. long. Flowers numerous, borne at the top,
blood red, 4 cm. across. A very desirable species.

var. **violacea** Frič. Flowers reddish violet.

Parodia catamarcensis Backbg. Northern Argentina (Catamarca).
Stem globular to short-cylindric, or elongated and curved, dark green.
Ribs 16 to 20, spirally arranged, divided into low flat tubercles. Areoles
4 mm. apart, at first with abundant white wool. Radial spines about
9, spreading laterally and downwards, white, up to ½ cm. long. Central
spines 4, spreading outwards, more or less curved, pure dark red,
the lowest bent downwards, thicker, hooked at the tip. Flowers 3 to
4 cm. across, whitish yellow.

Parodia sanagasta (Frič) Weingart = *Microspermia sanagasta* Frič.
Northern Argentina (Salta). Stem globular, often coppery red or
purplish, 4 to 5 cm. thick, with about 15 ribs, somewhat spiral, cut into
more or less angular tubercles, with round areoles, rather large, 5 to
7 mm. apart, at first with much white or whitish wool. The top of the
stem is covered with white wool. Radial spines 7 to 11, white, the
lower thicker and up to 8 mm. long. Central spines 4, the lowest being
the strongest, up to 1½ cm. long, hooked at the tip and directed downwards. At first the central spines are blood red, passing to white and
later to brown. Flowers yellow, the outer petals with a brown dorsal
band.

var. **albiflora** Hort. Flowers very pale yellow.
The following are other species in cultivation: **Parodia aurihamata**
Backbg., **P. jujuyana** Frič, **P. rigidispina** Frič and **P. rubrispina** Frič.

SPEGAZZINIA Backbg. (1933)

A new genus established to include two aberrant species from the
high arid ground along the Argentina-Bolivia boundary, and a third
species has lately been added. It is characterized by the presence of
a swollen root, separated from the body of the plant by a slender neck.
The plants are very spiny. The flowers are small, borne on the upper
areoles, near the centre, with a very short tube and a fully expanded
limb, which remains expanded on fading and persists on the fruit,
which is small, splitting at the base when ripe. The plants are not
affected by the recurrent sharp frosts of the cold regions where they
grow.

The genus is nearly allied to *Parodia*, if not quite identical with it;
but apart from the swollen root, the spines are thicker, and the flowers
are not borne on the central areoles. On the other hand, a similar
root, with a slender neck, is present in *Opuntia subterranea*, in
Neoporteria napina, in *Thelocactus subterraneus* and in *T. mandragora*,
plants of widely different affinities, and therefore cannot be taken as a
generic character of paramount importance.

Spegazzinia Fidaiana Backbg. Bolivia (southern province Potosi). Plant at first solitary, later throwing offsets from the upper areoles, greyish green, globular or oval or elongated, about 6 cm. thick, with about 15 deep ribs, notched into prominences on which are large, woolly, round areoles. Spines thick, but flexible, at first pale yellow, passing to violet black; 9 radials up to 3 cm. long; 3 or 4 centrals up to 5 cm. long, spreading, partly recurved. Flower cadmium yellow, 3 cm. long, and about as broad, with rounded petals, fully expanded. Ovary and very short tube scaly.

Spegazzinia Neumanniana Backbg. Same habitat. Similar to the preceding and possibly only a well-marked variety, but the flowers are orange red with pointed petals.

Spegazzinia Cumingii (Hopff.) Backbg. = *Echinocactus Cumingii* Hopff. = *Lobivia Cumingii* Br. et R. Slopes of the Andes in Bolivia and Peru. Stem of a lively green, globular depressed, about 10 cm. high. Ribs 18 or more, irregularly spiral, acute and notched. Areoles 2 to 3 cm. apart, round or oval, about ½ cm. long, whitish. Radial spines up to 20, spreading, the upper ones about 1 cm. long, the lower shorter. Central spines 2 to 8, longer, dark yellow or brownish, passing to grey, later developing minute hairs. Flowers borne on the sides or near the top, 2½ to 3 cm. long, funnel-shaped, orange red, with a yellow tube, scaly but not hairy. Stamens yellow. Stigma with 4 or 5 lobes. Very free-flowering, and capable of resisting low temperatures.

var. **flavescens** Poselg. Central spines pale yellow or white. Flowers pure yellow.

The genus *Weingartia*, established recently by Werdermann, is identical with *Spegazzinia* and includes the same species.

FRAILEA Br. et R.

Small plants, globular or cylindrical, often sprouting and forming groups, rounded at the top or depressed. Ribs many, low, notched into warts, with small slender spines. Flowers small, at the top of the plant, scaly, with wool and bristles; fruit likewise covered with scales, wool and bristles. Seeds black or brown, glossy, triangular, and con-cave on one side. The flowers are often cleistogamous (*i.e.* setting fruit without the flower opening). Includes 15 species, all miniature plants, natives of South America. All require half-shade, and grow better when grafted.

Frailea colombiana (Werd.) Backbg. = *Echinocactus colombianus* Werd. Colombia (near Dagua). Solitary or branching, forming flat groups; stem globular or oval, up to 4 cm. thick, glossy grass green. Ribs about 18, low, divided into low warts, up to ½ cm. apart, bearing minute areoles with whitish or brownish wool. Radial spines 15 to 20, bristle-like and flexible, less than ½ cm. long, spreading around almost comb-like, yellowish passing to greyish white. Central spines 2 to 5, hardly different from the radials, the lowermost just over ½ cm. long.

Ovary and tube with scales, having greyish wool and 1 or 2 dark brown bristles in their axils. Inner petals yellow, or yellow with a greenish sheen.

Frailea pumila (Lem.) Br. et R. = *Echinocactus pumilus* Lem. Paraguay and Argentina. Stem sub-globular, flattened and depressed at the centre, sprouting around the base, dark green, 3 cm. broad and 2 cm. high, with 13 to 15 flat ribs, very lightly notched. Areoles up to ½ cm. apart, round, small, with short brownish wool. Radial spines 12 to 14, up to ½ cm. long, greyish brown, mostly curved, quite soft. Central spines 1 or 2, similar to the radials, slightly longer and curved. Flowers many, cleistogamous, or opening only at midday, when the sun shines upon them. Petals brownish green, the inner ones spathulate, yellow. Stamens yellowish, style greenish, stigma with 5 yellow lobes.

Frailea pygmaea (Speg.) Br. et R. = *Echinocactus pygmaeus* Speg. Uruguay and Argentina. Stem globular, depressed at the centre, 1 to 3 cm. thick, dull dark green, freely sprouting, with 13 to 21 ribs, cut into warts. Spines 6 to 9, thin, bristle-like, whitish, tortuous and curved backwards, 1 to 4 mm. long. Flowers 2 to 2½ cm. long, mostly cleistogamous, with wool and bristles on the outer side; inner petals lanceolate, yellow; stigma with 6 or 7 yellowish lobes.

Frailea gracillima (Lem.) Br. et R. = *Echinocactus gracillimus* Lem. Paraguay. Stem globular to cylindrical, 4 to 10 cm. high, and up to 3 cm. thick, olive green or greyish green, often sprouting around the base, with 12 to 14 ribs, straight or slightly spiral at the centre, which is depressed. Ribs flat, divided into low round warts, bearing small round areoles, at first whitish, passing to brownish or greyish. Radial spines about 16, very short and curved, glassy white; central spines mostly 2, stronger and darker. Flowers 3 cm. long, with whitish wool and brown bristles; outer petals reddish on the outer side, inner petals linear, pale yellow, toothed, red at the throat. Stamens and style white, stigma with 13 white lobes. Seeds glossy yellowish brown, pitted.

Frailea Schilinzkyana (F. Haage jr.) Br. et R. = *Echinocactus Schilinzkyanus* F. Haage jr. Paraguay and Argentina. Plant freely sprouting around the base, with a thick conical tap root; stem globular, depressed, pale green passing to greyish green, 2 to 4 cm. across. Ribs 10 to 13, very flat, warts low, with small elongated areoles, less than ½ cm. apart. Spines 12 to 14, spreading, thin, 2 to 3 mm. long, black, curved backwards, falling off with age. Flowers 3½ cm. long, almost always cleistogamous. Ovary and tube with brown scales, white wool and 1 or 2 brown bristles: outer petals yellow, reddish on the outer side; inner petals spathulate-acute, sulphur yellow. Stamens yellowish, style and stigma white. Seeds brown, lightly pitted.

Frailea Grahliana (F. Haage jr.) Br. et R. = *Echinocactus Grahlianus* F. Haage jr. Paraguay. Plant freely sprouting around the base. Stem globular, flattened and depressed, 3 to 4 cm. thick, brownish green, with 13 straight ribs, very low, cut into round low warts, bearing oval areoles, with 9 to 11 curved spines less than ½ cm. long, at first yellow. Flowers 4 cm. broad, lively yellow. Fruit yellowish, with reddish brown scales, yellowish wool and small yellow bristles. Seeds glossy brown, lightly pitted. The form *rubrispina* Hort. has reddish brown spines.

Frailea Dadakii (Frič) Br. et R. = *Echinocactus Dadakii* Frič. Uruguay and Argentina. Similar to *F. pygmaea*. Stem with 12 ribs. Spines 8, brownish passing to white, curved backwards and twisted.

Frailea pulcherrima (Lem.) Br. et R. = *Echinocactus pulcherrimus* Lem. Paraguay and Argentina. Stem dark green, very freely sprouting at the base, 2 to 2½ cm. thick, depressed at the centre. Warts very low. Areoles small with greyish wool. Spines 14, pale brown, reflexed on the stem. One central spine, often absent, straight and stronger.

Frailea Knippeliana (Quehl.) Br. et R. = *Echniocactus Knippelianus* Quehl. Paraguay. Stem solitary, elongated, 4 cm. high, 2 to 3 cm. thick, glossy grass green, with 15 ribs divided into round low warts, bearing round areoles with yellowish wool and a few whitish bristles. Spines 16, amber yellow; the radials short and curved, the 2 to 4 centrals darker and longer, up to 1 cm. long. All spines later passing to greyish, and finally dropping off the corky areoles. Flowers up to 2½ cm. long, opening only when in full sun, outside streaked red, inside yellow. Seeds brown.

Frailea cataphracta (Dams) Br. et R. = *Echinocactus cataphractus* Dams. Paraguay. Stem globular, depressed, sprouting around the base, up to 4 cm. thick. Ribs 15, notched into low flat warts, with areoles about 3 mm. apart, with their lower half marked with a crescent-shaped brown or violet spot. Radial spines 5, directed backwards and laterally, slender, up to 2 mm. long, golden yellow, passing to greyish. Central spines absent. Flowers about 4 cm. long, and about the same across, mostly cleistogamous. Ovary and tube with brownish scales and greyish wool; outer petals greenish with a darker median band; inner petals pale yellow, pink at the throat. Stamens, style and lobes of stigma pale yellow. Fruit round, 4 mm. thick, with yellowish scales and pale brown hairs. Seeds large, glossy black.

Frailea caespitosa (Speg.) Br. et R. = *Echinocactus caespitosus* Speg. Uruguay (near Montevideo). Stem small, top-shaped or clavate, 4 to 7 cm. long, 1½ to 4½ cm. thick, depressed at the centre, half buried in the ground and sprouting very freely. Ribs 11 to 22, low, cut into low warts. Areoles round or oval, less than ½ cm. apart. Radial spines 9 to 11, very short, yellowish. Central spines 1 to 4, more or less curved, the longest 1 to 1½ cm. long. Flowers 3½ to 4 cm. long; inner petals yellow, lanceolate, acute; stamens yellow, style white, lobes of stigma purplish violet; scales of ovary and tube with greyish wool and bristles.

Other species in cultivation are: **Frailea castanea** Frič, **F. asterioides** Blossfeld, **F. phaeodisca** Speg. and **V. pseudopulcherrima** Frič.

MILA Br. et R.

(An anagram of Lima, Peru.)

A genus of small plants with cylindrical stems, branching from the base, with the habit of *Echinocereus*, having low ribs and needle-like spines. Flowers small, bell-shaped, yellow, borne at the top of the stems, with a short scaly tube and scaly ovary, having a few long hairs in the axils. Fruit small, roundish, glossy green, juicy. Seeds black, tuberculate. Originally included only one species, to which two more have been added recently. All natives of Peru.

Mila caespitosa Br. et R. A lowly plant, up to 15 cm. high, with stems 2 to 3 cm. thick, mostly prostrate, with about 10 ribs, with brown areoles, less than ½ cm. apart. Spines yellowish or whitish, tipped brown, the radials about 20, up to 1 cm. long, 1 central spine up to 3 cm. long. Flowers about 1½ cm. long, yellow. Thrives best in a sandy soil, in full sunshine.

Mila Kubeana Werd. et Backbg. About the same size as the preceding, and just as freely cespitose, often semi-prostrate, with about 11 ribs, slightly warty, with yellowish areoles, less than ½ cm. apart. Radial spines 9 to 12, white, spreading, bristle-like, up to 1 cm. long. Central spines 2 to 4, stronger, yellowish with a darker point, passing to grey, the lowermost up to 2 cm. long.

Mila Nealeana Backbg. Very much like the preceding, but growth is stronger. Plant freely cespitose, pale green. Stems up to 15 cm. long, often procumbent, and 2 to 4½ cm. thick, with about 11 low, flat ribs. Areoles round, more closely set, with yellow wool. Radial spines about 12, bristle-like, glassy white, up to 8 mm. long. Central spines 3 or 4, up to 1½ cm. long, flexible, straw-coloured, mostly directed downwards. Flowers pale yellow, 2½ cm. across, funnel-shaped, with a short tube, borne at the top of the stem. Just as easy to grow as *M. caespitosa*.

SCLEROCACTUS Br. et R.

Plant solitary or in clusters; stems with prominent warty or wavy ribs. Spines many, at least one of the upper centrals being papery, and at least one of the lower hooked. Flowers purple, borne on the central areoles. Ovary scaly. Fruit oblong or pear-shaped, almost bare, dry, opening by a basal pore. Seeds large, black, warty, with a large lateral scar.

Includes two species, North American.

Sclerocactus Whipplei (Engelm. et Big.) Br. et R. = *Echinocactus Whipplei* Engelm. et Big. New Mexico and Colorado. Plant solitary or slowly clustering; stem globular or oval, depressed and with white wool at the centre, 6 to 12 cm. high and 5 to 9 cm. thick, with 13 to 15 ribs, prominent, straight below, spiral above, sinuate and warty. Areoles 1 to 1½ cm. apart, round, with short whitish wool, later bare. Radial spines mostly 7, awl-shaped, spreading horizontally, whitish, straight or curved, up to 2 cm. long. Central spines 4, white, curved upwards, the uppermost straight, leaf-like, directed upwards, the lower one stronger, curved downwards, hooked at the tip. Flowers about 2 cm. long, borne on the central areoles; ovary with small, round, or kidney-shaped scales. Outer petals oval, obtuse; the inner oblong and acute, brownish outside, reddish green inside. Rather rare in cultivation.

var. **spinosior** Engelm. Radial spines more numerous (9 to 11), the lower ones brownish, the upper snow white. Utah and Colorado.

Sclerocactus polyancistrus (Engelm. et Big.) Br. et R. = *Echinocactus polyancistrus* Engelm. et Big. California and Nevada. Plant solitary, rarely sprouting at the base; stem oval to cylindrical, 8 to 20 cm. high and 6 to 10 cm. across, pale green, rounded at the top, with short yellowish wool and spines at the centre. Ribs 13 to 17, with narrow furrows beteen them, sinuate and lightly warty. Areoles 1 to 1½ cm. apart, round or roundish, the flowering areoles being elliptical, up to 1½ cm. long, with abundant brownish or yellowish wool, which drops off later. Radial spines 16 to 20, white, stiff, somewhat curved, the upper ones up to 4½ cm. long, tipped brown, the lower ones about 1 cm. long. Central spines often about 10, in groups of 2 or 3, the upper ones very long, up to 12 cm. long, leaf-like, straight or curved upwards, white, tipped brown; the lower 5 or more, cylindrical or slightly angular, purplish brown, up to 7 cm. long, straight or curved, the lowermost up to 3 cm. long, hooked at the tip. Flower 4½ to 5½ cm. long; ovary and tube with broadly oval scales; outer petals abruptly acute and ciliated; inner petals yellow, more lanceolate. Stigma with 9 or 10 lobes. Rare in cultivation.

UTAHIA Br. et R.

Small plants globular, with prominent warty ribs, spiny. Flowers small, yellow, borne on the central areoles; ovary and tube covered with dry, membraneous, imbricate scales. Includes only one species.

Utahia Sileri (Engelm.) Br. et R. = *Echinocactus Sileri* Engelm. Utah (between Cottonwood and Pipe Springs). Plant solitary, globular or slightly flattened at the top, where it is covered with whitish wool, and with a confused mass of white and black spines. The stem is about 10 cm. thick, with 13 to 16 ribs, more or less oblique, deeply divided into rhomboid warts 1 to 1½ cm. high. Areoles 1 to 1½ cm. apart, large, round, about 8 mm. broad, prolonged above the bundle of spines, with abundant whitish wool. Radial spines 13 to 15, spreading, awl-shaped, straight or arching; the uppermost pair, the longest, up to 2 cm. long, white, tipped brown. Central spines 3 or 4, the upper ones up to 3 cm. long, dark brown, almost black, straight or curved upwards; the lower ones shorter and lighter coloured, mostly straight. The flowers are 2½ cm. long, yellow.

This singular and aberrant species was listed in the catalogue of Friedrich Adolph Haage jr. in 1902, being then quoted at 10 to 20 marks, but was afterwards lost sight of. It was discovered again in 1931, but is still a great rarity. It is now being occasionally offered by dealers.

SUB-TRIBE V. CACTANAE

Plants globose or barrel-shaped, with straight spiny ribs. The flowering areoles at the top of the plant develop quantities of wool (and sometimes also bristles) forming a peculiar structure called *cephalium*. Flowers regular, embedded in the cephalium. Fruit a small naked berry. Includes two genera.

DISCOCACTUS Pfeiff

Plants small, globular more or less flattened, with low warty ribs, and spines more or less curved. The flower-bearing cephalium or crest, at the top of the plant, is made up of wool and bristles. Flowers nocturnal, large, white or pale pink, with a long tube and spreading limb. Ovary naked; tube with scales but without wool. Fruit small, naked. Seeds black, rough. Includes 7 species.

Discocactus Hartmannii (K. Sch.) Br. et R. = *Echinocactus Hartmannii* K. Sch. Paraguay. Plant solitary. Stem globular, flattened, glossy green, about 4 cm. high, or up to 6 cm., and up to 15 cm. across, with 12 to 16 rounded ribs, notched into conical warts, blunt or truncated at the top, bear a large oval dry scar, 1 to 2½ cm. apart. The lower areoles are very sparingly woolly, the upper ones developing a mass of whitish wool, and finally bare. Radial spines about 12, the lower 3 about 2 cm. long, the upper ones 1 to 1½ cm. long, awl-shaped, acute, cylindrical, curved on the stem, or straight, or strongly and irregularly curved, at first amber yellow, passing to brownish and greyish, finally dropping off. Central spine only one, up to 1 cm. long. The crest or cephalium is up to 4 cm. high, made up of white glossy wool, and a few yellow or brown spines or bristles. Flowers arising from the cephalium, up to 10 cm. long, with a cylindrical bare ovary, and with a long tube furnished with many linear, spreading, greenish white bracts, with a darker midrib; the limb is funnel-shaped, up to 5 cm. across, with linear pure white petals 3 cm. long, with a fringed edge. Stamens, style and stigma white. Fruit yellowish, immersed in the cephalium.

Discocactus alteolens Lem. = *Echinocactus alteolens* K. Sch. = *E. (Discocactus) tricornis* Monv. This last is probably a juvenile form. Brazil. Plant solitary; stem deep green, globular depressed or rather hemispherical, with a mass of greyish white wool forming the cephalium, about 1 cm. high, the stem being up to 7 cm. high, and 10 cm. in diameter. Ribs 9 or 10, straight, broad and rounded, cut into rounded warts with broad depressions on the top in which are situated the areoles. Radial spines 5 or 6, the upper one short and slender, the lower ones stronger, stiff and curved, about 2 cm. long; occasionally there is a small central spine, straight and erect. All spines dropping off with age, leaving a bare corky areole. Flowers few or solitary, occasionally as many as 3 or 4 together, up to 7 cm. long, partly immersed in the wool of the cephalium. Ovary elongated, bare. Limb funnel-shaped, like that of *Aporacactus flagelliformis*, but white and regular, with a white tube, naked below, above furnished with linear-lanceolate white leaf-like bracts, up to 2 cm. long, with a green midrib. Petals of similar shape, white and recurved. Stamens and style white, stigma greenish. Flower strongly perfumed.

Discocactus placentiformis (Lehm.) K. Sch. = *Cactus (Melocactus) placentiformis* Lehm. = *Echinocactus placentiformis* K. Sch. = *Melocactus Besleri* Lk. et Otto. = *Discocactus Linkii* Pfeiff. = *D. Besleri* Weber. Brazil (Rio de Janeiro). Plant solitary: stem light green or pale green, hemispherical, very flattened but raised at the centre, with a thick cephalium of whitish or yellowish wool, 2 cm. high, with spines or bristles, the stem being up to 6 cm. high and 15 cm. across. Ribs 10 to 13, straight, rather acute, broad at the base, notched into warts 1 to 3 cm. apart, like broad truncated cones, with a scar at the top, on which is situated the round areole, with greyish white wool when young, later bare. Radial spines 6 or 7, strong, awl-shaped, up to 3 cm. long, spreading, the upper ones short, straight or curved, the lower ones stronger and almost angular. There is sometimes one central spine, strong, mostly straight. All spines are at first reddish brown, passing to horny yellow and to grey, finally dropping off from the areole. Flowers one or few, on the cephalium, up to 7 cm. long, large. Ovary cylindrical, pale green or reddish, bare. Limb long and funnel-shaped; the tube is pink or carmine red, with linear recurved bracts of the same colour, up to 2 cm. long. Outer petals longer and more acute of same colour; the inner petals slightly shorter and more obtuse, of a paler colour. Stamens and style white, stigma with 5 flesh-coloured lobes.

The other species, very rarely met with in cultivation, are the following, all natives of Brazil:

Discocactus heptacanthus (Rodriguez) Br. et R. = *Malacocarpus heptacanthus* Rodriguez.

Discocactus Zehntneri Br. et R.

Discocactus subnudus Br. et R.

Discocactus bahiensis Br. et R.

Discocactus insignis Pfeiff., *and D. Lehmannii* Pfeiff. are probably the same as *D. placentiformis*.

Species of *Discocactus* are all very interesting, but they are also rarely grown.

CACTUS (L.) Br. et R.
(*Melocactus* Link et Otto)

As amended by Britton and Rose, the genus *Cactus* includes globular or short-cylindrical or barrel-shaped plants, with 9 to 20 ribs, more or less straight and spiny. Cephalium well developed at the top of the plant, bearing flowers year after year. The flowers are small, pink or pinkish, with a slender tube wholly immersed in the cephalium, and an expanded limb with few petals. Fruit naked, elongated, red, sometimes white. Seeds black. The flowers are diurnal, and the cephalium consists of a mass of wool and bristles or spines, developed from the central areoles in adult plants. The cephalium is more or less cylindrical in shape, often over 30 cm. long, and when it begins to form, the plant ceases to grow in size.

The genus is limited to the tropical regions of the West Indies and South America, and includes about 30 species.

The old genus *Cactus*, as established by Linnaeus, had no generic value, as it included species of *Opuntia*, *Selenicereus*, *Cereus* and also one of the species of this genus. In course of time the genus *Cactus* was discarded altogether, and the genus *Melocactus* was created by Link and Otto, and subsequently used by others, to include the species of the genus under discussion. It was, therefore, a happy thought on the part of Britton and Rose to amend and revive the old genus *Cactus*, practically under the same generic characters as *Melocactus*. Most European continental writers, chiefly in Germany, have stuck to the genus *Melocactus* as defined by Link and Otto, and a few have tried to distinguish between the two genera *Cactus* (as amended by Britton and Rose) and *Melocactus*, but the difference is so flimsy, that it is far more practical to consider the two genera as synonymous, thus following the lead of both Britton and Rose and of the German authors. Although the genus *Cactus* as amended by Britton and Rose, is in reality a new name, or rather a new entity, and therefore according to the laws of priority, must give place to *Melocactus*, on the other hand, in this particular instance, it is worth while to retain the popular generic name Cactus for the sake of old associations, as was done in other instances, and also as a tribute to Linnaeus, the author of the idea of generic names, to which Systematic Botany owes so much.

All species of *Cactus* (or *Melocactus*), known popularly by the name of "Turk's Cap Cactus," being natives of the tropical regions of the West Indies and South America, delight in a warm and moist atmosphere, and in full sun, at least during the growing or flowering season. Their root system is very poor, and very little soil or root space is required in their cultivation. In winter the temperature should not be allowed to fall for long periods below 20°C. = about 68°F., and then the plants should be kept comparatively dry, giving them only a little water now and then. The plants being mostly sea-side species, a slightly saline condition of the soil is rather beneficial than otherwise. Imported plants are always difficult to establish, but seedlings are now easily procured, and grow well in a mixture of gravel or sand with some leaf-mould. In any case, growth is always slow, but grafted plants make better growth and are more easy to handle.

Cactus Melocactus L. = *Melocactus communis* Link et Otto. West Indian Islands, chiefly Jamaica. Body short, cylindrical, up to about 1 m. high, glaucous green, with 12 to 20 acute and crenate ribs, 2 to 3 cm. high. Radial spines 8 to 11, awl-shaped, straight or arching; central spines 1 to 4, stronger, 4 to 6 cm. long. All spines are at first pale red or pinkish, passing to yellow or brownish. Cephalium up to 20 cm. high, and 10 cm. broad. Flowers pink, petals tipped carmine red.

PLATE XLVI

PLATE XLVII

Cactus macracanthus Salm-Dyck = *Melocactus macracanthus* Link et Otto. Venezuela (Curacao). Up to 30 cm. high, more or less globular, dark green, with 11 to 15 broad ribs. Spines at first brown, passing to yellow; radials 12 to 15 or more, spreading, awl-shaped, straight or a little curved, the lowermost up to 2½ cm. long; central spines 4 or more, thick, spreading, awl-shaped, angular at the base, dark brown red, up to 7 cm. long. Cephalium up to 20 cm. long, and 10 cm. across.

Cactus Lemairei (Monv.) Br. et R.=*Echinocactus Lemairei* Monv. = *Melocactus Lemairei* Miq. Haiti. Body conical, up to 30 cm. high, dark green, with 9 to 12 thick, obtuse, crenate ribs, with elliptical areoles 2½ to 4 cm. apart. Radial spines 11 to 14, very strong, awl-shaped, a little flattened or angular, straight or arching, up to 3 cm. long. Central spines 3 or 4, spreading, stronger and longer. All spines are at first wine red, passing to brown and white. Cephalium narrow, cylindrical. Flowers 2 cm. long, pink.

Cactus Ruestii (K. Sch.) Br. et R. = *Melocactus Ruestii* K. Sch. = *M. Brongniartii* Hildm. Honduras. Body short conical, 6 cm. high and 5 cm. thick, bluish green, with 15 low ribs. Areoles elliptical, about 1 cm. apart. Radial spines about 12, up to 1 cm. long, straight or curved. Only one central spine, curved upwards, up to 2½ cm. long. All spines are reddish white, tipped red brown. Flowers small, carmine red. Cephalium cylindrical, with white wool and blood red spines.

Cactus Maxonii Rose = *Melocactus Maxonii* Gürke = *M. guatemalensis* Gürke et Eichlam. Guatemala. Globular, a little depressed, grass green, up to 15 cm. high. Ribs 11 to 15. Areoles 2½ cm. apart. Radial spines 7 to 11, reddish, spreading, curved backwards, 1 to 1½ cm. long. Only one central spine, straight, up to 2 cm. long. Cephalium small. Flowers pink outside, white inside.

Cactus caesius (Wendl.) Br. et R. = *Melocactus caesius* Wendl. Venezuela (near La Guayra). Body globular or oval, bluish green or greyish green, 10 to 20 cm. high, and about 14 cm. thick, with 10 to 15 ribs. Areoles 2 to 3 cm. apart, with greyish wool. Radial spines 8, strong, spreading, pale red, up to 2½ cm. long. Central spines 1 or 2, slightly thicker, yellowish, curved upwards. Cephalium short but broad, greyish. Flowers small, of a lively pink.

Cactus melocactoides (DC.) Br. et R. = *Melocactus melocactoides* DC. = *M. violaceus* Pfeiff. = *M. depressus* Hook. Brazil, Rio de Janeiro to Pernambuco. Body short, conical, light green, about 8 cm. high, 15 cm. broad at the base, with 10 broad obtuse ribs. Areoles 1½ to 2½ cm. apart, small, round, with white wool. Radial spines 5 to 8, awl-shaped, angular at the base, spreading, straight or curved, whitish, later grey, up to 2 cm. long. No central spines. Cephalium low, broad, white, with short brown bristles. Flowers pink, with toothed petals. Fruit white or very pale pink, up to 2½ cm. long. *Melocactus violaceus* Pfeiff., from Rio de Janeiro, and *M. depressus* Hooker, from Pernambuco, are probably two distinct local varieties. The first

X

is more or less hemispherical-conical, up to 5 cm. high and 6 to 7 cm. across, with less obtuse ribs, somewhat spiral, with spines reddish to violet, passing to greyish. The second is globular-pyramidal or conical, 15 cm. across at the base and about 8 cm. high, with 10 ribs very obtuse and rounded; spines brownish or ash-grey, and cephalium only 1 cm. high.

Cactus obtusipetalus (Lem.) Br. et R. = *Melocactus obtusipetalus* Lem. = *M. crassicostatus* Lem. Colombia, near Bogota. Body globular-conical, greyish green, up to 22 cm. high, and 16 cm. thick, with 10 acute, prominent, straight ribs, 4 cm. high. Areoles 2 to 2½ cm. apart. Radial spines about 10, stiff, awl-shaped, spreading, ringed, white or brownish. Central spines mostly 2, the upper one straight, the lower curved downwards. Cephalium low, white, with purple red bristles. Flowers rather large, over 2 m. broad, pink, with oblong obtuse petals.

Cactus amoenus (Hoffmgg.) Br. et R. = *Melocactus amoenus* Hoffmgg. Colombia. Similar to the preceding. Body globular or almost, conical, dark glossy green, with prominent acute ribs. Spines strong, awl-shaped, mostly curved, at first red or reddish, passing to dark reddish brown, almost black, finally dark grey. Cephalium almost hemispherical, white with ruby red or purplish red bristles. The growing ribs are purplish. Grows very well from seed.

Cactus intortus (Mill.) Br. et R. = *Melocactus intortus* Mill. West Indies (coasts of various islands). Body up to 1 m. high, with 14 to 20 thin ribs. Spines 10 to 15, yellow, passing to brown or greyish, 2 to 7 cm. long. Cephalium cylindrical, tall, sometimes as tall as the plant. Flower about 2 cm. long, pale pink.

Cactus Neryi (K. Sch.) Br. et R. = *Melocactus Neryi* K. Sch. Brazil (Amazonas). Body globular-depressed, dark green, broad at the base, about 11 cm. high, with broad acute ribs. Areoles about 2 cm. apart. Radial spines 7 to 9, awl-shaped, straight or strongly curved upwards, yellowish brown passing to greyish, about 2½ cm. long; occasionally there are 1 or 2 short central spines. Cephalium 5 cm. high and 7 cm. thick, white, with red bristles 2 cm. long. Flowers about 2 cm. long and 1 cm. broad, pale pink. The berry is clavate, glossy carmine pink. A beautiful species.

Cactus Townsendii Br. et R. = *Melocactus peruvianus* Vaupel (not *Cactus peruvianus* L.). Peru (Chosica). Body globular, sometimes branching at the base, 10 to 15 cm. across. Ribs 12 or 13; areoles 1 to 1½ cm. apart. Radial spines 7 to 8, brownish. One central spine, often absent, up to 4 cm. long. Cephalium 6 to 8 cm. high, white, with reddish brown bristles. Flower 2½ cm. long, pink. Fruit red.

Cactus bahiensis Br. et R. Brazil (Bahia). Body almost hemispherical, 10 cm. high and 15 cm. across, dull green, with 10 to 12 broad ribs, 2½ cm. high. Radial spines about 10, up to 2½ cm. long, brown: central spines mostly 4, up to 3½ cm. long, same colour. Cephalium low, with many dark brown bristles. Flowers pinkish. Fruit red, clavate, 1½ cm long.

Cactus salvador (Murillo) Br. et R. = *Melocactus salvador* Murillo. Mexico, Vera Cruz, near Jalapa. Body globose, 30 to 40 cm. across, with 13 rounded ribs. Radial spines 8, awl-shaped, spreading and recurved. Central spines 1 to 3, awl-shaped, slightly stronger and longer, curved slightly downwards. Cephalium low, 8 cm. across; flowers rosy pink. A remarkably beautiful species.

Cactus Broadwayi Br. et R. West Indies (Tobago Island). Body globular to oval, 10 to 20 cm. high, pale green, with 14 to 18 ribs, 1 to 1½ cm. high, rounded, with narrow furrows between them. Areoles small, sunken, 1 cm. apart. Radial spines 8 to 10, horn-coloured, tipped darker, 1 to 1½ cm. long. Mostly 1 central spine, sometimes 2 or 3, thicker and longer, same colour or brown. Cephalium low, 6 to 7 cm. across, and 2 to 3 cm. high, white, with brown bristles. Flower small, purplish; fruit clavate, purple.

Cactus Harlowii Br. et R. Cuba, eastern coastal cliffs. Body slender, about 25 cm. high, pale green, with 12 narrow ribs. Areoles closely set, up to 1 cm. apart. Radial spines about 12, thin, 1 to 2 cm. long, reddish, passing to pale yellow. Central spines mostly 4, slightly thicker and longer. Cephalium small. Flowers deep rosy red, 2 cm. long. Fruit obovoid, 2 cm. long, deep red.

Cactus Jansenianus (Backbg.) = *Melocactus Jansenianus* Backbg. Peru (Pacific coast, at Lomas of Laredo). Stem solitary, globular, about 15 cm. thick, pale greyish green, with 9 or 10 straight ribs, 2 to 3 cm. broad, very flat, sometimes only marked out by vertical furrows between them. Areoles 1½ to 2 cm. apart. Radial spines about 8, blackish, awl-shaped, about 2 cm. long, recurved over the body. One central spine, dark brown or black, stronger, up to 3 cm. long, straight and directed outwards, or curved upwards. Cephalium cylindrical, up to 15 cm. high, and 5 to 6 cm. thick, reddish brown. Flowers small, red; fruits clavate, red. Seeds small, dull black. An interesting new species.

Cactus oreas (Miq.) Br. et R. = *Melocactus oreas* Miq. = *M. Ernestii* Vaupel. Brazil (Bahia). Stem globular, depressed, glossy grass green, 10 to 14 cm. thick. Ribs 16 to 20, prominent, rounded, slightly notched, bearing round yellowish woolly areoles in the notches, 1½ to 2½ cm. apart. Radial spines 10 to 16, spreading outwards, straight, yellowish passing to white, 1 to 2 cm. long. Central spines 1 to 4, 1½ to 3 cm. long, straight and erect, yellow. Flowers pale pink; fruit clavate, bright red.

var. **diamantinus** Werd. Brazil (Minas, near Diamantina). Body green to olive green, globular and very depressed at the centre, with 11 to 15 very prominent and rounded ribs. Areoles round, yellowish, with rounded chin-like prominences above them, 1½ to 3 cm. apart. Radial spines about 7, awl-shaped, pale yellow, yellowish red towards the tip, spreading outwards, mostly recurved, the lower ones the longest, up to 3 cm. long. Central spines 1 or 2, like the radials, but straight, slightly thicker and longer.

Cactus Miquelii (Lehm.) = *Melocactus Miquelii* Lehm. West Indies (Island Santa Cruz). Body oval, dark green, with 14 broad and crenate ribs, about 25 cm. high with the cephalium, up to 20 cm. thick. Areoles 3 to 3½ cm. apart, oval, at first woolly, later bare. Radial spines 8, spreading, slightly curved, dark brown, 1 to 1½ cm. long. Central spines 1 to 3, longer, straight. Cephalium cylindrical, 7 to 8 cm. long, white, 6 cm. thick, with short brown bristles.

Cactus Zuccarinii (Miq.) = *Melocactus Zuccarinii* Miq. Venezuela (Island Curaçao). Body conical, 22 cm. high with the ceph-alium, dark green, with 16 thick, obtuse ribs, notched, about 4 cm. high. Areoles oval, 2 to 2½ cm. apart, with white wool when young. Radial spines 18 to 20, almost pectinate, straight or slightly curved, yellowish grey, the lower ones up to 4 cm. long. Central spines 4 to 6, thick, awl-shaped, spreading, up to 7 cm. long, pale pink, bulbous at the base. Cephalium 4 cm. high, flat at the top, white, with bundles of stiff brown bristles. Flowers small, pale pink, 2 cm. long.

Cactus microcephalus (Miq.) = *Melocactus microcephalus* Miq. Venezuela (Island Curaçao). Body oval, up to 21 cm. high, and about 15 cm. across at the base, grass green, becoming corky and yellowish at the base, with 13 to 16 thick, obtuse and rounded straight ribs. Areoles elliptical, about 1 cm. long, and 1 to 2 cm. apart, at first with whitish wool, later bare. Radial spines 10 to 16, almost pectinate, the lower up to 3 cm. long, awl-shaped, straight or curved. Central spines 3 or 4, spreading, the lower one up to 4 cm. long. All spines are yellowish, tipped brown. Cephalium small, hemispherical, about 3 cm. high, whitish, with numerous brown bristles. Flowers 3 cm. long, petals lanceolate-obtuse, carmine red. Fruit dark pink.

Cactus matanzanus (Leon) = *Melocactus matanzanus* Leon. Mexico (Matanzan). Stem globular or slightly depressed, pale green, up to 9 cm. high, and 8 to 9 cm. thick. Ribs 8 or 9, straight, ½ cm. high, more numerous at the apex. Areoles about 8 mm. apart, with white and pink wool when young. Radial spines 7 or 8, up to 1½ cm. long, curved and almost depressed, the uppermost being shorter. Only one central spine, less curved and up to 2 cm. long. Cephalium 4 to 5 cm. high and 5 to 6 cm. thick, brilliant orange red. Flowers pink, embedded in the wool of the cephalium, opening in full sunshine during the afternoon. A very rare new species.

SUB-TRIBE VI. CORYPHANTHANAE

Plants more or less globular, spiny, low or elongated, with tubercles or warts arranged spirally. Areoles divided; the lower or spiny part of the areoles, bearing a tuft of spines, situated on the extremity of the wart or tubercle, and is connected by means of a groove, often very indistinct, along the upper side of the tubercle with the flowering part or upper part of the areoles, which is situated either half way to the axil or in the axil itself. The flowers are always solitary in their axils. The fruit is a greenish, yellow or red berry, fleshy or dry. The young seedling is club-shaped or globular, without any trace of cotyledons.

ANCISTROCACTUS Br. et R.

Small globular plants, with low spiral ribs bearing prominent tubercles grooved on the upper side. Central spines hooked. Flowers funnel-shaped, small, borne at the top of the plant. Ovary with small, thin scales. bare in their axils. Fruit oblong greenish, juicy, smooth and bare below, scaly near the top. Seeds round, large, with a bare hollow scar. Includes 3 species, natives of Mexico and Texas.

Ancistrocactus megarhizus (Rose) Br. et R. = *Echinocactus megarhizus* Rose. Mexico (Tamaulipas). Stem solitary or sprouting around the base, more or less globose, 4 to 5 cm. high, pale green, with long carrot-like roots. Ribs spiral, divided into conical warts. Areoles on the tips of the warts, prolonged in a woolly groove on the upper surface of the wart. Radial spines 20 or more, disposed comb-like, spreading, slender, yellowish passing to white. Central spines 4, the upper 3 like the radials, but hooked, the lower one thicker and more strongly hooked, brownish, spreading outwards, 1½ cm. long.

Ancistrocactus Scheeri (Salm-Dyck) Br. et R. = *Echinocactus Scheeri* Salm-Dyck. Northern Mexico and southern Texas. Stem mostly solitary, globular or conical, 3 to 7 cm. thick, green, strongly spined. Ribs 13, spiral, divided into conical warts, grooved on the upper surface, Radial spines 15 to 18, spreading, straw-coloured, passing to white, the upper ones about 1 cm. long. Central spines 3 or 4, 2 to 5 cm. long, the lower one strongly hooked, yellow, brown at the base. Flowers borne in the groove on the upper side of the wart, greenish yellow, 2½ cm. long.

Ancistrocactus brevihamatus (Engelm.) Br. et R. = *Echinocactus brevihamatus* Engelm. = *E. Scheeri* var. *brevihamata* K. Sch. Southern Texas. Differs from the preceding by its stronger growth, more numerous spines and pink flowers. The ribs are also closer together, and the groove on the upper side of the warts is continued down their to base.

THELOCACTUS (K. Sch.) Br. et R.

Plants globular, or somewhat depressed or elongated, sometimes very spiny: ribs low, often not well defined, divided into warts. Flowers diurnal, large, borne on the top areoles. Fruit mostly dry. Seeds black, with a large scar on the hilum.

Includes 27 species, almost exclusively Mexican.

Thelocactus hexaedrophorus (Lem.) Br. et R. = *Echinocactus hexaedrophorus* Lem. = *E. fossulatus* Scheidw. = *E. insculptus* Scheidw. Mexico (San Luis Potosi). Stem solitary, rarely branching, 15 cm. high, and about as thick, woolly at the top. Ribs about 12, spiral, entirely divided into plump six-sided warts, bluish green passing to greyish green, thickly packed together. Areoles 2 to 3½ cm. apart, displaced backwards. Radial spines 6 to 9, straight, 1 to about 2 cm. long, yellowish passing to pale brown, darker at the base and at the tip. One central spine, 2 to 3 cm. long, stronger, straight, of the same colour. Flowers large, borne at the top, 3½ to 4 cm. long; ovary with a few broad, fringed scales; tube short, scaly; outer petals pink or brownish edged white; inner petals white, minutely toothed. Stamens and style white, stigma with 6 to 10 yellowish lobes. A beautiful species of easy cultivation.

var. **major** Quehl. Plant larger; spines about 3 cm. long, of a lively red.

var. **Labouretianus** K. Sch. = *Echinocactus Labouretianus* Cels. Ribs more numerous and closer; spines lively red when young.

var. **Droegeanus** K. Sch. = *E. Droegeanus* Hildm. Warts ash-grey, very closely packed together.

var. **decipiens** Berger, probably = *E. fossulatus* Scheidw. A small form, dark green, with yellowish brown spines, curved backwards. Flowers almost white. = *T. fossulatus* Br. et R.

Thelocactus Saueri Böd. = *Echinocactus Saueri* Böd. Mexico (Tamaulipas). Solitary, globular-depressed, 3 cm. high and 5½ cm. thick, dull, greyish green, with white wool at the top. Ribs 13, divided into short conical warts, six-sided at the base. Areoles at the top of the warts, large, roundish, with white wool. Radial spines 14 to 18, spreading, recurved, glassy white or white, darker at the base, tipped brown, just over ½ cm. long, 3 or 4 of them almost centrals, up to 1 cm. long, straight or arched inwards, brown towards the tip. Central spines 1 or 2, straight or curved, about 1 cm. long, dark brown or black towards the tip. Flowers 2½ cm. long, borne at the centre, with much white wool; tube not scaly; outer petals whitish with deep red midrib, the inner petals longer and obtuse, minutely toothed, pure white, rosy at the throat. A pretty small species, very resistant.

Thelocactus rinconadensi (Poselg.) Br. et R. = *Echinocactus rinconadensis* Poselg. Mexico (Nuevo Leon, near Rinconada and Saltillo). Plant solitary, bluish green or greyish green, 6 to 8 cm. high, and up to 12 cm. thick, with 13 narrow ribs, divided into acute conical or pyramidal-sided warts. Areoles with whitish wool, later bare. Spines 1 to 3, or absent, straight, 1½ cm. long. Flowers 4 cm. long, borne at the centre, white, with lanceolate-acute petals.

Thelocactus lophothele (Salm-Dyck) Br. et R. = *Echinocactus lophothele* Salm-Dyck. Mexico (Chihuahua). Stem solitary or sprouting at the base, globose or short-cylindric, woolly at the top, glaucous or greyish green, up to 25 cm. high. Ribs 15 to 20, spiral, cut up into elongated warts, about 2 cm. long, bearing the areoles 4 to 5 cm. apart. Radial spines 3 to 5, spreading, mostly curved, amber colour, reddish brown below and bulbous at the base, up to 4 cm. long. Only one central spine, just longer, and often absent. Flowers 4 cm. long and 5 cm. broad. Ovary with a few broad scales. Petals lanceolate-acute, toothed, pale yellow, with a red midrib, reddish when fading; outer petals greenish with a red midrib. Stamens dark yellow, style and stigma pale yellow.

Thelocactus tulensis (Poselg.) Br. et R. = *Echinocactus tulensis* Poselg. Mexico (Tamaulipas, near Tula). Stem at first solitary, but branching at the top and sides when old, green to dark greyish green, globular to short-cylindric, up to 12 cm. high. Ribs spiral or oblique, wholly cut up into conical acute warts, up to 2 cm. high, rather closely packed together. Areoles elliptical, 1½ to 2 cm. apart, the woolly groove on the upper side of the areoles continuing for about 7 mm. Radial spines 6 to 8, spreading outwards, brown, 1 to 1½ cm. long. Central spines 1 or 2, often absent, thicker, darker at the base, up to 3 cm. long. Flowers 2½ cm. long, petals lanceolate acute, pink, with darker midrib.

Thelocactus phymatothele (Poselg.) Br. et R. = *Echinocactus phymatothele*. Poselg. Mexico. Stem semi-globular, rounded and woolly at the top, with 13 ribs spiral and cut into conical warts about 1 cm. high, pale greyish green. The plant is about 5 cm. high and 9 to 10 cm. broad. Areoles elliptical, 1½ to 2 cm. apart. Spines 3 or 4, bent upwards, 1 to 2 cm. long, at first reddish brown tipped yellow, often dropping off. Flowers 5 cm. long and 6 cm. broad: outer petals oval, brown, edged yellow: the next lanceolate, yellowish pink, the innermost pale pink. Stamens, style and 7-lobed stigma yellow.

Thelocactus Buekii (Klein) Br. et R. = *Echinocactus Buekii* (or *Buckii*) Klein. Mexico (Tamaulipas). Similar to *T. tulensis*, but smaller, with angular, acute, deep green warts. Spines about 7, reddish, spreading, slightly arching. Flower large, deep glossy pink.

Thelocactus nidulans (Quehl.) Br. et R. = *Echinocactus nidulans* Quehl. Mexico. Stem almost semi-globular, up to 20 cm. broad, bluish grey or grey, woolly at the top and very strongly spined. Ribs about 20, cut into acute warts 2 cm. high, with elliptical areoles almost bare. Spines about 15, brown or horny yellow, very thick and stiff, straight, erect, grey when old, and then becoming fibrous. Flowers 4 cm. long, yellowish white.

Thelocactus Roseanus Böd. = *Echinocactus Roseanus* Böd. Mexico (Coahuila). Stem solitary, or branching at the base, oval, 4 to 5 cm. high, 3 cm. thick, of a lively pale green, with short conical warts, 3 mm. high and broad, very much like a *Mammillaria*. Areoles elongated, at first with yellowish wool, afterwards bare. Radial spines about 15, slender, needle-like, spreading, the upper ones 1½ cm. long, the lower ones shorter, yellowish white passing to sulphur yellow. Central spines 5 to 6, like the radials, but thicker and longer, slightly curved. Flowers borne at the centre, pale pink.

Thelocactus Saussieri (Weber) Berger = *Echinocactus Saussieri* Weber. Mexico (San Luis Potosi). Stem globular-depressed, 15 to 20 cm. thick. Ribs spiral, cut into pale green conical warts, four-sided at the base. Areoles bare. Radial spines 9, spreading, silvery white, up to 1½ cm. long. Central spines 4, needle-like, brown or grey, 3 to 4 cm. long. Flowers 4 cm. long and broad, purple red, with narrow lanceolate petals; tube scaly, but without hairs or bristles. Stamens, style and stigma yellow.

Thelocactus leucacanthus (Zucc.) Br. et R. = *Echinocactus leuca-canthus* Zucc. = *E. Maelenii* Salm-Dyck. Mexico, near Zimapan. Plant at first solitary, afterwards freely proliferous. Stem oval to short-cylindric, pale green, with a thick root, up to 15 cm. high, and up to 8 cm. thick. Ribs 8 to 13, spirally arranged, entirely cut into conical oblique acute warts, about 1 cm. high, bearing roundish woolly areoles, 1 to 1½ cm. apart. Radial spines 7 to 20, spreading, up to 3 cm. long, pale yellow, passing to white or grey. Central spine only one, straight and strong, 4 to 5 cm. long. Flowers 4 to 5 cm. long, borne at the top, pale yellow, with lanceolate-acute, minutely toothed petals. Stamens yellow; style yellow, reddish at the base, stigma with 7 to 9 pale yellow lobes. A pretty resistant species of slow growth.

Thelocactus porrectus (Lem.) Br. et R. = *Echinocactus porrectus* Lem. Mexico (Zimapan and Ixmiquilpan). Similar to the preceding and often looked upon as a variety. Plant u.s., pale green, with 8 spiral ribs, divided into thick conical warts, oblique and rather obtuse, bearing areoles farther apart and slightly displaced towards the inner side of the wart. Spines 12 to 14, at first reddish, passing to yellowish and greyish, 2 cm. long, disposed like a brush, the side ones curved backwards. Central spines 4, spreading, the lower one stronger. Flower yellow.

Thelocactus Ehrenbergii (Pfeiff.) = *Echinocactus Ehrenbergii* Pfeiff. Mexico (Zimapan and Ixmiquilpan). Stem globular or oval, later cylindrical, at first solitary, later abundantly cespitose, 12 to 15 cm. high, and up to 7 cm. thick, pale green passing to greyish green, with white wool and yellowish spines at the top. Ribs 8 to 13, spiral, cut into oblique conical warts, about 1 cm. high, bearing elongated areoles with yellowish wool. Radial spines about 6, awl-shaped, straight, up to 2 cm. long, yellowish to yellowish grey. One central spine, like the radials, but brownish yellow. Flower 3½ to 4 cm. long, funnel-shaped, outer petals oval, pale pink with darker midrib; inner petals lanceolate, paler pink or white. Stamens white, style chrome yellow, stigma with about 10 reddish yellow lobes.

Thelocactus bicolor (Gal.) Br. et R. = *Echinocactus bicolor* Gal. = *E. rhodophthalmus* Hook = *E. ellipticus* Lem. From southern Texas to Central Mexico. A very variable species. Stem solitary, globular to oval or cylindrical, 6 to 10 cm. thick, bluish green or greyish green, woolly at the top and more or less strongly spined. Ribs 8, straight or slightly oblique, divided into oblique warts 1½ cm. high, bearing round or oval areoles about 1½ cm. apart, with short whitish wool, later bare. Radial spines 9 to 18, up to 2½ cm. long, awl-shaped, stiff, and very acute, spreading and slightly arched, white or red at the middle, with amber yellow point, red at the base. Central spines 4, the lowermost the strongest, straight, erect, or arched forward, up to 3½ cm. long, red, paler at the tip, passing to horny yellow; the others are like the radials, the upper one being angular at the base, later passing to greyish. Flowers large, 5 to 6 cm. long and broad; petals lanceolate-spathulate, acute, of a beautiful violet red. Stamens and style yellowish white, stigma with 10 brownish red lobes. A popular species of easy cultivation.

var. **bolanensis** K. Sch. Mexico (Bolanos). Written also *bolansis*, from Sierra Bola (Coahuila). Has stout milk-white spines, mostly directed upwards. A very striking variety.

var. **tricolor** K. Sch. Northern Mexico. Densely spiny, with lovely red spines, often red and white. A charming variety, free-flowering even when young.

Thelocactus Pottsii (Salm-Dyck) Br. et R. = *Echinocactus Pottsii* Salm-Dyck = *E. bicolor* var. *Pottsii* K. Sch. Mexico (Chihuahua to Coahuila). Stem globular-depressed, 15 to 20 cm. thick, with pale green conical warts, four-sided at the base. Radial spines 9, white, spreading, 1½ cm. long; 4 central spines, needle-like, 3 to 4 cm. long. Flower purple red, 4 cm. broad, with the inner petals narrow, lanceolate. Stamens, style and stigma yellow.

Thelocactus heterochromus Weber = *Echinocactus heterochromus* Weber. Mexico (Coahuila). Stem solitary, globular or globular-depressed, glaucous green, with whitish wool and many spines at the top. Ribs 9, straight, more or less rounded, cut into roundish warts. Areoles round, large, with white wool. Radial spines about 9, awl-shaped, up to 3 cm. long; the upper one flat and thin, white. Central spines 3, curved, flat on the upper surface, round on the lower, white, zoned brown. Flowers as in *T. bicolor*.

Thelocactus Gielsdorfianus Werd. = *Echinocactus Gielsdorfianus* Werd. Mexico (Tamaulipas). Stem solitary, rarely sprouting, globular to oval or short-cylindric, bluish green or greyish green, with white wool and black or brown spines at the top, 5 to 8 cm. thick. Ribs divided into broad, angular warts, about 6 mm. high. Areoles with white wool. Spines 6 or 7, all radials, white, spreading, about 2 cm. long, dark or black at the tip. Flowers borne at the centre, just over 2 cm. long, ivory white. Free-flowering.

Thelocactus hastifer Werd. et Böd. = *Echinocactus hastifer* Werd. et Böd. Mexico. Solitary, cylindrical or clavate, 10 to 15 cm. high, and 6 cm. thick, light green to green, with 18 to 20 ribs, divided into warts 4 to 8 mm. high. Areoles 1 to 1½ cm. apart, with white wool when young. Radial spines 20 to 25, spreading, glassy white, needle-like, recurved on the body, 1 to 1½ cm. long. Central spines about 4, milk white, the upper ones up to 2 cm. long, the lower ones up to 3 cm. long, curved upwards. Flowers at the centre, about 4½ cm. long; ovary and tube scaly; inner petals violet pink.

Thelocactus Smithii Muehlenpf. = *Echinocactus Smithii* Muehlenpf. Mexico (San Luis Potosi). Stem solitary, globular to short-cylindric, up to 7 cm. thick, glaucous green or bluish green, with white wool at the top. Ribs 21, divided into conical warts 5 to 6 mm. high, bearing elliptical areoles 1½ to 2 cm. apart, with white wool, later almost bare. Radial spines 20 to 27, spreading, straight or curved laterally, almost comb-like, white, the upper one up to 1½ cm. long. Central spines 4, straight or curved, white, up to 2½ cm. long, tipped brown or black, one of them being shorter, thicker and darker. Flowers borne at the centre, 3½ cm. long; outer petals linear-lanceolate, reddish; inner petals pale pink.

Thelocactus Knuthianus Boedeker = *Echinocactus Knuthianus* Boedeker. Mexico (San Luis Potosi). Stem solitary or proliferous at the base, forming groups, dark glossy green. Ribs divided into numerous slender warts. Areoles with white wool. Radial spines 18 to 20, stiff, needle-like, very slender, spreading horizontally, silvery white, less than 1 cm. long. One central spine, 1 cm. long, curved upwards. Flowers up to 2½ cm. long, pale pink.

Thelocactus conothelos Reg. et Klein = *Echinocactus conothelos* Reg. et Klein, on sandy soil in the north-east of Mexico, with a beautiful large purple violet flower, is now again in cultivation. The stem is ovoid to short-cylindric, 10 cm. high and up to 7½ cm. thick, greyish green. Ribs somewhat spiral, the lower tubercles 1 to 2 cm. long. Areoles oblique, with white wool when young. Radial spines 14 to 16, white, spreading or recurved, up to 1 cm. long. Central spines 2 to 4, erect or somewhat recurved, stronger and longer, 1½ to 3½ cm. long.

Thelocactus Viereckii Werd. = *Echinocactus Viereckii* Werd. Mexico (Tamaulipas). Stem solitary, globular to short-cylindric, dull green, with abundant white wool and dark spines at the top. Ribs 15 to 18, almost wholly divided into plump warts, 6 mm. high. Radial spines about 20, spreading, needle-like, glassy white, up to 1 cm. long. Central spines 4, thicker, spreading, white below, dark towards the tip, up to 2 cm. long. Flowers at the centre, 2 cm. long, pale violet red.

Thelocactus Valdezianus (Moell.) Böd. = *Echinocactus Valdezianus* Böd. = *Pelecyphora Valdeziana* Möller. Mexico (Coahuila). Stem mostly solitary, globular or elongated, very small, 1 to 2½ cm. in diameter, with a thick turnip-like root. Warts about 3 mm. long, glossy bluish green, more or less angular. Areoles minute, woolly. Spines about 30, all radials, hair-like, disposed more or less comb-like, white, up to 2 mm. long. Flowers at the centre, up to 2 cm. long, violet pink. Fruit very dark reddish brown. Very much like a *Pelecyphora* in appearance, and often classed as such.

Thelocactus Wagnerianus Berger = *Echinocactus Wagnerianus* Berger. Eastern Mexico. Stem elongated or cylindrical, 12 to 20 cm. long, and 5 to 6 cm. thick, proliferous at the base, forming small groups.

Ribs 13, straight or oblique, divided into prominent acute warts, bearing at the tip round or oval areoles, at first with white wool, prolonged slightly in a groove on the upper side of the wart. Radial spines about 20, spreading, comb-like, rather thick, reddish yellow, the upper one being straight or arched backwards. At first only one central spine, later 3 or 4, straight or slightly arched, bulbous at the base, 1½ to 2 cm. long. All spines are at first of a lively red, or yellow and red.

Thelocactus Mandragora (Frič) Berger = *Echinocactus Mandragora* Frič. Mexico. Plant with a thick turnip-like root. Stem globular, 4 to 6 cm. thick, entirely covered with spines, greyish green. Warts thickly packed, broad, four-sided, roundish at the top. Areoles roundish, with white wool when young. Radial spines about 12, subulate, white, arched inwards. Central spines mostly 2, thicker and longer, up to 2 cm. long, spreading, white tipped brown. Flowers at the centre, 2 cm. long and 2½ cm. broad; outer petals oblong-obtuse, green; inner petals white with a narrow dorsal pink band, green at the throat. Stamens greenish, style yellowish, stigma with 5 pale pink lobes.

Theolocactus subterraneus Backbg. North Mexico. A new species, remarkable as a curiosity. Plant solitary, with a round turnip-like root, with a long slender neck, and small globular plant on top, very spiny. Flower white.

Thelocactus Hertrichii Weinberg. = *Echinocactus Hertrichii* Weinberg. Arizona. Stem solitary, up to 1½ m. high and 60 cm. thick. Ribs 12 to 24. Radial spines 17 to 19, mostly bristle-like, up to 4 cm. long, the lower 3 up to 3 cm. long, stiff, reddish brown, ringed. Central spines 4, 4 to 6 cm. long, the lowermost curved like a hook. Flowers 6 cm. long, scaly on the outside; inner petals reddish brown with a darker midrib. Stigma with 16 to 20 lobes. A very problematic species, but hardly a *Thelocactus*.

NEOLLOYDIA Br. et R.

Plant rather small, more or less proliferous and forming groups, oval to cylindrical, with ribs arranged spirally, and divided into tubercles, very spiny. Flowers pink, yellow or purple, large, borne on the new areoles at the centre. Fruit deeply coloured, with a thin wall, becoming papery on drying, without scales, or only a few. Seeds dull black, with a large white hilum.

Includes 5 species, natives of North America, mostly with beautiful spines and showy flowers.

Neolloydia Beguinii (Weber) Br. et R. = *Echinocactus Beguinii* Weber = *Thelocactus Beguinii* Berger. Mexico (Zacatecas, Coahuila). Stem mostly solitary in cultivation, 10 to 15 cm. high, pale bluish green, entirely covered with spines. Ribs 13 to 21, wholly divided into low conical warts, rhomboid or four-sided at the base, closely packed, acute at the top, with oblong or elliptical areoles, furnished with short white wool when young. Radial spines 12 to 20, about 1½ cm. long, white, tipped black or dark, erect, or obliquely spreading, awl-shaped, very sharp-pointed; some being short (3 mm.), glassy white, tipped dark or black. Central spine 1, rarely 2, very stiff and sharp, up to 3 cm. long, obliquely erect on the upper end of the areole, straight, white, tipped dark or black. Flowers 3 to 4 cm. long, violet pink. Ovary without scales. Stamens, style and 7-lobed stigma white. A beautiful and popular species, free-flowering, thrives very well in cultivation.

var. senilis Hort. Plant somewhat thicker, spines longer and whiter. Central spines 2 or 3, one of them spreading outwards horizontally. Very attractive.

Neolloydia ceratites (Quehl) Br. et R. = *Mammillaria ceratites* Quehl = *Coryphantha ceratites* Berger. Not to be confused with *Eriosyce ceratites*. Mexico. Stem oval, greyish green, 6 to 10 cm. high, 5 cm. thick. Ribs wholly divided into transversely rhomboid warts, 1½ cm. broad and 1 cm. long, grooved on the upper surface, woolly in their axils. Areoles round, slightly woolly when young. Radial spines 15, spreading, stiff, 1½ cm. long, bulbous at the base, greyish white, often tipped darker. Central spines 5 or 6, stronger, up to 3 cm. long, straight, greyish, tipped black. Flowers 3 to 3½ cm. long, purple, with linear-lanceolate, acute petals.

Neolloydia conoidea (DC.) Br. et R. = *Mammillaria conoidea* DC. = *Echinocactus conoideus* Poselg. = *Coryphantha conoidea* Orc. Texas and eastern Mexico. Stem pale green to greyish green, cylindrical, 7 to 10 cm. high, 5 to 7 cm. thick, freely branching at the base and sides. Warts oval, obtuse and soft, with woolly axils. Areoles round or elliptical, with short white wool. Radial spines about 16, stiff, slender, spreading, up to 1 cm. long, white passing to greyish. Central spines 4 or 5, spreading, black, 1 to 3 cm. long. Flowers 6 cm. broad, reddish violet; petals linear-lanceolate, acute. Stamens yellow, red at the base, style and the 6- or 7-lobed stigma yellowish. Fruit globular, reddish yellow, later drying to brown and papery. According to Boedeker, **Neolloydia texensis** Br. et R. is the north Texas form of this species, and is of smaller size, with fewer and longer central spines.

Neolloydia grandiflora (Otto) Br. et R. = *Mammillaria grandiflora* Otto = *Coryphantha grandiflora* Berger. Mexico (Tamaulipas). Not unlike the preceding, with a similar habit. Stem cylindrical, with shorter warts, less oblique and closer together, with more abundant white wool in the groove of the wart, in the axils and on the young areoles. These are round and rather large. Radial spines up to 25, spreading horizontally or applied to the wart, white, dark at the tip. Central spines absent, or 1 or 2, spreading upwards, stiff, black. Flower large, broadly expanded, deep violet pink, with broader petals and more rounded at the tip.

Neolloydia horripila (Lem.) Br. et R. = *Echinocactus horripilus* Lem. = *Mammillaria horripila* Först. = *Thelocactus horripilus* Berger.

Mexico (Hidalgo). Stem globular to oval or cylindrical, about 12 cm. high and broad, bluish green, with whitish or greyish wool at the top, branching at the base, and sometimes also dichotomously at the top. Warts about 1 cm. high, close together, obliquely pointed upwards, with elliptical areoles, prolonged on the upper side of the wart, at first with snow white wool. Radial spines 9 or 10, the lowermost up to 1½ cm. long. Only one central spine, often absent, stronger. All spines are straight or slightly arching, stiff and sharp-pointed, snow white, tipped brown, passing to greyish and to chalky white. Flower 3 cm. long, funnel-shaped, with a globose bare ovary and short tube, this last with scales at the top, edged white and tipped brown; outer petals brownish pink; inner petals spathulate, carmine red. Stamens, style and 6-lobed stigma white. A very beautiful plant, with showy flowers cropping up twice or thrice during spring and summer. Thrives well in cultivation.

MAMILLOPSIS Weber

Small plants growing in large clusters, with a globular stem, entirely covered with dense white or whitish spines, with 4 to 6 hooked central spines. There is no trace of ribs, and the warts are not grooved, but have hairs or bristles in their axils. Flowers borne at the centre, from the axils of the new warts. Stamens and style longer than the perianth. Includes 2 species, quite like a *Mammillaria* in appearance and habit.

Mamillopsis senilis (Loddiges) Weber = *Mammillaria senilis* Loddiges. Mexico (Chihuahua and Durango). Plant freely sprouting and clustering when old. Stem globular to almost cylindrical, 6 cm. thick and up to 10 cm. high, covered all over with soft white spines. Warts closely packed, fresh green, up to 8 mm. long, obliquely pointed. Areoles with white wool, with numerous (about 40) radial spines, soft, bristle-like, 8 to 14 mm. long, and 5 to 6 similar central spines, the lowermost of these being longer (up to 2 cm.), thicker, pale yellow, hooked at the tip. Axils woolly. Flowers about 6 cm. long, and 4 to 5 cm. broad: tube long, trumpet-shaped, with broad round scales: petals spreading, long, obtuse, violet red, with a darker median band. Stamens in two bundles, one arising from the base, and the other from the tube, violet red, forming a brush around the style of the same colour, protruding beyond the flower. Stigma with 5 or 6 green lobes in a cluster. Flowers in May, the flower lasting for several days.

A pretty plant, deservedly popular. Cultivation is not difficult in a porous sandy and stony soil, fairly rich, with the addition of a little leaf-mould. Must have an open and exposed situation, with full sunshine at all times, and should be freely watered during the growing season of summer. In winter the plant may be sheltered under glass to keep off excessive rain during the period of rest, but in its native country the plant is usually covered with snow in winter on the heights of the Sierra Madre.

Mamillopsis Diguetii Weber. Mexico (Jalisco and Sinaloa on the Pacific). Is similar to the preceding, with stronger spines and smaller flowers, about half as large. Rare in cultivation.

Cochemiea (K. Brand.) Walton

Stem cylindrical, often elongated, like a *Mammillaria* or a *Cereus*, with spirally arranged tubercles, not grooved, nor milky, rather far apart on a broad base, mostly with 1 or more central spines hooked at the tip. Flowers borne in the axils of the upper tubercles, near the top, tubular, zygomorphic, two-lipped, curved; petals in two series; the red stamens and style exserted beyond the petals. Fruit oval or roundish, naked, red, a fleshy berry; seeds black, pitted. Includes 5 species, natives of Lower California.

An interesting genus, with flowers resembling those of *Zygocactus* and *Aporocactus*, but of course much smaller. All the species when aufficiently grown, sprout freely around the base, forming large clusters. The cultivation is easy, in full sun.

Cochemiea Halei (K. Brand.) Walton = *Mammillaria Halei* K. Brand. Lower California (Southern Islands). Stems 30 to 50 cm. high, and 5 to 7½ cm. thick, covered with spines. Warts short, axils woolly, Radial spines 10 to 20, stiff and straight, spreading, up to 1½ cm. long. Central spines 3 or 4, sometimes up to 6, stronger and up to 3½ cm. long, not hooked, but straight and very stiff. All spines are at first reddish brown, passing to yellowish and grey, always more or less darker at the tip. Flowers borne on the side axils around the top, 4 to 5 cm. long, scarlet red. Fruit a clavate berry, 12 mm. long.

Cochemiea Poselgeri (Hildm.) Br. et R. = *Mammillaria Poselgeri* Hildm. = *M. Roseana* K. Brand. = *M. longihamata* Engelm. = *M. Radliana* Quehl = *Cactus Roseanus* Coult. Southern part of Lower California. Stems numerous, often up to 2 m. long, sprawling or hanging, up to 4 cm. thick, bluish green to greyish green. Axils with white wool, occasionally with bristles. Warts conical, pointed, obliquely erect, broad and angular at the base, about 1 cm. high, with a round areole at the top, very woolly when young. Radial spines 7 to 9, spreading, stiff, the upper ones up to 1½ cm. long, at first dark yellow or red, passing to horny yellow and finally to greyish. Only one central spine, spreading outwards, up to 3 cm. long, much thicker and darker, strongly hooked at the tip. Flowers glossy scarlet, 3 cm. long, borne in the axils of the upper warts near the top. Frequently met with in cultivation.

Cochemiea Pondii Walton = *Mammillaria Pondii* Greene = *Cactus Pondii* Coult. Islands along the western coast of the northern part of Lower California. Stem up to 40 cm. high, 4 to 6 cm. thick, grass green, well covered with spines. Warts conical, short, obliquely erect, pointed, 6 mm. long, with large round areoles, with abundant white wool when young. Radial spines 15 to 25, spreading, slender, short, in 2 series, the outer white and shorter, the inner brown. Central spines 6 to 10, thicker, up to 3 cm. long, one or two of them hooked at the tip, dark brown in their upper part. The axils are woolly and with a few bristles. Flower 5 cm. long, slender, glossy pale scarlet. Fruit oval, scarlet.

Cochemiea setispina (Engelm.) Walton = *Mammillaria setispina*

Engelm. = *Cactus setispinus* Coult. Granitic formations in the south of Lower California. Plant forming large groups, up to 90 cm. across. Stems up to 30 cm. long, and 3 to 4 cm. thick, dull green. Warts short and broadly conical, almost four-sided at the base, obliquely erect, with woolly axils. Areoles round, woolly when young, later bare. Radial spines 9 to 12, slender, spreading, 1 to 3½ cm. long, variously curved, white, tipped black. Central spines 1 to 4, straight, spreading outwards, stiff, the upper one straight, up to 5 cm. long and hooked, the others shorter. Flowers borne on the side axils near the top, all round the stem, often over 6 cm. long, with a long trumpet-like tube, petals and tube scarlet red. Fruit oval, 3 cm. long, scarlet.

Cochemiea maritima Gates. Lower California. This is a new species, very much like *C. Halei*, but stronger, and with hooked centrals.

Neowerdermannia Frič

A new and aberrant genus of doubtful affinity, and its systematic position is still unsettled. It is inserted here tentatively close to *Coryphantha*. Includes only one species, native of the high regions of Bolivia, up to 5,000 m. above sea level, and the following description may be taken also as that of the genus.

Neowerdermannia Vorwerkii Frič. Stem more or less globular, green or pale green, 6 to 8 cm. thick, with a thick turnip-like root. Ribs about 16, divided into triangular warts, with a triangular upper side, and an acute, hatchet-like outer or lower side, more or less deeply notched into low tubercles like a molar tooth. The areoles large, round, at first with whitish wool, are situated at the base of the triangular upper side of the wart. Spines 7 to 10 or more, needle-like, thick, mostly curved and spreading star-like, at first brownish or purplish brown, passing to yellowish or horny greyish white, the upper ones straight, 1 to 1½ cm. long, the laterals slightly curved, 2 to 3 cm. long, occasionally up to 5 cm. long; the lower one thicker than the others, strongly curved backwards and hooked at the tip, 2 to 3 cm. long. Flower 2½ cm. long, funnel-shaped, with spreading limb, 2 cm. across; petals lanceolate-acute, white, with a lilac midrib. The fruit protrudes from the areole on ripening. The native name of this singular plant is *acka-kana*.

var. **Gielsdorfiana** Frič. Plant smaller, spines much shorter. Flower pinkish lilac; petals not acuminate. More frequent in cultivation.

Coryphantha (Engelm.) Lemaire
(Sub-genus *Eu-coryphantha* Berger)

Plant globular or cylindrical, solitary or sprouting from the base or sides, forming groups. Tubercles grooved along the upper surface from the tip to the base. Flowers large or fairly large, mostly yellow, sometimes red or purple, borne on the new areoles near the centre. Fruit large, oblong, green or yellow, ripening mostly in the following year. Seeds usually pale brown or black, with a thin shell.

Includes over 50 species, all North American, mostly Mexican, formerly included under *Mammillaria*.

All species are interesting and worth growing, for the beauty of their shape and spines, or for their flowers. Their cultivation is easy, and with ordinary attention imported plants do not fail to establish themselves, and soon make good growth. Propagation by seed is also easy, but as a rule seedlings grow slowly for the first 2 or 3 years. Should be kept dry or almost dry in winter, and any soil provided it is porous and moderately rich with the addition of some leaf-mould or old cow manure, and of some calcareous matter, will do for most species. Nearly all of them require full sunshine at all times.

Coryphantha macromeris (Engelm.) Lem. = *Mammillaria macromeris* Engelm. Mexico, western Texas and southern New Mexico. Freely clustering around the base and sides. Stem up to 20 cm. high and 7 to 8 cm. thick, pale greyish green. Warts 1½ to 3 cm. long, cylindrical, grooved on the upper surface to below its middle. Areoles woolly when young. Radial spines 10 to 17, awl-shaped, almost angular, at first reddish passing to white, tipped dark, 1 to 4 cm. long. Central spines 1 to 4, brown or black, 2 to 5 cm. long. Flowers up to 8 cm. broad, funnel-shaped, with numerous petals, the inner ones linear-lanceolate, acute, toothed, deep pink to carmine red. Ovary and tube with fringed scales. Stigma with 7 or 8 lobes. Fruit a green berry, 1½ to 2½ cm. long, juicy, sometimes with a few scales.

Coryphantha Runyonii Br. et R. Eastern Texas. Very similar to the preceding. Stem greyish green, less freely clustering, with short rounded warts and thick tuberous roots. Radial spines shorter. Central spines mostly 1, rarely 2 or 3. Flowers smaller.

Coryphantha elephantidens Lem. = *Mammillaria elephantidens* Lem. Mexico (Michoagan). A beautiful plant, at first solitary; when old freely sprouting from the warts and extending. Stem semi-globular or low globular, up to 14 cm. high, and 18 to 20 cm. broad, dark green, with white wool at the top and in the axils. Warts rounded, broad and plump, flat on the upper surface, where there is a deep woolly groove. Radial spines 6 to 8, strong, spreading, curved over the wart, brownish, tipped darker, up to 2 cm. long, at first pale yellow. No central spine. Flowers large, 8 to 10 cm. broad, with many lanceolate, toothed petals, pink, red, or carmine, with a darker midrib, and darker at the base. Stamens pink, style orange or yellow, stigma with 6 orange or yellow lobes. Fruit an oblong green berry, 2 to 3 cm. long, maturing the following year, growing out of the mass of wool at the time of ripening. Seeds pale brown.

Coryphantha Ritteri Boedeker. Mexico. A new species, very similar to the preceding, but smaller in size, of a paler and duller green, more easily sprouting around the base, and with yellow spines, reddish towards the tip.

Coryphantha bumamma (Ehrenb.) Br. et R. = *Mammillaria bumamma* Ehrenb. Mexico. Is also very similar, but of a duller green.

(b) ASTROPHYTUM MYRIOSTIGMA

(a) ASTROPHYTUM ASTERIAS

PLATE XLVIII

(b) ASTROPHYTUM CAPRICORNE
var. nivea

(a) ASTROPHYTUM CAPRICORNE

PLATE XLIX

Flower reddish yellow or yellow, about half as large as that of *C. elephantidens*, of which it is sometimes considered as a variety. Petals obtuse.

Coryphantha sulcolanata Lem. = *Mammillaria sulcolanata* Lem. = *M. retusa* (Scheidw.) Pfeiff. Mexico (Hidalgo). Globular-depressed, glossy dark green, at first solitary, sprouting at the base when old, 10 to 12 cm. thick, with abundant white wool at the top and in the axils. Warts large, 2 cm. long and 3 cm. broad, obtuse, more or less five-sided at the base, with a deep woolly groove. Areoles woolly at first. Radial spines 8 to 10, thick, the laterals about 1½ cm. long, at first yellowish white, tipped red, passing to brownish tipped darker, spreading over the wart. No central spine. Flowers up to 8 cm. broad, outer petals linear, acute, canary yellow. Stamens yellow, style and 9- or 10-lobed stigma whitish. Berry spindle-shaped, 3 cm. long, pale green.

Coryphantha cornuta (Hildm.) Berger = *Mammillaria cornuta* Hildm. Mexico. Stem globular-depressed, greyish green, 6 to 8 cm. thick, mostly solitary in cultivation. Warts large, obtuse, up to 17 mm. long and broad. Areoles round, at first with dirty white or yellowish wool. Radial spines 6 or 7, spreading, stiff, awl-shaped, straight or slightly curved, the lower 6 to 8 mm. long. One central spine, thicker and slightly longer, curved downwards. All spines horny yellow, tipped darker. Flowers pink.

Coryphantha cornifera (DC.) Lem. = *Mammillaria cornifera* DC. non Salm-Dyck = *M. daemonoceras* Lem. Central Mexico (Hidalgo). Stem globular or conical, mostly solitary, green to greyish green, about 12 cm. high, woolly at the top. Tubercles closely packed, rhomboid at the base, 1½ to 2½ cm. high and about as broad, with woolly axillae. Areoles woolly when young. Radial spines 7 to 12 or more, spreading, slightly curved, yellowish. Central spine only one, very thick, arching downwards, very stiff, at first red, passing to brown, tipped black. Flowers 7 cm. broad; outer petals brownish, the inner lanceolate, acute, lemon yellow. Stamens pink, style and 8-lobed stigma whitish.

var. **scolymoides** (Scheidw.) = *M. scolymoides* Scheidw. Tubercles more closely packed together, directed upwards, like the bracts of a globe-artichoke. Radial spines more numerous, curved upwards, 4 of them coloured darker. The bundle of radial spines on the top areoles is brush-like.

Coryphantha Borwigii J. A. Purpus. Mexico (Coahuila). Plant oval, bluish green to greyish green, 6 to 10 cm. high, and 5 to 7 cm. thick, with rhomboid obliquely conical tubercles, up to 1½ cm. high. Axils woolly when young. Radial spines on young areoles erect, in a brush-like bundle, 1 to 2 cm. long. Central spines on new areoles 3, stiff, bulbous at the base, the upper one curved laterally, and like the two others, dirty white to brownish, darker or black at the tip, 1½ to 2 cm. long. The wool in the new axillae is dirty white or brownish. Flower 6 to 6½ cm. long: outer petals greenish red below, purplish

Y

above, pointed red; the next row yellowish and toothed, with a red midrib; the inner row, broader, pale greenish yellow with darker midrib, with toothed margin and reddish at the base. Stamens red, style and 14-lobed stigma yellowish white.

Coryphantha reduncispina Böd. Mexico. Mostly solitary, globular to oval, almost flat at the top, deep green, 6 to 8 cm. thick. Tubercles in 8 or 9 rows, almost angular, keeled, but somewhat conical, up to 1 cm. long. Upper axils slightly woolly or hairy, the lower bare. Areoles at first with white wool, soon dropping off. Spines 2 to 5, thick, awl-shaped, the lower one curved downwards up to 1 cm. long, the others much shorter, straight; all spines horny white or horny yellow, tipped dark brown or black. Requires half-shade.

Coryphantha durangensis (Rge.) Br. et R. = *Mammillaria durangensis* Rge. Mexico (Durango). Plant freely clustering, greyish green, cylindrical, 10 to 15 cm. high, and 4 to 6 cm. thick, woolly at the top and axils. Tubercles rhomboid at the base, lozenge-shaped, obliquely pointed. Radial spines 6 to 8, spreading, slender, whitish, passing to grey, up to 1 cm. long. Only one central spine, straight, slender, black, slightly longer. Flowers up to 2 cm. long; outer petals narrow, reddish brown; inner petals creamy white to pale yellow.

Coryphantha chlorantha (Engelm.) Br. et R. = *Mammillaria chlorantha* Engelm. Southern Utah, Nevada and western Arizona. Plant u.s., stem 20 to 25 cm. high, and 8 cm. thick. Tubercles thickly set, and wholly covered by the densely matted spines. Central spines 3 to 5, more or less erect, white, brown towards the tip. Flowers 3 cm. long and 4 cm. across, with narrow yellowish petals, having an olive green midrib. Stamens yellowish white, style and 4-lobed stigma green. The rest as in the preceding.

Coryphantha Roederiana Boedeker. Mexico (Coahuila). Plant slowly clustering, oval, glossy green, 11 cm. high and 7 cm. thick woolly and spiny at the top. Tubercles conical, angular at the base with a narrow bare groove. Areoles very woolly when young. Axils hairy, without any gland. Radial spines 10 to 12, irregularly spreading, needle-like, sometimes arching, greyish tipped brown, 1 to 2 cm. long. Only one central spine, stiff, brown, often arched backwards, slightly shorter. Flowers 5 cm. broad; inner petals pale yellow to yellowish white, pale reddish at the base.

Coryphantha speciosa Boedeker. Mexico (Coahuila). Solitary, globular to oval, about 9 cm. high, and 8 cm. thick, glossy green or almost bluish. Tubercles fleshy, softish, conical or cylindrical, up to 2½ cm. long, slightly arching inwards, with a narrow bare groove. Areoles very woolly when young. Radial spines 7 to 9, spreading, about 1½ cm. long, ashy grey, tipped darker. Central spines 4, the upper one erect and directed upwards, the others like the radials. Axils at first hairy, later bare. Flowers about 6 cm. broad; inner petals golden yellow.

CEREEAE

Coryphantha obscura Boedeker. Mexico (Nuevo Leon). Stem solitary, very dark green, globular or elongated, 7 to 8 cm. thick. Tubercles conical, in 12 to 14 spiral rows, 2 cm. long. Radial spines 10, pale grey, tipped darker, up to 2 cm. long. Central spines 4, more rigid and thickened at the base, slightly longer, black above. Flowers 5 cm. across, funnel-shaped, orange yellow or brownish yellow; throat and stamens deep red, style pink below, yellow above, with 8 to 10 short yellow stigmas.

Coryphantha Werdermannii Boedeker. Mexico (Coahuila, Sierra de Paila). Solitary, rarely clustering. Stem globular, or almost oval, 6 cm. thick, greyish green or ashy green, spiny at the top. Tubercles about ½ cm. long, with bare areoles and bare axils. Radial spines 15 to 20, spreading comb-like, clear greyish white, about 6 mm. long. No central spines. When older, the plant develops tubercles 1½ cm. long, radial spines more numerous, 1½ to 2 cm. long, and 4 central spines, 3 of which are erect, and the fourth spreading outwards, straight, brownish or greyish, 2 cm. or more in length. Areoles and axils always bare. Flowers 5 to 6 cm. long, glossy pale golden yellow. A singular species, rare even in its native country.

Coryphantha radians (DC.) Br. et R. = *Mammillaria radians* DC. = *M. monoclova* Rge. = *M. pectinata* Engelm. Mexico (Hidalgo). Stem solitary, globular to oval or elongated, green, with wool and spines at the top, 5 to 6 cm. thick. Tubercles obliquely conical and obliquely pointed, with wool in the axils and in the areoles when young. Radial spines up to 20 or more, up to 3 cm. long, spreading comb-like or pectinate, and recurved on the wart, yellowish, tipped brown. No central spine. Flowers 6 to 7 cm. broad, with numerous linear-lanceolate acute petals, yellow, reddish at the base, the outer ones tipped reddish and with a greenish midrib. Stamens and style yellow, stigma with 8 to 10 lobes. A very variable species.

var. **pectinata** Engelm. = *Mammillaria pectinata* Engelm. Often listed as *Coryphantha pectinata* Engelm. Radials short, arranged comblike. Petals green at the base.

var. **impexicoma** K. Sch. = *M. impexicoma* Lem. Spines more numerous, longer, more erect.

var. **Altamiranoi** (Rose) = *Coryphantha Altamiranoi* Rose. With fewer spines.

var. **minor** Hort. A smaller plant, with smaller flowers, outer petals reddish green, inner petals straw-coloured.

Coryphantha Palmeri Br. et R. Mexico (Durango, Tamaulipas). Stem solitary or cespitose, globular-elongated, pale green, 8 to 10 cm. thick. Warts conical, erect. Areoles very woolly when young. Radial spines 11 to 14, slender, spreading, yellowish, tipped black. One central spine, thick, brown, hooked at the tip, 1 to 2 cm. long. Flowers 3 cm. long; outer petals linear-acute, yellowish white with a brown midrib; inner petals yellow. Stigma with 9 creamy white lobes.

Coryphantha Salm-Dyckiana (Scheer) Br. et R. = *Mammillaria Salm-Dyckiana* Scheer = *M. Scheeri* Auct. non Muehlenpf. Mexico (Chihuahua). Plant sprouting at the base, pale green, more or less globose, 10 to 15 cm. broad, with much white wool at the top. Warts almost rhomboid, 1 cm. long, obliquely pointed, with a deep bare groove. Areoles slightly woolly when young. Axils woolly. Radial spines 7 to 15, greyish or whitish 1 to 1½ cm. long, erect, often curved. Central spines 1 to 4, reddish to black, the upper 3 directed upwards, the lower thicker, 2 to 2½ cm. long, bulbous at the base, somewhat curved. Flowers up to 4 cm. long, outer petals greenish, edged reddish, the inner pale yellow, funnel-shaped. Stigma with 7 lobes.

Coryphantha Muehlenpfordtii Br. et R. = *Mammillaria Scheeri* Muehlenpf. non Auct. Mexico (Chihuahua, Sonora, and Coahuila, near Saltillo), New Mexico, Texas. Globular or oval, up to 20 cm. high and 7½ to 15 cm. thick. Tubercles softish, low and broad, passing to cylindrical, round at the top, up to 2½ cm. long, with several dark glands in the groove. Spines yellow to reddish, tipped brown or black; the radials 6 to 16, straight, up to 2 cm. long; the centrals 1 to 4, thicker, 3 to 3½ cm. long, straight or slightly arched, rarely hooked at the tip. Flowers 6 cm. long, yellow. Stamens white below, pink above; style greenish, stigma yellow.

Coryphantha Delaetiana (Quehl) Berger = *Mammillaria Delaetiana* Quehl. Mexico. Nearly allied to *C. Salm-Dyckiana*. Plant clustering into small groups; stem clavate to cylindrical, green, strongly spiny at the top. Warts 1 cm. long, closely packed, rhomboid at the base, with bare grooves. Areoles slightly woolly. Radial spines about 15, the upper 2 or 3 more erect and longer, the others 1 cm. long, spreading, bulbous at the base, diaphanous yellow, tipped darker. Central spines 1 or 2, stronger, curved downwards, 2 cm. long, black. Flower large, clear yellow.

Coryphantha pallida Br. et R. Mexico (Tehuacan). Plant solitary or clustering, globular, bluish green, up to 12 cm. thick, with closely packed tubercles. Radial spines about 20, whitish, spreading over the tubercles. Central spines 3 (only 1 in young plants), the upper 2 straight and erect, the lower one curved backwards, tipped darker. Flowers large, 7 cm. long, and as broad; outer petals narrow, greenish yellow with a red dorsal band; inner petals broader, acute, toothed, pale yellow. Stamens red, style and 9-lobed stigma yellow.

Coryphantha Andreae Böd. = *Mammillaria Andreae* Böd. Mexico (Vera Cruz). Stem globular or slightly elongated, glossy dark green, 9 cm. thick, axils and top very woolly. Tubercles thickly packed, plump, roundish, 2 cm. high and 2½ cm. broad, with a deep woolly groove. Radial spines about 10, yellowish grey, tipped brown, spreading, about 1 cm. long. Central spines 5 to 7, thicker and stiffer, up to 2½ cm. long, darker in colour, curved over the tubercle. Flowers 5 to 6 cm. broad, with narrow linear petals, acute, toothed, pale yellow. Stamens, style and stigma yellow.

(a) ASTROPHYTUM ORNATUM

(b) NOTOCACTUS CONCINNUS

PLATE L

(b) NOTOCACTUS LENINGHAUSII

(a) NOTOCACTUS SCOPA

PLATE L1

Coryphantha pycnacantha (Mart.) Lem.= *Mammillaria pycnacantha* Mart. = *M. Winkleri* Först. Mexico (Oaxaca). At first solitary, later clustering, oval to short-cylindric, bluish green, 8 to 10 cm. long, and 5 to 7 cm. thick, very woolly at the top and axils. Tubercles rhomboid at the base, 1 to 1½ cm. long, and about 2½ cm. broad, obtuse, obliquely pointed, at first woolly at the areole and groove. Radial spines 10 to 12, slender and slightly curved, yellowish, tipped darker, up to 1½ cm. long. Central spines 4, thicker and more curved, up to 2½ cm. long. Flowers about 4 cm. long and 5 cm. broad, with narrow acute lemon yellow petals. Stamens pale yellow, style whitish, stigma with 5 spreading yellow lobes.

Coryphantha conimamma A. Lke. = *Mammillaria conimamma* A. Lke. Solitary, rarely sprouting at the base, globular or oval, glossy dark green, up to 10 cm. thick, very much like *C. elephantidens* in general appearance. Warts conical, 1½ cm. long and as broad, with a deep groove at first slightly woolly, later bare. Areoles round, woolly, afterwards bare. Radial spines 6 to 9, stiff, spreading, up to 12 mm. long, slightly curved, amber yellow when young, passing to diaphanous yellow, tipped dark. Central spines 3 or 4, more strongly curved, about 2 cm. long. Flowers borne at the centre, freely, even on young plants, 5 cm. long, funnel-shaped; outer petals linear, greenish, with a reddish central band; inner petals linear-lanceolate, greenish yellow. Stamens red, and 5 lobed stigma and style yellow.

Coryphantha echinus (Engelm.) Br. et R. = *Mammillaria echinus* Engelm. = *M. radians* var. *echinus* K. Sch. Western Texas. Mostly solitary, globular or oval, pointed at the top, greyish green, 3 to 5 cm. thick. Warts conical, about 1 cm. long, rather closely packed. Radial spines 16 to 30, very stiff, needle-like, white, the upper ones longer, up to 1½ cm. Central spines 3 or 4, straight, thicker, spreading, 1½ to 2½ cm. long, bulbous at the base and dark brown. Flowers 5 cm. broad, yellow, outer petals linear-lanceolate, the inner more numerous and narrower.

Coryphantha sulcata (Engelm.) Br. et R. = *Mammillaria sulcata* Engelm. = *M. radians* var. *sulcata* K. Sch. South Texas. Stem greyish green, clustering, more or less globular, 8 to 12 cm. thick. Tubercles about 1 cm. long, soft-fleshed, somewhat flattened. Radial spines about 15, spreading almost comb-like, white. Central spines 1 to 3, often absent in young plants, curved outwards. Flowers 5 cm. broad; petals acute, toothed, yellow with a red central band; Stamens reddish, style greenish yellow, stigma with 7 to 10 yellow lobes.

Coryphantha vivipara (Haw.) Br. et R. = *Mammillaria vivipara* Haw. = *M. radiosa* Engelm. = *Cactus radiosus* Nutt. From Manitoba and Alberta (Canada), to Kansas, Colorado and northern Texas. Plant abundantly clustering, ashy green or greyish, globular to elongated, 2½ to 12 cm. high, with cylindrical tubercles and woolly areoles. Radial spines about 16, spreading, slender, white. Central spines 4 to 6, stronger, brownish, bulbous at the base. Flowers about 5 cm. broad;

outer petals greenish: inner petals reddish, ciliated at the margin. Stigma with 8 red acute lobes. A variable species; the stem may be 4 or 5 cm. thick, or up to 10, and is sometimes as low as 2½ cm., and occasionally up to 20 cm. high, always clustering.

Coryphantha neomexicana Br. et R. = *Mammillaria radiosa* var. *neomexicana* Engelm. Mexico (Chihuahua) to New Mexico and western Texas. Mostly solitary, very spiny, globular to short-cylindric, up to 8 cm. high. Radial spines very numerous, spreading, white. Central spines thicker, spreading outwards, whitish below, brown or black above. Inner petals broadly linear, acute, toothed. Lobes of stigma obtuse and white. The rest as in the preceding species.

Coryphantha arizonica (Engelm.) Br. et R. = *Mammillaria arizonica* Engelm. = *M. radiosa* var. *arizonica* K. Sch. Northern Arizona. Plant abundantly clustering, greyish green, with conical warts, 2½ cm. long, deeply grooved. Radial spines 15 to 20, white: central spines 3 to 6, deep brown above. Flowers 5 to 7 cm. broad. Petals numerous, linear, acute, pink, the outer ones ciliated. Stigma with 8 to 10 white lobes.

Coryphantha aggregata (Engelm.) Br. et R. = *Mammillaria aggregata* Engelm. Arizona and New Mexico. Stem freely clustering, globular, very spiny. Radial spines spreading, white, often tipped brown. Central spines 6 or more, spreading brush-like, especially at the top of the plant. Flower 5 to 7 cm. broad, red.

Coryphantha deserti (Engelm.) Br. et R. = *Mammillaria deserti* Engelm. = *M. Alversonii* Coult. = *M. radiosa* var. *Alversonii* K. Sch. Arizona, southern California and Nevada. A very beautiful species, at first solitary, afterwards sprouting at the base. Stem cylindrical, 10 to 14 cm. high, and 5 to 7 cm. thick, glaucous green, very densely covered with beautiful spines. Radial spines many, white, up to 1½ cm. long. Central spines 10 or more, at first red tipped black, passing to white tipped bluish, up to 3 cm. long, straight and spreading brush-like. Flowers 3 cm. broad, pale red.

Coryphantha difficilis (Quehl) Berger = *Mammillaria difficilis* Quehl. Mexico. Plant solitary: stem globular-depressed, greyish, with almost rhomboid tubercles up to 2½ cm. broad, more or less imbricate and directed upwards, with little wool in their axils. Grooves and areoles almost bare. Spines bulbous at the base: the radials 12 to 14, the upper ones up to 2 cm. long, tipped dark, the lower glassy white; the centrals 4, curved, horny yellow, tipped dark or black, 2 cm. long. Flowers yellow.

Coryphantha gladiispina (Böd.) Berger = *Mammillaria gladiispina* Böd. Mexico (Coahuila). Solitary, oval, 10 cm. high, 6 cm. thick, deep green passing to grey, very spiny at the top. Tubercles directed upwards, with bare grooves. Areoles round, bare. Radial spines 17 to 20, of which 7 or 8 upper ones forming a brush-like bundle, ashy grey, up to 2 cm. long, tipped black; the lower 10 to 12 shorter, 1 to 1½ cm. long, spreading, needle-like, glossy grey, slightly bulbous at the base. Central spines 4, the lower one 2½ cm. long, curved slightly backwards, the others curved upwards, all bulbous at the base, ashy grey, tipped darker. Flowers 4 to 4½ cm. broad: outer petals acuminate, chrome yellow, with a brown dorsal band, inner petals yellow. Stamens, style and 7-lobed stigma yellow.

Coryphantha Bergeriana Boedeker. Mexico (Neuvo Leon). Plant solitary, short-clavate, about 12 cm. high and 6 cm. thick, dull dark green, spiny at the top. Tubercles softish, conical, 10 to 14 mm. high, with a bare groove, in which there are 1 or 2 glands. Young areoles slightly woolly. Radial spines 18 to 20, spreading, greyish, needle-like, 1 to 1½ cm. long. Central spines 4, slender, yellowish, the upper 3 straight, obliquely spreading, about 12 mm. long, the other spreading outwards, often curved backwards, 1½ to 2 cm. long. Axils at first with whitish wool, later with one red gland. Flowers 4 cm. long, expanding to 7 cm., inner petals yellow.

Coryphantha Vaupeliana Boedeker. Mexico (Tamaulipas, near Jaumave). Globular or oval, dull bluish green, 7 cm. thick. Tubercles conical-triangular, 2 cm. long, 1½ cm. thick, with a narrow bare groove. Axils more or less bare, with red glands. Radial spines 15, the lower 8 or 9 slender, spreading, yellowish grey, 12 mm. long. the upper ones needle-like in a bundle. Central spines 4, thicker and longer, bulbous at the base, curved, greyish yellow, tipped brown. Flower large, yellow. Lobes of stigma white.

Coryphantha Georgii Boedeker. Mexico (San Luis Potosi). Solitary, glossy green, 4 cm. high and 7 cm. broad, spiny and woolly at the top. Tubercles softish, conical, up to 12 mm. long, with a narrow bare groove. Areoles at first very woolly. Axils more or less woolly, with a gland. Radial spines 8 or 9, needle-like, thin, radiating, greyish to whitish tipped brown, up to 12 mm. long. Central spines 1 or more, up to 4, about 2 cm. long, stiff, the longest often curved upwards. Flowers 2 cm. long, 3½ cm. broad; inner petals glossy creamy white to silvery white, with pale green throat.

Coryphantha clava (Pfeiff.) Lem. = *Mammillaria clava* Pfeiff. Mexico (Hidalgo). Mostly solitary, cylindrical, bluish green to greyish green, woolly and spiny at the top, up to 30 cm. long and 9 to 10 cm. thick. Warts obliquely conical, 1½ cm. long, obliquely pointed, with a pronounced groove. Groove and areoles woolly when young. Radial spines 9 or 10, radiating, up to 14 mm. long, yellow. Central spines 1 to 4, thicker, up to 2 cm. long, at first brownish, passing to yellow. Axils with white wool, and with 1 or 2 red or yellow glands. Flowers up to 8 cm. broad: outer petals green, pointed red; inner petals linear-lanceolate, toothed, glossy yellow, reddish on the dorsal side. Stamens yellow, style and 6- to 7-lobed stigma yellow.

Coryphantha unicornis Boedeker. Mexico (Coahuila). Stem clustering, globular, 6 to 8 cm. thick, glossy clear bluish green. Tubercles conical, softish, 1½ cm. long, obtuse, with a narrow bare groove. Axils woolly, with a red gland. Radial spines 7 or 8, sometimes 9, radiating, almost horizontal, needle-like, 1½ cm. long: only one central spine, up to 2 cm. long, straight. All spines are whitish, reddish brown towards the tip, more or less bulbous at the base.

Coryphantha octacantha (DC.) Br. et R. = *Mammillaria octacantha* DC. = *M. macrothele* Mart. Mexico (Hidalgo, Zimapan). A variable species, with a cylindrical stem up to 50 cm. high, bluish green to greyish green. Tubercles softish, 3 cm. long, obliquely pointed, spreading outwards or slightly backwards, with a bare groove, having one or more glands. Areoles woolly; axils woolly, with one or more glands. Radial spines 6 to 9, radiating, 1½ to 2 cm. long, yellowish tipped brown, spread over the tubercles. Central spines 1 or 2, thick, yellow, zoned brown, later more pale, 2 to 3 cm. long, straight, bulbous at the base. Flowers 5 to 6 cm. long; outer petals greenish, edged yellow, with a reddish dorsal band; inner petals glossy yellow. Stamens white or pale pink, style greenish, stigma with 10 yellow lobes.

Coryphantha Nickelsae (K. Brand.) Br. et R. = *Mammillaria Nickelsae* K. Brand. Mexico (Nuevo Leon). Plant globular, freely clustering, up to 7 cm. thick, green or greyish green, often reddish. Warts abroad, with glands in the groove behind the areoles. Radial spines 14 to 16, spreading, slender, at first yellowish, passing to whitish, 1 cm. long, the upper ones more or less in a bundle. Only one central spine, often developing later. Flowers 5 to 7 cm. broad, pale yellow, with red midrib.

Coryphantha asterias (Cels.) Boedeker = *Mammillaria asterias* Cels. Mexico. Mostly solitary, globular or elongated, greyish green, up to 12 cm. high, and 8 cm. thick. Tubercles thick, somewhat softish, groove often inconspicuous. Axils with white wool, hiding the red gland. Radial spines 9, radiating: central spines 1 or 2, the lower one hooked at the tip. All spines are stiff, bulbous at the base, yellowish, brownish at the tip. Flowers white to pink, stigma with 5 green lobes.

Coryphantha Ottonis Lem. = *Mammillaria Ottonis* Pfeiff. Central Mexico. Globular to short-cylindric, about 12 cm. high, greyish green. Tubercles thick, with a deep groove, almost dividing the tubercle into two lobes. Axils woolly, with a red gland. Radial spines 8 to 12 radiating, straight, up to 1 cm. long. Central spines 3 or 4, thicker and longer, yellowish, the lower one, the strongest, curved backwards. Flowers 4 cm. long, funnel-shaped, white; outer petals with a dark reddish dorsal band; the inner toothed. Stamens, style and 10-lobed stigma yellow.

Coryphantha longicornis Boedeker. Mexico (Durango). Plant mostly solitary, globular to short-cylindric, up to 20 cm. long and 10 cm. thick, glossy green to greyish green, spiny at the top. Tubercles conical, curved upwards and almost lozenge shaped, 1½ to 2 cm. long, with a narrow bare groove. Areoles woolly when young. Axils bare, with one gland. Radial spines about 12, diaphanous white, slender, straight or curved on the warts, up to 1 cm. long, greyish at the tip. Central spines 3, stiff, brown, the upper one about 1 cm. long, the lower thick and curved downwards, up to $2\frac{1}{2}$ cm. long. Flowers about $3\frac{1}{2}$ cm. broad; inner petals pure yellow. Fruit oblong, $1\frac{1}{2}$ cm. long, greenish yellow. Seeds yellowish brown.

Coryphantha recurvata (Engelm.) Br. et R. = *Mammillaria recurvata* Engelm. = *M. nogalensis* Rge. Arizona and northern Mexico (Nogales) Plant clustering abundantly, globular, 10 to 20 cm. broad, bluish green, covered with spines at the top. Tubercles conical, about 1 cm. long. Areoles bare. Radial spines 20 to 25, densely comb-like, yellow to grey, tipped darker, curved backwards, up to 12 mm. long. Central spine 1, sometimes 2, darker, up to 2 cm. long, curved backwards or laterally. Flowers $3\frac{1}{2}$ cm. long, funnel-shaped: outer petals lanceolate, yellowish brown; inner petals broader and toothed, yellow with a brown dorsal band.

Coryphantha Poselgeriana (Dietr.) Br. et R. = *Echinocactus Poselgerianus* Dietr. = *E. saltillensis* Poselg. = *Mammillaria valida* Purp. non Web. = *M. saltillensis* Böd. Mexico (Nuevo Leon, Coahuila, Zacatecas). Stem globular, up to 20 cm. high, often pointed at the top, where it is strongly armed with spines, bluish green. Warts large, 2 cm. long, rhomboid, angular, up to 4 cm. broad. Grooves woolly, with 3 or 4 glands. Areoles bare. Radial spines 5 to 7, stiff, 3 to 5 cm. long, slightly curved backwards, bulbous at the base, greyish, slightly reddish brown or black, the upper ones often collected in a bundle. Only one central spine, obliquely erect, straight or arching, 4 to 5 cm. long. Flowers 4 to 5 cm. long, and as broad, flesh-coloured or pink, rarely yellow, with spathulate toothed petals.

var. **Kieferiana** Berger = *Mammillaria Kieferiana* Hort. Stem greyish green, with large warts thickly set. Radial spines 8, three of which are more slender and directed upwards. One central spine. All spines spreading, thick, brown, darker at the tip, pale brown in the middle.

Coryphantha Guerkeana (Böd.) Br. et R. = *Mammillaria Guerkeana* Böd. Mexico (Durango). Plant glaucous green, strongly protected, with yellowish grey spines and prominent warts. Axils woolly, with a red gland. Radial spines 7, thick, besides 3 or 4 others, more slender in the upper part of the areole. Central spines 2 or 3, very strong, straight, hooked at the tip.

Coryphantha pseudechinus Boedeker. Mexico (Coahuila). Plant solitary or clustering; stem 5 cm. broad, and 6 to 9 cm. high, dull green passing to greyish green. Tubercles conical, pointed, 1 cm. high, rhomboid at the base, $1\frac{1}{2}$ cm. broad, with a narrow groove. Axils woolly. Areoles at first woolly, with 2 or 3 yellow glands in the groove, just above them. Radial spines 18 to 25, radiating, needle-like, stiff, straight, 12 to 15 mm. long, ashy white or grey. Only one central spine, more stiff, spreading outwards, bulbous at the base, 2 to $2\frac{1}{2}$ cm. long. In older plants there are 2 or 3 smaller central spines, like the radials. Flowers 2 cm. long and 3 cm. broad; inner petals linear, elongated, violet pink, paler at the margin, greenish or yellowish at the throat. Stamens whitish, style and 4- to 5-lobed stigma yellow.

Coryphantha echinoidea (Quehl.) Br. et R. = *Mammillaria echinoidea* Quehl. Mexico (Durango). Stem globular, dark greyish green, 5 to 6 cm. thick, entirely covered with spines Tubercles conical, 1 to 1½ cm. long and about as broad, obliquely pointed, with a red gland in the groove. Radial spines 20 to 25, in two rows, up to 1½ cm. long, radiating outwards, white, tipped brown. Central spines mostly 2, sometimes 1 or 3, about as long and of same colour. Axils woolly. Flowers 6 to 8 cm. broad, yellow, with linear-lanceolate toothed petals; outer petals greenish yellow with reddish dorsal band. Stamens white or pale pink, style and 11-lobed stigma greenish.

Coryphantha erecta Lem. = *Mammillaria erecta* Lem. Mexico (Hidalgo). Stem cylindrical, rounded at the top and furnished with white wool and yellow spines, up to 30 cm. high, 6 to 8 cm. thick, pale green. Tubercles obliquely conical and obtuse, 7 to 8 mm. long, 1½ cm. broad at the base. Axils very woolly, with a yellow or brown gland. Areoles at first woolly. Radial spines 8 to 14, straight, radiating horizontally or obliquely, at first amber yellow, passing to yellowish brown or greyish, about 1 cm. long. Central spines 2 to 4, the lower one up to 2 cm. long, curved backwards, same colour. Flowers 6 to 7½ cm. broad; petals narrow, lanceolate, pale yellow; inner petals canary yellow. Stamens yellow below, reddish above; style and 6-lobed stigma pale yellow. A beautiful species, usually with a solitary stem, but clustering in its native country.

Coryphantha raphidacantha (Lem.) Berger = *Mammillaria raphidacantha* Lem. = *M. clavata* Scheidw. = *Neolloydia clavata* Br. et R. Mexico (San Luis Potosi). Stem solitary, occasionally sprouting at the base, conical or cylindrical, bluish green, 15 to 30 cm. long, and 4 to 7 cm. thick. Tubercles obliquely conical, almost flat above, with a woolly groove. Axils woolly with a red gland. Radial spines 6 to 9, straight, spreading, white, tipped brown, at first red at the base, 8 to 15 mm. long. Only one central spine, stronger, up to 2 cm. long, yellow or brown, hooked at the tip, usually absent in young plants. Flowers 2 to 3 cm. long, glossy yellow, with linear petals, the outer pale brown with a red dorsal band, the inner more acute, yellow. Stamens orange red, style and 5-lobed stigma yellow. In the form *radicantissima* Quehl, the central spine is straight, not hooked. This species is certainly not a *Neolloydia*.

var. **ancistracantha** K. Sch. = var. *humilior* Först. Plant smaller, dark green; spines darker in colour; central spine always hooked at the tip.

Coryphantha Pottsii (Scheer) Berger = *Mammillaria Pottsii* Scheer. Mexico (Chihuahua). Plant clustering and branching; stem cylindrical up to 20 cm. high and 2½ to 3 cm. thick. Tubercles oval, obtuse, with a very narrow groove. Axils slightly woolly. Areoles bare. Radial spines numerous, slender, white, all equally long. Central spines stronger and longer, the upper one curved upwards, all bulbous at the base, tipped reddish brown. Fruit oval-elongated, reddish.

Coryphantha compacta (Engelm.) Br. et R. = *Mammillaria compacta* Engelm. Mexico (Chihuahua). Solitary, globular-depressed, 3 to 6 cm. high, 5 to 8 cm. broad; tubercles in 13 rows, closely packed, 8 mm. long, with a well-marked groove. Radial spines 14 to 16, stiff, flat upon the wart, whitish, 10 to 20 mm. long. Usually no central spine. Flowers 2 cm. long and broad, yellow. Fruit oval.

Coryphantha glanduligera (Otto et Dietr.) Lem. = *Mammillaria glanduligera* Otto et Dietr. = *Coryphantha exsudans* (Zucc.) Lem. Central Mexico. Stem oval-cylindrical, 4 cm. thick; tubercles ovate, thick, dull green, with pale yellow glands in the axils. Areoles woolly, later bare. Radial spines 6 or 7, 6 to 10 mm. long, slender, straight, spreading, yellow. One central spine, erect, yellow, brown at the tip, sometimes hooked. Flowers yellow. Requires half-shade. Another species requiring half-shade is **Coryphantha Vogtherriana** Werd. et Böd. a new species from Mexico.

NEOBESSEYA Br. et R.

Plant solitary or sprouting at the base. Tubercles spirally arranged or irregular, grooved on the upper surface as a *Coryphantha*. Flowers large, yellow or pink, borne on the upper areoles or grooves, near the top of the plant. Fruit globose, bright red, Seeds black, with a prominent white scar. Includes 7 species, all North American, formerly classed under *Coryphantha* or *Mammillaria*.

Neobesseya Wissmannii (Hildm.) Br. et R. = *Mammillaria Wissmannii* Hildm. = *Coryphantha* Berger. Central Texas. Plant freely clustering and branching. Stem more or less globular, up to 10 cm. high, bluish green. Axils with white wool. Tubercles cylindrical-conical, soft-fleshed, up to 2½ cm. long, 12 mm. broad at the base, directed upwards, with a groove on the upper side. Radial spines 15 to 20, radiating, yellowish white, tipped reddish, straight, up to 12 mm. long. Central spines often absent, or 1 to 3, thicker and just longer. Flowers 4 to 5 cm. long, funnel-shaped; outer petals yellowish brown; inner petals narrow, spathulate, acuminate, glossy pale yellow. Stamens pale green. Stigma with 5 to 7 yellowish green lobes. Fruit bright carmine red. Seeds glossy black.

Neobesseya similis (Engelm.) Br. et R. = *Mammillaria similis* Engelm. = *Coryphantha similis* Br. et R. Eastern Texas. Plant clustering, globular, deep green, 6 to 10 cm. thick. Tubercles cylindrical, obtuse, directed upwards, up to 2 cm. long. Areoles and grooves woolly at first. Spines 12 to 15, spreading, 1 cm. long, slender, often developing successively, whitish tipped brown, stiff, minutely hairy under a lens. Only one central spine, often absent, just thicker and longer. Flowers 5 to 6 cm. long, outer petals brown and green; inner petals narrow, acuminate, pale yellow. Stamens short, green; style and 4- to 6-lobed stigma green. Fruit globose or slightly oval, red. Seeds large, glossy black.

Neobesseya missouriensis (Sweet) Br. et R. = *Mammillaria missour-*

iensis Sweet = *Coryphantha* Br. et R. Dakota, Montana, Kansas and Oklahoma. Plant solitary or abundantly clustering, glaucous green to greyish green, globular, up to 5 cm. thick and 6 cm. high, with conical-cylindrical tubercles, 1 to 1½ cm. long, grooved on the upper side. Areoles and axils with white wool. Spines 10 to 20, needle-like, grey, up to 1 cm. long, straight or slightly curved, minutely hairy under the microscope. One central spine, often absent, up to 1½ cm. long, straight, its upper part brownish. Flowers 2½ to 3 cm. long, greenish yellow; outer petals narrow, lanceolate, brownish green, fringed; inner petals broader, acuminate, yellow. Stamens yellow, style and 2- to 5-lobed stigma green.

var. **Nuttallii** (Engelm.) = *Neobesseya Nuttallii* Br. et R. = *Mammillaria Nuttallii* Engelm. Petals with a red midrib. Stamens pink to violet. *Neobesseya Notesteinii* (Britton) Br. et R. = *Mammillaria Notesteinii* Britton, from Montana, is probably a synonym.

Neobesseya asperispina Boedeker = *Coryphantha asperispina* Boedeker. Mexico (Coahuila). Mostly solitary, globular, dark bluish green, about 6 cm. thick. Tubercles, conical, softish, pointed, about 18 mm. long, flattened on the upper side, with a superficial bare groove. Very young areoles slightly woolly. Axils bare. Radial spines 9 or 10, slender, stiff, greyish white, rough or hairy under a lens, up to 1 cm. long, at first spreading outwards, afterwards more radiating star-like. Central spine absent, or rarely appearing on young areoles. Flowers 3 cm. long and 2½ cm. broad; inner petals pale greenish yellow, with paler edge, and olive green midrib. Seeds round, glossy black.

Neobesseya odorata Boedeker = *Coryphantha odorata* Boedeker = *Neolloydia odorata* Backbg. Mexico (Tamaulipas, San Luis Potosi). Plant clustering; stem globular, 3 cm. thick, glossy dark green, with dark spines at the top. Tubercles cylindrical, about 1 cm. long, with a bare groove, and an axil with few hairs. Areoles with a little white wool when young. Radial spines 7 to 9, up to 1 cm. long, straight, slender, radiating, white tipped brown. Central spines 3 or 4, thicker, needle-like, at first red, passing to dark brown and dark honey yellow, all hooked, 2 to 2½ cm. long. Flowers small, 1½ cm. long, and 1 cm. broad; inner petals pale yellowish pink. Fruit small, pale greenish or reddish. The plant exhales a strong and pervading perfume.

Neobesseya filziane Boedeker = *Coryphantha filziane* Boedeker. Mexico (Coahuila). Plant slightly cespitose; stem short, cylindrical, 6 cm. high and 3½ cm. thick, glossy bluish green, spiny at the top. Tubercles oval, slender, about 1 cm. long, broad at the base, with a bare groove. Areoles and axils bare. Radial spines 12 to 15, radiating, stiff, needle-like, white, tipped brown, 1 to 1½ cm. long; there are 4 to 7 other spines in a bundle at the upper end of the areole. No central spines. Flowers 2½ cm. long, inner petals lemon yellow, tipped brown and with an olive green midrib. Fruit oblong or clavate, up to 2 cm. long, of a lively red. Seed small, glossy black, pitted.

Neobesseya rosiflora Lahman. Oklahoma. Plant more or less globu-

(b) BARTSCHELLA SCHUMANNII

(a) PARODIA CHRYSACANTHION

PLATE LII

(b) CORYPHANTHA CORNIFERA

(a) CORYPHANTHA ELEPHANTIDENS

PLATE LIII

lar, 7 to 9 cm. thick. Tubercles cylindrical or oval, about 1 cm. long, in about 15 rows, bearing areoles with much white wool and with 14 to 18 radial spines, straight, spreading star-like, white tipped black, up to 1 cm. long. No central spines. Flowers borne at the centre, funnel-shaped: perianth with numerous pink petals in two rows, linear-acute, very narrow, mostly reflexed, about 2 cm. long. Stigma with 5 to 7 lobes.

Escobaria Br. et R.

Plants mostly cespitose, with globular or cylindrical stems. Tubercles grooved on the upper side, becoming corky and persisting on the base of the stem when old. Spines not hooked. Flowers small, borne on the young tubercles around the sides of the stem, near the top. Fruit red, with the withered flower continuing attached on the top. Seeds brown or black. Includes about 11 species, all North American, remarkable for the beauty of their form and spines.

Escobaria tuberculosa (O. Ktze.) Br. et R. = *Cactus tuberculosus* O. Ktze. = *Mammillaria tuberculosa* Engelm. = *M. strobiliformis* Scheer. Better known under this last name. Northern Mexico, southern New Mexico and south-eastern Texas. Plant freely cespitose and branching. Stem cylindrical, 5 to 18 cm. long, and 2 to 6 cm. thick, bluish green or greyish green, with white wool and clustering spines at the top. Tubercles rhomboid at the base, obliquely pointed and directed upwards, 6 mm. long, with a woolly groove on the upper side. Areoles and axils with white wool. Radial spines 20 to 30, slender, needle-like, white tipped brownish, $\frac{1}{2}$ to 1 cm. long. Central spines 5 to 9, thicker and longer, pale bluish brown, or almost dark, the lower one often arched backwards. Flowers $2\frac{1}{2}$ cm. broad; outer petals lanceolate-acute, violet pink, fringed; inner petals paler. Stamens reddish, the inner ones white. Style whitish, stigma with 5 to 7, yellow lobes. Berry clavate, 2 cm. long, carmine red. A beautiful and variable species of easy cultivation.

The following varieties are the best known:

var. **caespititia** Quehl. Stems short and mostly globular, rather slender, densely cespitose. Radials wholly milk white; centrals white tipped brown. Outer petals pink, with a median brown band, fringed white; the inner pale pink, edged white. Stamens, style and 5-lobed stigma all white.

var. **rufispina** Quehl. Spines greyish white, tipped pink. Outer petals brownish.

var. **gracilispina** Quehl. Central spines very slender, diaphanous bluish white.

var. **pubescens** Quehl. Radials 30 or more, erect, soft, white, tipped reddish when new.

var. **durispina** Quehl. Radials more numerous, shorter, hard, easily breaking off, white, tipped reddish or brownish.

A cristate form is also cultivated

Escobaria dasyacantha (Engelm.) Br. et R. = *Mammillaria dasya-cantha* Engelm. = *Coryphantha* Berger. Texas and New Mexico. Slowly and sparingly cespitose. Stem globular to short-cylindric, up to 10 or 15 cm. high, and 5 to 8 cm. thick, pale glaucous green or greyish green, spiny at the top. Warts cylindrical, directed upwards and pointed, 7 to 9 mm. long and about 4 mm. broad at the base, with a woolly groove. Areoles small, round, those at the top of the plant with white wool, later bare. Axils with a little long white wool. Radial spines 25 to 35, white, bristle-like, soft, mostly spreading laterally on each side, often tipped brown, the uppermost up to 1½ cm. long. Central spines 7 to 13, stiffer and thicker, purplish brown to black, whitish at the base, the longest up to 2 cm. long, directed upwards. Flowers funnel-shaped, 3½ cm. broad; outer petals greenish brown, crisp-edged; the next white with a brown dorsal band; the inner white tipped pink, green at the base. Stamens pale pink, style and 5-lobed stigma white. A beautiful plant, but slow to propagate. Usually imported.

Escobaria Emskoetteriana (Quehl) Berger = *Mammillaria Emskoet-teriana* Quehl. = *Coryphantha* Berger. Mexico (San Luis Potosi). Plant cespitose. Stems dark green, oval or elongated, with conical acute warts 1 cm. high, directed upwards, softish and with a shallow groove. Areoles small, round, slightly woolly. Axils bare. Radial spines 20 or more, radiating, slender, bristle-like, white, mostly tipped dark, up to 2 cm. long. Central spines 6 to 8, white, tipped reddish, about 2 cm. long. Flowers 3 cm. broad; outer petals green, edged white; inner petals glossy whitish with a reddish green midrib. Stamens reddish, style and 6-lobed stigma pale yellow.

Escobaria Muehlbaueriana Boedeker = *Coryphantha Muehlbaueri-ana* Boedeker. Mexico (Tamaulipas). Stem oval or elongated, sparingly sprouting from the base, about 5 cm. high and 3 cm. thick, glossy dark green, spiny at the top. Tubercles softish, oval or conical, about 8 mm. long, with an almost bare groove. Axils bare or very slightly woolly. Areoles woolly only when very young. Radial spines 15 to 20, radiating, the upper ones hair-like, white; the lower slender and stiff, needle-like, whitish tipped brown, up to 8 mm. long. Central spines about 6, the upper ones up to 1½ cm. long, greyish, tipped reddish brown. Flowers 1½ cm. long, 2½ cm. broad; inner petals greenish yellow with a reddish midrib. Fruit globose, ½ cm. thick, red. Seed minute, glossy reddish brown, minutely pitted.

Escobaria Sneedii Br. et R. = *Coryphantha Sneedii* Berger. South-west Texas. A small plant, cespitose, with cylindrical stems 6 cm. long, and 1 to 2 cm. thick, entirely with small white spines. Warts numerous, 2 to 3 mm. long. Spines small, very numerous, covering the plant, white, slightly reddish when young. Flowers small pink. Fruit globose, small, deep pink.

Escobaria Runyonii Br. et R. = *Coryphantha Robertii* Berger. Mexico and Texas (Rio Grande). Plant densely cespitose, forming large groups, with globose or oblong heads, 3 to 5 cm. long, greyish green. Tubercles 5 mm. long, cylindrical, with a very narrow groove with white wool. Radial spines many, white, needle-like, 4 to 5 mm. long. Central spines 5 to 7, thicker, 6 to 8 mm. long, white tipped brown or black. Flowers 1½ cm. long, pale purple, petals with a dark purple median nerve and pale margins. Stamens purplish, stigma with 6 green lobes. Fruit globose or oblong, juicy, 6 to 9 mm. long, scarlet.

Escobaria bella Br. et R. Texas (Devil's River). Plant clustering freely. Stem cylindrical 6 to 8 cm. long; tubercles 1½ to 2 cm. long; groove with a brownish gland and white hairs. Radial spines few, up to 1 cm. long, whitish. Central spines 3 to 5, brown, 1 to 2½ cm. long. Flowers small, 2 cm. broad, borne at the top near the centre; petals linear-oblong, acute, pinkish with pale margin, outer petals ciliated. Stamens reddish, stigma with green lobes.

The following are other species rarely met with in cultivation:

Escobaria chihuahuensis Br. et R., **E. Chaffeyi** Br. et R., **E. Lloydii** Br. et R., from Mexico; and **E. Bisbeeana** Orc. = *Coryphantha Bisbeeana* Orc., and **E. Fobei** Frič. = *Fobea viridiflora* Frič, from Texas.

BARTSCHELLA Br. et R.

Plant cespitose, globular or oval, with large tubercles not grooved, rounded at the top, closely packed together and angular at the base. Central spines mostly hooked. Flowers large, pink or purple, borne around the top. Fruit small, at maturity remaining hidden or embedded between the tubercles. Seeds dull black, pitted, with a depressed scar at the hilum. Sufficiently differentiated from *Mammillaria* by the fruit not becoming elongated and protruding at maturity, as well as by the comparatively large flowers and tubercles. Includes one species.

Bartschella Schumannii (Hildm.) Br. et R. = *Mammillaria Schumannii* Hildm. = *M. venusta* K. Brand. Lower California. Plant freely cespitose, with oval greyish violet stems up to 10 cm. high, and up to 6 cm. thick, woolly at the top and in the axils. Tubercles rounded, four-sided at the base. Areoles woolly when new, afterwards almost bare. Radial spines 9 to 15, awl-shaped, stiff, straight, radiating, white, tipped dark or black, 6 to 12 mm. long. Central spines mostly 2, sometimes 1 or 3, the lower one black, strongly hooked, the upper ones straight and white, 1½ cm. long. Flowers on the new axils around the top, 3 to 4 cm. broad; perianth with about 10 lanceolate-acute purplish petals. Style whitish, stigma with 6 green lobes.

PORFIRIA Boedeker

Plant mostly solitary, with a thick turnip-like root, and a stem like a *Mammillaria*, flat at the top, exuding a milky juice when wounded. Tubercles somewhat flat at the base, directed upwards, bearing on top areoles with radial and central spines. There are no grooves. Flowers borne on the upper axils, like a *Mammillaria*. Ovary protruding. Fruit clavate, red, ripening in the following year. Seeds oblong, pale brown, pitted. Seedlings oval on germination. Includes only one species.

Porfiria Schwartzii Boedeker. Mexico (Coahuila). Plant solitary, roundish, 4 cm. thick, with fleshy, softish, bluish green tubercles, directed outwards and upwards, up to 12 mm. long, triangular at the base, where they are about 1 cm. broad, and about 4 mm. thick at the tip, which is more or less acute. Areoles elliptical, at first woolly, later bare. Radial spines 16, slender, greyish white, spreading, the lower up to 6 mm. long, the upper shorter. Only one central spine, brownish, 6 mm. long. All spines are rough and scaly, under the microscope. Flowers bell-shaped or funnel-shaped, fleshy at the base, up to 3 cm. broad, lasting for about 6 days: outer petals lanceolate, pale pink, with a broad dorsal brown band; the inner petals about twice as long, linear-acuminate, whitish, with a pink midrib. Stamens whitish, style pink, stigma with 5 pale yellowish green lobes.

var. **abliflora** Böd. = *Porfiria coahuilensis* Böd. = *Haagea Swartzii* Frič. Mexico (Coahuila). All petals white, with a brownish midrib.

PELECYPHORA Ehrenberg

Small, round or oval plants, more or less clustering, with tubercles compressed laterally or hatchet-like, hence the generic name, bearing an elongated or linear areole, with minute pectinate spines. The tubercles are not grooved, and the juice of the plant is not milky. Flowers borne in the axils at the centre, funnel-shaped, purplish, with a short tube. Fruit small, naked. Seeds small, round, dull black. Includes at least two species.

Pelecyphora aselliformis Ehrenberg. Mexico (San Luis Potosi). Stem globular to clavate, forming a cluster when old, 5 to 10 cm. high, and 2 to 5 cm. thick, greyish green. Tubercles arranged spirally, compressed laterally, elliptical or hatchet-like, 3 to 5 mm. high. Areoles linear-elliptical, with very numerous minute spines, arranged comb-like, united at the base and free only at the tip, not prickly. Flowers 3 cm. broad, surrounded with wool; segments of perianth in 4 rows; the outer whitish acute; the inner linear-spathulate, toothed, carmine violet. Stamens short and white, and white also is the style; the 4-lobed stigma is greenish yellow. The fruit is soft, hidden between the tubercles at the centre, maturing the following year and melting off. The seed is minute, kidney-shaped, black, smooth. There is also a rare cristate form in cultivation.

A singular plant of very slow growth, but of easy cultivation in full sunshine. Usually imported either single or in small cluster of 2 to 5 or more. Is frequently grafted to induce a quicker growth. Seeds germinate well, the seedlings being globose, about 2 mm. thick, but growth is very slow. The native Mexicans consider it as a holy plant; its native name *peyotl* or *peyote*, is shared with *Lophophora Williamsii*, and the plant is (or was) possibly used in the same manner.

Pelecyphora pseudopectinata Backbg. Northern Mexico (at Palmillas). Plant solitary, with watery sap; stem at first globose, later elongated, up to 6 cm. high and about 4½ cm. thick, hardly showing above ground, depressed and somewhat woolly at the top. Tubercles almost square at the base, compressed and hatchet-like above, bearing a linear areole with numerous short, white, slender, pectinate spines 1 to 1½ mm. long. Flowers 1 to 3 blooming together, on the newest areoles at the centre, pale pink, outer petals with darker midrib, inner petals very acute. This is evidently a species of *Pelecyphora*, although the appearance is that of a *Solisia*.

Pelecyphora Valdeziana Moeller, is the same as *Thelocactus Valdezianus* Boedeker.

SOLISIA Br. et R.

Very small, solitary plants, with a globular head, but when old may throw up one or more side branches from the base. Tubercles hatchet-like, or compressed laterally, with milky juice, bearing elliptical-elongated areoles with pectinate spines. Flowers yellow, small, borne in the axils of old tubercles on the sides of the stem. Axils bare. Fruit small, bare. Seeds black, dome-shaped, with a concave scar at the hilum. Includes only one species, formerly classed with *Pelecyphora* owing to the hatchet-like appearance of the warts.

Solisia pectinata (Stein) Br. et R. = *Pelecyphora pectinata* Stein = *Mammillaria pectinata* Weber. Mexico (Tehuacan). Stem globular or oval, 1 to 3 cm. broad, almost entirely covered with white spines. Warts compressed laterally, low, with narrow linear areoles, bearing 20 to 40 spreading white spines arranged comb-like, up to 2 mm. long. Flowers borne on the sides of the stem, around the top. Rather rare, even in its native country.

Usually grown on own roots, in a gritty porous soil, with some leaf-mould, in full sunshine. Thrives better when grafted. A pretty cristate form is also in cultivation, but rarely met with.

DOLICHOTHELE Br. et R.

Plants globular, solitary or clustering, with thick roots. Sap not milky. Tubercles not grooved, large, elongated, fleshy and soft. Flowers very large, yellow, borne in the axils of the side areoles around the top. Fruit smooth, green, red or purple. Seeds brown or black. Includes three species.

Dolichothele sphaerica (Dietr.) Br. et R. = *Mammillaria sphaerica* Dietr. Northern Mexico and southern Texas. Plant clustering, pale green; stem more or less globular, 4 to 5 cm. broad, with a thick root. Tubercles conical or cylindrical, 8 to 15 mm. long and 5 to 7 mm. thick, obliquely directed upwards, soft-fleshed. Axils bare or slightly hairy. Areoles at first woolly. Radial spines 9 to 15, spreading, slender, rather soft, up to 1 cm. long, greenish yellow passing to white. Only one central spine, shorter and just thicker, straight, yellow, reddish at the base. Flower large, showy, 6 to 7 cm. broad, funnel-shaped, sulphur yellow; inner petals lanceolate-acute, narrow and claw-like at the base.

Z

Stigma with 8 yellow or green lobes. Fruit oblong, reddish, sweet-scented. Seeds black.

Dolichothele longimamma (DC.) Br. et R. = *Mammillaria longi-mamma* DC. Central Mexico. Plant clustering from the base and branching into large clumps, green, with a thick root. Stem more or less globular, about 8 to 15 cm. high. Tubercles 2 to 7 cm. long, cylindrical, oval in section at the base, where they are 1 to 1½ cm. broad, soft-fleshed. Axils more or less hairy. Areoles at first woolly. Radial spines 5 to 7, radiating or spreading outwards, straight or arching, ½ to 2 cm. long, at first yellow, passing to white. Central spines 1 to 3, straight, ½ to 1½ cm. long, honey yellow, rough under the lens. Flowers funnel-shaped, 5 to 6 cm. broad, with a protruding ovary; petals lanceolate-acute, the outer greenish yellow, brownish on the dorsal side; the inner canary yellow, toothed at the tip. Stamens pale yellow, style and 5- to 8-lobed stigma yellowish green. Fruit oblong, yellowish; seeds dark brown, minutely pitted. A well known species, very free-flowering, easily grown in half-shade or in full sunshine.

var. **gigantothele** Berg. Tubercles 5 to 7 cm. long, cylindrical, often of a paler green.

var. **globosa** K. Sch. Tubercles green or dark green, about 4½ cm. long; axils woolly. Radial spines up to 12, and 2 or 3 central spines. There is also a cristate form; besides, many other horticultural forms are listed by dealers.

This species, in common with *Neobesseya Wissmannii* and other species, has the curious habit of sprouting into branches from the areoles, which become much thickened and woolly before the formation of branches.

Dolichothele uberiformis (Zucc.) Br. et R. = *Mammillaria uberiformis* Zucc. = *M. longimamma* var. *uberiformis* K. Sch. Central Mexico. Differs from the preceding species by its deep green colour, the broadly conical and acute tubercles more or less directed irregularly, outwards or laterally, with bare axils. Radial spines rarely more than 4, slender and short; no central spine. Less free-flowering; flowers smaller, yellow.

MAMMILLARIA Haworth
(*Neomammillaria* Br. et R.)

Plants mostly clustering or branching, low, globular or oval or cylindrical, sometimes much elongated, mostly with a watery sap, sometimes milky. There are no ribs. Tubercles more or less small, in spiral rows, without grooves, usually woolly or hairy in the axils. Spines various. Flowers mostly small, diurnal, bell-shaped, borne in the axils of the tubercles around the top of the stem, sometimes near the centre. Fruit usually clavate, bare, mostly red, ripening in the same season or shortly after flowering. Seeds small, black or brown.

This is a large genus, the number of recognized species at present amounting to well over 200, mostly North American, a few species being found in Venezuela and neighbouring islands; and fresh explorations are frequently resulting in the discovery of new species. They are most interesting plants, with a wide range of form and habit. The flowers, though small, are often very attractive, and the small club-shaped red fruits, protruding beyond the tubercles, often in a ring around the top of the plant, usually last for a long time, and are quite ornamental.

Most species are of easy cultivation in any good loamy soil, moderately rich; some of them inhabiting cold hilly regions, or the plains of the prairies, covered with snow in winter, are able to stand quite low temperatures, and are only injured by an excess of stagnant moisture in the pots in which they are grown. Other species prefer a more sandy soil, or even a soil stony and gritty, like that on the hillsides of their native haunts. Most of them prefer full sunshine; only a few, while capable of standing full exposure to the sun, prefer half-shade or some shading during the hottest period of summer. It should not be forgotten that besides the protection afforded by the spines against the effects of direct and prolonged sunshine, these plants in their native home are often partly shaded off by the dried grasses, and other dried up wild annual plants which had grown around them.

N.B.   In 1812, Haworth established the genus *Mammillaria*, deriving the word from *mammilla*, a teat or nipple, in allusion to the form of the warts or tubercles. Subsequent continental authors have dropped one *m* from the generic name, the Latin term being more frequently written *mamilla*. If there were in reality an orthographic mistake the correction would have been justifiable, but as there has been no mistake in adopting the less frequent mode of spelling, the suggested correction is uncalled for, and amounts really to the creation of a new genus altogether, and is therefore to be deplored. Accordingly, I am adhering to the old manner of writing this name, as written by Haworth, and as used in England and America.

On the other hand, Britton and Rose have created the new name *Neomammillaria*, on the ground that the generic name *Mammillaria*, as established by Haworth, could now be used only in a restricted or amended sense, and that the same name has been used by Stackhouse in 1809, for a genus of *Algae*. However, amended generic names are common enough in all families of plants and animals, even in this family of Cactaceae; and the old name *Mammillaria* as applied for *Algae*, has long fallen into disuse. For these reasons the new generic name *Neomammillaria* is now generally discarded for the old name *Mammillaria*, long sanctioned by use.

The species are too numerous for a detailed description of each to be given in this work, but a large proportion will be described, as well as their more important varieties. The following classification, slightly altered from Dr. Alwin Berger's work "Kakteen," as now generally followed, is given hereunder to facilitate the labour of identification. In the descriptions which follow, large use was made of Dr. Berger's admirable work, as well as of the works of other authors, including the recent contributions of contemporaries.

CACTI

SECTION I. HYDROCHYLUS K. Sch.

Species with watery sap. Stem green.

A. Stems clustering, cylindrical, slender, of unequal length. Spines radiating, yellow.　　　　　　　Series 1. LEPTOCLADODEAE K. Sch.

B. Stems clustering or solitary; stems of about the same height.

　　a. Radial spines very numerous, irregularly spreading, white, often entirely covering the stem, which is somewhat flattened at the top.　　　　Series 2. CANDIDAE K. Sch.

　　a.a. Radial spines less numerous, not irregularly spreading, stem often cylindrical.

　　b. Radial spines thin, often mixed with long hairs. Warts more or less cylindrical, or narrowly conical. Central spines straight, curved, or hooked. Series 3. STYLOTHELAE K. Sch.

　　b.b. Radial spines more stiff, awl-shaped, occasionally absent.

　　c. Radial spines very numerous, about 30, obliquely directed upwards. Central spines almost like the radials.
　　　　　　　　　　Series 5. POLYACANTHAE Salm-Dyck

　　c.c. Radial spines spreading outwards. Central spines differing markedly from the radials.

　　d. At least one central spine hooked.
　　　　　　　　　　Series 4. ANCISTRACANTHAE K. Sch.

　　d.d. Central spines not hooked, or exceptionally one of them is hooked.　　Series 6. HETEROCHLORAE Salm-Dyck

SECTION II. GALACTOCHYLUS K. Sch.

Species with milky sap. Stem more or less greyish green or grey, and firmer in texture.

C. Tubercles do not exude a milky sap when wounded, the milky sap existing in the inner parts of the stem. Radial spines very numerous, the centrals strong.　　　　Series 7. ELEGANTES K. Sch.

D. Tubercles exude a milky sap when wounded. (Compare with Series 2. Candidae.)

　　a. Radial spines radiating and spreading outwards, white, numerous, thin.　　Series 8. LEUCOCEPHALAE Lem.

　　a.a. Radial spines not so radiating and spreading. Tubercles large, more or less angular.

　　b. Axils bare.　　Series 9. MACROTHELAE Salm-Dyck

　　b.b. Axils woolly and with stiff bristles.
　　　　　　　　　　Series 10. POLYEDRAE Pfeiff.

SECTION I. HYDROCHYLUS K. Sch.
Series 1. LEPTOCLADODEAE K. Sch.
Stems clustering, cylindrical, slender, of unequal length. Spines radiating, yellow.

372

Mammillaria elongata DC. Mexico (Hidalgo). Abundantly clustering and branching. Stem cylindrical, erect, or more or less prostrate, 6 to 15 cm. long, 1½ to 3 cm. thick, fresh green, with conical warts, 2 to 4 mm. high. Axils slightly woolly. Areoles round, at first woolly, with 15 to 20 radial spines, radiating outwards, star-like, recurved, more or less yellow, 8 to 12 mm. long. Central spines 1 to 3, directed outwards, or absent. Flowers from the side axils, 1½ cm. long; petals white or yellowish, with darker or reddish central band, obtuse or acute, toothed. Stamens, style and 4-lobed stigma white. A pretty and popular species, of easy cultivation and of very fast growth; easily propagated. The least excess of moisture will cause it to rot off. To be kept dry, especially in autumn and winter. A variable species with many varieties.

var. **anguinea** K. Sch. = *Mammillaria anguinea* Otto. Tubercles higher; radial spines yellow, tipped brown; one darker central spine. Stems thicker and longer.

var. **echinata** K. Sch. = *M. echinata* DC. Stems stronger, erect, more freely sprouting. Radial spines about 20, yellow. Central spines 2 or 3, brown.

var. **rufocrocea** K. Sch. = *M. rufocrocea* Salm-Dyck. Stems prostrate. Radial spines yellow at the base, white in the middle, tipped brown; central spines mostly 1, sometimes 2.

var. **stella-aurata** K. Sch. = *M. stella-aurata* Mart. Stems slender, about 2 cm. thick, very freely sprouting, up to 12 cm. high. Radial spines golden yellow, or tipped reddish. Only one central spine. Very attractive.

var. **tenuis** K. Sch. = *M. tenuis* DC. Stems slender, 1½ cm. thick; spines shorter, one central spine.

var. **minima** Schelle = *M. minima* Reichb. Stems short and slender, 1 to 1½ cm. thick, up to 6 cm. high.

var. **Schmollii** Hort. Stems very slender, but up to 10 cm. long; spines deep yellow.

There are also various cristate forms.

Mammillaria microhelia Werd. Mexico (Queretaro). Stem solitary or sprouting, cylindrical, up to 15 cm. high, and about 4 cm. thick. Tubercles short, conical, 4 mm. high. Axils at first with dark wool, later bare. Areoles with white wool when young. Radial spines regularly radiating, about 50, bristle-like, but stiff, white, golden yellow or reddish brown at the base. Central spines 1 or 2, sometimes 3 or 4, absent from the lower areoles, erect at the top, red or reddish brown, about 1 cm. long. Flowers about 1½ cm. long and broad, glossy creamy white. A very fine species; makes quick growth, but must be kept rather dry; prefers full sunshine.

Mammillaria microheliopsis Werd. Mexico. Similar to the preceding, up to 8 cm. high. Radial spines 30 to 40. Central spines always present, 6 to 8, about 6 to 9 mm. long, pale grey to pinkish and dark brown. Flowers purplish red. Another beautiful new species, but unlike the preceding, still rare.

Series 2. CANDIDAE K. Sch.

Radial spines very numerous, irregularly spreading, white, often entirely covering the stem, which is somewhat flattened at the top.

Mammillaria candida Scheidw. Mexico (San Luis Potosi). Plant clustering when old, with a thick hemispherical stem, somewhat flat at the top, 6 to 8 cm. thick and 3 to 7 cm. high, woolly at the top. Tubercles slender, bluish green, about 1 cm. long, and 2 to 3 mm. thick. Axils with 4 to 7 white bristles and very woolly. Areoles round, with white wool. Spines about 40, bristle-like, radiating irregularly, unequal, white; central spines 5 to 9, like the radials but longer, up to 7 mm. Flowers small, whitish; petals acute with a broad dorsal pinkish band. Stamens pink, style dark pink, stigma with 6 purplish lobes. = *M. sphaerotricha* Lem. Prefers half-shade, and a rather moist atmosphere.

var. **rosea** Salm-Dyck. Central spines more slender, and about twice as long, pink or pale pink when young.

Mammillaria Humboldtii Ehrenb. Mexico (Hidalgo). Rare in cultivation. Similar to the preceding. Has glossy snow-white radial spines; no central spines; axils with wool and stiff bristles. Flowers carmine red. Lobes of stigma green.

Mammillaria lenta K. Brand. Mexico (Coahuila). Plant sprouting at the base and clustering densely. Stem hemispherical, up to 6 cm. thick and 3 cm. high, with white wool at the top. Tubercles up to 8 mm. long, slender, about 2 mm. thick, pale green. Axils very woolly. Areoles round, with white wool, and with 30 to 40 white radial spines, from 2 to 5 mm. long. Flowers small, petals white, acute. Growth is slow, but forms nice specimens. Prefers half-shade, like the preceding.

Mammillaria lasiacantha Engelm. Mexico (Chihuahua), Arizona, western Texas. A miniature plant, with a globular stem, solitary or rarely sprouting, pale green, 1 to $2\frac{1}{2}$ cm. broad, entirely covered with soft spines. Tubercles very small, 2 mm. long, with bare axils. Areoles roundish, at first woolly. Spines 40 to 60, in several rows, radiating, bristle-like or hair-like, 2 to 4 mm. long, rough under a lens. Flowers 12 mm. long, petals white with a reddish band. Rarely grown as a curiosity.

Mammillaria denudata Engelm. = *M. Rungei* Hort. Western Texas, Mexico (Coahuila). Another small species, but larger than the preceding, globular, 3 to 4 cm. thick, entirely without spines on the old areoles. Tubercles 5 to 6 mm. long; areoles with 50 to 60 white spines, 3 to 5 mm. long, dropping off after some time. Flowers small, petals obtuse, white, with a pale red midrib. Stamens white, style and stigma green. Rare in cultivation. According to Schumann this is only a local variety of the preceding.

Mammillaria Oliviae Orc. Southern Arizona. Stem slightly sprouting, more or less globular, entirely covered with spines. Axils bare. Radial spines 25 to 35, slender, 6 mm. long, snow white or brownish. Central spines 1 to 3, white tipped brown. Flowers 3 cm. broad, purplish red; petals acute, edged white.

Mammillaria Dumetorum J. A. Purp. Mexico (San Luis Potosi). Stem dark green, clustering, hemispherical or globular, with soft tubercles. Areoles very small. Radial spines very numerous, white, yellowish at the base, or entirely yellowish, more or less recurved, the outer row 4 to 6 mm. long, the inner row longer and thinner, bristle-like. Flowers 18 mm. long, white, the outer petals with a greenish brown band. Stamens and style white, stigma with 5 or 6 yellowish lobes.

Mammillaria cephalophora Quehl. Mexico (San Luis Potosi). Plant solitary, globular, glossy dark green, $7\frac{1}{2}$ cm. high, with yellow hairs and spines at the top. Tubercles 1 cm. long, 7 mm. thick at the base, cylindrical, directed upwards. Areoles round, bare. Axils bare. Spines up to 30, in 2 series, radiating, of various lengths up to $1\frac{1}{2}$ cm., bulbous at the base, diaphanous white with a golden yellow or brownish sheen, with the tip drawn out into silky yellowish white hairs or wool, covering the top of the plant. Flower 3 cm. long, pale pink. The root is long and turnip-like; the fruit is pinkish white. An interesting species, now frequently imported.

Mammillaria Baumii Boedeker. Mexico (Tamaulipas). Plant branching and clustering, glossy green; stems 8 cm. high and 6 cm. thick. Tubercles cylindrical-conical, softish, 8 mm. long and 5 mm. thick. Axils bare. Areoles roundish, at first with white wool. Radial spines 30 to 35, uneven in length, up to $1\frac{1}{2}$ cm., very slender or hair-like, white. Central spines 5 or 6, more stiff, straight, white, pale brown at the base, up to 18 mm. long. Flowers funnel-shaped, up to $2\frac{1}{2}$ cm. long: outer petals linear lanceolate, greenish yellow with a pink midrib; inner petals more acute, glossy yellow. Stamens yellow above, style greenish, stigma with 5 pale green lobes. Free-flowering and a fast grower.

Mammillaria Schiedeana Ehrenb. = *M. sericata* Lem. Central Mexico (Hidalgo). Plant dark green, freely clustering, with a globular flattened stem, soft-fleshed, more or less rounded at the top, 4 to $5\frac{1}{2}$ cm. thick. Axils with long white hairs. Tubercles slender, conical, about 1 cm. long. Spines 20 to 30, white, spreading, sharp, rough seen under a lens, mixed with numerous white hairs, yellow at the base, giving to the plant a frilled appearance. Flowers about $1\frac{1}{2}$ cm. long and broad; inner petals white, acutely toothed. Stamens and style white, stigma with 4 pale yellow lobes. A very pretty species, thrives well in full sunshine, but grows better in half-shade. Grows on limestone cliffs, and must have a very calcareous soil. Is perfectly hardy in the Mediterranean region, and is often grafted, as the offsets do not root readily. Flowers when quite young.

Mammillaria plumosa Weber = *M. lasiacantha* Hort. non Engelm. Northern Mexico (Coahuila). Grows in the fissures of calcareous rocks and on calcareous shingle, over which it spreads and binds together. Plant deep green, very freely clustering and spreading. Stem globular, 5 to 7 cm. thick, entirely covered with white feathery spines. Tubercles cylindrical, up to 12 mm. long. Areoles round; axils with long white wool. Spines all radial, up to 40, 3 to 7 mm. long, greyish white or white, minutely frilled and feathery. Flowers small, white, with a brown or reddish midrib. Seeds black. A most lovely species, deservedly popular, of easy cultivation in any calcareous soil, delighting in full sunshine. Should be kept rather dry from October to April. Clumps with 40 to 50 heads or stems are frequently imported.

Mammillaria Herrerae Werd. Mexico (Queretaro). Plant slowly clustering, with small, smooth, round or oval heads, like small balls of cotton. Axils bare. Warts very small. Spines all radial, very numerous, up to 100 or more, up to 5 mm. long, all alike, very evenly radiating star-like. Flowers 2 to 2½ cm. long; inner petals pale pink to purplish. Fruit small, white, almost globose. Seeds minute, dull black, warty. A small pretty plant of singular appearance. Requires full sunshine.

var. **albiflora** Werd. Stem often elongated and finger like, with little tendency to clustering. Flowers up to 3½ cm. long and broad, snow white.

Mammillaria Ortiz-Rubiona (Helia Bravo) Werd. Mexico (Guanojuato and Queretaro). Plant clustering and spreading, with white wool at the top, very similar to *M. Schiedeana*. Stems 6 to 8 cm. thick, globular, green, with cylindrical tubercles 1½ cm. long. Axils with numerous white bristles protruding beyond the tubercles. Areoles with white wool. Radial spines numerous, 12 to 15 mm. long, white, feathery, very evenly radiating. Central spines 4 to 6, as long as the radials, but thicker, white, tipped reddish. Flowers about 2 cm. long; petals yellowish pink, with a paler margin. Fruit carmine red. Seeds glossy black, pitted. Described originally by Helia Bravo under the generic name of *Neomammillaria*. A very desirable new species.

Series 3. STYLOTHELAE K. Sch.

Radial spines thin, often mixed with long hairs. Warts more or less cylindrical or narrowly conical. Central spines straight, curved or hooked.

(*a*) *Rectispinae*. Spines straight.

Mammillaria albicoma Boedeker. Mexico (Tamaulipas). A very small plant, clustering, with small warts. Radial spines 30 to 40, in two series, pure white, hair-like, glossy and soft, up to 1 cm. long. Central spines 3 or 4, often absent, about half as long as the radials, stiff, white, tipped brownish. Axils with white wool, and with a few long, white, hair-like bristles. Flowers borne profusely at the top, 10 to 13 mm. long and broad; inner petals glossy white or yellowish. Fruit very small. Seeds dark grey, pitted.

Mammillaria prolifera (Mill.) Haworth = *Cactus proliferus* Miller = *M. pusilla* DC. = *M. multiceps* Salm-Dyck. North-east Mexico, Texas, Cuba and Haiti. Plant very freely clustering and spreading. Stem dark green, globose or short-cylindric, 4 to 6 cm. long, and 3 to 4 cm. thick, rounded at the top. Axils with long, hair-like bristles. Tubercles soft-fleshed, slender, conical, 5 to 7 mm. long, and 4 to 5 mm. thick at the base. Areoles at first slightly woolly. Radial spines numerous, hair-like, white. Central spines 5 to 9, radiating, at first dark yellow, paler at the tip, rough under a lens. Flowers 13 to 14 mm. long; outer petals greenish yellow, oval, with a darker midrib, acute and fringed; inner petals broader and paler, not fringed. Stamens whitish, style pale yellow, stigma with 3 or 4 chrome yellow lobes. Fruit coral red, with a strawberry flavour. Seeds glossy black, pitted. The typical form is native of Cuba. A well-known species of easy cultivation and propagation.

var. **haitensis** K. Sch. Stem larger, up to 7 cm. thick, warts soft, bluish green. Spines more numerous, central spines at first yellow, passing to snow white. Less free-flowering. Haiti.

var. **texana** Engelm. Radial spines numerous, white. Central spines also white or tipped yellowish. Texas (Rio Grande).

var. **multiceps** (Salm-Dyck) = *M. multiceps* Salm-Dyck. Stem very slender, globose or short-cylindric, 1 to 2 cm. thick. Warts smaller; radial spines hair-like; central spines thickened at the base, yellowish, at first tipped red, passing to dark brown. Fruit dark red, longer. North-east Mexico.

Mammillaria pilispina J. A. Purp. Mexico (San Luis Potosi). Stem 4 cm. thick, hemispherical, dark green. Tubercles closely set, up to 1 cm. long. Areoles small. Axils with few hairs. Radial spines 4 or 5, stiff, 6 to 7 mm. long, associated all round with silky, snow white, hair-like spines. Only one central spine. All spines minutely hairy. Flower yellowish white.

Mammillaria Viereckii Boedeker. Mexico (Tamaulipas). Plant dark green, rarely sprouting at the base. Stem globose, 3 to 3½ cm. thick, covered with spines. Tubercles softish, slender, up to 1 cm. long. Axils slightly woolly, with about 10 long white bristles. Spines about 10, needle-like, 12 mm. long, yellow to golden yellow. Flowers few, 12 mm. long, creamy yellow, with greenish throat.

Mammillaria vetula Mart. Mexico (Hidalgo). Plant solitary, or sparingly sprouting at the base when old, pale green, up to 10 cm. high and 3 to 4½ cm. thick. Tubercles softish, conical, 9 mm. long. Axils mostly bare. Areoles round, at first woolly. Radial spines 25, later increasing to 50, radiating, slender, 3 to 8 mm. long, soft, white passing to greyish. Central spines 1 to 6, thicker and more stiff, up to 1 cm. long, reddish brown to dark brown. Flowers sparingly borne at the centre, 1 to 1½ cm. long: inner petals lemon yellow, outer petals with a red dorsal band. Stamens and style greenish white or yellowish, stigma with 5 whitish lobes.

Mammillaria sphacelata Mart.   Mexico (Oaxaca, Tehuacan).
Plant clustering, and sprouting from the sides of the stems, forming
large groups. Stems cylindrical, 10 to 20 cm. high, and 2 to 3 cm.
thick, pale green, often tortuous or sprawling. Tubercles conical, with
round woolly aeroles. Axils with short wool and a few bristles. Radial
spines 9 to 14, increasing to 20, radiating, needle-like, white, or tipped
reddish brown, up to 1 cm. long. Only one central spine, rarely 2 to
4, almost like the radials. All spines passing later to greyish. Flowers
small, borne on the sides of the stems; outer petals reddish brown,
inner petals deep red. Stamens and style reddish, stigma with 4 dark
red lobes.

Mammillaria viperina J. A. Purp. Mexico (Puebla). Plant clustering
and spreading, with the habit of *M. elongata*. Stems pale green,
sprawling, slender, 1½ to 2 cm. thick, very spiny. Tubercles ½ cm. long
and 3 mm. thick, with round, small, woolly areoles. Axils with hairs
and hair-like bristles. Spines numerous, densely clustering and covering
the stem, very thin, snow white to pale brown, or dark brown. Flower
1½ cm. long, and 2 cm. broad: outer petals olive green with reddish
brown midrib; inner petals carmine red. Stamens green below, red
above, style red, stigma greenish white.

Mammillaria Rekoi (Br. et R.) = *Neomammillaria Rekoi* Br. et R.
Mexico (Oaxaca). Stem globular to short-cylindric, up to 12 cm. long
and 5 to 6 cm. thick, sometimes milky. Tubercles green, cylindrical,
up to 1 cm. long. Axils with short white wool and with 1 to 8 long white
bristles. Radial spines about 20, white, needle-like, 4 to 6 mm. long.
Central spines 4, brown, thicker, 1 to 1½ cm. long, the lower one sometimes hooked. Flowers borne in the axils at the top, 1½ cm. long, deep
purple: inner petals narrow and acuminate. Stamens and style purplish,
stigma lobes greenish.

Mammillaria pseudorekoi Boedeker. Mexico. Stem cylindrical,
freely sprouting around the base, grass green, up to 15 cm. long and
2 to 3½ cm. thick, covered with whitish spines at the top. Tubercles
conical, 3 to 5 mm. long. Areoles small, with whitish wool. Radial
spines 25 to 30, diaphanous white or slightly flesh-coloured, bristle-
like, but stiff, 3 to 5 mm. long, radiating, mostly laterally. Central
spines 4 to 6 or more, all equal, ½ cm. long, spreading outwards more
or less star-like, whitish or flesh-coloured below, reddish or purplish
red above, passing to whitish. Flowers on the sides near the top, red.
Similar to, but larger than, *M. viperina*. Requires half-shade.

Mammillaria decipiens Scheidw. Mexico (San Luis Potosi). Plant
oval, rounded at the top, grass green, sprouting unevenly from the base
and sides, 6 to 10 cm. high, 5 to 7½ cm. thick. Axils with 2 or 3 stiff
white bristles. Tubercles cylindrical, about 1 cm. long and 3 to 4 mm.
thick, rounded at the tip, with a small areole. Radial spines 7 to 9,
radiating outwards, needle-like, white, tipped brown, up to 1 cm. long.
Only one central spine, erect, thicker, brown, 1 to 1½ cm. long. Flowers
1½ to 2 cm. long; outer petals green with a brown or reddish dorsal

band; inner petals more acute, white, toothed, with a dark midrib. Stamens and style white or reddish. Stigma with 4 to 6 yellowish lobes.

Mammillaria melaleuca Karw. Mexico (Oaxaca). Plant at first solitary, clustering when old, globose, dark green passing to greyish, with thick oval obtuse tubercles, at first glossy dark green. Axils bare. Areoles small, with white wool, later bare. Radial spines 8 or 9, radiating and recurved, the upper 4 longer and brown, up to 1½ cm. long, the lower ones white. Only one central spine (or none) slender, brown, straight, as long as the upper radials. Flowers borne sparingly on the sides near the top, about 4 cm. long, funnel-shaped, 4 cm. broad: outer petals oval-acute, pale green; the next lanceolate-acute pale yellow with a reddish midrib; the inner canary yellow. Stamens pale yellow, style pale green, stigma with 9 sulphur yellow lobes. A pretty species, often listed by dealers as a variety of *M. magnimamma* or as *M. centricirrha* var. *flaviflora* Hort.

(*b*) *Tortispinae*. Spines twisted or arching, not hooked.

Mammillaria camptotricha Dams. Mexico (Queretaro). Plant cespitose, forming large clumps. Stems broadly globose, deep green, 5 to 7 cm. thick. Tubercles conical and narrow, or cylindrical, often curved, up to 2 cm. long and 7 mm. thick at the base. Axils slightly hairy, and with about 15 white bristles. Areoles small, bare. Spines mostly 4, often 5 or more, slender, pale yellow, up to 3 cm. long, twisted or curved, clustering confusedly at the top. Flowers small, shorter than the tubercles, about 13 mm. long: outer petals greenish; the inner pure white. Stamens slender, white; stigma with 4 yellowish white lobes. A species of singular appearance, of easy cultivation in half-shade or even in full sunshine, sprouting freely from the base, and occasionally also from the upper areoles.

(*c*) *Hamatispinae*. At least one of the central spines hooked at the tip.

Mammillaria erectohamata Boedeker. Mexico (San Luis Potosi). Plant clustering around the base, glossy light green. Stem globular or slightly compressed, about 6 cm. thick, covered with white spines, and with dark red brown spines at the top. Tubercles cylindrical, about 8 mm. long. Areoles woolly only when young. Axils with a few white, hair-like, twisted bristles. Radial spines about 25, white, radiating, very slender, about 7 mm. long. Central spines 2 or 3, purplish red to dark brown, often golden yellow at the base, the upper erect and straight, the lower one up to 1½ cm. long, curved upwards and hooked at the tip. Flowers in a ring around the top, about 1½ cm. broad; inner petals glossy pure white. Fruit clavate, red, 12 mm. long. Seeds dark brown, pitted.

Mammillaria Schelhasei Pfeiff. = *M. Scheidweileriana* Dietr. Mexico (Hidalgo). Plant freely clustering, dark green or olive green. Stem globular, later cylindrical, 3 to 4 cm. thick. Tubercles cylindrical about 1 cm. long, slightly 4-angled at the base. Axils sparingly woolly. Areoles small, round, slightly woolly. Radial spines 15 to 20, stiff, slender, straight, white, up to 1 cm. long, directed outwards. Central spines 3, the middle one thicker, longer than the others, brownish, 1 cm. long, hooked at the tip. Flowers small, yellowish white, with a reddish midrib. Stamens and style white, stigma with 4 recurved whitish lobes.

var. **triuncinata** Salm-Dyck. The 3 central spines hooked.

Mammillaria phitauiana (Baxter) Werd. = *Neomammillaria phitauiana* Baxter. Lower California. Stem mostly solitary, rarely sprouting at the base, light green, cylindrical, about 15 cm. high and 4 cm. thick. Tubercles conical, 4 to 6 mm. long, in 13 rows, 1 cm. apart. Areoles bare or very slightly woolly. Radial spines about 24, straight, radiating, soft and bristle-like, white, 4 to 12 mm. long, at least one of them hooked at the tip. Flowers in a ring around the top, 1 to 1½ cm. long; inner petals white. Fruit globose or clavate, red, about 1 cm. long. Seeds black, oval.

Mammillaria pubispina Boedeker. Mexico (Hidalgo). Stem solitary, globular, dull light green, up to 4 cm. thick. Tubercles cylindrical, about 8 mm. long, with slightly woolly areoles. Radial spines about 15, radiating, thin, hair-like, mixed with curled hairs, white, about 1 cm. long. Central spines 4, sometimes 3, thin, needle-like, with short minute hairs under a lens, white, tipped brown, or reddish brown to dark brown, the lowermost directed downwards, hooked at the tip. Axils often pinkish at the bottom, slightly woolly and with a few whitish bristles. Flowers in a ring round the top, 18 mm. long: inner petals white or creamy white, with a pink midrib.

Mammillaria Zeilmanniana Boedeker. Mexico (Guanajuato). Stem mostly solitary, or slightly clustering, oval or short-cylindric, about 6 cm. high and 4½ cm. thick, glossy green, spiny at the top. Tubercles oval, about 6 mm. long. Areoles woolly when young. Radial spines 15 to 18, radiating, white, hair-like and soft, mostly straight, about 1 cm. long. Central spines 4, reddish brown, about 8 mm. long, the lower one slightly longer and hooked at the end. Axils bare. Flowers 2 cm. broad: inner petals pale violet to deep violet or purplish red. Fruit small, whitish green. Seeds dull black, pitted.

Mammillaria bocasana Poselg. Northern and central Mexico, especially Sierra de Bocas. Plant freely clustering and spreading, dark bluish green. Stem globular or short-cylindric, 4 to 5 cm. thick. Tubercles cylindrical, slender, up to 1 cm. long. Axils with very thin white hairs. Areoles round or slightly oval. Radial spines very numerous, radiating, white, bristle-like, ending in very fine silky hairs, up to 2 cm. long. Central spines 2 to 4, sometimes only one, needle-like, yellow or brownish, 2 cm. long, at least one of them hooked at the tip. Flowers 17 mm. long; petals reddish on the dorsal side; inner petals lanceolate-acute, yellowish white, with a red midrib, and tipped red. Stamens white, style and 4-lobed stigma green. Fruit clavate, red, with few seeds. A lovely and popular species, free-growing and resistant. A cristate form is also cultivated.

var. **splendens** Liebner. Plant slightly larger in all its parts, and perhaps with a more sturdy habit.

Mammillaria longicoma Br. et R. = (*Neomammillaria*). Mexico (San Luis Potosi). Radial spines 25 or more, hair-like and silky, straight or twisted, whitish. Central spines 4, 1 or 2 of which are hooked at the end. Petals more acute, pale pink or pink. The rest as in the preceding species.

Mammillaria multihamata Boedeker. Mexico. Stem dark green, globular, 5 cm. thick, slowly clustering. Axils with bristles only. Radial spines 25, thin, straight, spreading outwards, 8 mm. long. Central spines 7 to 9, bulbous at the base, longer and thicker, several of them hooked at the tip. Flower 1½ cm. long; inner petals whitish, with reddish midrib.

Mammillaria Kunzeana Böd. et Quehl. Mexico. Plant freely clustering and spreading, glossy green. Tubercles cylindrical, pointed upwards, about 1½ cm. long, with areoles woolly when young. Axils with long, curly bristles. Radial spines 25, mostly spreading laterally, about 1 cm. long, thin, white. Central spines 4, variously coloured, white to dark brown, or yellow to brown or reddish brown, rough under a lens, 2 or 3 about 1½ cm. long, directed upwards, the others directed downwards and hooked. Flower 2 cm. long and 1½ cm. broad, outer petals pink, edged yellowish, inner petals yellowish white. Stamens and style white, 4-lobed stigma creamy white. Fruit large, red.

Mammillaria Painteri Rose. Mexico (Queretaro). Plant small, solitary, globose, 2 cm. thick. Axils bare. Radial spines 20, stiff, white, minutely hairy. Central spines 4 or 5, dark brown, at least one hooked at the tip. Flower 1½ cm. long, greenish white; outer petals brownish.

Mammillaria hirsuta Boedeker. Mexico. Plant cespitose. Stems globose, 6 cm. thick; tubercles 1 cm. long, ½ cm. thick, rounded at the tip, dotted. Axils bare, but with 1 or 2 bristles. Areoles yellowish, not woolly. Radial spines 20 or more, thin, glassy white, 1 to 1½ cm. long, unevenly spreading. Central spines 3 or 4, rough under the lens, the upper 2 or 3 white tipped brown, straight; the lower one spreading outwards, thicker, 1½ to 2 cm. long, dark reddish brown, hooked at the end. Flowers 1 cm. long, pale yellow flushed pink, green at the throat. Stigma with 3 to 5 whitish lobes.

Mammillaria erythrosperma Boedeker. Mexico. Plant very freely clustering and spreading. Stems globular, 5 cm. high, dark green. Axils with hair-like bristles. Areoles bare. Tubercles cylindrical, glossy dark green, about 1 cm. long. Radial spines 15 to 20, straight, white, very thin, radiating star-like, up to 1 cm. long. Central spines 1 to 3, rarely 4, the lower one 1 cm. long, yellowish, reddish brown and hooked at the tip. Flowers of a beautiful carmine red, with darker midrib. Stamens, style and 3-to 4-lobed stigma carmine red. Fruit carmine red, as also the kidney-shaped seeds. A beautiful species of recent introduction, of easy cultivation and quick growth.

var. **similis** De Laet. Plant smaller. Central spines and flowers paler. Lobes of stigma yellow.

Mammillaria Seideliana Quehl. Mexico (Zacatecas). Stem solitary, rarely sprouting from the base, green, globular or short-cylindric, about 5 cm. thick, and 7 cm. high. Tubercles slender, cylindrical or, conical, 1 cm. long, $\frac{1}{2}$ cm. thick. Axils with a few bristles. Areoles oval, at first with white wool. Radial spines 18 to 25, hair-like, white, radiating, up to 8 mm. long: central spines 3, the lower one hooked at the tip, 1 to 1$\frac{1}{2}$ cm. long, white to brown. All spines are more or less hairy. Flowers numerous, 1$\frac{1}{2}$ to 2 cm. long; outer petals yellow, inner petals lanceolate, pale yellow. Stamens and style white, stigma with 3 to 5 yellow lobes.

Mammillaria glochidiata Mart. Mexico (Hidalgo). Plant thickly cespitose. Stems grass green, more or less globular, 2 to 3$\frac{1}{2}$ cm. thick. axils with few bristles. Tubercles softish, conical or almost cylindrical, with small areoles. Radial spines 8 to 20, radiating, bristle-like, white, up to 1 cm. long. Central spines 3 or 4, yellowish or reddish brown, the lower one 6 to 10 mm. long, hooked at the end, minutely hairy under the lens. Flowers 1$\frac{1}{2}$ cm. long; outer petals green and reddish; the inner lanceolate, pink or white with a pink central band. Stamens violet pink, style white, stigma with 4 yellowish lobes. Free-growing, but resents at once any excess of moisture.

var. **crinita** (DC.) K. Sch. = *M. crinita* DC. Inner petals white, with a yellowish central band.

var. **prolifera** K. Sch. Abundantly clustering. Stems smaller, radial spines fewer; only one central spine, pale yellow.

Mammillaria aurihamata Boedeker. Central Mexico. Plant clustering. Stems globular or elongated, glossy green, 6 cm. high, 4 cm. thick. Tubercles short-cylindric, 6 mm. long, 3 mm. thick. Axils with about 8 curly bristles. Areoles small, roundish, slightly woolly. Radial spines 15 to 20, up to 8 mm. long, yellowish white, at first spreading outwards, later radiating or partly reflexed. Central spines 4, thicker, bulbous at the base, the lower one 1$\frac{1}{2}$ to 2$\frac{1}{2}$ cm. long. spreading, hooked at the tip, the others straight; all at first glossy yellowish white, later golden yellow, sometimes brownish yellow. Flowers in a ring round the top of the stem, 1$\frac{1}{2}$ cm. long, and about 12 mm. broad: inner petals abruptly acute, more or less toothed, pale sulphur yellow. Stigma with 3 or 4 pale green lobes. Fruit small, red. Seeds dark brown.

Mammillaria Wildii Dietr. = *M. Wildiana* Otto. Mexico (Hidalgo). Abundantly clustering and spreading, dark green or bluish green. Stems cylindrical, 8 to 15 cm high and 4 to 6 cm. thick, erect or sprawling. Axils with a few bristles. Tubercles cylindrical, up to 13 mm. long, with round areoles, at first woolly. Radial spines 8 to 10, white, bristle-like, 5 to 7 mm. long. Central spines 3 or 4, thicker and longer, honey yellow, the upper one directed upwards and hooked, the others directed outwards and hairy under the lens. Flowers numerous, 1$\frac{1}{2}$ cm. long: inner petals acute, whitish; the outer with a deep red dorsal band.

Stamens white, style green, stigma with 4 or 5 yellowish lobes. A free-growing species. Requires a porous soil, sunshine and abundant watering in summer, and a warm and dry atmosphere in winter.

var. **rosea** Hort. Has pale pink flowers.

There is also a pretty cristate form.

Mammillaria pygmaea (Br. et R.) = (*Neomammillaria*) = *M. sinistrohamata* Hort. Mexico (Queretaro). A small plant with globose or cylindrical stems, 2 to 3 cm. thick, clustering. Tubercles small, obtuse. Radial spines 15, white, stiff. Central spines directed upwards, 5 to 6 mm. long, the lower one hooked. Flower 1 cm. long: outer petals reddish, the inner creamy white. Stamens and style greenish.

Series 4. ANCISTRACANTHAE K. Sch.

Radial spines spreading outwards. Central spines differing markedly from the radials: at least one central spine hooked.

Mammillaria fasciculata Engelm. = *M. Thornberi* Orc. Southern Arizona. Plant clustering. Stems slender, cylindrical. Radial spines 13 to 20, white, tipped brown. Only one central spine, occasionally 2 or 3, up to 18 mm. long, dark brown, one of them or all hooked at the tip. Flower large, 3 to 4 cm. broad, funnel-shaped, pink.

It is very much like a species of *Bartschella*.

Mammillaria mazatlanensis K. Sch. Mexico (Sinaloa, near Mazatlan). Plant freely cespitose and branching, greyish green. Stems cylindrical, 9 cm. long and 4 cm. thick. Tubercles low, softish, conical, 7 to 8 mm. long. Axils woolly and with a few bristles. Areoles round, woolly. Radial spines 13 to 15, spreading outwards, awl-shaped, white, 6 to 10 mm. long. Central spines 4, occasionally up to 6, thick, 1½ cm. long, glossy brown, white at the base, one of them, hooked at the tip. Flowers few, 4 cm. long, funnel-shaped; outer petals obtuse, white, with a broad brown central band; inner petals acute, reflexed, of a beautiful carmine red, paler along the margins. Stamens short, style long, both red, stigma with 5 to 7 green spreading lobes. A desirable species; requires warmth and sunshine.

var. **litoralis** (K. Brand.) = *M. litoralis* K. Brand. Growth stronger: central spines paler reddish brown; inner petals with a broad white margin. Fruit of a deeper red.

Mammillaria longiflora Br. et R. (*Neomammillaria*). Mexico (Durango). Stem globular, 5½ cm. thick, dark green. Tubercles up to 1 cm. long. Axils almost bare. Areoles oval, slightly woolly, later bare. Radial spines about 30, needle-like, spreading outwards, covering the stem, white, about 1 cm. long. Central spines 4, the lower one hooked at the end, reddish brown. Flowers borne near the centre, with a slender funnel-shaped tube, 3 to 4 cm. long and as broad. Petals lanceolate-acute, a lively light pink.

Mammillaria Sheldonii Br. et R. (*Neomammillaria*). Northern Mexico. Plant clustering, dark green or greyish green. Stems cylindrical, 5 to 8 cm. long, up to 3 cm. thick, with conical tubercles. Radial spines numerous, white tipped dark brown, spreading, $\frac{1}{2}$ to 1 cm. long. Central spines 2 or 3, reddish brown, whitish at the base, one of them up to 2 cm. long, hooked, directed upwards. Flower red.

Mammillaria microcarpa Engelm. = *M. Grahamii* Engelm. = *M. barbata* Engelm. Mexico (Chihuahua and Sonora), Texas, Arizona. Mostly solitary or sparingly sprouting, green to dark green, up to 8 cm. high, and 2 to 6 cm. thick, entirely covered with radial spines. Tubercles small, oval, with bare axils. Radial spines 15 to 30, radiating star-like, thin, white, 6 to 12 mm. long. Central spines 1 to 3, at first red, passing to dark brown, up to 18 mm. long, acutely hooked. Flowers 2 to 2$\frac{1}{2}$ cm. long: outer petals oval, obtuse, fringed; the inner pink or margined whitish. Stamens white, style red, stigma with 7 or 8 green lobes. Seeds black.

Mammillaria Goodridgei Scheer. Island Cedros, off the west coast of Lower California. Cespitose, more or less cylindrical, up to 10 cm. high, and 2 to 4 cm. thick. Axils bare or only slightly woolly. Tubercles cylindrical, closely set, rounded at the top. Areoles at first with short whitish wool, later bare. Radial spines 12 to 15, radiating, white, often tipped darker. Only one central spine, white below, brown above, hooked. Flowers 1$\frac{1}{2}$ cm. long; petals obtuse, yellow; the outer with a brownish red midrib. Lobes of stigma green and thin.

Mammillaria Carretii Reb. Mexico. Stem solitary, globose, slightly depressed, dark green, 5 to 6 cm. thick. Tubercles cylindrical, 7 to 9 mm. long, rounded at the top, directed upwards. Axils bare. Areoles round, at first sparingly woolly, later bare. Radial spines about 14, spreading horizontally, awl-shaped, slightly curved, yellow tipped brown, up to 13 mm. long. Only one central spine, directed upwards or outwards, straight, dark brown, paler at the base, about 1$\frac{1}{2}$ cm. long hooked at the tip. Flowers borne at the sides near the top, 2$\frac{1}{4}$ cm. long, funnel-shaped; outer petals pale pink, linear, acute, tipped pink; inner petals lanceolate-acute, whitish, with a pink midrib. Stamens white, style yellow, stigma with 5 or 6 greenish lobes.

Mammillaria trichacantha K. Sch. Mexico. Stem globular, mostly solitary, bluish green, about 5 cm. thick. Tubercles about 8 mm. long, clavate. Areoles small, round, with a little white wool. Axils reddish and bare. Radial spines 15 to 18, radiating, white, up to 8 mm. long. Central spines 2, the lower one hooked, 12 mm. long, at first reddish, passing to brown; the upper one shorter, straight, white, tipped brown. All spines are minutely hairy. Flowers are 1$\frac{1}{2}$ cm. long, yellowish, edged pink. Stamens yellowish, style light green, stigma white. Seeds black.

Mammillaria mercadensis Patoni. Mexico (Durango, at Cerro de Mercado). Stem globular or elongated. Radial spines numerous, radiating, white. Central spines 4 or 5, directed upwards, reddish brown, the lower one hooked, 2$\frac{1}{2}$ cm. long. Flower small, with obtuse clear red petals.

Mammillaria dioica K. Brand. = *M. Goodridgei* Engelm. non Scheer. California and Lower California. Plant dioecious, solitary

(a) CORYPHANTHA ERECTA

(b) CORYPHANTHA CLAVA

PLATE LIV

(b) DOLICHOTHELE SPHAERICA

(a) CORYPHANTHA VAUPELIANA

PLATE LV

or slowly clustering, globular or cylindrical, bluish green, rounded at the top, up to 25 cm. high, and 3½ to 6 cm. thick. Axils woolly and with a few long bristles. Tubercles thick, cylindrical, obtuse, 3½ to 5½ mm. long. Areoles round, bare. Radial spines 11 to 15, radiating, awl-shaped, stiff, white, tipped brown, or entirely reddish, 4 to 6 mm. long. Central spines 3 or 4, in young plants only one, brown, the lower one, the longest, up to 9 mm. long, hooked upwards. Flowers in a ring around the top, 12 to 20 mm. long: petals lanceolate, toothed, yellowish white with a red midrib. Style white, stigma with 6 yellow or brownish green lobes. Seeds black. The flowers of the male plant, bearing only stamens, are larger and more expanded. Prefers half-shade.

var. **insularis** K. Brand. Freely clustering. Axils more woolly. Radial spines more numerous, whiter and shorter. Centrals mostly straight.

Mammillaria Boedekeriana Quehl. Mexico. Globular, becoming elongated with age, dark green, 6 to 7 cm. high, and 4 cm. thick, somewhat flat at the top. Tubercles softish, cylindrical, 1 cm. long, somewhat flat on the upper side. Axils bare. Areoles small, slightly woolly when young. Radial spines 20, spreading star-like, glassy white, or with golden sheen, thin, 1 cm. long. Central spines 3 or 4, the middle one 13 mm. long, dark brown and hooked, the others more slender and paler; rarely with 2 or 3 hooked spines on the same areole. Flowers 2½ to 3 cm. long; petals lanceolate-acute, white, with a reddish brown midrib. Stamens whitish above, style white, lobes of stigma yellow. Flowers when quite young.

Mammillaria zephyranthoides Scheidw. = *M. zephyranthiflora* Pfeiff. = *M. Fennellii* Hopff. Mexico (Oaxaca and Hidalgo, at high altitudes). Stem solitary, globular depressed, 10 cm. thick and 8 cm. high, dark green. Axils almost bare. Tubercles softish, cylindrical-conical, somewhat flat on the upper side, obtuse, 2 to 2½ cm. long. Areoles round, with white wool. Radial spines 12 to 18, radiating, white, slender, up to 12 mm. long, rough under a lens. Central spines 2, sometimes only one, thicker, brown, paler towards the base, hooked. Flowers 3½ cm. long, fully expanded, 4 cm. broad; outer petals greenish brown, the inner lanceolate-acute, pale yellow or white, with a carmine red midrib. Stamens green below, carmine red above; style longer, with a 10-lobed green stigma. Fruit oval, green. A beautiful species, now frequently imported. Must be kept dry in winter.

Mammillaria Wrightii Engelm. New Mexico. Solitary, sub-globular, depressed, hemispherical above ground, very rarely throwing up one or two offsets, rounded or somewhat flattened at the top, 3½ to 7 cm. thick. Axils bare. Tubercles cylindrical, softish, rounded at the tip, mostly directed upwards, 6 to 11 mm. long, 3 to 4 mm. thick. Areoles round, slightly woolly when young. Radial spines 10 to 12, spreading star-like, thin but stiff, white, the upper 3 to 5 thicker and often tipped black, up to 1 cm. long. Central spines mostly 2, rarely 1 or 3, dark brown or black, all hooked, about as long as the radials.

Flowers about 2 cm. long, funnel-shaped: outer petals triangular, obtuse, fringed, green, edged purplish: the inner linear-lanceolate, acuminate, glossy purplish red. Stamens numerous, style longer than the stamens, stigma with 6 to 8 oblique lobes. Fruit oblong, 2 cm. long, purplish red. Seeds oval, black, pitted.

Mammillaria Wilcoxii Br. et R. (*Neomammillaria*) from southeast Arizona, according to Boedeker, is the same as *M. Wrightii*, or perhaps only a variety.

Mammillaria bombycina Quehl. Mexico. Stem globular, becoming elongated or cylindrical with age, 8 to 20 cm. high and 5 to 6 cm. thick, fresh green, clustering freely, at the top woolly and well furnished with beautiful reddish brown or yellow spines. Tubercles closely set, cylindric, obtuse, 1½ cm. long. Axils very woolly. Areoles round, bare. Radial spines 30 to 40, pectinate, spreading outwards, thin but stiff, glossy white, the side ones 1 cm. long. Central spines 4, crosswise, the upper 7 mm. long, the side ones 1 cm. long, and the lower up to 2 cm. long, stronger and hooked; all central spines are white at the base, glossy reddish brown or yellowish above. Flowers 1 cm. long, clear red, petals narrow, lanceolate. Fruit whitish, with minute black seeds.

var. **flavispina** Hort. Central spines yellow.

Mammillaria Moelleriana Boedeker. Mexico (Durango). Plant solitary, globular to oval, 6 cm. thick, glossy green. Axils slightly woolly, or bare. Tubercles oval, about 8 mm. long. Areoles oval, at first abundantly furnished with white wool, bare when old. Radial spines 35 to 40, radiating or spreading outwards, needle-like, very sharp, snow-white, slightly yellowish at the base, 7 to 8 mm. long, densely covering the plant. Central spines 8 or 9, rarely 10, the lower 4 hooked and up to 2 cm. long, the upper ones shorter, straight; all bulbous and paler at the base, above being glossy honey yellow, or dark reddish brown. Flowers in a ring around the top, 1½ cm. long; outer petals pale pink to brownish; inner petals pale pink or almost white, with a darker midrib. Stigma with 5 or 6 yellowish pink lobes. Fruit greenish white. Seeds glossy black. One of the finest recent introductions.

Mammillaria Verhaertiana Boedeker. Mexico. Stem solitary, cylindrical, pale green, 4 cm. thick. Tubercles conical, short, keeled, 7 mm. long. Axils with white wool and white bristles. Areoles roundish, with white wool. Radial spines 20 or more, thin, yellowish white, tipped darker, the upper ones about 1 cm. long, the lower up to 1½ cm. Central spines 4 to 6, straight, spreading, stiff, about 12 mm. long, yellowish white below, yellowish brown above, passing to white, at least one of them hooked at the tip. Flowers 2 cm. long, yellowish white or white, with a dorsal greenish band. Stamens, style and the 8- to 9-lobed stigma pink.

Mammillaria mainae K. Brand. State of Maine. Stem globular or elongated with age, 5 to 6 cm. thick. Tubercles softish, conical or elongated, up to 1½ cm. long. Axils bare, often red at the bottom. Radial spines 10 to 15, yellowish, ½ to 1 cm. long. Central spines mostly 1, sometimes 2, rarely 3, brown tipped dark brown, 1½ to 2 cm. long, curved, hooked at the tip. Flowers in a ring around the top, 2½ cm. broad, white; the outer petals with a brownish dorsal band; the inner with a reddish or pink dorsal band. Stamens pink, style longer and of the same colour, as also the 5 long lobes of the stigma.

Mammillaria armillata K. Brand. California. Stem cylindrical, sprouting at the base, up to 30 cm. long, and 4 to 5 cm. thick, with stiff conical warts, slightly angular. Axils with wool and bristles. Radial spines 9 to 15, white, 7 to 12 mm. long, sometimes greyish. Central spines 1 to 4, yellowish with brown zones or bands, 1 to 2 cm. long, the lowermost thicker, hooked at the tip. Flowers 1 to 2 cm. long, pale red or red. Fruit clavate, red, 1½ to 3 cm. long. Seeds dull black, pitted.

Mammillaria Gasseriana Boedeker. Mexico (Coahuila). Plant clustering. Stems globular or oval, 3 to 4 cm. thick, dull greyish green. Tubercles rather closely set, oval, 6 mm. long, minutely dotted. Axils bare. Areoles small, slightly woolly when young. Radial spines 40 to 50, pectinate, in 2 or 3 series, radiating outwards, 5 to 8 mm. long, white. Central spines 1 or 2, more stiff, 8 mm. long, white, dark brown above, hooked at the tip. Flowers small and few; petals broad, lanceolate, creamy white, with a brownish midrib, greenish at the base.

Mammillaria phellosperma Engelm. = *M. tetrancistra* Engelm. = *Phellosperma tetrancistra* (Engelm.) Br. et R. Arizona, California, Utah and Nevada. Plant solitary or clustering. Stem cylindrical, often up to 30 cm. long, densely spinous, pale green passing to greyish. Axils bare. Tubercles cylindrical, loosely set, often clavate, softish, round-topped, 7 to 13 mm. long, mostly directed upwards. Areoles very small, round, slightly woolly. Radial spines numerous, over 40, white, bristle-like, stiff, often tipped brown, 5 to 10 mm. long. Central spines 3 or 4, sometimes 1 or 2, thicker, 2 cm. long, dark brown, or black, all strongly hooked at the tip. Flowers borne on the sides near the top, 3½ to 4 cm. long: outer petals obtuse, fringed; the inner lanceolate-acuminate, fringed, reddish yellow. Stamens, style and 5-lobed stigma whitish or creamy white. Fruit clavate, 1 to 2 cm. long, red. Seeds glossy black, with a large corky pale brown hilum. The genus *Phellosperma* Br. et R. is based on the presence of this large dome-shaped corky hilum, as large as the seed itself. Requires an airy situation, half-shaded or shaded.

Mammillaria Gulzowiana Werd. Mexico (Durango). In appearance very like *M. bocasana*, but larger, and not so prone to form clusters. Stem green, almost globular, up to 7 cm. high, and 4 to 6 cm. thick, with bare axils. Tubercles soft, almost cylindrical, about 12 mm. long, and 5 mm. broad, with a round areole at first furnished with yellowish wool. Radial spines very numerous, 60 to 80, in 2 or more series, radiating obliquely outwards, white, bristle-like at the base and hair-like above, up to 1½ cm. long, curled or floccose. Only one central spine, reddish brown above, up to 1 cm. long, thin towards the tip, where it is hooked. Flowers few, on the upper axils near the centre, large, 5 cm. long, 6 cm. broad. Outer petals lanceolate, greenish or brownish with a pink margin, fringed white; inner petals linear-lanceolate, 2½ cm. long, 5 mm. broad, abruptly acute, deep purplish red. Stamens short, white, style shorter, stigma with 3 short greenish lobes. Seeds dull black, pitted, with a dark brown corky cap at the hilum.

Mammillaria balsasensis Boedeker. Mexico (Guerrero, near Balsas). Stem solitary, globular-depressed, about 6 cm. thick, soft-fleshed, glossy light green to dull deep reddish, with a thick tap-root, spinous and woolly at the top. Tubercles broadly conical, 6 to 7 mm. long. Axils slightly woolly. Areoles small, slightly woolly when young. Radial spines about 15, radiating star-like, straight, stiff, thin, needle-like, white, mostly tipped brown, up to 8 mm. long. Central spines 4, more stiff, straight, smooth, the upper ones up to 7 mm. long, the lowest up to 1 cm. long and hooked at the tip; all dark brown. Similar to *M. zephyranthoides:* grows on granitic lands, in warm and shaded localities.

Mammillaria Blossfeldiana Boedeker. Lower California. Mostly solitary, globular, dull green, 4 cm. thick, spiny at the top. Axils sparingly woolly. Tubercles softish, areoles woolly when young. Radial spines about 20, radiating, straight, stiff, needle-like, yellowish passing to greyish white, tipped darker, 5 to 7 mm. long. Central spines 4, like the radials but more stiff, straight, the longest about 1 cm. long, dark brown, hooked at the end. Flowers 2 cm. broad, inner petals carmine pink with a darker midrib. Fruit clavate, orange red. Seeds glossy black, pitted.

Mammillaria Patonii (Helia Bravo) Werd. = *Neomammillaria Patonii* Helia Bravo. Mexico (Islas Marias). Plant mostly clustering. Stems cylindrical, up to 15 cm. long, 4 to 5 cm. thick, olive green, sometimes bronze colour. Axils bare. Tubercles almost cylindrical, in 13 rows. Areoles with yellow wool when young. Radial spines 13 to 15 or more, greyish, tipped darker, up to 8 mm. long. Central spines 4, thicker, 12 mm. long, dark reddish passing to almost greyish, one of them hooked. Flowers borne at or near the centre, 3 cm. long, purple, the outer petals with a brown midrib. Stamens red, stigma with 8 olive green lobes. Fruit green. Seeds black.

Mammillaria Rettigiana Boedeker. Mexico (Hidalgo). Stem solitary, globular or oval, depressed, up to 4 cm. thick, glossy green. Axils bare or slightly woolly, without bristles. Tubercles thin, cylindrical, up to 1 cm. long. Areoles with white wool when young. Radial spines about 20, radiating, very thin, straight, white or glossy yellow, up to 1 cm. long. Central spines 3 or 4, more stiff, needle-like, reddish brown, the upper 2 or 3 spreading vertically like a fan, the lower one straight upwards, up to 1½ cm. long, hooked at the end. Flowers about 1½ cm. broad; inner petals glossy clear pink, edged paler. Fruit small, clavate, red. Seeds glossy dark brown, minutely pitted.

Mammillaria surculosa Boedeker. Mexico (Tamaulipas). Similar to *M. Carretii* Reb. Plant small, freely clustering, with a thick tap-root, glossy green. Stems 4 cm. high and 3 cm. thick, spinous at the top. Axils bare. Tubercles softish, short-cylindric, about 8 mm. long. Areoles small, at first with white wool, later bare. Radial spines about 15, radiating, stiff, very thin, mostly straight, glassy white, up to 1 cm. long. Only one central spine, mostly directed obliquely upwards, straight, amber yellow to brownish, up to 2 cm. long, hooked at the tip. Flowers few, in the upper axils, up to 18 mm. long; inner petals sulphur yellow, tipped reddish.

Mammillaria Saffordii Br. et R. = *Neomammillaria* Br. et R. Mexico. Plant freely cespitose. Stem olive green, globular to cylindrical, 4 to 8 cm. high, 1½ to 2½ cm. thick. Tubercles oval-cylindrical, 5 to 7 mm. long, and 3 mm. thick. Areoles round, yellowish. Radial spines 12 to 15, bristle-like or hair-like, of even length, about ½ cm., yellowish white, straight or slightly curved backwards. One central spine, rarely 2, up to 1 cm. long, reddish yellow or reddish, hooked at the tip. Flowers yellow, outer petals flushed reddish on the dorsal side. Similar to *M. surculosa*. Prefers half-shade.

Mammillaria jaliscana (Br. et R.) = *Neomammillaria* Br. et R. Mexico (Guadalajara). Plant cespitose, globose, bright green, 5 cm. thick. Tubercles in 13 rows, 4 to 5 mm. high. Radial spines 30 or more. Central spines 4 to 6, reddish brown, darker towards the tip, one of them strongly hooked. Axils bare. Flowers pinkish or purplish, 1 cm. broad, fragrant; outer petals ovate, toothed; inner petals oblong obtuse. Stamens pinkish, stigma with 3 or 4 white lobes. Fruit white, 8 mm. long; seeds black.

Series 5. POLYACANTHAE Salm-Dyck

Radial spines very numerous, stiff, more or less obliquely directed outwards. Central spines almost like the radials.

Mammillaria spinosissima Lem. = *M. polyacantha* Ehrbg. Central Mexico. Stem solitary, cylindrical, 4 to 10 cm. thick and up to 30 cm. high when old, dark green or almost bluish green, rounded at the top, and covered with wool and erect spines. Axils slightly woolly and with bristles. Tubercles conical, slightly angular, 4 to 5 mm. long. Areoles roundish at first slightly woolly, afterwards bare. Radial spines 20 to 30, radiating or spreading outwards, bristle-like, 2 to 10 mm. long. Central spines 7 to 10, thicker, 1 to 2 cm. long, bristle-like, stiff, but only slightly prickly, of varying colour from pure white to ruby red or dark reddish brown. Flowers in a ring around the top, 2 cm. long; outer petals brown, edged pink; inner petals fiery carmine, narrow, acute, minutely toothed. Stamens white or pink, style of the same colour, stigma with 7 or 8 greenish lobes.

This species is very variable, offering a large number of varieties, some of them being characteristic of the various districts where it grows, and might be considered as sub-species.

var. **auricoma** (Ehrbg.) = *Mammillaria auricoma* Ehrbg. Radial spines white, central spines white, tipped golden yellow.

var. **aurorea** (Dietr.) = *M. aurorea* Dietr. Radial spines pale yellow, central spines glossy golden yellow, darker at the tip.

var. **brunnea** Salm-Dyck. Spines reddish brown.

var. **castaneoides** (Lem.) = *M. castaneoides* Lem. Central spines maroon brown.

var. **flavida** Salm-Dyck. Central spines pale yellow.

var. **isabellina** (Ehrbg.) = *M. isabellina* Ehrbg. Spines pale brownish yellow.

var. **pretiosa** (Ehrbg.) = *M. pretiosa* Ehrbg. All spines pure white. Rare. There is also a cristate form of this variety.

var. **rubens** Salm-Dyck = *M. sanguinea* F. Haage jr. New Spines at the top intense blood red, passing to paler and dark reddish brown at the sides. A very remarkable variety.

Other varieties frequently listed by dealers are: var. **eximia** (Ehrbg.), **alba** Hort., **purpurea** Hort., **hepatica** (Ehrbg.), **Hermannii** (Ehrbg.), **caesia** (Ehrbg.), **Uhdeana** (S.-D.), **mirabilis** (Ehrbg.), etc.

Series 6. HETEROCHLORAE Salm-Dyck

Radial spines spreading outward. Central spines not hooked, or exceptionally one of them is hooked.

Mammillaria napina J. A. Purp. Mexico (Puebla, Tehuacan, on stony, chalky ground, in sunny localities). Stem globular, depressed, or hemispherical, pale green, with a thick fleshy turnip-like root. Tubercles conical, up to 1 cm. long. Axils mostly slightly woolly. Areoles bare. Radial spines 12, stiff, radiating, glassy white, yellow at the base, about 8 mm. long. No central spines. Flowers pink.

Mammillaria durispina Boedeker. Central Mexico. Solitary, globular to oval-elongated, 6 to 20 cm. high, 6 to 11 cm. thick, dull dark green. Axils at first with white wool, later bare. Tubercles closely set, 8 mm. long. Areoles at first slightly woolly, soon becoming bare. Radial spines 6 to 8, stiff, awl-shaped, straight, radiating starlike, 7 to 8 mm. long, the upper ones longer (1 to 1½ cm.), prostrate or reflexed on the stem; the lower ones directed more outwards. Central spines absent. Flowers in a ring around the top, 1½ cm. long, 12 mm. broad: inner petals of a beautiful deep carmine red, pale green at the throat. Stamens pale green, style pale green below, pink above; stigma with 5 short, thick, spreading, purple lobes. Fruit 2 cm. long, carmine red, greenish at the top. Seeds dull yellow.

Mammillaria bogotensis Werd. Colombia (near Bogotá). Stem mostly solitary, globular to short-clavate, up to 10 cm. high, and about 4½ cm. thick, white wool and short brown spines covering the top, fresh green passing to greyish green. Axils densely woolly, without bristles. Tubercles short-conical, not angular, 4 to 6 mm. high, 6 to 7 mm. broad at the base, obliquely pointed upwards. Areoles oval, small, with white wool when new, passing to yellowish white, afterwards quite bare. Radial spines 20 to 30, radiating very evenly, almost spreading outwards, bristle-like, stiff, straight, smooth, glassy white, 4 to 6 mm. long. Central spines 6, rarely only one, more or less radiating outwards, needle-like, straight, bulbous at the base, smooth, yellowish, tipped brownish, paler at the base, when new more brownish yellow, tipped darker, finally passing to dirty grey or brownish, 6 to 8 mm. long. This is the most southern species of *Mammillaria* so far known.

Mammillaria eriacantha Link et Otto. = *M. cylindracea* DC. Central Mexico (Jalapa). Mostly solitary, cylindrical, up to 15 cm. high or more, and 4 to 5½ cm. thick, fresh green, rounded at the top, with wool and short yellow spines. Axils and areoles only slightly woolly. Tubercles conical, almost four-sided at the base, 7 mm. long. Radial spines about 20, radiating, bristle-like, yellowish, minutely hairy, ½ cm. long. Central spines 2, awl-shaped, thick, with soft hairs, yellow, the lower one directed downwards and 1 cm. long, the upper one being shorter. Flowers in a ring around the top, 1½ cm. long; inner petals lanceolate-acute, yellow. Stamens and style yellow, stigma with 4 yellow lobes. Fruit clavate, 1 cm. long, yellowish to orange red. Seeds brown to black, pitted. A characteristic species. Requires warmth and full sunshine.

Mammillaria leona Poselg. Mexico (Nuevo Leon). Quite by mistake, often considered identical with *Coryphantha* (or *Mammillaria*) *Pottsii*. Stem cylindrical, solitary or sprouting from the base, bluish green, up to 12 cm. long or more, and 2 to 3½ cm. thick. Axils woolly. Tubercles conical; areoles at first woolly, afterwards bare. Radial spines about 30, bristle-like, spreading over the tubercles, about ½ cm. long, snow white, slightly yellowish at the base. Central spines 6 to 12, mostly 8, in a double cross, slightly thickened at the base, straight or slightly curved upwards, 1 cm. long, white, tipped a peculiar greyish violet. All spines passing to greyish and finally dropping off, the tubercles being reduced to scale-like prominences at the base of the stem. Flowers in a ring around the top of the stem, yellowish or reddish. A lovely species, desirable on account of the unusual colour of the central spines. Prefers full sunshine, and a soil composed of granitic sand or gravel, with much calcareous matter, mixed with some loam and leaf-mould.

Mammillaria gracilis Pfeiff. = *Neomammillaria fragilis* (Salm-Dyck) Br. et R. Mexico (Hidalgo). Plant most freely clustering and branching, with cylindrical stems, fresh green, up to 10 cm. high, and 3 to 4½ cm. thick, often sprawling and branching all over the sides. Tubercles 6 to 8 mm. long, 5 to 6 mm. thick; axils and areoles sparingly woolly. Radial spines 12 to 14, yellowish white, soon passing to milky white, stiff, bristle-like, 5 to 9 mm. long, spreading star-like over the warts. Central spines 3 to 5, up to 1½ cm. long, brown to dark brown. Flowers 17 mm. long, 13 mm. broad: outer petals lanceolate, yellowish white. Fruit 1 cm. long, pale yellowish red. The young offsets are globular or elongated, with low tubercles to which the radial spines are closely applied, without central spines. These offsets or branches drop off at the least touch, and root at once, but do not produce typical warts, with central spines and flowers, before the third year.

var. **fragilis** (Salm-Dyck) = *Mammillaria fragilis* Salm-Dyck. Plant smaller: central spines 2, white, tipped brown.

var. **pulchella** Salm-Dyck. Stems more slender, 2 to 3 cm. thick. Radial spines white, fewer, the upper ones brownish, the uppermost brown, slightly curved. Central spines absent. Fruit dark red, 1½ to 2 cm. long. The absence of central spines has caused it to be considered as only the juvenile form of the species.

Mammillaria fertilis Hildm. Mexico. Plant thickly clustering, dark green. Stems short-cylindric, 5 to 6 cm. thick. Axils slightly woolly. Tubercles thickly set, slender, 7 to 8 mm. long, slightly four-sided. New areoles woolly. Radial spines 8 to 10 or more, thin, transparent white, breaking off easily, the middle one up to 6 mm. long. Central spines 2 to 4, yellowish brown, tipped darker, 1 cm. long. Flowers in a ring around the top, 18 mm. long; inner petals acute, fiery carmine. Stamens, style and 4-lobed stigma fiery carmine.

Mammillaria rhodantha Link et Otto. Mexico (Hidalgo, on the high table-lands, in fertile soils). Plant dark green, cylindrical or clavate, repeatedly dividing itself dichotomously, in time forming large clumps, woolly at the top and very spiny, 10 to 30 cm. high, 7 to 8 cm. thick. Axils woolly. Tubercles conical, 6 to 9 mm. long. Areoles round, with short wool. Radial spines 16 to 20, spreading outwards, thin, needle-like, white or yellow, the lower ones up to 1 cm. long. Central spines mostly 4, sometimes up to 6, stiff, somewhat curved, yellow, red or brown, up to 2½ cm. long. Flowers numerous in a ring near the top, 15 to 18 mm. long, 12 to 13 mm. broad; outer petals reddish brown with a whitish margin, fringed; the inner lanceolate-acute, fiery carmine red. Stamens carmine red, style reddish or greenish white, stigma with 3 or 4 deep carmine lobes. Fruit clavate or linear, carmine red. Seeds few, yellowish brown, pitted. A very variable species, with numerous beautiful varieties, requiring half-shade, but easily grown in a good nourishing soil.

var. **Odieriana** (Lem.) = *Mammillaria Odieriana* Lem. Spines of uniform thickness: central spines pale yellow, slightly curved. Often considered as the typical form.

var. **callaena** K. Sch. Central spines pale brown.

var. **Pfeifferi** K. Sch. = *M. aureiceps* Lem. Central spines lemon yellow, all similar, slightly curved. Very distinct.

var. **rubra** K. Sch. Central spines red.

var. **ruberrima** K. Sch. Central spines longer and stronger than in other varieties, of a beautiful dark red colour.

var. **chrysacantha** (Otto) K. Sch. = *M. chrysacantha* Otto. Stem broader and lower. Radial spines yellow and curved. Central spines dark brown, the upper one long, thicker, slightly curved upwards.

var. **phaeacantha** (Lem.) = *M. phaeacantha* Lem. Spines brown.

var. **sulphurea** (Senke) K. Sch. = *M. sulphurea* Senke. Tubercles longer. All spines yellow, the radials slightly curved.

var. **stenocephala** (Scheidw.) K. Sch. = *M. stenocephala* Scheidw. Radial spines very short. Central spines 4, reddish brown, slightly curved.

var. **crassispina** (Pfeiff.) K. Sch. = *M. crassispina* Pfeiff. Central spines thick, yellowish brown, or reddish brown in the form *rufa* Hort.

var. **fulvispina** (Haw.) Schelle = *M. fulvispina* Haw. Central spines clear brownish yellow, radials yellowish.

var. **pyramidalis** (Lk. et Otto) K. Sch. = *M. pyramidalis* Lk. et Otto. Central spines all similar, at first ruby red, passing to dark brown.

var. **fuscata** (Otto) K. Sch. = *M. fuscata* Otto. Radials white passing to yellowish, centrals yellow, tipped brown. In the form *alba* Hort., the radials are white or very pale yellow, the centrals pale yellow to yellow.

There are also various cristate forms of great beauty, such as: *Odieriana cristata, crassispina cristata, rubra cristata, fuscata cristata,* etc.

Mammillaria Droegeana K. Sch. = *M. rhodantha* var. *Droegeana* K. Sch. Mexico (Puebla). Stem dark green, globular depressed, 6 cm. thick, wholly covered with spines. Areoles with brownish wool. All spines are bulbous at the base. Radial spines yellowish. Central spines 4 to 6, spreading, curved, pale brown, the lowermost dark brown, longer, straight, directed backwards. Flowers pink.

Mammillaria umbrina Ehrbg. = *M. Haynei* Ehrbg. Mexico (Hidalgo). Plant at first solitary, later cespitose, dark green, with cylindrical stems up to 10 cm. long, and 5 to 6 cm. thick, woolly at the top and with dark red spines. Axils bare. Tubercles conical, 7 to 8 mm. long, obliquely directed upwards. Areoles round, at first with snow white wool, later bare. Radial spines 18 to 20, bristle-like, white, $\frac{1}{2}$ cm. long, radiating, later passing to greyish. Central spines mostly 2, the upper one up to 2 cm. long, thick, often strongly arched upwards, the lower one shorter, both of a beautiful ruby red when new, passing to reddish yellow, tipped brown, finally greyish. Flowers in a regular ring round the top, 2 cm. long, $1\frac{1}{2}$ cm. broad: outer petals deep carmine with a paler margin; the inner fiery carmine red, acute, slightly toothed, white at the throat. Stamens and style white, stigma with 7 to 9 yellowish green spreading lobes. Requires half-shade.

Mammillaria Jossensiana Quehl. Mexico. Stem globular to elongated, pale green. Tubercles conical, acute, about 1 cm. long, at first directed upwards. Axils bare. Areoles round with white wool. Radial spines about 20, bristle-like, radiating, white, up to 1 cm. long, the upper ones shorter. Central spines 4 or more, stronger and longer, whitish, up to 1½ cm. long, often one of them curved or hooked. Flowers small, pale red, with a darker midrib. Style and 6-lobed stigma yellow.

Mammillaria discolor Haw. Mexico (Puebla). Stem globular to cylindrical, green or bluish green, somewhat woolly and depressed at the top, 5 to 7 cm. high, 4 to 5 cm. thick. Axils bare. Tubercles conical, 6 to 7 mm. long, pointing upwards. Areoles oval, at first with white wool. Radial spines 16 to 20 or more, radiating, thin, snow-white, the lower up to 1 cm. long. Central spines mostly 5, sometimes 6 to 8, thick, awl-shaped, spreading, pale yellow or dark yellow, 1 cm. long. Flowers in a ring around the top, 2 cm. long, and 1½ cm. broad; outer petals red, edged paler; the inner more obtuse and of a clearer red. Stamens and style white, stigma with 6 or 7 green lobes.

Mammillaria Mundtii K. Sch. Mexico. Stem globular depressed, 5 to 7 cm. thick, dark green, woolly at the top. Tubercles conical, 6 to 7 mm. long. Areoles round, at first with white wool, passing to yellowish, finally bare. Radial spines 10 to 12, thin white, up to ½ cm. long. Central spines 2, straight, spreading, brown, 1½ cm. long. Flowers numerous, slender, 2 cm. long: outer petals dark red, pink at the margin; inner petals lanceolate-acute, a beautiful glossy carmine. Stamens carmine, style and 4-lobed stigma white. The flowers are very freely borne in complete rings around the top of the stem.

Mammillaria Ruestii Quehl. = *M. Celsiana* var. *guatemalensis* Eichlam. Honduras and Guatemala. Stem globular to cylindrical, pale green, 4 to 7 cm. thick, up to 10 cm. high, with white wool and crimson spines at the top. Axils with bristles and very woolly. Tubercles conical, 6 to 7 mm. long. Areoles elliptical, with floccose white wool. Radial spines 16 to 20 or more, white, short. Central spines 4, awl-shaped, thickened at the base, 7 to 8 mm. long. Flowers small, hardly longer than the tubercles, pale pink with a pink midrib.

Mammillaria yucatanensis Br. et R. = (*Neomammillaria* Br et R.). Mexico (Yucatan). Plant cespitose, similar to the preceding species, pale green or dull green, globular to short-cylindric, 4 to 8 cm. thick. Axils very woolly, but without bristles. Areoles elliptical, woolly. Radial spines many, short, white. Central spines 3 to 5, crimson when young, passing to brownish, 6 to 10 mm. long. Flowers pink or pale pink. Prefers half-shade, and a sandy soil kept rather dry.

Mammillaria Graessneriana Boedeker. Mexico. Stem clustering, globular to oval, dark bluish green, about 6 cm. thick, densely woolly at the top. Axils woolly. Tubercles conical-pyramidal, four-sided at the base, 8 mm. long, 3 to 4 mm. thick. Areoles round, with long white wool. Radial spines 18 to 20, radiating, needle-like, glassy white, 6 to 8 mm. long, more numerous laterally. Central spines 2 to 4, rather thin, dark reddish brown, paler at the base, 8 mm. long. Flower small, red.

Mammillaria amoena Hopff. Mexico (Hidalgo). Plant cespitose when old, dark green. Stem globular to clavate, woolly at the top, 8 to 10 cm. high, 10 to 12 cm. broad. Axils with white wool. Tubercles conical, 5 to 7 mm. long, obliquely directed upwards. Areoles round, at first with white wool, later bare. Radial spines 20 or more, bristle-like but stiff, radiating, white, up to ½ cm. long. Central spines mostly 2, often up to 5, 1½ cm. long, slightly curved, and thicker, yellowish brown. Flowers in a ring at the top, 2 cm. long: outer petals brownish, fringed; the inner spathulate-acute, crimson. Stamens crimson, style reddish, stigma with 4 crimson lobes.

Mammillaria coronaria Haw. Mexico (Hidalgo). At first solitary, later cespitose. Stem green or greyish green, globular to cylindrical, 7 to 15 cm. high, 6 to 7 cm. thick, with white wool and erect dark red spines at the top. Axils bare. Tubercles conical, 8 mm. long; areoles elliptical, at first woolly. Radial spines 12 to 18, spreading outwards, transparent white, the lateral ones up to 1 cm. long. Central spines 6, spreading, at first dark crimson, later brown, passing to yellowish and grey, the upper one 1½ cm. long. Flowers in a regular ring around the centre, about 16 mm. long, brownish crimson on the outer side: inner petals lanceolate-acute, minutely fringed, clear crimson with a darker midrib. Stamens and style white, stigma with 4 yellowish green lobes. Fruit maturing in the following year, clavate, coral red.

var. **nigra** (Ehrbg.) = *Mammillaria nigra* Ehrbg. Central spines very dark brown or black.

var. **minor** (Haw.). Plant smaller and spines shorter.

This species is similar in appearance to *M. rhodantha*, and is almost as variable, presenting several varieties, which were described as distinct species.

Mammillaria Lesaunieri Reb. = *M. Lassaunieri* Hort. Mexico. Stem solitary, hemispherical to short-cylindric, dark green, 7 to 8 cm. thick, woolly at the top, with short, erect, brown spines. Axils bare. Tubercles conical, 1 cm. long. Areoles at first woolly. Radial spines 11 to 13, radiating, thin, awl-shaped, straight or slightly curved, white or yellowish, the middle and the lower ones 6 to 8 mm. long. Only one central spine, erect, slightly thicker, brown, about ½ cm. long. Flowers many in a ring at the top, 2½ cm. long, reddish brown outside, crimson inside. Stamens, style and 4-lobed stigma red. Requires warmth and sunshine.

Mammillaria Pringlei K. Brand. Mexico (San Luis Potosi). Plant mostly solitary, or dividing dichotomously, hemispherical to short-cylindric, dull greyish green, somewhat flat and woolly at the top, 8 to 12 cm. thick, entirely covered with long golden yellow spines. Axils with white wool and with a few white bristles. Tubercles broadly conical, closely set, four-sided at the base, 10 to 12 mm. long, spreading outwards. Areoles round, at first with white wool. Radial spines

20 to 30, radiating, bristle-like, straight or slightly curved, diaphanous white, up to 1 cm. long. Central spines 7 to 10, golden yellow, bulbous and reddish at the base, tipped reddish when new, $1\frac{1}{2}$ to $2\frac{1}{2}$ cm. long, straight or slightly curved, the upper one up to $3\frac{1}{2}$ cm. long, thicker and curved upwards. Flowers in a ring at the top, crimson. Fruit clavate, red, 1 cm. long. A most beautiful species of striking appearance, and easy cultivation in full sunshine.

Mammillaria densispina (Coulter) = *Cactus densispinus* Coulter = *M. pseudofuscata* Quehl. Mexico (San Luis Potosi). Plant solitary, dark green, similar to *M. rhodantha*, but does not divide itself dichotomously. Radial spines about 25, glassy white to yellow or brownish, up to 13 mm. long. Central spines 6, fuchsine red when new, passing to brown, slightly curved, bulbous at the base, the upper one darker, up to 2 cm. long. Flowers in a ring around the top; outer petals purplish red, the inner sulphur yellow.

Mammillaria albicans (Br. et R.) = *Neomammillaria* Br. et R. Gulf of California (Island Santa Cruz). Globular to cylindrical, 10 to 20 cm. long, about 6 cm. thick, covered with spines. Tubercles closely set. Areoles at first woolly. Radial spines very numerous, spreading outwards, short, white. Central spines many, short, straight, often tipped brown or black. Fruit clavate, red. Possibly a variety of the following:

Mammillaria Slevinii (Br. et R.) = *Neomammillaria Slevinii* Br. et R. Gulf of California (Islands of San Josef and San Francisco). Solitary, cylindrical, about 10 cm. high and 6 cm. thick, entirely covered with spines. Radial spines many, needle-like, spreading. Central spines about 6, slightly longer and thicker, pinkish and tipped brown or black when new, passing to white with age. Flowers 2 cm. broad, white, outer petals with a pinkish midrib; stamens pinkish, style and stigma white or whitish.

Mammillaria tetracantha Salm-Dyck = *M. dolichocentra* Lem. = *M. dolichacantha* Först = *M. longispina* Rehb. Mexico (Hidalgo). Stem mostly solitary, cespitose in its native country, dark glaucous green, globular to cylindrical, up to 30 cm. high, occasionally up to 1 m., brownish green when old, woolly at the top. Axils sparingly woolly. Tubercles 8 to 10 mm. long, conical, almost four-sided. Areoles small, with short white wool. Radial spines absent or reduced to a few bristles. Central spines 4, crosswise, rarely 2 or 5 to 6, one of them curved upwards, the lower one directed downwards, straight or slightly curved, 1 to $2\frac{1}{2}$ cm. long, at first yellowish brown, honey yellow at the base, passing to greyish. Flowers in a ring around the centre, 2 cm. long: outer petals lanceolate, reddish green, fringed; inner petals narrower; acuminate, carmine red. Stamens and upper part of style carmine, stigma with 4 pink lobes. Fruit clavate, dark red, about 2 cm. long. Seeds yellowish brown, smooth. Usually listed under the name of *M. dolichocentra*.

var. **Galeottii** (Scheidw.) K. Sch. = *M. Galeottii* Scheidw. Central spines dark brown or black.

Mammillaria polythele (Hort.) K. Sch. non Mart. Mexico (Hidalgo). Stem solitary, or sparingly cespitose, dark green or bluish green, elongated or clavate, up to 15 cm. long and 8 or 9 cm. thick. Axils with white wool. Tubercles conical, 1 cm. long, rhomboid at the base, obliquely directed upwards. Areoles oval, with floccose white wool, later bare. Radial spines few, bristle-like, up to $\frac{1}{2}$ cm. long, glassy white or white, often absent or dropping off. Central spines 4, spreading crosswise, the upper one and the lower about 2 cm. long, slightly curved, yellow or brown. Flowers in a ring, 18 to 19 mm. long: outer petals brown with a red margin; inner petals fiery carmine, acute. Stamens carmine, style greenish yellow, stigma with 3 or 4 reddish lobes. Fruit red.

Mammillaria hidalgensis J. A. Purp. Mexico (Hidalgo). Stem solitary, cylindrical, dark green, up to 30 cm. high, and 8 cm. thick, rounded at the top, woolly and with reddish brown spines. Tubercles conical, acute, 1 cm. long. Axils and areoles at first with floccose white wool, later bare. Radial spines mostly absent. Central spines 4, spreading crosswise, sometimes reduced to 2, all nearly equal, 1 cm. long, greyish white, tipped brown. Flowers 17 to 18 mm. long: petals narrow, lanceolate, acuminate, carmine red, paler at the base. Stamens, style and 5-lobed stigma reddish. A resistant species of easy growth, now frequently imported.

Mammillaria kewensis Salm-Dyck. First grown at Kew Gardens, probably native of Mexico (Hidalgo). Very similar to *M. hidalgensis*, with an elongated cylindrical deep green stem. Axils with curled white wool. Tubercles broadly conical, acute, with areoles at first woolly, soon becoming bare. Central spines 4 to 6, short, spreading star-like and recurved, very stiff, purplish brown, paler at the base, the upper and lower ones 10 to 11 mm. long, the laterals 5 to 6 mm. long. Flowers funnel-shaped, small: outer petals acuminate, pale red, inner petals deep pink. Stamens, style and 5-lobed stigma pink.

var. **albispina** Salm-Dyck = *M. spectabilis* Hort. Spines white, tipped brown.

Section II. GALACTOCHYLUS K. Sch.

Species with milky sap. Plant more or less greyish green or greyish, more solid-fleshed.

Series 7. ELEGANTES K. Sch.

The tubercles do not exude a milky juice when wounded, the milky sap being found only in the internal tissues. Radial spines very numerous. Central spines very prickly.

Mammillaria elegans DC. = *M. dealbata* Otto = *M. Klugii* Erhbg. = *M. acanthophlegma* Lehm. = *M. Peacockii* Rümpl. Central Mexico. Stem at first solitary, becoming sprouting and cespitose when old, globular to cylindrical, pale green or glaucous green, woolly and spiny at the top, 5 to 10 cm. high, and 5 to 8 cm. thick. Axils bare or more or less woolly. Tubercles closely set, oval-conical, almost four-sided at the base, 4 to 5 mm. long. Areoles at first densely furnished with white wool, later almost bare. Radial spines 25 to 30, radiating, stiff, bristle-like, white, 5 to 6 mm. long. Central spines 2, sometimes 1 or 3, one directed upwards and the other downwards, up to 1 cm. long, white, tipped brown. Flowers numerous, in a ring around the top, carmine red to violet red, 13 to 15 mm. long, 8 mm. broad. Stamens white at the base, carmine red above, style white, stigma with 5 to 7 erect, very short, yellowish lobes. A most lovely species of easy cultivation, with many varieties.

var. **supertexta** (Mart.) = *M. supertexta* Mart. A well marked and beautiful variety, freely clustering and sprouting. Stems more slender and rigid, sometimes globular, 2 to 2½ cm. thick, and sometimes becoming elongated and cylindrical, up to 15 cm. long. Centrals 2 to 4, more interlocked. Very free-flowering; flowers pale carmine red. Very resistant.

var. **dealbata** (Otto). Central spines pale yellow, stem more woolly at the top.

var. **Kunthii** (Ehrbg.) = *M. Kunthii* Ehrbg. Stem oval, 5 to 7 cm. thick, woolly at the top. All spines pure white, the centrals often just a little brownish at the tip.

var. **potosina** Hort. Stem oval, very glaucous, 4 to 6 cm. thick, woolly at the top. Central spines shorter, white, tipped yellow or yellowish. Free-flowering even when very young, flowers violet red.

var. **nigrispina**. Central spines black, whitish at the base, later passing to greyish; upper spine usually short, ½ cm.; lower spine 1½ cm. long.

var. **aureispina**. Central spines white below, golden yellow to honey colour above; upper spine 1 cm. long, lower spine shorter.

Mammillaria Haageana Pfeiff. Mexico (Vera Cruz). Sometimes described as a variety of the preceding. Stem globular to cylindrical, up to 15 cm. high, 3½ to 5½ cm. thick, sprouting at the base or sides when old; very rigid and erect. Axils slightly woolly. Tubercles very closely set, glaucous greyish green. Radial spines about 20, radiating, very thin and short (3 mm.). Central spines mostly 2, often 3 or 4, white or pale yellow at the base, black towards the tip, 6 to 12 mm. long. Flowers small, carmine red, in a ring below the top.

Mammillaria Donatii Berge. Mexico. Stem globular to oval-elongated, 8 to 9 cm. thick, pale bluish green, topped with wool and yellowish brown spines, mostly solitary, or sprouting when old. Axils and areoles woolly. Tubercles rather softish, conical, 8 mm. long. Radial spines 16 to 18, needle-like, glassy white, radiating star-like, up to 8 mm. long, the upper ones obliquely erect. Central spines 2, the lower one thicker, up to 1 cm. long, at first dark brown, passing to greyish. Flowers 1½ cm. long; petals lanceolate-acute, a clear carmine red. Stamens, style and 4-lobed stigma white.

Mammillaria conspicua J. A. Purp. Mexico (Puebla). Stem solitary, globular to cylindrical, 14 cm. high, about 10 cm. thick, greyish green. Axils woolly. Tubercles closely set together. Areoles small, at first woolly. Radial spines 16 to 25, radiating, white, bristle-like but stiff, the laterals about 6 mm. long. Central spines 2 to 4, spreading, 1 cm. long, thickened at the base, brown, with a white zone at the middle. Flowers about 2 cm. long, clear red.

Mammillaria Celsiana Lem. = *M. lanifera* Haw. = *M. Schaeferi* Fenn. = *M. Muehlenpfordtii* Först. Mexico (San Luis Potosi and State of Mexico). Stem solitary becoming cespitose when old, globular to cylindrical or clavate, flat at the top, where it is well furnished with white wool, glaucous green, up to 12 cm. high and 8 to 10 cm. thick. Axils well furnished with white wool. Tubercles conical, 6 to 7 mm. long. Areoles roundish, small, woolly. Radial spines 20 to 26, very thin, white, 6 to 7 mm. long. Central spines 4, sometimes 5 or 6, awl-shaped, straight, stiff, very prickly, dark yellow, tipped brown, the lowermost 15 to 18 mm. long, the others shorter. Flowers in a ring at the top, small, 11 mm. long: outer petals reddish brown; the inner lanceolate-acute, pink to fiery carmine red. Stamens and style white below and pink above, stigma with 4 pink lobes. A very lovely species; thrives well in half-shade.

var. **longispina** Hort. = *senilis* Hort. Has longer central spines.

Mammillaria Ochoterrenae (Helia Bravo) Werd. = *Neomammillaria Ochoterrenae* Helia Bravo. Mexico (Oaxaca). Stem solitary, globular-depressed, 8 cm. thick, grass green, spiny at the top. Warts close together, in 13 rows. Areoles slightly woolly when young. Radial spines about 17, white, bristle-like, spreading horizontally, and grouped in bundles laterally, 4 to 9 mm. long. Central spines 5, thicker, 1 to 2 cm. long, the lower one being the longest, straight, brown, tipped black when new, passing to yellowish grey, tipped reddish. Flowers in a ring at the top, 1 cm. long; petals pale pink with a dorsal reddish brown band. Stamens pink, style white, stigma with 5 or 6 yellow lobes. Seeds brown.

Mammillaria Schmollii (Helia Bravo) Werd. = *Neomammillaria Schmollii* Helia Bravo. Mexico (Oaxaca). Stem solitary, globular-depressed, about 6 cm. thick. Axils bare. Tubercles conical, in 13 rows. Areoles sparingly woolly when young. Radial spines 23 to 25, radiating, almost glassy white, 4 to 5 mm. long. Central spines 11 to 15, honey yellow, 7 to 10 mm. long, the middle one being the longest. Flowers in a ring at the centre, yellow.

Mammillaria collina J. A. Purp. Mexico (Puebla). Stem always solitary, globular, up to 13 cm. thick, with white wool and short brown spines at the top. Tubercles cylindrical, greyish green, up to 1 cm. long. Axils and areoles at first sparingly woolly, later bare. Radial spines

16 to 18, radiating, white, straight, up to 4 mm. long. Central spines 2, often only 1, white, tipped brown, one directed downwards. Flowers in a ring or crown, 1½ to 2 cm. long; petals broadly lanceolate, acute, of a lively pink red, with a paler central band. Stamens, style and 5-lobed stigma white. A beautiful free-growing and free-flowering species. Delights in full sunshine.

Mammillaria perbella Hildm. Mexico. Stem globular-depressed, greyish green, 5 to 6 cm. thick, woolly at the top, branching dichotomously and forming large flat groups. Tubercles conical, slender 4 mm. thick. Axils slightly furnished with white wool. Radial spines 14 to 18, white, bristle-like, up to 3 mm. long. Central spines 1 or 2, very thick and short, 4 to 6 mm. long, the upper one thicker and conical in shape, the smaller and lower one directed downwards. All spines are reddish white when new, later ivory white. Flowers in a ring, carmine red, 1 cm. long; inner petals lanceolate, abruptly acute. Stamens carmine red, as also the style and the 3-lobed stigma. A charming species of great elegance of form, requiring full sunshine.

Mammillaria microthele Muehlenpf. non Monv. Mexico. Plant cespitose, small, globular. Tubercles 6 to 7 mm. long. Axils at first woolly, bare when old. Radial spines 22 to 24, bristle-like, spreading outwards, white, 2 to 4 mm. long. Central spines 2, thicker, up to 2 cm. long. Flowers small, pale pink outside, white inside.

Mammillaria formosa Scheidw. Mexico (Nuevo Leon, near San Luis Potosi). Stem solitary or sparingly cespitose, globular or elongated, fresh green, up to 10 cm. high, and 6 to 7 cm. thick, with brown spines at the top. Axils bare. Tubercles closely set, narrow, pyramidal, four-sided, obliquely directed upwards 7 to 8 mm. long. Areoles small, round, at first lightly woolly, later bare. Radial spines white, 18 to 22, radiating, thin, 6 mm. long, often in bundles. Central spines 2 to 6, thicker, thickened at the base, at first pale red, tipped brown, passing to greyish, the lowermost up to 8 mm. long. Flowers small, up to 1 cm. long: inner petals lanceolate-acute, red, with dark red midrib. Stamens and style carmine red, stigma with 4 yellowish lobes. There is also a fine cristate form in cultivation.

Mammallaria crucigera Mart. Mexico. Oval to cylindrical, pale green, branching dichotomously, forming large rounded groups of great beauty, each stem being 6 to 7 cm. thick, with white wool at the top. Axils with abundant white wool. Tubercles very closely set together small, conical, four-sided at the base. Areoles with white wool. Radial spines 24 or more, bristle-like, white, spreading horizontally or reflexed on the warts, rough, 2 mm. long. Central spines 4, spreading horizontally crosswise, equally long, 2 or 3 mm. thickened at the base, stiff, waxy yellow. Flowers small, deep red, with narrow acute petals. Stigma with 4 or 5 red lobes.

Mammillaria Dyckiana Zucc. Mexico. Solitary, elongated or cylindrical, greyish green, with woolly axils. Tubercles short, conical, closely set. Young areoles with yellowish wool, later bare. Radial

(b) MAMMILLARIA SCHIEDEANA

(a) MAMMILLARIA CANDIDA

PLATE LVI

(b) MAMMILLARIA MELALEUCA

(a) MAMMILLARIA ALBICOMA

PLATE LVII

spines 16 to 18, radiating, glassy white, 4 mm. long. Central spines 2, horny yellow, tipped reddish. Flowers red.

Series 8. LEUCOCEPHALAE Lem.

Sap milky. Tubercles exude a milky juice when wounded. Stem more or less greyish green or grey, with firm tissues. Radial spines numerous, radiating, slender, white.

Mammillaria geminispina Haworth. = *M. bicolor* Lehm. = *M. nobilis* Pfeiff. = *M. eburnea* Miq. Central Mexico. (Hidalgo). A beautiful species long known in our gardens. Stem at first solitary, but soon sprouting and branching, resulting in large compact rounded clumps with 50 heads or more. Stem cylindrical, bluish or greyish green, spiny and with abundant white wool at the top. Axils furnished with white wool and bristles. Tubercles conical, 6 to 7 mm. long. Areoles with white wool. Radial spines 16 to 20 or more, bristle-like, radiating, pure white. Central spines 2 to 4, up to 2½ cm. long, white, almost flesh-coloured above when new, and tipped brown, the longest curved upwards. Flowers 17 to 19 mm. long: inner petals red, with carmine red midrib, lanceolate, minutely toothed. Stamens white or yellowish, style red above, stigma with 5 pink lobes. Fruit clavate, red. This is one of the finest species, of easy cultivation, of comparatively quick growth, and of easy propagation by offsets. It is also easily raised from seed. Delights in full sunshine.

var. **nivea** K. Sch. = *M. nivea* Wendl. Central spines longer, white, very pale brown at the tip, with a more snowy white appearance. Plant large, spines always straight.

There is also a very beautiful cristate form, grafted or grown on own roots.

Mammillaria pseudoperbella Quehl. Central Mexico. Stem globular or cylindrical, depressed at the centre, where it is snow white, 5 cm. thick, 7 to 15 cm. high, glaucous green, becoming corky at the base when old. Tubercles cylindrical 6 to 7 mm. long, 2 to 3 mm. thick. Axils slightly woolly. Radial spines 20 to 30, thin, radiating, mostly directed laterally on either side. Central spines 2, stiff; the upper one ½ cm. long, brown tipped black; the lower shorter with a transparent red tip. Flowers small, carmine red.

Mammillaria Klissingiana Boedeker. Mexico (Tamaulipas, on rocky hillsides of calcareous formations, in full sunshine). Globular to cylindrical, glossy green, entirely covered with white spines, up to 16 cm. high and up to 9 cm. thick. Axils very woolly. Tubercles small, very numerous and closely set together, 5 mm. long and 2 mm. thick. Radial spines 30 to 35, very thin, mostly directed laterally on either side. Central spines 2 to 4, spreading upwards, 2 to 4 mm. long, more or less tipped red when new. Flowers 1 cm. long, with acute lively pink petals. Very beautiful, often listed and sold instead of the following.

Mammillaria lanata Br. et R. = *Neomammillaria* Br. et R. Northern

Mexico. A rare species, very similar to the preceding, but more abundantly woolly in the axils and at the top. Stem short-cylindric. Spines 12 to 14, all radial, spreading, white, brown at the base. Flowers very small, 6 to 7 mm. long, immersed in a mass of long white wool or hairs. Inner petals oblong, mostly obtuse, red. Stigma with 3 short lobes.

Mammillaria Parkinsonii Ehrbg. Central Mexico. A very beautiful and popular species. Stem globular or clavate, depressed at the top, very richly furnished with snow white wool and white spines, bluish green, up to 15 cm. high and 6 to 8 cm. thick, repeatedly branching dichotomously, resulting in magnificent groups. Axils furnished with wool and bristles. Tubercles 6 to 7 mm. long, conical, slightly angular, exuding copiously a milky sap when wounded. Areoles woolly. Radial spines 20 to 30, bristle-like, radiating, white. Central spines 2, white, tipped dark brown, the upper one straight and erect, the lower about twice as long (2 cm. long), curved backwards. Flowers small, yellowish, copiously surrounded with wool, borne in a ring at the top. Fruit clavate, 1 to 2 cm. long, crimson red. Seeds brownish.

var. **Walthonii** Quehl. Central spines longer, the lower up to 4 or 5 cm. long.

There is also a superb cristate form (*cristata* Reb.).

Mammillaria Hahniana Werd. et Backbg. Mexico (Queretaro). One of the finest introductions of recent years, and among species of *Mammillaria* the white-haired counterpart of *Cephalocereus senilis* (Old Man Cactus). Stem globular, flattened at the top, 6 to 9 cm. thick, green, entirely covered with white spines and with long white hairs or bristles. At first solitary, later branching laterally and freely cespitose, resulting in large flat woolly or hairy masses. Axils with many hair-like long white bristles, up to 5 cm. long, covering the stem, which is globular or short-cylindric, flat at the top, 6 to 10 cm. thick. Tubercles conical-cylindrical, 6 to 9 mm. long, 3 to 4 mm. thick, with small, round, slightly woolly areoles. Radial spines about 30, white, thin, radiating, bristle-like, straight, mostly directed laterally on either side, 4 to 5 mm. long, the lower 1 or 2 thicker than the others. Central spines 2, straight, erect, diaphanous white, tipped reddish brown, more coloured when young, both equal, one directed upwards and the lower downwards, 5 to 8 mm. long. Flowers in a ring around the top, rather small, crimson: petals narrow, lanceolate, acute, with a deep crimson midrib. Stamens white, style white below and pink above, stigma deep crimson, with 2 or 3 short erect lobes. Grows freely, and flowers abundantly in full sunshine. Seedlings grow quickly, reaching a diameter of 5 cm. and flowering size in about 3 years.

var. **giselana** Werd. Hair-like bristles shorter, $1\frac{1}{2}$ to $2\frac{1}{2}$ cm. long.

Mammillaria leucocentra Bergm. Mexico. In appearance similar to *M. Parkinsonii*, with a solitary oval stem, deep green. Axils furnished with white wool. Tubercles closely set, oval-cylindrical, small. New areoles abundantly furnished with white wool, later bare. Radial spines numerous, radiating, thin, white, spreading laterally and covering the stem. Central spines 5 or 6, awl-shaped, stiff, straight, milk white, tipped brown, the lower one the longest, 12 to 15 mm. long, slightly curved downwards. Flowers in a ring at the top, small, of a lively carmine red.

Series 9.   MACROTHELAE Salm-Dyck

Plant with milky sap. Tubercles firm, exuding a milky juice when wounded, large, more or less angular; radial spines few, stiff, prickly, not radiating. Axils woolly, but without bristles.

(a) *Rectispinae*. Central spines not hooked.

Mammillaria simplex Haw. = *M. mammillaris* Karsten. = *Neo-mammillaria mammillaris* Br. et R.   Northern Venezuela, Curacao and neighbouring islands. Plant solitary, globular to short-cylindric, pale green, 4 to 6 cm. high. Axils woolly. Tubercles conical, 5 to 7 mm. long. Areoles at first densely woolly. Spines 10 to 12, all radials, needle-like, reddish brown, spreading outwards, 5 to 7 mm. long, the middle 3 or 4 longer and thicker. Flowers about 1 cm. long, creamy white: outer petals narrow, acuminate. Fruit 1½ to 2 cm. long, red; seeds minute, yellowish brown.

var. **flavescens** K. Sch. = *M. flavescens* DC. Spines slightly longer; flowers yellowish.

Mammillaria Brandegeei Engelm. = *M. Gabbii* Engelm.   Lower California. Plant at first solitary, later branching dichotomously, green passing to greyish green, globular, depressed at the top, 6 to 8 cm. thick, with white wool and brown spines at the top. Axils with white wool. Tubercles slightly angular, 1 cm. long, obliquely directed upwards. Areoles with greyish white wool. Radial spines 9 to 14, needle-like, spreading, white passing to greyish, up to 12 mm. long. Central spines 1 or 2, sometimes 3 or more, up to 2 cm. long, reddish brown, slightly curved. Flowers 1½ to 2½ cm. long; outer petals about 10, pale brown, dark-tipped, edged pale green and fringed; inner petals lanceolate, yellowish green with a narrow red midrib. Stamens white, style and 4-lobed stigma pale green. *Mammillaria arida* Rose, from the same country is very similar and hardly different.

Mammillaria petrophila K. Brand.   California,   Very similar to the preceding. Stem globular, depressed, rarely elongated, greyish green sprouting at the sides. Tubercles angular, acute, about 1 cm. long. Axils with abundant yellowish brown wool. Areoles small, with brownish wool. Radial spines mostly 10, often less, up to 2 cm. long, whitish, tipped chestnut brown, prickly. Central spines mostly 1, sometimes 2, thicker and darker and about twice as long. Flowers greenish yellow, with fringed petals. Stamens, style and 6-lobed stigma greenish yellow.

Mammillaria nivosa Link. = *M. tortolensis* Otto = *M. caracasana* Otto = *M. microthele* Monv. non Muehl.   West Indian Islands

CACTI

(Southern Bahamas, Mona Culebra, St. Thomas, Tortola, Antigua etc.). Plant cespitose, globular or elongated, dark green, often reddish or bronze colour, 18 cm. or more in diameter. Axils and areoles in old plants copiously furnished with white wool. Tubercles conical, 1 to 2½ cm. long, not angular. Spines about 14, of which 1 or 2 are central and similar to the others, pale yellow, awl-shaped, up to 1½ cm. long, often tipped brown, passing to brown. Flowers 1½ cm. long, lemon yellow, with narrow petals, the outer petals with an olive green midrib. A beautiful species, requiring warmth and sunshine; usually with a stem about 9 cm. thick, forming groups of 25 or more.

Mammillaria Macdougalii Rose. South-western Arizona. Plant solitary, globular-depressed or flattened, 12 to 15 cm. thick, and about 8 cm. high, dark green, with a thick turnip-like root. Axils woolly. Tubercles sharply angular, flat-topped. Areoles at first slightly woolly. Radial spines 10 to 12, spreading, white, tipped brown, up to 1 cm. long. One central spine, thick, straight, awl-shaped, slightly longer, brownish, tipped darker. Flowers 3½ cm. long, creamy white, outer petals short and fringed.

Mammillaria Zeyeriana Ferd. Haage Jr. North-western Mexico. Stem solitary, hemispherical or conical, pale greyish green, up to 15 cm. high and over 10 cm. thick. Axils sparingly woolly, later bare. Tubercles conical, very slightly angular, 10 to 12 mm. long, obliquely directed upwards. Areoles large, oval at first with white wool, later almost bare. Radial spines about 10, spreading, whitish, up to 1½ cm long. Central spines 3, more stiff, straight, 3 to 4 cm. long, brownish to violet, ruby red when young, finally passing to white, tipped black or dark brown. Requires warmth and a sandy soil, in full sunshine.

Mammillaria Heyderi Muehlenpf. = *M. declivis* Dietr. = *M. texensis* Lab. Northern Mexico, Texas. Stem hemispherical, flattened, later globular or elongated, up to 10 cm. high, 8 to 10 cm. thick, pale green, with a fleshy root, spiny at the top, mostly solitary. Axils and areoles at first woolly. Tubercles conical, angular. Radial spines 20 to 22, bristle-like, white, tipped brown, the outer ones up to 8 mm. long, the inner shorter. Only one central spine straight or slightly curved inwards, stiff, 6 mm. long, reddish brown, tipped darker. Flowers 1½ to 2 cm. long, with linear-lanceolate, obtuse petals, clear reddish, with a darker central band. Stigma with 5 to 8 red lobes.

Mammillaria hemisphaerica Engelm. Northern Mexico, south-western Texas. Very similar to the preceding. Stem globular, flat, dark green, woolly at the top, 8 to 12 cm. thick. Axils mostly bare; areoles at first woolly. Radial spines 9 to 13, brownish, needle-like, often tipped black, spreading outwards, the upper ones fewer. Only one central spine, brown, straight. Flowers cream-coloured, 1 to 1½ cm. long; inner petals acute. Stamens and style reddish. Stigma with 6 to 10 greenish yellow lobes. Fruit clavate, red.

Mammillaria applanata Engelm. Central and southern Texas. Also similar to the two preceding species. Stem globular, flattened, or hemispherical, dark green. Tubercles conical, acute, somewhat angular. Axils bare. New areoles very woolly, later almost bare. Radial spines 10 to 18, spreading laterally, brown, especially the lower ones. Only one central spine, very short, stiff, straight, brown. Flower bud greenish, acute: flowers 2½ cm. long; petals narrow lanceolate, acuminate, creamy white with a green midrib, greenish on the dorsal side. Stamens and style white, stigma greenish. Flowers when quite young.

Mammillaria Waltheri Boedeker. Mexico (Coahuila). Stem solitary more or less globular, dark green, 7 cm. thick, with bare axils. Tubercles four-sided, the lower angle more acute, roundish at the top, 8 mm. long, 4 mm. thick. Areoles small, round, at first slightly woolly. Radial spines 12 to 14, spreading irregularly, stiff, needle-like, greyish white, the upper ones thinner and shorter, and the lower ones longer, up to 7 mm. at first yellowish white, tipped darker or dark brown. One central spine, sometimes 2, more stiff, spreading outwards, thickened at the base, amber yellow to deep brownish violet or black. Flowers in a ring at the top, 1½ cm. long: petals whitish, 2 mm. broad, lanceolate-acute. Stamens white, style white below and pink above, stigma with 5 or 6 pale green lobes.

Mammillaria melanocentra Poselg. = *M. valida* Weber non Purp. Mexico (Monterey). Stem solitary, globular to cylindrical, rather flattened at the top, and with much white wool and long black spines, bluish green, 10 to 12 cm. thick. Axils and areoles at first copiously woolly. Tubercles pyramidal, almost four-sided, up to 2 cm. long, and 1½ cm. thick, obliquely pointed. Radial spines 6 to 10, straight, spreading outwards, stiff, needle-like, pale diaphanous yellow, passing to greyish, tipped black, the lower ones longer, 2 to 3½ cm. long. Only one central spine, at first black, 2 to 5½ cm. long. Flowers in a ring at the top, a lively pink, edged paler. A large and beautiful species, rather variable in regard to the size of the tubercles, the size and colour of the spines, and the quantity of white wool in the axils and areoles.

Mammillaria meiacantha Engelm. Western Texas, New Mexico. A quick-growing species, mostly solitary, greyish green. Stem globular. depressed, up to 13 cm. thick. Axils bare. Tubercles pyramidal, acutely four-angled, 12 to 16 mm. long, and about the same in thickness. Areoles at first slightly woolly, later bare. Radial spines mostly 6, sometimes up to 9, awl-shaped, spreading outwards, 5 to 9 mm. long, light coloured, tipped darker. Only one central spine, like the radials, straight or slightly arched. Flowers 2½ to 3 cm. long: inner petals whitish, with a broad pink central band; outer petals brownish green. Stamens white, style and 6- to 8-lobed stigma yellowish green. Fruit clavate, slender, curved, about 2 cm. long, carmine red. Seeds small, yellowish brown, minutely pitted.

Mammillaria crocidata Lem. = *M. Webbiana* Lem. Mexico (Hidalgo). Stem globular, dark bluish green, at first solitary, becoming elongated and cespitose when old, somewhat depressed at the top, and covered with floccose white wool, up to 10 cm. high, 7 to 8 cm. thick. Axils woolly. Tubercles pyramidal, four-sided, about 1 cm. long. Areoles very small, oval, at first very woolly, later almost bare. Spines mostly 4, sometimes 3, spreading outwards, the lower up to 1 cm. long, the upper smaller, diaphanous white, tipped brown, along with 1 or more thin and short subsidiary spines. Flowers in a ring near the top, 1½ cm. long; outer petals greenish white, fringed; the inner carmine red, edged paler. Stamens white, upper part of style pink, stigma with 5 reddish lobes.

Mammillaria Sartorii J. A. Purp. Mexico (Vera Cruz). Plant cespitose forming large clumps, dark bluish green. Stem globular or elongated, minutely dotted white, 8 to 12 cm. thick, depressed at the top, and furnished with white wool and short brown spines. Axils mostly woolly. Tubercles thick, pyramidal, four-sided, acute, 8 to 12 mm. long. Spines 4 to 6, all alike, 5 to 8 mm. long, whitish or brownish white, tipped brown. Only one central spine, like the radials, often absent. Flowers in a ring near the top, 2 cm. long, of a beautiful pale carmine red, with a darker central band, remaining open day and night for several days; petals linear-lanceolate with a fleshy tip, toothed; outer petals fringed. Stamens, style and 6-lobed stigma reddish.

Mammillaria roseo-alba Boedeker. Mexico (Tamaulipas). Stem mostly solitary, globular, flattened, bluish green, about 8 cm. thick. Axils at first bare, later woolly. Tubercles somewhat softish, pyramidal, four or five-sided. Areoles woolly when young. Radial spines 4 or 5, sometimes 6, about 8 mm. long, thin, awl-shaped, dark pink at the base, tipped white. Flowers few, up to 3 cm. long; outer petals brownish pink, edged paler, inner petals white with a pink midrib. Stamens white, style pink, with 6- to 7-lobed greenish yellow stigma. Fruit 1½ cm. long, red. Seeds minute, yellowish brown. A very beautiful species of recent introduction, with remarkably coloured spines.

Mammillaria phymatothele Berg. = *M. Ludwigii* Ehrbg. Mexico (Hidalgo). Stem dark greyish green, globular to clavate or cylindrical, at first solitary, later cespitose, 6 to 9 cm. thick, at the centre depressed and furnished with white wool. Axils and areoles woolly. Tubercles short and broadly conical, rounded above, angular or keeled on the lower surface, about 1 cm. long, obliquely pointed. Radial spines mostly 5, sometimes 3 or 4, or up to 7, awl-shaped, slightly curved, about 1 cm. long, the side ones being longer. Central spines 1 or 2, directed backwards, straight, up to 2 cm. long; dark red or orange yellow when new, passing to grey, tipped darker. Flowers 2 cm. long; outer petals dark brown edged paler, inner petals fiery carmine red. Stamens white, style yellowish below, pink above, stigma with 7 yellowish lobes.

Mammillaria magnimamma Haworth = *M. centricirrha* Lem. More commonly known under this name. Native of central Mexico, common over extensive areas. Plant freely cespitose, greyish green Stems globular, 10 to 15 cm. thick, with abundant white wool in the axils and areoles. Tubercles conical, slightly four-angled, 1 cm. long. Spines 3 to 5, of very unequal length, the upper ones short and straight, the lower 1 or 2 much longer, 1½ to 4½ cm. long, mostly curved backwards, or sometimes upwards, diaphanous yellow or whitish, tipped black. Flowers more or less creamy yellow, with a reddish midrib, the outer petals with a broader midrib. Stamens white, style white with the upper part pink, stigma with 5 or 6 yellowish or reddish lobes. Fruit clavate, 1½ cm. long, sometimes almost angular, carmine red. Seeds yellow to brown, smooth.

A very variable species, with a large number of varieties, which have been described under as many specific names. Of easy cultivation and propagation, thriving best in half-shade, and also easily grown from seed.

The typical form, to which the name *magnimma* Haw. properly applies, has a greyish dark green stem, with 4 yellowish white radial spines, tipped brown and recurved, the upper ones up to 1 cm. long, and the lower 1½ to 2 cm. long, thick and rigid, but no central spines.

var. **arietina** Salm-Dyck = *M. arietina* Lem. Plant larger and more vigorous. Areoles and axils very woolly. Areoles with 2 upper spines, small, and with 2 or 3 lower spines, white, thick, 4 to 6 cm. long, recurved and twisted like a ram's horn.

var. **lutescens** Salm-Dyck. Spines about as long as in the preceding variety, lemon yellow, tipped black.

var. **macrothele** Lem. non Mart. Plant more sturdy than the typical form, more bluish green; tubercles fewer, more angular, more acute at the tip. Spines shorter.

var. **Hopferiana** (Link) = *M. Hopferiana* Link. Plant smaller, tubercles smaller, spines more slender.

var. **Bockii** (Först.) = *M. Bockii* Först. Has a greyish green stem, with more acute angular tubercles, 4 radial spines, and 1 or 2 strongly curved, dark brown central spines.

var. **divergens** (DC.) = *M. divergens* DC. Stem greyish green, warts hardly angular; 4 radial spines almost always angular and recurved, at first yellow, passing to grey.

var. **Ehrenbergii** (Pfeiff.) = *M. Ehrenbergii* Pfeiff. Far less cespitose; tubercles oval-conical, deep green, slightly angular, covered with minute white dots. Axils and areoles very woolly, areoles later almost bare. Spines mostly reduced to 2, short, angular, about equal, white, tipped black, one directed upwards, the other downwards. Often considered as a distinct species.

var. **Krameri** K. Sch. = *M. Krameri* Muehlenpf. Warts brownish at the top, with sharp angles: radial spines 4 or 5, almost radiating horizontally. Only one central spine, up to 4 cm. long, curved downwards. All spines are at first yellow, passing to white. Flowers numerous, fiery carmine red. Probably a distinct species.

var. **recurva** K. Sch. = *M. recurva* Lehm. Stem very thick, warts dark brownish green, only slightly angular; radial spines 4, and 1 central spine, this last and the upper radial very thick and longer, honey yellow, the radial curved upwards, the central downwards.

There are over 100 varieties, with about 45 specific names.

Mammillaria macracantha DC. = *M. centricirrha* var. *macracantha* K. Sch. Mexico (San Luis Potosi). Similar to the preceding. Stem dark green, very thick, clustering when old. Tubercles large, oval, with sharp angles, four-sided. Young areoles and axils woolly. Radial spines 3 or 4, small, white, often absent. Central spines 2, yellowish brown, the upper curved upwards, the lower downwards, more or less angular. Flowers dark carmine red; petals linear. Stigma with 5 to 7 pink lobes. Possibly only a variety of the preceding.

Mammillaria Zuccariniana Mart. Central Mexico. Is an intermediate species between the preceding two, and often classed as a variety of *M. magnimamma*. Stem at first solitary, globular-depressed, later up to 27 cm. high, and up to 16 cm. thick. Axils at first woolly, later almost bare. Tubercles pyramidal-conical, 1 cm. long, with depressed areoles, almost bare. Central spines 2, ashy grey, tipped black, the upper one directed upwards, 9 mm. long, the lower directed downwards, up to 2½ cm. long, both arching. There are also 2 or 3 very short white bristle-like spines, often absent. Flowers more or less in a ring at the top, 2½ cm. long; outer petals purplish brown; inner petals longer, linear, acute, glossy purplish pink. Stamens white, style white below, pink above, stigma with 4 or 5 pink lobes.

Mammillaria Seitziana Mart. Mexico (Ixmiquilpan). A beautiful large species, free flowering, rather uncommon. Stem globular, passing to short-cylindric, about 10 cm. thick, and up to 25 cm. high, glaucous green, sprouting at the base and sides. Tubercles four-sided at the base. Axils with floccose white wool, and likewise the areoles when young. Spines 4, straight, the upper and lower of equal length, flesh-coloured or whitish, tipped black. There are also 2 central spines, about 1 cm. long, curved yellowish brown tipped black. Flowers in a ring at the top, 2 cm. long: petals linear-lanceolate, whitish, with a bright red midrib. Stamens white.

Mammillaria obscura Hildm. non Scheidw. Mexico. Stem solitary, dark green, globular-depressed, 9 to 11 cm. thick. Axils and areoles at first with white wool, afterwards bare. Tubercles pyramidal, four-sided, 7 to 8 mm. high. Radial spines 6 to 8, straight, awl-shaped, radiating, white, about 1 cm. long. Central spines 2 or 4, spreading, the lower 2 longer, up to 2 cm. long, slightly curved, all at first black, passing to grey. Flowers small, yellowish white, with a bright pink midrib.

Mammillaria Winteriae Boedeker. Mexico (Nuevo Leon, Monterey). Stem solitary, globular-depressed, up to 30 cm. thick. Axils at first slightly woolly, afterwards more densely. Tubercles fleshy and softish, large, four-angled, 1½ cm. long, 1½ to 2½ cm. thick at the base. New areoles woolly. Radial spines 4, crosswise, the laterals up to $1\frac{1}{2}$ cm. long, the others up to 3 cm. long, greyish red, tipped brown, thick, needle-like or rather thin and awl-shaped. No central spines. Flowers borne at or near the centre, about 3 cm. long: petals yellowish with a pink midrib. Stamens white below and violet pink above, style yellowish white, stigma with 5 or 6 yellowish green lobes. Fruit pale pink. Seeds dull reddish brown.

Mammillaria Zahniana Boedeker. Mexico (Coahuila). Stem mostly solitary, globular, more or less depressed, glossy dark green, about 10 cm. thick. Axils with floccose white wool. Tubercles softish, about 2 cm. long, four-angled, with a pronounced lower angle. Areoles with white wool when young. Radial spines 4, stiff, straight, diaphanous whitish, tipped dark, the upper ones about 8 mm. long, the lower ones up to 12 mm. long. No central spines. Flowers in a ring around the centre, about 3 cm. long: inner petals sulphur yellow, edged paler. Stamens yellowish white, style white, stigma with 8 to 10 pale green lobes. Fruit red; seeds reddish brown, rough.

Mammillaria carnea Zucc. $=$ *M. villifera* Otto $=$ *M. aeruginosa* Scheidw. Southern and central Mexico. Stem globular-elongated to cylindrical, dark bluish green or almost bronze colour, up to 10 cm. high, and 6 cm. thick, rounded at the top, sprouting from the base when old. New axils and areoles with white wool, later almost bare.

Tubercles rhomboid, four-angled, obliquely pointed, up to 1 cm. long, exuding a milky juice when wounded. Spines 4, spreading crosswise, the lower one the longest, up to 2 cm. long; all stiff, awl-shaped, straight or slightly curved, at first red, passing to dark brown, afterwards grey, tipped darker. Flowers in a ring at the top, 2 cm. long, $1\frac{1}{2}$ cm. broad, pale pink or pale carmine red. Stamens white, upper part of style pink, stigma with 4 greenish lobes.

Mammillaria Lloydii (Br. et R.) $=$ *Neomammillaria* Br. et R. Mexico (Zacatecas). Stem mostly solitary, at first globular-depressed, later short-cylindric, dark green. Axils at first slightly woolly, later bare. Tubercles very numerous and closely set together, four-sided, exuding a milky juice when wounded, 6 mm. long, 5 mm. thick, obliquely pointed. Areoles small, very slightly woolly when young. Spines 4, the lower 6 mm. long, the laterals shorter, all greyish white, the upper one erect, like a central spine, brown, tipped darker; 6 mm. long. Flowers numerous, in a ring at the top: outer petals dark red, edged paler; inner petals white or pink, with a dark red midrib. Upper part of stamens, style and stigma red.

Mammillaria flavovirens Salm-Dyck. Mexico. Stem globular to short-cylindric, 6 to 8 cm. thick, solitary or sprouting sparingly, glossy yellowish green. Axils and areoles almost bare. Tubercles pyramidal, four-angled, rather closely set, 10 mm. long. Radial spines 5, awl-shaped, $\frac{1}{2}$ cm. long, spreading outwards, yellowish, tipped reddish yellow, along with 2 smaller white subsidiary spines. One central spine, like the radials, up to 1 cm. long. Flowers about 2 cm. long and 12 mm. broad:

outer petals green with a reddish midrib; inner petals white with a pink midrib. Stamens and style white, stigma with 7 greenish lobes.

Mammillaria Trohartii Hildm. At first solitary, afterwards freely and densely cespitose, globular, slightly depressed, dark glaucous green, exuding a milky juice when wounded, with white wool and brown spines at the top, about 6 cm. thick. Axils bare. Tubercles conical, slightly angular, about ½ cm. long. Areoles small, round, at first with white wool, later bare. Radial spines 4 or 5, spreading, white, tipped brown, the lowermost and longest up to 8 mm. long. One central spine, often absent, stronger, straight or slightly curved, dark brown.

Mammillaria Wagneriana Böd. Mexico (Zacatecas). Mostly solitary, oval or short-cylindric, 6 to 9 cm. thick, slightly depressed at the top, pale glaucous green, with 8 or 9 spiral rows of obtuse-angled, almost conical tubercles 8 to 10 mm. long, slightly hairy in the axils. Areoles at first with white wool, later bare. Radial spines 10 to 12 spreading star-like, the upper ones bristle-like, white, 5 to 8 mm. long, the lower ones 1 to 2 cm. long, white, tipped reddish brown. Central spines at first 2, the upper curved inwards, the latter spreading outwards, later more numerous, purplish pink, darker at the tip. Flowers whitish pink. Prefers half-shade.

Mammillaria gigantea Hildm. = *M. MacDowellii* Heese = *M. guanajuatensis* Runge. Mexico (Guanajuato). Stem mostly solitary, globular-depressed, greyish green, 10 cm. high and 12 to 17 cm. thick, with white wool at the top. Axils with white wool. Tubercles numerous, up to 1 cm. long, thickly set together, four-sided. Areoles oval, at first copiously furnished with white wool, later almost bare. Radial spines up to 12, awl-shaped, straight, white, very short, about 3 mm. long. Central spines 4 to 6, very thick, mostly curved, the lowermost up to 2 cm. long, curved downwards, the others spreading, yellowish brown when new, tipped darker, passing to yellowish white, reddish at the base. Flowers greenish yellow.

Mammillaria sempervivi DC. Central Mexico. Stem solitary, or slowly sprouting from the base, dark green or greyish green, more or less globular or short-cylindric, with white wool and spiny at the top, about 7 cm. thick. Warts closely set together, short, about 9 mm. long, pyramidal, four-sided, sometimes five-sided, obliquely directed upwards. Axils woolly; areoles at first woolly, later bare. Radial spines in young plants 3 to 7, up to 3 mm. long, white, finally dropping off. Central spines 2, stiff, short, almost conical, slightly curved, the lower one, the longest, about 4 mm. long, reddish when new, passing to white or yellowish. Flowers numerous, at the top of the stem, about 1 cm. long, funnel-shaped; outer petals oblong, olive green or reddish; inner petals lanceolate-acute, dirty white with a red midrib. Stamens reddish, style white below and reddish above, stigma reddish with 4 or 5 spreading lobes.

Mammillaria caput-medusae Otto. = *M. sempervivi* var. *tetracantha* DC. = *M. staurotypa* Scheidw. Central Mexico. Stem mostly solitary, sometimes cespitose, globular-depressed to short-cylindric, about 6 cm. high and 7 cm. across, bluish green or greyish green, sometimes reddish, woolly and spiny at the top. Warts rather slender, conical, four-sided at the base, lower angle keeled, up to 1 cm. long. Axils woolly. Areoles small, at first woolly. Young areoles with 5 to 10 radial spines, white, bristle-like, 2 to 3 mm. long, soon dropping off, rarely persistent. Central spines mostly 4, spreading crosswise, sometimes 3 or 5, rarely 6 or 7, stiff, awl-shaped, white, all equal, about ½ cm. long; inner petals lanceolate-acute, flesh-coloured, with a darker dorsal band. Stamens and style white below and pink above, stigma with 4 or 5 whitish lobes.

Mammillaria Orcuttii Boedeker. Mexico (Puebla). Stem solitary, globular or short-clavate, glossy dark bluish green, with white wool and dark spines at the top. Axils very woolly, but without bristles. Warts softish, short, conical or oval, about 6 mm. long. New areoles densely woolly. Spines 4, rarely 5, strong, spreading outwards, straight, stiff, needle-like, at first pitch black or dark brown, passing to grey, the lowermost up to 2 cm. long, the upper 8 to 15 mm. long; along with these there are 6 to 8 white hair-like spines, about 2 mm. long. Flowers numerous, in a ring at the top, about 12 mm. long; inner petals pale carmine red, with a darker midrib.

Mammillaria Bachmannii Heese. Central Mexico. Similar to the preceding. Has a thick, dark green, globular stem, about 12 cm. thick. Warts large, conical, four-sided at the base. Areoles and axils woolly. Central spines 4, crosswise, black. Flowers small, pale pink.

Mammillaria Hamiltonhoytea (Helia Bravo) Werd. = *Neomammillaria* Helia Bravo. Mexico (Queretaro). Mostly solitary, rarely sprouting or branching. Stem globular, depressed at the top, olive green, up to 18 cm. in diameter. Axils bare. Areoles almost bare. Warts in 13 or 14 series, exuding a milky juice when wounded. Radial spines mostly 5, white, tipped brown, up to 8 mm. long. Central spines 3, stronger, the upper one up to 2 cm. long, the lower up to 3 cm. long and curved backwards, at first reddish, passing to ash grey. Flowers in a ring at the top, 2 cm. long, purplish, the outer petals more violet. Stamens white, style and 4- to 5-lobed stigma whitish.

(b). *Uncinatae.* At least one central spine strongly hooked.

Mammillaria uncinata Zucc. = *M. bihamata* Pfeiff. = *M. adunca* Scheidw. Central Mexico (San Luis Potosi, Hidalgo). Stem solitary, globular-flattened, depressed at the centre, bluish green, 3 to 8 cm. high, 5 to 10 cm. thick. Axils with white wool. Warts exuding a milky sap when wounded, regularly angular, 7 to 9 mm. long, 8 to 11 mm. thick. Areoles at first with short white wool, later bare. Radial spines 4 to 6, more or less spreading outwards crosswise, white, 4 to 5 mm. long. Central spines mostly 1, sometimes 2 or 3, much thicker, 12 mm. long, dark brown, strongly hooked at the tip. Flowers 2 cm. long: inner petals lanceolate-acute, pale red, with a darker midrib. Stamens and style whitish, stigma with 5 or 6 yellowish red lobes. An interesting and resistant species; prefers full sunshine.

Series 10. POLYEDRAE Pfeiff.

Tubercles firm, large, angular, exuding a milky juice when wounded. Axils with wool and stiff bristles.

Mammillaria Eichlamii Quehl. Guatemala, on sandy and stony soils. Plant freely cespitose, yellowish green, clavate or cylindrical, 15 to 25 cm. high and 4 to 6 cm. thick. with dirty yellowish hair at the top. Axils with yellowish wool and 5 or 6 whitish bristles. Tubercles conical, only slightly angular. Areoles small, with yellowish wool. Radial spines 6, sometimes 7 or 8, white, tipped brown, 5 to 7 mm. long. Only one central spine, yellowish, brownish red towards the tip, 1 cm. long. Flowers in a ring at the top, 2 cm. long: outer petals acute, yellow, with a brownish dorsal band: inner petals pure yellow. Stamens pale yellow, style yellow, stigma with 5 yellowish green lobes. The plant is profusely cespitose, growing into large rounded masses, the sprouts dropping off easily when handled, and quickly rooting. Full sunshine.

var. **albida** Hort. Axils and areoles with whitish wool.

Mammillaria chapinensis Eichl. et Quehl. Guatemala, in half-shaded localities. Profusely cespitose, dark green, woolly at the top. Stem globular to cylindrical, sprouting into broad clumps in the half-shade of bushes. Axils furnished copiously with white wool and bristles. Tubercles angular, about 1 cm. long, exuding abundantly a milky juice when wounded. Areoles oval, at first woolly, later bare. Radial spines 5 to 9, yellowish or white, tipped reddish brown, about ½ cm. long. Central spines 1 to 8, of various lengths up to 2 cm. yellow or reddish. Flowers 2 cm. long, yellow, the outer petals with brownish dorsal band. Stamens and style white, stigma with 5 yellowish lobes. A variable species.

var. **rubescens** Hort. Plant reddish or reddish brown.

Mammillaria Esseriana Boedeker. Southern Mexico. Stem solitary, clavate, almost rounded at the top, dull glaucous green, with erect yellow spines, repeatedly dividing itself dichotomously, resulting in large clumps with numerous heads, each head or stem about 10 cm. high and 6 cm. thick. Axils with white wool and with long bristles, up to 15. Tubercles four-sided at the base, keeled at the lower angle, more flattened at the upper, 8 mm. long and thick, obliquely pointed upwards. Areoles at first very woolly, later bare. Radial spines up to 10, directed laterally and downwards, white, stiff, almost needle-like, 3 mm. long, the lower ones up to 8 mm. long. Central spines 6, spreading upwards, awl-shaped or needle-like, the upper 7 mm. long, the lower up to 1½ cm., all diaphanous amber yellow, tipped reddish brown. Flowers 12 mm. broad: outer petals greenish with a brown midrib, toothed: the inner narrow, lanceolate-acute, fiery carmine, with a darker midrib. Stamens and style deep pink, stigma with 5 or 6 pale pink lobes.

Mammillaria tenampensis Br. et R. = *Neomammillaria* Br. et R. Mexico (Barranca de Tenampo). Stem globular, yellowish green, 5 to 6 cm. thick. Axils at first bare, developing yellowish wool and yellowish bristles when about to flower, the others developing white bristles. Tubercles pyramidal, acute, four-sided, 6 to 7 mm. long, exuding a milky juice when wounded. Young areoles with yellow wool, later bare. Spines 4 to 6, brownish tipped darker, spreading upwards, up to 1 cm. long, having along with them 8 to 10 small white bristles. Flowers borne at the centre: outer petals lanceolate, brownish, fringed or ciliated; inner petals purple red, toothed. Style and upper part of stamens reddish, stigma with 4 or 5 lobes. Prefers full sunshine.

Mammillaria polygona Salm-Dyck. Mexico. Stem solitary, almost clavate, dull green. Axils with white wool and white bristles. Tubercles large, four-sided, with a pronounced acute keel on the lower side. Radial spines 8, the upper 2 or 3 very small, the 4 laterals and the lower one longer. Central spines 2, often long and curved backwards, flesh-coloured, tipped brown. Flowers pale pink. Stigma with 5 or 6 lobes. Now rare in cultivation.

Mammillaria chionocephala J. A. Purp. Mexico (Coahuila). Stem slowly cespitose, globular, bluish green, up to 8 cm. thick, slightly depressed at the centre, entirely covered with short white spines and white wool. Axils copiously furnished with white wool and with numerous white bristles up to 2 cm. long. Tubercles short, slightly four-sided, abundantly exuding a milky juice when wounded. Radial spines 35 to 40, almost pectinate, spreading outwards, white, up to 8 mm. long. Central spines 2 to 7, shorter and thicker, white, tipped brown, spreading. Flowers 1 cm. long, of a lively pink or flesh colour. Fruit clavate, red. Requires a chalky stony soil, in full sunshine, and liberal watering in summer. The woolly growth at the top of the plant is rather poor on cultivated plants.

Mammillaria polyedra Mart. = *M. polytricha* Salm-Dyck. Mexico (Oaxaca). Stem solitary or slowly cespitose, globular or clavate, tender green passing to greyish green, 10 to 20 cm. high, and 7 to 12 cm. thick, depressed at the centre. Axils with whitish or yellowish wool and with many white protruding bristles. Tubercles exuding a milky juice when wounded, five-sided, upper and lower angles very acute at the base, with 2 angles on the lower side, and 3 or 4 on the upper, about 12 mm. long, acute at the top. Areoles round, with short white curly wool. Radial spines 4 or 5, straight, white, tipped brown, 2 to 5 mm. long, later up to 1 cm. long, spreading. Only one central spine, along with the radials, on the upper part of the areole, about 1 cm. long, later up to 2 cm. long, ivory white or flesh-coloured, tipped brown or black when new. All spines finally passing to greyish. Flowers in a ring, up to 2 cm. long, funnel-shaped: inner petals linear-lanceolate, pinkish, toothed; outer petals broader, acute, ciliated, reddish green, edged white. Stamens and style white, stigma with 8 yellowish green lobes. Fruit clavate, 2 cm. long, carmine red, juicy. Seeds very small, yellowish brown, pitted. A variable species. *M. subpolyedra* Mart., is a variety with a stem more flat at the top, warts with 5 or 6 angles, more irregular, flowers smaller but more expanded.

Mammillaria Karwinskiana Mart. Mexico (Oaxaca). Stem globular or short-cylindric, at first solitary, later repeatedly branching dichotomously, flat at the top, dark green or dark bluish green, 7 to 9 cm. high, and about equally thick. Axils woolly and with protruding bristles. Tubercles emitting a milky juice when wounded, about 12 mm. long, acute and angular, and furrowed underneath with two furrows, and also furrowed above with three of four furrows. Areoles roundish, woolly when young, afterwards almost bare. Spines 4 to 6, straight, greyish white, tipped darker, unequal, the uppermost being the longest and slightly curved, up to 12 mm. long. Flowers 2 cm. long, in a ring at the top, funnel-shaped: outer petals reddish green, the inner creamy white, acute and minutely toothed. Stamens and style white, stigma with 4 or 5 greenish yellow lobes. There is also a cristate form in cultivation.

var. **senilis** Hort. Axils with more abundant wool and more numerous bristles.

var. **centrispina** Salm-Dyck = *M. centrispina* Pfeiff. This is probably a distinct species. Stem 8 to 10 cm. thick, globular, solitary. Axils woolly, with a few bristles. Areoles woolly when young, later bare. Radial spines 6 or 7, stiff, white, tipped black, 4 to 9 mm. long, with 2 other smaller spines on the upper part of the areole. One central spine, thicker and longer, $2\frac{1}{2}$ to 3 cm. long, rarely absent. Flowers in a ring, pale pink, petals acute with a darker midrib. The name *centrispina* is also often given by mistake to *M. macracantha* and to *M. magnimamma* var. *Krameri*.

Mammillaria Fischeri Pfeiff. = *M. virens* Scheidw. Mexico (Oaxaca). Often considered as a variety of *M. Karwinskiana*. Has a similar branching stem, of a tender green; areoles with yellowish wool passing to whitish: axils with white wool and a few short bristles. Spines 4 to 6, pale reddish to pale brown, passing to grey, tipped darker. There is also usually a thick short central spine. The flowers are pale yellow with a pink midrib.

Mammillaria mystax Mart. = *M. mutabilis* Scheidw. = *M. maschalacantha* Cels. Southern Mexico, on heights up to 2,600 m. above sea level. Stem usually solitary, but occasionally sprouting, globular to short-cylindric, flattened or depressed at the top, dark greyish green, often reddish or purplish or bronze, slightly woolly at the top and covered with long variously twisted or curved spines, dull white or flesh-coloured. Axils woolly with long white bristles. Tubercles pyramidal, four-sided, with a prominent keel on the lower side, 10 to 12 mm. long. Areoles at first with white wool, later bare. Radial spines 1 ot 4 (sometimes 8 to 10), small, white, often absent.

Central spines 1 to 4, mostly 2 or 3, of which the upper one, and when there are, only 2, also the lower one, are 3 to 7 cm. long, angular, curved and twisted, at first red passing to dull white or flesh-coloured or grey, tipped darker, the upper one curved upwards or laterally, the lower one also downwards and laterally. Flowers numerous in a ring around the top, 1½ to 2½ cm. long: inner petals lanceolate-acute, minutely toothed, of a lively carmine red, paler at the base. Stamens white, style white below and pink above, stigma with 5 to 7 yellowish lobes. Berry short-clavate, crimson, juicy: seeds minute, yellow. One of the most beautiful species in this series, of easy cultivation in full sunshine. Offers several varieties.

var. **leucotricha** (Scheidw.) Monv. = *M. leucotricha* Scheidw. Axils with long bristles, entirely white. One central spine, sometimes 2, very long; radial spines more yellowish brown.

var. **xanthotricha** (Scheidw.) Monv. = *M. xanthotricha* Scheidw. The bristles in the axils are more numerous, and yellowish; radial spines yellowish brown; only one central spine, and rather short.

var. **autumnalis** (Dietr.) = *M. autumnalis* Dietr. The flowers are larger and make their appearance in autumn. Tubercles pyramidal, four-sided, with very pronounced angles and minutely dotted. Stamens purplish, style green.

var. **leucocarpa** (Scheidw.) = *M. leucocarpa* Scheidw. Fruit pale pink or whitish. Central spines more flesh-coloured.

var. **longispina** Hort. Central spines longer.

var. **rufispina** Hort. Central spines reddish to reddish brown.

Mammillaria compressa DC. = *M. angularis* Link et Otto = *M. cirrhifera* Först. non Mart. Central Mexico. A well known and variable species, better known as *M. angularis*. Plant densely and broadly cespitose. Stem globular-clavate, pale greyish green, somewhat flattened and with short white wool at the top. Axils with abundant white wool and with long white bristles. Tubercles short and thick, 8 to 10 mm. broad, and 4 to 6 mm. high, closely packed together, rhomboid, four-angled, keeled on the under side, rounded on the upper side, obliquely pointed. Areoles with white wool, later almost bare. Spines mostly 4, sometimes 5 to 7, the lower directed outwards or curved backwards, 2 to 7 cm. long, almost angular, the others shorter; all very stiff, at first reddish, passing to whitish, later greyish, tipped darker. Flowers rather rarely borne, in a ring around the top, 1 to 1¼ cm. long: outer petals somewhat fringed, inner petals pink with a darker midrib. Stamens and style pale red, stigma with 5 or 6 white lobes. A very resistant species, growing quickly into large clumps, and thrives well in half-shade as well as in full sunshine.

var. **compressa** K. Sch. Stem smaller, more flattened, up to 5 cm. thick. Axils less woolly. Tubercles more closely packed, angular above. Radial spines 5, white, tipped brown.

var. **fulvispina** K. Sch. Stem up to 8 cm. thick, as in the typical form, axils not very woolly, warts rounded above. Spines 5, yellowish brown, tipped black when new, the lower up to 3 cm. long.

var. **longiseta** Salm-Dyck. Strong-growing, up to 9 cm. thick, axils very woolly. Spines up to 7, and 1 central spine, up to 4 cm. long, white, tipped yellowish brown.

var. **triacantha** Salm-Dyck. Stem smaller, up to 5 cm. thick, axils very woolly; spines 3, white, tipped yellowish brown, the lower one up to 2 cm. long.

var. **rubrispina** Hort. Spines red, when new.

var. **brevispina** Hort. Spines only about 1 cm. long.

There is also a cristate form in cultivation.

Mammillaria Pettersonii Hildm. ═ *M. Heeseana* MacDowell. Mexico (Guanajuato). Stem mostly solitary, broadly globular, greyish green or glaucous green, later short-cylindric, up to 12 cm. thick, depressed at the centre, covered at the top, with long reddish brown spines and white wool. Axils with white wool and bristles. Tubercles pyramidal, four-sided, obtuse, obliquely directed upwards. Radial spines 10 to 14, the upper 3 white, up to 3 mm. long, the others up to 1½ cm. long, the laterals being the longest, white, dark-tipped. Central spines 4, chestnut brown, straight, thick, the lower one up to 4½ cm. long. Formerly rare in cultivation, now again frequently offered. Flowers said to be red. There is a form with spines up to 2 cm. and another with longer spines, up to 6 cm.

Mammillaria Knippeliana Quehl. Mexico. Stem solitary, globular, 7 cm. high, 6 cm. thick, tender green, occasionally branching dichotomously. Axils with white wool and white bristles. Tubercles 8 mm. long, pyramidal, with 4 or 5 angles. Areoles round, at first with white wool, later almost bare. Spines mostly 6, whitish, tipped red or brown, awl-shaped, spreading, the upper up to 3 cm. long, the lower up to 6 cm., often having along with them a few short white bristle-like spines. Flowers 1½ cm. long: outer petals red, fringed, edged yellow; inner petals yellow, with a reddish dorsal band, or yellow, tipped red. Stamens and style white, stigma with 6 pale green lobes.

Mammillaria Scrippsiana (Br. et R.) ═ *Neomammillaria* Br. et R. Mexico (Jalisco). Globular, later oval, glossy pale green or grass green, somewhat depressed at the top, 6 to 8 cm. thick, sprouting around the sides and forming groups. Tubercles in 8 to 10 spiral rows, pyramidal, four-angled, 8 to 10 mm. long, the lower angle more acute, with a small beak-like gibbosity below the areole, with woolly axils. Areoles with abundant white wool, and with 4 to 6 slender radial spines, white or glassy white, bristle-like, ½ to 1½ cm. long. Flowers small, 1 to 1½ cm. across, borne at or near the centre: petals narrow, mostly reflexed, pale pink or whitish, with a darker median line.

Mammillaria Praelii Muehlenpf. ═ *M. viridis* Salm-Dyck. Guatemala. Stem globular to short-cylindric, glossy dark green, freely cespitose when old, rather depressed at the centre, with abundant

(b) MAMMILLARIA GULZOWIANA

(a) MAMMILLARIA DIOICA

PLATE LVIII

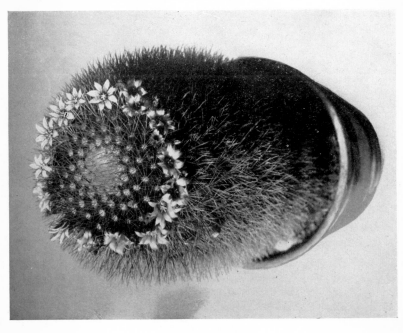

(a) MAMMILLARIA SPINOSISSIMA

PLATE LIX

white wool, and yellowish spines at the top. Axils with copious white wool and long protruding white bristles. Tubercles 9 mm. long, pyramidal, four-sided, obliquely pointed, with woolly areoles. Spines mostly 4, sometimes 5 or 6, more or less spreading outwards crosswise, needle-like, yellowish passing to white, tipped brown, the upper one and the lower longer than the others, up to 1 cm. Flowers in a ring around the centre, about 1½ cm. long, funnel-shaped: outer petals oblong-acute, yellowish white: the inner lanceolate, obtuse, recurved, pale yellow, with a narrow reddish dorsal band. Stamens and style white, 6-lobed stigma green.

Mammillaria Mendeliana (Helia Bravo) Werd. = *Neomammillaria* Helia Bravo. Mexico (Guanajuato). Stem solitary, globular, 8 to 9 cm. thick, dark olive green. Axils well furnished with white wool and white bristles. Tubercles roundish, in 21 rows, emitting a milky juice when wounded. Areoles slightly woolly when young, later bare. Radial spines short, bristle-like or hair-like, white. Central spines 4, crosswise, often reduced to 2 or 1, straight, the lower-most and longest 1½ to 2 cm. long, reddish to black when young, later greyish. Flowers said to be pink.

Mammillaria pyrrhocephala Scheidw. = *M. Senckei* Först. Mexico (Oaxaca, Hidalgo). Stem sprouting from the base and sides, globular to cylindrical, 8 cm. thick, green or greyish green, depressed at the centre and furnished with white wool. Axils with white wool and white bristles. Tubercles pyramidal, with 4 or 5 sides, strongly keeled on the lower side, 1 cm. long, 6 to 7 mm. thick. Areoles oval, woolly on the upper ones. Radial spines 6, star-like, 2 to 4 mm. long, at first black, passing to white, tipped brown, the lower one thicker and longer. Only one central spine, yellowish white, 3 mm. long, thicker than the radials, often absent. Flowers in a ring around the top, 2 cm. long, funnel-shaped: inner petals lanceolate-acute, glossy carmine red. Stamens reddish, style and 5-lobed stigma green.

var. **Malletiana** (Cels.) = *M. Malletiana* Cels. Plant more slender, tubercles more closely packed. Flowers yellow with a reddish midrib, Stamens yellow. Often considered as a distinct species.

var. **fulvolanata** (Hildm.) = *M. fulvolanata* Hildm. Axils and areoles with yellowish wool. Plant large, as in the typical form, less freely cespitose.

var. **Donkelaeri** Salm-Dyck. Plant larger than the typical form, of a paler green. Axils and areoles with white wool.

var. **confusa** (Br. et R.) = *Neomammillaria confusa* Br. et R. Plant smaller; flowers greenish yellow. Probably a distinct species.

This large genus includes also a considerable number of other species and varieties, many of which are now in cultivation. A selection is given in the following list, and except where otherwise stated, the species are Mexican.

Mammillaria bicornuta Tiegel, **M. Brauneana** Boedeker, **M. bucare-**

liensis Tiegel, **M. calacantha** Tiegel, **M. capensis** Gates, **M. Collinsii** Br. et R., **M. Conzattii** Br. et R., **M. Dietrichae** Tiegel, **M. Evermanniana** Br. et R., **M. Fraileana** Br. et R., **M. Gaumeri** Br. et R., **M. Hoffmanniana** Tiegel, **M. Johnstonii** Br. et R., **M. Martinezii** Tiegel, **M. Mieheana** Tiegel, **M. Milleri** Br. et R. (Arizona and California), **M. Morganiana** Tiegel, **M. multiformis** Br. et R., **M. Nealeana** Schmoll, **M. Nelsonii** Br. et R., **M. nidulata** Tiegel, **M. Nunezii** Br. et R., **M. occidentalis** Br. et R., **M. Ortegae** Br. et R., **M. peninsularis** Br. et R., Lower California, **M. roseocentra** Boedeker, **M. Solisii** Br. et R., **M. Swinglei** Br. et R., **M. tacubayensis** Br. et R., **M. Tiegeliana** Schmoll, **M. Vaupelii** Tiegel, and its variety **flavispina** Tiegel, **M. viridiflora** Br. et R. Arizona, and **M. xanthina** Br. et R.

SUB-TRIBE VII. EPIPHYLLANAE

Mostly epiphytic plants, growing on trees in the primeval forests, and also on the ground provided that it is rich in humus. These plants are generally spineless and much branched, with flat stems or branches, with areoles along the margin. The flowers may be regular or irregular and zygomorphic, usually with long protruding stamens and style, mostly large and showy. The fruit, red or purple, is generally bare, but may have areoles, either bare or furnished with hairs and bristles. The seeds are small and black.

These are mostly shade-loving plants, and although most of them will thrive well in half-shade, few of them will bear full exposure to the sun for prolonged periods without injury. A moist and warm atmosphere is necessary; and the soil should be very porous and well drained, but also substantial and nourishing, made up of crushed bricks and crushed charcoal, old leaf-mould, old cow manure and good granular garden loam, one part of each of these five substances. Instead of leaf-mould, fibrous peat may be used, and the addition of a little sharp sand is also beneficial.

ZYGOCACTUS K. Sch.

Stems much branched and jointed. Joints flat, 2-angled, flowering and branching more or less dichotomously from an elongated linear areole at the top of the joint, never or very rarely from the small areoles on each margin at the sides. Flowers irregular or zygomorphic. Stamens in two groups. Lobes of stigma close together in a round mass.

Zygocactus truncatus (Haw.) K. Sch. = *Epiphyllum truncatum* Haworth. Eastern Brazil (Rio de Janeiro); on stems of forest trees, and on shaded craggy shelves in hilly places and ravines. Plant hanging, of a lively green, where not exposed to the sun. Joints 4 to $5\frac{1}{2}$ cm. long, $1\frac{1}{2}$ to $2\frac{1}{2}$ cm. broad, flat, with 2 to 4 more or less acute teeth on each side, the upper tooth being always more pronounced. Flowers $6\frac{1}{2}$ to 8 cm. long, pink or deep red or claret. Ovary pear-shaped or oval, smooth; tube long, clad with segments of the perianth of the same size and colour, the tube terminating obliquely in a zygomorphic limb, looking downwards, with spreading segments, the lower or inner ones strongly recurved. Stamens and pistil exserted beyond the throat, the stamens of the inner group with an appendix at the base recurved backwards. Fruit oval or pear-shaped, very smooth, mostly dull vinous red.

A lovely plant, in many handsome varieties, flowering more or less profusely in October-January, very desirable for indoor decoration in a dull and flowerless period of the year; the flowers lasting for about 15 days. Full grown specimens, with 200 flowers or more, in bloom at the same time, are a sight to remember. May be grown on own roots as a hanging plant, but is mostly grafted on species of *Pereskia* (*P. aculeata*, etc.) or on *Hylocereus trigonus*, *H. undatus*, *H. triangularis* as a standard plant, as well as on columnar *Cerei*. *Selenicereus Macdonaldiae*, *S. Kunthianus*, *S. pteranthus*, and to a lesser extent other species of *Selenicereus*, are excellent grafting stock for growing standard plants. Should be kept in a shaded place in the open, not under glass, except in frosty weather, and should be syringed frequently throughout spring and summer. In late autumn, when the flower buds are forming, the plants may be taken into an airy and sunny greenhouse to avoid the danger of frost, and to develop their flowers to perfection. There are about 60 garden varieties or hybrids of this plant in cultivation.

var. **Altensteinii** (Pfeiff.) = *Epiphyllum Altensteinii* Pfeiff. From the same district in Brazil; differs from the typical form by the teeth on each side of the joint being more pronounced and acute. The flowers are of the same shape and size, or slightly larger, and the colour is carmine scarlet to scarlet, or brick red, or crimson. The habit of growth as a hanging plant is the same, but is distinctly more vigorous.

var. **delicatus** (N.E. Brown.)=*Epiphyllum delicatum* N. E. Brown. From the same district in Brazil. Has a more erect habit of growth. Joints narrower and longer, up to 7 cm. yellowish green or dull green, abruptly truncated at the top, with 3 or 4 very acuminate teeth on each side. Flowers in October-November, the buds are at first pure white, opening to a very delicate pink or flesh-colour; stamens white, style deep pink, with crimson stigma. In a shaded glasshouse the flowers are mostly of a pure glossy white, turning to flesh colour only when fading, sharply in contrast with the crimson ring at the throat and with the highly coloured style and stigma. More than of a distinct natural variety, the characters are those of a subspecies.

var. **crenatus** Borg. *n. var.* From the same district and often listed by dealers under the name of *violaceus* indiscriminately with horticultural varieties or hybrids of *Z. truncatus* of about the same shade of colour. Joints $1\frac{1}{2}$ to 2 cm. broad and up to 6 cm. long, greyish green, with 2 or 3, rarely 4, *crenate* teeth on each side, perfectly rounded or obtuse, not acute, each areole with 1 or 2 short white bristles; the top of the joint is more or less rounded, not abruptly truncated. The flower is slightly smaller than that of the typical *Z. truncatus*, with a more slender tube, but the same in form, and of bluish violet colour.

CACTI

The branches are more numerous and longer, and more decidedly hanging or pendulous. Flowers late in December or in January, and is exceedingly free-flowering. The fruit is more freely set, and is pear-shaped, 1½ to 2 cm. long, dull purplish violet, and the seeds reproduce the variety with all its characters. Indeed, it is more like a distinct species, than a subspecies or variety.

Latin diagnosis:

var. *crenatus Borg. A forma typica differt ramis longioribus, tenuioribus, magisque pendulis; articulis 1½ ad 2 cm. latis et ad 6 cm. longis, cineraceo-viridis, apice arcuato, non abrupte truncato; marginibus crenatis, 2 aut 3, rarius 4, denticulis late obtusis; flore coeruleo-violaceo, laciniis brevioribus et strictioribus, tubo tenuiore; fructu pyriformi-ovali, 1½ ad 2cm. longo, purpureo-violaceo.*

EPIPHYLLANTHUS Berger

Plants with the same habit of growth as the preceding, more or less branched, the joints being cylindrical or flattened, with areoles scattered all over the surface, like a miniature Opuntia; areoles minute, usually with 1 or 2 short white bristles or bristle-like spines. The joints are rounded at the edges, almost abruptly truncated or slightly rounded at the top, with a long linear areole from which 1 to 3 branches or joints are developed. The flowers are zygomorphic, exactly like those of *Zygocactus*, but only about ½ or ⅔ as large, purplish violet to white. Ovary angular. Includes 3 species natives of eastern Brazil.

Epiphyllanthus obtusangulus (K. Sch.) Berger = *Cereus obtusangulus* K. Sch. = *Epiphyllum obtusangulus* G. A. Lindb. Joints of oval shape, flattened, deep green, covered on both surfaces with minute whitish or greyish areoles, slightly raised above the surface, 2½ to 4½ cm. long, and 1 to 2 cm. broad. Flowers purplish violet, in spring or early summer, produced sparingly from the linear areole at the top of the joint, as in *Zygocactus*. Growth is slow. Requires the same treatment as *Zygocactus*. May be grown on own roots, but grows better when grafted.

The other species are:

Epiphyllanthus obovatus (Engelm.) Br. et R. = *Epiphyllum obovatum* Engelm. = *Epiphyllum opuntioides* Löfgren. With flattened joints, like the preceding, but larger, with purple flowers.

Epiphyllanthus candidus (Löfgren) Br. et R. = *Zygocactus candidus* Löfgren = *Epiphyllum candidum* Barboso-Rodriques. Has very slender, roundish, cylindrical joints, and small white flowers.

SCHLUMBERGERA Lemaire

Plants with the same habit of growth as *Zygocactus*, much branched. Joints mostly flattened, with acute sides. Flowers regular or actinomorphic, with a short tube, segments purple to scarlet. Ovary and fruit 5-angled, bare, with 5 scales at the top. Fruit oval or round, mostly red, with 5 wing-like angles.

Includes 2 species, natives of Brazil.

Schlumbergera Russelliana (Hook.) Lemaire = *Epiphyllum Russellianum* Hooker. Eastern Brazil. Joints oval or elongated, 2 to 2½ cm. long, 1 to 2 cm. broad, with 1 or 2 notches along the sides, with 1 or 2 bristles in each. Flowers 5 cm. long, 3 to 4 cm. broad, campanulate, regular, or very slightly irregular. Ovary with 4 angles, tube straight, not oblique at the throat, with about 20 acute, violet pink petals. Stamens in 2 groups, the outer, about 20, inserted on the tube, the others, about 10, on the ovary. Flowers in spring; rather rare in cultivation.

Schlumbergera Gaertneri (K. Sch.) Br. et R. = *Epiphyllum Gaertneri* K. Sch. = *E. Russellianum* var. *Gaertneri* Regel = *Rhipsalis* Vaup. = *Epiphyllopsis* Berger. South Brazil (Santa Catharina). Joints mostly 4 cm. long, sometimes up to 7 cm. and 2 to 2½ cm. broad, oval or oval-elongated, with acute side margins, having 3 to 5 notches with areoles on each, with 1 or 2 bristles in each areole. The joints are abruptly truncated at the top, with a long linear areole, bearing short yellowish bristles. Flowers borne profusely in spring (April-May) on the top areoles, perfectly regular or actinomorphic, star-like, 4 to 5 cm. broad, scarlet red, with a short tube. Petals numerous, acute, spreading all round, often almost recurved. Stamens inserted on the ovary, all equal, red. Style longer, white; stigma with 5 or 6 radiating lobes. Fruit scarlet, oval, acutely 5-angled, 1 to 1½ cm. long. A handsome species, very free-flowering, even on quite young plants, requiring the same cultivation and treatment as *Zygocactus*. Thrives better when grafted on a *Selenicereus* or on *Hylocereus undatus*.

var. **Mackoyana** W. Wats. Joints stiffer, with many stiff, thick, yellowish or brownish bristles, 1 to 2 cm. long, on the top areole.

EPIPHYLLUM Haworth
(*Phyllocactus* Link = *Euphyllocactus* K. Sch.)

Epiphytic plants with main woody stems, and flat leaf-like branches, variously toothed or notched on either side, sometimes 3-winged. Areoles small, situated in the notches, mostly bare, often associated with bristles, rarely with spines except when young. Flowers large and showy, mostly diurnal, furnished with a tube, often very long and slender. Ovary scaly or almost bare. Petals and stamens numerous. Fruit roundish or oval, rather large, red or purple, edible, often with a delicious flavour, smooth or with a few warts; pulp white or red; seeds black.

Includes 17 species.

Epiphyllum phyllanthus Haworth = *Cactus phyllanthus* L. = *Phyllocactus phyllanthus* Link. From Panama to southern Brazil, Bolivia and Peru. Stems numerous, with 3 or 4 angles: branches long, 3 to 7 cm. broad, thin, pale green, with a reddish margin, which later becomes almost woody, broadly serrated. Flowers 25 to 30 cm. long, with a very long and narrow tube. Petals 2 to 2½ cm. long, narrow, white. Style reddish, stigma with white lobes. Flowers nocturnal.

Fruit 8 to 9 cm. long, red, slightly furrowed. Seeds kidney shaped, pitted.

var. **boliviensis** Weber. Petals disposed star-like, 3 cm. long. Style lively red. Very free-flowering. Bolivia.

var. **paraguayensis** Weber. Style pale red, often almost white. Paraguay.

var. **columbiensis** Weber. Tube about 6 cm. long. Colombia.

Epiphyllum oxypetalum (DC.) Br. et R. = *Cereus oxypetalum* DC. = *Phyllocactus oxypetalus* Link. = *Ph. grandis* Lem. From Mexico to Brazil. Stems over 2 m. high, cylindrical. Branches thin, long, pointed, erect feather-like, often wavy. Flowers over 30 cm. long, and 12 cm. broad, with a green ovary, slightly angular, with short scales. Tube scaly below, brownish, about 24 cm. long, more or less curved. Outer petals narrow acute, reddish; inner petals broader, lanceolate, 9½ cm. long, pure white. Stamens and style white, lobes of stigma creamy white.

Epiphyllum latifrons (Link) Zuccarini=*Phyllocactus latifrons* Link. Mexico. Stems up to 2 m. high, erect, more or less cylindrical. Branches large, with shallow notches, few and far apart, obtuse at the top, green, with a more or less horny margin. Flowers 15 to 17 cm. broad; tube about as long, angular, green or reddish brown; outer petals linear, pink or pinkish; inner petals broader, greenish white on the dorsal side and slightly pink along the margin, white on the inner side. Style red, stigma with 8 yellow lobes. Often confused with the preceding, from which it is at once distinguished by the red style. Very free-flowering.

Epiphyllum stenopetalum (Salm-Dyck) Br. et R. = *Phyllocactus stenopetalus* Salm-Dyck. Mexico (Vera Cruz). Similar to the preceding in habit and branches. Flowers lasting only one night, 25 to 28 cm. long; tube 12 to 19 cm. long, with a few reddish scales. Petals fairly numerous; the outer ones more or less greenish white; the inner narrow, white, 5 to 8 cm. long, and 4 mm. broad. Stamens white, style very thin, carmine red; stigma with 12 to 14 golden yellow lobes. The plant is erect, very branched, with long, subserrate or crenate branches, up to 1 m. long.

Epiphyllum macropterum (Lem.) Br. et R. = *Phyllocactus macropterus* Lem. = *Ph. Thomasianus* K. Sch. Central America. A large plant about 3 m. high, much branched. Branches up to 40 cm. long, lanceolate, obtuse, pale green, 8 to 15 cm. broad, horny along the margin. Areoles in slight notches, 4 to 6 cm. apart. Flowers up to 30 cm. long, diurnal, very regular. Ovary almost cylindrical, with short triangular scales; limb broadly funnel-shaped, 15 to 20 cm. across; outer petals linear, acute, yellowish, with a reddish dorsal band; inner petals spathulate, pure white or slightly yellowish. Stamens chrome yellow, style white, stigma with 14 yellow lobes.

var. **Thomasianum** (K. Sch.). Branches narrower, 5 to 8 cm. broad, sometimes over 1 m. long, not horny along the margin. Areoles 3 cm. apart. Flowers as large or larger; same colour.

Epiphyllum strictum (Lem.) Br. et R. = *Phyllocactus strictus* Lem. Honduras and Guatemala. A large plant, about 2 m. high, with cylindrical main stems, and with narrow branches, pale green to bluish green, regularly notched along the sides. Flowers up to 25 cm. long, lasting only one night. Ovary and tube with a few scales: limb 10 cm. broad or slightly more. Outer petals narrow, linear, acute, pale green or brownish; inner petals narrow, linear-lanceolate, pure white. Stamens white, style white below and pink in its upper part. Stigma with 10 to 12 yellowish lobes.

Epiphyllum Ruestii (Weingt.) = *Phyllocactus Ruestii* Weingt. Honduras. Similar to the preceding, but the plant is shorter, up to 1m. high; stems more or less 3-angled. Branches lanceolate, up to 50 cm. long and 10 cm. broad, dark green, obtuse, leathery, lightly notched, with small areoles, occasionally with a small spine in the areoles of the main stems. Flowers about 29 cm. long: ovary oval-elongated, somewhat warty and with small triangular scales; tube pale yellow, scaly; scales more numerous and much longer near the top. Outer petals greenish white, the inner petals in 3 or 4 series, white, lanceolate, up to 14 mm. broad. Stamens pale yellow, shorter than the petals, style white, just longer than the stamens, stigma with 10 yellowish slender lobes.

Epiphyllum crenatum (Lem.) Br. et R. = *Phyllocactus crenatus* Lem. Honduras and Guatemala. Plant erect, densely branched, about 1 m. high, with cylindrical main stems. Branches stiff and thick, thin at the margin, lanceolate or broadly linear, up to 60 cm. long and 6 cm. broad, tender green or almost greyish green, with a thick median nerve, rather deeply notched. Flowers up to 22 cm. long, fully expanded, about 20 cm. across. Tube greenish below, reddish above. Outer petals broadly linear, greenish yellow; the inner spathulate, white or creamy white. Stamens pale yellow, style and 8-lobed stigma white. The flowers are diurnal and beautiful. This species is largely used in raising hybrids.

Epiphyllum Pittieri (Weber) Br. et R. = *Phyllocactus Pittieri* Weber. Costa Rica. Branches flat 30 to 40 cm. long, 3 to 4 cm. broad, more or less hanging, notched or serrated along the sides, thin. Flowers nocturnal, 10 to 13 cm. long: ovary and tube slender, pale green, with a few acute scales. Limb star-like, 6 to 8 cm. broad. Petals 25 to 30, linear, acute; the outer green and longer than the inner, which are white, in two series. Stamens in one group, on the throat of the flower, short, white: style pink or pale pink, of a deeper colour below the throat, within the tube; stigma with 10 lobes. Free-flowering; the flowers have the perfume of hyacinths.

Epiphyllum Hookeri Haworth = *Phyllocactus Hookeri* Salm-Dyck = *Ph. marginatus* Salm-Dyck. Northern Venezuela, Trinidad and Tobago, in large masses on the rocks and trees. Plant erect, much branched, with cylindrical stems. Branches tender green or pale green, 15 to 60 cm. long, 4 to 7 cm. broad, later passing to a dirty or bluish green, often edged reddish. They are oblong-linear, or lanceolate, rounded or acute at the top, serrate, with notches far apart. Flowers nocturnal, scentless. Ovary angular, with a few outspreading scales. Tube 11 to 13 cm. long, very slender, greenish, with few scales. Outer petals linear, reddish green, tipped pink; inner petals pure white, 5 cm. long, linear-acute. Stamens white; style yellowish below carmine in the middle and reddish above; stigma with 10 to 12 yellow lobes.

Epiphyllum Darrahii (K. Sch.) Br. et R. = *Phyllocactus Darrahii* **K.** Sch. Mexico, where it is also frequently cultivated. Plant bushy and much branched. Branches 20 to 30 cm. long, 3 to 5 cm. broad, rather thick, pale green, deeply notched or irregularly toothed, with rounded notches and teeth. Flowers 18 cm. long, sweet-scented. Tube up to 11 cm. long, 4 mm. thick, pale yellow or greenish, with a few linear scales. Limb 6 to 7 cm. across: outer petals linear-acute, lemon yellow; the inner lanceolate-acute, pure white. Stamens erect, white, inserted in a ring on the throat. Style and 8-lobed stigma white. Very free-flowering.

Epiphyllum anguliger (Lem.) Br. et R. = *Phyllocactus anguliger* Lem. = *Ph. serratus* Brongn. Southern Mexico. Plant bushy, erect, much branched. Branches lanceolate, rather fleshy, tender green, with a strong median nerve, with large teeth, more or less alternate on each side and more or less rectangular, with a deep rectangular notch between the teeth. Flowers 15 to 16 cm. long, sweet-scented. with a slender green or pinkish tube, often curved, slightly furnished with scales. Outer petals linear-lanceolate, yellowish flesh-coloured; inner petals lanceolate acute, toothed, pure white. Stamens, style and 8- to 11-lobed stigma white.

Epiphyllum grandilobum (Weber) Br. et R. = *Phyllocactus grandilobus* Weber. Costa Rica. Branches up to 25 cm. broad, moderately long, with long linear teeth or laciniae on each side. The middle nerve is as thick as a finger: areoles far apart. Flowers nocturnal, large, white. Ovary with few scales. Fruit bare, red. Style white.

Epiphyllum lepidocarpum (Weber) Br. et R. = *Phyllocactus lepidocarpus* Weber. Costa Rica. Plant small. Branches linear-lanceolate, acute, glossy green, 20 to 25 cm. long, about 3 cm. broad, with many hair-like white bristles when young. Areoles in shallow notches, 2 to 3 cm. apart on each side, with a few hairs. Flower up to 20 cm. long. Ovary long, reddish green, with many narrow fleshy acute reddish green scales, erect or reflexed. Tube pale red below and carmine in its upper part: outer petals long and narrow, pale carmine; inner petals white, broad, and few in number. Stamens in two groups, one inserted on the tube, the other on the throat, all white. Style white. Fruit 9 cm. long and 4 cm. thick, violet red, with many narrow fleshy scales, erect or reflexed. Pulp white, with an acid flavour.

Epiphyllum cartagense (Weber) Br. et R. = *Phyllocactus cartagensis*

Weber. Costa Rica (near Cartago). Plant tall, erect, much branched. Branches lanceolate, or linear-lanceolate, up to 30 cm. long, and 5 to 7 cm. broad, roughly serrated at the margin. Flowers about 20 cm. long, with a green ovary, 8 mm. thick, having 6 or 7 small scales. Tube slender, 6 mm. thick, pink or reddish, with 4 small scales. Limb 10 to 12 cm. across, with about 30 petals, 6 cm. long, linear-lanceolate: outer petals yellow or orange red, inner petals pure white. Stamens in one group, inserted on the throat of the tube, white, style and stigma more or less reddish.

var. **refractum** Weber. Outer petals strongly recurved.

Other species belonging to this genus are:

Epiphyllum pumilum (Vaup.) Br. et R. = *Phyllocactus pumilus* Vaupel, from Guatemala. Like *E. Pittieri*, with small sweet-scented flowers and white style.

Epiphyllum caudatum (Vaup.) Br. et R. = *Phyllocactus caudatus* Vaupel, from Mexico (Oaxaca), with small white flowers.

Certain other species, such as: *Phyllocactus macrocarpus* Weber, *Ph. costaricensis* Weber, both from Costa Rica, *Ph. caulorrhizus* Lem. from Honduras, and *Ph. acuminatus* K. Sch., from Brazil, are probably natural hybrids.

Epiphyllum Ackermannii Haworth = *Phyllocactus Ackermannii* Salm-Dyck, originally described as native of Mexico, is known to be a hybrid, raised in England, of a species of *Phyllocactus* with *Heliocereus speciosus*. The plant has all the characters of an *Epiphyllum* (*Phyllocactus*), but the seedling has a stem with white spines like one of the *Cerei*. It is the most free-flowering of all species and hybrids of *Epiphyllum*, and is deservedly popular on account of its large dazzling red flowers.

There are about 1,000 named varieties or hybrids of *Epiphyllum*, ranging in colour from pure white to flesh-colour, pink, yellow, mauve, brownish, red, dark red, crimson, carmine, brick-red, orange, purple and violet. They are mostly the result of crosses between *Epiphyllum crenatum*, or *Nopalxochia phyllanthoides* or *E. Ackermannii* with species of *Heliocereus* and *Selenicereus*, or with other hybrids. Their popularity is on the increase, and they have long ago taken their place among other florist's flowers, in more or less varied collections. The earlier hybrids were at first given Latin names, or names with a Latin declension, but the practice was objectionable, as the beginner might easily mistake them for true species. In order to avoid confusion, the older hybrids with Latin names are still catalogued under the name by which they were first offered to the trade. Among them we find:

Phyllocactus Ackermannii, described as a species by Haworth and by subsequent writers, *Ph. Pfersdorffii, Boothii, coccineus, colmariensis, Cooperi, Coswigii, Curtisii, Franzii, Jenkinsonii, kermesinus, Kleinii, Ludwigii, Mulhausianus, multiflorus, Newbertii, roseus, Reydii, Schmidtii, Smithii, splendens, superbissimus, Tettaui, tricolor, triumphans, Vogelii, Werneri*, and many others.

CACTI

Species of *Epiphyllum* and their varieties and hybrids, being epiphytic plants should be kept in half-shade or in the shade, throughout the year, although a little sun in winter and early spring will materially assist in inducing a good start of vegetation, with better prospects of an abundant crop of blooms. During summer and early autumn (June-October), the plants should be kept in the open, in the shade or half-shade, of tall trees, sheltered from high winds, and sprayed frequently or daily. The excessive heat of a greenhouse in summer, even if properly ventilated, may result in injury. The soil should be like that suggested for *Zygocactus*, very light and porous, but substantial and nourishing. Cuttings for rooting should not be taken at the lower or round part of the branch, but considerably above, where the stem is already broad, and after allowing the wound to dry for some days in the shade, may be planted off singly in small pots, in a mixture of sand and leaf-mould, with a little crushed charcoal. Cuttings are planted at any time during spring and summer, preferably from May to September. Grafting on *Hylocereus undatus* results in large sturdy plants, which flower very freely.

For the beginner who may be at a loss what varieties to have for his collection, the following list of 30 varieties is suggested.

Ph. Ackermannii majus, "Albert Gourant," "Bruxelles," *crenatus superbus,* "Dr. Boisduval," "Empereur," "Gloire de Poissy," "Imperator," "Alter Nicolai," "Joseph De Laet," *Laloyi,* "Grand Soleil," "Mons. A. Riviere," "Purpur Konig," *superbissimus,* "Toledo," "Triomphe de Authieux," "Bahia," "Alexandrine," *Feltoni,* "Francois Verhaert," "Raphael," "Dante," giant *coccineum,* "Goliath," "Freiherr v. Kapherr," *albus perfectus superbissimus,* "Pfersdorffii," *speciosus albus, albus candidissimus.*

DISOCACTUS Lindley
(*Disisocactus* Kunze)

Epiphytic plants, with the habit of *Epiphyllum.* Flowers small, red, diurnal. Ovary cylindrical, with a few small scales. Petals few, acute, arising from a short tube. Fruit globular or oval, not angular. Includes 2 species.

Disocactus biformis Lindley = *Phyllocactus biformis* Lab. Honduras. Stems cylindrical, 20 to 50 cm. long, with spirally arranged areoles. Side branches lanceolate, soft-fleshed, green, notched, with a pronounced median nerve. Flowers borne on the side areoles of the branches, near the top. The flower buds are acute, almost curved upwards, 4 to 5 cm. long. Flowers pale red, with 8 or 9 acute petals. Stamens and style red, stigma with 4 or 5 lobes. The stamens and style are slightly longer than the petals, and the areoles are 1 to $1\frac{1}{2}$ cm. apart, slightly woolly, with one or more bristles here and there. Fruit pear-shaped, $1\frac{1}{2}$ cm. long, wine red.

Disocactus Eichlamii (Weingt.) Br. et R. = *Phyllocactus Eichlamii* Weingt. Guatemala. Plant much branched from the base. Branches cylindrical below, flattened and lanceolate above, 20 to 30 cm. long, 3 to 5 cm. broad, tender green, notched with more or less acute teeth. Flowers borne on the upper areoles, very numerous, 4 cm. long, carmine red, with a slender, trumpet-like tube, the limb partly expanded, with exserted stamens and style. Fruit round, 1 cm. thick, red.

Both species require the same treatment as *Rhipsalis:* a warm and moist atmosphere, shaded or at least partly shaded by tall trees in summer, and a soil largely made up of leaf-mould, old cow-manure, crushed bricks and grit or sand, with a little garden loam, preferably topped with moss and kept rather moist.

CHIAPASIA Br et R.

Epiphytic plants, without spines, with crenate flat branches, thin, rounded towards the base. Flowers borne on the upper areoles, large, with a short tube and about 8 curved or partly recurved petals. Ovary with few scales. Includes only the following species.

Chiapasia Nelsonii (Vaup.) Br. et R. = *Phyllocactus Nelsonii* Vaupel = *Epiphyllum Nelsonii* Br. et R. = *Phyllocactus chiapensis* J. A. Purpus. Mexico (Chiapas). Stem erect, slender, wand-like, later hanging down, 60 to 120 cm. long, above branched spirally, with elongated or linear branches, flat and thin, 10 to 25 cm. long, and 3 to 4 cm. broad, notched or crenate. Flowers borne profusely on the side areoles of the upper part of the branches, 7 to 8 cm. long, sweet-scented, lasting for several days. Ovary bare; tube green, about 2 cm. long: limb funnel-shaped, almost lily-like. Petals partly expanded or recurved, carmine red, with the perfume of violets, inner petals broader. Stamens numerous, reddish below, white above; style slender, pale red, stigma with 5 white lobes. A very charming species, requiring the same treatment as *Epiphyllum*, and grows best when grafted.

ECCREMOCACTUS Br. et R.

Epiphytic plants with a hanging habit, with joints or branches up to 30 cm. long, and 5 to 10 cm. broad, flat and thick, notched, bearing areoles spiny in their native country, only slightly spiny in cultivation, with short white spines. Flowers on the upper areoles, with a short scaly tube, but without spines, the withered perianth persisting on the fruit, which is red, with a few spineless areoles. Seeds minute, black. Includes only one species.

Eccremocactus Bradei (Vaup.) Br. et R. = *Phyllocactus Bradei* Vaupel. Costa Rica. Branches dull light green, with a prominent median nerve, and wavy margins. Areoles small, with one short dark brown spine (rarely 2 or 3), 6 mm. long, passing to white. Flowers 6 to 7 cm. long, white, with obtuse fleshy petals, slightly reddish on the outer side, only partly expanded, nocturnal, withering off the next morning.

CACTI

NOPALXOCHIA Br. et R.

Epiphytic plants, abundantly branched, with flat lanceolate-acute, spineless joints or branches. Flowers borne copiously on the lateral areoles of the joints, with a tube as long as the limb. Includes only one species.

Nopalxochia phyllanthoides (DC.) Br. et R. = *Cereus phyllanthoides* DC. = *Phyllocactus phyllanthoides* Link = *Cactus alatus* Willd. non Swartz = *Epiphyllum speciosum* Haw. Mexico and Colombia. Plant bushy, erect, very thickly branched. Joints lanceolate-acute, obtusely toothed, cylindrical at the base, pale green or green, often somewhat reddish, with a prominent central nerve, and clearly defined side nerves. Flowers 10 cm. long, more or less campanulate. Ovary slender, with a few spreading scales, more numerous on the tube. Outer petals spreading, lanceolate; the inner lanceolate, obtuse, pink or pale red outside, paler inside. Stamens and style white, stigma with 5 to 8 white lobes. Fruit elliptical, angular, 3 to 4 cm. long, green, red when perfectly ripe. The plant grows up to 1 m. high, and is very free-flowering, lasting in bloom for 3 weeks or more, in spring.

It is long known in our gardens and deservedly popular. May be grown on own roots, but is best grafted on *Hylocereus undatus* or on *Opuntia ficus-indica*. Requires the same treatment as an *Epiphyllum*. The lovely variety "Deutsche Kaiserin," is that most commonly grown. The flowers are also sweet-scented. There are now also numerous hybrids, with larger flowers of various shades of pale pink, red or orange.

WITTIA K. Sch.

Epiphytic plants, with the habit of an *Epiphyllum*, with hanging stems and branches; these are leaf-like, long, notched along the sides. Flowers small, campanulate or funnel-shaped, red. Petals short and narrow. Stamens in two groups of unequal length. Ovary with small scales, but without hairs or bristles.

Includes 2 species, not yet in cultivation, viz:

Wittia amazonica K. Sch., from Peru.

W. panamensis Br. et R., from Panama and Colombia.

Wittia costaricensis Br. et R., originally described as a third species, was afterwards referred by the Authors to *Pseudorhipsalis himantoclada* Br. et R.

SUB-TRIBE VIII RHIPSALIDANAE

Much branched epiphytic plants, mostly living on trees. Branches alternate or in whorls, and are cylindrical, or angular or flat, or very slender. Spines mostly absent. The flowers are small, regular, with a very short tube, or without tube. The fruit is a small juicy berry, white, red or purple; the seeds are minute.

ERYTHRORHIPSALIS Berger

Differs from *Rhipsalis* by the numerous minute areoles, furnished with bristles or bristle-like spines.

Erythrorhipsalis pilocarpa (Löfg.) Berger = *Rhipsalis pilocarpa* Löfgren. Eastern Brazil. Branches cylindrical, 5 to 12 cm. long, 3 to 6 mm. thick, with 8 to 10 low furrows, mostly whorled. Areoles rather closely set, with 3 to 10 greyish bristles. Flowers mostly at the end of the branches, 2½ cm. broad, with numerous, lanceolate, spreading white petals, forming a short tube at the base. Stamens many, white; stigma with 6 or 7 lobes. Fruit oval, with a broad navel, wine red, furnished with bristles. A pretty species, flowering at Christmas.

RHIPSALIDOPSIS Br. et R.

Shrub-like, much branched, low, erect or hanging, up to 25 cm. long. Joints 3- to 5-angled, or flat, like a miniature *Zygocactus*, 2 to 4 cm. long, bearing areoles furnished with bristles. Flowers borne on the large elongated areole at the top of the joints, 3 to 4 cm. broad, perfectly regular, with a very short tube, rosy white or pink. Stigma with 3 or 4 white lobes.

The only species to which the above characters apply, is **Rhipsalidopsis rosea** (Lageh.) Br. et R. = *Rhipsalis rosea* Lageheim, native of the primeval forests of Parana, southern Brazil. A desirable species usually grafted like a *Zygocactus*, but thrives well also on own roots, in a compost made of leaf-mould, sand and crushed bricks.

PFEIFFERA Salm-Dyck

Epiphytic plants, woody at the base, with hanging branches mostly four-angled, and without aerial roots. Areoles spiny. Flowers inconspicuous, with a very short tube. Ovary spinescent. Fruit round, red, with areoles furnished with small spines. Seeds black.

An aberrant genus with only one species, which was originally described as a *Cereus* by Monville, and was afterwards included under *Rhipsalis*. Berger (1929) considered it as a primitive form of *Cereus*, and has accordingly classified it with the *Cerei*.

Pfeiffera ianthothele (Monv.) Weber = *Cereus ianthothele* Monville = *Rhipsalis cereiformis* Först. = *Pfeiffera cereiformis* Salm-Dyck. Northern Argentina (Tucuman), growing on trees. A plant of small growth, with 4-angled stems (sometimes 3-angled, or spiral), 15 to 50 cm. long, mostly about 30 cm. long, and 1½ to 2 cm. thick, pale green. Areoles on prominences along the angles, 1 to 1½ cm. apart, often reddish. Spines 6 or 7, thin, 4 to 5 mm. long, associated with brown bristles. Flowers 2 to 2½ cm. long, bell-shaped; ovary round, slightly warty, scaly and with small spines. Tube very short, almost absent. Petals in 2 series, only partly expanded; outer petals pale pink or purplish, paler inside; inner petals white. Stigma with 5 to 8 lobes. Fruit round, wine red, minutely spiny, as large as a small cherry. Requires the same treatment as a *Rhipsalis*; grows well as a hanging plant in a warm glasshouse, and is often grafted on a *Cereus*.

CACTI

ACANTHORHIPSALIS (K. Sch.) Br. et R.

A small genus of only 3 species, which differs from *Rhipsalis* mainly owing to the presence of spines in the areoles. The joints are flat or three-winged, crenate or toothed. Flowers borne on lateral areoles. Ovary with small scales, hairy in their axils. Seeds minute, black.

Acanthorhipsalis monacantha (Griseb.) Br. et R. = *Rhipsalis monacantha* Griseb. Northern Argentina (near Oran). A branched bush, about 1 m. high. Branches or joints leaf-like, linear, acuminate at the top, crenate, with well marked median nerve and secondary nerves. Areoles with yellowish wool, and with one (rarely two) dark brown stiff spine, 5 to 10 mm. long. Flowers white, about 1 cm. long; seeds small, round.

The other species are:

Acanthorhipsalis asperula (Vaup.) Br. et R. and **A. crenata** (Vaup.) Br. et R. formerly included under Rhipsalis.

PSEUDORHIPSALIS Br. et R.

Another small genus of epiphytic plants with thin flattened joints, and with tall wand-like stems, bearing solitary, but numerous flowers on the marginal areoles of the flat joints. Flowers small, greenish. Fruit round, with a few scales. Includes two species, formerly classed under *Rhipsalis*.

Pseudorhipsalis alata (K. Sch.) Br. et R. = *Rhipsalis alata* K. Sch. = *R. coriacea* Polak. Jamaica. A much branched shrub, up to 8 m. long, with cylindrical stems, and flat, thin, linear-lanceolate branches, obtuse at the end, and narrowed at the base to a cylindrical stem or peduncle $\frac{1}{2}$ to 8 cm. long; the branches are 15 to 25 cm. long, and up to 2 cm. broad, inserted mostly spirally or in parts, obtusely toothed, with a prominent median nerve. Areoles with short greyish wool, without bristles. Flowers borne on the marginal areoles, greenish white; ovary with 3 or 4 small scales. Fruit round, $\frac{1}{2}$ cm. thick, diaphanous white. Seeds oval, black, smooth.

Pseudorhipsalis himantoclada ((Gosselin) Br. et R. = *Rhipsalis himantoclada* Gosselin. *Wittia costaricensis* is referred by its Authors (Br. et R.) to this species. Costa Rica. Has erect or curved flat stems, with horizontal branches narrowed at both ends, with low serrate margins. Flower white; ovary, tube and sepals purplish.

LEPISMIUM Pfeiffer

Epiphytic plants, frequently also growing on rocks, with many long branches, hanging or creeping, flat and leaf-like, or three-winged, crenate along the margin, with a tuft of hairs in the areoles. Flowers in a small cluster at each areole, white or pink. Fruit round, smooth, purple. Seeds minute.

There are at least 4 different species, which were included by Britton

430

and Rose as subspecies or mere variations of one and same very variable species, under the name of *Lepismium cruciforme* (Vell.) Br. et R. but the evidence is in favour of their being specifically different, although closely allied, with several intermediate forms.

Lepismium commune Pfeiff. = *L. Mittleri* Först. = *Rhipsalis squamulosa* K. Sch. Eastern Brazil and Argentina, on trees and rocks. Plant hanging or creeping, with aerial roots. Branches three-winged, 10 to 30 cm. long, 1 to 2½ cm. thick, green or greyish green, reddish on their upper side, with acute angles, obtusely toothed. Areoles with a brush-like tuft of whitish wool and bristles. Flowers solitary or in pairs, from the side areoles, about 1 cm. long, with a short cylindric or roundish ovary: petals 10 to 12, campanulate, united at the base into a very short tube; outer petals oval, obtuse, green; inner petals oblong or linear-oblong, recurved, yellowish white, passing to canary yellow. Stamens shorter than the petals, diaphanous white, style white, stigma with 5 recurved white lobes. The fruit is violet red or purplish.

Lepismium myosurus Pfeiff. = *Rhipsalis myosurus* K. Sch. = *Cereus tenuis* DC. Eastern Brazil (Rio de Janeiro and Santa Catharina). Plant much branched, creeping, up to 1 m. long. Branches three-winged or four-winged, 10 to 25 cm. long, 5 to 12 mm. thick, narrowed to a point at the tip, hence the name *myosurus* = rat's tail, rather softish, green or greyish green. Areoles deeply set, with a tuft of wool and stiff grey bristles up to 1 cm. long. Flowers solitary on the side areoles, surrounded with stiff bristles, campanulate, with 10 petals. The outer petals are small, oval, scale-like; the next are almost triangular, fleshy, obtuse, reddish green; the innermost are oblong, white, tipped pink or reddish yellow. Style reddish, stigma with 2 to 4 recurved lobes. Fruit red.

Lepismium cavernosum Lindb. = *Rhipsalis cavernosa* Lindb. = *R. macropogon* K. Sch. Eastern Brazil (Rio de Janeiro and Minas Geraes). A shrub sparingly branched; joints flat or three-angled, linear-lanceolate, narrowed to a round stem at the base, more or less creeping, 15 to 25 cm. long, 2½ to 3 cm. broad at the middle, with straight acute angles, deeply notched. Areoles with a tuft of wool and long grey stiff bristles. Flowers 2 to 5 or more at each areole at the sides, 12 to 13 mm. long, with 9 petals, bell-shaped: outer petals obtuse, scale-like, greenish: inner petals oblong, white. Stamens white, shorter than the petals; style longer than the petals, also white; stigma with 4 recurved lobes.

Lepismium anceps Weber = *Rhipsalis anceps* Weber. Eastern Brazil (Sao Paulo). Plant abundantly branched. Branches usually flat, sometimes three-angled, lanceolate-acuminate, narrowed into a round stem at the base, 40 to 50 cm. long, 1 to 2 cm. broad, with a thick median nerve, green, often purplish along the margin, slightly notched. Areoles with long hairs or bristles, longer and stiffer in plants of flowering size. Flowers borne on the side areoles; inner petals violet, margined white, passing to yellowish. Fruit oval carmine red.

CACTI

HARIOTA DC.
(*Hatiora* Br. et R.)

Plants with slender, cylindrical, long stems, spineless. Joints more or less clavate or bottle-shaped, branching in whorls of 2 or 3, with minute areoles on the joints, and a woolly terminal areole at the upper end, from which new joints and flowers are developed. The flowers are yellow, with distinct sepals and petals. Ovary globose, bare. Fruit round, white.

There are 3 species, natives of eastern Brazil, often included under *Rhipsalis*.

Hariota salicornioides (Haw.) DC. = *Rhipsalis salicorniodes* Haworth = *Hatiora salicornioides* Br. et R. Brazil (Rio de Janeiro, Minas Geraes, Sao Paulo). An erect bush, or somewhat pendent, very copiously branched, pale green to deep green, up to 40 cm. high. Joints clavate or bottle-shaped, in whorls of 3 to 5, rarely 2 or 1, 1 to 3 cm. long, 4 to 7 mm. thick. Areoles with short white bristles. Flowers solitary or in pairs, on the top areoles of new joints, about 12 mm. long, funnel-shaped, 1 cm. broad; outer petals (or sepals) triangular, fleshy, yellowish green, slightly reddish outside; inner petals oblong obtuse, canary yellow or golden yellow. Stamens shorter than the petals, reddish; style and the 4- or 5-lobed stigma white. Fruit round, diaphanous white, reddish at the top.

Hariota bambusoides Weber. = *Hatiora bambusoides* Br. et R. Brazil, near Rio de Janeiro. Plant erect, up to 2 m. high; stem with thick nodes like a bamboo; joints larger. Flowers reddish yellow.

Hariota cylindrica (Br. et R.) = *Hatiora cylindrica* Br. et R. Brazil, near Rio de Janeiro. Branches 3 cm. long, almost cylindrical, pale green, dotted red, or reddish towards the top.

Hariota gracilis Weber, and **H. stricta** Weber = *Rhipsalis stricta* Cels., are varieties of *H. salicornioides*.

RHIPSALIS Gaertner

Plants with an epiphytic habit, living mostly on the mossy trunk of trees, or on ledges of rock in shaded or half-shaded ravines and hill sides, often emitting aerial roots, with an erect, or hanging or creeping habit of growth, very much branched. The branches or joints may be cylindrical or flat and leaf-like, or angular, the leaves being represented by minute scales. Areoles along the margins of flattened or angular joints, or more or less evenly distributed all round on cylindrical stems, associated with wool, hairs and bristles. Flowers usually solitary, sometimes clustered, on the marginal areoles in flat or angular joints, or on all the areoles in cylindrical joints, lasting for about 8 days or more, not closing at night. They are small, and the perianth has few segments. Fruit round or oblong, juicy, white, yellow or red, mostly bare. Seeds small.

There are about 60 species, ranging from Florida and the West Indies, through Mexico and down to Argentina. One or two species

(*a*) MAMMILLARIA HAHNIANA

(*b*) MAMMILLARIA PARKINSONII

PLATE LX

(b) MAMMILLARIA UNCINATA

(a) MAMMILLARIA SCHEIDWEILERIANA

PLATE LXI

exist in tropical West Africa, another in East Africa, another in Madagascar and neighbouring islands, and another in Ceylon, and these constitute the only exceptions to the rule that the Cactaceae are limited to the Western Hemisphere. One species, *R. prismatica*, is stated to be native of eastern Brazil and Madagascar, and unless there is a mistake of diagnosis, this curious fact must be attributed either to the agency of migratory birds, or of air currents, or sea currents, rather than to a parallelism of evolution.

The cultivation of species of this genus and of the foregoing closely allied ones in this sub-tribe, is often unduly neglected by the grower. It is true that they do not offer the singular attraction of form, and the fascinating beauty of the flowers of other Cacti, but the plant itself, and its habit of growth are often very interesting, and although the flower may be individually devoid of charm, its large numbers and even distribution, impart to the plant a peculiarly lovely and fairy-like appearance.

In regard to their cultivation, it should be remembered that these epiphytic plants are mostly denizens of the warm and moist primeval forests, where they live permanently in the shade of tall trees, or on ledges of rock in ravines and similarly shaded localities, and therefore too much exposure to the sun or to a dry atmosphere cannot fail to be injurious. The soil should be very porous, but also capable of retaining a certain degree of moisture, and of a rather rich composition. It may consist of equal parts by volume of leaf-mould, very old cow manure, good garden loam, sharp sand and crushed bricks or crushed charcoal. The addition of limestone gravel or other calcareous matter is not necessary, except in case that there is danger that the compost may become sour through over watering. The plants should be kept moderately dry at the roots, but should be frequently sprayed over-head with water which is not too cold.

I. *Species with a protruding or prominent ovary.*

A. *Eurhipsalis* K. Sch. Joints cylindrical, without bristles.

Rhipsalis Cassytha Gaertn. Florida to southern Brazil, also in tropical Africa and Ceylon. A hanging bush, over 1 m. long, very much branched dichotomously, or spirally, or in whorls, pale green. Joints 10 to 20 cm. long, rarely up to 50 cm., 2 to 4 mm. thick. Areoles small, at first with 1 or 2 very short white brisltes. Flowers borne along the joints, delicate, greenish or yellowish white, about $\frac{1}{2}$ cm. long, solitary on each areole. Ovary greenish, round, bare. Petals spreading: the outer about $\frac{1}{2}$ cm. long, triangular, green, slightly fleshy: the inner oblong, white or yellowish white. Stamens 9 to 12 whitish, short. Style longer than the petals, white; stigma with 3 to 5 reflexed lobes. Fruit round, $\frac{1}{2}$ cm. thick, white or rosy.

Rhipsalis cassythoides Löfgren. Brazil (Para). Joints more slender, 2 to 3 mm. thick. Flowers smaller, with 6 to 8 stamens. Fruit oblong, 4 mm. thick, greenish white.

Rhipsalis teres Steud. = *R. conferta* Salm-Dyck. Eastern and southern Brazil. Plant erect, tender green, much branched. Joints in whorls of 3 to 6 or more, 5 to 8 cm. long, 3 mm. thick. Areoles very small, often reddish, with whitish or greyish wool, and at first with 1 or 2 very short black bristles. Flowers copiously borne along the joints, about 10 mm. long and 13 mm. broad, yellowish white. Fruit round, disaphanous white, about 8 mm. thick.

Rhipsalis virgata Weber. Brazil. A bush much branched and hanging, about 1 m. long, with filiform branches, arranged spirally, rarely whorled, cylindrical, more stiff and more erect than those of *R. Cassytha*, wand-like, green, up to $\frac{1}{2}$ cm. thick, the secondary branches being $1\frac{1}{2}$ to 3 mm. thick, and 1 to 6 cm. long, thickly studded with areoles, which are very slightly woolly, and have 1 very short bristle when young. Flowers very numerous, on the side areoles, solitary or in pairs, up to 8 mm. long: outer petals or sepals 2, greenish like the ovary; inner petals 5, oval, recurved, dirty white. Stamens numerous, white; style white, stigma with 3 yellowish white lobes. Fruit only 3 mm. thick, white.

Rhipsalis Lindbergiana K. Sch. Eastern Brazil (Rio de Janeiro). Like the preceding, hanging, up to 2 m. long, side branches more rigid; the main branches dividing dichotomously, with secondary branches 8 to 16 cm. long, and 4 to 5 mm. thick. Areoles numerous and closely set, woolly, at first with a black bristle 2 mm. long, which soon drops off. Flowers solitary on the areoles of new twigs, about $\frac{1}{2}$ cm. long: sepals scale-like, fleshy, very short, 4 in number; inner petals obtuse, greenish or reddish. Stamens, style and 3- or 4-lobed stigma white. Fruit only 2 mm. thick, pale red.

Rhipsalis erythrocarpa K. Sch. East Africa (near Kilimanjaro). Like the preceding, hanging and much branched, over 1 m. long, pale green, branching dichotomously or in whorls of 3 or 4, branches 10 to 15 cm. long, 4 to 5 mm. thick. Areoles numerous, almost bare, with 1 very small bristle when young. Flowers borne chiefly on the areoles below the tip of new twigs, small, about 4 mm. long; inner petals oblong, obtuse, greenish outside, white inside. Fruit round, purplish red, 5 to 6 mm. thick.

Rhipsalis Shaferi Br. et R. Paraguay. Branches in whorls, 4 to 5 mm. thick. Flowers greenish white, 1 cm. broad. Fruit pale pink or white.

Rhipsalis grandiflora Haw. = *R. funalis* Salm-Dyck = *R. cylindrica* Steud. Eastern Brazil (Rio de Janeiro). An erect, much branched bush, up to 1 m. high. Stems up to 2 cm. thick, branching dichotomously, or in whorls of 3 or more. Branches or joints cylindrical, 5 to 15 cm. long, green, passing to greyish, reddish when young. Areoles slightly depressed, with a reddish ring. Flowers borne along the joints, about 2 cm. broad, with about 12 petals; the outer ones triangular, obtuse, whitish, with a green dorsal band; the inner petals oblong, lanceolate-acute, white. Stamens diaphanous white, 1/3 the length of the petals, stigma with 4 to 6 lobes. Fruit reddish, 6 to 7 mm.

thick. Grows into fine specimens grafted on *Hylocereus undatus*.

Rhipsalis clavata Weber. = *Hariota clavata* Weber. Eastern Brazil. A hanging bush, copiously branched. Joints of uniform length, pale green, sometimes reddish the lower ones about 5 cm. long, the upper ones 3 cm. long, more or less clavate, about 3 mm. thick at the top and 2 mm. below. Flowers borne mostly at the top of the joints, yellow in bud, white when in bloom, 1 cm. broad. Stigma with 4 thick white reflexed lobes. Fruit round, white or yellowish, 6 mm. thick.

Rhipsalis sansibarica Weber. Coast of Zanzibar. Looks like a robust variety of *R. Cassytha*, with lower and thicker joints, larger flowers with about 20 stamens, filaments and style greenish white, stigma with 3 thick recurved lobes. Fruit oblong, 7 mm. long and 6 mm. thick, white, very viscid, almost like a mistletoe berry.

Rhipsalis hadrosoma Lindb. = *R. robusta* Lindb. non Lem. Eastern Brazil (Sao Paulo). Has the same habit of *R. grandiflora*, to which it is very similar, but the joints are thicker, pale green, and the new areoles have a bristle about 1 cm. long. Flowers borne near the top of new joints, 2 cm. across; stamens about as long as the petals, white; style white, stigma with 3 to 5 recurved lobes.

Rhipsalis madagascariensis Weber = *R. pilosa* Weber. Madagascar (near Tamatave). A much branched bush, erect or partly hanging. Joints 8 to 10 cm. long, more or less cylindrical, 4 to 6 mm. thick, fleshy, brownish when young, passing to deep green and then to bluish green, slightly ribbed or furrowed. Areoles very sparingly woolly, later bare, but with a tuft of 15 to 25 whitish bristles, 2 to 4 mm. long. Flowers very numerous, along the new joints, up to 8 mm. long, and 5 mm. broad, with greenish erect petals. Fruit round, diaphanous white, 6 mm. thick.

Rhipsalis capilliformis Weber. Eastern Brazil. A hanging bush, very copiously branched, with long slender joints, like a wig. Joints of two sorts. Long ones, 10 to 15 cm. long, and 2 or 3 mm. thick; and shorter ones spirally arranged or in whorls of 3 to 7, thinner, pale green, with areoles slightly woolly, but without hairs or bristles. The flowers are almost terminal at the end of the joints, numerous, about 7 mm. long, glossy greenish white. Stamens and style white, stigma with 3 thick short lobes. Fruit round, about 5 mm. thick, white bare.

Rhipsalis prismatica Rümpl. = *R. tetragona* Weber. Brazil. Described also under the name of *R. Suareziana* Weber, from Madagascar. Has the same habit of growth as the preceding, but the joints are almost prismatic (four-angled), reddish, with tufts of small whitish or reddish bristles in the areoles. The smaller joints are 1 to 3 cm. long. Flowers small, whitish, borne along the whole length of the new joints.

Rhipsalis cribrata Rümpl. = *R. penduliflora* N. E. Brown = *Hariota cribrata* Lem. Brazil (Minas Geraes, Rio de Janeiro, Sao Paulo, Santa Catharina). A lively green bush, copiously branched, up to 30 cm. long. Joints of two sorts. Long ones, cylindrical, up to 15 cm. long, and up to 2 mm. thick: short ones, almost angular, 1½ to 2 cm. long, and 1 to 1½ mm. thick, quickly dropping off. Areoles on the long joints, with a little greyish wool and 1 or 2 small bristles. Flowers solitary or in pairs, at the tip of the short joints, and are about 12 mm. long, 7 mm. broad: sepals triangular, fleshy, green, tipped red; petals oblong, obtuse, white, ciliated at the tip. Stamens, style and 3-lobed stigma white. Fruit round or oblong, diaphanous white.

Rhipsalis cereuscula Haw. = *R. Saglionis* Otto = *R. brachiata* Hook. Eastern Brazil to Uruguay and Argentina. A much branched bush, lively green passing to dark green, growing into a globular mass, 60 cm. high. Joints of two sorts. Long ones, cylindrical, 10 to 30 cm. long, 3 to 4 mm. thick; and short ones, mostly arranged spirally or in whorls of 8 to 10, oblong or short-cylindric, 1½ cm. long. Areoles with short wool and with 2 to 4 very short bristles. Flowers borne at the tip of the short joints, solitary, rarely in pairs, about 1½ cm. long: sepals triangular, acute, fleshy green; petals oblong-lanceolate, acute, white with a yellowish band on the outer side. Stamens white, shorter than the petals, style white, stigma with 4 recurved white lobes. Fruit white.

Rhipsalis mesembryanthemoides Haw. = *R. echinata* Hort. Eastern Brazil (Rio de Janeiro). A much branched, erect, pale green bush, of globular shape, up to 40 cm. high, with two sorts of joints. Long joints cylindrical, 10 to 20 cm. long, 1½ to 2 mm. thick, furnished with numerous tubercles. Short joints very numerous, in spirals or in whorls, up to 1 cm. long, 2 to 3 mm. thick, somewhat club-shaped, 4 mm. at the tip, or cylindrical, often curved. Areoles woolly, those at the tip with 3 or 4 short bristles. Flowers solitary, at the tip of the short joints, about 8 mm. long and 1 cm. broad, with 10 petals: inner petals lanceolate acute, white, with a yellowish midrib. Stamens white, shorter than the petals, style white, stigma with 5 spreading white lobes. Fruit round, white.

B. *Ophiorhipsalis* K. Sch. Joints cylindrical or slightly fluted or furrowed, well furnished with long bristles.

Rhipsalis lumbricoides Lem. = *R. sarmentosa* Otto et Dietr. Uruguay and Paraguay. A much branched bush, creeping and rooting on moss-covered trunks of trees, pale green passing to greyish green, over 1 m. long. Main branches 14 to 20 cm. long, up to 8 mm. thick, cylindrical or slightly angular or furrowed. Areoles woolly, with 6 to 8 stiff, yellowish or brownish bristles, almost spinescent. Side joints often whorled, yellowish green to greyish. Flowers borne on the side areoles, 2 cm. long, creamy white, with the perfume of orange blossoms. Ovary oblong or cylindrical, bare. Petals 13; the outer oval obtuse, the inner lanceolate-acute, straw-coloured. Stamens greenish white, style white, stigma with 3 to 5 spreading greenish lobes. Fruit round, as large as a pea, at first green, passing to brownish and deep purplish brown at maturity. A pretty plant, still rare in cultivation.

Rhipsalis leucoraphis K. Sch. = *R. Buchtienii* Hort. Paraguay and northern Argentina. A much-branched bush, hanging, or climbing by means of aerial roots, up to 50 cm. long, tender green, passing to greyish green or grey. Joints cylindrical, up to 7 mm. thick. Areoles small, almost bare, with 1 to 5 spinescent bristles glassy white to dull white, up to 4 mm. long. Flowers mostly borne at or near the top of the joints, 1½ cm. broad: outer petals oval, greenish; the inner 10 petals up to 1 cm. long, white. Stamens and style white, stigma with 5 reflexed lobes. Fruit pale red.

Rhipsalis aculeata Weber. Paraguay and Argentina (Tucuman). A branched creeping bush, with the same habit as the preceding. Joints stiff, cylindrical, green, fluted or with 8 to 10 slight ribs. Areoles slightly woolly, with 8 to 10 white stiff spines or spiny bristles, spreading, 3 to 4 mm. long, more or less embedded in the areole. Flowers borne on the side areoles, 2 cm. long, 1½ cm. broad; inner petals oval, white. Stamens about 20, white, stigma with 3 reflexed white lobes. Fruit round, with few scales, dark wine red.

C. *Goniorhipsalis* K. Sch. Joints cylindrical, clearly ribbed or angular.

Rhipsalis pentaptera Pfeiff. = *R. pentagona* Först. Southern Brazil and Uruguay. An erect bush with many stems, pale green to dark green, up to 40 cm. high, and 1 m. across. Joints 7 to 12 cm. long, with 5 angles, rarely with 6, angles pronounced, winged, toothed, branching dichotomously, sometimes in whorls. Areoles in the notches between the teeth of the wings, almost bare, but with a few small bristles. Flowers on the upper part of the joints, about 8 mm. long, with 11 petals: outer petals or sepals triangular, fleshy, green; inner petals oblong, obtuse, white, with a green dorsal band. Stamens and style translucent white, stigma with 3 or 4 short erect lobes. Fruit round, white or pale pink.

Rhipsalis sulcata Weber = *R. micrantha* Hort. non DC. Probably native of Ecuador. A bush up to 1 m. long, pale, green, more or less erect. Joints 5 to 8 cm. long, 3 to 5 mm. thick, five-angled. Areoles in notches far apart along the angles or wings, mostly reddish, almost bare, with 1 or 2 bristles. Flowers borne on the side areoles, solitary, about 12 mm. long, white to reddish.

Rhipsalis micrantha DC. = *Cactus micranthus* H.B.K. Ecuador and northern Peru. A branched hanging bush, of a lively green. Stems with 4 obtuse angles, rarely with 5 angles. Joints triangular, sometimes with two angles (flat), angles acute, up to 1½ cm. broad, remotely crenate. Areoles small, with short wool. Small joints mostly two-angled, rarely with 3 angles, 5 to 8 mm. thick. Flowers solitary in the areoles, associated with 1 or 2 spinescent bristles. The flowers are 7 mm. long, with 7 petals, white. Stamens about 25, white, stigma with 3 reflexed lobes. Fruit round or oval, ½ cm. long, with the withered perianth persisting upon it.

Rhipsalis Tonduzii Weber. Costa Rica. A bushy plant, erect or hanging. Joints 6 to 10 cm. long, 1 cm. thick, green, with 4 or 5 angles, the lower joints being mostly 5-angled, the upper 4-angled, or rarely 3-angled. Ribs or angles acute, with notches 2 cm. apart, areoles with bristles when young. Flowers small, whitish. Fruit round, about 8 mm. thick, white.

D. *Phyllorhipsalis* K. Sch. Joints flat, leaf-like, sometimes three-winged.

Rhipsalis gonocarpa Weber = *R. pterocarpa* Weber. Southern Brazil (Sao Paulo). A much branched plant, erect or hanging, up to 50 cm. long. Stems and joints 3-winged, or 3-angled, up to 30 cm. long, and up to 3 cm. broad, reddish along the wings, but otherwise of a lively green, notched along the margins of the wings. Areoles with a little white wool, without bristles. Flowers borne along the wings, 1½ cm. long; ovary with 4 or 5 acute angles; outer petals short, green; inner petals (7 or 8) lanceolate-acute, dirty white. Stamens 20 to 30, short, white; style pale pink, stigma with 3 or 4 yellowish or reddish reflexed lobes. Fruit copiously produced, round, slightly angular, 1 cm. thick, dark purple.

Rhipsalis Warmingiana K. Sch. Eastern Brazil (Minas Geraes). Similar to the preceding. Joints and stems 10 to 30 cm. long and about 2 cm. broad, flat, or with 3 or 4 angles, crenate, with slightly woolly areoles, but without bristles. Flowers borne along the side areoles, about 1 cm. long; ovary with 5 or 6 angles; the 2 or 3 outer petals or sepals triangular, acute, green; the inner petals, about 10, oblong, white, minutely toothed. Stamens and style white, stigma with 3 or 4 spreading lobes. Fruit with 4 or 5 angles, dark violet.

Rhipsalis ramulosa (Salm-Dyck) Pfeiffer = *Cereus ramulosus* Salm-Dyck = *Hariota ramulosa* Lem. Costa Rica (in the forests near San José). A branched bush, more or less erect, up to 30 cm. long, woody at the base. Joints up to 12 cm. long, and 2½ cm. broad, pale green, leaf-like, broadly linear, obtuse above, narrowed to a cylindrical peduncle below, with a prominent median nerve, remotely notched and crenate along the margin, with areoles in the notches, slightly woolly and without bristles. Flowers in the side areoles, solitary, small (6 to 7 mm. long), greenish white, with oblong petals. Stamens very short, white, style whitish, stigma with 4 lobes. Fruit round, white.

Rhipsalis angustissima Weber. Costa Rica (near Cartago). A much branched hanging bush, up to 40 cm. long. Lower stems round, glossy brown, with spirally arranged green side shoots, often whorled, with a cylindrical glossy brown peduncle, 1 to 1½ mm. thick. The side shoots are leaf-like, green, linear or narrowly lanceolate, remotely toothed along the margin, 8 to 10 cm. long and 5 to 6 mm. broad. Flowers small, whitish. The upright primary stems are glossy pale brown.

Rhipsalis Purpusii Weingt. Mexico (Chiapas) and Guatemala. Stems long, wand-like, cylindrical. Secondary joints flat, hard, leathery, lanceolate, acuminate, dark green, 8 to 20 cm. long, and up to

(b) EPIPHYLLUM DARRAHII

(a) ZYGOCACTUS TRUNCATUS

PLATE LXII

(*a*) SCHLUMBERGERA GAERTNERI

(*b*) EPIPHYLLUM ACKERMANNII

PLATE LXIII

3 cm. broad, notched far apart. Flowers small, 11 mm. long, greenish white. Fruit round, white.

Rhipsalis Wercklei Berger. Costa Rica. Bush much branched, 1½ m. long, tender green. Lower stems three-angled, the next in whorls of 3 to 5. Secondary joints 1 or 2, sometimes 3, from the same areole, flat, linear, with 2 wings or angles, 15 to 20 cm. long, 12 to 18 mm. broad. Areoles slightly depressed in the notches, 4 cm. apart. Flowers 8 mm. broad, whitish.

Rhipsalis linearis K. Sch. Southern Brazil and Uruguay. A bush about 80 cm. long, very much branched, mostly hanging. Stems cylindrical or almost two-winged. Secondary joints leaf-like, narrowly linear, acute, 5 to 20 cm. long, 5 to 7 mm. broad, narrowed almost to a cylindrical peduncle at the base, with a prominent median nerve, without lateral nerves. Areoles slightly woolly, without bristles. Flowers on the marginal areoles, about 18 mm. long, with 12 segments; the sepals being triangular, acute, fleshy, green; the petals lanceolate-acute, white or yellowish. Stigma with 3 or 4 reflexed lobes. Fruit round, translucent white.

Rhipsalis Houlletiana Lem. = *R. Regnellii* Lindb. Eastern Brazil (Minas Geraes). Copiously branched, 1 to 2 m. high, with tall cylindrical stems, and joints of two sorts: cylindrical ones, stiff and erect, about 2 mm. thick, and others leaf-like, flat, stiff and leathery, pale green, lanceolate-acute at both ends, 10 to 20 cm. long, and 2½ to 3½ cm. broad, sometimes reddish, roughly toothed, the teeth 2 to 3 cm. long and up to 1 cm. broad. Flowers borne abundantly from the marginal areoles, about 18 mm. long, campanulate, with 12 segments, the inner ones or petals being lanceolate-acute, yellowish white, tipped greenish. Stigma with 4 or 5 reflexed lobes. Fruit round, carmine red.

Rhipsalis rhombea Pfeiff. = *R. Swartziana* Pfeiff. Brazil (Sao Paulo). A bush 80 cm. high. Stems cylindrical or slightly angular. Joints flat, rarely three-winged, narrowed to a short cylindrical peduncle at the base, with a strong median nerve, and with lateral nerves, oval or lanceolate-rhomboid, obtuse at the top, 3 to 12 cm. long, up to 5 cm. broad, green or reddish, toothed on the margins. Areoles with a little greyish wool, and with 1 or 2 bristles, which soon drop off. Flowers borne along the margin, 1 cm. long, with 10 petals: inner petals oblong, obtuse, pale yellow passing to canary yellow on fading. Stigma with 3 or 4 reflexed lobes. Fruit round, red.

Rhipsalis crispata Pfeiff. = *Epiphyllum crispatum* Haw. = *R. rhombea* var. *crispata* K. Sch. Brazil (Rio de Janeiro). Joints pale green, obtuse at the top and also at the base, without a cylindrical peduncle, elongated or roundish, wavy along the margin, stiff, 6 to 12 cm. long, up to 7 cm. broad. Flower yellowish, about 1 cm. long. Fruit white.

Rhipsalis elliptica Lindb. Eastern and southern Brazil. A branched bush, 50 to 60 cm. long. Joints leaf-like, elongated-elliptical, 6 to 15 cm. long, 2½ to 6 cm. broad, obtuse or acute at both ends, dark green, slightly notched along the margins, with a pronounced median nerve, and often also with lateral nerves. Flowers 9 mm. long, on the marginal areoles, associated with 1 or 2 bristles: inner petals oblong, obtuse, whitish. Stigma with 4 white lobes, collected in a globular mass. Fruit round, $\frac{1}{2}$ cm. thick, pink or red.

Rhipsalis chloroptera Weber. Brazil. An erect branched bush; stems mostly triangular, with acute angles, almost winged, sparingly toothed. Joints leaf-like, spathulate, or oval-oblong, or lanceolate-acute, narrowed at the base, tender green, passing to greyish, 8 to 16 cm. long, $1\frac{1}{2}$ to 6 cm. broad, often reddish along the margin, which is notched. Areoles slightly woolly, with 1 or 2 short transparent spinescent bristles. Flowers rather few, $1\frac{1}{2}$ cm. long, borne on the marginal areoles, with 9 petals, pale yellow. Stigma with 5 recurved lobes. Fruit very small, round. The flowers on fading turn to deep yellow.

Rhipsalis pachyptera Pfeiff. Brazil (Rio de Janeiro, Sao Paulo, Santa Catharina). An erect branched bush, up to 1 m. high. Joints rarely 3-winged, usually leaf-like, flat, rather thick, oblong or broadly elliptical, obtuse at either end, or narrowed at the base, often concave-convex, dark green, roughly notched, often margined purplish red, with a thick middle nerve, and pronounced side or lateral nerves, 8 to 20 cm. long, 5 to 12 cm. broad. Flowers on the marginal areoles, solitary or in clusters of 2 or more, about $1\frac{1}{2}$ cm. long, with 10 petals: inner petals elliptical, obtuse, canary yellow, tipped reddish. Stigma with 3 or 4 reflexed lobes. Fruit red. Areoles slightly woolly, without bristles.

Rhipsalis robusta Lem. = *R. pachyptera* var. *crassior* Salm-Dyck. Brazil (Rio de Janeiro). Plant larger in all its parts, except the flowers. Lower joints mostly three-winged. Upper joints more stiff and thicker. Flowers as in the preceding, but more numerous, and in clusters of 5 to 8 from the same areole.

Rhipsalis platycarpa Pfeiff. = *Cereus platycarpus* Zucc. Brazil. An erect branched bush, about 1 m. high. Joints leaf-like, elongated, linear-oblong, obtuse, narrowed at the base, 8 to 30 cm. long, and 4 to 5 cm. broad, with a broad and thick median nerve, and pronounced lateral nerves, crenate or toothed, dark green, often reddish along the margin. Areoles slightly woolly, usually without bristles. Flowers solitary, on the side areoles, about 18 mm. long, with 10 petals: inner petals oblong, obtuse, yellowish. Stigma with 5 spreading lobes. Fruit hemispherical, greenish white.

II. *Species with depressed ovary, that is partly sunk into the areole.*

A. *Calamorhipsalis* K. Sch. Joints cylindrical.

Rhipsalis floccosa Salm-Dyck. Brazil (Minas Geraes). Moderately branched, mostly hanging or creeping on mossy trunks of trees, about 1 m. long, stems about 8 mm. thick. Joints 10 to 30 cm. long, 4 to 5 mm. thick, arising singly or in whorls of 2 or 3, from the upper end of the stems and other joints, dull dark green, or greyish or reddish, perfectly cylindrical, acute at the tip. Areoles irregularly distributed along the joint, slightly depressed, with a little greyish wool and with 2 to 4 dark bristles. Flowers about 14 mm. broad, usually surrounded with many bristles. Outer petals triangular, obtuse, green: the inner oblong, obtuse, greenish white. Stamens diaphanous white; style white, thick, spindle-shaped; stigma with 4 or 5 erect, thick, white lobes. Fruit white, about 6 mm. thick, embedded in the wool of the areole.

Rhipsalis tucumanensis Weber. Argentina (Tucuman). Sparingly branched. Joints cylindrical or very slightly angular, green, of varying length, ½ to 1 cm. thick, acute at the tip. Areoles on flowering joints slightly woolly. Flowers on the side areoles, about 12 mm. long, with the ovary embedded in the wool of the areole. Outer petals 4, rounded, concave at the tip, white, tipped pink; inner petals 8, lanceolate, white, tipped reddish. Stamens very numerous, white; style white, stigma with 4 or 5 thick reflexed lobes. Fruit round, depressed, up to 1 cm. thick, white flushed pink.

Rhipsalis Neves-Armondii K. Sch. Brazil (Rio de Janeiro). Copiously branched, hanging bush, dull green, at first erect, with two sorts of joints: the lower ones erect, cylindrical, up to 20 cm. long, 4 to 5 mm. thick; the upper ones in whorls mostly of 5 to 7, 3 to 10 cm. long, slightly angular and thinner. Areoles very small, disposed spirally on the longer joints, and along the angles of the shorter joints, having 3 to 5 very small bristles embedded in the tissues. Flowers solitary or in pairs, near the top of the joints, on more woolly areoles, about 13 mm. long. Ovary round, white, embedded in the areole: petals 8 to 10, oblong, obtuse, white. Stamens and style diaphanous white, stigma with 5 reflexed fleshy lobes. Fruit greenish or red, 8 mm. thick.

Rhipsalis gibberula Weber. Eastern Brazil, mostly on ledges of rock. Moderately branched, and low growing. Joints cylindrical, pale green to greyish green, 10 to 20 cm. long, or shorter and slightly five-angled, branching in whorls. Areoles small, slightly woolly, mostly without bristles or with 1 to 4 very short ones, the joints slightly thickened below the areoles. Flowers numerous, borne along the sides of the joints, 9 mm. long, up to 14 mm. broad. Ovary depressed in the areole, surrounded with wool: sepals 4, oval, greenish, tipped red: petals 8, oval, concave at the top, more or less erect, white. Stamens white, style thick, white, stigma with 4 to 6 white lobes. Fruit round, depressed, up to 1 cm. thick, white.

Rhipsalis pulvinigera Lindb. Brazil. A branched and hanging bush, up to 80 cm. long. Stems or joints glossy dark green, cylindrical, 40 to 60 cm. long, 5 to 7 mm. thick, branching in whorls of 3 to 5. Areoles on small prominences surrounded by crescent-like, toothed scales, with a little greyish wool, and 1 or 2 very short bristles. Flowers solitary, 2 cm. long, and up to 22 mm. broad. Ovary depressed, green. Petals greenish white, fading to yellowish. Stamens and style white, stigma with four reflexed lobes. Fruit round, diaphanous purplish red.

Rhipsalis megalantha Loefgren. Brazil, Sao Paulo (Island of San

Sebastian). Similar to *R. tucumanensis*. A tall erect bush, moderately branching, later branching from the base and extending, finally hanging, dull greenish grey. Stems long, branching in whorls, about 1 cm. thick, cylindrical or fluted. Joints branching dichotomously or in whorls of 3 to 6, cylindrical or furrowed, 8 to 15 cm. long, at first pale green and with white hairs. Areoles only slightly depressed, with oval brown scales, very minute, with yellowish wool, and 1 or 2 very small yellowish white bristles. Flowers very numerous, with an embedded or depressed ovary, corolla up to 4 cm. across; inner petals oblong, obtuse or acute, yellowish white. Stamens very numerous, less than 1 cm. long, spreading, orange red at the base, pink above; style thick, white, stigma with 6 to 8 recurved lobes. Fruit oval, pointed, 1 cm. long, white flushed pink, with the withered perianth attached to it.

Rhipsalis dissimilis K. Sch. Eastern Brazil (Sao Paulo). Bush much branched, at first erect, later hanging; stems and joints very different. Stems erect, tall, cylindrical-angular, with 6 or 7 low angles, about 1 cm. thick, dark green, with areoles closely set along the angles or ribs, and rather deeply embedded, with short wool, and with 14 or more bristles, 3 to 5 mm. long. The joints, also long, and thinner, with areoles arranged spirally, also furnished with bristles. The upper joints are up to 15 cm. long, and 5 to 7 mm. thick, mostly triangular, with acute angles, branching in whorls, with areoles along their sides. Flowers borne along the upper joints, red when in bud, about 13 mm. long; ovary depressed into the areole; petals 10, oval, obtuse, pinkish outside, white inside. Stigma with 4 or 5 reflexed lobes. Fruit red.

var. **setulosa** Weber. Upper joints five-angled, not three-angled.

Rhipsalis pacheo-leonii Leofgren. Eastern Brazil. Like the preceding. Irregularly branched, and with smaller flowers.

Rhipsalis puniceo-discus Lindb. Eastern Brazil. Stems long, hanging, moderately branched, soft and flexible, 5 to 7 mm. thick, pale green or yellowish green. Joints cylindrical, 7 to 10 cm. long, 4 mm. thick, glossy dark green, with areoles spirally arranged each surrounded with a reddish border, very slightly woolly, without bristles. Flowers borne along the joints, 1½ cm. long, with a depressed ovary: petals oblong-lanceolate, acute, white; stamens and style purplish below, pink above; stigma with 4 or 5 recurved lobes. Fruit at first black, passing to golden yellow.

var. **chrysocarpa** (Leofgr.) = *R. chrysocarpa* Leofgren. Style white. Fruit pale orange red.

Rhipsalis epiphyllanthoides Backbg. A new species, recently discovered in southern Brazil, growing erect in pockets of tufaceous rocks. Growth similar to that of *Epiphyllanthus candidus*. erect, with few stems. Joints one above the other, 2 to 4 cm. long, cylindrical, slightly angular when dry, at first with weak ribs below the areoles, the ribs terminating in a reddish prominence bearing the areole, which is furnished with short white wool, and with about 12 thin white bristles up to 4 mm. long, directed upwards, which soon drop off. Flowers about

(b) RHIPSALIDOPSIS ROSEA

(a) CHIAPASIA NELSONII

PLATE LXIV

PLATE LXV

3 cm. broad, yellowish white: outer petals oval, tipped darker; inner petals lanceolate and narrower; stamens many, white, shorter than the petals.

B. *Epallagogonium* K. Sch. Stems three-sided, jointed, twisted at each joint, so that there is an angle above and below each flat side alternately.

Rhipsalis paradoxa Salm-Dyck = *R. alternata* Lem. Brazil (Sao Paulo). Moderately branched, 30 to 50 cm. high, jointed, pale green to dark green, often overlaid reddish, especially along the angles. Joints branching dichotomously, sometimes in whorls of 3, 10 to 18 cm. long, with 3 acute angles, twisted into lesser joints at intervals of 2 to 5 cm. bearing a scaly areole at the top of each angle (or at the base of each flat side). Areoles slightly woolly, and with 1 or 2 small bristles when young. Flowers solitary on the upper areoles of the joint, about 2 cm. long, with a bare depressed ovary and with 8 petals; outer petals oval, obtuse, white with a green dorsal band; inner petals the same or pure white. Stamens and style white, stigma with 4 or 5 white recurved lobes. Fruit reddish. A species of very curious aspect.

C. *Trigonorhipsalis* K. Sch. Joints always triangular, with very acute and straight angles; without bristles.

Rhipsalis trigona Pfeiff. Eastern Brazil (Rio de Janeiro). A strong growing, much branched bush, about 1 m. high, dark green, passing to greyish. Joints 3 to 9 cm. long, 1½ to 2 cm. thick, with 3 acute angles, and with flat or slightly concave sides, slightly notched along the angles, bearing areoles, at first sparingly woolly, becoming hairy when flowering. Flowers borne copiously along the angles of the upper and new joints, about 2 cm. broad: inner petals (7 or 8) oval, obtuse, white. Stamens, style and 4-lobed stigma white. Fruit globular, about 1 cm. thick, wine red.

CONCLUSION
SUMMARY OF CULTURAL HINTS

Cacti are highly specialized plants, and almost all of them are specialized to sustain a prolonged period of drought, whether in full sun or in the shade. Some of them are specialized for an epiphytic life, like most Orchids and Bromeliads, living on the mossy trunks of trees or on shaded or half-shaded ledges of rock, and therefore they require shade or half-shade, with well defined periods of drought, relieved only by more or less heavy falls of dew, or by the invisible condensation of atmospheric moisture in the soil; but being of rather quick growth, they require more space for their roots and a more nutritious soil than Orchids and Bromeliads. Others are specialized for a life in the half-shade of the undergrowth on the outskirts of forests, in a soil made up largely of leaf-mould and of other decaying vegetable matter, and they have also well defined periods of rest and growth, although it is known that a soil of that type is capable of condensing and retaining much atmospheric moisture. Others are specialized for an existence on the alluvial soil of the pampas and prairies, where the soil is more or less loamy, and often flooded in the rainy season, and during the long periodical droughts they are partly shaded off by the dried vegetation around them. But most of them are denizens of the exposed, arid, sandy and stony wastes of desert regions, under a broiling sun; or of the craggy and almost bare slopes of hills and valleys, often at high altitudes, where they are usually covered with snow in winter, and these, although they may at first thrive wonderfully in a milder climate and more nourishing soil, are bound to resent a long continued course of good treatment, and unless they are allowed proper periods of rest and short commons, in which to mature their growths, they generally succumb suddenly to rot, as a result of surfeit and plethora. Thus warned, the reader will understand better the advice conveyed in the following hints for each tribe and genus, and will soon acquire enough practice to be able to act correctly on his own initiative, when modifications of the line of treatment become necessary to suit special circumstances.

Tribe I. PERESKIEAE

Pereskia. These species are the least specialized of all Cacti. They thrive well in any porous soil, moderately rich, and are able to stand periods of drought and also a great deal of neglect. They require warmth and full sunshine, with abundant watering during the growing season. Are easily propagated by cuttings in late spring and summer, and are mostly of fast growth and large development. Only 2 or 3 species are of real ornamental value.

444

SUMMARY OF CULTURAL HINTS

Tribe II. OPUNTIEAE

Pereskiopsis. The same treatment as Pereskia.

Quiabentia, Pterocactus. Soil sandy and gritty and very porous, with some old leaf-mould. Full sunshine or half-shade, but in an open and well ventilated situation. Keep rather dry, even during growth. *Pterocactus* requires more warmth and sunshine, and is best grafted on Opuntia (*O. Ficus-indica*), but grows well also on own roots.

Tacinga. Very rare in cultivation; mainly of botanical interest. Compost made of equal parts of sand and leaf-mould. Half-shade, Water moderately and spray frequently.

Maihuenia. Opuntia, Nopalea, Grusonia. Soil very porous and calcareous, made of garden loam and old cow manure roughly powdered, 2 parts of each, old mortar roughly powdered or hard limestone gravel and crushed bricks or grit, 1 part of each. Species of *Maihuenia,* of *Opuntia* of the sub-genus *Sphaeropuntia,* and of *Grusonia,* have a comparatively weak root-system, and for them the addition of sand is desirable (sand, loam, limestone gravel or old mortar, cow manure or leaf-mould in equal parts). Other species of *Opuntia* and *Nopalea* have a powerful root system, and will thrive well in any porous calcareous soil with a fair quantity of old cow manure.

Many species of the sub-genus *Platyopuntia* are quite hardy, and will bear unscathed several degrees of frost. Others require more warmth or even a tropical climate, and are liable to suffer severely from exposure to cold, even in comparatively mild climates. *Maihuenia,* and most species of the sub-genus *Cylindropuntia,* will thrive well in half-shade. A few species, such as *O. clavarioides, O. vestita, O. floccosa, O. Spegazzinii,* require half-shade. All other species thrive best in full sunshine, with abundant water during the growing season. Keep almost entirely dry in autumn and winter. Spray frequently during summer.

Tribe III. CEREEAE
Sub-tribe I. *Cereanae*

Cereus (Piptanthocereus), Lemaireocereus, Stetsonia, Acanthocereus, Haageocereus. For species of these genera the soil may consist of a mixture of good garden loam somewhat clayey, sand or limestone gravel, crushed bricks or crushed hard limestone or crushed old mortar, and leaf-mould or old cow manure, in equal parts by volume. A good soil is also made by mixing equal parts of sand and very old and exhausted cow manure or leaf-mould, and limestone gravel or roughly powdered old mortar, to which some crushed charcoal may be added. The presence of limestone or old mortar or other calcareous substance is necessary for the full development of the spines. Most species require full sunshine in a sheltered situation, with some slight shading in the case of plants grown in pots. *Cereus azureus, C. coerulescens, C. chalybaeus* and *Lemaireocereus Beneckei* prefer half-shade. Should be abundantly watered and sprayed frequently during the season of growth, but the new growth should be matured and hardened off by

445

reducing the amount of water early in autumn, and must be kept almost dry throughout the winter, in a dry atmosphere, giving just enough water now and then to keep the roots alive and to prevent the plant from shrivelling too much. They are usually grown on own roots, either from seed, or from cuttings made early in summer.

Pachycereus, Lophocereus, Espostoa, Oreocereus, Cephalocereus, Browningia, Machaerocereus. Should have a warm situation in full sunshine. *Cephalocereus Palmeri, C. Sartorianus, C. euphorbioides* and *C. rhodanthus* (*Arrojadoa*) prefer half-shade. The soil may be more stony or gritty and more proous, with less leaf-mould or cow manure, and on the whole poorer and less nourishing. A good compost would consist of garden loam and sand 2 parts of each, limestone gravel or crushed old mortar and old manure or leaf-mould, 1 part of each. *Machaerocereus* prefers a more sandy soil with more calcareous matter. *Pachycereus columna-trajani, Browningia candelaris* and certain species of *Cephalocereus*, as well as species of *Espostoa* and *Oreocereus*, are often grafted, but they grow also quite well on own roots, although growth may be slower. They all require a soil rich in lime, and this is best supplied either as roughly powdered old mortar or as hard limestone gravel or limestone sand or hard limestone or marble chipped or crushed.

Arthrocereus, Monvillea, Harrisia, Corryocactus. Arthrocereus microsphaericus is often grafted on species of *Cereus*, but grows well on own roots in a mixture of equal parts of sand and leaf-mould, with the addition of a little garden loam and some limestone gravel and crushed charcoal. Requires half-shade and warmth. All the others thrive best in full sunshine, in a warm and sheltered situation, in a soil of the same composition but with more garden loam and with some old manure, and also with a good allowance of calcareous matter, particularly for species of *Harrisia.*

Leocereus, Heliocereus, Cleistocactus. The species of the first two genera require a soil heavily charged with leaf-mould, and may consist of leaf-mould and sharp sand 2 parts of each, crushed bricks, crushed charcoal, peat and old manure 1 part of each; the addition of a little charcoal dust will keep the soil porous and sweet. They thrive better in half-shade. *Cleistocactus* grows well in a mixture of garden loam, sand or limestone gravel, crushed bricks and leaf-mould or old manure, in equal parts, and flowers more freely in full sunshine.

Species of *Borzicactus* and *Nyctocereus* thrive best in full sunshine, in a soil made as suggested for *Monvillea*, with a more liberal proportion of limestone gravel.

Bergerocactus, Peniocereus and *Wilcoxia* require a very sandy and porous soil, made up of 2 parts sand, 1 part leaf-mould or very old mnaure, and 1 part gravel or finely crushed bricks, with the addition of a little garden loam and charcoal dust. *Peniocereus* grows best in half-shade, the others in full sunshine. *Peniocereus* is often grafted, as it usually makes slow growth on own roots. Species of *Rathbunia* thrive well in the same soil and in full sunshine, but the proportion of garden loam should be increased, and some limestone gravel added.

Trichocereus, Binghamia. Some species of *Trichocereus,* such as *T. strigosus, T. tephracanthus, T. thelegonus, T. macrogonus, T. pasacana,* etc., delight in a sandy and stony soil, with the addition of some leaf-mould or old manure, but will also grow quite well in a mixture of garden loam, sand and leaf-mould, always with the addition of crushed old mortar or limestone gravel. For other species, such as *T. Spachianus, T. lamprochlorus, T. Schickendantzii,* the soil should be more nourishing and less calcareous. *T. pasacana, T. Terscheckii, T. cephalopasacana, T. cephalomacrostibas, T. Werdermannianus, T. strigosus, T. chiloensis, T. fascicularis,* etc. delight in full sunshine, the others thrive just as well, or better, in half-shade. Species of *Binghamia* require a soil heavily calcareous, with some leaf-mould or old manure added, and prefer full sun. All species of *Trichocereus* and *Binghamia* should be liberally watered and sprayed frequently during the season of growth.

Sub-Tribe II. *Hylocereanae*

All species of *Hylocereus* require warmth, and most of them require half-shade. The soil should be rich in humus. A few species, such as *H. trigonus, H. undatus, H. Napoleonis, H. extensus,* will grow well in garden loam, with a liberal addition of sand and leaf-mould or old manure. Others, like *H. Purpusii* and *H. Lemairei,* are more exacting, requiring a rather rich compost made up of broken peat, leaf-mould or old manure and sand in equal parts, with the addition of some crushed bricks and charcoal dust. In their case the addition of calcareous matter had better be avoided. Keep almost dry during the period of rest, or just moist enough to keep the roots from dying off, but water abundantly and spray frequently from May to September.

Mediocactus and *Deamia,* and other allied genera, may have the same soil as suggested for *Heliocereus,* and must be kept in half-shade, or even fully shaded.

Selenicereus and *Aporocactus* will grow well in a mixture of garden loam, sand and leaf-mould or old manure, in equal parts, with the addition of some hard limestone gravel or crushed old mortar and of a little crushed charcoal. They require a warm, sheltered and half-shaded situation, or where they are exposed to full sunshine for only 3 or 4 hours every day; and should be watered freely and sprayed frequently during the summer months. Certain species which are exclusively epiphytic, such as *Selenicereus Donkelaeri, S. Murrillii, S. vagans,* etc. thrive best in a soil made of 2 parts leaf-mould, 1 part sand, with some crushed charcoal and old manure, and must be kept in a warm and shaded situation. Species of *Aporocactus* are best grafted as standards on *Selenicereus Macdonaldiae* or other suitable species, and trained on an umbrella-like wire support; but they grow and flower well also on own roots, as hanging baskets.

Sub-Tribe III. *Echinocereanae*

All species of *Echinocereus* thrive well in full sunshine, but a few species, such as *E. Viereckii, E. Blanckii, E. pentalophus, E. cinerascens, E. Knippelianus, E. amoenus, E. pulchellus, E. paucispinus, E. Hempelii, E. Salm-Dyckianus*, thrive and flower as well also in half-shade. For most species the soil should be sandy and calcareous, with the addition of leaf-mould or old manure. For a few species, such as *E. acifer, E. Baileyi, E. Knippelianus, E. Weinbergii, E. Roetteri*, etc., the proportion of leaf-mould should be greater. Keep dry during winter, close to the glass, in full sunshine, and water liberally in summer, but see that the growths are properly matured early in autumn. *Echinocerei* are very generally grown on own roots, but *E. papillosus, E. caespitosus, E. pectinatus, E. Fitchii, E. Fendleri* and the various cristate forms are often grafted.

Austrocactus, Chamaecereus, Rebutia and *Lobivia*, mostly delight in full sunshine, but thrive well also in half shade. A few species of *Rebutia*, viz; *R. minuscula, R. pseudo-minuscula* and 1 or 2 others require half-shade, as also *Lobivia Pentlandii* and its varieties, *L. cinnabarina, L. longispina, L. caespitosa, L. Bruchii* and a few others. A few species of *Lobivia* (*L. Backebergii, L. rebutioides*, etc.) must have full sunshine at all times. *Chamaecereus* flowers better in full sunshine. The soil should be substantial, consisting of peat, sand, leaf-mould or old and thoroughly exhausted manure, with some crushed old mortar and crushed charcoal added. Some limestone gravel or crushed old mortar is always beneficial.

Most species of *Echinopsis* prefer half-shade, but a few, such as *E. Bridgesii, E. Silvestrii, E. formosa*, prefer full sunshine at all seasons. A few species, such as *E. calochlora, E. cordobensis, E. leucantha, E. obrepanda, E. Spegazziniana*, prefer a soil predominantly sandy; for the others the soil may consist of equal parts of garden loam, sand, crushed bricks, old manure and old leaf-mould. Many species will thrive satisfactorily in a soil containing much garden loam, along with leaf-mould or old manure, and some grit or hard limestone gravel, but too much lime in the soil, especially in a too soluble form, is definitely injurious for *Echinopsis*, as it may cause a state of chlorosis, to which the plant often succumbs. A few species, such as *E. albispinosa*, and the various cristate forms, are often grafted; the others are generally grown on own roots, whether propagated by offsets or by seed. Keep rather dry from October to April, but water liberally during the season of flowering and growth. Spray with care, and only in the morning, so that the small accumulation of moisture which may collect in the depression at the top of the stem may have time to evaporate during the day.

Sub-Tribe IV. *Echinocactanae*

Denmoza rhodacantha and *D. erythrocephala* will grow well in a mixture of equal parts of sand, good garden loam and leaf-mould, with the addition of some hard limestone chips, and of some crushed bricks and crushed old mortar, or of a limestone gravel. When fully established a dressing of old manure may be given, but too much nourishment should be avoided. Place in full sunshine, with occasional morning sprayings during the growing period, but watering should be done sparingly, especially in winter.

Ariocarpus, Encephalocarpus, Lophophora, Aztekium, Pediocactus, Copiapoa, Neoporteria, Toumeya, Epithelantha and *Oroya* inhabit sandy and stony districts and therefore must have a soil decidedly sandy in character. They grow well in a mixture of 3 parts sand, 1 part grit or finely crushed bricks, 1 part leaf-mould, 1 part good garden loam, with a little old manure. Species of *Ariocarpus, Encephalocarpus* and *Lophophora*, having a long turnip-like root, must be planted in deep pots. Water moderately during the growing season, and keep almost completely dry in winter. They require warmth and full sunshine. *Lophophora* sprouts very freely around the base and forms a large clump in a few years. It has a tendency to shrivel too much in winter, but soon recovers in spring. Species of *Copiapoa* and *Neoporteria* are often less satisfactory. In particular, the interesting *Neoporteria nidus* and its variety *N. senilis*, soon establish themselves and make good growth, but often die off after 2 or 3 years, and are therefore best grown grafted. The beautiful *Oroya peruviana* is much more resistant, and imported plants, as well as seedlings, do very well on own roots. For *Oroya*, as well as for *Matucana Haynei, Leuchtenbergia principis* and species of *Hamatocactus*, the soil may be richer, with a greater proportion of leaf-mould and with a little old manure, as well as with a larger allowance of calcareous material. They are all sun-loving plants, delighting in an airy and open situation, and should be well watered during summer.

Most species of *Stenocactus* (*Echinofossulocactus*) prefer a soil well charged with humus. A mixture made of equal parts of leaf-mould, sand and garden loam, with a good sprinkling of crushed old mortar or limestone gravel, has proved very satisfactory. The proportion of sand may be increased, or that of loam reduced, for *S. hastatus, S. crispatus, S. multangularis, S. gladiatus* and *S. dichroacanthus*. They thrive better in half-shade than in full sunshine.

Species of *Ferocactus* are sun-loving plants, and thrive best in a sandy and stony soil of rather poor quality. A substantial and nourishing soil should be avoided. The following mixture will be found satisfactory for most species, 3 parts sharp sand with some stone chips, 1 part crushed old mortar or hard limestone gravel or crushed white marble, 1 part good garden loam and 1 part old leaf-mould or old manure. *Ferocactus crassihamatus, F. melocactiformis, F. glaucescens* and *F. flavovirens* thrive well also in half-shade, in a soil with more leaf-mould and less sand. Avoid excessive watering, even in summer, and spray only in the morning, for the reason mentioned under *Echinopsis*. Species of *Ferocactus, Hamatocactus, Stenocactus* and *Leuchtenbergia* are best grown on own roots.

Most species of *Echinomastus, Gymnocalycium, Echinocactus, Homalocephala, Eriosyce* and *Astrophytum* delight in full sunshine and in an airy situation, in a sandy soil as recommended for *Ferocactus* but with a little more leaf-mould or old manure, and may be freely watered in summer, but should be kept comparatively dry in winter. A few species of *Gymnocalycium* (*G. gibbosum*, *G. Netrelianum*, *G. Mihanovichii*, *G. Spegazzinii*, etc.) prefer half-shade and a richer soil with more leaf-mould. *Astrophytum asterias* thrives best in a sandy soil, but other species of *Astrophytum* and *Aztekium Ritteri*, should have a soil heavily charged with crushed old mortar or limestone gravel, and a fair proportion of leaf-mould and some old manure. *Echinocactus Grusonii* is easily scorched in full sunshine, and should be kept half-shaded, or in the shade of trees.

Sub-Tribe V. *Cactanae*
Species of *Cactus* or *Melocactus*, should be watered rather sparingly in summer and kept almost dry in winter. When grown on own roots, their roots are few and superficial, and occupy very little space. Shallow pots, well drained, are the best for them. They are sea-side plants mostly and for most of them sandy soil with crushed bricks and crushed old mortar and a fair allowance of leaf-mould will prove satisfactory. A few species, such as *C. amoenus*, *C. salvador*, *C. Townsendii*, *C. macracanthus*, prefer a richer soil, with about one-third old leaf-mould, and with some old manure. All require full sunshine, and the winter temperature should not be less than 20°C. The same soil and treatment are suitable for species of *Discocactus*.

Sub-Tribe VI *Coryphanthanae*
The pretty *Mamillopsis senilis* thrives better in full sunshine and in exposed situations, and requires a soil composed of equal parts of sharp sand, limestone gravel and leaf-mould, and should be only moderately watered in summer and kept almost dry in winter, but should be sprayed frequently in summer. It is always a difficult plant to deal with, and for this reason, it is frequently grafted on *Trichocereus Spachianus*.

Most species of *Thelocactus*, *Neolloydia* and *Cochemiea*, thrive best in a sandy soil, made up of 3 parts sharp sand and grit, with some stone chippings, 1 part garden loam and the same quantity of crushed old mortar and of leaf-mould, and a little old manure may also be added. Most of them thrive best in full sunshine. A few species, such as *Thelocactus lophothele*, *T. rinconadensis*, *T. Lloydii*, prefer half shade, and these also prefer a soil with more leaf-mould and garden loam. For species of *Neolloydia* and *Cochemiea* the addition of limestone gravel, with an equivalent reduction of sand, is desirable. They should be kept rather dry, even in summer, but frequent sprayings are recommended.

Obregonia and *Neowerdermannia* should have rather deep pots for their tapering roots, and the soil may consist of equal parts of sand, garden loam and leaf-mould, with some limestone gravel and crushed charcoal. They prefer full sunshine.

SUMMARY OF CULTURAL HINTS

Species of *Coryphantha* are mostly sun-loving plants, preferring a soil decidedly sandy and gritty, and therefore may consist of 2 parts of sharp sand, 1 part crushed bricks, 1 part crushed old mortar or limestone gravel, 1 part garden loam and 1 part leaf-mould or old manure, with the addition of some crushed charcoal or charcoal dust. The soil should be kept rather dry; and plants in pots may be watered twice a week in summer, and in very hot weather even thrice a week, but should be kept dry or almost dry in winter. *Coryphantha clava, C. Georgii, C. echinoidea, C. Poselgeriana, C. Salm-Dyckiana, C. Vaupeliana, C. pycnacantha, C. reduncuspina* and a few others, thrive best in half-shade, and their soil should contain a larger proportion of leaf-mould.

Neobesseya and *Escobaria*, require the same arid or semi-arid conditions of soil and treatment. The soil should have more limestone gravel or other calcareous matter in its composition.

Pelecyphora aselliformis and *Solisia pectinata* require full sunshine and sandy calcareous soil with some leaf-mould.

Species of *Dolichothele* thrive best in half-shade, in a sandy and calcareous mixture, somewhat clayey or retentive, made up of 2 parts good garden loam, 1 part sand, 1 part limestone gravel and 1 part leaf-mould or old manure. Water sparingly, particularly in autumn.

The species of *Mammillaria* which thrive best in half-shade are about as numerous as those which prefer full sunshine. The beginner will therefore do well to stand all species in a sunny place, with some slight shading, or in a place where the plants are exposed to continuous full sunshine only for 2 to 4 hours every day in summer, preferably in the morning, and he will soon find out for himself which species seem to revel in the sun, or to demand a little more shade. Of course in the half shade of tall trees, where sunshine and shadow are continually moving along over the plants, these will have the full benefit of half-shade throughout the day. A few species have a large tap-root, like a *Coryphantha*, and these of course must have rather deep pots; the others will do well in shallow pots, well drained. For some species, such as *M. Parkinsonii, M. compressa, M. geminispina, M. chionocephala, M. perbella, M. carnea, M. Boedekeriana, M. Hahniana,* etc., the soil should be well charged with hard limestone gravel or other calcareous material, with a good proportion of leaf-mould. Species like *M. elongata* and its varieties, *M. spinosissima* and its varieties, *M. simplex, M. meiacantha, M. vetula, M. Zeyeriana, M. Wagneriana,* etc., prefer a more sandy soil, a mixture of 2 parts sand, 1 part garden loam and 1 part leaf-mould. Most other species are satisfied with a mixture of garden loam and sand, like the alluvial soils of their native home, but there should be always an allowance of limestone gravel or crushed old mortar, as well as a proportion of leaf-mould or old manure, about one-fifth of the total volume. For a few species like *M. plumosa, M. Schiedeana, M. Herrerae,* the soil should be predominantly calcareous, consisting for about two-thirds of hard limestone gravel and chipped or crushed limestone rock.

Watering must be done very carefully. It is advisable to soak the plants thoroughly, and then allow them to dry properly before watering again. Spray frequently, but lightly, preferably in the morning. When in doubt about watering, it is better to stir the surface soil in the pot, and to put off watering till next day or the day after. Many species, like *M. elongata*, *M. microhelia*, *M. Schiedeana*, *M. plumosa*, etc., which will stand a lot of drought and neglect, will soon perish if allowed too much moisture. Species of *Mammillaria* with a solitary stem, and also many cespitose species of rather delicate nature, are often grafted on *Trichocereus Spachianus* and other *Cerei*, but it is always better and more instructive to grow these plants on own roots. Slow-growing seedlings of certain species, may be grafted to induce a quicker development.

Sub-Tribe VII. *Epiphyllanae*

All species and varieties of *Epiphyllum*. *Zygocactus*, *Schlumbergera*, *Chiapasia*, *Epiphyllanthus* and *Nopalxochia* require half-shade, in summer the shade of tall leafy trees being admirably suited. They will grow well in situations so shaded that the sun hardly ever reaches them, but then most of them are far less free-flowering, even though they may have the requisite degree of warmth. The soil should consist of leaf-mould and sharp sand in equal parts, with the addition of some crushed bricks and crushed charcoal, and with some old manure. Of course, grafted plants should have a soil suitable to the stock on which they are grafted. *Zygocactus* is best grafted on *Selenicereus Macdonaldiae* or on *Hylocereus undatus* or on species of *Pereskia*, but will also grow well or own roots in hanging baskets, shrivelling considerably after flowering in winter, but soon recuperating and starting fresh growth in spring. The joints will turn reddish, and soon lose their healthy aspect on exposure to full sun even for a few days. During the flowering season these plants should be watered liberally, giving them a short rest after flowering, but continuing the sprayings. *Schlumbergera*, *Chiapasia* and *Epiphyllanthus* may have the same treatment as *Zygocactus*. Species and varieties of *Epiphyllum* and *Nopalxochia* are mostly grown on own roots, from cuttings taken about halfway up the joint (discarding the narrow lower part), in spring and summer, and after curing for a few days in the shade, they are potted off separately in small pots, in sand or in a mixture of sand and leaf-mould. Grafting on *Hylocereus undatus* results in free-flowering plants of sturdy growth. They are huge feeders, and the soil should be very nourishing. The soil may consist of equal parts of sand or of loam, crushed bricks, leaf-mould and old manure, or a mixture of equal parts of sharp sand, leaf-mould, old manure, peat and crushed charcoal, this last will prevent the compost from getting sour. For grown up plants the proportion of old cow manure may be increased without any injurious results, and it is necessary to keep the plants somewhat dry, particularly in autumn and winter, but frequent light sprayings are beneficial at all times. For species of *Disocactus*, which are rarely met with in cultivation, the soil should have a larger proportion of loam and less old manure.

Sub-Tribe VIII *Rhipsalidanae*

With very few exceptions all species of this Sub-Tribe dislike direct sunshine, even for short periods, and thrive best in perfect shade. Most of them grow into very fine specimens when grafted on species of *Cereus*, especially on *Hylocereus undatus*. The soil for plants grown on own roots may consist of a mixture of sharp sand and leaf-mould in equal parts, with the addition of a little old manure and some charcoal dust or crushed charcoal. Several species, such as *Rhipsalis trigona*, *R. paradoxa*, *R. grandiflora*, *R. salicornioides* and the new species *R. epiphyllanthoides* will also thrive well in a mixture of equal parts of garden loam, crushed bricks and grit, and leaf-mould, with the addition of crushed charcoal and some old manure. The last mentioned species happens to be one of those few species which will stand exposure to full sunshine for prolonged periods, All species require a warm and airy situation, without excessive damp.

The flat secondary joints of a number of species, which normally have tall cylindrical wand-like stems or leaders, will strike root with ease, but often fail to throw up leaders, and therefore are difficult to grow into fine specimens as when propagated by seed, or by cuttings of the cylindrical stems, or by division of the rootstock.

General Hints. A plot of ground, sloping towards the east, southeast or south, with a high wall or a belt of leafy trees for protection from the cold northerly winds, or rather from prevailing cold and high winds, would be ideal for most species of Cacti. Of course many species will require the shelter of a glass structure in winter, and in case of lean-to structures, these should likewise face the east, south-east or south. Span-roofed structures may have their long axis directed north, so as to have the sun on one side in the morning, and on the other side in the afternoon, although if their long axis is directed towards the east, the northern and shaded side would suit very well those species requiring shade or half-shade, such as the *Epiphyllanae* and *Rhipsalidanae*.

A locality near the sea, provided that it is not too exposed or within the reach of wind-borne sea spray, is very eligible for Cactus-growing, owing to the more equable temperature of seaside places, and the particularly bracing air, the slight salinity of the atmosphere being rather an advantage than a drawback, and promotes sturdy growth and immunity from disease, as I had occasion to notice on many occasions.

In handling Cacti grown in pots, it is important to remember not to change the direction of the pots in moving them from one place to another, particularly when the plants are making new growths or when the growths are still tender. For this purpose it is advisable to mark the side of the pot towards the north: a small disk or dot, about 1 cm. in diameter, made neatly with a small brush or with a cork dipped in oil paint, would provide a permanent mark for the guidance of the gardener.

It is always most important that the soil should be porous and the pots well drained. Drainage is best secured by means of crocks, well placed, covering the drainage holes with a large curved crock, which would not obstruct the quick outflow of surplus water. Instead of crocks, broken bricks chipped into pieces of convenient size, or thick gravel or shingle may be used, but should be washed to remove all traces of salt. Within certain limits, the composition of the soil may be varied without injury to the plant, so long as the fundamental qualities of the soil in its native habitat are kept well in view. The soil should be essentially sandy for plants living on a sandy soil; stony and calcareous for plants growing on a stony calcareous soil; loamy and somewhat clayey for plants inhabiting the alluvial deposits of the prairies and pampas; rich in humus or leaf-mould for epiphytic species generally, and for species living in the undergowth on the outskirts of forests. In these last two cases the addition of sand or fine gravel or crushed bricks is necessary to keep the soil in an open and porous condition, and the addition of crushed charcoal or charcoal dust prevents the soil from getting sour and also increases its porosity.

Leaf-mould should be old and thoroughly consumed. It is a good practice to pass it through a sieve, in order to separate the bits of stems, etc., which may ferment or putrefy and cause trouble. Leaf-mould, even if very old, is liable to clog and become sour, and also to breed worms, and this tendency is corrected by the addition of a little charcoal dust and sharp sand.

Organic manure—and here preference should always be given to cow manure, free as much as possible from straw and other litter—should be very old and thoroughly fermented, and its fertilizing qualities reduced by long exposure to damp and atmospheric action for at least one year. Cow manure, one or two years old, which was continually exposed to atmospheric action, and in the meantine has been turned over several times, may be used instead of leaf-mould or along with it, or mixed with peat, in making the various composts, but of course is always more nourishing for the plant than mere leaf-mould or peat, and its too liberal use, particularly for species requiring arid or semi-arid conditions, may prove dangerous.

For watering or spraying use rain water if available, and see that the water is of about the same temperature as the soil, or slightly warmer. Do not water unless there is a real need; when in doubt stir the surface of the soil to ascertain its condition, or withhold water for a day or two, even in the hottest days of summer, especially in the case of plants in large pots, which usually take many days to dry. Water and spray preferably in the morning, before the sun has reached the plants. Spray carefully and lightly, better with a syringe, and avoid wetting the stems of Cacti too frequently. An occasional spray with a good insecticide or fungicide, especially in warm and moist weather of early autumn, will help in preventing or controlling outbreaks of insect pests and plant diseases.

A SHORT BIOGRAPHY OF THE AUTHOR

BY BEATRICE BORG

Following the publication in 1937 of the first edition of "Cacti" by Professor John Borg, M.A., M.D., naturalists and Cactus lovers expressed the wish to know something about the author—"a short story of his life and career in the Government service, so as to give a picture of the author in his various human bearings and surroundings." With the publication of the second edition revised and enlarged by the author before his death and the continued success met by the work which essentially supplies the knowledge necessary for successful cultivation and classification of Cacti, the need for a biography of Professor J. Borg became even more evident.

And so it is my pleasant task to supply this more general knowledge of my husband—the man who gave the best years of his life in an effort to leave his island home a more beautiful place than formerly. By so doing I feel many readers, who may already feel acquainted with him through his work, will come to look upon him as a trusted friend.

EARLY YEARS

John Borg was born on November 9, 1873, at Balzan, a small inland village of Malta. His parents were Mr. and Mrs. Angelo Borg. He was their eldest son and had two brothers and a sister.

His first years of learning were spent at the village school, where he remained until the age of ten. His progress showed he was a studious lad, eager to grasp knowledge. In 1883 he entered the Lyceum, the government grammar school in Valletta, where he started a more advanced course of studies which led to matriculation for the University.

After successfully matriculating in 1891, John entered the University to take the seven years' course for the medical profession. Natural History was one of the subjects of the first years of this course, and so this was a source of considerable pleasure to him, for from early childhood he had shown a leaning towards nature and his free moments were always spent in gardening or in reading books on his favourite pursuit. In 1893 he won a prize for the best Herbarium of the course, and the following certificate was awarded:

"It is certified that Mr. John Borg, Student in Arts and Sciences in the Royal University, has presented to the Society of Natural Sciences a Collection of dry indigenous plants in the form of a Herbarium, made by him, which was judged worthy of praise and of the prize promised by this Society."

In the following year, 1894, he gained the degree of M.A., with honours in Latin, English and Italian Literature, Philosophy and Mathematics. In 1896 he obtained a certificate showing he had successfully undergone a course of Pharmacy, and on August 27, 1896, he was granted a warrant to practise as an apothecary. From that time he started to earn his first salary by attending a pharmacy as a professional apothecary after University lectures.

In 1898 he graduated in Medicine, and in 1899 acquired a warrant to practise as physician and surgeon. He at once began to practise, devoting his whole time and energy to his patients, and by the end of the year his practice was considerable. In this year's work as a doctor he was able to grasp the full meaning of the life of a conscientious general practitioner, the strain attached to it and the constant closeness to the misery and suffering of humanity. He was thorough in everything he undertook: had he been less so, he might not have decided on the action he was about to take.

SUPERINTENDENT OF PUBLIC GARDENS

In 1900 he gave up his practice in Medicine, and accepted the important post of Superintendent of Public Gardens, choosing to dedicate himself to the career of the cultivation and study of plant life for the improvement and embellishment of the Island.

At the time when Dr. Borg took over this post, there were practically no public gardens in Malta, except San Antonio Gardens, adjacent and leading to the Palace built by Grand Master de Paule at Attard in the year 1625.

The gardens and plantations came under the Public Works Department, and had been sadly neglected. It would be robbing Dr. Borg of one of his settings if special mention were not made of the Boschetto which, as its name implies, was a small wood or forest in the neighbourhood of Rabat. This was the first Public Garden in Malta and had been planted by Grand Master Hugh Loubens de Verdalle towards the close of the XVI century. It is renowned for the gigantic ash-trees in the valley, famous for the vivid green foliage which must be more than 350 years old, and was the place Borg visited every week for the best part of his life.

This semi-wild and lovely place, the home of the tall white Asphodels (sweet-scented narcissi), once an ancient holy Grove, the native place of the evergreen oak (*Quercus Ilex*) and of another holy tree "*Callitris quadrivalvis*" which supplied the famous "Citron" wood of the ancients; and of the Aleppo pines (*Pinus halepensis*), descendants and survivors of native pine groves—was not frequented by the public on account of its distance from the nearest town, except for the annual festivity of St. Peter and Paul (Mnarja) when young and old met beneath the trees.

At San Antonio Gardens, the main types of trees were three kinds of Cupressus, viz: Monterey Cypress, Nootka Sound Cypress and Evergreen Cypress: three kinds of Casuarina, viz: the "He Oak", the

"Iron Wood of the South Sea Islands" and the "Erect She Oak" "*Callitris quadrivalvis*"—the jointed *Arbor vitae*—besides a row of wild olive trees, originally planted as a windscreen across the entire breadth of the Gardens, and vines flanking the path ways. The remainder was mainly an orchard of orange trees of old ordinary varieties of low commercial value.

Plantations were almost non-existent so Dr. Borg had the hard task before him, for which he was most fitted, to renew and transform what had a bare existence, to create new gardens in the Islands besides planting numerous trees throughout all Malta and Gozo, not neglecting the small Island of Comino in the Channel between Malta and Gozo. In the year 1900 Borg made a comprehensive Report on the "Present Decay of San Antonio Gardens" with suggestions for improvements which, as Superintendent, it fell to him to put into effect. From this Report we gather that the trees were at the mercy of imported pests, the gardeners had no instructions and were without means of combating insects and diseases, and no nurseries existed. It is evident from the Report that financial considerations curtailed improvement and planning of the gardens, so that his plans for reforms had to be modified, subject to the small capital and little money at his disposal. Notwithstanding these difficulties, the Government eventually saw its way to providing adequate funds.

Now let us forget the precarious and difficult circumstances under which Dr. Borg began his career as Superintendent of Public Gardens and look back with appreciation on what he was able to achieve.

In Valletta, Hastings Gardens were considerably extended. The Garden at the Upper Baracca containing the tomb of Sir Thomas Maitland, where a lovely view of the harbour is enjoyed, was extended and well cultivated. The garden at the Lower Baracca containing the monument to Sir Alexander Ball, facing the outward side of the harbour and the Three Cities and commanding a fine view, was planted and adorned; the pond was furnished with ducks and geese. The bastion overlooking the inner side of the harbour on the south east of Floriana was converted into a secluded garden named Piazza Miratore Garden, and Blata l-Bajda Gardens outside Porte des Bombes, along the road to Marsa, came into being. Extensive areas were adorned with flower-beds and a fine collection of palms and ornamental trees.

Besides improving and enlarging the small gardens, one of his chief tasks was planting and furnishing the two fine extensive cemeteries, the Addolorata Cemetery and "Ta Braxia" Cemetery with ornamental trees, chiefly cypress trees and their many varieties, Aleppo pines, stone pines, *Arbor vitae*, *Araucarias*, palms and vines.

In 1909, Dr. Borg created a new garden, just outside Valletta, on the east side of the Palm Avenue, called King Edward VII Avenue, now much restricted to afford traffic facilities. This was named after the then Governor, "Rundle Gardens". He planned another one in Victoria, Gozo, bearing the same name, which is very extensive and affords a place of relaxation to the population. On the marshes at Gzira, between Valletta and Sliema, he laid out a garden which has much improved and embellished that part of the Island; likewise Sa Maison Garden in the outer part of Floriana. In 1923-24 when he was Superintendent of Agriculture he undertook the planning of Howard Garden at Notabile. This was laid out in difficult circumstances as many gaps had to be filled in and high ground levelled, but the final results are beautiful.

The south side of the Island was not neglected, for besides extensive plantations of trees on Santa Margherita Hill at Cospicua in 1926, an ancient Government Garden "Tal Cmand" at Zeitun, which at the time of the Knights belonged to the Commander of the District, was converted into a charming Public Garden and named "Luqa Briffa Garden". It is a great pleasure to see people in the neighbourhood availing themselves of its amenities on Sundays, as also on weekdays.

In a report made in 1925, he mentions the extensive plantations of ornamental trees in the Public Gardens at Verdala Park, Boschetto, San Antonio, the Valletta and Floriana Gardens as well as along roads and open spaces in Malta and Gozo. Even so, he deplores the fact that "our Islands are practically treeless", and says that "notwithstanding the many groves and orchards existing in both Islands, the generally bare aspect of our hills and countryside is greatly regretted for aesthetic as well as economic reasons."

Many trees were planted along the roads to form avenues; a few species of Ficus such as *Ficus elastica; F. rubiginosa; F. lucida; F. Citrifolia; F. dealbata; F. Magnoliaefolia* cultivated for their luxuriant evergreen foliage; and oleanders with their fine masses of bloom that adorn several highways and squares. In the neighbourhood of towns and villages fine avenues of false pepper *"Schinus Molle"; Schinus teribinthifolius* were also planted. Besides the noble avenues of palms near Valletta, thousands of trees were planted on the road to Boschetto and on the hilly ground above it, also pine trees on the way to Mellieha and Selmun. Numerous Agaves and Aloes were planted in the crevices of rocks on the road of Bahar ic-Ciak to Salina Bay, and many trees were also planted in Gozo. Besides these material benefits which Malta received from Dr. Borg's able and enthusiastic directoshsip of the gardens and plantations, enjoyed by the whole population and visitors alike, first and foremost he is to be praised for his initiative in educating and instructing the gardeners—"armed with much patience" as he himself declares, for they had been sadly neglected.

Once a week he gathered all the gardeners for a course of instruction. On a Friday they would gather full of enthusiasm to learn, paper and pencil in hand, for, in order to be sure they understood him, he would make them sketch, as he did himself whenever necessary to clarify the subject in question. Although his lessons, filled with all kinds of knowledge, were fit for people of higher education than the apprentices, yet his explanations were adapted to his audience and were understood and enjoyed by all.

RECOGNITION OF HIS WORK

As early as 1903 recognition of his work is recorded when His Excellency the Governor-General Lord Grenfell of Kilvey, G.C.B., G.C.M.G., was pleased to show his sympathy with Dr. Borg's task. On March 5, 1903, before relinquishing his high office, he requested his A.D.C., Colonel Biancardi to forward to Dr. Borg a book "which His Excellency hopes you will accept as a mark of his appreciation of the way you have done your duty as Superintendent of Public Gardens and of the improvements in same."

Also in 1903 we find some correspondence in connection with the King's desire to have some fair sized orange-trees of good shape and as nearly matched as possible (about 24 or 30) for his orangery at Windsor. In a letter from Windsor Castle, dated November 15, 1903, to the Superintendent of Public Works and signed "Esher" we read:

"The King desires me to express to you His Majesty's thanks for the trouble you have taken in obtaining the orange trees for the orangery at Windsor; and H.M. desires that you will also thank the Superintendent of Public Gardens at Malta for his kindness in the matter."

The knowledge of Dr. Borg's achievements reached other countries, and in 1907 we find him in correspondence with the Horticultural Society of Alexandria which requested all sorts of information, and his detailed and scientific answer on fertilization in plant life and caprification is worthy of note.

In 1908 Dr. Borg was elected a member of the Società Botanica Italiana, and in a letter dated March 14, 1909, the renowned botanist, Sommier, of the Società Italiana d'Antropologia acknowledged receipt, with much pleasure, of two letters from Dr. Borg and a small box of "Melitella" which, he said, arrived perfectly fresh. (The *Melitella pusilla* is a small stemless flat annual plant indigenous to the Maltese Islands—an alley plant which, rather than rising from the ground prefers being trodden, first found by Dr. Sommier in Gozo in 1906. In 1909 Dr. B rg found it in other localities in Gozo and afterwards in Malta). Sommier wrote that he would be reading Dr. Borg's letters at the next meeting before giving them to the press.

In 1916 he was requested by the Ministry of Agriculture in Cairo, Egypt, to give information on Caprification and he wrote a further treatise detailing all the sorts of caprifigs, explaining the action of the insect and what may interfere with the success of the operation.

Space does not permit the complete account of Dr. Borg's works. I will however give a short account of his hobbies, his leisurely pursuits —Cacti and his own garden.

PRIMORDIAL COLLECTION OF CACTI

Ever since childhood Cacti had held a fascination for him and as a lad he formed a numerous collection which he duly classified in 1896, giving the scientific as well as the popular name of his plants. This was an arduous task, since at that time reference books appertaining to Cacti were non-existent. Unfortunately, this first collection was almost all destroyed by hail in 1900.

Here is the complete list:

1. **Cereus** Ackermanni
2. coccineus Salm-Dyck
3. eburneus
4. Eyriesii, Hort. Bert=Echinops. Eyriesii Pfeiff & Otto.
5. flagelliformis, Mill. (Rat's tail Cactus)
6. grandiflorus, Mill. (Night flowering Cereus)
7. multiplex, Hort. Berol.=Echinopsis multiplex, Pfeiff & Otto.
8. peruvianus, Mill. (Thorny Reed of Peru)
9. McDonaldi Hook. B.M.
10. rostratus, Lem.
11. serpentinus, D.C.
12. triangularis, Mill. (Strawberry Pear)
13. Quillardetii, Hort.
14. variabilis, Pfeiff.=speciosum, Sweet. Hort. Brit.

15. **Echinocactus** Decaisnei, Steud=Echinopsis Decaisneana, (Hedge-hog Cactus)

16. **Echinopsis** Eyriesii Pfeiff et Otto.
    multiplex Pfeiff et Otto. (See Cereus)

17. **Epiphyllum** truncatum, Haw (common winter Cactus)

18. **Mammillaria** (Nipple Cactus) Conopsea, Scheidn.
19. gracilis, Pfeiff.
20. pusilla, Sweet.=stellaria, Haw.
21. simplex, Haw.
22. tenuis, D.C. not=stella aurata Mart.

23. **Opuntia** amyclaea, Tenore
24. andicola, Hort. Angl.
25. brasiliensis, Haw.
26. curassavica, Mill.
27. Dillenii, Haw
28. elatior, Mill.
29. ferox, Haw.
30. Ficus Indica, Mill.
31. fragilis, Haw.
32. microdasys, Pfeiff.
33. monacantha, Haw.
34. var. variegata, Hort.
35. polyantha, Haw.
36. Salmiana, Parm ex Pfeiff.
37. ovata, Pfeiff.

38. **Pereskia** grandifolia, Haw. (Barbados Gooseberry)
39. **Phyllocactus** (leaf Cactus) Ackermannii, Walp.=Cereus Ackermanni, Salm Dyck.
40.   Hookeri, Walp.
41.   phyllanthoides, Link.= Cactus speciosum Bonpl. =Cereus phyllanthoides, D.C.
42.   phyllanthus, Link.

PRIVATE GARDEN

It had always been his wish to plan a garden of his own, and like many a famous man build his home in it. In 1904 he set about realizing his dream by leasing a plot of ground, an acre in area at Attard close to the residence attached to his official post.

He began by sinking a large well, and with the stones quarried he built a high wall dividing the ground, for the purposes of sheltering the trees. A wide passage 60 metres long ran the length of the larger division which was flanked by grape vines whose clusters hung on arched trellis. He built a spacious room and furnished the garden with ponds and conduits for irrigation purposes. An order for pears furnished him with rare varieties such as *"Passe Crassane"*, *"Angelique de Rome"*, *"Clapp's Favourite"*, *"Fondant de Bois"*, *"General Totleben"*, *"Sucre de Montlucon"*, *"Baronne de Mello"*, *"Doyenne d'Automne"*, *"De Cure"*, *"Passatutti"*, *"Saint Germain d'Hiver"* and *"Belle Poitvin"*: each having a special time for cutting and ripening, so that his table might be furnished with pears all the year round.

He planted a great number of citrus trees, principally egg-blood oranges and seedless oranges including "Thompson's Improved", "Golden Nugget", and "Golden Buckeye", a few sweet oranges and some mandarins. He planted lemons all along the boundary wall; also seedless lime, Pomelo or grape fruit in three varieties, Valencia Oranges, Citrus in two varieties, Bergamot, Piret and sweet lime.

He also planted a good number of pomegranates, "The Santa Rosa", "Santa Caterina", "The blood red Pomegranate" and the Mule's tooth variety, with very large fruit, peaches (early and late varieties), nectarines, loquats, apples, apricots, and plums, soft shelled almonds, a mulberry tree, a guava, custard apple, bananas and oriental trees, such as Philodendrons and Kaki or Chinese Date Plum.

He reared a great variety of strawberries in pots, all with different tastes and shades, and his vines included such delicate varieties as "To-Kay Musque", "Black Frontignan", "Black Muscat of Alexandria", etc.

He did not neglect the aesthetic side. He knew in detail where the different plants would best thrive, and he utilized climbers to cover the bare garden walls. Among annuals, pride of place was given to the very elegant Cypress-vine, Ipomoea, which properly treated develops enormously, flowering in profusion. The pretty *Bryonopsis laciniosa erythrocarpa*, ornamental both on account of its elegant vine foliage as well as for the clusters of small round scarlet fruits with longitudinally arranged silvery white blotches, which remain long after the plant has died in late autumn, had practically naturalized itself in his garden, and was adopted to cover stems of trees; as also *Humulus japonicus* with its very ornamental foliage variegated white. But as all these summer annual climbers require much watering, perennials were his preference. Among those with voluble stem, *Stephanotis floribunda*, rich in satin-like deep green foliage and in pure white clusters of small trumpet-shaped flowers, was planted along walls, balustrades and trellises, and its sweet-scented flowers in bloom from June to September were ideally suitable for decorating flat bowls in the home. There was also *Jasminium officinale* a very popular plant in Malta. The white flowered climbers were contrasted with *Tecoma Capensis* of fiery red flowers, *Plumbago* with its light blue clusters, and the *Antigonon leptopus*, a truly elegant climber, producing large panicles of rose-pink flowers throughout the summer and autumn.

Among the foliage climbers there were *Ampelopsis veitchii* whose green red foliage covered a whole wall in Autumn, *Asparagus plumosus*, *Asparagus Bonplandi* and *Smilax*.

Having provided suitable climbers to cover the boundary walls, he next thought of planting shrubs and perennials along the boundaries of the garden and orchard. He made a good choice. His garden became, and still is, famous for the well-known Frangipani *Plumeria alba* and its congeners *P. acutifolia*, *P. bicolor*, *P. rubra* (the last a later addition sent from Italy by a colleague, an Italian Professor). A specimen of *Plumeria alba* is now about 30 feet high, and is quite an artistic feature of the garden. The *Strelitzia Reginae*, with their strange yellow and blue flowers, were quite at home in his garden though they are difficult to establish. Borg had a great love for *Heliotropium Peruvianum* with its lovely vanilla scented pale and dark blue flowers. He had many kinds of the popular Hibiscus plants: *Hibiscus mutabilis* with its large double white flowers produced in autumn turning red within twenty-four hours and the many single and double varieties of *Hibiscus altea*, as well as the elegant *H. schizopetalus*. He also grew *Aloysia citriodora*, the tall *Ferdinanda eminens* with effective large white flowers, the scarlet flowered *Salvia splendens*, and the more sober lilac flowered variety. Of course, the white broom *Genista alba* could not be forgotten as it is very beautiful with bright coloured flowers for vases and bowls, though, certainly no plant could beat *Poinsettia pulcherrima* for home decoration so gorgeous at Christmas time.

"The old tag that the Rose is Queen of Flowers is amply justified at least as regards the Rose in our gardens. In fact there is no species of rose, and hardly any variety or hybrid, which given adequately favoured conditions as regards soil and treatment does not do well with us" wrote Professor Borg in "Gardening in Malta", and in the acre of ground at his disposal he cultivated the rose extensively. To mention a few varieties which flowered and throve splendidly: the "Noisette" Roses; "Allister Stella Gray"; "Rêve d'or" and particularly

"William Allen Richardson"; the Tea Roses and the Hybrid Teas, all of them more or less perpetual flowering, and usually producing as large an autumn growth of flowers as the spring blooming, comprised the bulk of the roses cultivated and there were also "Archiduchesse Marie Immaculata"; "Auguste Comte"; "Beauté Inconstante"; "Mme. Constance Soupert"; "Marie Von Houtte"; "Mamman Cochet" and its white form "Papa Gauthier"; "Sapho"; "Souvenir de Pierre Notting" and "Adèle Hameau", which is quite superb in Autumn: and among the Sarmentose or Climbing Tea roses: "Marechal Niel"; "Duchesse D'Auerstaed"; "Reine Marie Henriette"; "Gloire de Dijon"; "Mme. Jules Graveraus"; "Lady Hillingdon", etc. The bush or Dwarf Hybrid Teas were "Antoine Rivoire", an admirable rose of sturdy constitution, with large flowers of a delicate flesh colour: "Charles Levegue"; "Etoile de France"; "Gloire Lyonnaise" which is practically thornless; "Jonkheer J. L. Mock", a magnificent rose; "La France", a well known rose exquisitely scented; "Laurent Carl" with large damask-red flowers; "Mme. Caroline Testout"; "Madame Jules Grolez". The magnificent class of hybrid Perpetuals included "Captain Christy"; "Commandeur Felix Faure"; "Frau Karl Druschki"; "Louis Van Houtte"; "Paul Neyron"; "General MacArthur" and others.

And since roses do not resent the neighbourhood of bulbs, and bulbs are indispensable in any garden, beneath the roses there was a profusion of all kinds of Hyacinths, narcissi, daffodils, Freesia, *Iris hispanica*; *Iris germanica* and *Lillium candidum*.

Apart from these decorative plants, he had a wonderful collection of medicinal plants such as *Absynthe* (white herb) *Salvia officinalis L.* (common sage) *Mentha virides L.* (mint) *Origanum marjorana* (marjoram) *Thymus vulgaris* (thyme) *Melissa officinale* (balm) chives, estragon, hyssop, sorrel, rosemary, lavender, coriander, water cress, wild or bitter fennel, borage, capsicum, etc.

*   *   *

It is to be mentioned here that he did much useful work while Secretary of the Economic Agrarian Society. This Agrarian Society, encouraged by Government, was composed of members who had at heart the interests of farmers, and they organized yearly shows of vegetables, fruits and livestock at Boschetto and kept a model farm at Attard.

John Borg was for many years Secretary of this Society and for 18 years Director of the Experimental Farm for which worthy services and in recognition of his agrarian work he was in 1917 awarded the coveted silver medal of the Society. This Society was the means of bringing to light much erudition otherwise latent in Dr. Borg for he was their spokesman.

A lengthy note was sent to him in 1906, making much fuss about a supposed American Invention of an artificial fertilizer of the soil by means of bacteriological culture. This invention which was approved by the United States Consul in Malta, who advised the Society to make direct appeals to the Minister of Agriculture in Washington for a sufficient quantity to fertilize a good portion of land, was dealt with by Dr. Borg in a most enlightening and lucid explanatory answer.

After acknowledging the importance of bacteriological culture in rural economy, the results of which had already been known from time immemorial by Maltese farmers, and which had been accurately studied during the last two decades, he explains that the nodules that develop in the roots of leguminous plants are due to a bacillus *Rhizobium leguminosarum* or *Bacillus radicicola* which feeds on the texture of the roots and compensates by fixing the element nitrogen from the air contained in the soil, and transforming it into an azotate quaternary substance (amide) which can be easily assimilated by the host plant. (The other necessary substances for the development of the Host Plant—phosphorus, potassium, calcium, silica, magnesium, iron, etc.—are already in the soil and are taken directly by the plant). It is a reciprocity, a sort of vegetable communism, useful to the parasite, as also to the host plant.

Now, he continues, besides the native leguminous plants, many annual leguminous vegetables are cultivated in these Islands. But it is interesting to record that the microbe differs according to the plant it lives on, so that almost every leguminous plant has a special microbe of its own; and as all these leguminous plants are successfully cultivated in Malta, since ancient times, it is clear that the soil in our fields swarms with spores and bacilli of all the varieties of *Rhizobium leguminosarum*, and therefore we are in no need of importing them from abroad. A handful of earth from our fields contains thousands of these microbes. He adds that our farmers, although they lack instruction, know full well that, after a crop of a leguminous plant, the soil rich in the microbe that had advanced the preceding crop, gives marvellous results, being utilized by the subsequent product.

He ends by assuring the members of the Society that the microbes cultured in Germany and America are the very same existing in the countries washed by the Mediterranean, and affirms that the microbes distributed by the Americans originate from our Island, Tunis and Algeria. "However", he concludes, "I must make it clear that in the countries where our leguminous plants have not been cultivated as in many regions of America and Australia, it is almost useless to cultivate them if the soil is not inoculated with the necessary microbe."

Another letter relating to the expediency of planting in Malta *Rhus Coriaria* and thus encouraging arboriculture sent to Dr. Borg by the Secretary of the Society in 1920 resulted in an extensive elucidation on Arboriculture in Malta as compared with other countries, by him, in his official capacity of Superintendent of Agriculture.

Coming to later years, neither stress of work nor poor health prevented his being useful to anybody in whatever line he was consulted.

BIOGRAPHY

In 1934, Robert Theodore Gunther, M.A., Hon. LL.D., F.R.G.S., F.L.S., F.Z.S., a Fellow and Tutor of Magdalen College, Oxford, and a member of the Athenaeum until his death in 1940, took in hand the publication of the English version of the Discorides which had lain so long in Magdalen College, Oxford, but his difficulty was that he did not know how far the drawings were correct. So the book was brought over from London by Sir D'Arcy Power to be shown to the Maltese botanist, and Prof. Borg "greatly helped him out of this difficulty."

In returning the Herbal of Discorides with accompanying notes Prof. Borg wrote:

"I hope, Sir, that you will not think that I have commented upon the work of Discorides; a thorough study of this work requires a long time, and I am afraid that even after a long study many of the problems will remain unsolved. Of course, Discorides is not responsible for the figures, and no blame can attach to him if they do not always agree with the descriptions. But the descriptions are too often very incomplete and inaccurate and leave much doubt as to the identity of the plants described, so that we must also absolve the commentator who is responsible for the figures. Some of these, however, are very good indeed, and as such can hardly be improved upon."

In answer, by letter from "The Athenaeum"—Pall Mall, London, Prof. Gunther wrote:

"I am exceedingly grateful to receive your names of the Discoridean figures and text, which have been forwarded to me by Sir D'Arcy Power. Your notes are very valuable, and I am greatly impressed with the speed with which you have put them together. I hope to write to you again later from Oxford."

Less than five months before his death we find him in detailed and instructive correspondence with Colonel C. E. Gresham, who being much interested in the wild flowers of Malta, and having read with much appreciation Professor Borg's "Flora of the Maltese Islands", from which "excellent book" he derived much pleasure, sought through correspondence "an intimate knowledge of this fascinating subject" and at the same time looked forward to the pleasure of his acquaintance. Owing to Professor Borg's critical state of health a meeting never took place, although he wrote many helpful letters and was asked to run his eye over and comment on some notes which Colonel Gresham thought he might publish in the "Journal of the Royal Horticultural Society", and which Professor Borg considered quite comprehensive.

SUPERINTENDENT OF AGRICULTURE

In 1911 a Royal Commission, recognizing the paramount importance of the agricultural industry to Malta, recommended that the small Agricultural Department be further developed and the field of its activity extended, and Dr. Borg was asked to organize the Department.

CACTI

In 1919 he was appointed by the Government to be Superintendent of Agriculture, and to his reforms we owe the set up of the Department as it is today. On his recommendation, the Government Experimental Farm was transferred to the site it now occupies at Ghammieri and new farming implements were imported and demonstrated on the Farm for the benefit of local farmers. He also established a Pathological Section of the Department and founded a Review, the "Melita Agricola", in which his own contributions figured conspicuously.

In the same year (1919) Borg concerned himself with the formation of the "Farmer's Union" and it is to him, as its Founder, that Malta owes the creation of this Union. Soon after a scheme was submitted for the formation of an Agricultural Bank which he considered urgently needed, but, notwithstanding promises, years elapsed without anything being done in this direction.

Borg was thoroughly convinced that the main industry of the Maltese Islands was Agriculture, and insistently urged the Government to adopt a rational and vigorous agricultural policy, and to spend money where it was so much needed, particularly on Animal Husbandry and Viticulture.

1919 was destined to be a very busy and eventful year in the annals of Agriculture in Malta, for it was in that same year that the much dreaded Phylloxera was detected in Gozo, and almost simultaneously in Malta. Since John Borg's appointment to the post of Superintendent of Public Gardens and Plantations (1900) and through his subsequent Report on San Antonio Gardens, he had recommended the planting of American vines, in order to be prepared should the Phylloxera make its appearance. Twenty years later the dreaded parasite appeared.

Government immediately established extensive nurseries of American vines of sorts suitable for the Malta types of soil. Originally, they were two in number, one in Malta and another in Gozo. They were subsequently expanded in size, and increased in number to three in Malta and two in Gozo.

They were all formed by Dr. Borg with the assistance of the Plant Pathologist, and on several occasions he had the whole hearted approval of the best experts including Professor Paulsen an expert of European fame and Director of Vine Nurseries in various parts of Sicily. In 1932-33 the number of rootlings and graftlings supplied by these Nurseries amounted to over 177,000.

When it was realized that only American vines could combat the dreaded disease and that Maltese literature on the subject was sadly lacking, Borg set himself to write a book on American vines "Dwieli Americani fil-Gzejjer Taghna", reprinted three times, of the greatest use to the viticulturists, through which not only was the necessary scientific knowledge imparted in the language everybody could grasp, but it was of paramount importance as all other books written about the subject elsewhere would not hold good for the climate, soil and water— highly charged with lime—of the Maltese Islands.

466

In the meantime Borg was encouraging enthusiastically the Wine Making Industry which was still in its infancy, by recommending the standardizing of the industry.

He regretted that the original scheme (1920) of Lord Blight, Head of Gilbey's wine business, a firm of world-wide importance and associations, that Malta should become the emporium of the Empire's trade in fortified wines—was allowed to fall through. This scheme was prepared by Borg in furtherance of Lord Blight's suggestions: the acreage of vineyards in both Islands was to be increased ten times with the assistance of loans and grants; the above-mentioned firm would establish nurseries for the supply of a yearly average of one quarter of a million graftlings on American stock of such type of wine grapes as would be considered suitable for the purpose; and special arrangements were also considered for the cultivation of the vines and for the purchase of the produce. The adoption of the scheme and its successful working would have meant an unprecedented era of prosperity for the farmers, but the matter was allowed to drop (1921) and a splendid opportunity was thus lost.

We cannot end this epoch of Dr. Borg's career without mentioning the amount of study and research work he spent on the possible introduction of the silk-industry in Malta.

SILK-WORM INDUSTRY

Various previous attempts had previously been made to establish the silk-worm industry.

On December 30, 1909, Signor Carlo Tosolini of Udine, Italy, submitted a communication containing an offer to assist the Government in establishing sericulture in Malta, accompanied with information and suggestions. John Borg was called upon to express his views on the matter. He submitted in a Report that the soil of Malta was suitable for the growth of the White Mulberry tree wherever it is sufficiently deep and well drained; and therefore if the white mulberry trees were grown for the purposes of the silk industry, they should be planted in large numbers on suitable agricultural land.

At the conclusion of the 1914-18 War, when in all countries a general revival of industry was expected, some of the local residents of Malta urged once more the advisability of establishing the silk-worm industry in these Islands; and several persons again began to rear the silk-worm on a small scale. The matter was brought for consideration before the Committee appointed by the Government for the fostering or development of local industries; and Borg was asked to attend at one of these meetings to give his views on the possibility of establishing sericulture on commercial lines. He submitted a Report dated January 5, 1923, stating that the Industry could be established in these Islands (if financed by the Government, and if suitable agricultural land were devoted to the planting of mulberry trees); and continued that, if it was proposed to start the industry on a fairly large commercial scale, it was unnecessary to go through an experimental stage because that had already been done long ago and had given satisfactory results. In order to establish the silk-worm industry on something like a firm footing it would be necessary to have about 100,000 mulberry trees which could be planted in about ten years' time at the rate of 10,000 every year. In about three years, it would be possible to raise any number of mulberries in the Government nurseries. A mulberry tree of average size will yield 10 kilograms of foliage throughout the season and as from 15 to 25 kilograms of foliage are required to produce 1 kilogram of cocoons, 1 metric ton (1,000 kilograms) of cocoons require the foliage of 1,500 to 2,000 trees of average size, so that 100,000 trees mentioned above will produce from 40 to 66 tons cocoons.

After stating that it was always advisable for the Government to encourage and finance a new industry which has a good chance of success, and which as a secondary occupation for the household of the small farmers would prove a real boon to many people, he continued that as, moreover, heavy expenditure was already being incurred for relief work, it would be more rational to prevent unemployment and poverty by establishing new industries which would afford permanent employment, and encourage export trade; but the one point which required consideration was whether it would not be easier and cheaper to develop and organize in the first instance such industries as were already in existence, but which were in a precarious and unsatisfactory condition, owing to lack of co-operation and organization or to lack of some measure of encouragement and assistance. He continued: "Among the Agricultural industries which are already established, or partly established, but which require the guiding hand of the Government to become a great source of national prosperity and give ample profitable employment to many thousands of people, I may mention viticulture and cheese making, meat production and poultry breeding, as well as the canning and the textile industries."

As a supplement to the above Report, at the request of the Head of the Ministry, Dr. Borg prepared a scheme for the gradual planting of mulberry trees on suitable agricultural land belonging to the Government providing for the planting of 100,000 mulberry trees, 70,000 in Malta and 30,000 in Gozo at an approximate rate of 7,000 trees in Malta, and 3,000 in Gozo a year.

However, as good and drained agricultural land such as the mulberry tree required is very valuable, it was not deemed advisable to proceed with the scheme, which would be an expensive adventure, the result of which appeared to be doubtful. So he again confirmed that viticulture and dairying appeared to be destined to become the main agricultural industry in Malta.

Dr. Borg was very active in making suggestions in the annual Reports of the Department of Agriculture and in other Reports concerning the revival and extension of the canning industry, for better export channels, and the improvement of the potato crop, also giving advice with regard to the exportation of onions, cumin seed and cotton. He desired the cultivation of oranges and fruit trees to be extended and, though satisfied with the considerable improvement in the supply of vegetables, he still hoped that an encouragement of the canning industry might react favourably also on the successful cultivation of vegetables.

He was very keen on agricultural instruction in the practical knowledge of diseases and pests, and in modern viticulture; and in both cases the necessary instruction was imparted by the plant pathologist and his staff who carried on numerous practical demonstrations in both Islands with a liberal distribution of leaflets in Maltese. He declared that animal husbandry had been a desideratum for many years, and hoped that when the Experimental Farm was properly organized it would be possible to start these short courses of practical instruction in the various branches of farming for intending emigrants, but he deplored that many of his recommendations had remained a dead letter for lack of interest; and hoped that circumstances might compel those that controlled expenditure to respond more generously to the requirements of agriculture.

One of his last acts before relinquishing his office was a Memorandum, published in the Government Gazette on July 19, 1933, listing historical trees in the Island as having an antiquarian importance. It included those of at least two hundred years of age and also memorial trees that were to be protected by law.

On relinquishing his post of Superintendent of Agriculture he received an official communication from his successor dated January 1934, which said:

"I am directed by His Excellency the Governor to communicate to you the expression of thanks and appreciation of the Government for the valuable services you have rendered to Agriculture in Malta."

"I avail myself of this opportunity to convey to you the feelings of my deep regards, sincerely wishing you a long enjoyment of your well merited pension."

Another letter (in Italian) said:

"Now that you are leaving the Department of Agriculture, which you have created, and for so many years directed with lavish care and affection, the technical staff, the other workers and I beg you to accept this small token in memory of the work accomplished by you and as a perennial symbol of our deep gratitude."

A pair of silver candelabra was presented, and this circumstance afforded the opportunity to Professor Borg of saying an official good-bye to all the officers and men of the Department at a farewell party he gave them at his residence— Villa "La Fiorentina" Attard.

CACTI

In 1921 Dr. John Borg, Superintendent of Agriculture, was offered the Professorship of Natural History at the Royal University of Malta, which he accepted.

During the twelve years Professor Borg held this important post he arranged the Botanical and Zoological courses, and especially the course of Medical Botany. He introduced many medicinal plants, which were cultivated in the Botanical Gardens, so that the Students could understand better through seeing the living plant, and he often used to give demonstrations in practical Botany at the University and at the Argotti Botanical Gardens. He also organized Botanical and Zoological excursions.

At this time Professor Saccardo of Padova University—the best authority on "Fungi"—as a sign of due respect to his colleague Professor John Borg of the Royal University of Malta decided that some of the Fungi found by Professor Borg should be named after him, as follows:

1. Physolospora Borgiana Sacc.
2. Venturia Borgiana Sacc.
3. Didymosphaeria Borgii C.G. et Sacc.
4. Plenodomus Borgianus Sacc.
5. Glocosperium Borgianum Sacc.

The following are wild plants found by Professor J. Borg and listed as such in *Flora Melitensis Nova* by Sommier and Caruana Gatto.

1. Coronilla Emerus L.
2. Abutilon Avicennae Gaertn.
3. Paronychya argentea Lam.
4. Trifolium echinatum Marsh.
5. Lathyrus inconspicuus L.
6. Rosa sempervirens v. floribunda Guss.
7. Launaea resedifolia L.
8. Plantago stricta Schoubs.
9. Convolvulus silvestris Waldst.
10. Origanum Dictamnus L.
11. Iris Sicula Todars.
12. Silene gallica L.
13. Agrostemma Githago L.
14. Fumaria capreolata L. var. speciosa Borg.
15. Vicia pannonica Crantz. var. Stricta M.B.
16. Vicia monantha Retz.

So far Professor John Borg has only been considered as it were officially, in his professional capacity, his work and worth, but it is fitting that we should be acquainted with his inner self, the spiritual facet of his life, his character, his ideals and his views. Nothing can so

470

well revive my husband's personality as quotations from his own intimate letters.

As we shall see, he always associated Nature with high ideals and spiritual values.

"It is a pity that flowers are so perishable, and their beauty only lasts for a short time. This is the common lot of everything upon the earth. But our spirit—the spirit which moves the mind—is immortal, and its origin is therefore not earthly, and we shall be mistaken if we take too much delight in earthly things for themselves" he wrote.

His religious outlook is revealed here: ". . . . . If I take so much delight in earthly things, it is because I am always anxious to know myself, and the reason of my being. The truths of Nature are the clearest mirror of the Origin of all truth. Let us therefore soar above the Earth, and hail its Author, who is the true Sun of the Universe and source of our life;" and again: "I never understood what is the popular meaning of 'luck'. Whatever luck may be I do not believe in it, as I know that our Protector, the supreme ruler, is infinitely good, and disposes everything to our good. This is my faith—the humble and simple faith of a child. No wonder, because we are His children, though often rebellious and always unworthy, and He is our Father."

"I advise you to read frequently the Gospel. No other book is so well calculated to enlighten the mind and ennoble the heart. No other book gives us a clearer view of our duties and our rights. . . . . . May the infinite goodness of God dwell with us for ever! And may we do always our very best to deserve it!

"Our only God is the true God of love and his Son our Redeemer, is Love itself. Therefore when we take the holy Eucharist, we take the Author of Love, who created us from the mud of the earth and made us his companions and his friends and brothers—a living example of infinite love."

On another occasion he writes: "When cares and troubles come my way I turn to my trees and flowers, and I am soon refreshed by their silent greetings and innocence, and I resume my work with renewed joy.

"I take no delight in the noise and fuss of pageantry. I am a simple quiet man, and I am most pleased and happy when I am in the midst of peace and simplicity"—he said truly of himself. Often he sought solitude. "Yesterday evening I passed some time in my garden enjoying the solitude, and am glad that the vines do not show any marked tendency to disease. . . . . . I've been to Boschetto and between the precipices on the steep sides of the hill I have seen a heap of '*Ornithogalum arabicum*', which the English call Star of Bethlehem, and we Maltese, with more exactness call 'halib it-tajr'—(the bird's milk). How very beautiful it was, and romantic! What snowy whiteness, and what scent!"

This plant is cultivated in many gardens on the Continent, but in Malta we can boast of its growing wild.

There are many more quotations I could give showing how deep were my husband's reflections on religion, Nature and philosophy, but space does not allow me to do so.

It was my privilege to share his anxieties and success throughout 36 years of marriage from our wedding in 1909 to his death. His love of Nature was founded on his deep religious convictions seeing in all the Creator's hand. His outstanding characteristic was uprightness in his dealings with all.

He was always intent in imparting knowledge as also in absorbing it, ready to learn from the experience of others, and was extremely generous, sparing neither time nor labour in the interests of his fellow men. Beloved by all, he had a few intimate friends, akin to him in character, who could really count on his deep esteem.

CACTUS COLLECTION

Now as Professor Borg's busy and fruitful long stretch of public service drew near to its end his old love of cacti began to reassert itself. His public duties coupled with his writings had left him little spare time to devote to other interests. But retirement would afford him ample time for the care of cacti, those beautiful and often bizarre plants from another Continent.

From the beginning he had definite ideas as to how his collection should be built. He decided that it would not be haphazard. A south-facing wall in the garden of the Villa was chosen as the site of the collection affording the greatest amount of sunshine.

A shed for housing the plants in winter was essential and Prof. Borg could not seriously proceed with the collection before this had been erected. The Maltese climate obviated the need of a greenhouse. The greatest danger to cacti is frost, and in Malta the temperature never falls to freezing point. So cactus collectors have no heating problems in winter. What cacti need is protection from the winter rains which are a feature of the Mediterranean type of climate.

The climate of Malta is rather dry with an annual rainfall of about 20 inches, mainly in winter. The period of rainfall thus coincides with the period of rest for cacti, and a spell of cold wet weather can easily play havoc with a collection. Hail is also a hazard to be taken into consideration.

The shed still stands on the right-hand side of the Villa Garden, as you enter from the road, and runs longitudinally from north to south. It is 13 metres long, about 3 metres wide, and 2 metres high where the glass roof projects out in front. It is supported by a row of eight thick square wooden pillars embedded in stone rings. This row is repeated about 1½ metres inside the shed, and these pillars uphold another longitudinal bar of wood running the length of the shed and supporting the transverse slabs of wood on which the glass rests.

Two ridged shelves, one above the other, were placed between these two rows of pillars and ran along the whole length of the shed, except for a gap 1 metre wide in the middle where the entrance to the shed was situated. The lower shelf is completely shaded by the other shelf above and except for the outer space which, facing the sun, could well be utilized for delicate cactus, could only be used for storing dormant cacti in winter. However it was here the Professor had always to hand different sizes of pots for potting cactus plants ready filled with a mixture of soil passed through a sieve with the addition of fine garden loam, and rough sand or gravel.

Against the wall at the back of the shed was built a bench of stone slabs, resting on stone pillars reaching up to one's waist, and it is here in a reserved empty corner that all the potting and repotting took place. The space beneath this bench was used for storing loam, leaf mould, sand, and empty pots of all sizes.

Wire was stretched longitudinally on the wall and trailing cacti were trained on them. On the entrance the Inscription was inscribed in bold letters: "*Magna Opera Domini*". On a smaller adjacent shed that had been not long ago a hot house for ferns, but now adapted and arranged as an additional shed for cactus plants, the Inscription ran: "*Pinguescent Speciosa Deserti*".

These sheds in winter were filled to capacity with thousands of all sizes of pots, with all sizes of cactus plants; and it was a wonderful sight to view them from a terrace nearby, which being on a higher level afforded the opportunity of seeing the whole at one glance.

With the shed completed, Professor Borg could set about building his collection. The collections in the Island were rather poor, and it was to dealers abroad that he had to turn. For eight years, from 1932 until the outbreak of the Second World War, the postmen each spring and summer delivered a stream of parcels with postmarks from Italy, Germany, Great Britain and Czechoslovakia.

The first orders went to neighbouring Sicily, to the firm of Allegra. Professor Borg had previously had dealings with Allegra when he had ordered an assortment of Cacti and other succulents for San Antonio Gardens, just across the road from Professor Borg's home. The plants ordered and received from this source included some rare plants, such as *Leuchtenbergia principis; Obregonia denegrii; Pelecyphora aselliformis* and *Pilocereus hoppenstedti*.

Next year saw the Professor casting his net further afield. His orders had exhausted Allegra's lists, and German dealers were sending illustrated catalogues offering new discoveries from South America. These dealers included such famous names as Friedrich Haage, Junior, Graessner and later Wentzel. Robert Blossfield, realizing he was searching for more rare varieties in 1933, sent him the first seedlings raised in Europe of *Cereus Trollii*. In December 1934 in full winter, taking advantage of a moderate climate and not having patience to wait till spring, he placed large orders with "Stern" of San Remo. In 1935-36 Neale's vast resources were also tapped, when he had already a large collection of nearly 3,000 plants purchased from various Continental firms, knowing that Neale could still supply something quite different from Continental dealers.

CACTI

Many a time bulky consignments, in large baskets, arrived from abroad. This was indeed a thrilling business as the Professor, pipe in his mouth, note-book and pencil in hand unfolded, admired and chuckled as some specially longed-for specimen unfurled itself under his eyes, criticized and many a time corrected the name under which it was sent.

He never failed to praise the plants where praise was due, but dealers had a hard time with him as he complained of the plants when not satisfactory and deliberately contradicted some of the names under which the plants had been sent.

Sergeant Bugeja, a great enthusiast of Cacti in Malta, who used often to call on the Professor and admire his collection was struck by the fine specimens of *Espostoa Dautwitzii* or *melanostele* which, furnished with very silky pale yellow or even golden yellow hair veiling the stem very lightly, resulted in a fascinating transparent effect—as also *Ariocarpus fissuratus, Mammillaria Baumii; Cochemia Poselgeri; Harrisia gracilis; Obregonia Denegrii*, Fric.

Professor Borg also made frequent orders for succulents, of which he had a large collection. Succulents interested him, and we find literature about them among his papers, especially on the genus Euphorbia which includes not less than 700 species, mostly natives of the old world, mentioning different species and reporting on their irritant poisonous milky juice composed of starch granules. He was not the type of collector who collected only those plants which are attractive in appearance. His training in botany made him see in a plant more than meets the eye, and some plant would attract him for some feature of botanical interest.

His aim was not a specialized collection; the orders placed at the time and also later included plants from all tribes and genera, and ranged from Opuntias to Zygocactus. He was aiming at a representative and comprehensive collection. This wide range of genera he was later to find very useful in providing first hand knowledge about a large number of plants when he came to compile his book about Cacti.

Next to the shed he took care to plant a pecan nut to afford some shade to a good part of the shed, and it was useful too, to keep cactus plants and all kinds of succulents under its spreading branches. A plot of ground paved in slabs not far from the shed and the flanks of wide pathways gave summer hospitality to the cactus plants. This operation of shifting plants from the shed towards April and arranging them in serried ranks in the open became a very laborious business, as the cactus plants were continually repotted in larger pots as soon as they outgrew their residence and were not denied comfortable space; pots measuring one foot in diameter and more were certainly not an exception. Taking the cactus plants back to the shed was begun and continued by the month of October.

Naturally a different system of watering the cactus plants had to be observed. During summer when the plants were growing water was liberally given, whilst in winter, when the plants were resting comfortably in the shed, water was rigidly withheld.

As early as in 1932 the Professor became interested in growing Cacti from seeds and it is interesting to note that between December 1932 and May 1933 the following varieties were sown:

1. Ferocactus robustus
2. F. Colvillei
3. F. hamatacanthus
4. F. Wislizenii
5. F. Emoryi
6. F. acanthodes
7. F. Lecontei
8. Echinocactus pumilus
9. E. Ottonis paraguayensis
10. E. Leninghausii
11. E. Saglionis
12. E. Caesius (Melocactus)
13. E. Schumannianus
14. E. pygmaeus
15. Lophocereus Schottii
16. Phyllocactus hybridus
17. Mammillaria macromeris
18. Neomammillaria
　　　　　　　Macdougallii
19. Opuntia camanchica
　　　　　　　longispina
20. O. camanchica albispina
21. O. camanchica major
22. O. camanchica pallida
23. O. Rafinesquei arkansana
24. O. Lindheimerii
25. O. discata
26. O. humilis
27. O. versicolor
28. O. leptocaulis
29. O. laevis
30. O. Engelmannii
31. Echinocereus rigidissimus
32. Peniocereus Greggii
33. Echinocereus polycanthus
34. E. Fendleri
35. E. Boyce-Thompsonii
36. Coryphantha Palmeri
37. 　　　,, 　　radians
38. 　　　,, 　　Andreae
39. Mammillaria rhodantha
40. M. bocasana

41. M. Hahniana
42. M. elegans
43. Astrophytum myriostigma
　　　　　　　potosina
44. Echinocactus ceratistes
　　　　　　　Sandillon
45. E. grusonii
46. Mammillaria candida
47. Echinopsis formosa
48. E. rhodacantha
49. E. campylacantha
50. Echinocereus pectinatus
　　　　　　　rigidissimus
51. E. De Laetii
52. Cereus pruinosus
53. C. marginatus
54. C. Strausii
55. Pilocereus chrysacanthus
56. P. Trollii
57. Cephalocereus Palmeri
58. C. senilis
59. C. Hoppenstedtii
60. C. Pilocereus (mixed).
61. Aloe variegata
62. Opuntia cardona
63. Ferocactus latispinus
64. Astrophytum myriostigma
65. A. ornatum v. Mirbellii
66. Opuntia aoracantha
67. O. floccosa
68. O. diademata
69. Astrophytum capricorne
70. A. capricorne senilis
71. A. myriostigma tetragona
72. A. mixed
73. Leuchtenbergia principis
74. Mammillaria Zahniana
75. M. Pfeifferi
76. Pilocereus sp. nov. poco
77. Pelecyphora pectinata
78. Haagea Schwartzii
79. Echinopsis potosina

CACTI

80.	Echinocactus Fordii	85.	E. Beguinii senilis
81.	E. Matthsonii	86.	E. uncinatus Wrightii
82.	E. electracanthus	87.	E. (Eftus) lamellosus
83.	E. Haselbergii	88.	Opuntia erinacea
84.	E. senilis	89.	O. basilaris

Later he was very keen to collect seeds from his own plants, and to be able to gather them at the appropriate moment. He kept the husk under rigid observation—inspecting it at different times during the day especially in the hot days of summer when growing became accelerated. He would then cautiously and carefully break open the pod when he was satisfied it was perfectly ripe and put the tiny black seeds on a piece of white cloth to dry and afterwards to be sown. He invariably gave the pan or shallow pot containing the sown seeds, water from the outside, and many a time you could see him fondly and patiently bent on the ridge of the pond, the pan in both hands waiting for the water to go up and find its way to the surface. The pans containing the seeds were kept in special glazed garden frames 1m. 35cm. long, 1m. wide, 55 cm. high at the back, 30cm. at the front covered with a square piece of glass—generally on two pieces of narrow cane or bamboo for ventilation purposes; and the glass roof of the frame was opened by day in several dimensions as required according to season, weather and the growth of the seeds, It was invariably closed for the night to keep off the coldish night air, as also any unwelcome visitor, but care was taken that it was opened very early in the morning.

Grafting from October to April was a very interesting business, and one which he practised very successfully, being observant about the question of greater or less affinity of the stock and the scion.

He always kept himself provided with good stock such as *Selenicerei*, thick stemmed *Cerei*, and it was his habit to roam in the country fields and choose flat jointed pads of *Opuntia Ficus-Indica* to be grafted on.

Cacti had always been John Borg's passion since he was a boy; the frequent pricks with which these proud plants often repay their lovers did not in any way diminish his attraction, nor did the adverse forces of nature cool his ardour; in fact the destruction by hail of his first collection developed in his stern, strong-willed character the impetus to defend and safeguard his plants.

At a time when cactus literature was certainly very scarce or nonexistent, he as a lad could term the cactus plants in his collection by their scientific nomenclature as also by their popular name.

For fifty years his interests in this direction apparently remained dormant, but his constant enthusiasm and industry in gathering information and amassing literature on the subject was such that he was able to produce "Cacti" in about six months, as we gather from his interesting correspondence with Dr. Harold Unwin, O.B.E., specialist in tree planting of Nicosia, Cyprus.

We give a few notes from the above mentioned correspondence which might interest cactus lovers:

The family Cactaceae includes about 1,500 known species and they are exclusively American. The following are the only exceptions to this rule: *Rhipsalis Cassytha*, native of America, as well as of Tropical Africa and Ceylon; *Rhipsalis erythrocarpa*, native of East Africa near Kilimanjaro; *Rhipsalis sansibarica*, native of the Coast of Zanzibar; *Rhipsalis Madagascariensis*, native of Madagascar and *Rhipsalis prismatica—R. tetragona*, native of Brazil and Madagascar.

A few species of Prickly-pears (Opuntia) have now become acclimatized in other countries since the discovery of America (1492).

Other species, such as *O. tuna; O. vulgaris*, etc. are also naturalized in the Mediterranean region, but these species and also other species such as *O. aurantiaca; O. tomentosa*, etc. have become veritable pests over extensive districts in South Africa, India and Australia, propagating and extending with alarming rapidity.

Species of Cacti are found all over the American Continent and the Islands from the cold regions of Missouri and Nebraska down to Chili and Patagonia, but, for abundance of species and great variety of size and form, the Mexican region (including Mexico, California, New Mexico, Arizona and Texas) may well be called the classic home of Cacti, notwithstanding the recent discoveries of many species in the region of the Andes.

Cacti are found in sandy and stony deserts, in the rich alluvial pampas, in torrid regions, on high mountains where they are covered with snow in winter, and also in the primeval forests of Brazil, in many instances altogether shaded off from the sun.

On the other hand the Succulents, as distinct from Cacti, include a great number of species distributed in many families of the Vegetable Kingdom. Thus the genus *Euphorbia* (fam. Euphorbiaceae) comprising over 700 species, includes quite a considerable number of cactus-like species some of which are quite tree-like in growth, inhabiting Africa (from Morocco to Abyssinia and South Africa) and Arabia.

Practically all species of the family *Crassulaceae* (to which Ventinant had given the name of Succulentae) inhabiting the Old World, and *Aizoaceae* with their numerous mimicry forms, mostly South African denizens of desert regions, are all Succulents. Numerous species of *Amarillidaceae* of the genus (Agave) natives of America, are also Succulents and so are numerous species of *Lilliaceae* of the genus *Aloe* (Gasteria, Haworthia, etc.), mostly natives of Africa. To these may be added some species of *Portulacaceae*, many species of *Asclepidaceae* (*Stapelia, Caralluma, Heurnia Piaranthus, Hoodia*, etc.) a few species of *Apocynaceae* (*Pachypodium*) and quite a good number of Compositae (*Kleinia, Senecio*, etc.) a few Geranieae, etc.

*   *   *

It is interesting to hear what Professor Borg's views about manure for Cacti are.

CACTI

A letter from A. Wm. Vass, Brooklyn, New York, U.S.A., dated 17th January, 1940, soliciting advice says:

"In your book 'Cacti' you recommend the addition of cow manure to the soil mixture for some species of Cacti. Would it be advisable to use dehydrated cow manure for this purpose?

I have a copy of your 'Cacti' and must say it is the best of its kind I have yet seen."

Professor Borg answers:

"With reference to your note of the 17th January just received, I may point out that dehydrated manure offers the great advantage of a considerable reduction in bulk and in weight, but is sure to start a fermentation as soon as it comes in contact with moisture and organisms of the soil.

It is also comparatively rich in fertilizing qualities. Both the fermentation and the excess of nourishment should be avoided in the cultivation of most Cacti. If *old* and thoroughly *consumed* cow manure is not available, it is better to use only old-leaf-mould which any nurseryman can supply. The addition of some crushed charcoal is recommended. It is known that charcoal (as well as the humus in leaf mould and in manure) has the power to fix and oxidize atmospheric nitrogen (and ammonia) transforming it into nitrates, so that no other organic manure is needed. An excess of nourishment such as that obtained from bonemeal, brings about a remarkable spurt of growth, but the Cacti thus forced are very liable to rot off very suddenly."

LAST YEARS

When the war broke out in 1939 John Borg was making the most of his time rewriting and reviewing his last great work "Cacti", and intent in the pursuit of cactus culture, although it is quite amazing that such a placid distraction as cactus culture could even be considered in such uncertain conditions.

Towards the end of the war his health began to give way and he had to undergo a major abdominal operation which was performed by Professor P. P. Debono, a well known surgeon who had been a student of his, assisted by two other doctors also his students; but, of course, this was hardly remarkable, as he had been examiner and teacher continuously at the University for nearly 45 years. However, what shows his great power of detachment is his declining a general anaesthetic during the operation and having only a local injection he coolly observed the progress of a lengthy operation on his own person.

Although the operation was successful it was only for a short span he could be himself again. However, this brief year of convalescence was fully utilized by Professor Borg to give a new home to his numerous collection of Cacti and Succulents, considered one of the best in Europe, consisting of over 4,000 plants, 600 different species comprising some very fine and rare specimens and especially the tall columnar Cacti that would be the pride of a collection anywhere. He had already willed this collection to the Argotti Botanic Gardens, but now feeling his health failing he consigned it himself, supervising its transfer and naming some plants that had escaped being labelled.

In the short period intervening between this transfer and his death, he twice visited the collection and followed his Cacti with shrewd observations and keen advice. His intimate association and full knowledge of his plants on one of these visits made him detect amongst his numerous collection a stranger plant which, as soon as detected, he immediately pronounced as not belonging to him, which the curator and gardener, in amazement, had to confirm.

On another occasion he humbly asked for a cutting of *Opuntia Santa Rita* from his own collection, to have together with the few cactus plants I had kept, and which he termed "his wife's collection", and which true to himself he was daily increasing and multiplying, and even declared he would make as numerous as the other one. But his intention was not carried out, for his illness was getting the better of him, and at the end of April, 1945, he received the last Sacraments.

Even to his very last days his religion was coupled with his interest in natural history. He devoutly partook of the Holy Viaticum with the humble idea playing in his mind, that he was "a Zaccheus receiving the Lord into his house with joy;" and in the short talk he afterwards had with the priest administering the Sacrament, he gave him the name of the plant that had been used by Pilate's soldiers forming the crown of thorns to put on the head of Our Saviour, saying it was "*Nummularia*".

On Friday, May 4, 1945, at the words uttered by the parish-priest on his behalf "In manus tuas commendo spiritum meum" John Borg passed away peacefully.

His funeral was a very quiet affair, just as he had lived and as he had arranged beforehand. The Honourable Rector of the Royal University and the Librarian of the Royal Malta Library and a few intimate friends joined the family circle. A cross surmounts his simple grave at the Addolorata Cemetery with a bronze head of Christ wearing the crown of thorns. A simple inscription reads: "Scio quod Redemptor meus vivit" (I know that my Redeemer liveth).

Following his death, the local newspapers contained appreciations of "this scholar of high-repute, this self-made man, with no other influences to spur him on in his untiring and inexhaustible passion for scientific detail and accuracy save the love of his country and the sympathy and collaboration of his wife."

The donation of the fruits of his life-long labour—a magnificent collection of thousands of specimens of Cacti and Succulents to the Argotti Botanic Gardens; the presentation of his Research Microscope and Histology Bench to the Biology Section of the Royal University; and the bequest stipulated jointly with his wife of a substantial scholarship in Biology, as also his extensive collection of books on Natural

History and other subjects willed to the Royal Malta Library, were considered of the greatest value to the nation and the forging of other links with posterity.

It is the lot of man, when deprived of the spark of life, in the ever changing vicissitudes of the world to fall gradually into oblivion. However, great men never die, and it seems we have now a case in point, inasmuch eight, even ten, years after the death of John Borg we still find he is vividly remembered and put forward for the admiration of the public in broadcasts and journals commemorating the date of his death. Scarcely a year passes without his name appearing in the Press, in one way or another.

PUBLICATIONS

This short biography could in no way be complete if his various and numerous publications were not at least touched upon.

From 1896 when he was a young man of 23 up to his old age, he produced one or more contributions every year, ranging from detailed catalogues, informative articles, meticulous reports, interesting pamphlets to well over 50 books of considerable proportions.

His mind was vast and fertile, and his swift and fluent pen kept pace with it, while his interests were many and varied. The gifts of nature developed by his education, perfected by experience, and aided by his methodical mode of life concurred to make him a unique personality as an author.

His writings, although moving in the same orbit, had each and separately a distinctive note and were adapted to the class of readers for whom they were destined. As science was such an intimate part of his being, it was throughout a distinctive note. For half a century he poured out his learning and experience for the benefit of his fellow men, giving fully of all he had to give.

Prominence of place must be given to the books which have distinguished him as a scientist and author and have made his name well known far beyond the shores of Malta.

The Cultivation and Diseases of Fruit Trees, dedicated by the author "To my Comrades, The Noble Toilers of the Soil", attracted attention in all the countries bordering on the Mediterranean and spread to all Southern Europe.

The Flora of the Maltese Islands, dedicated "To my Wife, Beatrice, a constant companion and assistant in my botanical rambles" is a work of high botanical order which has proved interesting to agriculturists and horticulturists alike in such places as London, Kew, Berlin, Zurich, Muncheberg, Mark and lately Oslo.

Written in encyclopaedic form, *Gardening in Malta* and *Semina di Prodotti Orticoli ed Agricoli*, are important for the information they give, as are the various comprehensive pamphlets on the orange and the vine.

BIOGRAPHY

Finally, the publications he wrote of a more recreative nature should be noted, such as:

Traces of the Quaternary Ice Age in the Maltese Islands
Remains of Prehistoric Flora in Malta
The Avocado Pear
Witches' Brooms
Bulbs

and also the very attractive books dealing with insect life.

It is remarkable that in his writings there should be such a combination of scientific fact and theory, shrewd observation and general knowledge; these, aided by the reader's imagination of the bygone days, makes them a source of instruction and pleasure.

Malta, 1958.

BIBLIOGRAPHY

1859   Engelman, G. *Cactaceae of the Boundary* (Mexico- United States.)
1860   Labouret, J. *Monographie de la Famille des Cactées.*
1863   Lemaire, Ch *Les Cactées*
1889   Watson, W. *Cactus Culture for Amateurs.*
1898   Schumann, Dr. Karl. *Gesamtbeschreibung der Kakteen.*
1923   Britton, Dr. N. L., and Rose, Dr. J. N. *The Cactaceae.* (4 volumes).
1926   Berger, Dr. Alwin. *Die Entwicklungslinien der Kakteen.*
1926   Schelle, Ernst. *Kakteen.*
1928   Haage jun., F. A. *Haages Kakteenzimmerkultur.*
1928   Haage jun., F. A. *Kakteen im Heim.*
1929   Kupper, W. *Das Kakteenbuch.*
1929   Berger, Dr. Alwin. *Kakteen.*
1929   Roeder, Dr. W. *Der Kakteenzuchter.*
1930   Houghton, A. D. *The Cactus Book.*
1930   Haage, Walther. *Die Welt der Pflanze, III Kakteen.*
1930   Backeberg, Curt. *Kakteenjagd.*
1931   Knuth, F. M. *Der Stora Kaktusboken.*
1932   Marggraf, M. *Anzucht und Pflege der Kakteen und Sukkulenten.*
1933   Werdermann, Dr. E. *Brasilien und seine Saulenkakteen.*
1933   Backeberg, Curt. *Neue Kakteen.*
1933   Higgins, Vera, M. A. *The Study of Cacti.*
1934   Haage jun., F. A. *Bluhende Kakteen Neuheiten Bildkatalog.*
1935   Neale, W. T. *Cacti and Other Succulents.*
1934-7 Backeberg, Curt. *Blätter fur Kakteenforschung.*
1941   Taylor Marshall, W. and Bock, T. N. *Cactaceae* (Supplementing the work of Britton and Rose).

481

INDEX

The names in italics are synonyms. The figures in brackets indicate illustrations.

INDEX

CACTI

485

INDEX

INDEX

INDEX

INDEX

CACTI

CACTI

INDEX

INDEX

CACTI

INDEX

INDEX

CACTI

Neoporteria—*contd.*
  nidus senilis, 268
  nigricans, 269
  occulta, 269
  Odieri, 270
  Odieri Mebbesii, 270
  Pepiniana, 270
  Reichii, 271
  subgibbosa, 270
  villosa, 271
  villosa nigra, 271
  villosa polyraphis, 271
Neoraimondia macrostibas, 200
  macrostibas gigantea, 200
  macrostibas roseiflora, 200
Neowerdermannia Vorwerkii, 351
  Vorwerkii Gielsdorfiana, 351
Nopalea Auberi, 122
  coccinellifera, 112
  dejecta, 122
  dejecta Guarnacciana, 122
  guatemalensis, 122
  inaperta, 122
  Karwinskiana, 122
  lutea, 122
  moniliformis, 73
Nopalxochia phyllanthoides, 428 (443)
Notocactus apricus, 320
  concinnus, 315 (356)
  floricomus, 319
  Graessneri, 319
  Grossei, 319
  Haselbergii, 318
  Leninghausii, 318 (357)
  mammulosus, 317
  muricatus, 318
  napinus, 271
  Ottonis, 316
  Ottonis brasiliensis, 316
  Ottonis Linkii, 316
  Ottonis multiflorus, 316
  Ottonis paraguayensis, 316
  Ottonis tenuispinus, 316
  Ottonis tortuosus, 316
  Ottonis uruguayensis, 316
  pampeanus
  Reichii, 271
  rubriflorus, 317
  Schumannianus, 319
  Schumannianus nigrispinus, 319
  scopa, 316 (357)
  scopa candida, 316
  scopa ruberrima, 316
  submammulosus, 317
  tabularis, 320
  Velenowskyi, 315
Nyctocereus guatemalensis, 173
  Hirschtianus, 172
  Neumannii, 173
  oaxacensis, 173

Nyctocereus—*contd.*
  serpentinus, 172
  serpentinus ambiguus, 172
  serpentinus splendens, 172
  serpentinus strictior, 172
Obregonia Denegrii, 263
Opuntia acanthocarpa, 107
  aciculata, 95
  affinis, 85
  agglomerata, 112
  airampo, 76
  albisetacens, 75
  alcahes, 110
  Alexanderi, 116
  amyclaea, 89
  anacantha, 91
  andicola, 119
  andicola minor, 119
  angustata, 98
  aoracantha, 117 (79)
  aquosa, 68
  arborescens versicolor, 109
  arbuscula, 106
  Archavaletai, 91
  arenaria, 79
  argentina, 72
  atacamensis, 120
  atrispina, 98
  atropes, 85
  atrovirens, 78
  atroviridis, 103
  Auberi, 122
  aurantiaca, 92
  aurea, 121
  australis, 116
  austrina, 75
  azurea, 98
  bahamana, 74
  bahiensis, 72
  Ballii, 99
  basilaris, 81
  basilaris albiflora, 82
  basilaris cordata, 82
  basilaris nana, 82
  basilaris ramosa, 82
  Beckeriana, 94
  bella, 78
  Bergeriana, 93
  bernardina, 107
  Bigelowii, 108
  Boldinghii, 93
  bolivensis, 121
  borinquensis, 75
  brachyarthra, 79
  Bradtiana, 123
  Brandegeei, 68
  braziliensis, 72
  Bruchii, 118
  brunnescens, 93
  bulbispina, 113

503

CACTI

INDEX

CACTI

INDEX

BORG'S CACTI

'In the second edition of *Cacti* a further 312 species have been added, bringing the total number of species described to 1,500, and there are 36 additional illustrations. . . .

This book will be of the greatest assistance to growers of Cacti and its scientific accuracy will also commend it to botanists interested in these plants.'